LET'S GO: FRANCE

is the best book for anyone traveling on a budget. Here's why:

No other guidebook has as many budget listings.

In Paris, we list over fifty places to stay for less than $8 per night; in tho countryside, we found hundreds more for much less. We tell you how to get there the cheapest way, whether by bus, plane, or thumb, and where to get an inexpensive and satisfying meal once you've arrived. There are hundreds of money-saving tips for everyone plus lots of information on special student discounts.

LET'S GO researchers have to make it on their own.

No expense accounts, no free hotel rooms. Our student researchers travel on budgets as limited as your own.

LET'S GO is completely revised every year.

We don't just update the prices, we go back to the places. If a charming cafe has become an overpriced tourist trap, we'll replace it with a new and better listing.

No other budget guidebook includes all this:

Coverage of both the cities and the countryside; in-depth information on culture, history, and the people; distinctive features like rail, city, and regional maps; tips on work, study, hiking and biking, nightlife and special splurges; and much, much more.

LET'S GO is for anyone who wants to see the real France on an inflation-fighting budget.

LET'S GO:

The Budget Guide to France

1983

Robert M. McCord, Editor

Written by Harvard Student Agencies, Inc.

St. Martin's Press
New York

ISBN: 0-312-48212-4

First Edition
10 9 8 7 6 5 4 3 2 1

Let's Go: France is written by Harvard Student Agencies, Harvard University, Thayer Hall-B, Cambridge, Mass. 02138.

Editor: Robert M. McCord
Assistant Editor: Judith A. Rosen
Managing Editor: Christopher Billy
Publishing Manager: Stacey M. Lewis
Advertising Representatives: Karen P. Chen, Geralyn White
Advertising Coordinator: Sesha Pratap
Researcher/Writers:
  Pico Iyer: *Corsica, Cote d'Azur*
  John Lear: *Alps, Burgundy, Dordogne, Loire Valley, Massif Central, Provence*
  Joshua Leiderman: *Alsace-Lorraine, Brittany, Champagne, Comte Jura, Paris*
  Jon Serbin: *Basque Region, Languedoc, Pyrenees*
  Mary Yntema: *Atlantic Coast, Loire Valley, Normandy, the North, Paris*
Staff Assistants: Miriam Roberts, Efrat Levy, Holly Billy, Beth Vangel, Chris Caldwell, Johnnie Moore, Allison Taylor

Proofreaders: Regina Arnold, Alisa Clements, Susan Hegeman, Clare McHugh, James Millward, Phuong Pham, Janet Savage, Sue Ellen Webber, Susan Chaffin, Isabel Holland, Rebecca Sheridan, Vijaya Ramachandran
Maps: Jeanne Abboud
Legal Counsel: Harold Rosenwald

Acknowledgments

The most lovable, creative crop of workers ever to congregate in a dungeon contributed to this book. Only the *Let's Go* staff could successfully reincarnate a boasting boxer, a Soviet songster, a spitting llama, and a fainting pig. Remarkably, this staff also produced *Let's Go: France*. For this feat, my first, greatest, and yet most insufficient thanks go to Judy Rosen, the assistant editor who did far more than assist. Judy's skill with words and tenacity with work made her the ideal partner. And her familiarity with France allowed her to write a magnificent introduction and fill many of the holes left by my own gaping ignorance.

Buckets of coffee, thousands of pages, and plenty of sleepless nights now blur in my memory, but I clearly recall the joy and the support which Andrea Blaugrund brought, the smiles which Karen Baker carried, and the sparkling wit which Gideon Schor offered. Nor will entertaining images of Gary Marx, master of the imperative, ever fade.

Researchers, past and present, gave this book substance and life. I thank the researchers who most recently scurried around France in a mad search for information. John Lear covered nearly half of France, and his outstanding work fills much of this edition. Josh Leiderman literally zigzagged around the country to produce his thorough and insightful research; and Jon Serbin and Mary Yntema managed to produce crucial copy, even though they were fairly well catapulted around the continent. Making it all look easy, Pico Iyer graced many of the following pages with his lovely, flowing prose.

Relief as well as gratitude still fill me when I recall the last-minute aid of two super workers. Efrat Levy churned through miles of red-rimmed scrawl and produced pristine typed copy, and Holly Billy, who had already contributed a loved one and several tons of food to the cause, also contributed hour after productive hour at the typewriter.

Four people deserve special, overarching thanks. Together, Chris Billy, Stacey Lewis, Miriam Roberts, and Linda Haverty served as the heart of *Let's Go* this year. While I hid in safe libraries, cafes, and airports, these people kept the swirling, pressure-filled office ticking. As an organizer, editor, and friend, Chris Billy performed Herculean tasks with Herculean perseverance. Stacey Lewis proved equally wonderful as she shifted her boundless energy to any and every task at hand. Performing the work of ten, Stacey could manage finances, laugh at bad jokes, and wrestle with an IBM Selectric all at the same time. Miriam Roberts tolerated the mayhem and offered epic efficiency, enduring insight, and an uncanny ability to infuse confidence, energy, and love. Fellow editor Linda Haverty served as companion, critic, friend, and hero. With beguiling charm and wisdom, Linda inspired.

Resources, work, and kindness poured into the *Let's Go* office from other corners of Harvard Student Agencies and the rest of the "outside world." I owe special thanks to Christa Kuljian, Jackie Green, David Stoddart, and Alison Taylor. They tolerated my amoeba-like mess and brightened the office with their humor, energy, and affection. Thanks also to Maura Gorman and Dan Del Vecchio who offered friendliness and crucial material support, even as we remained rather raucous and stubbornly immune to the lures of corporate cleanliness.

I thank St. Martin's Press, and particularly Ashton Applewhite, for providing the magic publicity and printing which brings this book to the stand.

Finally, I thank Leigh, who once again stayed with me as I lurched from procrastination to obsession. And I owe my deepest appreciation and acknowledgment to my parents, who prepared me for this job by passing on their taste for travel, their respect for words, and their love of laughter.

RMM

These are times when only the best will do!

and the time is now.

France's TGV, the world's slickest and fastest train, is a symbol of Europe's modern and convenient rail system. There is no better way to discover and enjoy la belle France and her neighbors than to travel the rail way.

And we offer you the best in rail values with EURAILPASS and EURAIL YOUTHPASS. These prepaid tickets will give you unlimited rail travel on the networks of France and 15 other Western European countries, plus *free* travel on the TGV, on many steamers, ferries and buses. A 1st class EURAILPASS costs $260 for 2 weeks, with other tickets available for 21 days, 1, 2 and 3 months at higher fares. The 2nd class EURAIL YOUTH-PASS, for the under 26 traveller, is priced at $290 for 1 month and $370 for 2 months.

For more information on these outstanding train travel features, consult your travel advisor.

French National Railroads

CONTENTS

10   **Contents**

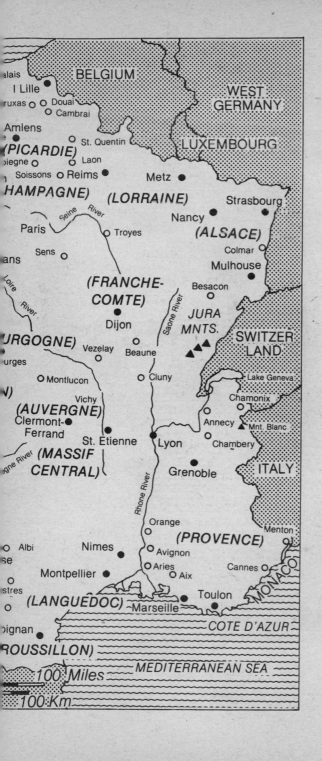

LET'S GO: FRANCE

The French sense of self-importance has both attracted and irritated foreigners for centuries. It is hard not to envy France's confidence in her own culture, the ease and the zest with which politics becomes a passion, passion a national pastime, and eating an event. It is also hard not to sympathise with Horace Walpole, an eighteenth-century English author, who wrote that he disliked the French not from "the vulgar antipathy between neighboring nations, but for their insolent and unfounded airs of superiority." If the French pride is occasionally insolent, however, it is certainly well-founded. This is the nation which gave the world so many of its "isms" and its "ists"—Impressionism, Fauvism, Existentialism, and Structuralism, to name just a few—and which boasts the architecture of Versailles, Chartres, and the Loire chateaux, the thought of Descartes, Rousseau, and de Tocqueville, and the cuisine and vinyards of, well, the French. Even today, in trying to define what is stylish, sophisticated, romantic, and beautiful, it is France that we turn to, and advertisers still try to capture our confidence by inscribing "French-style" on their yogurt and "French-cut" on their jeans.

In the past several years, however, this collective self-confidence has been somewhat shaken. Beneath the charmed and often charming exterior is a modern, industrialized nation with vast employment problems and a generation of pessimistic young people who have too many degrees and too few satisfying jobs. Deep-seated political unrest and hope for a new political and economic order swept the Socialists to power in 1981, but now hope is fading and dissatisfaction growing as inflation continues to rise and the value of the franc continues to fall abroad. Don't let the Gallic effort to define themselves by what is best about their past blind you to the realities of their present. You will undoubtedly find France a land of great beauty and excitement, but you should open your eyes to her troubles as well as her much-touted triumphs.

Using Let's Go

If you want to see France but have a limited budget, *Let's Go* can be a helpful companion. Our researchers travel on a shoestring budget, so their concerns are the same as yours: how to eat, drink, see the sights, entertain themselves, and sleep, in the most economical way possible. We list the least expensive accommodations and restaurants in each town and tell you how to cut costs at every corner.

Let's Go can also guide you through the maze of tasks that need to be done before you go. We can help you decide what kind of trip you want—whether to stay in hostels or homes and whether to travel by train, bus, or thumb—while our regional introductions to each province of France give you the flavor of the areas you might choose to visit.

Once you're there, *Let's Go* details what there is to see and do in France. We cover the sights in each city and suggest possible day-trips to surrounding areas. We mention festivals and concerts, monuments and museums. And for

15

those who don't stop when the sun goes down, we tell you where to find the nightlife.

Let's Go tries to lead you to new and unexplored places. We cover remote villages in the Pyrénées, lesser-known vineyards in Burgundy, and the bustling Parisian marketplaces. As you familiarize yourself with the territory, you will want to put our guide away and explore on your own. Some of the most exciting discoveries will be those you make yourself.

Finally, a word of warning. Healthy skepticism will serve you better than blind faith in using any guidebook. The book was researched in the summer of 1982, and since then, the world has not stood still; prices have risen, hostels have moved, and restaurants have closed. Save youself unnecessary legwork by calling ahead before trekking out to the hostel on the outskirts of town. After all, that's what the telephone numbers are for.

A Note on Prices

$1U.S. = 7.09F   IF = $.14

We quote prices in effect in summer 1982. Given the current rate of inflation in France, however, 1983 travelers should expect increases of 10-15% over our prices.

Planning Your Trip

One of the most geographically diverse countries in Europe, France has something to please almost everyone. There are the snow-capped mountains of the Alps and the Pyrénées, the rich, rolling vinyards of Burgundy, and the cliffs and windswept coasts of Brittany. The Côte d'Azur offers beaches of imported white sands, while Corsica possesses mountains and coastlines of a wilder beauty. The river valley of the Loire is studded with chateaux and flooded with tourists, but Central France, with the prehistoric caves of Périgord and the mountains and forests in the Massif Central, remains virtually untouched by the invading hordes.

The French people are almost as culturally diverse as their countryside. Rural Brittany has long maintained a rich Celtic heritage in its distinctive language, music, and regional customs. Southwestern France, encompassing the Pyrénées and the Basque Country, is imbued with a strong Spanish influence and a fierce separatist drive, while the German heritage in Alsace is reflected everywhere in the region's architecture, language, and cuisine.

How and When

One basic consideration when planning your trip is whether to travel alone or with others. Traveling alone can result in a sense of isolation, but affords you greater independence and the incentive to meet people. Going with others helps you save money on accommodations and store-bought food, and the companionship may be comforting, especially if this is your first trip abroad.

Another idea is to travel during the off-season. Fall wine harvests, Paris in winter, Provence in the spring—all are lures of non-summer travel. Air fares are cheaper, and flying standby, except around major holidays, is simple.

Getting around is easy too: you don't have to compete with the hordes of summer tourists crowding hotels, sights, and train stations and driving up prices and local tempers.

On the other hand, there are drawbacks to off-season travel. Winters in France are usually fairly mild, but their frequent rain and overcast skies can dim your spirit. Camping, when possible, will be less appealing; one compensation is that campgrounds are less crowded in the winter. Many hostels and some hotels are closed, museums and tourist offices keep shorter hours, and the streets are more subdued.

If you do plan to travel during peak season, however, be forewarned; all of France seems to go on vacation at the same time, with the bulk of departures concentrated between June 28 and August 11. Getting anywhere during the final few days of July and August (in addition to the first few days of August and September) is almost impossible: If you must travel then, you should reserve seats on trains or watch for posters advising motorists when to avoid the roads.

Useful Addresses and Organizations

The best way to ensure a relaxing, trouble-free trip is to do your research early. Below we list addresses you should use for information. (These organizations are listed throughout the chapter.)

French Government Tourist Office, 610 Fifth Ave., New York, NY 10021 (tel. (212) 757-1125). This is the American office of the French National Tourist Board. Write for information on any region of France.

Council on International Educational Exchange (CIEE), 205 E. 42nd St., New York, NY 10017 (tel. (800) 661-0311 or (212) 661-1414), for mail or phone inquiries; New York Student Center, 356 W. 34th St., New York City, for in-person inquiries; or 312 Sutter St., San Francisco, CA 94108 (tel. (415) 421-3473. CIEE is a non-profit organization providing work, study, and travel services throughout the world for students and other budget travelers. CIEE also has offices in Berkeley, Boston, Los Angeles, Miami, San Diego, and Seattle; address all informational inquiries to their offices in New York. For a list of their Paris offices, see the "Useful Addresses" in the Paris introduction. You can pick up CIEE's annual *Student Work, Study, Travel Catalog* for free at most student travel offices.

United States Student Travel Service (USSTS), 801 2nd Ave., New York, NY 10017 (tel. (212) 867-8770). Write for their catalogues on low-cost camping tours and work abroad.

Canadian Universities Travel Service (CUTS), 44 St. George St., Toronto, Ont., M5S 2E4, with branches in Halifax, Ottawa, Saskatoon, Edmonton, Vancouver, and Montreal. Inquire about their student rates and special programs for Canadian citizens or landed residents.

Harvard Student Agencies (Travel Division), Harvard University, Thayer Hall-B Cambridge, MA 02138 (tel. (617) 495-5230). International Student Identity Cards, Eurailpasses, Youth Hostel card, etc.

Educational Travel Centre, 438 N. Frances St., Madison, WI 53703 (tel. (608) 256-5551). Eurailpasses. Write for their bulletin, *Taking Off*, with information about tours and flights.

Forsyth Travel Library, 9154 W. 57th St., P.O. Box 2975, Shawnee Mission, KS 66201, a mail-order service, stocks a wide range of city, area, and country maps, as well as guides for rail and boat travel in Europe. They are the sole North American distributor of the Thomas Cook Continental and Overseas Timetables for trains. Write for their catalogs (enclose $.25 for postage).

Should you need help or information on passports and visas, the French consulates in the U.S. are located at 934 5th Ave., New York, NY 10021 (tel. (212) 535-0100; 2570 Jackson St., San Francisco, CA 94115 (tel. (415) 922-3255; 8350 Wilshire Blvd., Suite 310, Beverly Hills, CA 90211 (tel. (213) 653-3120. The American Embassy in Paris is at 2, ave. Gabriel-Peri (tel. 365-74-60; Métro Concorde).

Budget travelers seldom make effective use of tourist offices. All of the towns in France which attract a significant number of visitors have a tax-supported office called the **syndicat d'initiative** to provide information on the town and the surrounding area. The syndicats d'initiative are listed in the Practical Information section of each town. Each of these offices has stacks of brochures on the attractions of its town and lists of its hotels and restaurants. In addition, there are numerous **Maisons des Provinces de France** with offices in Paris; these offer information on lodging, tourism, and activities particular to the provinces they represent. Their addresses are:

Maison des Alpes-Dauphine, 2, place André Malraux 75001 Paris (tel. 296-08-56 and 296-08-43; Mo. Palais-Royal). Open 9:30am-7pm, Sat. 10am-6pm.

Maison d'Alsace, 39, Champs Elysées, 75008 Paris (tel. 225-93-42; Mo. Franklin Roosevelt). Open 9am-7pm, Sat. 11am-5pm.

Maison d'Auvergne, Bourbonnais, Velay, 194*bis*, rue de Rivoli, 75001 Paris (tel. 261-82-38; Mo. Tuileries). Open 9:30am-1pm and 1:30-6:30pm, Sat. 10am-1pm and 2-5pm.

Maison de Bretagne, 17, rue de l'Arivée, Boîte 1006, 75737 Paris Cédex 15 (tel. 538-73-15; Mo. Montparnasse-Bienvenue). Open daily 10am-7pm.

Maison de Corse, 82, blvd. Haussman, 75008 Paris (tel. 239-45-50; Mo. St.-Lazare). Open 10am-6pm, Sat. 10am-1pm.

Maison des Hautes-Alpes et de l-Ubaye, 4, ave. de l'Opéra, 75001 Paris (tel. 296-01-88 and 296-05-08; Mo. Palais-Royal). Open 10am-7pm, Sat. 10am-1pm and 2-7pm.

Maison du Limousin, 18, blvd. Haussmann, 75009 Paris (tel. 770-32-63 and 246-60-76; Mo. Chausée d'Antin or Richelieu Drouot). Open daily 10am-7pm.

Maison du Lot et Garonne, 15-17, passage Choseul, 75002 Paris (tel. 297-51-43 and 296-51-43; Mo. 4 Septèmbre or Pyramides). Open Mon.-Fri. 10am 7pm.

Maison de la Lozère, 4, rue Hautefeuille, 75006 Paris (tel. 354-26-64; Mo. St.-Michel). Open 10am-6pm, closed Mon.

Maison de Normandie, 342, rue St.-Honore, 75001 Paris (tel. 260-68-67; Mo. Tuileries). Open 10am-7pm and Sat. morning.

Maison du Périgord, 30, rue Louis le Grand, 75002 Paris (tel. 742-09-15; Mo. Opéra). Open 10am-1pm and 2pm-7pm, closed Sat. and Sun.

Maison du Poitou-Charentes-Vendée, 4, ave. de l'Opéra, 75001 Paris (tel. 296-01-88 and 296-05-08; Mo. Palais-Royal). Open 9am-7pm, Mon. and Sat. 10am-1pm and 2-7pm; closed Sun.

Maison des Pyrénées, 24, rue du 4 Septèmbre, 75002 Paris (tel. 742-21-34; Mo. Opéra). Open 10am-1pm and 2-7pm, closed Sat.

Maison du Rouergue, 3, rue de la Chaussée d'Antin, 75009 Paris (tel. 246-94-03; Mo. Opera or Chaussée d'Antin). Open 10am-6pm, Sat. 2-6pm.

Maison de Savoie, 16, blvd. Haussmann, 75009 Paris (tel. 246-59-26 and 770-76-84; Mo. Chaussée d'Antin or Richelieu Drouot). Open daily 9am-7pm.

Maison du Tarn, 34, ave. de Villiers, 75017 Paris (tel. 763-06-26 and 766-55-90; Mo. Villiers).

Documents and Formalities

Passports

A valid passport is necessary in order to enter any European country, and to reenter the U.S. or Canada. You can obtain a U.S. passport, now good for ten years (five years for anyone under 18), at any U.S. Passport Agency, or you can apply at any clerk of court or post office. To locate the nearest agency, check the local telephone book under "U.S. Government, Department of State," or call the local post office or clerk of court. If this is your first U.S. passport, or if your current passport is more than eight years old or was issued before your eighteenth birthday, you must apply in person; otherwise, you can apply by mail. You must submit a completed application form, proof of U.S. citizenship (either a certified copy of your birth certificate, under the seal of the official registrar, naturalization papers, or a previous passport issued no more than eight years ago), identification (such as a driver's license), and two

identical, recent photographs (two inches square on a plain white background). The fee for the new ten-year passport has not been set as we go to press. Processing of the application usually takes from two to three weeks (longer through a clerk of court or post office) but it's wise to apply several months before your expected departure date. If you are leaving within 48 hours, a "rush" service is provided by the Passport Agency while you wait, but you must have valid proof of your departure date and arrive in the office before 2pm. For more details, write to the Office of Passport Service, Department of State, Washington, DC 20524 for their free pamphlet, *Your Trip Abroad*.

If you lose your passport abroad, notify the U.S. Consulate and local police immediately (it's a good idea to record your passport's number and date and place of issue in a separate, safe place). The U.S. Consulate can now issue you a temporary passport for $15 on a same-day basis—usually within a few hours of application.

Canadian passports, also valid for five years, can be obtained by mail from the Passport Office, Department of External Affairs, 125 Sussex Drive, Ottawa, Ont. K1A OG3, or in person at regional passport offices, post offices, and travel agencies), evidence of Canadian citizenship, two identical photos, and $20 cash or certified check. Passports will usually be issued three to five days after receipt of the application. More information can be found in the booklets *How to Obtain a Canadian Passport in Canada,* and *Bon Voyage, But . . .,* available free from the Passport Office. The useful pamphlet, *I Declare,* is available across Canada at customs offices, travel agencies, or at Revenue Canada, Public Relations Branch, Customs and Excise, 600 Mackenzie Ave., Connaught Bldg., Ottawa, Ont. K1A OL5. Canadian citizens residing in the U.S. should apply at the nearest Canadian consulate.

Visas

A visa is an endorsement or stamp placed in your passport by a foreign government which permits you to visit that country for a specified period of time. Americans or Canadians planning to stay in France longer than three months will need a visa, which is also the prerequisite to obtaining a work permit, student registration, *au pair* status, or the *carte de séjour* (residency permit). You must submit a valid passport, one or two passport-type photographs, and proof of financial resources. This proof can be in bank statements, letters from banks confirming a transfer of funds from a U.S. account to a French one, letters from family or a host family, or a *certificat d'hebergement* (certificate of lodging) from the French family or friends with whom you will be staying. (All letters must be notarized.) Applicants under 18 also need written permission from parents or guardians.

Students intending to study in France for more than three months must also obtain from the French university or school a letter of admission or other evidence of registration. Workers need to have their prospective employer submit a contract to the French Ministry of Labor for approval before their visa and subsequent work permit can be processed. The *au pair* needs a copy of a work contract or agreement, signed by both parties and approved by the French Ministry of Labor. All three types of applicants need a medical examination no more than three months prior to their application date.

Please note that as a non-member of any Common-Market country, it is not possible to come to France as a tourist without a visa and then regularize your status as a worker, a student, or a resident. If you change your mind and wish to get a visa, you will have to return to your home country and apply for one there.

Student Identification

The **International Student Identity Card (ISIC)** is often required for certain student flights, trains, and clubs. The card can usually get you discounts on museum admission, theater tickets, transportation, and more; get into the habit of asking about student discounts wherever you go. Even if you only get a few reductions with your ISIC, the card is also useful as an extra ID, especially in those instances when no other student ID works. Finally, the $6 fee provides you with medical insurance coverage up to $1000.

Among the student travel offices which issue the ISIC are CIEE, Canadian Universities Travel Service, and Harvard Student Agencies (see the Useful Addresses section). The card is also obtainable at many campus travel offices. When applying for the ISIC, you must supply all of the following: 1) current *dated* proof of your *full-time* student status (a letter on school stationary, signed and sealed by the registrar, or a photocopied grade report; 2) a vending-machine-sized photo with your name printed on the back; 3) proof of your birthdate and nationality (xerox of birth certificate). The card is good until the end of the calendar year in which you bought it. Unfortunately, those taking a year off from school cannot purchase a new card in January unless they were in school during the fall semester. If you have just graduated, you may still obtain an ISIC card during the year in which you graduated.

With the increase of phony ISIC cards and improperly issued ones, many airlines and some other services require double proof of student identity. Therefore, we strongly recommend that you take with you to Europe a signed letter with the school seal from the registrar testifying to your student status.

If you are going to be studying at a French university, you will be given a student card *(carte d'étudiant)* by the enrollment office at your school upon

You can replace a lost Citicorp Travelers Check in places that've never heard of meter maids.

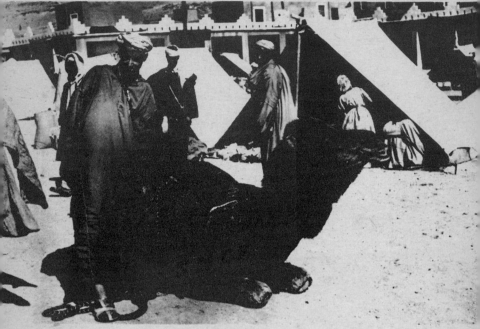

Imagine being lucky enough to visit a place where you don't have to be bothered with double parking, exact change lanes and speeding tickets.

The fact is, you never know where you might end up. That's why Citicorp has tens of thousands of convenient refund centers throughout the world (with emergency funds in the U.S. through 8,500 Western Union locations, many of them open 24 hours a day, 365 days a year).

So don't worry if you're visiting a part of the world where if they say "fill 'er up," it means with water. Because you can get a refund on a lost Citicorp Travelers Check even there.

Travel the world with Citicorp—America's leading financial institution, worldwide.

CITICORP ✦®
TRAVELERS CHECKS

presentation of a receipt for your university fees and your residency permit (see the Visas section).

If you don't qualify for the ISIC or *carte d'étudiant* and are under 26 years of age, don't hesitate to ask about youth discounts wherever you go. Your passport is adequate proof of your age, but you should also consider applying for the **FIYTO** card, available to anyone under 26 and obtainable in most student travel bureaus in Western Europe (you will need your photograph, passport number, and proof of your age to apply). A FIYTO card can get you reductions on certain transportation and accommodations throughout France. An IYHF card offers similar reductions (see the Hostels section).

Driver's Licenses

An **International Driving permit** is suggested for driving in France. It is available from any local office of the **American Automobile Association** or at the main office, **AAA Travel Agency Services**, 8111 Gatehouse Rd., Falls Church, VA 22047. It is also obtainable from the **American Automobile Touring Alliance (AATA)**, 888 Worcester St., Wellesley, MA 02182 (tel. (617) 237-5200), or the **Canadian Automobile Association (CAA)**. You will need a completed application, two passport-sized photos, a valid U.S. driver's license (which must always accompany the International Driving Permit) and $5.

If you are going to drive, buy a car, or borrow one that is not insured, you will need a "green card" or International Insurance Certificate. Most rental agencies include this coverage in their prices; if you buy or lease a car, you can obtain a green card through the dealer, from an office of the American Automobile Association, the Canadian Automobile Association, or from some travel agents. Check to see that your insurance applies abroad. If not, you can take out short-term policies (contact AAA Travel Services about their liability insurance program).

Money

Travelers Checks, Credit Cards

Nothing is likely to cause more headaches than money—even when you have it. Carrying large amounts of cash is extremely risky. Travelers checks eliminate most of the risks. Although not all banks accept travelers checks, especially in the smaller towns, the occasional inconvenience is a small price to pay for peace of mind. **American Express** travelers checks are one of the most widely accepted and the easiest to replace if lost or stolen. In addition, American Express provides five valuable services free of charge to travelers whose checks have been lost or stolen. Local American Express Travel Service offices will cash personal checks up to $200 (including foreign checks), have stolen credit cards cancelled, arrange to obtain a temporary I.D., help change airline, hotel, and car rental reservations, and send a Western Union mailgram or international cable to one individual. These extras can help prevent a holiday from turning into a nightmare. **Citicorp** travelers checks are sold in financial institutions throughout the U.S. and in more than 150 countries worldwide, and can be easily replaced if lost or stolen. For refund information and assistance in the U.S., dial toll-free 1-800-632-6388. **BankAmerica** travelers checks can be obtained and refunded at numerous banks throughout the States and in Europe. For claims and refund information while abroad call either the San Francisco or London BankAmerica Customer Service Center collect. (San Francisco 415-622-3800, London 01-629-7466.)

Two British-based institutions, Barclay's Bank and Thomas Cook Travel

Money

Travelers checks

Nothing is likely to cause more headaches than money—even when you have it. Carrying large amounts of cash, even in a moneybelt, is just too risky. Travelers checks are the safest and least troublesome means of carrying your funds. They are sold by several agencies and major banks, usually for a fee of 1% of the value of the checks you are buying.

American Express Travelers Cheques are perhaps the most widely recognized abroad and the easiest to replace, if lost or stolen. They are sold, exchanged, cashed and refunded at offices throughout the world. In addition, American Express provides five valuable services, free of charge, to travelers whose checks have been lost or stolen.

Local American Express Travel Service Offices will cash personal checks up to $200, have lost or stolen credit cards cancelled, arrange to obtain a temporary ID, help change airline, hotel and car rental reservations, and send a Western Union mailgram or international cable to one individual. These extras can help prevent a holiday from turning into a nightmare.

*

Thanks a lot "Let's Go, Europe." We couldn't have said it better ourselves.

Agency, issue travelers checks in dollar and sterling (£) denominations. **Barclay's Visa** checks are sold free of commission in New York and at many regional offices. **Thomas Cook** sells travelers checks in dollars commission-free, and charges 1% for sterling. They can be purchased at Thomas Cook offices, banks, as well as at local offices of the American Automobile Association (AAA).

Deak-Perera, a foreign exchange with offices throughout the U.S. and Canada, offers Thomas Cook and Visa travelers checks commission-free in dollars and in a number of foreign currencies.

Whether you should buy checks in U.S. dollars or in a foreign currency depends largely on the current exchange situation. If you do buy your checks in francs, you can often use them to pay directly for hotel rooms and purchases, especially in the bigger cities. In any case, buy in small denominations ($20), so if the exchange rate is unfavorable and you need cash quickly, you won't have to change more than you need.

Be sure to keep the receipts for travelers checks and a record of which ones you cash in a safe place separate from the checks. If you do need replacement checks, the receipts will speed up the process dramatically, although full replacement is rarely as instantaneous as the companies promise. American Express is the most reliable: they promise full replacement within 24 hours.

Charge cards are generally useless for the budget traveler as far as purchases go—the cheap places just don't honor them. But they are useful in case of financial emergency. If you don't have a round-trip ticket, you can charge your flight back. American Express will allow cardholders to cash a personal check drawn on a North American bank (up to $1000 on a green card and $2000 on a gold card in any 21-day period, payed out in a mixture of cash and travelers checks)—the money comes directly out of our account at home. With other credit cards, such as Bank of America-issued Visa or MasterCard, you can get an instant cash advance, essentially a loan on which a transaction fee is charged, up to your credit limit. If you are a student or your income level is low, you will of course have difficulty acquiring your own international credit cards. But if someone in your family already has a card, it is often easy to get additional, joint-account cards for other members of the family.

Sending Money

Sending money overseas is a costly and complicated process; to avoid problems, carry a credit card or a separate stash of 500F to be saved for emergencies.

If you anticipate needing money while in France, you can save yourself a lot of trouble with a little advance planning. Visit your bank before you leave and get a list of its correspondent banks in France. You can arrange to have your money sent to you at a specific correspondent bank in either of two ways. The fastest way is by cable transfer. Contact your home bank by letter or telegram and state the amount of money you need and the name and address of the bank to which your money should be cabled. This service takes about 48 hours—a bit longer if you're not in a major city—and costs about $20 for amounts under $1000.

A cheaper but slower way of receiving money is by bank draft. Your home bank sends a draft (make sure it's in your name) by air mail (preferably registered) to a specified correspondent bank; you pay a commission charge of about $10 and postage costs. You can have a friend at home buy the draft and send it to you, or you can write directly to the bank, or tell them before you leave to process drafts from your account and send them when and where you want them.

Another possibility is to have someone at home cable you money through American Express at a cost of $15 (more for amounts over $500 and that person must be an American Express card holder). It takes from one to three days for the money to reach you, with the first $200 payable in local currency and the remainder in U.S. travelers checks.

Finally, if you are stranded with no recourse at all, a consulate will wire home for you and deduct the cost from the money you receive. They are often less than gracious about performing this service, so you should turn to them only in desperation.

Currency and Exchange

The basic unit of currency in France is the franc, which is divided into 100 centimes and is issued in both coins and paper notes. The new Franc, equal to 100 old Francs, was issued in 1960, but old habits die hard, especially in the provinces; so if an elderly waiter demands "mille (1000) francs" for two cups of coffee, relax—10F should cover the bill.

Always check the exchange rate before changing money in France. Banks usually offer the best rates with no commission charge; an exchange office at the airport or the train station might take 25 centimes per dollar in return for remaining open late and on weekends; at a hotel or restaurant, you could lose as much as half a franc for every dollar changed. The difference between 5.8F and 6.1F to the dollar might not seem like much, but be careful—small losses add up fast.

Packing

The most effective way to pack is to set out the items and clothes you think you'll need for your trip. Then cut the amount by half and pack the bare minimum. The convenience of an easily transportable pack or suitcase is well worth the inconvenience of a small wardrobe.

Whether or not you use a backpack depends on the kind of traveling you'll be doing. If you will be visiting cities and towns only, you might want to consider a light suitcase. If you plan to cover a great deal of ground or to do a lot of camping, it is more efficient to carry a backpack (for advice, see Camping section). In addition, a small daypack is useful for carrying your lunch, maps, and poncho on short day-trips or city excursions; those who wish to travel unobtrusively might choose a large shoulder bag that zips or closes securely.

Choose dark, perma-press clothes that won't show the wear you'll be giving them. It's wise to dress on the neat and conservative side; you'll fare better when hitching and dealing with elderly hotel owners. Instead of jeans, you might want to bring a pair of sturdy cotton-blend pants or, for women, a wide skirt—both are cooler and look more polished. Shorts above the knee are inappropriate for touring cities and towns, especially for women, and will brand you instantly as a foreigner. Since laundry service in France is expensive and inconvenient, take clothes that you can wash in a sink and that dry both quickly and wrinkle-free. Also keep the weather in mind when planning what to pack. France is generally fair and warm in summer (especially in the south), with temperatures in the mid-to-upper 70° F (around 24° C). Winters are mild, averaging in the 40° F (about 5° C) during the day.

Footwear is the crucial item on your packing list. Running shoes or sandals are fine for touring cities, but for country travels, walking shoes are essential. Sturdy rubber-soled, lace-up shoes or lightweight hiking boots are advisable. Always break your boots in *before* you go; stiff boots and tender feet are a painful combination that can ruin any trip. A double pair of socks—light, absorbent cotton inside, and rag wool outside—will cushion your feet and keep them dry. (Sprinkling talcum powder on your feet and inside your shoes or sandals helps prevent uncomfortable rubs and sores, while moleskins relieve any blisters that do develop.) It's good to have a pair of light shoes or sandals, which can serve as dress shoes and which ease your feet on long train trips.

A rain poncho is a very useful item. If you plan to do any camping, it's worth paying a little more for a lightweight poncho that unbuttons to form a ground cloth. Make sure the poncho will cover both you and your pack.

Have some sort of pouch or money belt to hold your money, passport, and articles that you'll want with you at all times. The most theft-resistant are necklace pouches that slip under your shirt. A nylon or leather pouch with slits on the back to loop your belt through may be more convenient; it sits over your front pocket, where you can keep an eye on it and reach what you need with ease.

It's better not to take anything electric with you when travelling abroad. But if you can't bear to leave your blow dryer behind, remember that in most European countries, electricity is 220 volts AC, which is enough to blow out any of your appliances. (North American electricity is 110 volts AC.) If you can use batteries, you'll save money; if you can't, you'll need an **adapter** to change the shape of the plug. In France, as in most of Europe, there are mainly two-pin round plugs, while in some places, such as Britain, there are three-pin plugs. If you do not have a dual voltage shaver or hair dryer (which can save you a lot of trouble), you'll also need a **converter** to change the voltage. But remember that you can only use these converters in areas with AC current. They will not work in certain places in Germany, Greece, Morocco, Portugal, and Sweden which use DC current. You can buy adapters and converters when you get to Europe, or order them in advance from the Franzus Company, 352 Park Ave. S., New York, NY 10010 (tel. (212) 889-5850).

Finally, here's a checklist of sundry items you should consider taking: a jackknife, first-aid kit (see Health and Insurance section), needle and thread, string, a small flashlight, cold-water soap (for you and your clothes), plastic bags (for damp clothes or messy foods), mess kit, matches, small notebook, and travel alarm clock. If you take expensive cameras or equipment abroad, it's best to register everything with customs at the airport before departure. Since color film is more expensive in France, consider buying it before you leave.

Customs

Upon reentering the U.S., you must declare all articles acquired abroad. Keep all receipts. You can bring in $300 worth of goods duty-free, and then must pay a flat 10% duty on the next $600 worth. The duty-free allowance includes forty ounces of liquor and fifty cigars or two hundred cigarettes (you must be 18 to bring liquor into New York, 21 elsewhere in the U.S.). All items included must accompany you; they cannot be shipped separately. And remember that "duty-free" only means that you did not pay local taxes in the country of purchase. You have to pay duty on your purchases if they exceed your allowance. There is no duty, however, on personal goods of U.S. origin that are marked "American goods returned." But if you send back European goods worth more than $25, the Postal Service will collect the duty plus a handling charge when they are delivered. (Perfume, tobacco products, and liquor are taxed in any quantity.)

To avoid problems when carrying prescription drugs, label bottles clearly and carry your written prescriptions or a doctor's certificate along with you.

For a detailed description of U.S. customs regulations, write to the Department of the Treasury, U.S. Customs Service, Washington, D.C. 20229. Their Traveler's Packet, which includes the pamphlet *Know Before You Go,* is extremely helpful.

Canadian customs regulations are somewhat different. Once every calendar quarter you can bring in goods to the value of $50. Once every calendar year, you're allowed $150. However, these two allowances can't both be claimed on the same trip. Anything above the duty-free allowance is taxed at 25% on the first $150, and at varying rates afterwards. For a more comprehensive coverage of customs regulations, see the Canadian government's pamphlet *I Declare,* available from Revenue Canada—Customs and Excise, Connaught Bldg., Ottawa, Ont., K1A 0L5.

When entering France, travelers under 18 might wish to carry their parents' written approval of their work, study, or travel plans.

Getting There

Travel to Europe

By Air. Air travel still accounts for the largest single expense of a European trip, and only detailed calculations and advance planning can uncover the best way to go. Since deregulation was instituted in 1978, the trans-atlantic flight situation has been in a perpetual state of flux. Price wars among airlines and fluctuating fuel costs exert such radical influences on fares that as we go to press it is impossible to predict prices for 1983.

Off-season travelers will enjoy lower fares and face much less competition for inexpensive seats, but you don't have to travel in the dead of winter to save. Peak-season rates are set on either May 15 or June 1 (departure) and run until about September 15 (return). If you can arrange to leave in May and return in late September, you can travel in summer and still save. When planning your trip, try to keep your schedule as flexible as possible; an indirect flight to Brussels or Luxembourg could cost considerably less than a direct flight to Paris. The four budget flight options outlined below differ from one another in economy, flexibility and security. The simplest and surest way to decide among them is to find a travel agent who keeps abreast of the chaos in airfares and who is committed to saving you money. Don't hesitate to shop around—travel agents are by no means the same. Commissions are smaller on cheaper flights, so some agents are less than eager to help you find the best deal. The travel section of the Sunday *New York Times* or another major newspaper is a good place to start looking for bargain fares, but be sure to read the fine print on restrictions and cancellation procedures. Start looking early; some popular bargain fares are fully booked by May.

After a short period of decline due to cut-rate fares on scheduled flights, **charter flights** are again emerging as the most economical option. Rules governing charters were recently liberalized, so on most charters you can now book up to the last minute (though most flights fill up well in advance of the departure date). Charters do not permit flexibility; you must choose your departure and return dates when you book, and you lose all or almost all of your money if you cancel your ticket. In addition, charter companies reserve the right to change the dates of your flight, cancel the flight, and add fuel surcharges after you have made your final payment. Beware of fares that sound too good to be true, as not all charter companies are entirely honest or reliable. A good travel agent can help you choose a charter wisely and will usually try to find you protection against a cancelled flight or a last-minute change of date.

CIEE, the granddaddy of the charter scene, has been offering dependable service out of New York and the West Coast for years. It is the largest U.S. charter operator (twice weekly from May until October) to Paris. Their charters are extremely popular, so make your reservation as early as possible. For prices and schedules tel. (212) 661-1414. Tickets are available from March— naturally you save by flying before peak-season. Travac and the Davis Agency are also among the more reliable charter companies. There are countless other companies of varying degrees of dependability; just be certain you know what you're getting for your money and always read the fine print on the contract before making your final payment.

For the last-minute traveler or for those who don't want to commit themselves to a set schedule, the cheapest way to go is generally to fly **standby.**

Standby fares have risen substantially since Laker Airline's unfortunate demise (especially fares to London), but during off-season, flying standby can still be a budget-traveler's dream. During high season, however, the dream can turn into a nightmare of uncertainty and frustration, as hordes compete for a diminishing number of available seats. You can purchase standby tickets in advance, but you are not guaranteed a seat on any particular flight. Seat availability is known only on the day of departure, though some airlines will issue predictions (usually erring on the pessimistic side) of your chances of success on a given day. The system of assigning standby seats varies from airline to airline. Get the official story from each company—find out where seats are assigned and what time the office opens. If you want to fly on a particular day, buy a ticket for the earliest departure and keep an eye on other airlines that have competitive fares for standby flights leaving later the same day. In 1982, **Capitol Airways** (to Brussels and Frankfurt) and **Metro International** (to Brussels) offered the cheapest standby fares from New York to the Continent. Another airline to check for good standby fares is **Icelandic** (to Luxembourg). **TWA, British Airways,** and **Northwest Orient** have cheap standby fares from Boston and New York to London.

The **Advanced Booking Excursion Fare (APEX)** is the most flexible of the reduced fares—it provides you with confirmed reservations and is not as restrictive as charters in terms of cancellation penalties and adjusted travel dates. The "open-jaw APEX" will even allow you to return from a different city from the one into which you originally flew. However, APEX does have drawbacks; you must fly back within a specified period of time, usually 7-60 or 22-45 days after leaving; payment is due three to five weeks in advance; and APEX fares are considerably higher in peak-season. Somewhat cheaper "super APEX fares," available on some routes, work in the same way. A $50 cancellation fee applies for both APEX and super-APEX. Book APEX flights early; by early June you may have difficulty getting your desired departure date.

Another option is to investigate unusual airlines that try to undercut the major carriers by offering special bargains on regularly scheduled flights—and to watch for those major carriers who fight back by offering special bargains of their own. Most of these special fares are in effect for short periods only, so watch for advertisements in the pages of the major national newspapers.

The days when you had to travel to New York city for a cheap flight are over. Reasonably direct flights are available from nearly twenty gateway cities scattered across the U.S. Inexpensive flights from Canada are substantially higher than the lowest fares from the States. Otherwise, be sure to investigate flights from Toronto to London offered by the **Canadian University Travel Services,** 44 St. George St., Toronto, Ontario M55 2E4 (tel. (416) 979-2806).

By Boat. If you want to travel in the grand old style and have a few extra days and many extra dollars, the **Cunard Line's Queen Elizabeth 2** still plies the waters between New York and Southampton, calling at Cherbourg in northern France to discharge passengers to the Continent. One-way youth fare (ages 12-26, traveling without parents) for the five-day crossing was $485 last summer, including food, accommodations, and entertainment on board, but not the port tax, which was an extra $45. Availability is limited (only sixteen places are reserved), so write or call early; you'll probably be wait-listed., A $50 deposit is required when booking. Contact Cunard's main office at 555 Fifth Ave., New York, NY 10017 (tel. (800) 221-4770) or consult your travel agent. **Polish Ocean Lines** has crossings between Montreal and London ($610 and up one-way; a 25% discount on round-trip fares). For more information, contact

McLean Kennedy, Ltd., 410 St. Nicholas St., Montreal, Quebec H2Y 2P5. In addition, **freighters** occasionally take on passengers for a trans-atlantic crossing; for a complete list, write for *Ford's Freighter Travel Guide*, 22151 Clarendon St., Woodland Hills, CA 91365.

Travel Within France

By Train

Most European trains are all that American trains are not: fast, punctual, and convenient, with lines stretching to rural areas as well as major cities. An occasional overnight train trip is a good way to save money on accommodations, although you might wish to spend a few extra dollars for a berth in a bunkbed *couchette* car to ensure more than a few snatches of sleep. Bring your own food and drink, which will be much cheaper and tastier than that served in the restaurant cars. If you'll be travelling during a peak period and don't want to risk standing for hours, you should reserve a seat in advance. Otherwise, if you are leaving from a main station and embarking from the train's starting-point, be sure to arrive early; the train will often wait at the platform for a full hour before departure.

Always remember to validate your ticket *(compostez votre billet)* by inserting it in the post-like machine at the entrance to the platforms. Failure to do so could result in a considerable fine. If you break your journey, you must validate your ticket again after your stopover. And always keep your ticket with you, as you may have to present it both during your trip and as you leave the train upon arrival at your final destination.

If you are under 26, you can use **Transalpino BIGE** tickets which cut 20-40%

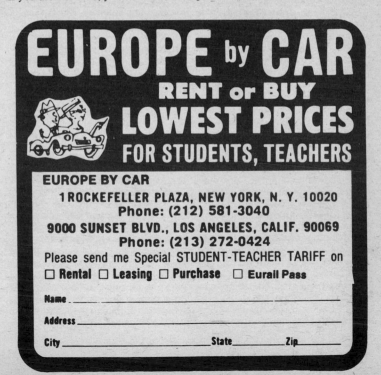

off standard, second-class rail fares to over one-thousand European destinations. Tickets are valid for two months (tickets to Istanbul are valid for six months), and free stopovers along a direct route are allowed, except in Belgium. For example, you can go from Paris to London for about $30. For travel within France you must buy round-trip tickets and have an ISIC card. Transalpino has offices in Paris, Lyon, and Amiens as well as 23 other European cities. The offices in Paris are at 36*bis,* rue de Dunkerque, 9*ème* (tel. 878-05-77), near Gare du Nord, and at 14, rue de Lafayette, 9*ème* (tel. 247-12-40). For information and tickets, write to **Express International, Inc.,** Main St., P.O. Box A, Saltillo, PA 17253 (tel. (814) 448-3941), or to Transalpino Ltd., 71-75 Buckingham Palace Rd., London SW1 (tel. 834-9656).

If you wish to fit a lot of cities and kilometers into your trip, you should consider purchasing a railpass. The **Eurailpass** is valid for unlimited rail travel in all Western European countries, including the Republic of Ireland, but not Great Britain or Northern Ireland.

Those under age 26 can buy the **Eurail Youthpass,** good for one month of second-class travel for $290, or two months for $370. If you are 26 or over, you must purchase the first-class Eurail pass, which costs $260 for 15 days, $330 for 21 days, $410 for one month, $560 for two months, and $680 for three months. You must buy your full or Youth Eurail pass in North America; they are available from a travel agent, CIEE, the Educational Travel Centre, or Harvard Student Agencies. Canadian Universities Travel Services gives a free copy of *Let's Go: Europe* with every Eurailpass they sell.

One possible—if precarious—alternative for those under 26 years of age who are planning to travel hard for a single month, or who are traveling in countries not covered by the Eurailpass, is the **InterRail pass.** It is good for one month of unlimited second-class travel in all countries covered by Eurail, plus Great Britain, Morocco, Yugoslavia, Romania, and Hungary. The pass, sold in major rail stations throughout Europe for approximately $230, is officially for European residents only. This rule is inconsistently enforced, and you can always give the address of a European friend or invent one if you have to. Just remember that you'll be running a risk and that you won't be able to buy a Eurail pass abroad if the InterRail falls through. There is one further catch; the pass gives you only a 50% reduction in the country you buy it in, so you should try to buy it outside of France.

The French National Railroad offers its own rail pass, called **France Vacances,** valid for French trains, 4-7 days unlimited travel on the Paris bus or metro systems, Orly- or Roissy-rail (linking downtown Paris to its airports), a 10% discount on French railroad bus travel throughout France, and admission to the Centre Georges Pompidou in Paris. Last summer, this smorgasbord cost $115 for 7 days, $150 for 15 days, and $230 for a month. You must purchase the Vacances railpass outside of France (it is available from CIEE, Harvard Student Agencies, your travel agent, or from the French National Railroad Office, 610 Fifth Ave., New York, NY 10020 (tel. (212) 582-2110). Since it is rather expensive, decide how many of the fringe benefits you will make use of when comparing it with a Eurail or an InterRail pass.

Other reduced rates are available through **Eurotrain,** a group of nine student organizations in Europe offering point-to-point rail tickets for those under 26 years. The reduction is 30-50% depending on the route, and tickets are valid for up to two months. Eurotrain tickets are sold at local student offices in France or from Eurotrain in Paris. CUTS now sells vouchers that can be redeemed for tickets at the Eurotrain office in Paris.

By Bus

In France, buses are generally used for tour groups or to fill in gaps in the train service rather than for long-distance, inter-city transportation. When buses and trains do cover the same routes, the bus is usually less expensive, if somewhat slower. For information on routes and fares, check at the local *syndicat d'initiative* or *gare routiere* (usually next to the railway station).

Europabus, run by the European Railways, serves major European cities and offers a wide variety of tour packages. For more information, contact Europabus, % German Rail, 747 3rd Ave., New York, NY 10017 (tel. 1-800-223-6036 outside New York State, (212) 308-3100 in New York State only). In France, call the Europabus office at the Gare St.-Lazare in Paris (tel. 293-35-67) or in Nice, at the railway station (tel. 88 89 91).

Magic Bus, an off-beat and often-used company with offices throughout Europe, offers inexpensive transport to major cities in Europe and beyond; the Paris to London run costs approximately $25. For information, contact one of the following offices: 16, rue de Rivoli, Paris 75004 (tel. 27-12-333); 15600, Roscoe Blvd., Van Nuys, CA 91406 (tel. (213) 994-0329); 67 New Oxford St., London WC1 (tel. 836-77-99).

There is also a **Relais Bus Pass** available which gives unlimited travel in France for 15 to 60 days. Contact the Federation Inter-Jeunes France Europe at 218, rue St.-Jacques, Paris 75005, for information on this and other special bus fares.

By Air

Air fares are exorbitant within Europe, but there are two types of less expensive (although not cheap) flights that can save you hours of grueling train travel.

Student Air Travel Association (SATA) flights are student charters leaving on specified dates. You can book SATA flights through CIEE, CUTS, Harvard Student Agencies, and other student travel offices in the U.S. and abroad (listed in CIEE's *Student Work, Study, Travel Catalog*—see our Useful Addresses section). To qualify, you must be a full-time student under age 30 with a valid ISIC card, or an accompanying spouse or child of an eligible person. Flights are limited, so you should book well in advance.

There are also youth and student fares available on the regularly scheduled flights of most European airlines. **British Airways** and **Air France** offer London-Paris service ($106 in 1982). Air France and Air Inter have many youth discounts on domestic flights. Check at the nearest Air France office to see which of these discount tickets can be purchased in the U.S.

Several charter airlines fly to a wide range of destinations, including several in Africa and Asia. Two of the better-known charter organizations are **Club Partir,** 28, rue du Pont-Louis-Philippe, Paris, 4*ème* (tel. 887-69-77; Metro Pont-Marie) and **Nouvelles Frontiers,** 37, rue Violet, Paris 15*ème* (tel. 578-65-40; Metro Emile-Zola).

By Car

If you are traveling with a companion or in a group, renting or leasing a car may be the most enjoyable way to see France. You won't have to conform to train schedules, and you can get off the main roads and really explore the countryside. On the other hand, you ought to consider the cost of this convenience. Renting costs about $200 per week for a four-seater, not including taxes or deposit, and gas in France runs about $3.50 a gallon. Your car can also be a nuisance in congested cities where parking is expensive. Nevertheless, the cost falls dramatically when three or more people share the expense, making the troubles easier to put up with.

For three weeks or under, the only option is to rent; if you want the car for longer periods, leasing is the most economical plan. Most firms lease to 18-year-olds, while rentals have an age minimum of 21 and up.

Most companies also require that you have a major credit card. Several U.S. firms offer rental and leasing plans in France. Send away for their catalogs, and if you are a student or faculty member, ask whether there are any special discounts. Compare prices carefully; they may vary substantially between firms. Among the major firms renting in the U.S. are **Europe by Car,** 630 Fifth Ave., New York, NY 10020 and 9000 Sunset Blvd., Los Angeles, CA 90069; **Kemwel Group, Inc.,** 106 Calvert St., Harrison, NY 10528; **Foremost Euro-Car,** 5430 Van Nuys Blvd., Van Nuys, CA 91401; and **Driving Abroad Inc.'s France-Auto-Vacances,** 420 Lexington Ave., New York, NY 10017. CIEE, France-Auto-Vacances, and Harvard Student Agencies have discounted rental and leasing plans for students and faculty members.

You can also wait till you get to France to make arrangements. **Avis, Hertz, Eurocar,** and **Solvet** are major companies with agencies all over the world. The **French National Railroad (SNCF)** has a train-plus-car rental package available in about 200 cities which you can also investigate in France. Many firms in the U.S. and France rent campers (sometimes called "motor caravans") overseas, which can also be practical when the cost is split among several people.

Once you have a car, you'll have to adjust to the French road system. The speed limit on the *autoroutes* is 130kph, which means that traffic moves at almost 80mph. Somewhat slower, but no safer due to the driving habits of French motorists, are the *Routes Nationales* which run through towns. For a synopsis of French driving regulations, write to the French Government Tourist Office (see the Useful Addresses section) for the pamphlet *Motoring in France.*

The best road maps are the Michelins, available in book stores and kiosks. The large map, number 989, is especially useful. Stick to the suggested roads (drawn in yellow) which supposedly bypass congested areas.

By Thumb

Hitching in France takes patience. The drivers you meet can be very interesting, but if you are pressed for time or wish to follow a rigid itinerary, you should probably use some other means of transportation. France is among the worst countries for hitching in Europe. Getting out of big cities such as Lyon, or traveling along the Riviera can be almost impossible.

The system of primary roads consists of *Autoroutes* (designated by A) and the *Routes Nationales* (the N roads). For long-distance rides the autoroutes are best, but you must stand on the entrance ramp to get a ride. Traffic on the nationales is generally short range, consisting of cars going from one small town to the next. If you are more interested in the experience than in where you are going, the nationales are the best bet.

It is simply not safe for a woman to hitch alone in France. Two women are safer; one male and one female is probably the safest and most reliable combination. A man alone may encounter difficulties as well (both in getting picked up and in not getting picked up). But whatever the case, you should refuse rides in the back of a two-door-car. Don't lock the door and keep your luggage handy—don't let it be thrown in the trunk if you can avoid it. In an emergency, open the car door. This usually surprises the driver enough to make him slow down. In any case, if you start feeling uneasy about the ride for any reason—and this applies to men as well—get out at the first opportunity or firmly demand to be let out.

The lighter you travel, the better your luck will be. Pick a place where the driver can stop easily and can get back on the road safely. A destination sign may help you get longer rides and avoid the ten-minute lifts. You may be able to find rides (or hitching companions) by checking message boards in student travel offices or in student gathering places.

ALLOSTOP, 65, passage Brady, Paris 10ème (tel. 246-00-66), with offices in Strasbourg, Toulouse, Bordeaux Lyon, Marseille, and elsewhere in France, is a service which brings together drivers with riders who share expenses. For would-be passengers, the service costs 28F for a single trip or 100F for unlimited use of the service for a year; the fee for drivers is 30F annually. Telephone a few days in advance, if you can.

By Moped

Mopeds (and their ancestors, motorized bicycles) have long been popular for short-distance transport in Europe and are just beginning to catch on in the U.S. The reason—their great fuel economy and the fact that Europeans have always paid over twice what Americans have paid for gasoline. Mopeds offer a wonderful way to tour the countryside, particularly where there's little automobile traffic. They cruise at about 35mph, and are easily put on trains and ferries. But unless you want to have a close encounter with a hospital, play it extremely safe on a moped; they're dangerous in the rain and on rough roads or gravel. You should not ride them wearing a backpack, and you'd be wise to wear a helmet. Some other drawbacks of mopeds; the spark plugs need frequent attention, you can't carry much luggage, and long journeys are tiresome. But mopeds can still be a good compromise—especially for the solo traveler—between the high cost of car travel and the limited range of bicycling. Rental runs about 55F per day from many bicycle and motorcycle shops.

By Bicycle

Cycling is an excellent way to see the countryside and endear yourself to the French. Ride on the backroads and early in the morning or evening when you have the road to yourself and it's still cool. You need special preparation for a short, afternoon cruise, but some advance planning for longer tours is absolutely necessary.

French roads, with a wealth of well-paved minor routes, are generally fine for cyclists. Avoid the main roads (marked in red on Michelin maps) in favor of the secondary roads (marked in yellow) or the local roads (marked in white). The Michelin green guides are useful, with information on the areas you will be passing through, and are available in bookstores throughout France. In addition to your Michelin maps, you may want the larger-scale and more expensive (12F) maps from the **Institut National Geographique (IGN).** Outstanding touring regions include: the Loire Valley, Normandy, Brittany, Provence, the Massif Central, and the somewhat mountainous Jura. In the Pyrénées and the Alps, you can often take a train up the mountains and then cycle down.

For touring information, first consult the tourist bureau annexed to most French embassies, or the **Office de Tourisme de Paris,** 127, Champs Elysées, 75008 Paris. The **Fédération Francaise de Cyclotourisme,** 8, rue Jean-Marie Jego, 75013 Paris, is a non-profit, member-supported liaison between 2000 cycling clubs of France. Although they are not a travel agency or tourist information bureau, they will advise foreign cyclists on a limited and friendly basis. The **Cyclist's Touring Club**, Cotterell House, 69 Meadrow, Godalming, Surrey GU27 3HS, U.K., offers annual membership for £10 (age 21 and over), £6 (18-21), or £4 (under 18). They can provide members with an information sheet on France, route sheets for popular touring areas in France, and a dictionary of French mechanical terms for bicycles, among other services.

For the last few years it has been possible to count a bicycyle as your second free piece of luggage on transatlantic flights, but policies vary. Some airlines will have you fit the bike into a crate (which involves removing the pedals and front wheel); carry a wrench to the airport and know how to make adjustments on the spot if necessary. French threads and rim sizes differ from English sizes, but bicycles made in Italy and England are becoming more popular, and spare parts in English sizes are available in many towns. Even so, you ought to carry one or two extra inner tubes and a spare tire if you plan on a long ride, and tape a few spokes to the body. You can buy an excellent bicycle in France and have it shipped back home (see the Paris Shopping section for information on sales tax rebates), but if you do, make sure you get one fitted for export, as French parts are even harder to find in the U.S. than English ones are in France.

Once in France, you can easily combine biking with train travel. Regardless of how far you go, it costs 18F to register a bicycle as baggage for transport. On some trains, you can check the bicycle car into the baggage car *(fourgon)* yourself for free: inquire at the train station.

You can rent bicycles in many of the larger towns, and it is usually possible to get a serviceable ten-speed model. **Paris-Vélo**, rue du Fer-à-Moulin (tel. 337-59-22) and **Loca-Cycles**, 3, rue du Vieux Colombier, are good places to try in Paris. The French National Railroad provides a service called Train + Bicycle through 121 railroad stations in France. With a valid passport and a 150F deposit, you can rent a one-speed (only occasionally a five-speed) bicycle. When you return the bicycle to any participating station, you pay 20F for a full day or 14F for a half day.

If you have never done any cycling before, take it slowly at first (about 30km the first day). Although biking offers the chance to make real contact with the countryside, there is always a temptation to treat the ride as an end in itself.

By Foot

If you have more time than money and prefer countryside to monuments, you may be interested in hiking France's extensive network of long-distance footpaths. The **Fédération Française de la Randonnée Pedestre**, 92 de Clignancourt, 75883 Paris (tel. 259-60-40) provides topographical maps *(topo-guides)* for 32,000km of footpaths. Huts or mountain hostels which usually serve meals are staggered along many of the suggested routes. The member organizations of the Fédération organize group trips through the countryside.

Proper hiking gear is essential. Lightweight, leather hiking boots with sturdy rubber soles are the most critical item, though in summer you can get by with good sneakers if you're not in the mountains. You will also need a warm sweater, a water-proof poncho, a change of socks, long pants (in addition to your shorts), and a comfortable pack with a hip belt (see the Camping section for advice on backpacks). Depending on how far away from restaurants you'll be, you may want to carry a light butane or white gas stove and a mess kit.

To find out about climbing in France, contact the **Club Alpin Francais**, 7, rue la Boetié, 75008 Paris (tel. 742-36-77). The club runs several centers in the Alps which provide instruction in Alpine technique.

By Boat

France has more than seven thousand miles of navigable rivers, canals, lakes, and sea coast. To float through the countryside or take better advantage of your time at the seaside, contact the **Syndicat National des Loueurs de Bateaux de Plaisance**, Port de la Bourdonnais, 75007 Paris (tel. 555-10-49). They'll set you up in whatever region and boat (canoes to yacht cruiseboats to dinghies) interests you. **Nautic Voyage**, 8, rue de Milan, 75009 Paris (tel. 280-04-96 or 526-60-80) can arrange the rental of a houseboat. For information on routes and waterways suitable for canoeing, contact the **Fédération Francaise de Canoe-Kayak**, 87, quai de la Marne, 94340 Joinville (tel. 889-31-31) or the **Group du Canoe-Kayak, Touring Club de France**, 6-8, rue Firmin-Gillot, 75737 Paris (tel. 532 22-15).

Accommodations

Hostels

Most French Youth Hostels are operated by the **Fédération Unie des Auberges de Jeunesse,** the French branch of the **International Youth Hostel Federation (IYHF)**. In each Accommodations section, *Let's Go* distinguishes between IYHF-affiliated "Youth Hostels" or "Hostels," and non-IYHF "youth hostels" or "hostels." To stay in an IYHF Hostel, you will need to become a member of the International Youth Hostel Federation. The IYHF card costs $14 ($15 in Canada) for those age 18 or older, $7 ($9 in Canada) for those younger than 18, and $21 ($30 in Canada) for a family membership. You can get one from the American Youth Hostel Association in most major cities, or from the **AYH headquarters** at 1132 'I' St., NW, Suite 800, Washington, DC 20005 (tel. (800) 424-9426), or the **Canadian Hosteling Association** at Place Vanier, Tower A, 333 River Rd., Vanier City, Ottawa, Ont. KIL 8B9. You can get an IYHF card in France at the Paris office of any Hostel. The very useful *International Youth Hostel Handbook*, vol. I (available from AYH for $7.50) details locations of each Hostel in Europe and the Mediterranean countries and includes a basic map. For a more detailed list of Hostels in France, which includes the dates each Hostel is open and many helpful maps, contact the Fédération Unie des Auberges de Jeunesse at 6, rue Mesnil, 75116 Paris (tel. 261-84-03; Metro Victor-Hugo).

A night in a French Youth Hostel, or **auberge de jeunesse,** is roughly half the price of a hotel stay—prices range from 13.50F to 22.50F, with breakfast an additional 7F. Accommodations usually consist of bunk beds in single-sex dormitories, and most Hostels either serve evening meals or have kitchen facilities that you can use. Quality varies widely; some Hostels are extremely well-kept and well-situated, while others are in run-down barracks far from the center of town.

Hostel life has its drawbacks: an early curfew (10 to 11pm for most Hostels, midnight to 2am for those in Paris), lack of privacy, prohibitions against smoking and drinking, a lock-out from 10am to 5pm, a three-day limit to your stay, and hordes of vacationing school-children. But the prices can't be beat, and many Hostels fill quickly in July and August. Only some Hostels accept reservations—it's a good idea to try, in any case—so arrive early, if you can.

All Hostels require sheet sleeping sacks, which they rent or sell for a nominal cost. You can also make your own from a folded white sheet sewn shut on two sides (at least 2'7" wide and 7' long, including a 13½" pocket to cover the Hostel's pillow and a 1'11½" flap to protect the blanket). If you intend to bring a sleeping bag, make sure it fits inside the sleeping sack.

A smaller network of youth hostels is run by the **Ligue Francaise pour les Auberges de la Jeunesse (LFAJ)**, 38, blvd. Raspail 75007 Paris, 7ème (tel. 548-69-84). These are more expensive, about 22-25F per night, but the hostels are often in excellent hiking or skiing regions. An LFAJ membership costs 20F and is available from the Paris office (minimum age 14 years).

Hotels

French hotels can be a bargain, and rates are generally lower in the country-side than in cities. The French government uses a star-system for classifying hotels: 4L (luxury), 4, 3, 2, 1. Most hotels listed in *Let's Go* are one-star or unclassified, though sometimes we list two-star establishments with inexpensive rooms. Expect to pay 40 to 60F for a single and 50 to 70F for a double. Frequently, hotels offer only rooms with a double bed, which rent for the same amount whether one or two persons occupy them. Likewise, doubles are often equipped with two double beds which can accommodate three or four.

When looking at hotels, remember that in France the ground floor is called the *rez-de-chausée,* and the second floor is called the first *(premier étage).*

Most hotels serve a *petit déjeuner obligatoire,* a required breakfast, which costs 9 to 13F. Since the local cafes also serve croissants and coffee for fewer francs, you may want to opt out of breakfast, if possible.

If you plan to visit a popular tourist area, especially during a festival, it is advisable to make a hotel reservation by letter. (Be sure to include an International Reply Coupon for a prompt reply by airmail.)

Camping

Camping liberates you from hostel regulations and drab hotels. There are campgrounds all over France, and many are situated by lakes, rivers, or the ocean. Be aware, however, that the vacationing French often arrive at campgrounds with their trailers, radios, and a great deal of cooking paraphernalia—and there usually isn't much space between sites. In August you might have to arrive well before 11am to insure yourself a spot.

French campgrounds, like hotels and restaurants, are classified by a star system. The fewer the stars, the fewer the amenities and the cheaper the site. Three- and four-star sites are usually large, grassy campgrounds with hot showers, bathrooms, a restaurant, or store, and often a lake or swimming pool nearby. Occasional student discounts are offered to those with student ID's.

You might want to combine lightweight camping with bicycling. Pace yourself so that you will arrive at your next destination by late afternoon, since you will have to move on to another campground if there is no vacancy.

It is also possible to camp unofficially. Any inconspicuous plot of ground will do. (Within sight of a farmhouse you should ask permission.) Leave the site just as spotless as you found it, both for the sake of the landowners and for those who will follow in your path.

In addition to your backback, you will need only three items for camping; a sleeping bag; an ensolite pad; and a tent, tarpaulin, or bivouac sac to protect you from the rain or heavy dew. The **sleeping bag** need not be down; Polarguard or a good synthetic fiber is almost as warm and, more importantly, dries much more quickly than down. For three-season camping (spring, summer, fall), a 2½-pound down bag ($130 and up) or a 3½-pound synthetic bag ($95 and up) should be more than adequate. At an average of $9, an ensolite pad (much warmer than foam rubber) is a real bargain, providing crucial protection from a cold, damp, and often rocky ground. Good tents have become very expensive, however, ($120 and up for a two-person nylon tent with a rain fly), but are a sound investment. In the U.S., **Eastern Mountain Sports,** with locations mainly in the Northeast, has quality camping equipment at very reasonable prices. Send for their mail-order catalog to Eastern Mountain Sports, Inc., Vose Farm Rd., Peterborough, NH 03458.

Backpack. Purchase your pack before you leave—American packs are generally more durable and comfortable than European makes, and often less expensive. Backpacks come with either an external frame or an internal X- or A-shaped frame. If your load is not extraordinarily heavy and you plan to use the pack mainly as a suitcase, an internal-frame model is preferable. It will be less cumbersome and awkward, which is especially important if you'll be hitching or traveling on crowded trains, and will be less likely to be mangled by the airlines or rough handling. A good pack costs at least $100.

Student Accommodations

Short-term accommodations are available during the summer in the dormitories of most French universities. We list the addresses of the **Centre Regional des Oeuvres Universitaires (CROUS)** offices for many universities (see Study section). Those interested in summer housing can also contact the Cité Internationale Universitaire de Paris, 19, blvd. Jourdan, 75014 Paris (tel. 589-68-52).

Foyers, youth halls of residence, are a good bet in Paris. These single-sex dormitories require a three-night minimum stay. You can find a bed through the **Accueil des Jeunes en France,** opposite the Pompidou Museum at 119, rue St.-Martin, Paris, 4*ème* (tel. 277-87-80; Metro Rambuteau); at the main concourse of the Gare du Nord, facing platform 19 (tel. 285-86-19); or at the Hotel de Ville, 16, rue du Pont Louis-Philippe, 4*ème* (tel. 278-04-82; Metro Hotel de Ville). According to one of A.J.F.'s leaflets, "these three offices guarantee that they will find every young traveler who visits one of them decent and low-cost lodging with immediate reservation." AJF runs four youth hotels in the center of Paris. One offers shared rooms at 30F per night, the other three at 46F, breakfast included. AJF also provides valuable information about jobs, courses, budget travel, sports events, and cultural holidays in France.

Alternative Accommodations

For a rural experience, **Logis** and **Auberges de France,** found off the main roads or between towns, are hotels and restaurants roughly comparable to country inns. The food is usually excellent, the accommodations reasonably priced and comfortable. Any tourist office will provide a list for the region that will enable you to plan a stop along your route and in line with your budget. To obtain a booklet giving a list of these establishment write to **La Féderation Nationale des Logis de France,** 25, rue Jean-Mermoz, 75008 Paris (tel. 359-86-67).

Gites de France are also rural accommodations—furnished lodgings in farm houses, cottages, small villages, even campsites—conforming to fixed standards of comfort, facilities, and price. They are intended especially for stays of two weeks or more, particularly in areas where you might hike, sail, or ski. The **Fédération des Gites de France,** 35 rue Godot de Mauroy, Paris, 9*ème* (tel. 742-25-43) handles inquiries and dispenses booklets on each region.

Monasteries can be an alternative for those seeking spiritual solace. Those interested should write for reservations in advance. For a list of the monasteries in France, write to Repertoire de l'Hospitalité Monastique, Abbaye St.-Martin, 86240, and enclose ten IRC's to cover postage.

International Host Organizations

Servas is a membership organization devoted to promoting understanding among people of different cultures. Traveler members may stay free of charge in host members' homes in eighty countries. You are asked to contact hosts in advance, and be willing to fit into the household routine. Stays are limited to two nights unless you are invited to stay longer. Prospective traveler members are interviewed, and are asked to contribute $30 and a refundable $15 fee. You then receive a directory of host members in countries you will be visiting, with short self-descriptions of those listed. Write Servas at 11 John St., Room 406, New York, NY 10038.

Similar to Servas, **Travelers' Directory,** prints a semiannual registry of its members, which lists names, addresses, ages, interests, and specific offers of hospitality to other members of the organization. Membership is primarily North American and Western European, and you must be willing to host other members in your home. The donation for annual membership for those living in North America is $15 ($20 outside North America). Write Travelers' Directory at 6224 Baynton St., Philadelphia, PA 19144

Work

Finding work in France is extremely difficult. With unemployment so high, the French government is understandably wary of hiring foreign workers; before you can obtain a work permit, your employer must be able to convince the French Ministry of Labor that there is no native capable of filling your position. Even when a foreigner is being considered, Common Market country members get priority. If you're a specialist in a needed field—a computer expert, a doctor, a teacher—you may have better luck.

Except for *au pair* jobs, it is illegal for foreign students to hold term-time jobs. Students registered at French universities may get work permits for the summer with a valid visa, a student card from a French university, and proof of a job. But if you have not spent the year in a French university and are seeking summer employment, you have other sources available to you. The fact sheet *Employment in France* put out by the **Cultural Services of the French Embassy,** 972 Fifth Ave., New York, NY 10021 (tel. (212) 570-4400), gives basic information about work in France and also lists government-approved organizations through which foreign students must get their jobs. CIEE is the only U.S. organization so approved. If you are a full-time student, a resident U.S. citizen, and have a good working knowledge of French (at least two years of college French), CIEE will issue you a summer work permit for $60. Under this system, you do not need a job prior to obtaining a work permit. Once you have the permit, you are on your own, as CIEE's Work Abroad Program does not place people overseas.

Nevertheless, CIEE does offer helpful advice on where to start your job search. Their *Whole World Handbook* ($5.95, including postage), which is available in bookstores or from any CIEE office, gives leads but not individual job listings. For specific opportunities, consult CIEE's *Emplois d'Eté en France* ($7.95 plus $1.50 postage) or *The Directory of Overseas Summer Jobs* ($7.95 plus $1.50 postage, available from CIEE or from Writer's Digest Books, 9933 Alliance Rd., Cincinnati, OH 45242), which lists 50,000 openings world-wide, volunteer and paid, with firms that ask to be included. Once in France, check the help-wanted columns in the newspapers, including the English-language *International Herald Tribune.* In Paris, there are also bulletin boards with job listings at the Alliance Francaise, 101 blvd. Raspail, 75006 Paris, and at the American Cathedral, 23, ave. George V, 75008 Paris.

When writing to a French employer, send a cover letter, resume, and two International Reply Coupons to guarantee a rapid reply by airmail.

A number of programs offer practical experience for people with technical and business skills. **AIESEC-US**, 622 Third Ave. New York, NY 10017, organizes an exchange program that places qualified students in management positions including marketing, accounting, and computer science. All positions pay a stipend to cover living expenses. Applications are accepted in early January only from students at colleges with AIESEC membership. (Canadians should write to **AIESEC-Canada**, 1411 Crescent St. Suite 408, Montreal, Quebec H3G 2B3. The **Association for International Practical Training (AIPT)** offers on-the-job training for agriculture, architecture, math, engineering, and science students who have completed two years at an accredited four-year institution. Apply by December 15 for summer placement, six months in advance for other placement, to IAESTE Program, % AIPT, 217 American City Bldg., Columbia, MD 21044. (Canadians should write to IAESTE-Canada, P.O. Box 1473, Kingston, Ont. K7L 5C7.

Summer positions as group leaders are available with **American Youth Hostels (AYH)** and with the **Experiment in International Living (EIL)**, Brattleboro, VT 05301. For either, the minimum age is 21. AYH requires a week-long leadership course, and you must lead a group in America before taking one to Europe. EIL requires leadership ability and extensive overseas experience. Applications are due by early December.

Teaching positions are another possibility. The French government, in cooperation with the **Institute of International Education (IIE, 809 U.N. Plaza,** New York, NY 10017) dispenses forty assistantships through an annual competition to graduating seniors and others with a B.A. from an American university. With a masters degree you may be able to find an assistantship yourself. Write to the U.S. Department of Education, 400 Maryland Ave. SW, Washington, DC, and International Schools Services, P.O. Box 5910, Princeton, NJ 08540.

There are several opportunities for volunteer work. The **Service Civil International**, 129, rue du Faubourg Poissoniere, 75009 Paris (tel. 874-60-15), runs various work camps throughout France. For work in the great outdoors, try a *vacance en chantier*—a work camp geared towards young people interested in improving the environment or reconstructing old buildings. Write to **Etudes et Chantiers**, 33, Campagne Premiere, 75014 Paris (te. 322-15-61) for more information about their year-round programs in France. You might also try **Club de Vieux Manoir**, 10, rue de la Cossonnerie, 75001 Paris, which works to restore historical churches, castles, and fortresses throughout France. The Club offers summer- and year-long programs, and anyone over 15 years of age is eligible to apply. The application fee is $5. If working on an **archeological dig** interests you, contact **Le Conservateur**, Musee de Nogent-sur-Seine, 10400 Nogent-sur-Seine, France. M.Piette offers volunteer work during the summer from July 4 to the end of the month or from August 1 to August 15. There is a registration fee of 50F for insurance and subscription to the archeological club.

If you like wine and hard work, then the fall grape harvest may be for you. You get little more than transportation, room, and board, but it's worth it. In Paris, contact the **Centre d'Information et de Documentation Jeunesse (CIDJ)**, 101, quai Branly, 75015 Paris (tel. 566-40-20; Metro Bir-Hakeim). There are also agencies listed in the Burgundy and Bordeaux sections of *Let's Go*.

And then there is always the old standby, *au pair* work. The positions are primarily reserved for single young women aged 18 to 30 (though some men are employed) with a minimum knowledge of French. The au pair is responsible for helping his or her French family by taking care of the children and helping with light housework for five or six hours each day (one day off per week), while taking courses at a school for foreign students or a French university. You'll receive room, board, and a small monthly stipend. Always determine the details of pay and obligation *before* settling in with your family, and contact the local police for a residency permit within one week after arriving in France. The **Cultural Services of the French Embassy** offer a detailed information sheet on au pair jobs. Organizations recommended for placement in au pair positions include: **Acceuil Familial des Jeunes Etrangers** (requires a six-month commitment), 23, rue du Cherche-Midi, 75006 Paris (tel. 222-50-34); **Amitié Mondial,** 39, rue Cambon, 70001 Paris (tel. 260-99-68); and **L'ARCHE,** 7, rue Barque, 75015 Paris (tel. 273-34-39).

Study

Studying in France can be more than a simple extension of your American education; it is also a chance to participate in an educational system radically different from your own. The strengths and weaknesses you observe in the French system will teach you a great deal about French culture and values. The emphasis of a French education is on preparing students for a series of standard examinations they must pass in order to proceed from one level of instruction to the next. Courses are demanding and strictly regimented. As a result, the French student seems to command an awesome store of factual information. But if you find such people enviable or intimidating, remember this—French students are far less comfortable with abstract or revisionist thinking, and they have had far fewer opportunities to develop their own interests outside of class or to shape their own curriculum.

A good place to start investigating different programs for study abroad is *The Whole World Handbook* (see the Work section). The Institute of International Education (see the Work section) prints several useful publications, including *Basic Facts on Foreign Study,* which covers everything from Visas to tax returns; *Vacation Study Abroad* ($8, plus $.75 postage), which lists unusual semester programs; and *U.S. College-Sponsored Programs Abroad: Academic Year* ($8 plus $.75 postage), a thorough guide to university-level study in Europe, with information on scholarships and work opportunities. *Study Abroad* (23rd edition, 1981-83, $12.95 from UNESCO) Publication Center, 345 Park Avenue. S., New York, NY 10010) lists fellowships, scholarships, and awards for study and travel opportunities. For free pamphlets and much useful advice about study in France, contact the Cultural Services of the French Embassy (see the Work section).

Perhaps the most intellectually challenging and culturally rewarding way to study in France is to enroll as a regular student in a French university. Furthermore, as tuition is low in France (at least by American standards), you may cut your overall college costs by spending a year abroad. For details on application procedures, contact the cultural services office at the closest French consulate or embassy. The application period is between February and May of the year in which you wish to attend.

As a student registered in a French university, you will be given a student card *(carte d'étudiant)* by your school upon presentation of your residency permit (see the Visas section) and a receipt for your university fees. In addition to the student benefits to which the *carte d'étudiant* entitles you, there are also many benefits administered by the **Centre Regional des Oeuvres Universitaires et Scolaires (CROUS)**. This division of the *Oeuvres Universitaires*, founded in 1955 to improve the living and working conditions of the students in its membership, welcomes foreign students. A CROUS card entitles you to subsidized student rates for restaurants, accommodations, and various social and cultural services. The card is issued annually by the nearest CROUS office. In Paris, the Regional centre is at 39, ave. Georges-Bernanos, 75231 (tel. 329-12-43). The Paris address of the Service d'Accueil des Étudiants Etrangers (CROUS foreign students welcome center) is 6, rue Jean-Calvin, 75005 (tel. 331-56-54). Also, write for their helpful guidebook, *I'm Going to France* (20F).

Another way to study in France is to enroll in a year-abroad program run by an American university. If you want to meet French students and experience French culture, however, be wary of American university-sponsored programs that cater mainly to Americans; you may find them little different from studying in the U.S.

If your main object is to learn the language—and there's no place like France for learning French—you might wish to investigate an institute for foreigners run by a French university or special language courses offered by various institutions. After all, there's no place like France to learn French. The **Alliance Francaise, École Internationale de Langue et de Civilisation Francaises,** 75006 Paris (tel. 544-38-28; Métro Notre-Dame-des-Champs or Métro Rennes), is the best-known, cheapest, and least intimidating language school in Paris. It is open all year, gives classes at all levels, and lets students start on the first and fifteenth of every month. The main problem with the Alliance is that most classes progress very slowly, since in any given class of twenty students about fifteen different nationalities are represented. The school building, with a student restaurant and book store, is filled with students of all ages throughout the day, and there are bulletin boards with news of vacant apartments and temporary employment prospects.

The **Institut Catholique de Paris,** 21, rue d'Assas, 75270 Paris (Métro St.-Placide), also has classes at all levels, though their schedule is less flexible than the Alliance's: students must register for three months, although there is a summer course.

The **Sorbonne** has been giving its French Civilization course for a long time. As well as an academic year course (which can be taken by the semester), the Sorbonne has four-, six-, and eight-week courses, with both civilization and language classes at various levels and a special course in commercial French. In all, approximately 2500 students enroll each semester. Write to: Cours de Civilisation Francaise, 47, rue des Ecoles, 75005 Paris. If you are in Paris, see: Sécretariat des Cours de Civilisation Francaise, 17, rue de la Sorbonne, Galerie Richelieu (tel. 329-12-13, ext. 3858).

Orientation to France

Avoiding Trouble

Simple caution should allow you to hold on safely to your possessions. Take the precautions that you would take in any large American city. Professional thieves tend to frequent public transportation lines and large, crowded streets, often diverting their victims with street acts or card games while an accomplice picks pockets. Carrying money and valuables in a pouch around your neck or in a money belt is one precaution, though you should avoid carrying large sums of money with you in any case. Always keep travelers checks separate from their identifying numbers, and keep a separate record of your passport number. Save receipts for all railpass and airline ticket purchases, too. If robbed, contact the local police and the nearest American embassy immediately.

Women traveling in France—especially those traveling alone—will experience more problems than men. A woman cannot expect to hitchhike and stay in rock-bottom hotels with the ease and safety of a man; she will probably end up spending 25% more on accommodation and transport than he would. Forego cheap dives and city outskirts in favor of university accommodations in a youth hostel or a foyer (in some cities, you can obtain a list of all-women foyers from the tourist office), and remember that centrally-located accommodations are usually safest and easiest to get back to at night. In general, two women traveling together will be safer, as will a woman traveling with a man.

The major tourist areas of Paris are reasonably safe at night; in fact, if you don't venture out in the evenings you'll miss a major reason for being in Paris. Avoid empty Métro stations late at night, and never enter an unoccupied–subway car. In particular, steer clear of the Bois de Boulogne at dusk, when most of the action is illegal, and the Place Pigalle and Madeleine districts after dark.

Foreign women in France, especially Americans, are frequently beset by unwanted and tenacious admirers. French men in the presence of foreign women often try to bank on their suave image, and their advances can become unpleasant. Be warned: you cannot change an entire culture in one short visit, and you shouldn't waste your time trying. Your best answer to harrassment is no answer at all, since street admirers are often encouraged by the slightest sign. Seek out a policeman (or a passer-by) before a crisis erupts, and don't hesitate to scream for help. (It's a good idea to carry enough extra money for a phone call, bus, or taxi, in case you feel threatened.) The Practical Information section for every large city lists emergency, police, and consulate phone numbers.

Sensitivity to a culture can often prevent threatening situations from arising. Cut-offs (in fact, shorts in general), T-shirts, and halter tops advertise your nationality and invite unwanted attention. Watch the behavior and dress of the local women and follow their example.

Health and Insurance

Before you go, check your insurance policy (or your parents' if it includes you) to see whether it includes medical care abroad. Many university health plans cover foreign travel. If yours doesn't, you may want to purchase a short-term policy for your trip. (Remember that your ISIC card provides you with $1000 accident and sickness insurance from the time you purchase it through December 31, 1983.) CIEE has an inexpensive plan including medical treatment and hospitalization, accidents, lost baggage, and even missing a charter flight due to illness.

Canadian health insurance plans generally cover foreign travel, but the details vary from province to province. Check with the provincial Ministry of Health for details.

A self-assembled traveler's kit should include soap (both mild and antiseptic), an extra pair of eyeglasses, multiple vitamins, aspirin, sunscreen, something for diarrhea, something for motion sickness, some antibiotic, and bandages.

If you know that you will require medication while you travel, obtain a full supply before you leave, since matching your prescription with a foreign equivalent is not always safe or even possible. (It is a good idea to leave your medicine or eyeglass prescriptions with a friend at home so they can be filled in the U.S. and sent over to you if necessary.) You should always carry your written, up-to-date prescriptions and/or a statement from your doctor, especially if you will be carrying insulin, syringes, or any narcotic drug. Finally, keep all vital medicines in your carry-on bag when traveling to ensure a constant supply if your luggage is lost.

Few areas of France are so isolated that you will have to worry about finding competent medical help in an emergency. Keep in mind, however, that your best chance of finding a good doctor (and the comfort of an English-speaking one) may well be at the emergency room of a university hospital. A list of English-speaking doctors world-wide is obtainable from the **International Association for Medical Assistance to Travelers (IAMAT)**, 350 Fifth Ave., Suite 5620, New York, NY 10001 (tel. (212) 279-6465).

Travelers with a medical problem or condition that cannot easily be recognized (e.g. diabetes, allergies to antibiotics, epilepsy, heart conditions) should seriously consider obtaining a Medic Alert identification tag. This internationally recognized emblem communicates vital information in emergency situations. In addition to indicating the nature of the medical problem, the tag provides the number of Medic Alert's 24-hour hot-line, through which attending medical personnel can obtain information about the member's medical history. Membership is $15; write to Medic Alert Foundation International, P.O. Box 1009, Turlock, CA 95381 or (tel. (209) 668-3333).

Travel for the Disabled

The physically disabled person can enjoy travel with the proper precautions and some careful advance planning. Try to make arrangements with your airline or hotel well ahead of time, and specify exactly what you are unable to do and what you need. If you give these places time to prepare and then check personally that the arrangements have been carried through, you should have no problem.

Air travel is becoming more accessible and less threatening to the disabled traveler. Try to find out in advance what sort of facilities are available at airports here and abroad. Your airline may require a traveling companion or doctor's letter certifying to your flying fitness. If you have a wheelchair, find out if there are airlines whose bathroom doors will accommodate your chair. If you normally use a battery-powered wheelchair, consider traveling with a manual one instead (they're easier to transport), or at least get a non-spillable battery. Make your flight more comfortable by ordering ahead for special foods to meet your dietary restrictions. Most airlines offer anything from low cholesterol to hypoglycemic meals.

Cruise travel is a good, if costly, alternative to flying. When you choose a ship line, ask about ramps, doorways, and special services. Most ships require a doctor's letter of reference.

Blind travelers with seeing-eye dogs must be sure to have a current certificate of the animals' rabies, distemper, and contagious hepatitus innoculations, as well as a veterinarian's letter attesting to the dogs' health.

Planning your itinerary will be much simpler if you have a guide of access to the regions you intend to visit. These booklets describe what a city or area offers in the way of accessible hotels, restaurants, toilets, campsites, theaters, and other sights. One of the most helpful sources of information for planning your trip is the *1982-83 International Directory of Access Guides*, which tells you where to get accessibility guides to facilities in 25 countries around the world. For a free copy of the booklet, write to Travel Survey Dept., Rehabilitation International USA, Dept. TL, 20 W. 40th St., New York, NY 10018. Louise Weiss' book, *Access to the World: A Travel Guide for the Handicapped* (Chatham Square Press, $7.95), is also helpful. To begin touring France, write the Comité National Français de Liaison pour la Réadaption des Handicapés, 38, blvd. Raspail, 75007 Paris, for their book *A Guide to France for Disabled Persons* (32F plus postage). Also try the Association de Paralysés, 27, ave. Mozart, 75016 Paris. For a donation to cover the cost of mailing, the Pauline Hephaistos Survey Projects group will send you a guide to Paris and several French regions detailing hotel and hostel accommodations and access to points of interest. Write to them at 39 Bradley Gardens, West Ealing, London W13, England. Another useful book, the *Disabled Traveler's International Phrasebook*, is available for £1 from the Disability Press, 1 Farthing Grove, Nettlefield, Milton Keynes, MK6 4JP England.

Once you've arrived in France, consider traveling by rail. Write to the French National Railroad, 610 Fifth Ave., New York, NY 10020 and ask for their list of train stations which accommodate wheelchairs. There is a special service provided by the SNCF (with a specialized train compartment and an escalator for boarding) available only between Paris and Brest, Toulouse, or Nice, but it is worth writing to the train station at your particular destination to alert the conductor as to your specific needs. In Paris, travel by Métro is made more possible by the wider seats reserved for the handicapped, although many stations have stairs rather than escalators or elevators.

Drugs

If you're caught with any quantity of drugs in France, you'll be kicked out of the country immediately. Never bring anything across borders. International express trains are not as safe as they might seem: you and your belongings may be searched thoroughly while on board. The assistance available from the U.S. consulates to nationals arrested is minimal: consular officers can visit the prisoner, provide a list of attorneys, and inform family and friends. However, as a State Department bulletin indicates, "U.S. officials cannot ask for or obtain different treatment for American citizens than that given to others under the laws of the country concerned. You're virtually 'on your own' if you become involved, *however innocently*, in illegal drug trafficking."

Staying in Touch

Sending Mail

Between France and the East Coast of the U.S., air mail averages five to seven days and is fairly dependable, although the post services seem to be less careful with postcards. Send mail from the largest postal office in the area. Surface mail is considerably cheaper, but takes one to three months to arrive. It is adequate for getting rid of books or clothing you no longer need in your travels. (Check the Customs section for details about sending things home duty-free.)

If you have no fixed address in France, you can receive mail through American Express or through the post office's Poste Restante (general delivery) service. If you are a customer, American Express will receive and hold mail for up to thirty days (after which they return it to sender). Most big-city American Express offices will hold mail for you free of charge if you have their travelers checks, but some require that you be an American Express Card holder; American Express travel agency representatives in smaller cities are less willing to hold mail, even for customers. If you don't have checks or a card, you may be charged a couple of dollars to pick up whatever mail they've held. Only some offices will forward mail (usually for a fee). A free pamphlet, *Services and Offices*, contains the addresses of American Express offices everywhere, and can be obtained from any branch or from **American Express International Headquarters**, 65 Broadway, New York, NY 10006.

Alternatively, make use of the system of **Poste Restante** for any place in France with a post office. In major cities the central post office handling Poste Restante is open long hours and weekends. You have to pay a nominal fee for every letter received. Forwarding is possible from most post offices to Poste Restante anywhere else in France. Avoid long lines at the *PTT* by purchasing stamps at local *tabacs*.

Telephone and Telegram

You can make phone calls from phone booths, cafes, and post offices with PTT *(Poste, Telegraphe, Telephone)* signs. In cafes, you'll need to purchase a *jeton* (token) from the counter (60c-1F).

You can make intercontinental calls from the post office. The clerk will assign you to a phone from which you can usually dial direct, and will collect your money upon completion of your call. In many towns, you can dial directly overseas from a corner phone booth. If you only have a brief message to deliver and want to avoid the temptation of talking too long, use the payphone; when your coins drop out of sight, the call is over, and the line goes dead. On the other hand, you might find one of the fabled broken phones, which let you talk overseas for hours on a single franc.

An international operator, often English-speaking, is available in large cities by dialing 12. To call long-distance within France, dial 16 and then the appropriate area code, which is listed in the Practical Information section of each town. *En PCV* (pronounced "pay-say-vay") is a collect call, and a call made *avec préavis* is person-to-person.

Telegrams to the U.S. can be sent from any post office in France. Rates are 25F for the first 21 words (the address counts as text) and 3F for each additional word.

Life in France

Food

A Frenchman doesn't eat, he dines. There may be a McDonald's on the Champs Elysées, but fast food is still a fling for foolish youth, not a national habit. Most families shop daily for fresh food, and the idea of eating one's meals from bottles and cans still raises a pitying smile. In a country like this one, you should make food a priority in your budget.

The French breakfast is usually small, consisting of bread (*pain,* sometimes *croissants* or a *brioche*—fancy rolled breads) and *café au lait* (espresso and hot milk). The largest meal of the day is eaten at noon, and most shops and businesses close down for two hours at this time. Dinner begins quite late—many restaurants don't begin serving until 7:30pm—and is also a meal to be lingered over.

Many restaurants offer a *prix fixe* menu, which includes appetizer, main course, and cheese or dessert, and is cheaper than ordering *à la carte*. But two leisurely restaurant meals a day will quickly exhaust any budget. Make a virtue of necessity and assemble a gourmet (yet inexpensive) meal of your own.

Sample the enormous range of cheeses that France has to offer—more than four hundred varieties—and the many delicious *patés*, the cheapest of which is *paté de campagne*. Bread and wine are staples of the French diet; their prices are controlled by the government, so you can afford to indulge with every meal.

You can add items to the basic bread-and-cheese meal as funds and fancy permit. You may have to do some running around to assemble your picnic; the French food industry, unlike the government, is decentralized. A *charcuterie*, the French version of the delicatessen, offers cooked meats, pates, and sausages. *Crémeries* sell the varied dairy products that account for the richness of French cuisine, and your street-corner cremerie will stock over one hundred kinds of cheese, ranging from old favorites like *Camembert* and *Brie* to *Emmenthal* (Swiss cheese), *Boursin*, and the smelly *Boursault*. A *boulangerie* sells bread and some pasteries, while a *patisserie* sells pastry and candy and a *confiserie* sells candy and ice-cream. For the more adventurous, a *boucherie chevaline* sells horse-meat (look for the gilded horse-head over the door); the more timid can stick to familiar steaks and roasts at regular *boucherie*.

If you don't have the patience for gathering your fare in the specialty shops, *supermarchés* do exist. Look for the small foodstore chains like **Monoprix, Prisunic,** and **Felix Potin,** where prices are lower than most. *Epiceries* (grocery stores) also carry staples, wine, produce, and a bit of everything else. But the open-air markets, held at least once a week in every town, village, and market, are the best places to buy fresh fruit, vegetables, fish, and meat. Prices here are usually low, as there may be a half-a-dozen fruit-sellers trying to outdeal one another. If you understand French, pay attention to the colorful sales-patter.

You can also save money by eating strategically. Each region has its specialties, and the cost of certain foods varies from region to region. Eat *camembert* cheese in Normandy and sample seafood on the coast. Crêpes were first folded in Britanny, and are a real bargain there. Wine-based dishes are best in Burgundy (home of *boeuf bourguignon*), whereas vegetable dishes (such as *ratatouille*) can be found in Provence. For heavier German foods, head for Alsace-Lorraine. The southwest of France offers excellent Spanish cuisine, including *paëlla*, a rice-and-seafood specialty.

The café epitomizes the French delight in savoring the moment. Hardly a corner or square in any sizeable city is without one, and the price of a cup of coffee gives you leave to sit and rest, read and write, or just watch life go by. When choosing a cafe, you will be paying in part for its location. Those on a major boulevard with a good view of the crowd can be much more expensive than smaller establishments a few steps down a side street. If you're simply thirsty, go inside to the bar to order your drink—prices are ⅓ to ½ cheaper. Coffee, beer, and *Pernod* (licorice-flavored and alcoholic) are the staple drinks; *citron pressé* (our lemonade—*limonade* is a soda) and *diabolo menthe* (peppermint soda) are among the most popular non-alcoholic choices. This is also the place to have a Coke, if you want one—never have Coke with a meal, unless you're eating at McDonald's—but be prepared to pay twice what you would in America. Cafés are not really suited to cheap eating. A *croque monsieur* (grilled ham-and-cheese sandwich), a *croque madame* (the same with a fried egg), and assorted omelettes cost about 12F, and rarely make a filling meal.

Wine

Wine is one of the great and civilized pleasures of the world. It symbolizes joy, friendship, good living, and romance. French wine production, like

French cooking, is an intricate and regionalized affair, involving great care and hard work. There is an elaborate, often pretentious vocabulary used to describe a wine's appearance, taste, and smell—but you don't have to play that game. Wine-tasting needs no special ceremonies or rigid rules.

Since 1935, when France passed the first comprehensive wine legislation, the *Appellation d'Origine Controlée* (AOC or "controlled place of origin" laws), regulations have been enforced to ensure the quality and to uphold the fine reputation of French wines. All wines are categorized according to place of origin, alcohol content, and wine-making practices, and only about 16% of France's wines make the top classification. Other categories include *Vins Délimités de Qualité Supérieure* (VDQS or "restricted wines of superior quality") and *Vins de Pays* (country wines), which each have restrictions on growing factors. (The more grapes there are per acre, the more the concentration of taste per grape is affected.)

One way to discriminate among the bewildering range of wines in France is to examine the varieties of grapes that go into their production. Just as different wines are suited to different foods, different grape varieties are suited to different vinifications. All true Burgundies, for example, are made from only *Pinot Noir* grapes, while Bordeaux wines are different mixtures of four varieties of grape, the *Cabernet Sauvignon* being the dominant variety. The whites are usually made from *Chardonnay* or *Chenin Blanc* grapes and are occasionally mixed with minor varieties in the Champagne region.

When shopping for a fairly expensive wine, it is important to study the label carefully. The majority of wines are matured by shippers who buy young wines from the growers and mix them to achieve the blend they desire. In general, the label will indicate that a product is from a region such as Bordeaux, but not the specific grower. Look for the term *"mis en bouteille au domaine"* if you want to make sure the wine was estate bottled.

Labels have little meaning for ordinary French table wines, which are sound and simple products. The real mongrels, like those made from the grapes of "various Common Market countries," can cost as little as 6F a bottle. Remember, though, that the enjoyment of wine is ultimately in the drinking. All you can really expect from wine is good taste, and of that only you are the judge.

Politics

Remember that you are not simply traveling in France, but in the Republic of France. The present regime is the fifth in a sporadic series of republics dating back to the French Revolution, and only the second that did not result from a popular uprising. The revolutionary spirit still manifests itself in a numbing patriotism (some might say chauvinism) that injects politics into every walk of life. The clothes you wear, the newspaper you read—the little things will brand an individual as a member of a certain political group.

Politics is even more of an issue at present, because the French government is once again undergoing a kind of revolution. France, like much of Western Europe, has been riddled with double-digit inflation and rising unemployment. The hardest-hit industries have been steel, coal, and automobiles, and this has staggered the industrial North of France, where unemployment often reaches 40%. Employment opportunities for university students have also become scarcer. In 1981, deeply dissatisfied with Giscard d'Estaing, and his autocratic personality, his Gaulist policies, and frustrated by the nation's economic stagnation, students and labor banded together to elect the Socialist Francois Mitterrand as president—the only time since 1958 that control of the Government has passed from right and center-right groups to the left. The Socialists won a solid majority in the National Assembly the following June, assuring Mitterrand full government power and confirming the shift to the left.

Mitterrand's early policies have been ambitious indeed. Within his first two months in office, he raised the minimum wage, instituted a mandatory fifth week of vacation, and shortened the working week to 35 hours. He has also called for a transfer of power from departmental prefects to regional councils, a plan that would dismantle the strongly centralized political system that has dominated France since the time of Napoleon. A centralized government has necessitated a sizeable bureaucracy, and this has been the perpetual Achilles' heel of the French political system. Everything from university regulations to tourist offices has been controlled by an intricate and highly frustrating network emanating from Paris to each department. In addition, centralization has also been at odds with the country's great regional diversity, especially since certain provinces have traditionally suffered from Parisian neglect. Brittany, the Basque country, and the Languedoc region around Toulouse are presently fostering separatist movements which have met with begrudging conciliation from Paris. In each case, the issues combine cultural and linguistic differences with economic complaints. The political lines of the occasionally violent separatist movements are well drawn, and you should be aware of them (for your own safety as well as edification) as you travel through these regions.

Another major change has been the nationalization of a huge slice of the country's privately-owned banks and industries, the most extensive Government takeover of private industry since World War II. Mitterrand considers nationalization essential to economic development and has committed some $7 billion to compensate stockholders for the takeover, as well as an additional $1.6 billion to finance the newly-controlled industries.

But the inflation rate (at this writing) is up significantly since the Socialists came to power, unemployment has not fallen, and high interest rates have undercut Mitterrand's plans to stimulate the French economy with spending programs. In July of 1982, the President abruptly changed course. He has now decided to battle inflation head-on, imposing a four-month freeze on wages and prices (to end in October, 1982). The freeze is bound to hurt Mitterrand's crucial labor constituency; it has already angered businessmen, who insist that price controls do not combat the real cause of inflation. Mitterrand is caught between France's ailing economy and his own ambitious plans for political reform. To avoid massive budget deficits and higher inflation, the President must cut government spending—and that could mean sacrificing much of his cherished social programme. In amy case, as the country's future becomes more puzzling, the volume of political discussion in cafes will surely increase. Listen closely and you will learn much, but don't be afraid to add to the conversation—the republican spirit allows everyone to join in.

Public Holidays and Closing Days

French holidays are a blessing for the natives, but can cause the traveler endless trouble unless he is well-warned in advance. The following days are public holidays, when banks, museums, and other public buildings are closed: January 1, Easter Monday, May 1 (Labor Day), May 8, Ascension Day (five weeks after Easter), Whit Monday, July 14 (Bastille Day), August 15 (Assumption Day), November 11 (Armistice Day), and December 25. When a holiday falls on a Tuesday or Thursday, the French often take Monday or Friday as a non-work day also (called *faire le pont*—to make a bridge). Be sure to note that banks close at noon on the day or the nearest working day before a public holiday.

Also keep in mind that most food stores close on Mondays, though they remain open on Sunday mornings. Stores and smaller businesses also close for a few weeks in July or August; they will post the names of similar stores open in the area on their door. Almost all museums close on Tuesday.

Festivals and Sports

France blossoms with festivals. Throughout the year, and especially in the summer, local *fêtes* are celebrated in almost every town. Expressions of civic pride, these *fêtes* often include carnivals, markets, and folk dancing. Most famous are expensive gatherings like the **Cannes Film Festival** in May, the **Nice Jazz Parade** in July, and the **Avignon Drama Festival** and **Aix-en-Provence** music festival in July and August. In addition, there are at least a hundred smaller music festivals every year, as well as other events that combine music with dance or drama, such as the Paris Festival du Marais in June. (For a list of music festivals, write to the French Tourist Office, 610 Fifth Ave., New York, NY 10020, for *Musique en France: calendrier des festivals.*)

Holidays, both legal and religious, and are another consideration to make when planning your itinerary. Try to be somewhere special for **Bastille Day** on July 14 (when the French celebrate the founding of the First Republic)—the parade down the Champs Elysées in Paris is a military spectacle. May 1, **La Fête du Travail** (French Labor Day), is a socialist celebration all over the country. For **Jeanne d'Arc Day** (the second Sunday in May), Orléans has a commemorative celebration. The **Feux de St. Jean** is a rural holiday combining John the Baptist's Day (June 24) with the ancient Celtic summer solstice observance; bonfires are lit throughout the countryside. Brittany is famous for its *pardons*—festivals held to honor a parish's patron saint.

Two special sporting events are **Le Mans,** a famous 24-hour car race on the second weekend of June, and the **Tour de France,** a three-week bicycle race in July traversing most of France. Check out the set itinerary to see if they cycle past one of your stopovers. For more information on holidays and special events, send for the French Tourist Office's pamphelt *Events in France.*

Language, or If You Don't Speak French

> *Never go to France*
> *Unless you know the lingo*
> *If you do, like me*
> *You will repent, by jingo.*
> Thomas Hood, 1839

Everything you've heard is true: traveling in France can be difficult if you don't speak French. Language is at the core of a very real cultural chauvinism in France, and the same scenarios of short-tempered telephone operators and sneering waiters are replayed year after year, especially in Paris. You may be trying hard, but if you were foolish enough to have been born in the wrong country, *tant pis* (tough).

With a little effort and the proper attitude, though, travel in France is not only possible for those who don't speak French, it is vastly educational and often downright funny. The French are inveterate teachers—don't get angry when they incessantly correct your articles, tenses, and pronouns, just remember it for future use. And don't feel insulted when they (especially the students) respond in a halting English: they are just as eager to try out their linguistic abilities as you are.

In fact, the French speak a lot more English than they care to let on—much of it culled from American TV series. The country is gradually, if unwillingly, adapting to an ever-increasing number of English, American, and German tourists, and you will find multi-lingual signs in airports, train stations, and major tourist sites. In the larger cities, the tourist office staff almost always speaks passable English, and at sites where the guided tours are in French, there is usually a printed English translation available. Just remember that the French dislike the common American assumption that everyone can—and should—speak English. You will find people much more helpful if you ask "Parlez-vous anglais, Madame/Monsieur?" before addressing them in English.

It is in every-day activities, such as shopping and catching buses, that you will find language a frustrating barrier. For these times, you will want to buy a phrasebook and perhaps an English-French dictionary before you leave home. Browse around the travel section of any large bookstore; you'll probably find something you're comfortable with. Larousse publishes a thick, pocket-sized dictionary, but you need eagle eyes to read the fine print. Berlitz publishes a phrasebook that's not much help in social situations, but which is packed with useful words and phrases for getting you through customs, booking a room in a hotel, and deciphering train schedules. Use these tools only when necessary: if they become a crutch, you will miss the chance to widen your cultural horizons. Don't be afraid to ask *"qu-est-ce que c'est?"* (what is it?) or *"Comment s'appelle-t-il?"* (What do you call it?). Gesticulating or pointing to what you want to buy usually succeeds and brings many laughs as well.

In your day-to-day contact with French proprietors or waitresses don't forget the common courtesy of saying *"Bonjour madame/monsieur"* before you ask *"combien?"* (how much?). Above all, keep trying, and resist the temptation to lapse into English if you can. The similarities between the two languages are often greater than their differences, and your ability to speak will undoubtedly improve with time. Buy a phrase book, learn a few phrases and French gestures, and don't be afraid to act like a ham. It's bound to pay off.

Helping Let's Go

Each year hundreds of readers send us suggestions and corrections—from two-word postcards to ten-page letters. These invaluable suggestions are often used in our next edition. To share your discoveries with our readers and to help us improve *Let's Go,* please send the tear-out postcard in the back of the book (or a letter) by Decmeber 31, 1982. Mail it to *Let's Go* Staff, Harvard Student Agencies, Thayer Hall-B, Harvard University, Cambridge, MA 02138.

PARIS

Don't listen to what some provincial New Yorkers say; no city in the western world truly rivals Paris. Whatever your obsession, generations of the similarly-inclined have indulged here before you. This city is a haven for aspiring revolutionaries and aristocrats—aristocrats by birth, by virtue, and by vice.

A plethora of intellectual movements received their first airing in Paris. Marxism, existentialism, and structuralism have been among the less ephemeral. Music, theater, and art flourish, from the classical to the avant-garde and beyond. Paris has harbored great exiled writers as diverse as Heinrich Heine and F. Scott Fitzgerald, Gertrude Stein and Ernest Hemingway. And in recent times, Paris has become home for South American writers and Eastern European artists. The Centre Pompidou has revived French curatorship for contemporary art, providing the facilities and the excuse to mount major retrospectives of twentieth-century artists and art movements. And of course the other museums of Paris—first among them the Louvre, Jeu de Paume, and the Orangerie—remain collections that art lovers long to see.

These are impressive traditions and achievements, but they are not the only reason to visit Paris. You can come here simply to enjoy the raw feel of the place. Hemingway described Paris as a moveable feast, a city with qualities so infectious that once you visit it, you carry bits of the experience around with you forever. It is also something of a giant, all-night carnival, a never-ending collection of delights and eccentricities.

For there is a vibrancy here that is missing almost everywhere else. It is apparent in the flair of the luxury stores, the airs of expensive restaurants, and the brashness of the new public spaces, the Centre Pompidou and the Forum of Les Halles. But this vibrancy is most apparent in the Parisian people. Parisians seem to do everything with a certain sense of purpose, a stylish self-consciousness and confidence—little wonder that fashions of all types, whether in clothing, art or cuisine, catch on with such a vengence here. It's a game, partly, but a game the Parisians take very, very seriously. Whether you call their studied casualness style, panache, or just plain "cool," it makes Paris one of the world's most diverting places in which to watch people.

Unfortunately, the Parisian style is accompanied by a snobbism and general orneriness which seldom goes unnoticed. Popular opinion holds that the average Parisian's demeanor runs the gamut from shades of condescension to rudeness, with an extra edge of contempt reserved for those who speak no French.

Yet you should at least try to understand the people here, who see millions of strangers tramp through their city each day, asking annoying questions and adding to the congestion. Remember that this is their home, and don't demand that they conform to your customs and expectations. Speaking even a little French can help a great deal. Learn to ask whether someone speaks English ("Parlex-vous anglais, Madame/Monsiur?") and learn to apologize in French for speaking French so poorly—even if you speak it impeccably. Parisians can

Paris

1 Palais de Chaillot
2 Tour Eiffel
3 Les Invalides
4 Musee Rodin
5 Grand Palais
6 Petit Palais
7 Elysee Palace
8 Orangerie
9 Musee du Jeu de Paume
10 Madeleine
11 American Express
12 Opera
13 Sacre-Coeur
14 Musee du Louvre
15 Comedie Francaise
16 Post Office
17 Centre National d'Art et Culture
    (Beaubourg/G. Pompidou)
18 National Archives
19 Musee Carnavalet
20 Sainte Chapelle
    and Palais de Justice
21 Notre Dame
22 Musee de Cluny
23 Sorbonne
24 Arenes de Lutece

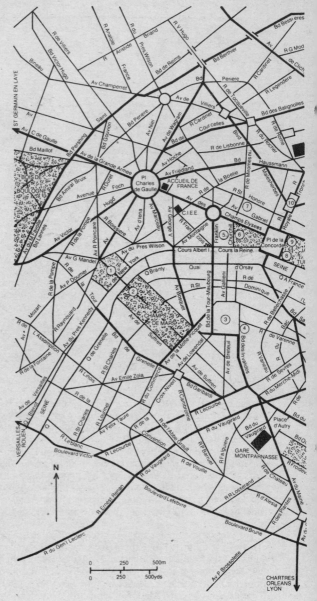

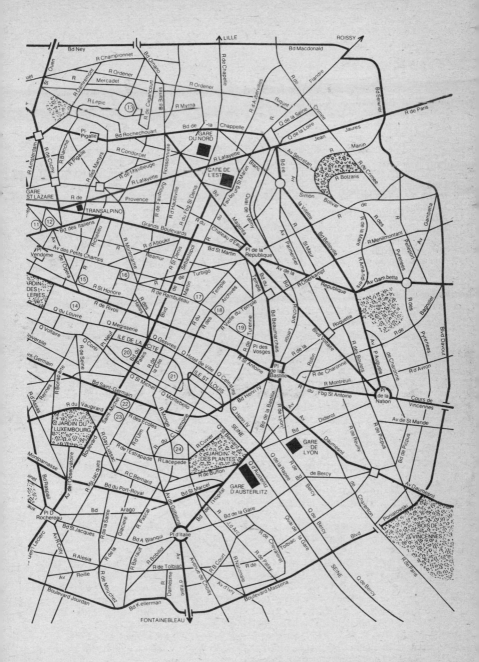

be warm, friendly, and generous, but you must realize that they are part of a much more formal society, and it takes much longer to make friends with them than with Americans.

Remember also that thousands of those in Paris are not Parisian or even French. Polish and Russian newspapers, bookstores, and political and literary groups abound. And as the capital of an Empire that once stretched from Tunis to Hanoi, Paris has been the adoptive home of people from around the world. From around the world, Paris still draws students to the universities, musicians to the conservatories, and artists to the garrets. Millions of visitors sense the attraction of this city and gain the feeling that they too could make Paris their home. Yet as a new arrival, you may feel intimidated by the city's pride and confidence in rich historical and cultural tradition. Don't let intimidation spoil appreciation; a surrender to Paris can be the sweetest of defeats.

Orientation

Getting into Paris

By Air. Most transatlantic flights land at the **Roissy-Charles de Gaulle** airport located about fifteen miles north of Paris. Charter flights usually fly into **Orly Sud** airport (about seven miles from the city), except during the airport's curfew hours when they are diverted to Roissy. Paris also has a third airport, **Le Bourget,** which primarily serves the French provinces. For flight information at Roissy, call 862-22-80; for Orly Sud, call 687-12-34 or 853-12-34.

To get into the city from Roissy, the cheapest and fastest method is to take the **Roissy Rail** bus-train combination to the Gare du Nord Metro stop. A second-class ticket costs 17F, and the trip takes 35 minutes. Leave from Charles de Gaule Aérogare 1 gate 30, arrival level, or Aérogare 2 gate B6 or B7. A shuttle bus will take you to the aérogares for free. The Gare du Nord stop lies on the Porte de Clignancourt-Porte d'Orléans line that runs directly to the prime hotel areas around the St. Michel and Odéon stops.

Several other, more expensive forms of public transportation take you to the Gare du Nord. **RATP buses** #30 and #351 both cost six Metro tickets (3F each, second-class), run from about 6:30am to 9pm, and take a bit under an hour to make the trip. The #30 bus may be more useful, since it goes to Gare de l'Est on the Porte de Clignancourt-Porte d'Orléans line. It leaves from the *Boutiquaire* floor exit. Bus #351 goes to the Nation Metro stop, a less central location in the eastern part of Paris. **Air France buses,** which guarantee you a comfortable seat, go to the Porte Maillot—the least convenient terminus. Finally, there are **taxis** for the affluent. On an average day, the trip to Roissy will take about an hour and cost roughly 100F (more in the evening).

Orly Sud airport is served by **RATP buses** #215 and #285, both costing three Metro tickets. Bus #215 runs from Denfert-Rochereau, convenient to several *foyers*, between 6:20am and 8:40pm, and #285 from Porte d'Italie between 4:45am and 12:30am. The **Air France bus** costs 18F and goes to the Invalides stop from Orly Ouest gate E every twenty minutes from 7am-11:20pm, and from Orly Sud gate J every twenty minutes from 7:10am to 11:30pm. There is a **shuttle** between Orly Ouest and Sud, and the same Air France guarantee as above applies. **Orly Rail** takes you by bus from Orly Ouest gate F, arrival level, or Orly Sud gate H to the Orly station every 15 minutes between 5:30am and 8:50pm, every half hour from 8:50pm to 11:20. From there, you take the RER train into Paris. You can get off at St.-Michel or any other stop on the line for the same price (14F). **Taxis** cost at least 65F and take about 45 minutes to reach the center of town. From Le Bourget, you can take RATP bus #350 to Gare de l'Est (for three Metro tickets).

By Train. The arteries of France are made of steel. Generations of French people have entered and left their capital through the vast, bustling train stations. Each is a community on its own, with resident bums and policemen, cafes and restaurants, tabacs and banks. Locate the ticket boxes *(guichets)* and platforms *(quais)* and you will be set. All stations are located on at least one Métro line and the Métro station bears the name of the train station. For general train information dial 261-50-50 when the stations are open, between 8am-10pm. The information numbers of the individual stations (see below) operate 8am-8pm each day. There is a free telephone with direct lines to the stations on the right hand side of the Champs Elysées tourist office.

Gare du Nord (tel. 280-03-03). Trains to northern France, Belguim, the Netherlands, Scandinavia, USSR, northern Germany, and Britain.

Gare de l'Est (tel. 208-49-90). Eastern France (Champagne, Alsace, Lorraine), Luxembourg, parts of Switzerland, southern Germany, Austria, Hungary.

Gare de Lyon (tel. 345-92-22). Southern and southeastern France (the Riviera, Provence) parts of Switzerland, Italy, Greece, and points east.

Gare d'Austerlitz (tel. 584-16-16). Southwestern France (Bordeaux, the Pyrénées, the Loire Valley), Spain, and Portugal.

Gare St.-Lazare (tel. 538-52-29). Normandy, including the port at Le Havre, where ships leave for North and South America and England.

Gare de Montparnasse (tel. 538-52-29). Western France, including Versailles, Chartres, and Brittany.

Having a ticket does not guarantee you a seat on the train, and during vacation and holiday periods almost half the passengers travel standing up (or lying down) in train corridors. If you are traveling during one of these peak periods, it is worth making a train reservation: 8F for a seat and 63F for a *couchette* (one of six quite comfortable sleeping shelves per compartment) in supplement to first- or second-class tickets. Berths, or *wagon-lits*, probably exceed your price range: 213F extra for half of a double and 385F for a single. You can reserve a couchette up to two hours before departure (but no later than 6pm) and up to two months in advance. You should try to leave half a day for a seat reservation. You can make reservations by phone, letter, or in person.

With the new **Carte Jeune,** anyone under 25 can benefit from reductions of up to 50% between June 1 and September 30 on train trips in France, except on commuter trains, weekends, and during the *période bleu* of heavy traffic. You can buy the Carte Jeune at the Office de Tourisme Universitaire for 100F. Student rail tickets are available at the Council for International Educational Exchange (CIEE), Accueil de Jeunes en France (AJF), and Office du Tourisme Universitaire (OTU). (See the Student Services section under Useful Addresses in the general Introduction.) **Transalpino,** 14, rue Lafayette, 9ème, Mo. Chausée d'Antin (tel. 247-12-40) will also give you big reductions on all international train rides (approximately 30% outside France, 25% in the country). Reductions on runs within France are often limited to round-trip tickets. Open Mon.-Fri. 9am-7pm, Sat. 9:30am-6:30pm. Be prepared to wait in line.

By Thumb. Hitching out of Paris is very difficult, as the competition for rides is overwhelming, although certain tricks can give you the advantage in this game. First of all, do not wait at any of the *Portes* (gates to the city) where the major *autoroutes* radiate from the city, as you'll inevitably find there a long, wavering line of wayfarers who all look as though they've been standing there for at least two days. Avoid this vacationer's purgatory and pull out your map of Paris public transportation. Figure out which *autoroute* you need to catch to get to your destination, then trace the train or bus line until it approaches this route—that is where you should start your hitching. The few extra francs you'll spend to get away from the city could save you hours of frustration. The following suggestions will help get you started:

Towards the South and Spain: Take the Métro Ligue de Sceaux to Fontaine Michalon. From here you can easily pick up the N20 which feeds into the A1, and you are on your way.

Towards Switzerland and Italy: Get off the Métro at Alfort-Ecole vétérinaire and walk to ave. du Général de Gaulle. Hitching from here will get you on *autoroute* N5.

Towards the Netherlands: Take bus #302 (except on Sundays) from Porte de la Chapelle to stop Général-Leclerc. Follow the street opposite this stop to the service station on the *autoroute* and catch a ride there.

Study the map carefully and you're bound to get the hang of it. In general, the more original and inventive your method of reaching an entrance to an *autoroute* outside of Paris, the less chance that there will be other hitchhikers on your path. Hold up a sign designating your destination, include the word "S.V.P." *(s'il vous plait),* and say *fromage.*

If you have a little money and want to save some time, try **ALLOSTOP,** 84, passage Brady, 10*ème,* (Mo. Strasbourg-St.-Denis; tel. 246-00-66). Open Mon.-Sat. 9am-7:30pm. They will try to match you up with a driver going your way. The cost for finding a ride is 28F, and if you plan on using this service more than two or three times, it pays to spend the 100F for one year's worth of rides. They also have offices in Strasbourg, Toulouse, Bordeaux, Lyon, Marseille, and other cities throughout France.

Layout of Paris

Paris is divided into *arrondissements* which spiral clockwise from the Louvre *(1er)* to the Porte de Vincennes (20*ème).* All street addresses in the Paris section are immediately followed by arrondissement number, to ease your hunting. The Métro and buses provide rapid transport to all the arrondissements, but for the center (arrondissements one through eight), it is often more convenient and pleasant to walk. You are closer to almost everything if you base yourself near the center, but this is by far the most touristy part of town and in the summer it can be unpleasantly crowded with foreigners. You will also find higher prices here. If you want to see more of Paris than just the sights and the tourists, try exploring parts of the 18*ème* around Montmartre and Pigalle (the red light district), the 10*ème* along the quiet banks of the St. Martin Canal, or the "grands boulevards" in the 9*ème.*

Another important distinction is that between the Right Bank *(la rive droite)* and the Left Bank *(la rive gauche)* of the river Seine. The Sorbonne area, Quartier Latin (5*éme)* and the student-artsy-chic areas of Odéon and St.-Germain (6*ème)* have earned the Left Bank a reputation for a bohemian lifestyle, student-oriented activities, and low costs. The 16*ème,* the Faubourg St. Honoré, and the Champs Elysées put the Right Bank in the look-but-don't touch category, but low-cost neighborhoods like the Marais (4*ème),* Belleville (20*ème),* and the area around the canal St.-Martin (3*ème* and 11*ème)* exist here too—usually without the mobs of Left Bank tourist. For navigation, by far the

Paris
Arrondissements

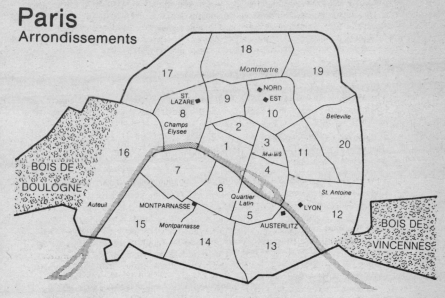

◆ = Stations (Gares)

best map is the 35F *Plan de Paris par Arrondissements,* which includes a detailed street map for each arrondissement, a Métro map, a list of bus routes, and a wealth of up-to-date miscellany. These useful little red books are available in most bookstores, *papeteries,* and news kiosks.

Useful Addresses

(Note: In the listings below and throughout the Paris section, a Métro stop is indicated by the abbreviation Mo.)

Tourist Offices

Bureau d'Accueil Central, 127, ave. des Champs-Elysées, 8*ème* (tel. 723-61-72; Mo. Etoile). Provides general tourist information for Paris, as well as for the rest of France. They have a hotel-finding service covering all price ranges. Open Mon.-Sat. 9am-10pm; Sun., holidays, and Nov.-March 9am-8pm. Usually jam-packed in summer. The other, smaller **Bureaux d'Accueil** operated by the Office de Tourisme de Paris are located in the train stations and provide similar services.

Bureau Gare d'Austerlitz, Porte 15, 13*ème* (tel. 584-91-70; Mo. Austerlitz). Open Mon.-Sat. 8am-10pm, closed Sun. and holidays.

Bureau Gare de l'Est, 10*ème* (tel. 607-17-73; Mo. Gare de l'Est). Open Mon.-Sat. 8am-1pm and 5-10pm, closed Sun. and holidays.

Bureau Gare de Lyon, 12*ème* (tel. 343-33-24; Mo. Gare de Lyon). Open Mon.-Sat. 8am-1pm and 5-10pm, closed Sun. and holidays.

Bureau Gare du Nord, 10*ème* (tel. 526-94-82; Mo. Gare du Nord). Open Mon.-Sat. 8am-10pm, closed Sun. and holidays.

Provincial Tourist Offices: In Paris there is a special office devoted to each French province, with information on regional tourism, lodging, and activities. For addresses of the various offices, see the "Planning your Trip" section of the Introduction.

Student Services

Acceuil des Jeunes en France (AJF), has three locations. 119, rue St.-Martin, 4ème (tel. 277-87-80; Mo. Rambuteau), across the pedestrian street from the Centre Pompidou. Open Mon.-Sat. 9:30am-7:30pm. 16, rue de Pont Louis-Philippe, 4ème (tel. 278-0482: Mo. Pont Marie), near the Hôtel de Ville. Open Mon.-Fri. 9:30am-6:30pm. Also at the Gare du Nord (tel. 285-86-19; Mo. Gare du Nord), opposite track #19. Open Oct.-June Mon.-Fri. 9:15am-6:15pm, and July-Sept. 9:15am-9pm daily. The staffs dispense information, sell ISIC cards, and find you a place in one of their excellent *foyers* (free of charge) or somewhere else (for a portion of the room price). The office at rue St.-Martin also sells reduced-price student train tickets. AJF can help you out if you plan to study in France or have questions regarding an extended stay. For a stay of any length, ask for the booklet "Paris Welcomes Young People," the best compendium of useful listings and information on Paris that exists (includes a section on what to do if you get bored!).

Centre d'Information et de Documentation Jeunesse (CIDJ), 101, quai Branly, 15ème (tel. 566-40-20; Mo. Bir-Hakeim). An information clearinghouse that specializes in sending you to exactly the right place for employment, recreation facilities, and some long-term accommodations. Jobs for non-French are scarce, but this is certainly a place to try. CIDJ also offers pamphlets on camping and tourism throughout France. Open Mon.-Sat. 9am-7pm.

Council on International Educational Exchange (CIEE), 51, rue Dauphine, 6ème (tel. 326-79-65; Mo. Odéon). English-speaking, young people's travel agency. Books flights all over the world and sells student train tickets, guidebooks, and ISICs. Also sells the discount BIGE/Transalpino rail tickets (about 25% off in France, 35-50% international). If you have lost a CIEE ticket, these people can telex the U.S. to authorize a substitute. Also at 16, rue de Vaugiraud (tel. 634-02-90; Mo. Odéon). Another office, the Centre Franco-Americain, at 1, place de l'Odéon (tel. 634-16-10), specializes in work and study opportunities for American students in France (the first two offices are concerned only with travel services).

Office de Tourisme Universitaire (OTU), 137, blvd. St. Michel, 5ème (tel. 329-12-88; Mo. Port Royal), is a French student travel office which provides much the same services as CIEE; somewhat less crowded, though less complete. Open Mon. 11am-6:45pm, Tue.-Sat. 10am-6:45pm.

Alliance Française, 101, blvd. Raspail (tel. 544-38-28; Mo. Raspail). The Alliance teaches French to foreigners at all levels, from the beginner who knows not a word to the fluent who are working for a teaching certificate. Also has excellent resources for lodgings and stays in Paris, including places with families. There is also a restaurant here (next to nothing for Alliance students, 12-16F a full meal for non-students). An excellent place to meet foreign students from absolutely everywhere.

Guarding your Money

One drawback to life in Paris is that it costs. Paris is an excellent city for the rich, but it is also very well suited for the marginally solvent. There are enough interesting walks to keep you busy for a week, enough bakeries selling 2F *baguettes* (French bread) to keep you alive, and enough places where people congregate at night that you will not have to endure your poverty alone. Street corner fire-eaters, musicians, and escape-artists provide some of the most exciting shows in Paris. Paris' nightlife can be wild. Enjoy it, but take care. Although it is usually safe to walk around at night in most *quartiers,* always try to anticipate potential dangers. Even during the day, men should carry their wallets in a front pocket and women should carefully guard their purses, especially while on the crowded Métro. Purses with zippers or very secure clasps are the best defense against pickpockets. This is basic advice, but it's all too easy to forget in the hustle and bustle.

When you do spend, expect to be challenged—prices are often double those in the provinces. You can still find adequate inexpensive hotels and good restaurants serving generous portions at low prices, if you take time to explore. Don't sit down at a cafe on a main thoroughfare without first consulting the menu prices. A cup of coffee could set you back 12F, so beware; but since all prices are clearly posted outside, you shouldn't make too many expensive mistakes. Métro prices have gone up recently, but if you buy a *carnet* of ten tickets and try to walk as much as possible, you'll save money and gain a much better sense of the capital's diverse neighborhoods. Shopping in Paris is almost certain to be expensive; if you're determined to buy something, look for *soldes* (sales) and check out flea markets on weekend mornings.

Practical Information

American Express: 11, rue Scribe, 9*ème* (tel. 266-09-99; Mo. Opera). The banking service is open Mon.-Fri. 9am-5pm, closed Sat. and Sun. Not a bad place to meet people. From the Left Bank, take bus #21, 27, or 81 from the place St.-Michel, get off at the Opéra, and walk one block left on rue Auber to rue Scribe; AmEx is right across from the Opera. They will hold mail for you free of charge if you have either their card or travelers checks; 5F per inquiry otherwise. No matter what business you plan to transact here, don't forget to bring your passport along.

All-Night Post Office: 52, rue du Louvre, 1*er* (tel. 233-71-60; Mo. Louvre). All General Delivery Mail (Poste Restante) is held at this post office unless otherwise specified. The branch at 71, ave. des Champs Elysées, 8*ème* (Mo. Georges V), is open Mon.-Fri. 8am-11:30pm, Sat. noon-11pm, and Sun. and holidays 10am-noon and 2-8pm.

Late Money Exchange: 125, Champs Elysées, 8*ème,* Mo. George V. Open Mon.-Fri. 8:45am-5:15pm; Sat. and Sun. 10:30am-1pm and 2-4pm.

Money Exchange at the Train Stations: Gare d'Austerlitz, 13*ème* (tel. 584-91-40), Mon.-Fri. 9am-7pm; **Gare de l'Est,** 10*ème* (tel. 206-51-97), Mon.-Sat. 7:30am-8pm; **Gare St.-Lazare,** 8*ème* (tel. 387-08-53), Mon.-Fri. 7:30am-8pm; **Gare de Lyon,** 12*ème* (tel. 628-29-51), 6:30am-11pm daily; **Gare Montparnasse,** 15*ème* (tel. 566-48-19), 9am-7pm daily; **Gare du Nord,** 10*ème* (tel. 526-96-22), 6:30am-10pm daily.

Money Exchange at the Airports: Orly, 6:30am-11:30pm: **Roissy-Charles de Gaulle,** 6:30am-1:30am.

Police Headquarters: Central Police office at 9, blvd. du Palais, 4*ème* (tel. 260-33-22 or 277-11-00; Mo. Cité). **Service des Etrangers** (Foreign Service), 7-9, blvd. du Palais, 4*ème,* (tel. 329-21-55) for visa problems, if you're robbed, etc.

Emergency Dial 17.

SOS Ambulance: (tel. 707-37-39). **SOS Médecin:** (tel. 707-77-77), Emergency medical help 24 hours a day. **Emergency Medical Association of Paris** (Association pour les Urgences Médicales de Paris): (tel. 578-61-38), provides a list of doctors and pharmacies that are open late.

All-Night Pharmacies: Pharmacie Dhery, 84, ave. des Champs Elysées, 8*ème* (tel. 256-02-41), open 24 hours. **Proniewski Pharmacy,** 5, place Blanche, 9*ème* (tel. 874-77-99). Open 24 hours.

Hospitals: Hospitals in Paris are numerous and efficient. They will generally treat you whether or not you can pay in advance. Settle with them afterwards and don't let the fear of foreign medicine or financial uncertanties cause you to ignore a serious problem. **Cochin Hospital,** 27, rue du Faubourg St.-Jacques, 14*ème* (Mo. Denfert-Rochereau), is very reliable. **L'Hôpital Américain de Paris,** where English is spoken, is at 63, blvd. Victor Hugo, Neuilly (tel. 747-53-00; Mo. Sablons or bus #82). A visit costs at least 250-500F, more expensive than most hospitals, but you can pay in dollars. They can also direct you to the nearest English-speaking doctor and also provide dental services. **Hôpital Franco-Britannique de Paris,** at 48, rue de Viliers, Levallois-Perret (tel. 757-24-10; Mo. Anatole-France), provides complete services.

Down and Out: Services and aid for the desperate, drugged out, and destitute in Paris are split up among a number of organizations. If you are in real financial straits, the **American Aid Society** can help. Though their offices are in the U.S. Embassy, the Society is an independent organization (Embassy tel. 296-12-02 and 261-80-75, extensions 2717 and 2932 for the Aid Society). You can borrow money interest-free here, based on a personal interview. For any sort of personal counseling (psychiatric or emotional, for everything from pregnancy to serious homesickness), go to the two services based at the American Church (65, quai d'Orsay, 7*ème*, Mo. Invalides or Alma Marceau), the **International Counselling Service** and the **American Student and Family Service.** These two groups share the same staff and provide access to psychologists, psychiatrists, social workers, and a pastoral counselor. Payment is voluntary and geared to the capacity of the patient. The ICS has regular hours in the morning (Mon.-Fri. 9am-noon), the ASFS in the afternoon (2-5pm); other hours by appointment. (Tel. for both is 550-26-49 at the Church). Job and housing difficulties should be referred to Mrs. Boyd at the **American Center,** 261 blvd. Raspail, 14*ème* (Mo. Raspail), a cross-cultural center for students and artists in Paris. Organizes concerts, art exhibitions, theater, and art classes. Open Mon.-Fri. 10am-10pm, Sat. 9am-2pm; (tel. 633-51-26 or 321-42-20).

SOS Help Crisis Line: (tel. 723-80-80), daily 3-11pm. English-speaking. For anything you need help with: emotional distress, where to find a VD clinic, you name it.

Drug Problems: Hôpital Marmottan (tel. 574-00-04).

American Church in Paris: 65, quai d'Orsay, 7*ème* (tel. 705-07-99; Mo. Invalides). As much a community center as a church. Nondenominational. Bulletin board stocked with information on jobs, rides, etc. Also the home of *Free Voice,* a free, English-language monthly specializing in cultural events and classifieds. After church on Sunday, there is a coffee half-hour and then a filling, friendly, inexpensive luncheon at 12:30pm (17F for students, 25F for adults). A counseling service is also offered; if you are down and out, you might come here for advice.

U.S. Embassy: 2, ave. Gabriel, 8*ème* (tel. 296-12-02 and 261-80-75; Mo. Concorde). Open Mon.-Fri. 9am-6pm. Office of American Services open Mon.-Fri. 9am-4pm.

Canadian Embassy: 35, ave. Montaigne, 8*ème* (tel. 225-99-55; Mo. Franklin-Roosevelt). Open Mon.-Fri. 9am-12:30pm and 2-5:30pm.

Lost Property: If you lose something on the Métro or on a bus, go to the **Bureau des Objets Trouvés**, 36, rue des Morillons, 15*éme;* Mo. Convention. Open weekdays 8:30am-5pm. For things lost in the street (tel. 531-14-80); in the Métro (tel. 828-32-36); on the bus (tel. 828-97-30).

Public Baths: If your hotel charges 10F for a shower, and you're not far from the place de la Contrescarpe, try the municipal baths. A shower, soap, and towel cost only 3.20F. Located at 50, rue Lacepède, 5*ème* (tel. 331-44-44; Mo. Monge). Open only Thurs. noon-7:30pm, Fri. and Sat. 7am-7pm, and Sun. 8am-noon. Another public bath is at 8, rue des Deux Ponts, 4*ème*, on the Ile St.-Louis (tel. 354-47-40; Mo. Pont Marie), with the same hours and prices.

Laundromats: The average price is around 17F to wash and dry one load; check in the yellow pages under *Laveries Automatiques* to find one near your hotel. Outside of Paris there are fewer laundromats, so you might want to do your laundry before leaving. In the Latin Quarter try: 72, rue Monge, Mo. Monge; 3, rue de la Montagne-Ste.-Geneviève, Mo. Maubert-Mutualité; 60, rue Guy Lussac, Mo. Luxembourg; 113, rue Monge, Mo. Censier Daubenton; 91, rue de la Seine, Mo. Mabillon.

The American Library in Paris: 10, rue du General-Camou, 7*éme* (tel. 551-46-82; Mo. Alma-Marceau). Primarily for Americans living in France or American students enrolled in French universities. A permanent address in France is required. Open Tues., Thurs., and Fri., 2-7pm; Wed. and Sat. 10am-7pm. Closed Sun., Mon., holidays, all of Aug., and the first week of Sept. A full year membership costs 220F. You might also try the public library, one of the few in Paris, at the **Centre Pompidou** (Mo. Rambuteau), which has some English language books and magazines and popular listening room. It's free! Open Mon., Wed., Thurs., Fri. noon-10pm; Sat. and Sun. 10am-10pm.

Telephone Code: (01).

Getting Around

The Métro. The Paris Métro is one of the most useful and efficient urban subway networks in the world: you are never more than half a mile from a station and the travel time between any two points is rarely more than forty minutes, usually far less. The first trains start running at 5:30am; the last leave for their final trips at 12:30am. Free Métro maps are available at many stations, and display maps are posted in all stations. Connections to other lines are indicated by signs marked *correspondance,* and Métro lines are named after their last destinations. The blue *Sortie* signs indicate exits.

Second-class Métro tickets, which can also be used on buses, cost 3F each or 20F for a book *(carnet)* of ten, and are sold at Métro stations and in some *tabacs.* Each journey on the subway costs only one ticket. Every Métro has at least one first-class car distinguished from the others by its color; first-class tickets cost 5F each and 30F for a *carnet* of ten. Riding in a first-class car with a second-class ticket can incur a fine except between 9am and 5pm, when all Métro cars are made equal. (The Socialist government cut back the hours of first-class service last spring. Old habits die hard, however, and the first-class cars are still fairly empty in off-hours.) No matter what class you ride, hold on to your ticket until you have passed the doors marked *Limite de Validité de Billets,* for you may be checked by a uniformed RATP *controleur,* and fined—starting at 40F. Being a foreigner is no excuse. Besides, some *correspondances,* especially those with the *Réseau Express Régional,* or RER

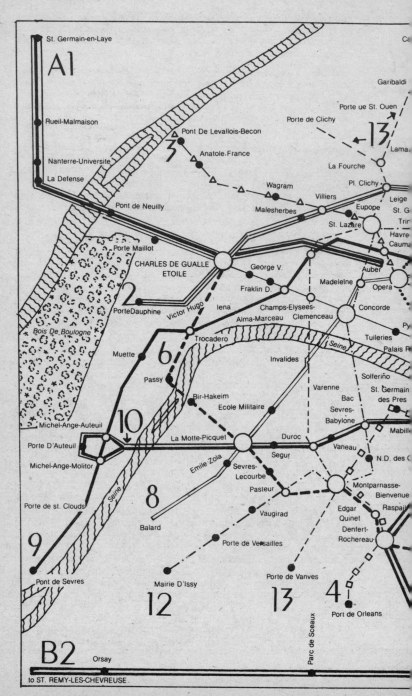

St. Germain-en-Laye

A1

Rueil-Malmaison

Nanterre-Universite

La Defense

Pont de Neuilly

Pont De Levallois-Becon

Anatole-France

Wagram

Villiers

Malesherbes

St. Lazare

Porte Maillot

CHARLES DE GUALLE
ETOILE

George V.

Fraklin D.

Madeleine

Porte Dauphine   Victor Hugo   Iena   Champs-Elysees-
                                      Clemenceau

Alma-Marceau

Concorde

Bois De Boulogne

Muette

Trocadero

Seine

Tuileries

Palais R

Passy

Invalides

Solferiño

St. Germain
des Pres

Bir-Hakeim

Ecole Militaire

Varenne

Bac

Sevres-
Babylone

Mabille

Michel-Ange-Auteuil

10

Porte D'Auteuil

Michel-Ange-Molitor

La Motte-Picquet

Duroc

Vaneau

N.D. des (

Seine

Emile Zola

Sevres-
Lecourbe

Segur

Pasteur

8

Montparnasse-
Bienvenue

Porte de st. Clouds

Vaugirad

Edgar
Quinet

Raspail

Balard

Denfert-
Rochereau

9

Porte de Versailles

Pont de Sevres

Mairie D'Issy

12

Porte de Vanves

13

4

Port de Orleans

Parc de Sceaux

B2   Orsay

to ST. REMY-LES-CHEVREUSE

Garibaldi

Porte ue St. Ouen

Porte de Clichy

13

Lama.

La Fourche

Pl. Clichy

Leige

Eupope

St. G

Trin

Havre

Cauma

Auber

Opera

Py

3

PARIS MÉTRO

○ connections

4 Line number

4 de Clignancourt

12 Porte de la Chapelle

7 Porte de La Villette

Marcadet-Poissoniers

Eglise de Pantin 5

Chateau Rouge Stalingrad

Porte de Pantin

Anvers

Jaures

alle Barbes-Rochechouart

Louis Blanc

Gare du Nord

11

Lorette

Gare del'Est

Pl. des Fetes

Mairie Des Lilas

'Antin
Rue Montmartre

Pyrenees

Porte des Lilas

Strasborg St. Denise

Bellieville

Sentier

Republique

Gallieni 3

eamur-
abastopol
e Marcel
vre

Temple

St. Maur

Gambetta

Porte de Bagnolet

Arts et Metiers

Oberkampf

Pere Lachaise

Halles

St. Sebastien-frissard

9

telet

Hotel de Ville

St. Paul

Cite

Pont-Marie

Bastille

Sully-Moreland

Ledru-Rollin

Faidherbe-Chaligny

NATION

1

uubert-
Mutualite
ardinal-Lemoine

Reuilly Diderot

Picpus

Chateau de Vincennes

Jussieu

Gare de Lyon

6

Monge

Gare D'Orleans Austerlitz

Daumnesnil

St. Marcel

Gobelins

Porte Doree

Bois de Vincennes

Porte de Charenton

Pl. D'Italie

Liberte

Porte de Choisy

Porte d'Ivry

Porte de Italie

7

Marie D'Ivry

aplace

to CRETEIL 8

(rapid train to the suburbs, also useful for Nation-Chatelet-Etoile trips), require you to put your validated (and uncrumpled) ticket through a turnstyle. Special tourist tickets *(Billets de Tourisme)* are also for sale but at inflated prices.

The *Carte Orange* is by far a better deal if you're planning to stay in Paris for more than a couple of weeks. For 100F you are granted a calendar month (from the first day of one month to the first day of the next) of unlimited travel on the Métro and the buses within Paris and the immediate suburbs. *Cartes* that allow you to travel farther outside Paris are also available, but are only worthwhile if you plan to go to the environs every day. To buy a card, take a small identification photograph to any Métro office (photo machines are located in many Métro stations if you don't have an extra one) and ask for a two-zone *Carte Orange* which will allow you to travel anywhere inside the city limits. Zones 3, 4, and 5 are for the suburbs. But remember to retain the little orange ticket each time you use it since it is good until the end of the month.

Buses. Bacause the Métro is so efficient and easy to use, the Paris bus system is unjustly ignored by many visitors. It shouldn't be, for buses are often less crowded than the Métro and in Paris it is a waste to spend extra hours underground. Free bus maps, the *Autobus Paris-Plan du Réseau,* are available at some Métro information booths, and the routes of each line are also posted at each stop. Buses take the same tickets as the Métro—short trips cost one ticket and longer trips two. Once on the bus, punch your own ticket by pushing it into the canceling machine by the driver's seat. If you have a *Carte Orange,* flash it at the driver but don't insert the ticket into the machine. As on the Métro, there are sometimes *controleurs* (transit inspectors) who will ask to see your ticket, so hold onto it until the end of the ride. For more information, call the RATP office (tel. 346-14-14).

Most buses stop running at about 8:30pm, though some, marked *Autobus de Soir,* continue until midnight, and a few others, the *Autobus de Nuit,* run all night. The night buses all start their runs at Châtelet. Only a few buses run on Sunday. If you are planning extensive touring by bus, it might be worth investing in a copy of *Le Plan de Paris par Arrondissements* (on sale at most newsstands and bookstores), which contains detailed diagrams of the bus routes.

The pamphlet printed by the RATP, *Billet de Tourisme* (free at RATP stations) lists several bus routes which pass through interesting neighborhoods and by the main sights of Paris. It also lists directions to major museums, churches, and monuments. One thing to remember when puzzling out bus routes is that buses traveling within Paris have two-digit numbers, while those traveling to the *banlieux* (suburbs) have three digits.

Some bus routes pass by enough interesting sights to make them mini-tours in themselves. Buses worth riding from start to finish include:

> **Bus #95:** From Montparnasse Tower via St.-Germain-des-Près, the Louvre, Palais Royal, the Opéra, and to Montmarte, near Sacre-Coeur.

> **Bus #96:** From Montparnasse via St.-Michel, the Palais de Justice on the Ile de la Cité, Châtelet, and the Hotel de Ville.

> **Bus #69:** From the Champs de Mars via the Eiffel Tower (just behind), Hotel des Invalides, Palais Royal, Châtelet, Hotel de Ville, the Marais, the Bastille to Père Lachaise, Paris' most famous cemetery.

Taxis. According to an AJF estimate, the average cost of a taxi trip is between 15 and 30F, but their estimate is uselessly low. Rates vary according to time of day and geographical boundaries crossed. (If you go out to the *banlieux,* or suburbs, the highest rate is in effect, meaning that you should be prepared to turn over your first-born child if you take a taxi to or from a Paris airport. Tarif A, the basic rate, is in effect from 6:30am-10pm; Tarif B from 10pm-6:30am and during the day from the airports; Tarif C, the highest, is in effect from the airports 10pm-6:30am. All taxis have lights on top which indicate the rate being charged, so you can check to see that the driver is playing it straight. At any rate, taxis will always be offensively expensive. If you must take one, try waiting at a stand *(arrêt taxis, tête de station)*, hailing from the sidewalk (unless you are within 50 meters of a stand), or calling a radio-cab, which is then dispatched to your address. The last is the most expensive, as you must pay for the distance the cab drives to pick up up. Dial (tel. 200-67-89, 739-33-33, 203-99-99, 656-94-00, or 281-44-44).

Bicycles. The center of Paris, with its narrow, congested streets and its ill-tempered drivers, is not the place for a leisurely afternoon pedal. Still, a few intrepid tourists do see Paris that way, the parks, especially the Bois de Boulogne and the Bois de Vincennes, can be enjoyable when explored on two wheels. Try first: **Paris-Velo**, 2, rue de Fer-à-Moulin, 5*ère*, Mo. Censier or St.-Marcel (tel. 337-59-22), an exceptionally friendly place (open 9am-7pm in summer). Three types of bikes ranging from about 50F for a day, 130F for one week, and 200F deposit. Open Mon.-Sat. 9am-1230pm, 2-7pm. Try to book in advance and ask for any accessories you'll need. Also take a look at their cycling book and maps. The **Bicy Club de France**, 8, place de la Porte Champerret, 18*ème*, Mo. Porte de Champerret (tel. 766-55-92) also rents bikes.

Mobilettes. There is a catch to renting mobilettes in Paris. One agency in Paris does rent mobilettes (scooters), but French law requires that you wear a helmet—and you cannot rent helmets anywhere. So, if you have your own or can borrow one, rentals are 65F per day, 325F per week, with a 1000F deposit at the **Autothèque**, 80, rue Montmartre, 2*ème*, Mo. Sentier (tel. 236-87-90).

Cars. Paris is difficult to drive in. Parisian drivers are notorious for their *"systeme D"* (i.e., do whatever works); street parking is hard to come by and garages are expensive. *Priorité à droite* gives the right of way to the car approaching from the right, regardless of the size of the streets, which makes driving quite exciting for those who are not familiar with the system. The Parisian driver makes it an affair of honor to take his right of way even in the face of grave danger. Of course, you are not allowed to honk your horn within city limits unless you are about to score by hitting a pedestrian. Flashing your headlights is the recognized sign for anger at the wheel. If you're still set on driving, you can rent a Renault 4 for 78F per day with a mileage charge (80C per km) from either one of these two agencies; **Inter Touring Service**, 117, blvd. Auguste Blanqui, 13*ème*, Mo. Glacière (tel. 588-52-37) open Mon.-Sat. 8:30am-6:30pm; and **LUT**, 4, rue Camille Desmoulins. 11*éme*, Mo. Voltaire (tel. 379-45-53).

Books About Paris

The green *Guide Michelin* (available in French or English, 34F) is by far the best source of information for the museums, history, and architecture of Paris. Providing detailed maps, descriptions, and architectural plans for many of the sights, this guide is invaluable for visitors who want to understand as much as possible about what they are seeing. The *Guide Michelin* features a number of interesting walking tours as well. (The green guide is also available for each of the French provinces and offers the same in-depth coverage.) For the famous and respected restaurant stars, you must turn to the pages of the red, hardcover *Michelin* for France (64F), or buy its Paris section, published separately in a thin paperback.

The *Blue Guide to Paris and Environs* (about $10) is more expensive and less interesting, but remains an excellent reference book for history, art, and architecture.

The *Gault-Millau* guide to Paris (95F) is perhaps more informative in its listings. It is not aimed toward the budget-minded either, but it will help you get the best for your money.

The *Plan de Paris par Arrondissements* for 35F is the best map of the city, complete with Métro and bus routes as well as an exhaustive street index. With this little tome in hand, you can no longer get lost.

Nairn's Paris (Penguin, recently out of print) would be fun to have, if you can find it. English architecture critic Ian Nairn is the author of this witty, insightful, and totally personal guide to his favorite Parisian buildings. An example of his style: "Never for a minute does the Eiffel Tower bear down on the city or its visitors; never does it endorse the puniness of man. Instead, it enlarges the viewer, gathers him up in its colossal size . . . and declares that the sky is not terrifying at all but was meant for our enjoyment along with Pernod and Coquilles Saint-Jacques."

Pariswalks, by Alison and Sonia Landes (New Republic Book Company, $6.20), takes you step-by-step on four walks around the Latin Quarter, and one around the place des Vosges in the Marais, explaining odd street names and telling good historical stories all the way. The prose is too cute, and the suggestions often ignore the privacy of the occupants of interesting houses, but the walks are well-chosen and fun.

If you read French and want another all-purpose budget guide, *Guide de Paris en Jeans* (Hachette, 39F) gives all the addresses and phone numbers you'll need to find anything—goods, services, cultural enlightenment, entertainment—and is especially helpful for longer stays. *Paris Pas Cher* (Ballard, 55F) is a street-by-street guide to inexpensive shops, boutiques, and galleries, as well as to restaurants and clubs. If you have lots of money, this book will help you decide how to spend it.

To find out what is going on in Paris (museum exhibits, festivals, movies, nightlife, restaurants, and cultural events), buy either one of the informative weekly guides to Paris, *Pariscope* (2.50F) or *Officiel des Spectacles* (2F) available at all newsstands. The listings are in French, but are very clear even for the non-French speaker. Non-French speakers, especially, will be interested in the various English publications in Paris, among them *The Paris Free Voice,* a weekly newspaper concentrating on arts and cultural events, is published by the Cooperative for Better Living in Paris at the American Church and is available free at the church (65, quai d'Orsay, 7ème, Mo. Invalides) and at many foreign student centers. More trendy and expensive (4F) is *Passion,* a weekly on sale in some English bookstores (try MacDougall, 8, rue Casimir-Delavigne, 6ème, Mo. Odéon) with extensive arts coverage and club listings.

Accommodations

Even in Paris, you have to sleep occasionally (or at least have a place to leave your bags while you are out defying fatigue), so chances are you'll have to pay for some sort of accommodations. Parisian hotels are usually terribly expensive, and it's all too easy to get stuck paying a lot of loot for a shabby room. If the places listed below are full, be sure to visit your room before you spend more than 50F per night on it. There are four basic types of Parisian accommodations: hostels, student *foyers*, hotels, and the bridges and parks.

Since the two IYHF Hostels are relatively expensive and far from the center of town, the bridges are usually full and the parks dangerous, most visitors will limit their options to the *foyers* and the hotels. If you are alone and would rather not be, the *foyers* are the better choice; fairly inexpensive for one person (with breakfast and shower included), they also give you an opportunity to meet other travelers. Couples will fare better in a hotel, and groups of three and four will do especially well in multi-bedded rooms. (In a hotel, you will not have to observe the curfew often imposed in *foyers*.) If you know when you will be in Paris before you leave home, make reservations in advance. Inquire first and then send one night's rent for confirmation. Alternatively, you can book a room through the Accueil de Jeunes en France (AJF) who run four hotels in Paris (46F per night, showers and breakfast included), with priorities to groups and people under thirty; For information write to AJF at 119, rue St.-Martin, Paris, 4*ème*. Many *hoteliers* will accept reservations over the phone, though equally many no longer do so, because they say callers never show up. If you call, be courteous and don't make reservations you don't truly need, or you'll make life more difficult for the multitudes who will follow.

Hostels

Ever since the inhospitable **Auberge de Jeunesse** on blvd. Kellermann went up in smoke a few years back, Paris has been without its own Youth Hostel. There are two Hostels in the suburbs, but both are inconvenient and often crowded with noisy groups of schoolchildren. When transportation costs are taken into account, you will find that you are paying more for a bed in a Hostel than at a foyer or budget hotel in Paris. Also, remember that trains and buses travel infrequently at night, and that hostels' curfews may restrict your nightlife.

If you forgot to buy a **Youth Hostel card** in the U.S., several Hostel association offices in Paris sell them. The cards, valid throughout the world, cost 86F for foreigners of any age, and are available at the **Fédération Unie des Auberges de Jeunesse**, 6, rue Mesnil, 16*ème*, (tel. 261-84-03); Mo. Victor Hugo), which will also provide you with a French Youth Hostel handbook free of charge. **La Ligue Française des Auberges de Jeunesse**, 38, blvd. Raspail, 7 *ème*, (tel. 548-69-84); Mo. Sèvres-Babylon) runs a smaller network of youth hostels in France. Take along a small photo and some form of ID to get LFAJ membership card, along with 30F if you're under 26, and 50F if you're older.

Auberge de Jeunesse Rueil-Malmaison (IYHF), 4, rue des Marguerites, Rueil Malmaison (tel. 749-43-97). Take the train for 3.50F (rail passes valid) from the Gare St. Lazare to the Gare de Suresnes (15 minutes), then follow the signs for another 15 minutes. 25F for breakfast and a place in a nine-bed room. Camping 17.50F, breakfast included. Sleeping sacks 8F. Cold dinner available for 15F, hot for 23.50F. The desk is open from 8-10am and 5-10pm; the Hostel shuts its doors at 1am.

Centre de Séjour de Choisy-le-Roi, ave. de Villeneuve St.-Georges, Choisy-le-Roi (tel. 890-92-30). Take the RER train for 5.50F (railpasses valid) from the St.-Michel train station to Choisy-le-Roi, then cross the bridge over the Seine. Take the road immediately to the right and follow the signs. Dorm beds from 50F with shower and breakfast included; double with obligatory *demi-pension* (breakfast and dinner included) 74F; 283 beds. No curfew, no reservations.

If apartment-hunting by poring through *Le Figaro* isn't bringing you success, try the **Fédération Nationale des Etudiants de France (FNEF)**, 120, rue

Notre Dame-des-Champs, 6ème, (tel. 633-30-78; Mo. Port-Royal). Their hours
are Mon.-Fri. 2:30-6pm, open until 8pm on Wednesday, but be prepared to get
there early and to struggle with many other students looking for apartments.
For a 50F initial fee, a student ID, and a photo they will provide you with a list
of available rooms. Don't forget to check the apartment listings at the Centre
d'Information et de Documentation Jeunesse (see the Useful Addresses section).

Foyers

Parisian foyers are generally a lot of fun: French youth groups stay in them
all the time, as does a fairly diverse youth community from all over the world.
They are a good deal for someone traveling alone; two or more can often find a
hotel room for less, though it may not be as clean or as friendly. Some of the
foyers are inconveniently located, but there are a few in the center of town.
During the summer months, the best way to find a bed in a foyer is to phone
or visit the **Acceuil des Jeunes en France (AJF),** 119, rue St.-Martin, 4ème (tel.
277-87-80; Mo. Rambuteau), right across from the Centre Georges Pompidou
(also called the Centre Beaubourg). Even in the busiest months, the AJF
seems to be able to find places for everyone who visits them—in fact, they
guarantee finding you "decent and low-cost lodging with immediate reservation." You must pay the full price of the foyer room when you make your
reservation. AJF can also help you find a hotel room. Open Mon.-Sat. 9am-
10pm, Sun. 9am-8pm. Another office is located in the **Gare du Nord,** across
from platform 19 (tel. 285-86-19; Mo. Gare du Nord), and open daily 9:15am-
9pm July-Sept., Mon.-Fri. 9:15am-6:15pm Oct.-June. There is a third office at
the **Hôtel de Ville,** 16, rue du Pont Louis-Philippe, 4ème (tel. 278-04-82; Mo.
Hôtel de Ville), open Mon.-Fri. 9:30am-6:30pm. The **Acceuil Room Service** at
the main tourist office (127, ave. Champs Elysees, 8ème, Mo. Etoile), offers
further room-finding services.

Hôtels des Jeunes (AJF): 11, rue le Fauconnier, 4ème, (tel. 272-72-09 and 274-23-
45; Mo. St.-Paul). Friendly, English-speaking staff. There are 131 beds at 46F
each; doors close at 1am. The same managements runs other similar establishments at 12, rue des Barres; Centre Maubuisson; 6, rue Francois Miron; and 6, rue
de Fourcy—all located in the 4ème (Mo. St.-Paul) and very close to one another.
These stars of the foyer system are all in historic buildings; Le Fauconnier may be
the most attractive, but really, you can't miss. One usually goes through AJF to
obtain a place (they will book you for free), but you can try showing up at the
foyer before 11am or after 3pm. All cost 46F per person, breakfast and shower
included, in two- to eight-bed rooms. 1am curfew. Be warned that AJF gives
priority to groups which, unlike individuals, can make reservations.

Centre International de Jeunesse (BVJ), 20, rue Jean-Jacques Rousseau, 1er (tel.
261-66-43 or 236-88-18; Mo. Louvre). An old hotel converted into a foyer; good
location near Tuileries, Louvre, les Halles. 50F per person, breakfast and shower
included, in one- to eight-person rooms. *Demi-pension* (room plus one meal
daily), 70F. No individual reservations; maximum stay two weeks. 2am curfew.
There is a brand new place run by the same management at 11, rue Jean-Jacques
Rousseau, 1er (tel. 260-77-23; Mo. Pyramides).

Foyer Franco-Libanais, 15, rue d'Ulm (tel. 329-47-60; Mo. Cardinal Lemoine or
Luxembourg). Clean, in an excellent location. When the students clear out, you
can get a room; but the management says that because of the situation in Leba-
non, the foyer will be full for a long time. Still worth a try—you might write well in
advance. Rooms 45F without shower, 60F with. Studios at 110F. In theory, open
for *résidents passagers* (transients) from July 1-Sept. 30.

Centre International de Séjour de Paris, 6, ave. Maurice Ravel, 12ème (tel. 343-19-01 or 343-29-28; Mo. Porte de Vincennes). A big place with excellent facilities. Dormitories with eight beds at 44.50F each, 55F in rooms with three to five beds and shower; singles 60.45F, doubles 71.50F. Has a bar, restaurant, self-service (meals 28F), and access to a pool, but the location is far from central.

Foyer International d'Acceuil de Paris, 30, rue Cabanis, 14ème (tel. 584-99-15; Mo. Glacière). Monolithic, modern, and clean. Rooms with four to six beds are 41.50F per person; doubles without shower 43.50F per person, 46.50F with shower; singles 46.50F. Prices slightly higher in their annex. Generally takes groups rather than individuals. Equipped for the handicapped. Complex includes self-service (25.50F meal) and bar, with breakfast 7F. The none-too-helpful management expects prices to rise by 15% in Sept.

Maison des Clubs UNESCO, 43, rue de la Glacière, 13ème (tel. 336-00 63, Mo. glacière). Modern, well-cared for, with a friendly, English-speaking staff. Will accept short-term reservations by telephone. 100 basic dorm-room places for 41F, breakfast and shower included. Maximum stay usually not more than one week. Closes at 12:30am, and they don't hand out the key. During the summer months, UNESCO also runs **Foyer Jemmapes**, 152, quai de Jemmapes, 10ème (tel. 607-90-76; Mo. Luxembourg or Odéon), same conditions, and 13, rue Vaugirard, 6ème (tel. 326-50-78; Mo. Luxembourg or Cluny), also the same.

Maison Internationale des Jeunes, 4, rue Titon, 11ème, (tel. 371-99-21; Mo. Faidherbe-Chaligny). 150 beds in rooms of three to six for ages 16-30. 50F, showers in hall. The building closes at 1am, but you can obtain a key from the doorman. Rooms are locked during the day, 10am-6pm, and the office is open all day, 8am-1pm.

Foyer des Jeunes Ledru Rollin, 151, ave. Ledru Rollin, (tel. 379-56-91; Mo. Voltaire). The doors close at 11:30pm. Open July-Sept. 10. Men only. One- and two-bedded rooms for 43F.

Le d'Artagnan, 80, rue Vitruve, 20ème (tel. 361-08-75; Mo. Porte de Bagnolet). In a fancy, modern building beside the slums. 200 beds, which cost from 38F for a place in a eight-bed dorm (these fill up fast) to 65F for a single. Doubles, triples, and quads also exist. Breakfast and shower included. No minimum or maximum stay; takes short-term reservations by phone.

Foyer International des Etudiantes, 93, blvd. St.-Michel (tel. 354-49-63; Mo. Luxembourg). From Oct.-June, takes only women who are in Paris to study or teach, but in summer takes both sexes, with the only prerequisite that they stay at least five nights. Singles 65F, doubles 47F per person. Showers included in the price, but there is no breakfast.

YWCA, 22, rue de Naples, 8ème, (tel. 522-72-70; Mo. Europe). Women only. This foyer is similar to the YWCA in the U.S. but is not affiliated with the American association. 100 beds for women 18-24. The rooms start at 44F per night, with breakfast and dinner. Monthly rates start at about 1000F. Reserve a month in advance if you plan to stay here in summer. Convenient location for the Gare St.-Lazare and the busy commercial districts, but in a dull neighborhood.

For Longer Stays:

The Cité Universitaire, 19, blvd. Jourdan, 14ème, (tel. 589-68-52; Mo. Cité Universitaire). Singles in this city of university housing run 44F; singles also available by the month for 1230F. By reservation only. For details, in the summer, American students should contact: La Fondation des Etats-Unis, 15, blvd. Jourdan, 14ème, (tel. 589-35-79; Mo. Cité Universitaire). For housing at any of the other halls at the cité, write to M. le Délégué Général de Cité Internationale Universitaire de Paris, Fondation Nationale, 19, blvd. Jourdan 75690 Paris Cedex 14. There are at least a dozen other foundations with beds (prices vary).

Association des Etudiants Protestants de Paris (AEPP), 46, rue de Vaugirard, 6ème (tel. 633-23-30 or 354-31-49; Mo. Luxembourg or Odéon). Located directly across from the Luxembourg Palace and Gardens, the AEPP has been judged one of the best and cheapest of the student foyers. Unfortunately, beginning in the fall of 1982, they will have less space for short-term visitors. Still worth a try, especially if you may be in Paris for six months to a year. The minimum stay is still five days; rooms about 40F per night, including breakfast. Cafeteria and kitchen facilities available. Reception Mon.-Fri. 8am-noon and 3-7pm, Sat. 8am-noon and 6-8pm, Sun. 10am-noon.

Hotels

Finding a hotel room in Paris might be a thoroughly disheartening affair, were it not for the excellent reservation service provided by the **Accueil des Jeunes en France,** 119, rue St.-Martin (Mo. Châtelet-Les Halles or Hôtel de Ville). Open Mon.-Sat. 9:30am-7:30pm. Also at Gare du Nord, opposite track 19; open July-Sept. 9:15am-9pm daily, Oct.-June Mon.-Fri. 9:15am-6:15pm. The days when you could breeze into Paris and find some small but charming hotel on an ancient side street are just about over—at least if you arrive during the peak tourist season (May through October, Christmas and Easter). But the people at AJF have taken a lot of the pain out of the hotel search. No longer is it necessary to take the long, discouraging walk from one less-than-charming place to the next, where you receive nothing but a curt "complet!" (full). AJF has some remarkable bargains in private hotels and in the four new youth hotels they have recently opened (prices start at about 46F, breakfast and shower included). Furthermore, they do not charge any commission for their efforts. A similar service is provided by the **Office de Tourisme de Paris,** 127, ave. des Champs Elysées, 8ème (Mo. George V). Open Mon.-Sat. 9am-10pm, Sun. and holidays 9am-8pm; off-season 9am-8pm daily.

If you want to stay in a particular Parisian hotel and you prefer to arrange everything beforehand, reserve your room at least two weeks in advance (and more time is safer). Some hotels will hold a room for you if you merely ask for one in writing, but most places require a deposit of one night's rent. Most large American banks can make out international money orders in French currency; enclose International Reply Coupons (sold at U.S. post offices). Never send more than one night's rent, otherwise you might wind up stuck in a place you don't like and struggling to get any money back.

If you prefer to look on your own, or if you are unable to make a reservation, try to arrive as early in the day as possible (though before 10am many hotels won't know whether they will have space, as lodgers often decide to stay or check out in the morning). Hotels fill up quickly after morning check-out, and by late afternoon most rooms are gone. Even if the *complet* sign is up, try reserving for the next night. It's best to try the Latin quarter (Mo. St.-Michel or Odéon), which has a high concentration of relatively inexpensive hotels— the streets radiating off of rue l'Ancienne Comédie and rue Dauphine, the rue des Ecoles, rue du Sommerard, rue Cujas (Mo. Luxembourg) and rue Victor-Cousin (which becomes rue de la Sorbonne) are all possibilities. Predictably, these are also the first hotels to fill up, and it could be much more fruitful to go to the Canal St.-Martin area (10ème, near the Gares du Nord and de l'Est).

A more costly alternative is to try the Right Bank, where hotels cluster like moths along the rue de Rivoli near the Hotel de Ville, and on some of the nearby side streets like rue du Temple. Finally, Pigalle, the sad, touristy, red-light district, specializes in cheap hotels, though their rooms are more often rented by the hour than by the day. The area is seamy and it's not the safest part of town, but as a last resort, try investigating the side streets around the Pigalle or Barbès-Rochechouart. (One word of advice: always ask to see the room before you take it—this is standard procedure and acts as a guard against any unpleasant surprises.)

The hotels below are listed geographically, beginning with the Left Bank (south) and the Right Bank (north). They have been further grouped according to neighborhood and Métro stop. The Food section is divided into corresponding districts, so check there for eateries once you've found a room.

A note on hotel prices: under the Socialist Mitterand government, there is a scheduled inflation rate of 11% per year, which is usually made in two (non-compounded) installments during January and June. Thus prices are likely to go up 5-6% before your very eyes if you are traveling in France at the end of June and the beginning of July.

Left Bank

Made up of the neighborhoods of St. Michel, the Sorbonne, Place de la Contrescarpe and Luxembourg, the Latin Quarter has a character entirely of its own. Students make up the greater part of the crowd that course its busy streets, but in summer you'll have to compete with wall-to-wall visitors for rooms in budget hotels. The Latin Quarter was once the only campus in Paris; its name reflects the fact that only Latin could be spoken by the intellectuals inhabiting its winding streets. Well into the twentieth century, this *quartier* preserved its young, but scholarly air: students made up the larger part of the crowd that coursed its busy streets and the *Boule Miche* was crowded with small, friendly bookstores. Over the last decade, however, the area has greatly changed in character. After the riots of '68, the university was quickly decentralized and the Latin Quarter lost in one blow a large portion of its traditional inhabitants. Then, the tidal wave of tourist gold washed over the area and crushed the ancient booksellers, leaving large industrial bookshops in their stead.

Today, boulevard St. Michel is still a lively place, but it is crowded now with boutiques and tourists and students you'll encounter in the cafe are more often German or Swedish than French. The Latin Quarter is now, as always, something emphatically worth seeing, but if you want to get close to Parisian life, you would do better to go out to the quieter streets of St. Martin, or to the wild but closer-to-home haunts of Montparnasse.

St. Michel is the district north of blvd. St.-Germain and east of St.-Michel (at Mo. St.-Michel and Mo. St.-Germain). These narrow winding streets host a number of simple but fairly comfortable hotels in this area, only a few minutes walk from the round-the-clock activity in the place St.-Michel.

Hôtel Henri IV, 9, rue Saint-Jacques, *5ème,* (tel. 354-51-43; Mo. St.-Michel). If you want to sleep cheaply and are not intimidated by dingy corridors and sinister back rooms, this does the job. The mattresses are lumpy and the curtains are torn, but the sheets are clean. Singles 35-50F, doubles 50F. Ask to see a room before you take it, so you know what you are in for. No breakfast or showers.

Le Petit Trianon, 2, rue de l'Ancienne Comédie, *6ème* (tel. 354-94-64; Mo. Odéon). Right off blvd. St.-Germain. A small, easily overlooked hotel in the middle of it all. Singles 65F, including required breakfast. Doubles with shower 110F (otherwise showers 10F). Guests say the owner can be very short-tempered.

Hôtel le Regent, 61, rue Dauphine, 6*ème* (tel. 326-76-45; Mo. Odéon). Functional hotel in a great location. Singles 47-74F, none with shower. Doubles 59F, 74F for two beds, 115-130F with shower. No breakfast, showers 9F. Some rooms are dark and stuffy. Reservations accepted by phone.

Hôtel Nesle, 7, rue de Nesle, 6*ème,* off the rue Dauphine (tel. 033-62-41; Mo. Odéon). A funky, if ramshackle cure for the bored and lonely traveling blues. Renée, the owner, admits that you will love it or hate it. Not the cleanest, and the WCs are a bit grim, but these purple, red, and pink rooms certainly are "special." 42.50F for a single, 55F for two, 35F for an extra bed. Showers 6.50F. Breakfast, by now a tradition with incense and Arab music, is included. Garden, six cats, corner of nirvana included. No reservations, so go early.

For those who are seeking more than the basics and have the money to spend, the following splurges will do the trick:

Eugènie Hôtel, 31, rue St.-André-des-Arts, 6*éme* (tel. 326-29-03; Mo. St.-Michel). An exquisite two-star hotel on an old and picturesque side street. The building is 200 years old, and the staircase is recognized as a historical monument. Two singles at 55F, doubles 85F (double bed) to 184F (with shower and WC). Required breakfast 13F. Shower 9F. English spoken.

Hôtel du Vieux Paris, 9 rue Git-le-Coeur, 6*ème,* (tel. 354-41-66; Mo. St. Michel). This quaint hotel is in a sixteenth-century building and boasts a long history— Henry IV himself slept here. Because of its historical charm and recent publicity in U.S. magazines, this hotel costs a bit more, but it's worth it. Singles start at 105F with breakfast, doubles start at 140F. English spoken. Reservations usually necessary.

Hôtel des Marronniers, 21, rue Jacob, 6*ème,* (tel. 325-30-60; Mo. St.-Germain-des-Pres). "Hotel of the Chestnut Trees," which are actually there in the garden. Clean hotel and lovely staff, but does not usually cater to students. Breakfast served either in the garden, salon, or your room. Quiet expected after 11pm. The hotel has recently undergone a change of ownership. Most rooms are 210F (for two) and up, breakfast 16F. Reservations necessary.

Hôtel du Quai Voltaire, 19, quia Voltaire, 7*ème,* (tel. 261-50-91; Mo. Palais-Royal). Truly fine hotel with only moderately inflated prices; view over the Louvre and the Seine. Singles start at 120F, doubles at 180F. Breakfast is included and can be taken in bed.

Plaisant Hôtel, 50, rue des Bernardins, 5*ème,* (tel. 354-74-57; Mo. Jussieu). Deserves its name. The rooms are very French: clean and pretty, with sculpted plaster ceilings. The management is friendly. Singles are 85F, doubles are 90-160F. Obligatory breakfast 11.70F. Showers 9F. English spoken.

Place de la Contrescarpe is less touristy and more bohemian than much of the rest of the Latin Quarter. The rue Mouffetard, which runs downhill from the place, has a food market most days of the week and more small, inexpensive to medium-priced restaurants than anywhere else in the city. Hotels are also plentiful in the area, but some are of questionable character. Check around the rue Monge or try these hotels. (Metro stops: Monge, Censior Daubenton, Cardinal-Lemoine, and Jussieu).

Grand Hôtel Orientale, 2, rue d'Arras, 5*ème,* (tel. 354-38-12; Mo. Jussieu or Monge). A kind proprietor and comfortable, pretty rooms. Singles from 85-95F, doubles from 95F-110F with showers. Breakfast included.

Hôtel Studia, 51, blvd. St.-Germain, 5ème, (tel. 326-81-00; Mo. Maubert). This two-star hotel is relatively inexpensive for the quality of lodging you find there, but it is popular, so reservations are necessary two months in advance for the summer. Singles start at 70F; doubles at 76F. Showers 7F.

Luxembourg, with its lovely gardens and elegant artists' *ateliers,* is as lively as neighboring St. Michel, but you might have trouble finding a room here. If you do, the rue St.-Jacques beyond the rue Soufflot (away from St. Germain) is a wonderful place for charcuteries and crèmeries, with a real small town feel to it.

Hôtel de la Faculté, 1, rue Racine, 6ème (tel. 326-87-13; Mo. St.-Michel or Odéon). As usual, it pays to go as a pair. Rooms start at 100F for one or two people, breakfast included. Showers 10F for the cheaper rooms without shower or bath.

Hôtel de Medicis, 214, rue St.-Jacques, 5ème (tel. 326-14-66; Mo. Luxembourg). One of the best small, cheap hotels in Paris. The proprietor of this family-run hotel is friendly, and the price is reasonable. Singles 38-41F, doubles 53F, three people 70F. The showers are an unusual 5F, because Mme. Rault knows that Americans take showers every day and doesn't believe she should exploit it.

University Hotel, 160, rue St.-Jacques, 5ème, (tel. 354-76-79; Mo. Luxembourg). The street-side rooms are noisy, but the others are quiet and clean. Singles 55-95F, doubles 90-120F, extra bed (for third person) 32F. Breakfast 11F, showers 8F. Longer stays get a reduction. English spoken.

Hôtel de Nevers, 3, rue de l'Abbe-de-l'Epee, 5ème, (tel. 326-81-83; Mo. Luxembourg). Nice and very clean on a pleasant side street. Friendly management. Singles with breakfast 46F, doubles 56F and up, extra bed 30F. Showers 8F, breakfast 11F.

Hôtel de l'Avenir, 52, rue Gay-Lussac, 5ème, (tel. 354-76-60; Mo. Luxembourg). One-star and a value. Prices decrease with the number of stairs you are willing to climb. Singles 48F, doubles 60-95F. Showers 8F; breakfast is 11F and more or less obligatory. Television and radio available, but the management is rather unpleasant. Also try **Hôtel du Progrès** next door. Singles 38-55F, doubles 80F, breakfast 11.50F.

Grand Hôtel Gay-Lussac, 29, rue Gay-Lussac, 5ème, (tel. 354-23-96; Mo. Luxembourg). Decent hotel, but located on a busy street. Singles 60F, doubles 90F, triples 130F, breakfast included. No deposit required for reservations. Space may be limited, because the proprietor is now working with a Danish agency which books groups.

Sorbonne Area, south of blvd. St. Germain (Mo. Maubert). The original heart and soul of the *quartier Latin,* named after the priest, Robert of Sourbon, who convinced his king to found a college for poor students on the southern bank of the Seine. Bookstores and movie theaters abound, as well as costly hotels and restaurants. Several less expensive hotels can be found along rue du Sommerard and rue des Ecoles.

Hôtel Marignan, 13 rue du Sommerard, 5ème, (tel. 354-63-81; Mo. Maubert). Right in the heart of the Latin Quarter on a quiet street between blvd. St.-Germain and rue des Ecoles, this is one of the nicest hotels in the area. March-October singles 60-75F; doubles 100-120F. That rare find, a triple with three beds, is 140-165F; a four-bed room is 200-220F. Breakfast and showers down the hall are included with all rooms. Prices are lower the rest of the year, and you may use the laundry room and kitchen as well. A babysitter will even be provided for a reasonable fee. English spoken.

Grand Hôtel de la Loire, 20, rue du Sommerard, 5ème, (tel. 354-47-60; Mo. Maubert). This is one of the least expensive hotels in Paris, but with one catch: you must stay at least five nights. Singles at 40F, doubles at 49F. No breakfast, showers 8F. The beds are not the softest, but the floors are of real wood and the rooms are clean. The owner is helpful even when he has no rooms left. No reservations accepted.

Hôtel Excelsior, 20, rue Cujas. 5ème, (tel. 634-79-50; Mo. Luxembourg). On a quiet street near the Luxembourg Gardens. Fairly clean and very cheerful, with bright wallpaper and friendly management. Some of the rooms have recently been redone. Singles 48F, doubles 60F and up. Non-obligatory breakfast 10.50F, showers 8.50F. Your dog is welcome as well if you are willing to pay 10F more. Open all night.

Hôtel Cujas, 18, rue Cujas. Another good choice on a very profitable street for hotel-hunters. 50 rooms, so you should find something. Rooms with double bed 48-75F; mostly rooms with shower at 58F. Triples 125F. No breakfast, showers 9.50F. Open all night. English spoken.

Hôtel de Flandres, 16, rue Cujas, 5ème, (tel. 634-67-30; Mo. Luxembourg). A good deal for two. Singles 50-55F, doubles 77F. Showers 8F and breakfast 10F. Open all night.

Hôtel Cluny-Sorbonne, 6, rue Victor-Cousin, 5ème, (tel. 354-66-66; Mo. Luxembourg). Could be cleaner, but the management is very pleasant and helpful. Only one single. Doubles 75-102F, triples 120-153F, quads 140F. Breakfast included, shower 9F. Try to make reservations at least a week in advance. The **The Hôtel de la Sorbonne** is at the same address, right across from the Sorbonne (tel. 354-58-08; Mo. Luxembourg). One of the nicer hotels in the area, but with somewhat higher prices. Singles 64-86F, doubles 85-97F, triples 130-150F, breakfast included. Shower 9F.

Hôtel du Commerce, 14, rue de la Montagne Ste.-Genevieve, 5ème, (tel. 354-66-66; Mo. Luxembourg). Not the cleanest of places, but the management is very pleasant and helpful. Singles 38F, doubles 58F, showers 10F. No breakfast given, no reservations taken.

Hôtel de Monaco, 11, rue Champollion, 5ème, (tel. 354-50-64; Mo. St.-Michel. On a dingy street off blvd. St.-Michel. Nice management, clean rooms, and slightly higher prices. Singles start at 60F, 80F for double occupancy. Showers 12F, non-obligatory breakfast 10F.

Montparnasse, south of the Latin Quarter in the sixth arrondissement, near the Montparnasse train station (Mo. Montparnasse-Bienvenue). The nightlife is lively here, with well-known cafe-theaters and movie houses and some seedier entertainment along rue du Gaieté. (Women, take care.)

Celtik-Hôtel, 15, rue d'Odessa, 6ème, (tel. 320-93-53; Mo. Montparnasse-Bienvenue or Edgar-Quinet). Close to the Montparnasse Tower, but also convenient to the fascinating blvd. Montparnasse, rue des Rennes, and blvd. Raspail. Comfortable, fairly clean and not a bad price for the area: singles 58F, doubles 97F., breakfast 7F. Showers 10F.

Kenmore-Hôtel, 37, blvd. de Montparnasse, 6ème, (tel. 548-20-57); Mo. Montparnasse-Bienvenue). Singles with breakfast 69F, doubles 80F. There are no showers, but you can take a bath for an extra 12F.

Modern Hôtel Maine, 71, ave. du Maine, 14ème, (tel. 326-91-11; Mo. Montparnasse-Bienvenue). Convenient to the Gare Montparnasse and across from the infamous Tower. Singles 60F, doubles 82F, showers 8F. Triples 142F with shower and WC.

Hôtel de l'Etoile d'Or, 2, rue de L-Abbé Grégoire, 6ème (Mo. Vaneau). Rooms come with no more than the basic amenities and the WC (bathrooms) smell a bit, but the beds are large and the place is fairly clean. Double-bedded with their own (un-smelly) WC cost 65F. If you are willing to use the one in the hall, both singles and doubles cost 53F, which, you will observe, is a great deal for a couple. Showers 5F, and breakfast 9.50F. May close in 1983.

Ile de la Cité

Paris was born on *Ile de la Cité;* the heart of the city, with its winding streets and its monuments is still found here. The cafe, restaurant, and hotel prices are inflated because this is prime tourist territory, but there does remain one stalwart survivor of modern-day inflation:

Hotel Henri IV, 25, place Dauphine, 1er (tel. 354-44-53: Mo. Pont-Neuf or Cité). One of the best and least expensive hotels in all of Paris, and consequently quite crowded. Located on a pretty and tranquil little square right behind the Palais de Justice and the Conciergerie, this hotel has singles for 53F, doubles for 66-76F, triples for 97, quads for 110F. Breakfast included; showers 9.50F. You must reserve a month or two in advance in order to get a room here.

Right Bank

Le Marais, a district which stretches from the rue du Renard to the Bastille, derives its name ("the swamp") from the marshy ground that was drained to extend the land available to the city in the thirteenth century. Over the years, the district that grew upon it changed hands many times. The elegant town houses *(hôtels)* for which the area is famous, were once the sole property of the aristocracy. During the seventeenth and eighteenth centuries, hosts such as Mme. de Sevigné invited the most prominent literary and artistic figures to their *salons,* which became a vital part of Parisian cultural life (her house has since been converted into the gorgeous Musée Carnavalet). After the Revolution and the destruction of the Bastille, the aristocracy fled the area, and members of the working class took up residence in the crumbling mansions. Today there is a large and longstanding Jewish community around the rue des Rosiers, which is filled with synagogues and schools, kosher butchers and *boulangeries.* In the last few years, parts of the Marais have again become fashionable; the wealth of Paris is once again taking up residence in the grand old houses. Don't let the cracked exteriors fool you, for behind many of these worn facades lie some of the most expensive real estate in Paris. The area is still one of contrast rather than uniformity, however, and among the three-star hotels you will find some surprising bargains.

Grand Hôtel du Loiret, 8, rue des Mauvais-Garcons, 4ème, (tel. 887-77-00; Mo. Hôtel de Ville). Its dingy interiors and lukewarm water are no recommendation for a comfortable stay, but the hotel is fairly cheap: 53F singles, doubles 66F. Breakfast included. Also try **Hôtel Rivoli** at #2. Singles 45-70F, doubles 60-110F, breakfast and showers 10F. A little dingy, but serviceable.

Hôtel de l'Quest, 144-146, rue St.-Honoré, 1er, (tel. 260-29-89; Mo. Louvre). Basic, almost clean, and a nice location. Singles 50-60F, doubles with showers 65-85F. Showers 10F. No breakfast.

Hôtel de Nice, 42*bis,* rue de Rivoli, 4*ème,* (tel. 278-55-29; Mo. Hôtel de Ville). A little more expensive than most, but clean and cheerful rooms near the Ile de la Cité and the Centre Pompidou. Reservations highly recommended here. Singles 69F, doubles 80-140F, breakfast included. Showers 12F.

Grand Hôtel Malher, 5, rue Malher, 4*ème,* (tel. 272-60-92; Mo. St.-Paul-le-Marais). Well-placed on a street that connects Rivoli with the heart of the Jewish quarter. Management very friendly and helpful. No singles as such, though one person can take the smaller double (one large bed) in a pinch. Doubles start at 61F. Larger rooms with more beds (for up to four people) range from 88-144F; higher priced rooms with WC and bath.

Hôtel du Progrès, 7, rue Pierre-Chausson, 10*ème,* (tel. 208-16-55; Mo. J.-Bonsergent or République). One star, but a little cheaper than most. Small singles for 50F, doubles 60-140F (more expensive doubles could sleep three or four). Breakfast and showers 10F each; elevator.

Hôtel de Nevers, 53, rue de Malte, 11*ème,* (tel. 700-56-18; Mo. République). A pretty, one-star hotel, complete with elevator. Singles 52F and doubles 70F. Showers 10F and breakfast 12F. The management is a bit unpleasant.

Hôtel Lafayette, 198, rue La Fayette, 9*ème,* (tel. 607-44-79; Mo. Gare du Nord or Gare de l'Est). Yet another one-star hotel, not ravishing but very serviceable; singles at 70F, doubles at 120F, and showers 12F more. You pay here for the location. Doors lock at 1am. No elevator, but two rooms on the ground floor.

Near the Bastille are a few gritty places, some of them residential, all in working-class neighborhoods. Try them if you are stuck or you want a sootier taste to your Parisian experience:

Hôtel du Chemin de Fer, 6 rue de Charenton, 12*ème,* (Mo. Bastille). Not the prettiest nor the cleanest, but inexpensive: 37-40F for a single or a double; 50-65F if you want a shower in the room. No breakfast, but there are plenty of cafes around where you can get one. If this place is full, there is another hotel next door of approximately the same quality and price.

Hôtel des Alliés, 90, rue Faubourg Saint-Antoine, (Mo. Bastille). A basic, service-able place, with singles starting at 45F, doubles 55F. The rooms are clean but very small. No breakfast, and the hotel lock-up varies according to the proprietor's bedtime (usually 10:30-11pm).

Hôtel St. Armand, 6, rue Trousseau, 11*ème,* (Mo. Ledru-Rollin). It is not apparent that the *hôteliers* really want anyone to stay here, but it is clean and very cheap. Singles and doubles 39-42F. No breakfast.

Opéra

Opéra-St.-Lazare. Close to the Pigalle and Montmartre area, walking distance from the *Grands Magasins,* and on a direct Métro line to the Left Bank, this district is centrally-located and alive with business and commercial activity.

Hôtel de Nantes, 55, rue St.-Roch, 1*er,* (tel. 261-67-78; Mo. Tuilleries). Excellent location near the church of St.-Roch. Single bed from 75F, 105F, with WC; two beds 95F, 125F with shower or bath. Breakfast included. Showers 10F if not in rooms.

Hôtel des Trois Poussins, 15 rue Clauzel, 9*ème,* (tel. 874-38-20; Mo. St. Georges). This is one of those finds that are becoming rarer: a family hotel whose owners are eager to go out of their way to make their guests feel at home. Ask M. Desforges to show you the rooms he has remodelled himself. The prices are a bit steep: doubles start at 80F, 120F with shower; 190F for a triple with bath and kitchen. Extra child's bed 30F. Showers 12.50F, breakfast 10F. If you are planning to stay more than a few days the Desforges are willing to negotiate a price. No reservations by phone.

Hôtel de Berne, 30, rue de Chateaudun, 9ème, (tel. 874-37-66; Mo. Notre-Dame de Lorette). Clean and attractive, but on a busy street which can be a bit noisy. Pleasant management. One bed: (1-2 people) 52-125F, two beds (2-4 people) 125-130F. Breakfast 12F, shower 10F.

Camping

Camping is not the way to stay in Paris; this is a city which should be taken in from its midst. Besides, there are very few available spaces in the campgrounds near Paris during the summer, and it is probably best to avoid camping here if at all possible. If you are determined to join the mob and pitch your tent anyway, contact either the **Touring Club de France**, 65, ave. de la Grande-Armée, 16ème, (tel. 502-14-00; Mo. Porte Maillot), or the **Camping Club of France**, 218, blvd. St.-Germain, 7ème, (tel. 548-30-03; Mo. Rue du Bac) for a list of nearby campgrounds. The **tourist office** at 127, ave. Champs-Elysées, 8ème, Mo. George V, can usually provide campground information as well. Michelin map #96 is useful for locating the following sites. Note that all but the first site are a considerable distance from the city.

Camp TCF (Touring Club of France) Bois du Boulogne, Route de Bord de l'Eau, 16ème, (tel. 506-14-98; Mo. Porte Maillot). Off route N185. The only campsite in Paris and an extremely huge operation with store, laundry and warm showers. From the station, take the summer "Camping TCF" bus (5F) to the campground.

Camping du Tremblay (TCF), quai de Polangis, 94500 Champigny-sur-Marne (Val de Marne), Mo. RER Champigny (tel. 283-38-24) is 14km east of Paris on the N4 and A4.

Camping du Camp des Cigognes, bord de Marne Créteil, Val de Marne (tel. 207-06-75). Can be reached by the RER Créteil l'Echat stop.

Camping Municipal de Porchefontaine, 31, rue Berthelot, 78000 Versailles (tel. 951-23-63) is 22km west of Paris. Near the N10 in the Bas Meudon (if biking, be prepared for some steep hills on the way).

Down and Out

If you are really down-and-out and need some help, contact:

The American Aid Society, in the U.S. Embassy, 2, ave. Gabriel, 8ème, (tel. 296-12-02; Mo. Concorde). Open weekdays in the morning; for Americans only.

Armée du Salut (Salvation Army) for cases of real desperation: Main office, 76, rue de Rome, 8ème, (tel. 387-41-19; Mo. St.-Lazare). **Asile Flottant** near 93, quai de la Gare, 13ème, (tel. 584-34-00; Mo. quai de la Gare) or **Cité de Refuge Hommes Femmes,** 12, rue Cantagrel, 13ème, (tel. 583-54-00; Mo. Porte d'Ivry or Chavaleret) or at the **Aisle Nicholas Flamed,** 63, rue des Rentiers, 13ème (tel. 583-20-20).

If you have tried everything, we suggest as a last resort—for men only—a few bridges and parks, conveniently located and cheap, but more than a little risky:

Quai d'Orléans, quai de Béthune, Mo. Maubert-Mutualité. On a clear night, this is probably your best bet. There are trees, benches, and steps available, most with a view of Notre Dame's flying buttresses. Sometimes the smell can be a problem. Several bridges are nearby in case it looks like rain.

Square de l'Ile de France, Mo. Sully-Morland. Although well guarded, this park has good potential and the view of Notre Dame is unbeatable. Crowded on November 11, Armistice Day.

Pont Neuf, Mo. Pont-Neuf. If you get settled early enough, or slip by late when no one is looking, you can sleep in the small square du Vert-Galant right below the statue of Henri IV. If the police bother you, appeal to the king. Somewhat public, and not a place to go if it looks like rain.

Bois de Boulogne, Mo. Porte d'Auteuil, Porte Maillot, Sablons, or Pont de Neuilly. This park stays open legally all night, but most of what happens there after dark is illegal. Some idea for **Bois de Vincennes,** Mo. Chateau de Vincennes, place Bérault, Porte Dorée or Liberté. If you stay in the Bois de Boulogne, sleep near the campground, for the comfort it provides.

For women who have no place to stay late at night, the best best is to go to the Police—they will keep you safe for the night, if not extremely comfortable. If you can't bring yourself to go to them, then the train stations are your best bet: in the summertime there are plenty of people in them all night long, and scores of sleeping-bag-cocooned travelers stretched out on the ground.

Food

Eating in Paris should always be a pleasure. Good food and drink contribute as much to the character of the city as do the *hauts couturiers* and the Métro. So try not to succumb to the comforting familiarity of MacDonald's (there are seven) or the impersonal convenience of Les Selfs (self-service restaurants). Even the strictest budget wil allow a wide range of adventurous experiments.

While the famous multi-starred restaurants cost about as much as they do at home, you can still eat an unforgettable restaurant meal for 30F, especially if you go light on wine. Some very cheap French restaurants hide in quiet corners of the city, but the more obvious inexpensive choices (especially those in the Latin Quarter) represent a dizzying range of other cultures—Greek, Italian, Vietnamese, and North African, often all crammed together on one small street. Just don't try to cut too many corners. Here food is something to be treated with respect, not to be scrimped on. Flaunt too many culinary conventions, and you'll be made to feel like the ugliest American ever, with shovels for hands and a tiny little tightwad in your pocket. If you don't have much money, avoid restaurants altogether. A little bit of food costs a lot, and anyway, cafes are much better suited to *les petits* faims (little hungers).

If you do decide to eat out, remember that dinner is served quite late here—between 7pm and 10pm. A fine, and very Parisian dish to try is a *gratinée*, or French onion soup, with a bread and cheese crust, for about 10F at any medium-sized cafe. To avoid trouble, look for *prix fixe* (fixed price) menus and *service compris* (service counted into the total price). Salade (just lettuce and vinaigrette, if not otherwise noted), generally follows the main course to clear the palate for dessert, which is often cheese. Generous helpings of bread accompany the meal, almost always for free. To finish comes tar-black espresso, served in lethal little cups.

Most of the time, of course, you will be fending for yourself. You will do very well, as Parisian open markets are everywhere, very colorful and offering an awesome variety of food. The French style of shopping is ideally suited to picnic meals; storeowners are used to people buying a small slice of paté or enough salad for two. In markets and specialty stores, you usually point and the salesperson gets, while supermarkets often leave you to serve yourself. Market hours vary, but *épiceries, boulangeries,* and other small stores seldom close before 7pm; almost everyone closes for a few hours in the afternoon. At any time of day, you can fall willing prey to vendors selling crêpes for about 6F, candy, roasted chestnuts in winter, and ice cream in any season. You can even take full meals home with you from *charcuteries,* couscous joints, and Chinese restaurants. Look for the words *à emporter* (to carry away).

Restaurants

The restaurants listed below follow the same basic organization as our Hotels section. Left Bank restaurants are clustered in the St.-Michel area north of blvd. St.-Germain and in the Contrescarpe district. On the Right Bank, most of the restaurants are in the Marais and St. Lazare-Opéra areas, but some are located in the Montmartre area further north.

Left Bank

St.-Michel, Odéon, Luxembourg

Restaurant des Beaux-Arts, 11, rue Bonaparte, 6ème (Mo. St.-Germain-des Près). Usually crowded, and for a very good reason. Menu for 33F, beverage and service included, the mainly traditional food is good, and relatively inexpensive. *Poissons au gratin* (fish and cheese casserole) and the *tarte à la maison* are highly recommended. Located right across from the Ecole des Beaux-Arts. Open daily noon-2:30pm and 7-10:30pm.

Les Balkans, 33, rue St.-Jacques, 5ème (Mo. Maubert-Mutualité) and also at 3, rue de la Harpe, 5ème (Mo. St.-Michel). An old standby in the Latin Quarter featuring "Eastern Specialties" including shish kebab, *couscous,* and good vegetable dishes. *Menu* at 28.20F. Both branches are open Sun.

La Mazarinade, 4, rue J. Callot, 6ème (Mo. St.-Germain-des-Près). A corner cafe-restaurant with outdoor seating 30F menu as familiar as the candledrip bottles on red-checkered tablecloths—but the quality and quantity of the food served makes it a bit special. Check out the generous salad bar with a 15F unlimited hors d'oeuvres plate.

Le Jardin de Grégoire, 10, rue Grégoire de Tours, 6ème (Mo. Odéon). One of the few French restaurants that has an unlimited salad bar, but salads are only endless for those who order the excellent 38F *menu* (including roast veal). There is also a 30F*menu.* Add 15% service. On a street with a dozen good, inexpensive restaurants.

Les Byzantins, 33, rue Dauphine, 6ème (Mo. Odéon). A well-touristed, but unspoiled bar-restaurant featuring Greek specialties between 19-42F. *Menu* 27F, not including service or beverage.

La Procope, 13, rue de l'Anclenne Comédie, 6ème (Mo. Odéon). Well-known restaurant dating from 1686 and boasting to be the oldest in the world. Clientele has included the likes of Voltaire, Ben Franklin, and Robspierre. Luckily, past glories have not spoiled Procope, and it still serves very good French food. Not a budget restaurant, but a healthy lunch menu is served for 27F, not including tips and drinks. Otherwise, the menu is 61F. The large *à la carte* menu offers traditional fare: onion soup *gratinée* (14F), duckling with cherries (30F), and *truite meunière* (22F). Open noon-2pm, closed on Mon. and in July.

A La Bonne Crêpe, 11, rue Grégoire de Tours, 6*ème*, serves crêpes and crêpes only. Start with a *galette*, a dinner crêpe filled with ham, egg, or spinach ("Le Popeye"), and for dessert try one with chocolate, marmalade, or Grand Marnier *flambé*. Cider is the customary accompaniment to Breton crêpes, and is served in traditional ceramic bowls for 4F. Crêpes run 15F a piece, but a *menu* is available at 26F. This is a fine place for a light meal or snack; just walking down this street is a treat. Open noon-10:30pm, closed Sun.

La Microbiothèque, 17, rue de Savoie, 6*ème* (Mo. Odéon). A health food restaurant serving walnut and apple yogurt, salad (10F), zucchini, and brown rice (12F) and lots else. All greens are unsprayed, but unfortunately the management isn't as pleasant as the cuisine it prepares. The menu is 28F, beverage and service included, no liquor. A small health food store is at the front of the restaurant.

Crèmerie-Restaurant Polidor, 41, rue Monsieur-le-Prince, 6*ème* (Mo. Odéon). Between blvd. St.-Michel and the Odéon Theater. Hemingway and Chagall dined in this atmospheric old restaurant. It is still a very popular place, so be prepared to wait a few minutes for a table, especially if you arrive late. Lunch menu with service, no beverage, 26F. Dinners, including wine, for about 40F. *Boeuf bourguignon* and *sauté d'agneau* are the house specialties. Open noon-2:30pm, 7-10pm. Closed Sun.

Luxembourg

La Godasse, 38, rue Monsieur le Prince, 5*ème* (Mo. Odéon). The name is slang for "old shoe," but have no fear: the food they serve can in no way be described as tasting like leather. The *menu* at 36.50F offers unlimited hors d'oevres. All sorts of meats grilled on a wood fire.

Zero de Conduite, 64, rue Monsieur le Prince, 6*ème* (Mo. Luxembourg). Frequented by Parisians. The atmosphere may not be fancy, but the place is lively and the 36.80F *menu* (service included) is of consistently high quality.

Aux Charpentiers, 10, rue Mabillon, 6*ème* (Mo. Mabillon). This restaurant caters to students, but has a good reputation among Parisian grownups as well. Large quantities of unmistakably French food. No *menu,* but reasonably priced. Closed Sundays.

Place de la Contrescarpe

The rue Mouffetard, a market street teeming with stalls and shoppers by day, is an international diner's paradise by night. Many of the restaurants are Greek, a few are Vietnamese, some are North African, and a couple are French. Most charge 30-45F a meal. Shop around before choosing. For before or after dinner drinking, the cafe right on the *place*, the **Chope,** offers maximum visibility, but beware of prices.

If you're living hand-to-mouth, the nearby Luxembourg Gardens are scattered with benches on which you can guzzle your Perrier or wine, and munch on the take-out Greek sandwiches, 8F, sold everywhere.

Restaurant My-Vi, 6, rue des Ecoles, 5*ème* (Mo. Cardinal Lemoine). This is the cheapest and highest quality menu in the Latin Quarter. (The owner claims that he can keep his prices low because of the volume of *Let's Go* business.) 20.50F (service included) for hors d'oeuvres or soup, entrée, rice, and dessert. Chinese-Vietnamese specialties *à la carte*. The friendly management speaks English. Open noon-2:30pm and 6:30-10:30pm every day except for lunch on Sun.

Tay-Do, 16, rue des Ecoles. If the crowd at My-Vi is too much for you, try walking down the street to this place, which serves similar fare on a 25F *menu* and has specialties from 20-28F. Open 7-11pm daily except Tuesday.

L'Ecurie, 2, rue Laplace, *5ème* (Mo. Cardinal Lemoine). A place of dark wood, low ceilings, and French countryside. Small wooden tables outside look onto a tiny quiet old street, near the Ecole Polytechnique. Specialties, including mussels and andocuilettes, 18-42F; a few vegetarian dishes also available.

Le Volcan (Chez Bali), 10, rue Thouin, on the corner of rue Descartes, *5ème* (Mo. Cardinal Lemoine). Another Left Bank standby. A large restaurant, a 31F *menu* (drink and service included) with considerable variety, featuring decent French and Greek food, reasonable prices, fast service, and lots of customers. The *brochettes* are consistently good.

La Droguerie, 1, rue Mouffetard, *5ème* (Mo. Cardinal Lemoine). Decorated with colorful cartoons of octopi and fishnets on its walls. Lunch *menu* 32.50F, dinner a pricey 42.50F but with an exceptionally wide variety. The 32.50 menu includes service and beverage. Highly recommended are *truite* (trout) and *tarte à la maison*. Outside seating and a large *à la carte* selection are available. Open daily noon-2pm, 7:30pm-midnight.

Crêperie de la Mouff, 9, rue Mouffetard, *5ème* (Mo. Cardinal Lemoine). Delightful aroma in a clean, white-curtained setting. Good for a snack or meal. Crêpes and *galettes* (13F) made in front of you. A meal can cost you 18-30F if you're not a heavy eater. Try the smoked salmon crêpes for 19F. Closed Sun., open Mon. for dinner only.

Le Poele, 47, rue Descartes, *5ème* (Mo. Cardinal Lemoine). A tiny place always uncomfortably crowded, but serves gargantuan portions of French food with a Mediterranean influence. Their chicken dishes are original and good; steak-lovers should try their *poivre*. Fixed-price *menus* at 29 and 35F (plus service). Often a line after 7:30pm. Closed Mon.; open other days till 2am. Outdoor seating.

La Culotte, rue Pot de Fer, *5ème* (Mo. Monge) is a friendly little place that serves a good French *menu* for 38F. Closed Sun. Nearby, the **Tire-Bouchon** serves mouthwatering fondue for under 50F.
Aux Savoyards, rue des Boulangers, *5ème* (Mo. Jussieu), is a homey French place which serves home-cookd French food, with a menu for 35F, drink and service included. Closed Sat. afternoon and Sun.

Montparnasse

When the Bretons come down to Paris from their homeland in the north, they disembark at Gare Montparnasse. And with them they bring their seafood specialties—crabs, oysters and pretty *bigournots* (sea snails). Be sure to check the prices before you enter, as they can be quite high.

Taverne du Maître Kanter, 68, blvd. du Montparnasse, *15ème* (Mo. Montparnasse-Bienvenue). A huge place with balconies and two main levels, all decorated in an Austrian style. The specialty of the house, a huge plate of *choucroute* (a fancy variety of sauerkraut) with sausage or ham, costs 33F. For a real treat order the *Plateau de Fruits de Mer* (seafood) for 56F which is enough for two.

Les Bistros de la Gare, 59, blvd. Montparnasse, one of several scattered around the city. Bought up by the son of a famous French chef and turned into a French *"chaine"*. The food is standardized but tasty; elegant turn-of-the-century atmosphere. The food served is classically French—creamy and rich. The *menu* is 42.50F, not including drink or service. For dessert, order *la jatte*, the biggest helping of chocolate mousse you've ever seen, for 12F. (Don't ask for extra spoons—they'll charge you for them). You will find other Bistros de la Gare at 38, blvd. des Italiens, 9*ème*; and at 73, Champs Elysées.

Le Petit Parnasse, 138, rue de Vaugirard, 15*ème* (Mo. Pasteur). This little restaurant is always crowded, and for good reason: it serves three high-quality menus, at 40F (noon only) and 52.50F. Main service included. Excellent French food, and quite a bit of it; if that sounds good to you, you should try to reserve a table. Closed Sundays.

Northwest of Montparnasse

U Sampieru Corsu, 12, rue de l'Amiral Roussin, 15*ème* (Mo. La Motte-Picquet). An anarchist restaurant run by a Corsican. You are served large quantities of whatever's available that day; 21F is the suggested payment. (You put your money in a large drawer and payment is by honor.) On nights when there is entertainment (usually politically-minded), a few francs is added to the meal cost to help support the artist.

Le Commerce, 51, rue du Commerce, 15*ème* (Mo. La Motte-Picquet). Same management as Le Drouot and Le Chartier, with the same delicious food, although the decor is not as fancy. *Menu* is 27F, drink included. This is the place to go after seeing the Eiffel Tower or wandering the Rodin museum. After supper take a walk along the fascinating rue du Commerce.

On or near L'Ile de la Cité

Tabac Henri IV, place Dauphine, 1*er* (Mo. Pont-Neuf). Right off the Pont Neuf and across from the hotel of the same name, this is a friendly, wooden tavern offering interesting French menus for 24F (service not included). Open Mon.-Fri. 11:30am-10pm. Saturday noon-3pm. Closed Sun.

Le Menestrel, 51, rue Saint-Louis-en-l'Ile, 4*ème* (Mo. Sully-Morland). A small, friendly restaurant with a familiar menu (chicken and steak). *Menu* at 35F, service included. Closed Sunday nights and Mondays. For desert, try the ice cream at **Berthillon,** right up the street at #31. Spectacular ice cream and very cheap. Seating inside, take-out window on the street. Open Wed.-Sat. 1-10pm, Sun. 2-10pm; closed Mon. and Tues.

Le Saint-Antoine, 21, rue des Prêtres-St. Germain l'Auxerrois, 1*er* (Mo. Pont-Neuf). This restaurant has a simple but hearty *menu* which has remained the same for years and years, and has pleased enough people to win the *imprimateur* of a number of serious international dining clubs. *Menus* at 42F (pork), 45F (beef), and 48F (veal)—which gives you the approximate class hierarchy of French meats. Service not included. Closed Mon.

Right Bank

There are several inexpensive restaurants in the rue Vivienne area of the 2*ème*, but it is not the most comfortable place for a woman to walk alone. Be prepared to encounter a superabundance of sleazy massage parlors and sleazier men.

South of Montmartre. These restaurants are only a ten-minute walk from Les Halles, but already in a residential neighborhood, with lots of places to choose from.

Tout au Beurre, 5, rue Mandat 2ème (Mo. Sentier). Serves wholesome food at reasonable prices, if one sticks with the *menu.* For 31F (beverage and service included) you'll receive a full meal, which changes daily. Open Sundays.

La Tourtière, 11, rue Mandar, 2ème (Mo. Sentier or Les Halles). An intimate restaurant run by a woman with a culinary mission: to bring back the art of French tart-making to include *"tartes salées"* (those made with salt instead of sugar, something like pizza, but lighter and obviously French). Main courses are *tartes salées* with various combinations of meat, vegetable, and cheese toppings; for dessert, *tartes sucrées,* sweet with fruit toppings. *Menus* at 25F and 36F. You can also buy tarts of either variety by the slice to eat there or take out. Closed Sun. and Mon.

Les Halles—Marais

Restauranteurs here are more than aware that tourists throng to the Centre Pompidou and have jacked up their prices accordingly. An omelette eaten with a privileged view of the steel and glass structure can cost three times as much as one bought in a less-touristed area farther south. The Centre's own penthouse cafe offers a spectacular view of the city, but its prices are just as spectacular. Bring your own edibles or head for the section behind Beaubourg towards the Marais. The Marais has a sizeable Orthodox Jewish community, and bagels, lox, and kosher corned-beef share space with *baguettes, éclaires,* and more standard French fare. (Tragically, this was the scene of last summer's terrorist attacks, but there is no clear reason why you should avoid the area altogether.) If you are at the Louvre, head towards the Left Bank, or eat at one of the North African restaurants in the area.

Restaurant Le Smalah, 9, rue de la Verrerie, 4ème (Mo. Hotel de Ville). Rumored that the *couscous* here, which starts at 28F, is better than at other restaurants who celebrate the specialty in their name. Open daily all summer for lunch and dinner.

Le Refuge, 4, rue des Halles, 1èr (Mo. Chatelet). Nothing fancy, but good for a budget meal. Choice of Italian or Spanish menu for 23F with service, beverage extra.

Goldenberg's, 7, rue des Rosiers, 4ème (Mo. Saint-Paul). This kosher-style deli, with Jewish foods from all over the world, is almost an institution in its own right. Strictly kosher *(cacher)* food around the area.

Le Roüergue, Chez Julien, 23, rue Herold, 1er (Mo. Les Halles). A bar-restaurant whose wooden-beam cave atmosphere survives the pinball machines in front. The food is good and the *menu* 27F. Beverage and service included. Fish and meat entrees. Open only for lunch from 11am-3pm; closed Sun.

Mini-Ferme, 40, rue St.-Honore, 1er (Mo. Louvre or Les Halles). This new restaurant serves 100 varieties of omelettes. It has a slightly fast-food aura, but where else could you get omelette with morels? Prices range from 8-40F, with most 12-25F. Dessert omelettes also available. Open daily 8am-10pm.

Aquarius, 54, rue Ste.-Croix de la Bretonnerie (Mo. Hôtel de Ville or Rambuteau). This small vegetarian restaurant is run by the Rosicrucians and serves completely vegetarian fare *à la française,* including omelettes, salads, and *quenelle de soja* (soy), all made with *légumes biologique* (organically grown vegetables) and without preservatives. *Menu* 30F, service included. Also sells its own bread and has a small Rosicrucian bookstore. Restaurant open daily noon-9:30pm, except closed Sun.

Opéra and St. Lazare

Although this area is full of expensive restaurants and food stores, there are a few fine, inexpensive restaurants for the budget-minded.

Le Richelieu, 103, rue de Richilieu, 2*ème* (Mo. Richilieu-Drouot). Only a 15-min. walk from the Louvre. The atmosphere is lively and the prices are relatively low. The *menu* is a bit expensive, but most of the main dishes cost about 17F, so you can eat *à la carte* (and drink) for about 27F, not including service. **Le Chartier,** 7, Faubourg-Montmartre, 9*ème* (Mo. Montmartre) is owned by the same people as Le Drouot and offers the same quality food in a somewhat more formal setting, but for the same low prices. Open every day 11am-3pm and 6-9:30pm.

Ma Normandie, 11, rue Rameau, 2*ème* (Mo. Pyramides). Right down the street from the Bibliotheque Nationale and close to both the Opera and the Louvre. This is a great place for lunch with a 27F *menu* including drinks and service. The menu changes every day and offers a wide variety of entrees, including salmon. There are several rooms to accommodate the huge numbers of people who frequent this place. Open Mon.-Fri 11am-2:30pm

Chez Stella, 3, rue Thérèse, 1*er* (Mo. Palais-Royal or Pyramides). A tasty array of hors d'oeuvres, entrees and desserts offered on a 28F *menu* service but not beverage included. Main dishes 20-30F. Open noon-2pm and 7:30-9pm. Closed weekends and holidays.

L'Incroyable, 26, rue de Richelieu, 1*er*, (Mo. Palais-Royal). The food is simple and good, and the price is a bit unbelievable, with *menus* at 29F and 35F, service included. A pretty, turn-of-the-century dining room, with a tiny covered terrace, and a regular clientele.

Restaurant André Fauré, 40, rue du Mont-Thabor, 1*er* (Mo. Tuilleries), is a splurge place that specializes in farmer-sized meals. The 40F *menu* is feeble by comparison; the real reason to come is the 63F don't-eat-for-another-week *dîner fermier,* which has four courses, including unlimited hors d'oevres and wine. This is the place to try rabbit stew (really). Popular, so you may have to wait. On the same street at #28 is **Le Petit Ardechois,** one of those rare places where you can get food 24 hours a day, including such basic fare as onion soup (20F) and *omelette paysanne* (25F). Avoid the expensive *menu,* though

Southwest of St. Lazare

Le Grand Chinois, 6 ave. de New-York, 16*ème* (Mo. Alma-Marceau). An elegant Chinese restaurant (for a change), in an elegant quartier of Paris. Get the *menu* for 46F service included, sit in the comfortable dining room and look out at the beautiful garden. Run by the daughter of the man who owns the excellent **Pagoda Restaurant,** 50, rue de Provence, 9*ème;* this restaurant has a 40F *menu* that is worth trying as well.

Le Volnay, 6, rue de Labords, 8*ème* (Mo. St.-Lazare or St.-Augustin). For 35F, drink and service included, one can have beef bourgignon or *coq au vin* along with other carefully prepared dishes. Less crowded in the evening than at lunch. Closed Saturday night and Sunday.

Farther north of St. Lazare

La Bonne Cuisine, 17, rue Biog, 17*ème* (Mo. Clichy). Fish is the specialty here; stick to the 30F *menu*, service included, or else you could drop well over 55F per person. Closed. Tues. evenings and Wed.

" A La Bonne Table, 5, rue Seveste, 18*ème* (Mo. Anvers). A 200-year-old family tradition featuring equally traditional food on a three-course, 35F *menu* and a four-course, 39F *menu*. At the foot of Sacré Coeur.

University Restaurants

Institutional food—even in France—is poor, but it is inexpensive. Eating in one of the Restaurants Universitaire (Resto-U) provides the opportunity of meeting French students. Students with an International Student Identity Card or a valid American College ID may purchase *passager* (transient) meal tickets for 11F each. If you know some French students, you can buy tickets from them for less: they pay only about 5F.

Most university restaurants are open from 11:30am-2pm for lunch and 6-8pm for dinner. Many are closed on weekends and only a few stay open in the summer. The Accueil des Jeunes, 119, rue St.-Martin, 4*ème*, Mo. Rambuteau (tel. 277-87-80) or CROUS, 39, ave. Georges Bernanos, 5*ème*, Mo. Port-Royal (tel. 329-12-43) will provide you with the summer schedule.

Albert Chatelet, 10 rue Jean Calvin, 5*ème*, Mo. Censier-Daubenton.

Alliance Française, 101, blvd. Raspail, 6*ème*, Mo. St.-Placide, has a restaurant with better than average student food for 18-20F (dinner), 12-16F (lunch). A good place to meet students from all over the world.

Assas, 92, rue d'Assas, 6*ème*, Mo. Notre-Dame-des-Champs.

Bullier, 39, ave. Georges Bernanos, 5*ème*, Mo. Port-Royal.

Censier, 3, rue Censier, 5*ème*, Mo. Censier-Daubenton.

CHU Necker, 15, rue de Vaugirard, 15*ème*, Mo. Pasteur.

Citeaux, 4, rue de Citeaux, 12*ème*, Mo. Reuilly-Diderot.

Concordia, 41, rue Tournefort, 5*ème*, Mo. Monge.

Cuvier, 8*bis*, rue Cuvier, 5*ème*, Mo. Jussieu.

Grand-Palais, Cours-la-Reine, 8*ème*, Mo. Champs Elysées-Clemenceau.

La Table D'Hôtel, 16, rue du Pont Louis-Philippe, 4*ème*, Mo. Pont-Marie, is the restaurant run by the Accueil. Full meals for under 26F. Tickets are sold about an hour before the meal.

Mabillon, 3, rue Mabillon, 6*ème*, Mo. Mabillon.

Cafés

Cafés are a valuable public service, and an integral part of Parisian social life. The vast majority are unfancy corner "locals," like British neighborhood pubs, that cater to a loyal local clientele, and are reasonably priced. Some, however, are famous, chic, and expensive (or simply expensive), and it pays to understand the law of café prices. Basically, the cost of a drink in a café is determined by real estate values. If the café is situated on a busy thoroughfare, especially a fashionably busy thoroughfare (e.g. the Champs Elysées, blvd. St.-Germain, rue de la Paix), prices will be astronomical—in the neighborhood of 10-15F for a cup of coffee. A café half a block away, down a side street, will charge a half or a third as much, simply because its location offers less visibility. But no matter how posh or pedestrian the café, buying one drink enables a customer to sit for quite a while. The price of the drink is considered rent on the chair, and you can stay as long as you want. Cafés are required to post their prices, so look first to avoid paying more than you should. Drinks at the bar are about a third cheaper than drinks served to a table. A tip at the bar used to be left to the customer's discretion, but is now beginning to be included on the bill. Service charges are usually included on the bill at a table.

In addition to serving drinks and food, cafés provide two other essential services: telephones and toilets. Every café possesses at least one public phone, and charges 80 centimes-1F centimes for a call, twice as expensive as in a post office. The toilets are often of the Turkish variety, also known as "squatters," with two marks for your feet and a hole in the center. It's a good idea to bring your own toilet paper, since you never know what the café owner will provide (if anything). The conveniences are always located near the telephones, and are almost always free. If you are passing a café and need to use the facilities but don't want to buy a drink, simply walk in as if you are going to use the telephone—the ploy almost always works. In expensive cafés and restaurants, an attendant sits outside the bathroom and expects a tip: leave about half a franc. A red, diamond-shaped sign outside a café signifies that it is a tabac as well, and sells cigars, cigarettes, matches, postage stamps, and a selection of other useful items like batteries, razor blades, Métro tickets, and lottery tickets. Stamps are no more expensive in tabac than in a post office.

Cafés also serve excellent sandwiches for as little as 9F. They consist of about ⅓ of a baguette filled with ham, cheese (usually *camembert*), or paté. A lot less filling is the *croque-monsieur,* a grilled ham and cheese sandwich, while a *croque-madame* is the same with an egg. In the cheaper cafés a sandwich, wine, and coffee will usually cost less than 18F at the counter or a bit more sitting down.

In Paris, most beer on tap is lager, and a glass of draught is called *une pression* or *une demie.* Bottled beers, foreign and domestic, are available as well. *Monaco* is beer with grenadine syrup mixed in. *Kir* is white wine with *cassis* (black currant syrup). *Anis* is the traditional licorice-flavored apertif that turns cloudy when water is added: familiar brands are Pernod and Ricard. Cinzano and Dubonnet are sweetish apertifs. Mixed drinks, of the American cocktail lounge variety, are almost never served in cafés. If you crave a Tom Collins or a Manhattan, you will have to go to one of Paris' American bars (see Entertainment).

You will have no difficulty finding one of the hundreds of neighborhood cafés which charge very reasonable prices for their drinks and food. A tried-and-true establishment is *La Tartine,* 24, rue de Rivoli, 4*ème* (Mo. St.-Paul). Catering to a very local clientele, this turn-of-the-century café charges 5-8F for sandwiches, and is located on a very busy thoroughfare close to the Marais. Or, on the Left Bank, try the venerable **La Pallitte,** 16, rue J. Callot, on a street filled with galleries near the Ecole des Beaux Arts. Its clientele is as interesting as the murals over the bar. If you're looking for something a little more chic and are willing to pay the inflated prices, here are a few suggestions:

La Coupole, 102, blvd. du Montparnasse, 14*ème,* Mo. Vavin, at the intersection of the blvd. du Montparnasse and blvd. Raspail. One of the most famous cafés in Paris. Open daily from 8am-2am; in Aug., Tues.-Sat. 11am-1pm.

La Closerie des Lilas, 171, blvd. du Montparnasse, 14ème,Mo. Port-Royal. A beautiful atmosphere with foliage-covered private areas. You are definitely contributing to the gardener's paycheck when you come here. Very expensive. Open daily for lunch, dinner, and drinks.

Aux Deux Magots, blvd. St.-Germain, 6ème, Mo. St.-Germain-des-Près. A very chic café and former hang-out for Sartre and Hemingway. In the center of the St.-Germain evening "scene."

Café de la Pais, place de l'Opera, 9ème, Mo. Opéra. A super-sophisticated café right in the middle of the busy Opéra district, it offers a front-row center view of Parisian life.

Café de Paris, in the Arcades des Champs Elysées, 8ème, Mo. George V. For luscious desserts (creative ice cream sundaes, 18-25F, indescribably elaborate pastries and tortes 15-20F in a trendy and well-known arcade secluded from the traffic on the Champs Elysées. A good place to splurge on your way to the post office (across the street at #71).

Building the City

Stand by Notre Dame on the **Ile de la Cité,** where Paris began, and imagine a Roman temple in place of the twin-towered Cathedral. To the north lies marshland or *marais;* to the south are the Roman forum and baths. As the years pass, Paris becomes the capital city of the Franks, but the Roman palaces will stand until the thirteenth century. Under Philippe Auguste, a wall springs up to protect the city; the slender **Tour de Nesle** raises itself to the sky, reflected on the Right Bank by the first building of the **Louvre.** Soon **Notre Dame** makes her grand début, while **Les Halles** becomes the central marketplace and hospitals and aqueducts appear all over the city. Over on the Left Bank, students are officially made members of the **University of Paris** in 1215, but it is another forty years before they are granted their own building, **The Sorbonne.** Over on the middle of the island, a new **Palais de Justice** appears, and within it the gothic miniature **Sainte-Chapelle,** seemingly held up by the light streaming through its brilliant stained-glass windows.

The fourteenth century brings Charles V, who has the swamp drained and transforms **The Marais** into the chic place to live. A little later, an old dump by the banks of the Seine becomes an elaborate garden and palace, the **Tuileries,** built by the cultivated Marie de Medici. Her husband, Henry of Navarre, equally determined to recreate the city, has the arcaded **Place des Vosges** built like a symmetrical outpost in the Marais.

Paris continues to spread, and soon the new Ile St.-Louis is contructed—an aristocratic neighborhood where Voltaire, Ingrès, Baudelaire, and Cézanne are all eventually to live. The **Palais Royal** appears for the comfort of the implaccable Richelieu, the **Palais de Luxembourg** for Marie de Medici. Suddenly, the sun rises over Paris, and under Louis XIV, the Sun King, the city radiates with magnificent buildings and gardens: the **Champs-Elysées,** the **Place Vendôme,** the **Observatoire,** and, most impressive of all, the new royal residence of **Versailles** and its incomparable gardens take shape. Despite all this rich construction, a slum bubbles and seeps from Notre Dame to the Palais de Justice. Class tension and elite privilege prove too much, and in the north the **Bastille** is stormed; the guillotine is erected and takes over 1300 lives, including those of the King and Queen. The Place de la Révolution (formerly Place Louis XV), the scene of so many executions, is hopefully renamed **Place de la Concorde** after the end of the Terror.

After a lull, as life settles down, arches are erected to Napoleon Bonaparte, who crowns himself emperor in Notre Dame. The grand **Arc de Triomphe** goes up on the hill of Chaillot. The Rue du Rivoli grows its arcades, and fancy cemeteries flower with elaborate tombs outside of town.

In the nineteenth century, Napoleon III lets Baron Hausmann loose on the city. He mows down the slums, replacing them with broad and elegant boulevards. The ornamental Opéra is born, the **Bois de Boulogne** made into a park, and under the streets the celebrated sewers are constructed. The Louvre is finally completed in the form we find it today. The 1870s bring turmoil and destruction. The newly elected commune is formed in response to the German invasion, and the Communard flames soon devour the Tuileries, the Palais de Justice, and the Hôtel de Ville. On May 28, 1871, the rebels are cornered and shot at the cemetery of **Père Lachaise,** which becomes the site of an annual political pilgrimage. The Tuileries are never to regain their former glory, but a series of exhibitions sweeps Paris, leaving in their wake the **Eiffel Tower** (considered the monstrosity of its age), the grand **Petit Palais,** and the flat-topped **Palais de Chaillot.** Add **La Défense** to the west and the **Tour Montparnasse** to the south, and you can set your imagination to rest. All skyscrapers are relegated to the suburb of La Defense, and yet right in the middle of the twelfth-century village of **Beaubourg** springs up the futuristic **Centre Georges Pompidou,** a surrealist steel arts complex as controversial as any building in Paris, past or present. Nearby is the **Forum of Les Halles,** Beaubourg's fellow creature, a tubular steel and glass shopping mall which supplanted the area's old market sheds.

Sights

Even in a lifetime devoted to nothing else, you could probably never see everything that Paris has to offer. And if you try to accomplish the impossible in a short visit, armed with a list of spots to tick off, you may miss the greatest sight of all—the city itself. So while you'll certainly want to see the Eiffel Tower or tour the Louvre, take time to visit nearby attractions, and walk between them, don't take the Metro. You'll come away with a better feel for the piece of Paris you have seen, and with a better sense of how the piece fits into the city as a whole.

One of the best ways to gain a perspective on Paris is to view the city from above. Climb high above the hectic pace for a detached view of how the different parts are related. Since all of the skyscrapers (except the Tour Montparnasse) are located outside of the city limits, nothing will block your view of the famous monuments. It is relatively easy to pick out the Eiffel Tower, the immense Louvre stretching down the Seine's Right Bank, Notre Dame on the Ile de la Cité, and the somewhat incongruous Beaubourg—as well as many other Parisian landmarks.

Paris' most unforgettable visual trademark, and the classic place to Paris-watch, is the **Eiffel Tower,** 7ème, (Mo. Bir-Hakeim), open every day (10am-11pm in the supper and 10:30am-6pm in the winter). Gustave Eiffel's "300-meter flagpole" offers a great view of the city and charges 6F for an elevator ride to the first level, 13F to the second, and 18F to the third. In the evenings (6:30pm-11pm) the price rises to 10F to the first stage by elevator and 14F to the second. (During the day, you can also walk up to the first level for 4F and to the second level for 6F). Rivaling the Eiffel Tower is the **Tour Montparnasse,** 15ème, (Mo. Montparnasse-Bienvenue). For 14.50F you can ride up to the 56th and 59th floors; 11.50F for the 56th floor only. Open every day from 9:30am-11:30pm.

Circle the **Arc de Triomphe,** place de l'Etoile, 8ème, (Mo. Etoile-Charles-de-

Gaulle), on foot a few times before going to the top, just to experience Napoleon's conception of grandeur. This triumphal arch commemorates the military victories of the First Empire and provides a superb view of the Champs Elysées and the eleven other avenues radiating from the star-shaped place de l'Etoile. The Arc de Triomphe also houses the tomb of the unknown soldier. Open daily 10am-5pm; admission 9F, 4.50F on Sunday and anytime with student ID. The fifth floor of the **Pompidou Center,** rue Rambuteau, 4ème, (Mo. Rambuteau), offers a free view of Paris. The exposed escalators on the outside of the building make the ride up as enjoyable as the view once you arrive. On clear days, the view here is as fine as that from the Eiffel Tower, and in the summer you are provided with a bird's-eye view of the mimes, fire-eaters, and crowds down below in the "plateau Beaubourg." Open weekdays except Tuesday noon-10pm, weekends 10am-10pm.

If you want the chance to see some gargoyles close-up, follow the little old man up the rickety stairs of **Notre Dame's belltower,** Ile de la Cité, 4ème, Mo. Cité). The guide gives his tour in French and you can tip him what you want for the experience. Open daily 10am-4:30pm; admission 8F, 4F on Sunday and holidays and with student ID. 2F for photograph privileges. Or, view Paris from the "Butte" of Montmartre on the **Terrace of Sacré-Coeur,** 18ème, (Mo. Anvers). You can either walk up a very steep hill or take the cable-car (funiculaire) from the top of rue Steinkerque. Get there about an hour before sunset and watch the lighted city unroll before your eyes.

Two Paris department stores offer great views of the city and both vistas are free. From the sun terrace of **Galeries Lafayette,** 40, blvd. Haussman, 8ème (Mo. Chausée d'Antin), you can look over at the gargantuan Opéra across the street and spot other important buildings as well. There is also an open-air cafe with reasonable prices on the terrace, but you don't have to buy a thing. Open Mon.-Sat., 10am-6pm. Closer to the Seine on the Right Bank is the **Samaritaine** department store, rue du Pont-Neuf, 6ème (Mo. Pont-Neuf), which also has a moderately-priced terrace on the tenth floor of building #2. You can sit for hours (except during busy lunch times) and contemplate the city. There is a free observation deck one flight up from the cafe. Open during the warm months (May through October) Mon.-Sat. mornings and afternoons only.

Paris is a collection of distinctly different neighborhoods, each exhibiting its own personal style and charm. There is the Marais, with its mixture of wealth and working class, Arab and Jew; the Opera, with its opulent stores and residences; Montparnasse, with its undying vestiges of Bohemian life; the Latin Quarter, where the small town feel of the residential streets meets the cafes, bookstores, and institutional buildings (universities and lycées) of student life. Walking is probably the best way to acquaint yourself with Paris in all her guises. The places we list below have been grouped into loose categories which will take half a day to cover. But don't follow our suggestions too faithfully. The old truism is indeed true; the best sights are those that you discover yourself, probably when wandering or lost—the peaceful side street, the shuttered houses on some unimportant square, or your own bridge across the Seine.

The first walk covers the two islands, Ile de la Cité and Ile St.-Louis, as well as the Latin Quarter. The second continues along the Left Bank, passing Les Invalides, the Ecole Militaire, and the Eiffel Tower. The third district described stretches from the Arc de Triomphe down the Champs Elysées to the Louvre, the Marais, and the Bastille. The northerly parts of Paris, including the Opéra, the busy Grands Boulevards, and Montmartre are grouped together in a fourth walk.

Ile de la Cite, Ile St.-Louis, and the Latin Quarter

Paris was founded in the third century B.C. with the settlement of the Parisii tribe along the Seine. Threatened by the Goths in the third century A.D., this Celtic people took refuge on the Ile de la Cité (called Lutèce). This island and the Ile St.-Louis are the only two remaining of the original eight islands in this part of the Seine. Although only about two-and-a-half miles long, Ile de la Cité is thick with historical spots and points of interest. On the western point of the island, the *Pont Neuf* (1578-1604—the oldest bridge in Paris, despite its name) connects the Right Bank with the Ile. Near the bridge is the **Square du Vert-Galant** and the famous statue of Henry IV, the first Bourbon King of France. **Place Dauphine,** nestled behind the busy Palais de Justice and the Conciergerie, still retains two rows of houses dating from the reign of Louis XIII (1601-1643). It is a peaceful shaded area, great for a bread and cheese break before you move on to the **Palais de Justice** and its Salle des Pas Perdus, where judges, lawyers, and prosecutors mill around, and clerks hurry from door to door. If you are interested, you can sit in on a public trial (but the more inconspicuous you try to be, the better).

Inside the Palais je Justice is **Ste.-Chapelle,** a small church begun in 1246 to house the Crown of Thorns, and finished in a record 33 months. It is said that St. Louis, King of France (1226-1270) gave away so many thorns as political favors that very few remain intact. Frequently hailed as the supreme achievement of Gothic architecture, St.-Chapelle appears to be supported by the streams of light from the stained glass windows rather than by the airy masonry which frames them. From the outside, the building looks tall: in fact, it consists of two stories of chapels; the lower, darker one for servants, the magnificently ornate upper one for the nobility. This upper chapel is adorned with fifteen thirteenth-century, partially restored stained glass marvels portraying more than 1100 scenes from the Old and New Testaments. Open daily 10am-5pm; admission 9F, half-price Sunday and holidays.

Just around the corner is the **Conciergerie,** 1, quai de l'Horloge, where the famous prisoners of the Revolution—Marie Antoinette, Danton, and Robespierre—were confined before execution. A genuine guillotine is on display, as is the escape message pinpricked by Marie Antoinette. It is still used as a temporary prison by those about to go to trial in the Palais de Justice, a purpose it has served throughout much of France's long history. While most of the rooms are remarkable primarily for the heavy stone ribbed vaulting, the so-called **Galerie des Prisonniers** is particularly remembered for the part it played in the Reign of Terror: from here nearly 2600 prisoners departed for the guillotine between January 1793 and July 1794. Open daily 10am-6pm; admission 9F, half-price on Sundays and holidays. The 1370 clock in the tower on the square (corner of the quai and the boulevard) is the oldest municipal timepiece in Paris.

Near the Métro stop is the **Marché aux Fleurs,** where every day except Sunday flowers are bought and sold. Making your way past the formidable **Préfecture de Police,** you will approach Paris' most photographed and visited sight: the **Cathédrale de Notre Dame.** Built from 1163-1330 on the plans of the Bishop Maurice de Sully, Notre Dame was heavily vandalized during the Revolution when it was rededicated to the cult of Reason, and its interior "redecorated" as a storage area. The cathedral found a prison in the Citizen King, Louis Philippe, and an able restorer (1844-64) in Viollet le Duc, whose controversial work (he added a spire) changed, but saved, the cathedral. The impressive interior height of the building and the grace of the interior supports are made possible by the exterior flying buttresses (best seen from the square

Discover *Le Journal Français d'Amérique*. It keeps you in touch with the French world for only $16.50 a year (24 issues). Each issue has 20 to 32 pages of news from France, interviews of French personalities, travel tips, food and wine features, movie reviews and much more. *Tout en français.*

☐ Please enter a subscription for :

Name _____

Address_____

_____

Starting_____

Gift from_____

☐ My check for $16.00 is enclosed.

☐ Bill me.

PLEASE follow these instructions carefully- incomplete applications will be returned.

Application for International Student Identity Card enclose: 1) Dated proof of current student status (copy of transcript or letter from registrar stating that you are a full time student). The proof should be from a registered educational institution and CLEARLY indicate that you are currently a full time student. 2) One small picture (1½ X 1½) signed on reverse side.

Railpass application: passport number _____

Last Name _____
First Name _____Middle Initial___
Street _____
City _____
State _____Zip___
Date of Departure from U.S. _____
 month/day/year

Date of Birth_____Citizenship___
School/College _____

WELCOME TO THE
LET'S GO Travel Store
"The Filene's Basement of the Travel Industry"

Please send me:

$6.00 International Student I.D.

$14.00 American Youth Hostel Card
(add 50¢ for plastic case)

_____ **Eurail Pass (First Class)**
15 day- $260, 21 day-$330, 1 month- $410, 2 month- $560, 3 month- $680

_____ **Eurail Youth Pass (under 26 years)**
1 month- $290, 2 month- $370

Free! More information on charter flights, commission-free currency, discount car rental, Britrail Passes, France Vacance, and MORE!

$2.00 Certified mail and handling

_____ **TOTAL**
Please send a postal money order (for fastest service) or a personal check payable to:
LET'S GO Travel Services
Harvard Student Agencies, Inc.
Thayer Hall-B/Harvard University, Cambridge, MA 02138

de l'Archéveque, behind the church). Before you decide that the interior is dark and gloomy, give your eyes time to adjust, and recall that the revolutionary achievement of Gothic architecture was letting in more light. For a close look at the Gothic towers, griffins, and gargoyles climb the worn steps to the left of the main portal. The Tower is open daily 10am-4:30pm, and admission is 8F, half-price on Sunday. Free organ concerts are held every Sunday throughout the summer at 5pm (tel. 354-23-88 for details). Remember that Notre Dame is a church and perhaps the best way to appreciate it is to go Sunday morning. The square of *"parvis"* in front of Notre Dame is the geopolitical heart of the country: all distances in France are measured from this spot.

Try to struggle through the busloads of tourists to the little park behind the cathedral, **Square Jean XXIII**, where there is an excellent view of the Left Bank and the Ile St.-Louis. Across the street and down a narrow, stark flight of steps is the **Memorial de la Déportation**, erected in remembrance of the 20,000 French victims of Nazi concentration camps. Modern and abstract, the memorial is hauntingly moving.

Cross the Pont St.-Louis to the other island, **Ile St.-Louis**, a much smaller and more intimate area where such luminaries as Voltaire, Mme. de Châtelet, Daumier, Ingres, Baudelaire, and Cézanne all once resided. While you're in the area, you might as well take advantage of one of the best and cheapest ice cream parlors in Paris, **Berthillon**. It's on rue St.-Louis-en-l'Ile, but you'll have no trouble finding it—just look for the line.

Crossing over the Left Bank by the Pont-au-Double will take you to the Church of St.-Julien-le-Pauvre (rebuilt in the twelfth century) and the **Square René-Viviani**, with one of the best views of Notre Dame. It's also a very peaceful little square where you can sit back and contemplate the fact that you're in Paris. Right around the corner is rue Galande, one of Paris' oldest streets. Across the rue St.-Jacques stands St.-Séverin, a Gothic church noted for its flamboyant interior. Organ concerts are often given in St.-Séverin, providing much-needed relief from the swarming activity out on rue de la Huchette and St.-Séverin. You will find countless eateries in these streets—Greek, North African, and Italian. Nestled away on the rue de la Huchette is Paris' smallest theater. **Théatre de la Huchette,** where Ionesco's *La Cantatrice Chauve (The Bald Soprano)* has been playing for over two decades. On the other side of the blvd. St.-Michel *(Boul-Mich),* you will find much the same atmosphere—discos, jazz clubs, and restaurants, with inexpensive hotels sprinkled in between. If you head down rue St.-Andre-des-Arts (it later turns into rue de Buci) and then follow the tiny rue de Bourbon-le-Chateau, you will arrive at one of the most pleasant little squares in all of Paris, near the rue de Furstemberg. Now the center for many expensive art galleries, this area was once home to Eugène Delacroix. You can visit his **Atelier** (workshop) at 6, place de Furstemberg. Open 9:45am-5:15pm every day but Tuesday; admission 6F, 3F Sunday and for students, free on Wednesday.

South of here is the busy blvd. St.-Germain. The church of **St.-Germain-des-Près,** at the intersection with the rue de Rennes, is paris' oldest church and one of the few Romanesque structures still standing in the area. Of special interest are the eleventh-century nave and, in the second chapel on the right, a stone marking the interred ashes of Descartes. Nearby, at #170, is the famous cafe, **Aux Deux Magots,** once frequented by Jean-Paul Sartre. **Café de Flore** at #172 is similar in style. South of the Odéon Métro stop on blvd. St.-Germain is rue Monsieur-le-Prince, a street boasting August Comte, Saint-Saens, Longfellow, and Pascal among its former residents. Near the intersection of the street with rue Racine.is the **Théatre National de l'Odéon,** located a short distance from the

Palais du Luxembourg (1615-1627), once a royal residence. After the death of her son, Henry IV, Marie de Medici tired of living in the Louvre and had a palace built to remind her of the Pitti Palace in Florence, the city of her birth. Architecturally, the palace is an interesting mix of French and Tuscan styles. She gave the adjacent **Petit-Luxembourg** to Cardinal Richelieu in 1626, and it now serves as the residence of the President of the Senate. Actually more compelling than the palaces is the **Jardin du Luxembourg** adjoining them. It was originally laid out in the seventeenth century, but was destroyed in 1782 and 1867. Now in its third incarnation it still provides a colorful and attractive setting for marionette shows, games of *pétanque,* and other activities.

The **Sorbonne** occupies a large part of the area across the blvd. St.-Michel from the Luxembourg Gardens. Reputedly the oldest university in Europe, dating from the first decade of the twelfth century, the Sorbonne has undergone numerous changes in its curriculum and organization in the last eight hundred years, the most recent being the decentralization of the university into thirteen autonomous campuses following the student riots of May 1968. The Sorbonne presently comprises Paris III and Paris IV Universities. Feel free to wander through the old courtyards and peek into the lecture halls. If the university is in session while you are there, try to get the name of a good lecturer from one of the students, and you will see how different the French style of education is from the North American.

Perched on the highest and most central point (200 feet) of the Left Bank is the **Panthéon,** built in the shape of a Greek cross. The crypt of the Pantheon houses the heart of Léon Gambetta (in an urn) and the tombs of Victor Hugo, Voltaire, Rousseau, Louis Braille, and Emile Zola, as well as a host of Napoleon's flunkies. The rest of the cavernous, heavily Neoclassical building is empty save for late nineteenth-century paintings of mythical scenes from Paris' early history. Open daily except Tuesday 10am-5:30pm; admission 9F, 4.50F on Sunday and with student ID. Across the place Ste.-Geneviève, the levity of the **Eglise St.-Etienne-du-Mont** contrasts with the Panthéon's sobriety. Lopsided and overdone, the church is the only one in Paris with a walkway raised above the congregation, supported by two ornate spiral staircases.

Following the rue Clovis over the rue Cardinal Lemoine, you can still see a remaining fragment of Philip Augustus' perimeter wall. This wall, constructed between 1180 and 1210, girded a recently enlarged Paris: swamps had been drained, fields cultivated, and a river harbor established by this great Capetian monarch. Retracing steps, the rue Descartes leads into the fascinating rue Mouffetard, an ancient narrow market street passing by the place de la Contrescarpe. Heading east on rue Rollin, across rue Monge, are the ruins of the **Arènes de Lutèce,** a Roman amphitheater discovered only in 1870. Here you can sit in one of the many stone-enclosed box seats and observe the games of neighborhood children. Across the rue Livré is the **Jardin des Plantes** with its many gardens and museums (see the Out-of-doors section). Then, suddenly, you will come across **La Mosquée,** 39, rue Geoffrey Saint-Hilaire, 5ème, Mo. Monge. Paris' Muslim mosque (1922-1925) is an impressive Hispanic-Moorish building, partially inspired by the Alhambra in Granada, with lovely carved wooden ceilings, mosaics, and hidden gardens. After the guided tour, have mint tea and North African pastries in their tearoom. Open daily except Friday, 10am-noon and 2pm-5:30pm; admission including tour 6F, 4F with student ID.

Eiffel Tower to Les Invalides

The Eiffel Tower (Mo. Bir-Hakeim) is no longer the world's tallest freestanding structure as it was upon its completion in 1889. Nor is it the only terminal for transatlantic radio-telephone connections as it was in 1916. Still, no self-respecting tourist would miss its steel lacework. And yet the Eiffel Tower was not always so popular. Among the Parisians to protest its erection were Maupassant, Dumas, Coppée, and Gounod. One of the best views of the tower is from the far end of the adjacent **Champs de Mars.** This park was originally planned in the eighteenth century as a parade ground, and was made into a park in 1913. It was the site of many revolutionary festivals and aeronautical experiments.

At the other end of the Champs de Mars is the **Ecole Militaire,** France's military academy (Mo. Ecole Militaire) an interesting example of eighteenth-century military-minded building style. Among its alumni it numbers a Napoleon Bonaparte, class of 1785, lieutenant in the artillery. Across the street, **UNESCO House** (1958) is one of Paris' most famous twentieth century buildings, place de Fontenoy, 7ème (Mo. Cambronne). Inside the building are murals by Miro, a fresco by Picasso, a Calder mobile, sculpture by Giacometti, and other works of art. Open Mon.-Fri. 9am-noon and 2-6pm; admission free.

Many critics consider Napoleon's red marble resting place, **Les Invalides,** to be the finest example of monumental architecture in Paris. It is located an easy walk toward the center of town from the Eiffel Tower or at Mo. Varenne or Ecole Militaire. Napoleon's remains were transferred from St. Helena, his second island of exile, to this church in 1840. He lies in the crypt of the Eglise du Dôme, one of two chapels in the complex, in the innermost of six successive coffins. (See the Museums section for information on the hours of the emperor's tomb.)

Arc de Triomphe to the Bastille

The Right Bank is a totally different side of Paris. Start out at the **Arc du Triomphe** (Mo. Etoile) the world's largest triumphal arch, containing since 1923 the Tomb of the Unknown Soldier. Four sculptured groups, each by a different artist, tell the history of France in allegory: Departure, Resistance, Triumph, and Peace. Rudé's "The Departure of the Volunteers in 1792" or "Marseillaise" is commonly considered the best of the lot. From the Etoile, gaze down the spectacular **Champs Elysées,** lined with chic boutiques, airline offices, international banks, and cinemas. Walking down the Champs, you might even see someone you know, since there are always lots of tourists staked out in the prime-sight cafes, ogling the other tourists promenading past. Running down from the Etoile, the avenue reaches the **place de la Concorde,** where the "nation's razor" provided free public entertainment during the Reign of Terror (1793-1794) in the square that had recently been consecrated to Louis XV. The architectural grandeur of the square is now somewhat diminished by the constant flood of Fiats, Citröens, and Peugeots that pours through it. The American Embassy is located off Concorde on ave. Gabriel on the corner of a grassy park area. Proceeding up to the Tuileries Gardens, you will find the **Jeu de Paume** on the left corner and the **Orangerie** on the right (see Museums). The **Tuileries** makes a great place to walk, rest, watch the fountains, or catch a bite to eat in one of the outdoor cafés. Be sure to check the prices beforehand though, since one of the cafés charges a hefty 2-3F more for their sandwiches and crêpes than the other two. At the far end of the gardens is the **Arc de Triomphe du Carrousel,** inspired by the Arch of Septimus Severus in Rome, and built in 1806-8 to commemorate Napoleon's victories of 1805. At one time, the four bronze horses from St. Mark's in Venice graced this little arch; Napoleon borrowed them when he conquered the Veneto. Past the arch stretches the **Palais du Louvre,** constructed initially under Philip Augustus as a military fortress but converted during the fourteenth century into a residence by Charles V. This combination fortress and royal palace was abandoned by the nobility in 1682 when Louis XIV moved the court to Versailles. The idea of transforming this, the largest royal palace in Europe, into a museum was the brainchild of Louis XVI, and the Grand Galerie opened its doors to the public on August 10, 1793, a few months before his execution.

Napoleon had the good taste to extract the very best artwork from the lands he conquered, thus greatly expanding a collection which has swollen to 400,000 entries owing to gifts, legacies, and purchases. (See the Museums section.) Walking east on the ritzy **rue de Rivoli** (catch a glimpse of the Place Vendome on rue Castiglione when you pass by; it's an architectural master-piece in the Louis XIV-style, now the center for many luxury shops and the Ritz), you will run into the **Hôtel de Ville** (Paris' city hall). To get an idea of the monumental architecture of the early years of the Third Republic, tour the Hotel de Ville, with its lavish Neo-Renaissance/Belle Epoque styling and its 136 statues. Although Paris' city administration has been located on this spot since Louis IX first appointed councillors in 1260, the former Hôtel de Ville was put to the torch during the overthrow of the Paris Commune in May 1871, and this new one was erected.

From the Hôtel de Ville, take the rue du Renard to the **Centre Georges Pompidou,** an ultra-modern building located in an old market and artisan neigh-borhood. The Center houses the Musée National de l'Art Moderne and the Bibliothéque Publique d'Information (public library), and it sits on a vast cement plaza that rings with the sounds of street musicians. A few hundred yards away is the **forum des Halles,** an immense, subterranean shopping com-plex containing branches of Paris' chicest shops. The streets around Les Hal-les are home to a number of old, pre-chic restaurants, popular American student bars, new wave clothing stores, and fast-food joints. If you walk west along the rue des Francs Bourgeois, into the heart of the **Marais,** you will discover the **Musée des Blancs Manteaux.** Occupying a central position in the Marais is the ancient **place de Vosges,** preserving its original buildings of stone and brick from the times of Henri IV. Although none of the buildings are precisely alike, the classical lines of the square give an impression of fine unity to his sixteenth-century residence. The Hôtel de Chaulnes, at #9, is now the Academy of Architecture; the Marquise de Sevigny lived at #1*bis* and Cardi-nal Richelieu at #21. At #6 is a small but entertaining **Victor Hugo Museum.** Closed Monday; admission 7F; free on Sunday and half-price with student ID.

A short walk from place de Vosges is the **place de la Bastille,** Mo. Bastille, the location of the riot of July 14, 1789. Four hundred idealistic proletarians liberated a few forgers and lunatics, and a young nobleman whose father had requested that he be incarcerated. Only the ground plan of the famous prison remains, marked by a line of stones. As for political prisoners, the Bastille had at different times such inmates as Voltaire and the Marquis de Sade.

Opéra District and Montmartre

A good place to start exploring this quadrant is the **Palais-Royal,** a peaceful collection of buildings and galleries opening onto a garden of roses and foun-tains. Cardinal Richelieu had a "palais cardinal" raised in 1620. It became a "palais royal" when Anne of Austria, regent for Louis XIV, established resi-dence there. Accessible by numerous passageways, this area played an impor-tant role during the period of the Revolution, as well as occupying a central place for social circles of the late eighteenth and early nineteenth centuries. On the southwestern corner of the Palais-Royal is the **Comédie Française** (See the Entertainment section), built in the late nineteenth century and restored in the twentieth century after a fire. As you proceed north on the rue Richelieu, notice the **Bourse** (stock exchange) on the right, down rue de Colonel Driant. Continuing along rue Richelieu will take you past the **Bibliothèque Nationale.** Competing with the British Museum for the title of largest library in Western Europe, the library contains seven million volumes, including two Gutenberg Bibles and first editions of famous French authors from the fifteenth century on. You must have two photos and a letter of recommendation if you wish to use this massive resource.

A little further, the rue du Quatre Septembre crosses rue Richelieu. The Second Empire building housing the **Opéra** lies to the west. If you have time, go inside the Opéra and see its interior (see the Entertainment section) and decor. Be sure to note the Chagall ceiling (1964). The busy and crowded **Grands Boulevards** lined with large department stores are always hustling with frenzied activity during the week. Off the main drag (blvd. Haussmann) the pace continues on a smaller scale in the St.-Lazare and Lafayette business districts.

Montmartre, or *"mont des martyres,"* is so named after three saints beheaded here in 272 A.D. One, St. Denis, promptly picked up his head, washed it off in a nearby fountain and walked away. He ultimately expired four miles away, the legend tells us, and the **Basilique St.-Denis** stands on this spot today.

To visit Montmartre, walk north or take the Métro to Anvers, Blanche, or Abbesses. This area is certainly worth a visit, but don't expect to find artists and writers starving in their garrets, turning out tomorrow's masterpieces. The area, though still living off its bohemian heritage, is nowadays about as artistic as Baltimore. But even though the real artists are gone, the area still charms with its winding roads, steep staircases etched into the sides of the hills, and famous views of the city. If your legs are in good shape, start from the Anvers, Pigalle, or Blanche Métro stops and head uphill. Enjoy the place du Tertre (just to the west of Sacré-Coeur) for what it is—a touristy marketplace for ready-made shlock art. If, by any chance, the Urchins-With-Big-Eyes drawings or paint-by-numbers Paris street scenes turn you on, remember that the "artists" here usually start by asking several times what they think they can get.

Sacré-Coeur, the most visible landmark of the Montmartre area, is an oriental-looking white church in the Romanesque-Byzantine style, constructed after the Franco-Prussian war of 1870-71 with cupolas, a great dome, and a 336-foot belltower. From here, you will see a marvelous view of Paris far below.

Paris has several ethnic neighborhoods seldom visited by tourists. Among these is **Belleville,** a multi-ethnic working-class neighborhood a bit like New York's Lower East Side. Tunisian Jews sell kosher *(cacher)* couscous while a few doors down Arabs bargain over the price of silk caftans and Maoist students look for converts in cafes filled with Greeks. Get off at Métro stop Belleville or Couronne, then walk around the streets that run toward the rue des Pyrénées. The cheapest street market in Paris is the Marché d'Aligre, a 20-minute walk east from the Bastille, Mo. Ledru-Rollin, a heavily North African neighborhood.

Museums

If you have a special interest, there's probably a museum in Paris devoted to it. The following list represents a fairly broad range of appeal, but there also exist many smaller museums retrospectives, and special exhibitions which you will find listed either in the *Pariscope* or *Officiel des Spectacles.* There is also a useful pamphlet, *Musées de la Ville de Paris,* available from the tourist office. The most comprehensive listing is *Musées, Monuments, Expositions de Paris et de l'Ile de France,* published by the Musées Nationaux de la France and available at the Hôtel de Sully in the Marais, 62, rue St.-Antoine, 4*ème* (Mo. St.-Paul). This leaflet has hours and prices for almost every museum in Paris as well as a brief description of their collections. In general, French National museums are open every day except Tuesday. Entrance is free for those under 18 years of age, half-price for people 18-25 and over 65, and free either on Wednesday or Sunday. Photographic privileges are free (5F for the use of a tripod); no flash or other lighting permitted. It's hard to go wrong if you let your interests guide you, but keep a few rules of thumb in mind; Don't try to see too many museums in a short amount of time; and if you only have one or two hours for a major museum, concentrate on a limited part of the collection and really enjoy it.

Not all works of art hang in a museum, and Paris is a great center of contemporary art. The city's private galleries are rivaled only by New York's in the extent to which they are in tune with current artistic tastes. As well as presenting the new styles of up-and-coming unknowns, these galleries sell the works of established artists, some of which are extremely valuable. Even if there's no room in your budget for your very own minor masterpiece, it is still fun to look in the galleries, since they are always free. Many are located on or near the rue de Seine, 6*ème*. Mo. St.-Germain-des-Pres or Odeon: another group of them cluster in the streets around the Miromesnil and St.-Philippe Metro stops, 8*ème. Le Guide des Arts,* published monthly and on sale at most newsstands, lists current gallery shows.

To see what Parisian art students are doing, walk around the **Ecole des Beaux-Arts,** on 14, rue Bonaparte at the corner of quai Malaquais, 6*ème,* Mo. St.-Germain-des-Pres; it's Paris' best-known art school. For information about the changing exhibition, hours, and entrance fees, call (tel. 260-34-57) or check *l'Officiel.*

Permanent Collections

Musée de Louvre, place du Carrousel, 1*er,* (Mo. Louvre or Palais-Royal), occupied the opposite end of the Tuileries from the place de la Concorde. A truly enjoyable visit to the Louvre requires careful planning and a general sense of the museum's organization. You might otherwise be overwhelmed by the enormity of the place and find yourself utterly confused and lost in the seemingly endless maze of galleries (225 actually). If you don't have the green *Guide Michelin* to Paris, it is worthwhile to invest in one of the museum guides sold near the entrance and available in several languages.

If the sheer size of the Louvre doesn't get to you, the number of tourists probably will. The museum is packed, particularly on Sunday when admission is free, making it difficult to see some of the more popular exhibits. Don't try to see too many galleries in one visit. If you have time, try to make several trips to the Louvre and concentrate on only a few areas at a time. Better to enjoy a small part than to succumb to utter exhaustion while gaining a superficial familiarity with the whole.

Although the exhibits do rotate, the layout of the museum remains basically the same. Sculpture is found in the Pavillon de Flore in the Tuileries, extending across the street from the major part of the Louvre. Representative pieces from France's Romanesque, Gothic, Renaissance, and Neoclassical periods are exhibited here, as well as Italian sculpture of these periods. Search out the two slaves by Michelangelo on the ground floor. These sensual figures were originally intended for the tomb of Pope Julius II. A collection of busts by Jean-Antoine Houdon, master of French sculpture in the late eighteenth century, includes portraits of Voltaire, Rousseau, Washington, and Franklin.

Paintings are included in several parts of the museum according to school. Spanish (El Greco, Goya, Ribera), Italian (Guardi, Botticelli, Bellini, Fra Angelico, Giotto), Flemish (Van Dyck), and Dutch schools are on the second floor of the Pavillon de Flore and Pavillon des Etats. The Medici Gallery contains a cycle of 21 paintings by Peter-Paul Rubens commissioned by Marie de Medici, Queen of France, and originally hung in the Luxembourg palace. French paintings of·the fifteenth to nineteenth century (Le Nain, De La Tour, Poussin, Le Brun, Watteau, Van Loo, Greuze, and David) extend the length of the second floor of the Grande Galerie (almost a quarter of a mile). Also on the second floor, in the Salle des Etats, is Leonardo de Vinci's *La Joconde* (*The Monu Lisa*, 1503-1505). Glass-enclosed and heavily guarded, this work is often difficult to view because of the flocks of tourists. Nevertheless, do push yourself through the crowds to glimpse the over-familiar yet still enigmatic portrait of the wife of a rich Florentine. English painting from the seventeenth to nineteenth century is housed on the third floor of the museum. This includes the famous portraits of the English court by Holbein and Van Dyck.

Greek and Roman, as well as Egyptian and Oriental, antiquities occupy the first (ground) floor of the museum. Follow the crowd to the **Winged Victory of Samothrace** (third century B.C.) on the landing of the Daru staircase, and the **Venus de Milo** (second century B.C.) located beyond the Winged Victory in the Pavillon des Arts. The Greek, Roman, and Egyptian collections also extend to the second floor of the museum.

Also on the second floor are *objets d'art* and furniture. The Louvre possesses a fine collection of Gobelins tapestries as well as the Maximilian Tapestries. The Apollo-Gallery houses the Crown Jewels and the Regent diamond.

The Louvre operates a very good museum shop, with an extensive book section, postcards, posters, and reproductions, in the entrance foyer. An often overlooked area of the museum is the **Chalcographie** department located beyond the museum shop on the second floor. Here you can purchase five engravings from original plates: choose from over 14,000 engravings by such artists as Dürer, Delacroix, Matisse, and many others. Although they are priced higher than the reproductions in the shop below, they are considered genuine works of art and are worth the expense. The Chalcographie department is open daily except Tuesdays, 10am-1pm and 2-5pm.

The Louvre is open daily except Tuesdays from 9:45am-5:15pm, some rooms open till 6:30pm. Admission is 11F, 5:50F for those agest 18-25 and free on Sunday for everyone. The museum also gives tours in English daily except Sunday and Tuesdays from 10am-4pm for 7F.

Jeu de Paume, Jardin des Tuileries, 1er (Mo. Concord or Tuileries). The Jeu de Paume, which houses one of the world's foremost collections of Impressionist painting, is one museum you shouldn't miss. Much smaller than the Louvre, it is located in a former tennis-court building of 1861, on the corner of the Tuileries facing place de la Concorde. You can easily manage to see all of the works here in an enjoyable two or three hours, since there are only two floors of rooms.

On the first floor are Degas' studies of dancers and landscapes by Picasso, Corot, and Sisley. In the Salle Manet is *Dejeuner sur l'Herbe* and *Olympia*, two works which provoked scandals when first exhibited. Paintings by Monet, Van Gogh, Gauguin, Cézanne, and Seurat are also on display on the ground floor.

On the second floor are Monet's celebrated studies of the cathedral at Rouen. Take some time to view these five studies of the great cathedral's portal from different distances and angles. Monet painted a series of canvases at different times of day to watch the play of light and shadow. Many of his water lilies are in the Salle Caillebotte, along with some portraits by Renoir. Works by Cézanne (*The Card Players* and some still lifes), Van Gogh (from his years in Arles), Gauguin, and Henri Rousseau (*The Snake Charmer*) all together under one roof make this rich collection a "must-see." Open daily except Tuesday from 9:45am-5:15pm. Admission 8F, 4F on Sunday or with student ID, and free on Wednesday. The Gallery Shop, which sells post cards, posters, and guidebooks, is a bit expensive.

Centre National d'Art et de Culture Georges Pompidou, (Beaubourg), rues Rambuteau, St.-Martin, and Beaubourg, 4ème (Mo. Rambuteau, Hôtel de Ville, or Chatelet; tel. 277-11-12 for recorded information in French on the week's exhibits and events; tel. 277-12-33 for general information). Nobody would deny that successful architecture should be impressive and memorable, but few buildings have tried as hard as the Pompidou Center. Since opening a few years ago, it has become France's number one tourist attraction (Versailles is second) and has revitalized the area around the Beauboug. Even so, the controversy has not ended. The provocative Leger-like steel and glass exterior with its fully exposed and brightly painted ventilation ducts may be read as a celebration of the building-as-organism, whose inner workings we are allowed to see. Or it can be thought of as alien and deliberately ugly. Decide for yourself.

The center houses numerous exhibits and small shows which change frequently. A lot of these exhibits are free, although the major and longer-running ones charge a 10F admission fee. Since there are so many movable interior walls, exhibitions can be mounted with a great deal of freedom and creativity. The center's approach to art is interdisciplinary: it has a cinema which shows all kinds of films, including the most avant-garde; a non-circulating library (**Bibliothèque Publique d'Information**) which has open stacks, a rarity in France and in Europe generally; a computer room; a room where you can read the latest editions of newspapers from around the world; a free stereo center (on the ground floor) where you can listen to popular or classical music; and countless other forms of cultural entertainment. There's even a language lab, if you want to improve your French.

The **Musée National d'Art Moderne** is the center's main permanent collection, containing a rich selection of twentieth-century art, from the Fauves and Cubists to pop and conceptual art. Admission 11F, 5.5F for those between 18-25, under 18 free; free to all on Wednesday. There is also a fairly large bookstore in the center with books on art, architecture, and design.

The center is a fun way to spend an afternoon. The external escalator will take you up to each level while providing a marvelous view of the city and festivities in the Plateau Beaubourg below. Open Mon.-Fri. (closed Tuesday) noon-10pm; Saturday and Sunday 10am-10pm. The library, including the language labs, is free. You can buy an all-day pass (*laissez-passer*) for the entire museum for 18F. Otherwise there are separate admissions to the major exhibits (usually 10F, 5F for students). A laissez-passer good for one year costs 78F, 55F for students. In addition, there are guided tours every day except Tuesday at 3:30pm (11am on Sun.) for 12F. For information on weekly events (tel. 227-11-12).

Musée d'Art Moderne de la Ville de Paris, 11, ave. du President Wilson, 16ème; (tel. 723-61-27; Mo. Alma Marceau or Iéna). Not as impressive as the Musée National, but houses good selections of Dufy and Roualt and frequent exhibits of very recent, very bizarre works. Open 10am-5:30pm every day except Monday; until 8:30pm Wednesday. Admission 9F, 4.50F for students, and free on Sundays.

Musée Rodin (Hotel Biron), 77, rue de Varenne, off rue dès Invalides, 7ème, (tel. 705-01-34; Mo. Varenne). The works of France's greatest sculptor are displayed here in an elegant eighteenth-century hotel. The central foyer on the main and first floor contains some of the most famous of Rodin's sensual sculpture: *The Kiss, The Hand of God,* and *The Cathedral.* Throughout the rose-filled gardens are such works as *The Thinker* and *The Door of Hell.* The sculpture garden frequented by nursemaids, small children, and young couples, is a good place for picnickers as well. There is a cafe on the side for cold drinks. The gardens and museum stay open from 10am-6pm (though they rush you out by 5:45) daily except Tuesday. Admission 8F, 4F for ages 18-21 and over 65, under 18 free. All are admitted free on Wednesday.

Musée de Cluny, 24, rue du Sommerard (at the intersection of the blvds. St.-Germain and St.-Michel), 5ème (tel. 325-62-00; Mo. St.-Michel or Odéon). This is Paris' museum of medievaliana, the most famous of whose treasures is the six-wall tapestry *La Dame à La Licorne (The Lady and the Unicorn).* A group of tapestries such as this is called a *chambre,* or room, as medieval rooms were tapestried primarily to retain heat. Recently unearthed and exhibited here is *La Galerie des Rois de Judas,* a set of statues of kings which were sheltered above Notre Dame's portals before the revolutionaries of 1793 shattered them as part of their battle against any Gothic or classical representation. Don't walk by some of the less obvious treasures of the museum: the Book of Hours, gold *ostensoirs* and *encensoirs.* Half of the museum is in a late Gothic hotel, while the other half occupies the remains of the baths of Roman Paris. A must, especially since it is so accessibly located in the center of the Latin Quarter. Open daily 9:45am-12:30pm and 2-5pm, closed Tuesday. Admission 8F, 4F on Sunday; free on Wednesday. Tours in French every Wednesday at 3pm.

Musée Carnavalet, 23, rue de Sévigné, 3ème (tel. 272-21-13; Mo. St.-Paul). Housed in a building that was the home of the famous letter-writer Madame de Sévigné from the 1670s to 1690s, the museum of the city of Paris includes paintings, objects, and letters from the city's past. All the exhibits are interesting and tastefully arranged on the first floor—especially the documents from the Revolution and the *objects d'art of* lovers Georges Sand and Frederic Chopin. Both floors are open daily except Monday, 10am-5:40pm. Admission 9F. 4.50F with a student ID, free on Sunday.

Musée des Arts Décoratifs, Pavillon de Marsan, 107, rue de Rivoli, 1er, (tel. 260-32-14; Mo. Palais-Royal or Tuileries) exhibits furniture, *objets d'art,* china, and other such household items from the Middle Ages to the present. Open 2-5pm, closed Tuesday; admission 5F, 2.50F with student ID.

Musée Marmottan, 2, rue Louis-Boilly 16ème; (tel. 224-07-02; Mo. Muette). Near the Bois de Boulogne. Originally a private collection that concentrated on the First Empire period (paintings of Napoleon, sculpture, furniture), the Marmottan inherited the legacy of Michel Monet, which includes many of his father's paintings and several by other impressionists. It is one of the best collections of Impressionism outside the Jeu de Paume. Open daily except Monday 10am-6pm; admission 15F, students 6F.

Musée Cognacq-Jay, 25, blvd. des Capucines, 2ème, (tel. 742-94-71; Mo. Opéra). Not far from the American Express office. It contains the collection of the founder of the Samaritaine department store, who filled his house with eighteenth-century paintings, furniture, and *objets d'art.* Rosy-cheeked ladies and trinkets abound. Open 10am-5:40pm except Monday. Admission 7.50F, 3.50F with a student card, free on Sunday.

Musée Jacquemart-André, 158, blvd. Haussmann, 8ème, (tel. 562-39-94; Mo. St.-Phillipe de Roule) houses collections of Italian Renaissance (Uccello, Botticelli, Titian) and eighteenth-century French paintings (Watteau, Boucher, Greuze). It also exhibits tapestries and antique furnishings. Open daily except Monday and Tuesday. 1:30-5:30pm; admission 8F, 4F with a student ID. **Musée Nissim de Camondo,** 63, rue de Monceau, 8*ème,* Mo. Villiers (tel. 563-26-32). This opulent Louis XVI mansion houses a considerable collection of eighteenth-century art including priceless Chinese vases, Aubusson tapestries, and Sèvres porcelain. Open Wed.-Sun. 10am-noon and 2-5pm. Admission 8F. **Musée de L'Affiche,** 18 rue de Paradis, 10*ème,* (tel. 824-50-04; Mo. Poissonière), is a museum devoted to the art of the poster, housed in a turn-of-the-century crockery shop. Exhibits have shown works by French masters of poster and print-making, including works by Daumier, Toulouse-Lautrec, and Magritte. Open daily noon-6pm, closed Monday and Tuesday. Admission 7F, 3.50F students.

Arts and Letters

Several museums in Paris house impressive collections of Oriental art. The **Musée Guimet,** 6, place d'Iéna, 6*ème,* (tel. 723-61-65; Mo. Iéna), has one of the best collections of Asian art in the Western world. There are works from India, China, Japan, Cambodia, Vietnam, Korea, and Nepal. Open daily except Tuesday, 9:45am-noon and 1:30-5:15pm; admission 8F, 4F with a student ID, free on Wednesday. The **Musée Cernuschi** specialized in ancient Chinese art. It is located at 7, ave. Velasquez, 8*ème* (tel. 563-50-75; Mo. Villeurs), and is open from 10am-5:40pm daily except Monday, admission 7.50F, 3F with a student ID and free on Sunday. A smaller and free collection of Japanese and Chinese art, the **Musée d'Ennery,** 59, ave. Foch, 16*ème* (Mo. Porte Dauphine) is open only on Sundays and Thursdays 2-5pm. Free admission.

Paris also has a number of "Great Men" museums. A favorite is the **Maison de Victor Hugo,** 6, place des Vosges, 4*ème,* (Mo. St.-Paul). The house was Hugo's home from 1832-1848. The collection contains photographs, manuscripts, letters, even the Master's pen and inkwell. Open 10am-5:40pm daily except Monday; admission 7F, 3.50F with student ID, free on Sunday). The **Musée Balzac,** 47 rue Raynouard, 16*ème,* (Mo. Passy or Mo. La Muette) houses similar memorabilia from the life of Honoré de Balzac, who wrote the last part of *The Human Comedy* there from 1840 to 1847. Open 10am-5:40pm except on Monday, admission 7F, 3.50F with student ID, free on Sunday. Not far away the **Musée Clemenceau,** 8, rue Franklin, 16*ème* (Mo. Passy), was once the apartment of the French statesman of the World War I era who was Woodrow Wilson's antoganist at the Versailles conference (open 2-5pm Tuesday, Thursday, Saturday, and Sunday only; admission 4F, 2F with student ID). **Delacroix's** apartment and *atelier* (studio) have been made into a museum at 6, place de Furstemberg, 6*ème,* Mo. St.-Germain-des Près, (open 9:45am-5:15pm except Tuesday; admission 4F, 2F with student ID, under 18 free). So has the *atelier* of **Gustave Moreau** the nineteenth-century symbolist painter who was the teacher of Matisse, Roualt, and many other Fauvists—14, rue de la Rochefoucauld, 9*ème,* Mo. Trinité (open 10am-1pm and 2-5pm except Monday and Tuesday; admission 6F, 3F with student ID, closed in August.

Opera buffs should visit the **Musée de l'Opéra,** in the rear of the Opéra building, 1 place Charles-Garnier, 9*ème* (Mo. Opéra), Open 11am-4:30pm except Sunday; admission 6F with student ID. The museum contains the ballet slippers of Nijinsky, the crown of Pavlova, sketches of famous costumes, and other operalia. If you are interested in old instruments, the **Musée Instrumental,** with its lutes, lyres, harpsichords (one made for Marie de Medici), bagpipes, and many other ancient instruments is a must. Open only Wednesday and Saturday 2-6pm, free; located at 14, rue de Madrid, 8ème, Mo. Europe; closed in August.

History and Science

The **Musée de l'Histoire de France,** located in the building of the French Archives, 60, rue des Francs-Bourgeois, 3ème (tel. 277-11-30; Mo. Rambuteau), contains historic documents from the Merovingian era to World War II. The material is displayed in an informative manner. Open daily except Tuesday from 2-5pm. Admission 4F, 2F on Sunday or with student ID.

Musée National des Arts et Traditions Populaires, 6, route du Mahatma Gandhi, Bois de Boulogne (tel. 747-69-80; Mo. Sablons). One of Paris' newest, most innovative museums, it explores the roots and evolution of cultural habits. The excellent collection of tools and everyday artifacts illustrates what rural French life was like before the industrial revolution. Every Wednesday at 3pm, there is a guided tour in French. Don't miss the audio-visual presentations held daily. Open daily except Tuesday from 10am-5:15pm. Admission 8F, 4F on Sunday and holidays and with student ID. Free on Wednesday and to those under 18. The library is open from 9:30am-5pm, weekdays only.

War buffs will enjoy the **Musée de l'Armée,** located in one wing of Les Invalides, 7ème (tel. 551-92-84; Mo. Latour-Maubourg or Varenne). It features a collection of weapons, armor, uniforms, and numerous bits of First Empire trivia, including the Emperor's tomb (located in a different part of the building, but the 10F or 5F student admission entitles you to see it). Open daily 10am-6pm, closed holidays. Also, the naval museum, **Musée de la Marine,** in the Palais de Chaillot, 16ème (tel. 553-31-70; Mo. Trocadéro), displays ships, flags, the history of the French Navy, and other things maritime. Open daily except Tuesday and holidays 10am-6pm; 8F or 4F with a student ID. The **Musée National de la Legion d'Honneur et des Ordres de la Chevalerie,** 2, rue de Bellechasse, 7ème, Mo. Solferino (tel. 555-95-16) is devoted to France's Legion of Honor and to foreign orders of chivalry; medals, ribbons, plaques, decorations. Open daily except Monday 2-5pm; admission 6F, 3F with student ID, free on Sunday.

The **Musée de l'Homme,** in the Palais de Chaillot (only several minutes away from the Eiffel Tower on foot). 16ème (tel. 553-70-60; Mo. Trocadéro), has a well-displayed collection of archeological finds which will delight anyone interested in anthropology. Illustrating human origins and various tribal stages, the colorful anthropological exhibits include masks from Africa, Maori carvings from New Zealand, and pre-Columbian relics, along with helpful maps and occasional audio-visual presentations. There are also some French monuments, murals, and sculpture. Beware of the museum's restaurant and snack bar, which charge exorbitant rates. Open daily 10am-6pm except Tuesday. Admission 10F, 6F with student ID.

Special Interest

Stamps, Coins, Movies, and Foxes: Paris has a museum for almost everyone with a hobby. Philatelists should stop by the **Musée Postal,** 34, blvd. Vaugirad, 15ème (tel. 320-15-30; Mo. Montparnasse-Blenvenue), open daily 10am-5pm except Thursday and holidays; admission free. Coin collectors will enjoy the **Hotel de la Monnaie de Paris,** 11, quai de Conti, 6ème, Mo. Pont-Neuf (tel. 329-12-48), with a display of medals as well as money. Open daily except Saturday, Sunday, and holidays 11am-5pm; admission free. Even the Parisian police have their own museum, the **Musée des Collections Historiques de la Prêfecture**

de Police, 1*bis,* rue des Carmes, 5*ème,* Mo. Maubert-Mutualité, open Wednesday and Thursday 2-5pm; admission free. Exhibitions of film paraphernalia are displayed at the **Musée du Cinema** in the Cinémathèque, Palais de Chaillot, 16*ème,* Mo. Trocadéro (tel. 533-21-86), open daily except Monday from 10am-noon and 2-5pm; admission 10F. Open to guided visits only at 10am, 11am, 2pm, 3pm, and 4pm. Those who love hunting might enjoy the **Musée de la Chasse et de la Nature,** 60, rue des Archives, 3*ème* (tel. 272-86-43; Mo. Rambuteau or Hôtel de Ville), open daily except Tuesday and holidays from 10am-5pm, admission 8F with paintings and tapestries illustrating the hunt and the hounds. **Musée des Gobelins,** 42, ave. des Gobelins, 13*ème* (Mo. Gobelins). The famous Gobelins tapestry factory (a state institution for over three hundred years, still retaining some of its seventeenth-century buildings) gives guided tours of the museum and factory on Tuesday, Wednesday, and Thursday from 2-4pm. Admission 8F, 4F with student ID.

The Out-of-Doors

The **parks** of Paris are an integral part of the city and are used heavily by young and old, by students and bums—and by the dogs. You will learn to use the park as the Parisians do, as a haven, a shelter from the traffic and the cars—not as a rediscovery of nature, but as a temporary refuge of peace and (relative) quiet. Though walking in the parks is free, sitting down sometimes costs. The chair franchise is run by tough little old ladies who extort about one franc a seat. The benches are generally free. If you have taken up residence in Paris for any length of time, you may want to try to join a game of *boules* in one of your neighborhood parks: usually at lunch-time, or after work, a group of serious players gathers in some sandy alley of the local park. Approach with tact and a pair of boules (60F), and you should find yourself a game. Avoid betting for at least one week.

Bois de Boulogne, past the 16*ème* arrondissement, Mo. Porte Maillot, Sablons, Pont de Neuilly Porte Dauphine, or Porte d'Auteuil. A vast, wooded area, with lakes, restaurants, horse races, and bicycle races—even a baseball diamond in the corner of the Bagatelle soccer and rugby fields. One of the most enjoyable attractions is a small zoo and amusement park in the **Jardin d'Acclimation** (Mo. Sablons), admission 4F. For a pleasant stroll, walk along the **Lac Inferieur** (lower lake), down the route de Suresnes from the Porte Dauphine (Mo. Porte Dauphine). The restaurant in the middle of the lake can only be reached by rowboats, which you rent by the hour. Or, visit the **Bagatelle,** once a private estate within the Bois, now a well-preserved flower garden famous for its water lilies and an exhibition of roses every June. (Mo. Pont de Neuilly, then bus #43; open 9am-5pm except during the summer when it is open until 8pm; admission 1F). The nighttime Bois is quite different from the Bois during the day. When the moon comes out, so do the prostitutes—male, female, and transvestite.

Bois de Vincennes, 12*ème* (Mo. Porte Dorée or Château de Vincennes). Less famous and less classy than the Bois de Boulogne, but more interesting in many ways; the zoo and amusement park are bigger and better. There is also a real castle: the Château de Vincennes, a medieval fortress which long served as a prison. (Closed for renovation, though it should be open by summer 1983. Call 328-15-48 for hours.) The Vincennes Zoo is considered the best in France; uncaged animals wander around in relatively natural surroundings. In the center of the zoo wild goats make their homes on a 72-meter-tall artificial rock. (Mo. Porte Dorée, open daily 9am-6pm; admission 15F.) The horticultural displays of the **Floral Gardens** are in blossom year round (open daily 9:30am-

6:30pm; admission 3.20F: walk from the chateau down the rue de la Pyramide). During the spring an amusement park is set up near the Porte Dorée entrance. Finally, the **Lac Daumesnil** must be one of the most graceful, peaceful bodies of water in France.

Jardin des Plantes, 57, rue Cuvier, *5ème* (Mo. Jussieu) contains a park, botanical gardens, and a small zoo. There is also a lovely, shady alleyway for strolling which runs parallel to rue Buffon. The garden is open daily except Tuesday 9am-5pm, while the zoo is open daily 9am-5:30pm. Admission to the garden's botannical exhibits is 6F, students 4F; entrance to the zoo is 10F, students 7F. There are also mineralogy and paleontology exhibits at the **Musée Nationale d'Histoire Naturelle** inside the park, open every day except Tuesdays 10am-5pm; 10F, 6F for students.

Jardin du Luxembourg, 6*ème* (Mo. Luxembourg) is as integral a part of the Latin Quarter as the Sorbonne or the cafes. For a look at a dying art, join the kiddies at a marionette show—it does not matter if your French is nonexistent. Shows on Wednesday, Saturday, and Sunday at 2:30 and 3:30pm.

Buttes-Chaumont, 19*ème* (Mo. Buttes-Chaumont or Botzaris) looks more rugged than the city's other parks, but yields a good view of Paris from the top of the tallest hill. Unfortunately, it is out of the way and not particularly close to anything else of interest. If you go, take note of the logs along the path—man adding a little insult to injured nature.

Parc de Monceau, 8*ème* (Mo. Monceau) is a lush park in a prosperous neighborhood bordered by well-preserved townhouses. Although it's not worth the trip just to see the park, across the street are two fine museums, the **Musée Nissim de Camondo** (furniture and *objets d'art*) and the **Musée Cernuschi,** housing Oriental art (see Museums section).

Park Monsouris, 14*ème* (Mo. Cité Universitaire) contributes an attractive, peaceful, hilly landscape to the neighborhood of the Cité Universitaire across the street. It includes a nice pond where large fish rise to the surface and swans and ducks preen themselves on an island in the center.

Cemeteries

Père Lachaise Cemetery, 20*ème* (Mo. Père-Lachise). The grandfather of Paris' cemeteries and one of the city's most beautiful open spaces, with tree-lined promenades, melancholy hills, and lonely paths running between the graves. Many spots in the cemetery feel miles from civilization. On the tombstones are names like Molière, Comte, Piaf, Colette, Balzac, Bizet, Apollinaire, Proust. And some foreigners are buried here, too—Chopin, Oscar Wilde (with a Jacob Epstein memorial), Gertrude Stein (whose birthplace, Allegheny, PA, is misspelled on the tombstone), Alice B. Toklas, and even Jim Morrison, lead singer of the Doors, who died in a Paris hotel. (His grave, which none of the cemetery attendants seem to know about, is located in the northwest corner of the Sixth Division, not far from the intersection of paths where the 14th, 16th, and 6th divisions come together.) Some of the graves are ostentatious, with private chapels and exquisite stained glass windows, while others, tombstones crumbling into the earth, have a more mournful appearance. The last members of the 1871 Paris Commune were killed in the northeast corner of Père Lachaise against the **Mur des Federés** and are buried beneath it. You can view the city from the terrace in front of the chapel: the last scene of *Jules and Jim* was also filmed on that hill. The guards dispense useful maps with the famous graves marked, for which they expect a 1 to 2F "donation." Open 7:30am-6pm Mar. 16-Nov. 5, and 8:30am-5pm Nov. 6-Mar. 15. Open Sundays from 9am-5pm.

Paris' other cemeteries: Though not as physically impressive as Père Lachaise, Paris' two other major cemeteries have their share of interesting monuments and residents. **The Montmartre Cemetery,** entrance from rue Caulaincourt, 18*ème,* (Mo. place Clichy), is the final resting place of Stendhal, Dumas, and Berlioz, among others. The **Montparnasse Cemetery,** entrance from blvd. Edgar Quinet, 14*ème,* (Mo. Edgar-Quinet or Mo. Raspail), contains the graves of Baudelaire, Maupassant, Saint-Saens, and Tristan Tzara, the Father of Dada. Both are open from 9am until sunset and are free.

Cat and Dog Cemetery, 4, Pont de Clichy, Asnières (Mo. Asnières). Dating from the 1890s, this cemetery is the resting place of many a faithful pet: tiny tombstones mark the passing of Zouzou, Phiphi, Zazie, Poupette, Loulette, and even, oddly enough, Iowa. A bird or two is interred as well. On its own island in a lonely stretch of Seine, the cemetery has a kind of lugubrious beauty. Allow about thirty minutes from the center of Paris. Open Mon.-Sat. 9-11:45am, 2-5:45pm, Sunday and holidays, 2-5:45pm. Admission 8F.

Waterways

Once crowded with barges, Paris' canals are now usually quiet, fished by old, hopeful fishermen and sketched by art students. The best known canal (thanks to Dubuffet's oil paintings) is the **Canal St.-Martin,** which runs from place de Stalingrad, 10*ème,* (Mo. Jaurès or Stalingrad) to the square Frédéric-Lemaitre, near the place de la République, (Mo. République), where it disappears underground. The area along the banks is mostly commercial and pleasantly dilapidated. The canal continues on the north side of the place de Stalingrad, as the Bassin de la Vilette, in more industrial surroundings. To get to this section, you can also take a boat from the Pont Neuf to the *écluses* (locks) on the canal.

Though you'll be elbow-to-elbow (or camera-to-camera) with other tourists, cruising down the Seine on a *bâteau-mouche* is one of the best ways to see Paris. Boats leave from several places: a boat departs from the **Pont de l'Alma,** 8*ème,* on the Right Bank (Mo. Alma Marceau; tel. 225-96-10) during the summer every half hour from 10am-noon and 2-7pm, and several times at night (9pm, 9:30pm, 10pm, 10:30pm). During the winter there is only one trip each morning and each afternoon, 00F before noon, 00F after noon. From the **Pont Neuf,** 1er, on the tip of the Ile de la Cité (Mo. Pont Neuf, tel. 633-98-38), there are departures almost every half hour 10am-6:30pm, and rides at night at 9, 9:30, and 10pm. Boats also leave from the quai de Montebello, 5*ème* (Mo. Saint-Michel; tel. 551-33-08) during the summer every twenty minutes from 9:30am-noon and 2-5pm, and nightly at 9pm (no 9pm sailing in winter). The boats charge about 15F for their standard morning trip (20F in the afternoon and evening); some also offer musical voyages and even dinner cruises at outlandish prices.

Festivals, Fairs, and Other Annual Events

French panache and love of celebration is most evident in Paris, where the slightest provocation brings masses of people into the streets to drink, dance, and generally lose themselves in the spirit of the *fête* (festival). Parisians like the size of crowds to be in the hundreds of thousands: the gatherings in Washington on the Fourth of July or in Times Square on New Years's Eve are piddling in comparison to the assemblages of humanity on hand for Bastille Day fireworks, the coming of the New Year, or political demonstrations. The **Tourist Office** (127, Champs Elysées, 8*ème,* Mo. George V) has a booklet that lists all of the celebrations, large and small, that take place in every month of the year.

Easter

Foire du Trône, Reuilly Lawn of the Bois de Vincennes (Mo. Porte Dorée). A gigantic amusement park with roller coasters, side-show fat ladies, pony-rides, fortune-tellers, funhouses, and enough toffee apples, cotton candy *("barbe*à papa"),* donuts, and waffles to keep the most gluttonous junk-food junkie happy for days. Lasts two months; jammed on warm weekends.

La Foire à la Ferraille et au Jambon ("Scrap-Iron and Ham Fair"). Porte de Pantin (Mo. Porte de Pantin). A centuries-old market with antiques, bric-a-brac, and food. Takes place the week before Easter, and again in October.

May

Festival de l'Ile St.-Louis. Singing, dancing, and theater on the smaller of the two islands in the Seine. Lasts about a month (Mo. Pont-Marie).

Foire du Trône continues.

Festival de l'Ile de France. Concerts, and walking tours of the châteaux and parks in the Ile de France. Continues for two months into July. For information, call (tel. 723-40-84).

Festival de Versailles. Two months of operas, concerts, and theater in Versailles. For information, call (tel. 950-36-22).

June

Festival du Marais. Music (classical and jazz), theater, exhibitions. Many of the events are outside, in courtyards or renovated Renaissance buildings in the Marais. The classical concerts tend to be expensive, but some of the other events are free. Mid-June through mid-July (Mo. St.-Paul, Pont-Marie, or Hotel de Ville). For information, call (tel. 887-74-31).

Festival of St.-Denis. Dance and music festival, held in the church during the month of June (tel. 243-30-97).

Festival de la Foire St.-Germain. Art exhibits, concerts, and theater productions in the St.-Germain Forest. Take the RER from Etoile to Mo. St.-Germain-En-Laye (tel. 329-12-78).

Festival du Palais-Royal. A ten-day festival in the garden of the Palais-Royal, 1er (Mo. Palais-Royal; tel. 296-20-00).

Fêtes du Pont Neuf. The bridge is closed to traffic and opened for dancing, music, street artists, and minstrels. A weekend in late June (Mo. Pont Neuf; tel 277-92-26).

Foire du Trône, Festival de l'Ile de France, and **Festival de Versailles** continue.

July

Bastille Day, July 14. Big-time celebrations nationwide. *Vive la République* and pass the champagne. The day starts with the army parading down the Champs Elysées and ends with fireworks at Montmartre, the Parc Montsouris, the Palais de Chaillot. The traditional street dances are held on the eve of Bastille Day at the tip of the Ile St.-Louis (the Communist Party always throws their gala there), the Hôtel de Ville, the place de la Contrescarpe, and, of course, the Bastille, where it all started. Dancing continues the next night.

End of the Tour de France, a few days after Bastille Day. thousands of spectators turn out along the Champs Elysées to watch the finish of the month-long bicycle race, which attracts as much attention in France as the World Series does in the States. Get there early and bring something to stand on.

Festival Estival. Classical music: opera, chamber music, recitals in churches, palaces, and concert halls throughout the city. (Tickets about 30F, less with student card.) Until mid-September. For information (tel. 227-12-68).

Fête des Loges, in the Foret Saint-Germain-en-Laye (RER train from the Etoile suburban train station). Another fun-fair/amusement park. Until mid-August.

Festival de Musique de Sceaux. A mixture of chamber music and popular music held in the orangerie of the Château de Sceaux on weekends from mid-July until October. For exact location and times call 660-07-79.

Festival du Marais and **Festival de l'Ile de France** continue.

August

Festival de Montmartre. This month-long festival begins during the last week of August and features dancing, music, theatre, and cinema. Information (tel. 606-50-48).

Festival Estival, Fête des Loges, and **Festival de Sceaux** continue.

September

Festival d'Automne. Dance, theater, expositions, and music at various locations around Paris. End of September through beginning of December (tel. 296-12-27).

Fête de l'Humanité, parc de la Courneuve (Mo. Porte de la Villette, then special buses), the second or third week of the month. The annual fair of the French Communist Party, and like nothing you have ever seen. A million people show up to hear debates, ride roller-coasters, sample regional specialties, and collect Marxist-Leninist leaflets. Entertainers in recent years included Charles Mingus, Marcel Marceau, the Bolshoi Ballet, and radical theater troupes. Communist parties from all over the world distribute literature and sell their native food and drink. A cross between a state fair, the Democratic Convention, and Woodstock, and you don't have to be a Communist to enjoy it. (*Humanité* is the name of the French CP's newspaper.)

Festival de l'Ile de France. Another phase of the Ile de France festival, including concerts in churches and monuments in the area. Lasts until November (tel. 359-31-13).

Festival International de Danse de Paris. Many internationally famous troupes performing around Paris, including the American Ballet Theater with Baryshnikov. September 27-October 31 (tel. 723-40-84).

Festival de Musique de Chambre de Paris. Chamber music in churches around Paris, mid-September (tel. 260-12-27).

Festival Estival, Festival de Sceaux, and **Festival de Montmartre** continue.

October

Festival de Jazz de Paris. There's so much jazz in Paris anyway that this is hardly necessary, but it makes things official. Everybody on the European circuit (Nice, Antibes, Montreux, etc.) should be here (tel. 783-33-58).

Fête des Vendanges á Montmartre, rue Saules, 18ème, (Mo. Lamarck-Caulaincourt). Usually the first Saturday in October. The celebration of the harvest of the vineyards on Montmartre. Though it is not France's best-known wine-producing region, Montmartre still bottles enough wine to warrant setting aside a day for celebrating its accomplishment.

Foire à la Ferraille et au Jambon, Porte de Pantin. See the listing under "Easter."

Festival d'Automne, Festival de l'Ile de France and **Festival International de Danse** continue.

November

Armistice Day, November 11. Military parade from the Arc de Triomphe to the Hotel des Invalides.

Festival d'Automne continues.

December

Festival de Musique Sacré. Sacred music at churches around Paris, including Notre Dame (tel. 277-92-26).

Christmas Eve. At midnight, with the celebration of the Christmas Eve Mass, Notre Dame becomes what it only claims to be the rest of the year; the cathedral of the city of Paris. Thousands of people fill the church, making it, for a few hours, a very human place. Many of the neighboring cafes stay open late for those who want to start celebrating Christmas early.

New Year's Eve. When the clock strikes midnight, the Latin Quarter erupts: strangers embrace, motorists find people dancing on their hoods, and for an hour the boulevard St.-Michel becomes a pedestrian mall, much to the dismay of the *agents de police* who are still attempting to direct traffic. Much the same scene occurs on the Champs Elysées.

Entertainment

When the sun goes down, Paris comes alive. If you station yourself on a bridge or quai on the Seine a little before sunset, you can capture one of the best views of the city. Pont de la Concorde, Pont des Arts, Pont Neuf, and quai St.-Michel all offer wonderful vantage points. The areas around the Champs Elysées, Beaubourg (the Pompidou Center) and place St.-Michel all become hives of intense activity which lasts until 1 or 2am in the summer; some spots stay lively until dawn. Movies run from 2pm to 1am, theater and concerts usually take place between 7pm and midnight (some Sunday and Wednesday matinees), while most *boîtes de nuit* (nightclubs) stay open until early morning, although the Métros don't (they stop running by 12:45am). The *Pariscope* (comes out Wednesday for the following week) or the *Officiel des Spectacles* list events from Wednesday through the following Tuesday and are available at all newsstands. Both have complete listings of movies, plays, and concerts for the week, as well as museum and show information.

Unfortunately, most of Paris' after-dark attractions are expensive. Ticket prices for movies, plays and music are not much cheaper than those in New York City: the run-of-the-mill dinner spectacle costs a dazzling 170F. Still, there is plenty of free or pay-as-you-can entertainment. On warm evenings, the Latin Quarter becomes a stage for street musicians, wandering mimes, and the occasional fire-eater or sword swallower, not to mention the dressed-up Parisians themselves. Some bars have jazz or folk groups whom you can hear perform for the price of a cup of coffee. Whether you splurge on an evening in a restaurant or at a show, or wander around just observing the nightly festivities, you're sure to find the Parisian nightlife every bit as *gai* as it's made out to be.

Cinema

Paris may well be the movie capital of the world. As well as screening the latest European and American big-budget features, Paris' cinemas show classics from all countries, avant-garde and political films, and little-known or forgotten works. Ever since the New Wave crested, French interest in American film has been nothing short of phenomenal; in fact, many American films play here which are rarely seen in the U.S. First-run, big-studio films are shown in the large, sumptuous, expensive theaters on the Champs Elysées, while more artsy offerings are screened in the little theaters on the side streets of the Left Bank.

To find out what is playing, pick up a copy of *Pariscope* or *L'Officiel des Spectacles*. The notation "V.O." (short for *version originale*) after a non-French movie listing means that the film is being shown in the language in which it was made, while "V.F." (for *version francaise*) signifies that it is dubbed. Almost all cinemas offer card-carrying students a 3-5F discount off their regular 18-25F admission, but only on weekdays and sometimes only before 5pm. In many cinemas, the prices are several francs lower on Mondays. In almost all Parisian theaters you will be greeted by an usher who tears your ticket, escorts you to your seat, and expects 1F per person. Ushers who don't get tipped are liable to be nasty.

The **Cinémathèque Française** is inside the Palais de Chaillot, at the corner of aves. Président-Wilson and Albert de Mun, 16*ème*, Mo. Trocadero (tel. 704-24-24) (take bus #82 at the Gare du Luxembourg). A "must" for serious film buffs, the government-supported theater shows three to five different films daily, many of them classics, near-classics, or soon-to-be classics. Admission is only 5F, but expect long lines: at screenings of popular films the tail of the line usually doesn't get in. No screenings Mondays.

The **Pompidou Center** has two cinemas which screen avant-garde and experimental films as well as some classics. All are free. For film times, call the center (tel. 278-35-57) or stop by for a program (rue Rambuteau, 4*ème*, Mo. Rambuteau or Hotel de Ville). No showings on Tuesdays. (Note that the Cinémathèque and Beaubourg are listed under "Cinémathèques" in Pariscope, separate from commercial theaters.) The **Olympic**, 10, rue Boyer-Barret and 7-9, rue Francis-de-Pressensé, 14*ème*, (tel. 542-67-42; Mt. Pernety) is another new-concept theater, boasting no fewer than five different small rooms for intimate viewing. It is located in a lively but somewhat seedy area (Mo. Montparnasse).

Theater

Theater in Paris is not just Molière, Corneille, and Racine. The classics are there if you want them, and so are the moderns (Anouilh, Giradoux, Sartre, Ionesco), but there are also Broadway-type comedies and musicals, experimental plays, and political satires to choose from. Occasionally, even *commedia dell' arte* is performed in the courtyard of the Bibliothèque Nationale, harlequin costumes glittering in the twilight. Prices vary, but tickets generally cost between 15 and 55F, and some theaters sell any tickets that are left half an hour before the performance to students at half-price. The student organization, **COPAR**, 39, ave. Georges Bernanos, 5*ème*, (tel. 325-12-43; Mo. Port-Royal), has some reduced-price tickets available and publishes a monthly list of shows for which these tickets may be obtained. Complete listings of current shows can be found in *Pariscope*.

Some of the best productions in Paris are staged at the state-subsidized national theaters. The **Comédie Française**, place du Théâtre-Français, 1er (tel. 296-10-20; Mo. Palais-Royal), the grand showcase of French theater, presents a mixture of old and new. Tickets are moderately priced (14-50F) and not that difficult to obtain. Plays at the **Odéon** (officially the **Théâtre de France**) place Paul-Claudel, 6ème (tel. 325-70-32; Mo. Odéon), are of an equally high caliber; the **Petit Odéon**, in the same building, stages new and experimental pieces, and student tickets there cost only 10F. Another well-known theater for avant-garde productions is the **Théâtre National Populaire** in the Palais de Chaillot, place du Trocadéro, 16ème (tel. 727-81-15; Mo. Trocadéro). Keep an eye out for posters with the TNP logo, since the troupe at times stages productions elsewhere.

Two theaters at the place du Châtelet, Mo. Châtelet, the **Théâtre du Châtelet** and the **Théâtre de la Ville**, specialize in light musicals, star performers (popular and classical) and shows of the 500-dancing-Romanian-bears variety.

Paris' small avant-garde theaters are about as stable as France's political coalitions, but a few have been in existence for several years and show signs of continuing health. The **Théâtre d'Orsay**, Gare d'Orsay, 7, quai Anatole-France, 7ème (Mo. Solferino), originally under the direction of Jean Louis Barrault (the mime in *Les Enfants du Paradis*) and Madeleine Renaud, has a reputation for creativity. If you want to spend a lively evening at the theater, try to get tickets for Eugene Ionesco's *La Cantatrice Chauve* (The Bald Soprano) and *La Leçon* (The Lesson), which have been playing non-stop for over twenty years at the tiny **Théâtre de la Huchette**, 23, rue de la Huchette, 5ème, (Mo. St.-Michel tel. 326-38-99). Tickets for 38F are on sale Mon.-Sat. 3pm-10pm; performances are at 8:30pm. 28F tickets for students go on sale a half-hour before the show but are sometimes gone by late afternoon (no shows on Sundays).

A uniquely Parisian institution is the café-théâtre, consisting of caustic, comic (often political) satire delivered through skits and short plays, but puns and double-entendres abound, so unless you are up on French *argot* (slang) and politics, you'll probably miss a lot of the fun. Among the better café-théâtres are: **Au Bec Fin**, 6, rue (Thérèse, 1er, (Mo. Palais- Royal; tel. 296-29-35); **Leo Blancs-Manteaux**, 15, rue des Blancs-Manteaux, 4ème, (Mo. Rambuteau; tel. 887-15-84); **Le Café de la Gare**, 41, rue Temple, 4ème (Mo. Hotel-de-Ville; Tel. 278-52-51); **Le Splendid**, 10, rue des Lombards, 4ème (Mo. Châtelet; tel. 887-33-82); **Le Café d'Edgar**, 58, blvd. Edgar Quinet, 14ème (Mo. Edgar Quintet; tel. 320-85-11); and **La Cour des Miracles**, 23, ave. du Maine, 14ème, (Mo. Montparnasse; tel. 548-85-60). Most charge at least 35F (sometimes 30F with a student ID) for admission and a drink.

The musical cousin of the café-théâtre is the *chansonnier* (cabaret), where French folk songs are performed and the audience is invited to join in. Again, a good knowledge of French is needed. One popular *chansonnier* is located in Montmartre at the top of a very steep hill beyond the place du Tertre; **Au Lapin Agile**, 22, rue des Saules, 18ème (Mo. Lamarck-Caulaincourt). Try to get there before 10pm for a good seat; it's usually very crowded. 40F covers admission and drink.

Finally, a word about those big, bouncy, brassy places that Paris is famous for among the package tour set. The **Folies Bergère** and the **Moulin Rouge** (once the haunt of Toulouse-Lautrec) now cater to busloads of Instamatic-toting tourists and put on shows reminiscent of the dancing routines on '50s comedy shows. At the more chic spots, like **Crazy Horse**, the **Lido**, and **Alcazar**, the staging is more creative, the bodies more symmetrical, and the proportion of exposed flesh greater, but ticket prices are astronomical: getting through the door costs upwards of 120F, and drinks (champagne often obligatory) don't come cheap. It's a little bit of Las Vegas in Paris.

Classical Music

If you want to hear some classical music in Paris, don't be discouraged by the high-priced tickets. If you get to the box office early enough, there are often some reduced tickets available. Also inquire about rush tickets, on sale the morning of a concert.

Recitals are given in Paris' churches, especially St.-Germain-des-Pres. St.-Sulpice and St.-Severin, and ticket prices are affordable. Free organ concerts are given every Sunday at **Notre Dame** at 5pm as the setting sun filters through the great stained glass windows. Look on walls in the Latin Quarter for posters advertising concerts; also, check under "Concerts" in *Pariscope*. **Ste.-Chapelle** and the **Conciergerie** also have inexpensive concerts in the summer. Check the posters around town for more information or go to the box office at 4, blvd. du Palais, 1er (Mo. Cité). Open daily from 11am-6:30pm.

COPAR, a student agency, sells tickets at reduced prices for many concerts, even during the summer. Their ticket agency (Service des Activités Culturelles) is at 39, ave. Georges Bernanos, 5ème (Mo. Port-Royal; tel. 329-12-43).

The Paris **Opéra,** place de l'Opéra, 9ème (Mo. Opéra; tel. 742-57-50) has been called a "declamatory roulade of allegory that would pump up a sense of occasion into the limpest libretto" (Ian Nairn, British architecture critic). It is also where the French elite come to display themselves to each other during intermission. Most tickets cost 130-300F, but reductions are available for some productions. You may not be able to see from the cheapest seats, but the acoustics are fine and you will be a lot closer to the enchanting Chagall ceiling.

Some of the most enjoyable and least expensive music you'll find echoing through the major Métro stations such as Châtelet. Here young street musicians from all over the world set up their loudspeakers or their music stands to play for the coins dropped by the passersby. Admittedly, some of them are better off drowned out by the incoming trains, but others are really good, and a pleasant concert atmosphere can grow up among the pillars.

Jazz

Paris is no longer the jazz center it once was. The big names find it more profitable to play the huge summer festivals in the south of France and in Switzerland, and the small club scene has moved north to Copenhagen and Oslo. Still, some clubs are left: for the most complete listings of who is playing where, pick up a copy of the monthly *Jazz Magazine,* the weekly *Passion,* or *Pariscope.* Here are a few old reliables and affordable places:

Jazz O Brazil, 38, rue Mouffetard, has excellent samba guitarists and other groups (sometimes dancing). Up to 20F. A very small and very inviting place. Come for an "apéritif musical" Fri.-Sun. 6-8:30pm (20F first drink) to hear new artists.

Caveau de la Huchette, 5, rue de la Huchette, 5ème. (tel. 326-65-05; Mo. St.-Michel). The Caveau has been Paris' semi-official student club for ages. Their jazz is often the sort you can dance to. Admission is 25F; drinks 7F and up. Open 9:30pm-2:30am (until 3am on Saturday). You need a student ID and 18 years of life experience to get in.

Le Petit Journal, 71, blvd. St.-Michel, 5ème (tel. 326-28-59; Mo. Luxembourg). A "serious" jazz cafe in a small, relaxed setting. Past performers include the Claude

Bolling trio and the popular Haricots Rouges. First required drink 45F, 35F after that. In the restaurant you can get a light meal for 35F if you're careful.

Caveau de la Montagne, 18, rue Descartes. *5ème* (tel. 354-82-39; Mo. Cardinal-Lemoine). Three levels, often with a different group on each level. All kinds of jazz. Open 9:30pm-2am nightly.

Slow Club, 130 rue de Rivoli, *1er* (tel. 233-84-30; Mo. Chatelet). Miles Davis says this is his favorite jazz club in Paris. It's big, and it attracts big names, so be prepared to part with at least 40F. Drinks 4F and up. Open Tues.-Sat., 9:30pm-2am. Closed Sun. and Mon.

New Morning, 7-9, rue des Petits Ecuries (tel. 523-51-41; Mo. Château d'Eau), may be the place where the jazz stars really shine in Paris (Art Blakely, John Hammond, and Betty Carter, to name a few). Admission hovers around 70F, including the first drink. From 9pm nightly.

Le Petit Opportun, 15, rue des Lavandières, Ste.-Opportune, off the rue de Rivoli, *1er* (tel. 236-01-36; Mo. Châtelet). Jazz groups; first drink 40F. Open as a nightclub Sun.-Thurs. from 11pm-3am; Fri. and Sat. holds concerts at 11pm and 1:15am. Bar open nightly 9pm-4am.

Chez Eugène, 17, place du Tertre, *18ème* (tel. 258-02-26; Mo. Abbess). Traditional jazz until 2am. Drinks from 30F.

Discos

The discos that are "in" (or even in business) change drastically from year to year. Many Parisian clubs are officially private, which means they have the right to pick and choose their clientele. The handleless front doors of these clubs are fitted with one-way peep holes through which prospective customers are judged. Many of the smaller places in the Latin Quarter admit almost anyone who is dressed up enough. People in Paris tend to dress up more for a night on the town, but leather never seems to go out of style. To gain entry into one of the more exclusive places you have to be accompanied by a regular and many clubs reserve the right to refuse entry to unaccompanied men (women often get a reduction or get in free). Private clubs are expensive—admission and a drink can cost more than 75F. The following discos are somewhat less exclusive and less expensive:

Le Palace, 8, Faubourg Montmartre, *9ème* (tel. 246-10-87; Mo. Montmartre). The funkiest disco place in Paris; immense, multi-leveled dancing and drinking in a hollowed-out building that used to be an Art Deco theater. The 75F entrance includes one drink; thereafter booze is 15F a glass. Dancing Wed.-Sat. 11pm-5:30am. Also big-name concerts.

Club Zed, 2, rue des Anglais, *5ème* (tel. 354-93-78; Mo. Maubert-Mutualité). Dancing, often to live bands. First drink 60F, 30F after that. About 35F; open 10:30pm-dawn every day except Mon. and Tues. Proper dress required.

Riverside, 7, rue Grégoire-de-Tours, *6ème* (tel. 354-01-72; Mo. Odéon). Heavy pick-up scene (reductions to unaccompanied women and foreigners, except Fri., Sat., and holidays); lots of foreigners. Open every night, 10pm-dawn.

Le Tabou, 33, rue Daphine, *6ème* (tel. 633-33-95; Mo. Odéon). Open every night from 9:30pm on. Entrance 35F on weekdays, 40F on weekends, includes one drink. Matinees on Sundays and holidays at 2:30pm, 30F.

Les Bains-Douches, 7, rue du Bourg l'Abeé, 3ème (tel. 887-34-40; Mo. Les Halles or Réamur Sebastopol). How's your "look"? Here, they care. Dancing nightly till dawn. Entrance: first drink 70F, after that 40F. Special dances for very cool teenagers on Saturday afternoons between 2 and 7pm, 35F.

Bars

Like the hotdog, the bar is an unabashedly American export that has successfully sunk its roots into French soil. The difference between a cafe and a bar is the difference between a room surrounded with plate glass windows, open to the world passing by, and a room that is closed and dim. Most of all, the difference is between crowds that are French and crowds that are American or who would like to think of themselves as American. The bars which have sprung up in the recent decade around Les Halles are all American-owned, serve American food and play American music for a largely American expatriate clientele. The people often belong to the poor-yet-beautiful set, including photographers, models, out-of-work actors and the stray writer or artist. Bars are good places to find out about possible apartments for rent, jobs, and other information that only hip residents are privy to.

Joe Allen's, 30, rue Pierre-Lescot, 1er (Mo. Etienne). The first of the Les Halles American bars, opened in 1972. Sophisto-chic crowd; meals and snacks as well as drinks. Meals run about 70F, but salads are a better buy at 15-45F. Carlsburg draft 10F; gin, scotch, etc. 18F.

Parrot's Tavern, 17, rue de L'Ancienne Comédie, 6ème (tel. 329-38-70; Mo. Odéon), in the arcade. A ritzy English place off a very old and unrenovated alley which boasts that it is the largest pub in Europe; 7 rooms, 132 types of whiskey, 200 different kinds of beer, homemade ice cream, and an English-style breakfast. Open day and night and full of punked-out teenagers. Menu at 50F, beverage and service included, but other side dishes are more reasonable (23-28F). The type of place that takes credit cards.

Top Banana, 46, rue des Lombards, 1er (Mo. Chatelet). Cheesecake, Heinz ketchup, attempts at San Francisco ambience. Cocktails around 20F (all drinks half-price 6:30-8pm daily), hamburgers 23-31F.

Rosebud, 11bis, rue Delambre, 14ème (Mo. Edgar Quinet or Mo. Vavin) in Montparnasse. Semi-bohemian, semi-intellectual crowd. Good jazz records. Beer 14F, scotch 25F, vodka 29F, 15% service not included.

Le Sept, 7 rue Ste.-Anne, 2ème, (Mo. Palais-Royal) and its two neighbors, **The Bronx** (drinks from 24F) and **The Colony** (drinks 36F; on weekends 40F), are male gay bars. Lesbian bars include **Katmandou,** 21, rue de Vieux-Colombier, 6ème (Mo. St.-Sulpice), where no men are admitted, or **Elle et Lui,** 31, rue Vavin, 6ème (Mo. Vavin), which is also a nightclub. 100F first drink for the club, 60F at the bar. Proper dress.

Other Things to Do at Night

Every evening after sunset and until midnight (1am on Saturday) Paris lives up to its reputation as the City of Lights. The **Arc de Triomphe** (Mo. Etoile), **Notre Dame** (Mo. Cité), the **Eiffel Tower,** (Mo. Bir-Harkeim), **Place de la Concorde** (Mo. Concorde), and the **Hôtel de Ville** (Mo. Hôtel de Ville) are illuminated and provide a truly dazzling sight. In the summer, the historic buildings of the **Marais** (Mo. St.-Paul) are some of the buildings and gardens of **Montmartre** (Mo. Anvers or Abbesses) are lit up as well. A night ride on the *bâteaux-mouches* gives an excellent opportunity to see many of these buildings. One ride costs about 17F and leaves every half hour (with a dinner break) from the Right Bank pier on the Quai d'Alma (tel. 359-30-30, 225-22-56, for information).

A French art form: take an impressive building, add a light show, superimpose a recorded message about the glorious history of the building, or the region, or the county, and voilà: **son-et-lumière.** It sounds tacky, and it is, especially the commentaries that absolutely drip with grandeur. Still, the light shows are fun, and the buildings are usually impressive. In Paris you can see one during the summer months (April 1 through mid-October) at **Les Invalides,** (Mo. Invalides) with shows at 11:15pm and commentary in English: at 10:15pm in French (admission 20F). The show is entitled "Shades of Glory."

Shopping

Paris is not a bargain for shoppers, although certain things (such as perfume and Adidas) can be found at a good price. But the Parisians have elevated window dressing to the level of an art form, and exploring the Left Bank boutiques near St.-Germain-des-Près or the fashionable designer shops in the Faubourg St.-Honoré, rue de Rivoli, and the 16ème can be a fun and interesting way to pass an afternoon.

Toward the river on the Left Bank, the rue Bonaparte is lined with antique stores containing furniture, books, and art works. The streets around the Opéra and the Gare St.-Lazare (9ème, Mo. Opéra or Havre-Caumartin), known as the Grands Boulevards, contains a number of large department stores. On blvd. Haussman, 8ème, 9ème (Mo. Chausée-d-Antin) are the Macy's and Gimbel's of Paris: **Galeries Lafayette** and **Printemps.** These rivals are located right beside each other and across the street from the British **Marks and Spencer.** All three carry an extensive selection of merchandise, including food. For trendy clothes, look at the stores on St.-Germain, but buy on rue St.-André-des-Arts, around the rue de Seine, and the upper part of St.-Michel. The rue de Rivoli and the little streets around (not in) Les Halles also offer some good deals.

At Galeries and Printemps, a foreigner can easily receive a rebate of around 20% on purchases over 600F. In order to get this rebate, you need to spend over a period of six months at least 600F in the same store and have each saleslip marked by the cashier for detaxé. For some purchases like perfume, the salespeople are often willing to subtract the tax right away; in any case, you must save the receipt given you by the store and have it stamped by Customs and mailed back to the place of purchase before you leave the country.

A detaxé savings may also be gained when purchasing bicycles or cars, though the paperwork can be a hassle. If your dealer is familiar with foreigners, you can get 17% back on bicycles purchased in France and 33% back on cars. The dealer must prepare the appropriate pink, green, and blue carbon forms for French Customs (douanes). Upon returning to the U. S., you must pay customs if purchases amount to over $300, but often this fee is less than the rebate returned by French Customs.

Along the Seine, the **Samaritaine** (named for the large pumphouse that once stood there and which supplied the Louvre and Tuileries with water; Mo. Pont-Neuf) and the **Bazaar de l'Hotel de Ville** (Mo. Hotel de Ville) carry everything you think you want and many things you know you don't. Across the river, at the intersection of rue des Sèvres and rue de Babylone, is the **Bon Marché,** one of the earliest of department stores (founded in the reign of Louis Philippe) and a good place to shop for clothes.

For bargains on books and records, go to **FNAC** (rue des Rennes), where the selection is extensive and where there are always crowds. For bargains on French goods, go across the street to **TATI.** And no matter where you are in the city, you will find, a few blocks away, a **Monoprix, Uniprix,** or **Prisunic—** all three good discount department stores which sell food as well.

A fairly large selection of English books can be found in several local book- stores: **Nouveau Quartier Latin,** 78, blvd. St.-Michel, 6ème (Mo. Luxem- bourg), has a wide assortment of Penguin paperbacks and guidebooks (including the *Let's Go* series). The more celebrated **Shakespeare and Co.,** 37, rue de la Bûcherie, 5ème, is a place with not only new books for sale, but used ones in the back; a library upstairs for your use; poetry readings on Monday nights, and a fascinating history which includes such *habitués* as F. Scott Fitzgerald, Ernest Hemingway, and James Joyce. You can also try: **Bren- tano's,** 37, ave. de l'Opéra, 2ème, (Mo. Pyramides); **Brown's Bookshop,** pas- sage Dauphine, between rue Mazarine and rue Dauphine, 6ème (Mo. Odéon); and **W. H. Smith,** 248, rue de Rivoli, 1er (Mo. Concorde). If you feel like checking out a good (though huge) French bookstore that stocks everything from wonderful guidebooks to full-color cookbooks and the latest novels, go to **Librairie Gilbert** on blvd. St.-Michel. The staff is helpful, despite any first impressions you might have, so don't be shy to ask them for help or advice.

Flea Markets and Others

The largest flea market *(marché aux puces) in Paris and one of the largest in Europe is held by the* **Porte de Clignancourt** Métro stop every Saturday, Sun- day and Monday morning and afternoon. It is vast, with hundreds of stalls selling antiques and junk, old and new clothes, records, and food. Since it is not always cheap, never pay the first price asked, and get there by 9am for bargains. For junkier stuff, and a better chance of walking off with a steal, try the flea market at the **Porte de Montreuil** (Mo. Porte de Montreuil) early on Saturday and Sunday mornings. Also visit the market at **Porte de Vanves** Métro stop, held every Saturday and Sunday 8am-7pm. Lastly, the **Marché d'Aligre** on rue d'Aligre near the Bastille is one of the cheapest of the flea markets (Sat. and Sun. all day), and its colorful stalls are worth a visit.

The Carreau **Marché du Temple,** blvd, du Temple, 3ème (Mo. Filles du Calvaire), is not a fleamarket, but a beautiful building where new clothes are sold at wholesale prices. (Open Tues.-Sat. 9am-7pm with the requisite lunch break; Sun. 9am-1pm.)

Every day but Sunday from 9am-6pm, the place Louis-Lépine, in the midst of the Ile de la Cité, blooms with color as the **Flower Market** takes over the small square. On Sundays the colors really come alive, as the plants are replaced by hundreds of birds. The **Bird Market** (a truly charming sight) is at the place Louis-Lépine on Sunday. Dogs are marked at 106, rue Brancion, 15ème, Mo. Convention, Sunday 2-4pm; horses, donkeys, and the occasional mule are sold at the same place Monday, Wednesday, and Friday morning. Stamp collectors and postcard collectors get together every Thursday, Satur- day, Sunday, and holidays 10am-nightfall, at the **Stamp Market** on the corner of ave. Gabriel and ave. Marigny, 8ème, Mo. Champs-Elysées-Clemenceau. And if you're looking for old books or posters, don't forget to check out the *bouquinistes'* stalls located on the quais of the Seine, starting at the Louvre and running up to the Hôtel de Ville. You might just come across a treasure.

For some real bargains, and lots of free entertainment, stop by Paris' largest auction house, the **Hôtel Drouot,** Mo. Richelieu-Drouot, which deals in both collectors' pieces and odd lots of toilet plungers. Sales practically daily.

Paris' street markets are a special event and sight: each neighborhood has at least one market weekly (inquire at any of the *petits commerçants* for the day and location). Early in the morning, the merchants set up their stands: the care and attention that goes into the presentation extends far beyond cellophane wrapping. In the livelier markets (the one on rue Mouffetard at Mo. Censier-Daubenton is especially good), some merchants put on a real show. At the end of the market time, the prices go down, and the goods that will not keep until the next morning are thrown out. (One note: watch out for the little old ladies with their rolling carts. They're fast and furious, and they'll mow you down if you're not careful.)

Environs of Paris

The **Ile de France,** the regional *département* of which Paris is the center, offers a wealth of palaces, monuments, museums, and cathedrals in all of France. These sites are easily accessible from Paris by train, bus, or car and make excellent daytrips.

Versailles, the magnificent palace of Louis XIV, fairly represents the absolute power of the Sun King. Disliking Paris for its association with the power struggles of his youth, Louis XIV turned his father's small hunting chateau into his royal residence and capital. Louis was not content merely to construct the finest palace in Europe—he transformed the shape of the land as well. Hills were leveled, gardens laid out, entire forests transplanted, water channeled from the Seine to supply the fountains. The court became the center of noble life and status, where more than a thousand of France's greatest feudal lords vied for the King's favor. Louis hoped to control the often wayward nobility by keeping them at Versailles—where his eye was upon them. Court life also destroyed the financial independence of the nobility by forcing them to pay crippling taxes to support Louis' lavish expenditures.

The guided tour of the interior leads through those apartments and halls that are presently restored, including the royal bedroom; the **Galerie des Glaces** (Hall of Mirrors), where the Treaty of Versailles was signed in 1919; and the *petits appartements,* the private royal chambers. Open daily except Monday, 9:45am-5pm; admission 11F, 5.50F on Sunday or for those under age 25 or over 65. Free on Wednesday. Take the tour and then go out to the spacious grounds. The park still has many of its original *bosquets,* or groves, first planted in the seventeenth century. The fountains are operated only at limited times, royal extravagance not being suitable to these democratic days. Be sure to see the Trianons and Le Hameau. The **Grand Trianon,** the royal guesthouse built for Louis XIV by Mansart, has pink and white marble wings joined by a colonnade. The **Petit Trianon,** built under Louis XV, is famous as Marie Antoinette's play palace along with **Le Hameau,** the hamlet where the Queen amused herself by pretending to live the peasant life. The Grand Trianon is open daily except Monday from 9:45am-5pm; admission 8F, 4F on Sunday and for those under age 25. The Petit Trianon is open Tues.-Fri. 2-5pm; admission 6F, under age 25 3F. Tickets to both Trianons cost 10F, 5F half-fare. The park, open until nightfall, is free. On the first and third Sunday of each month from May-Sept. at 4pm, the park features **Les Grandes Eaux,** an elaborate (and free) display of the water fountains. Plan ahead to visit Versailles on one of these Sundays. Versailles also hosts a series of **Fêtes de Nuit** at Neptune's Pond during the summer. Fireworks, fountains, and lights are all combined in a multi-hued extravaganza that serves the same purpose as a *son-et-lumière,* but on a Versaillian scale. Derived from the "Grandes Fêtes" given in the Park at Versailles by Louis XIV, the shows run regardless of the weather on three Sundays in summer. Tickets cost between 30-125F and go on sale at the **tourist office** in Paris (Gare St.-Lazare) and Versailles a month before each festival.

You can also write Tourist Office, 7, rue des Reservoirs, 78000 Versailles; include an additional 12F for postage.

You can reach Versailles (twelve minutes away) by train from the Gare Montparnasse, les Invalides, and Gare St.-Lazare, or more cheaply by taking the Métro to Pont de Sèvres and transferring to bus #171 there. For those who prefer a quicker pace, you can take the same train from the Gare Montparnasse to Chartres (one hour; 56F round trip, about 45F with BIGE student reductions) and visit both the Cathedral and Versailles in one day. For more information on tours of the old section of Versailles, the town, and *visites commentées* on individual sections of the palace, call on the **syndicat d'initiative,** 7, rue des Réservoirs, a five-minute walk from the palace (tel. 950-36-22). Open 9am-noon and 2-6:30pm, Sunday 9:30-11:30am and 2:30-6:30pm in season.

Fontainebleau, older than Versailles, was favored and frequented by some of France's most famous rulers, many of whom added a wing or altered the palace. François I transformed the château into a Renaissance palace, bringing Italian artists to decorate the interior with paintings and mosaics. Louis XIII and Napoleon I also made substantial alterations. It was Napoleon's principal residence for much of his reign; the cour des Adieux was the scene of his dramatic farewell in 1814. The palace is open daily except Tuesday, 9:45am-12:30pm and 2-5pm. Admission to the Grands Appartements if 9F, small apartments 6F; twin ticket 10F, 4.50F Sunday. Students half-price, free to all on Wednesday. As splendid as the palace is the **Forest of Fontainebleau,** a thickly wooded, beautiful preserve with hiking trails, and the famous sandstone rocks used for training alpine climbers. The train from Gare de Lyon takes about 45 minutes and costs 52F round trip (about 40F for student fare). Near Fontainebleau, **Château de Fleury-en-Biere** has a nice park.

The **Château de Vaux-le-Vicomte,** a masterpiece designed by Le Vau, decorated by Le Brun, and with magnificent gardens by Le Notre, was built for Fouquet, the Minister of Finance under Louis XIV. The château's elegant grandeur hastened its owner's downfall. Young King Louis, received for a feast here in 1661, was enraged at being outshone and stripped Fouquet of power. Appropriating Vaux-le-Vicomte's artists and eventually some of its works, Louis embarked on the construction of his less-balanced and gaudier Versailles. The château is open to visitors from April-Nov. 1, 10am-6pm daily; Nov.-April 2-5pm; closed end Dec. through Jan. The water fountains go on from 3-6pm the second and last Saturday of each month. Admission to chateau and garden 20F, 15F for students; garden and museum 25F, 19F for students. Take the train from the Gare de Lyon to Melun (44F roundtrip full-fare, about 36F students) and the bus from there.

Set in beautiful surroundings at the edge of the Foret de Chantilly, **Chantilly** is a double château with a fine park and sumptuous museum. The chateau was in the hands of the Condé family from the seventeenth century until its bequest to the Institut de France in the late 1800s. The most renowned of the Condé family was the grand Condé, celebrated victor of Rocroi and cousin of the Sun King. An example of how seriously Chantilly's owners took their entertaining is shown by the following story of a little family gathering. King Louis decided to visit his cousin's delightful castle and arrived accompanied only by his immediate personal entourage of several thousand courtiers and retainers. Condé's chef Vatel was called upon to demonstrate his reputation as France's finest and most efficient chef on the shortest notice. All was going well if frantically, when Vatel heard that the fish, which he had been expecting as the final flourish, would not arrive. Rather than face his disappointed masters, Vatel retired to his chambers and did the honorable thing. At the loss of so great a talent, the court was uncharacteristically aghast, especially upon learning that the fish had indeed arrived after all. The **Musée** in the château bears testament to this substantial and lavish style in which the princes lived. Magnificent furnishings and vast numbers of master paintings fill the chambers. The library holds tens of thousands of volumes and more than a thousand manuscripts, among them the beautiful *Trés Riches Heures du Duc de Berry*. Open daily except Tuesday, 10:30am-6pm; admission 12F, no student discount.

More lavish and interesting than any château of the Loire, Chantilly is overrun with tourists, particularly on Sunday. Visit also the **Grandes Ecuries**, great stables capable of housing 240 horses and hundreds of hounds for stag and boar hunts in the forest. The stables are open from Easter-Nov. 1; Thursday, Sunday, and holidays only from 2-5pm. The park is open Thursday and Sunday afternoons, year round. Two of France's premier horseraces are held here in June—the *Prix de Diane* and the *Prix du Jockey Club*. The park, stables and chateau are closed during race-meetings. Take the train from Gare du Nord (38F full-fare, round trip).

Not far from Chantilly is **Senlis** with its handsome Gothic cathedral of influential sculpture and design. The **Royal Castle** housed kings from Charlemagne to Henri IV and now has a unique hunting museum. The remains of its Gallo-Roman fortifications still surround the town. Open daily except Tuesday and Wednesday morning from 10am-noon and 2-6pm. Admission 5F. Take the train from Gare du Nord for about 15F.

The **Cathédrale St.-Pierre** in **Beauvais** boasts the tallest Gothic chancel in the world, and is the product of architectural ambition pushed beyond what was feasible and reasonable. Begun in 1225, the chancel was completed in 1272, but survived only twelve years in its original state, until, too top-heavy for the supporting columns, it collapsed in 1284. Rebuilding began immediately and continued until the sixteenth century, when chancel and transept were completed. The date each vaulted arch was completed is inscribed in the ceiling. In the 1560s, however, an additional central spire was built above the intersection of transept and choir, again over-burdening the supporting pillars and resulting in the disastrous collapse of 1573. So much time and money was then spent on rebuilding and strengthening the chancel again (see the complex of flying buttresses around it), that the construction of the nave was never begun, and the opening from the transept has been bricked up for the last four hundred years. Stand back from the cathedral and try to imagine its immense proportions if the nave had been built.

The **Church of St.-Etienne,** south of the place de la Hachette, is a fascinating combination of Roman nave and Gothic choir, with some beautiful stained glass. Open daily.

In 1664, the only branch of the great **Gobelins tapestry factory** of Paris was opened in Beauvais. It was concerned mainly with weaving tapestry for furniture and using pastoral scenes rather than historical or mythological themes. Located next to the cathedral, the modern **Galérie Nationale de la Tapisserie** houses an interesting collection of tapestries, ancient and contemporary, and a workshop for demonstration. Open daily, except Monday, 9:30am-12:30pm and 2-6:30pm. Admission 7F, 3.50F with student ID. The **Festival of Jeanne Hachette,** the last Sunday in June, celebrates with medieval costumes and processions through the streets the gallantry of the women of Beauvais in resisting the onslaught of the Burgundian army of Charles the Bold. Inexpensive accommodations are rare, but you can lunch reasonably at the cafes across from the cathedral.

The **syndicat d'initiative,** 6, rue Malherbe (tel. 445-08-18), across from the cathedral, is open April 15-Oct. 7. There is another **Bureau de Tourisme** at 37, rue Bureaugard (tel. 448-13-82). From the Garde du Nord, round-trip full-fare ticket to Beauvais costs 62F.

Try to make time to head farther north to the beautiful Forest of **Compiègne**. The train car in which the 1918 Armistice was signed still stands on its tracks, documents arranged on the authentic desks inside. In World War II, the Germans forced the French to capitulate at this location. A palace and more extensive museum of military memorabilia is nearby. The **Château of Blerancourt** not much farther northwest now houses the **National Museum of Franco-American Friendship** (admission 6F, 3F Sunday, and free on Wednesday). The countries' *amitié* is documented from Ben Franklin's times, through literary, scientific, and political intrigues, to the World War volunteers who served in the others' armies. The apartments of the château and the **Musée du Second Empire** are open daily except Tuesday from 10am-noon and 2-5pm; admission 7F, 3.50F on Sunday. There are many country inns and pleasant picnic spots along the 100km route from Paris to Blerancourt (about 1½ hours away by car). Train from Gare du Nord, 66F full-fare round-trip.

St.-Germain-en-Laye has a remarkable rooftop view of Paris, and its château was the birthplace of Louis XIV. The chateau houses the **Musée des Antiquités Nationales** containing prehistoric, Gallo-Roman, and Merovingian artifacts. Open daily except Tuesday, 10am-noon and 1:30-5pm; admission 8F, 4F on Sunday or with student ID. Free on Wednesday. Take the RER or bus #158 from La Défense.

Malmaison is a lovely palace displaying the apartments of Napoleon and Josephine. Open daily except Tuesday, 10am-12:30pm and 1:30-5:30pm, and until 4:30pm Oct.-March; admission 9F, 4.50F on Sunday or with a student ID. Take the RER to La Defense, then bus #158 to the Danielle Casanova stop.

Saint-Cloud, just outside Paris proper, was the scene of the assassination of Henri III in 1589 and the coup d'etat of 18 Brumaire in 1799, among other notable occurrences. Nothing remains of the castle but the magnificent park, by Le Nôtre, which preserves lakes and 100-foot *jet d'eau* fountains, statues, arbors, and an English garden. Take bus #72 from the Hôtel de Ville or #52 from the Madeleine.

St.-Denis, to the north of Paris, is the site of the **Abbey** housing the tombs of the kings of France. Suger, minister of Louis VII, built the Gothic church that inspired the achitects of Chartres and Senlis and hence much of Gothic everywhere. The tombs can be visited daily except Sunday mornings, 10am-4pm daily. Admission 8F, 4F Sunday and holidays. Take the Métro to St.-Denis-Basilique.

Chartres

Perched high above the river Eure and the flat plain of Beauce, **Chartres Cathedral** stands as one of the finest specimens of medieval architecture and artistry, a testament to the primacy of religion in medieval France. The architecture incorporates the newly developed techniques of using flying buttresses and ribbed vaults, creating the first Gothic structure of truly dazzling height and lightness. Consequently, this otherwise sleepy town has become a pilgrimage site for lovers of medieval architecture, history, and spirituality.

Where the Cathedral now stands, there was originally a Romanesque cathedral built to house a garment believed to have been worn by Mary at the time of Christ's birth. A huge fire in 1194 destroyed almost all of this building, but the holy relic was miraculously saved, and the thankful and astonished clerics resolved to rebuild the Cathedral on a scale worthy of the event. The current

Cathedral is thus dedicated to Mary as the "earthly palace of the Queen of Heaven."

Start your visit to the Cathedral by following the guided tour (at noon and 2:45pm) given by the splendidly eccentric Malcolm Miller, who for the last 23 years has been opening the eyes of English-speaking visitors to the wealth of exquisite detail in the Cathedral. Miller makes the symbolism of the fine stained glass windows and the portal statuary come alive with an affection that is hard to resist. Afterwards, take plenty of time to discover the wonders of this building for yourself.

Built in less than thirty years, the building's architecture, sculptures, and windows have an astonishing coherence (despite the mismatching towers, the shorter surviving from the earlier structure). Unlike most others in the region, the Cathedral has lasted through the turbulent periods of French history virtually unscathed. The original stained glass, an exceptionally complete collection, is an encyclopedia of the sculptures and of life in biblical times. The windows of Chartres are famous for their use of the distinctive "Chartres blue," a dark, richly textured color which takes on different shades with the changing light. Most of the glass is from the thirteenth century and was preserved through two World Wars by the town authorities, who dismantled more than three thousand square yards and stored it piece by piece until the end of the hostilities. The Cathedral is open daily 7am-7pm, till 6pm in winter. It is also possible at certain times to view the ancient crypt and to climb the **Jehan-de-Beauce** (north) tower. There are organ recitals on Sunday afternoon and, in September and October, *samedis musicaux*, Saturdays at 9pm.

Though the Cathedral is unquestionably the town's main attraction, take a walk through the hilly, narrow streets of Chartres' old quarter. Here you will find some well-restored medieval houses and constant, beautiful glimpses of the Cathedral through gates and alleyways. The new international **stained-glass center** (Centre International du Vitrail, 5, rue de Cardinal Pie) is also well worth a visit, housing small, but impressive rotating exhibits of stained glass by artists from all over the globe. Open Mon.-Fri. except Weds. 10am-noon and 2-5pm; admission 5F). Also notable are the **Eglise St.-André,** a stately Romanesque structure by the narrow and beautiful Eure River, and the **Eglise St. Pierre,** a delicately-supported edifice of the thirteenth century. A climb up the rue St.-Pierre brings you once again to the *ville haute*.

Practical Information

Chartres is easily accessible from Paris: frequent trains from Montparnasse take less than an hour. Bicycling and hitching are also possibilities, but getting out of Paris is a nuisance. Once in Chartres, look for the famous Cathedral spires at the center of town; nearby are the post office and the prefacture at the Place des Espars. The train station is to the west of the Cathedral.

Office de Tourisme: In front of the Cathedral's main entrance (tel. 21-54-03). They will find you accommodations for a 5F fee plus a 20F deposit on a room. Procure tickets (usually 25F) and information on *samedis musicaux* here. Open Mon.-Sat. 9:30am-12:30pm and 2-6pm, Sun. 10am-noon and 3-6pm.

Post Office: At Place des Epars, on the blvd. de la Résistance. Open Mon.-Fri 8am-7pm, Sat. 8am-noon.

Police: 2, rue Chanzy (tel. 21-47-06).

Boat Rentals: For a *promenade en bâteau* on the river: **La Petite Venise,** just off the blvd. de la Courtille, near the stadium. Canoes and pedal-boats 24F per hour.

For more information, call the proprietor, M. Dauimartin's, neighbor at (tel. 34-05-76).

Bike Rental: Bikes available at the train station, place Pierre-Sémard (tel. 28-50-50).

Market Days: Open-air market Tues. and thurs. at Place Billaird. Larger market on Sat. on the Promenade des Charbonniers.

Telephone Code: (37).

Accommodations

Unless you write or call ahead, hotel accommodations may be hard to find, especially in the summer. The hotels listed below accept peak-season reservations and are open year round.

Auberge de Jeunesse (IYHF), 23, ave. Neigre (tel. 34-27-64). Lock-out 10am-6pm. 2km south from the station—go past the Cathedral and over the river by the Eglise St.-André, then follow the signs. Newly renovated with excellent showers and kitchen facilities. 22F per person, sheets 8F extra. Breakfast 7F, dinner in the cafeteria 23.50F.

Foyer des Jeunes Travailleurs, 9, rue du Pot-Vert (tel. 34-36-23). On a small street across the river from the Eglise St. André. A large establishment run by a friendly proprietor, primarily for working students, but with a few rooms for transient guests. 42F for a single room with breakfast, 37F after three days. *Foyer* is clean and includes bar, TV room, and a darkroom.

Hôtel St.-Jean, 6, rue de Faubourg St.-Jean (tel. 21-35-69). Two lefts from the train station. Quiet rooms overlook a pleasant courtyard. Friendly proprietor with a great collection of cats (but beware of the dog!). Singles and doubles 45-69F. Breakfast 9F and worth it. Showers 6F.

Hôtel de l'Ecu, 28, rue du Grand Faubourg (tel. 21-34-59). Singles 50F, doubles 60F or 75F with shower.

Hôtel de la Poste, 3, rue de Général Koenig (tel. 21-04-27). Across from the post office at the place des Epars. A large hotel with ten double beds for 65F (without shower), breakfast 16F.

Camping: May be your best bet. the **Municipal des Bords de l'Eure** on rue de Launay, 1 km southeast of Chartres, (tel. 28-79-43). Beautiful sites beside the river. Open April-Oct.; 5F per tent, 5.50F per person.

Food

Restaurants are generally over-priced and menus are poor. If possible, do your own food-shopping and cooking. The covered market on the place Billard opens early on Tues., Thurs., and Sat., closing around 3pm. Alternatively, there is a **Monoprix** supermarket on rue de Bois Merrain, with many small food shops nearby.

For regional specialties you can't cook yourself, try **La Fringale,** one block from the Cathedral at 6, rue du Cheval-Blanc, which offers a tasty *plat du jour* for 25F or a fixed menu for 35F. **Le Penalty** at 4, rue de la Poissonerie, two blocks from the Cathedral, is a small, cozy restaurant serving a 40F menu that changes daily.

Normandy

A green, fertile province to the northwest of Paris, Normandy's history separates it from the rest of France. Seized by raiding Vikings in the ninth century, Normandy was officially recognized as an independent province in 911 A.D. when the French king acknowledged the domination of the Norsemen (a name later corrupted to "Normans"). The great age of Norman independence lasted from the tenth to the thirteenth centuries. Meanwhile, the Normans continued to expand their territory, invading Britain in 1066 and pillaging the lands of the French kings. During this period, Norman architecture flourished. The established Romanesque style, characterized by pillars and walls thick enough to support the weight of the roof, was slowly replaced by the more elegant and ornamented Gothic architecture. The new twelfth-century style used cross-vaulting and flying buttresses to help carry the roof, and allowed for thinner, more refined walls and pillars for an airier effect inside the building. Gothic style was intended to "reflect the walls of the kingdom of heaven within the kingdom of man," and with this in mind, builders developed a wonderful range of surface decoration, from stained glass and statuary to bas-reliefs and tapestry.

The French throne regained control over Normandy in 1204, but lost the area to the invading English in the fourteenth century. The Hundred Years' War brought Normandy to the fore again, as Joan of Arc, captured by the English, was brought to Rouen for trial and execution; traces of the British presence are evident throughout this part of the province. In the present century, Normandy again played an important role in the fight for France's freedom. The Allied forces landed here on June 6, 1944—D-Day.

Rouen, capital of Upper Normandy, was the province's ducal seat from the earliest days of its existence, and the town retains fine Gothic monuments as well as an interesting old quarter. The city also serves as a touring center for the abbeys and parks of the Val du Seine and for the coastal resorts of **Dieppe, Fécamp,** and **Etrétat.** Capital of Lower Normandy, and William the Conqueror's favorite city, **Caen** has preserved its architectural heritage despite the bombing of World War II. It lies close to the decadent but elegant seaside resorts of **Beauville, Trouville,** and **Cabourg.** To the west, **Bayeux** exhibits its famed eleventh-century tapestry, a graphic representation of the 1066 invasion of Britain.

North of Bayeux are the British and Commonwealth D-Day landing beaches, with a battle museum at **Arromanches,** and, further west, the American landing sites at **Omaha** and **Utah** beaches. This is the beginning of the rugged and less-touristed **Cotentin Peninsula** with its magnificent craggy cliffs and savage tides. On the other side of the peninsula stands **Mont St.-Michel,** an eleventh-century abbey built on its own sea-encircled rock, where tourists outnumber the monks by a thousand to one.

Accessible by ferry from England and Ireland and by hovercraft from England, the Norman ports of **Le Havre, Dieppe,** and **Cherbourg** greet travelers coming to France. Within Normandy, major towns are connected by rail, but

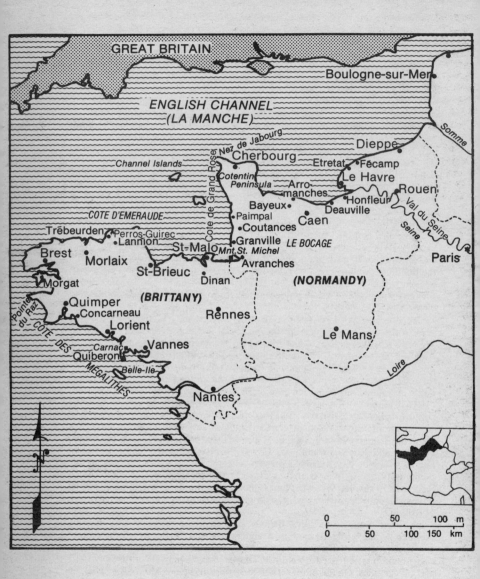

you're better off taking buses if you want to visit the smaller villages. (Compagnie Normande d'Autobus connects coastal towns with a regular, if expensive bus service.) Since many of the nicest spots are off the main roads, it is helpful to have a bike or car for extended touring in Normandy. If bicycling, remember that the roads are hilly and the coastal winds blow roughly west-to-east.

Famous for its produce and dairy products, Normandy supplies a large percentage of the nation's butter. Try the creamy, pungent *camembert* cheese, but be sure it's ripe. The province's traditional drink, *cidre*, is a hard cider that comes both dry *(brut)* and sweet *(doux)*. *Calvados* is apple brandy that has been aged twelve to fifteen years, and it ranks with the finest of cognacs.

Rouen

Rouen seems to have the best of both worlds: a rich historical and architectural legacy combined with a flourishing present. A large, bustling, industrial city, its vital center is still the old town—a lively conglomeration of half-timbered Norman houses, Renaissance residences of well-to-do merchants, and exquisite Gothic churches. The businessmen, students, tourists—and the inflated prices—constantly remind you that this is no provincial town. Rouen is big enough, however, to provide some cheaper options in the quieter side streets, which are actually more interesting than the main touristed area.

For three hundred years, beginning in the tenth century, Rouen enjoyed great prestige and power as capital of a large Norman empire that controlled much of France and spanned the channel to England. During this time, Gothic architecture blossomed; today's visitor cannot help but admire the hundreds of spires, gargoyles, and gables which embellish the Rouen skyline.

Rouen's history is closely linked with the name Joan of Arc. Held prisoner here by the English after her great campaign across France, she was interrogated and tried for heresy by the French clergy. Joan stood firm for three months, but finally faltered, retracted her belief, and was sentenced to life imprisonment. Still not satisfied, the English pressed for a heavier punishment, and in May 1431 Joan of Arc was burned at the stake in the place du Vieux Marché at Rouen.

In a more recent war, Rouen was badly damaged by both German and American bombing. The current reconstruction of nearly every church and dozens of medieval houses makes Rouen a haven for stonemasons.

Practical Information

Syndicat d'Initiative: 25, place de la Cathédrale (tel. 71-41-77). Opposite the Cathedral. The helpful staff speaks English and will book you a room for 6F. If you plan a long stay, pick up the restaurant and leisure guide, Le P'tit Normand (15F). Open daily 10am-noon, and 2-6pm. From Sept. 15 until Easter, closed Sundays. Also changes money, but only cash.

Post Office: 45, rue Jeanne d'Arc (tel. 88-81-20). Open Mon.-Fri. 8am-7pm, Sat. till noon. Telephone: Teleboutique on rue Thiers between rue des Carmes and rue de la République; for long-distance calls, direct dialing Mon.-Thurs. 8:30am-12:30pm and 1:30-5:30, Fri. till 5:30pm, closed Sat. and Sun. The cashier makes change during office hours; use the telephones outside Sun. 7:30pm-8am Mon. for half-price calls within France.

Train Station: SNCF, rue Jeanne d'Arc past the tower (tel. 98-50-50). Express trains from Rouen to Paris take about an hour. BIGE/Transalpino tickets sold at Voyage Wasteels (tel. 71-92-560), up the street at #111 *bis*.

Bus Station: rue des Charettes (tel. 71-81-71), on the river near the Pont Jeanne d'Arc. Buses to coastal towns and resorts. Ask about student discounts. CNAA, at the Gare Routière next to the SNCF station, has excursion packages.

Hitching: For Paris and Caen take bus #12 to the end. For Dieppe, take bus #2 or 8 to Deville; for Le Havre, get on the **autoroute du Havre** which starts in the center of town (you'll still have to wait.). For locations on the right bank of the Seine (Duclair, Jumièges, St. Wandrille), take bus #19 (Mesnil-Esnard) to Canteleu. Cheer up, this goes faster. Or try Allostop, 70, rue d'Amiens (tel. 71-45-10). Open Mon.-Sat. 2-7pm. Coordinates riders with drivers for 28F for one journey, or 100F for a year-long subscription.

Laundromat: 79, rue Beauvoisine, is fairly central and open daily 7am-10pm. Or if you like to hike, try the laundromat two minutes from the Place Beauvoisine on the rte. de Neufchâtel.

Police: place General de Gaulle (tel. 89-81-22). Emergency: (tel. 17).

Telephone Code: (35).

Accommodations

Auberge de Jeunesse (IYHF), 17, rue Diderot (tel. 72-06-45). On the Left Bank, 2km from the station. Take bus #12 to rue Diderot. 22.50F per person includes breakfast. Modern and chaotic; often full of schoolchildren. Get there by 5pm to be assured of a place.

University Housing: available through CROUS, 3, rue d'Herbouville (tel. 98-44-50). Open June-Sept. 33F per night, but the Cité Universitaire is far from the center of town in Mont St. Aignan. You will need a student ID, and an extra photo; take bus #11 from the center.

Hôtel de Touraine, 10, rue de la Cigogne (tel. 71-46-12). Off the rue Thiers between rue des Carmes and place de Général de Gaulle. A small hotel on a quiet street with charming rooms. 42F singles, 47F double beds, 52F for two beds, 75F for triples. Showers 8.50F, breakfast 10F. Proprietors speak good English.

Hôtel Monopole, 44, place des Carmes (tel. 71-46-12). Great location, very nice rooms. Singles 48F, doubles 63F and up. Breakfast 10F, showers 8F. Outside door is locked at 10:30pm, but you can let yourself in with a night key.

Hôtel Normandya, 32, rue du Cordier (tel. 71-46-15). In a quiet area down the rue du Donjon from the rue Jeanne d'Arc. A very nice place, complete with fresh flowers and jam at breakfast, but the proprietor is strict. Double bed for one or two 55-60F, two beds 70F. Breakfast 12F, showers an incredible 15F. Door is locked at 8pm, but they'll give you a night key.

Hôtel le Regent, 132, rue Beauvoisine (tel. 71-84-03). You should know right away that this place is a dive, without showers or breakfast. On the other hand, the rooms are un-numbered; instead, they're named after great French authors, and the decor is quirky and amusing. Singles 45.50F, and doubles 47.70. Closes at 8pm, but you can get the key.

Hôtel la Cache-Ribaud, 10, rue du Tambour (tel. 71-04-82). Central location, right off the rue du Gros Horloge. Often full. There are six double-bedded rooms at 45F, and bigger doubles and triples at 65F, and the 10F breakfast is obligatory; showers 8F. The 50F menu is the closest you'll get to Norman *haute cuisine* at a decent price.

Hôtel St. Ouen, 43, rue des Faulx (tel. 71-46-41). On a park-like street with superb views of the Eglise St. Ouen. Nice rooms, less nice management. Singles 49F, doubles 58F, breakfast included. Showers 10F. Closes at 9:30pm. but they give you the key. No reservations.

Camping: at Deville, 4km from Rouen; take bus #2. (tel. 74-07-59).

Food

Rouen is a gastronomical bonanza—this is one town where eating well can be a bargain and is definitely part of the total picture. Local specialties include duck pâté, *sole normande,* sheep's feet, and *tripes à la Normandaise* (intestines Norman-style). There is a mouth-watering range of fish, cheese, fruit, and vegetables available from the *traiteurs* (food vendors) in and around the place du Vieux Marché (the Old Market)—go before noon if you are preparing your own food.

Self Flunch, 60, rue des Carmes. Serves cheap, typical cafeteria meals for around 23-28F.

La Galette, 168, rue Beauvoisine. Crepes and *galettes* (whole-wheat crepes) with a wide variety of fillings including *crevettes* for 13F, and *andouille* for 23F. Closed Sat. lunch and all Sun. Or try **Normandie-Bretagne,** 52, rue Cauchoise, which serves its 27F *menu* that includes a *bolée* of cider, until 9pm, but continues service à la carte (for about 25F) until 11pm. Closed Weds. and Sat. lunch.

La Marmite, 100, rue Ganterie, may be the place to try out Norman cuisine. Skip the rather dull 33F *menu,* and splurge on any of four trout dishes (31-36F), *Raie au buerre noire* (35F), or *andouillette au vin blanc* (26F). Closed Sun. and Mon.

La Rotonde, 61*bis,* rue Saint Sever, and the **Bar des Fleurs,** which sometimes has live music on fine evenings, are both popular lunch spots, and evening gathering-places.

Sights

With its central spire piercing the sky, the **Cathédrale de Notre Dame** dominates the center of old Rouen. Begun in the twelfth century and completed in the sixteenth, it incorporates nearly every intermediate style of Gothic architecture. Observe the ever-changing patterns of shadow and light on the western facade which Monet strove so to capture on canvas. Also noteworthy are the left portal of St. John (thirteenth century), and the central portal of St. Stephen (sixteenth century). Inside, the four-story nave and lantern tower culminate in the noble, pure line of the choir.

Victor Hugo called Rouen the city of a hundred spires, and the epithet still rings true. Behind the Cathedral is the flamboyant **Eglise St.-Maclou.** Dating from the fifteenth century, its curved west front has one of the greatest collections of gables and sculpture of any Gothic church. Beyond the church, turn left into 186, rue de Martinville, where a small passageway leads to the **Aitre St.-Maclou,** the church's former charnel house. It saw much use during the great plagues of the Middle Ages, and the wooden beams bear a gory fifteenth-century frieze of the *Danse Macabre.* Today, in a happier incarnation, it houses Rouen's Ecole des Beaux-Arts. Up the rue Damiette, next to the Hotel de Ville, is the **Eglise St.-Ouen** (begun in 1318), the purest expression of Gothic architecture in Rouen. Its towering vaults are second only to those of Beauvais in height, and the choir contains some of the finest carving in France. The entrance, somewhat difficult to find, is around the side through the Marmoset Portal.

Most unusual of Rouen's churches, the **Eglise Jeanne d'Arc** was built on the site of the Maid's execution. Opened in 1979 by former president Giscard d'Estaing, it is a whimsical, modern structure. This monument to the city's patron saint, though not entirely in harmony with its surroundings, serves as a focal point for the daily market activity under the shadow of its tent-like roof. (Open 10am-1pm, 2-6pm. Closed Fri. and Sun. morning.) The presence of Joan of Arc is felt everywhere in Rouen. The **Tour Jeanne d'Arc** on the rue du Donjon (walk up the hill along the rue Beauvoisine) is the last remaining tower of the chateau where Joan was imprisoned. The tower contains a display of material relating to the trial which fills in the background to the events. (Open daily 10am-noon and 2-5pm; admission free.) Throughout the summer concerts are held in various churches and chapels around Rouen, and to keep up, you should get the free *Programme de Spectacles* at the Tourist Office.

On the rue Thiers is Rouen's superb **Musée des Beaux Arts.** The galleries are filled with the works of artists from Rubens to Monet, including many local Impressionist paintings. The collection of Rouen *faience* (pottery) is one of the most important in France. (Open 10am-noon and 2-6pm; closed Tues. and Wed. morning. Admission 4F, free with student ID.) Right next door, housed in a fifteenth-century church, is the **Musée de Ferronnerie Le-Secq-des-Tournelles** (rue Jacques-Villon, same hours and admission price as the Beaux-Arts), an unusual collection of fancy grillwork, locks, keys and other household objects in iron, from the third to nineteenth centuries.

The **Musée des Antiquités,** in the Cloitre Ste.-Marie, 198, rue Beauvoisine, has a fascinating collection of relics from Gallo-Roman, Merovingian, and Renaissance times, mostly from local sources. Mosaics, bronzes, earthenware, carvings, and the magnificent, fifteenth-century tapestry *Winged Stags* are among the exhibits. Open daily except Thurs., 10am-noon and 2-5:30pm. Admission 3F, free for students. Antiquity buffs may be interested in the new discovery of an eleventh century *Monument Juif,* which can only be seen on a guided tour arranged with the Tourist Office, Saturdays, at 2pm, for 15F, or 11F for those under 25 and over 65 years.

Two writers with strong Rouen connections have museums in their honor here. Novelist **Gustave Flaubert**'s childhood home is at 51, rue de Lecat (Open Tues.-Sat. 10am-noon and 2-6pm; admission free). If you're truly devoted to Flaubert, make the pilgrimage to Roisset, where you'll find the unexciting library and the remains of the estate where Flaubert wrote *Madame Bovary.* Take bus #9 (10F), for a twenty-minute trip. Plan carefully and get hours from the bus station because the bus has the same hours and admission as Flaubert's house.

Rouen's finest treasures are in its narrow streets. Walk along rue aux Juifs to find the elaborately decorated **Palais de Justice.** Restored from World War II damage, its facade crawls with gargoyles. Parallel to it is the rue de Gros Horloge, once Rouen's main shopping street and now a crowded, noisy pedestrian precinct crammed with shops and cafes. Halfway down the street is the **Gros Horloge** itself, built into a bridge spanning the thoroughfare and telling the time with charming imprecision. The platform above the clock offers a good view of the Cathedral and of the city. (Open daily 10am-noon and 2:30-5:30pm. 4F buys you a combination ticket for this and two other museums; free with student ID.) For amusement in the evening, you could relax in an outdoor cafe-bar like the **Bar des Fleurs,** place des Carmes, **"Brasserie Bavaroise" Taverne Walsheim,** 260, rue Martainville, or **La Rotonde,** 61*bis,* rue Saint Sever. For great music, trek to **Studio 44,** 6km to the south of Rouen, a discotheque and club that in the past has welcomed such greats as Graham

Parker and Stray Cats, in addition to many reggae groups. This will be an adventure without a car: take bus #5, get off at place des Chartreux, in Petit Quévilly in Petit Quevilly, and stick your thumb. To return, you're on your own, as buses stop at 10pm.

Near Rouen

From Rouen to Le Havre, the Seine meanders through forest preserves and apple orchards. Here the Benedictine monks founded their great abbeys in the seventh century, and many lovely ruins still stand today. Three exceptional sights are accessible from Rouen by one bus serving the villages along the D982. The twelfth-century **Abbaye St.-Georges** in St. Martin de Boscherville is a masterpiece of Romanesque architecture. In Jumièges, about 4km off the main road, a majestic eleventh-century Romanesque church sits in a half-forgotten pastoral landscape. (Open daily except Tues., 10am-noon and 2-6pm; admission 7F, 3.50F for those under 25 years.) You may have to walk the 4km if the bus takes you only as far as Yainville.

About 10km further down the D982 in the tiny village of St.-Wandrille is the **Abbey of St.-Wandrille.** There's no need to imagine the ancient atmosphere here—the monks still live, work, and perform their devotions according to the 1500-year old Benedictine rule. Mass is performed in Gregorian chant in a simple building next to the ruins of a Gothic church (Sundays at 10am, weekdays at 9:15am; vespers are at 5pm Sun. and holidays, 5:30pm Mon.-Sat., except Thurs.). There are guided tours of the cloister and other buildings (4F).

Both Jumièges and St.-Wandrille are situated within the **Parc naturel regional de Brotonne,** a protected area of forests and hills, ideal for camping, fishing and riding. There is an outdoor recreational center at Jumièges-le-Mesnil (tel. 91-93-84), and camping at Jumièges. For full information on opportunities, contact Maison du Parc, 2, Rond-Point Marbec, 76580 Le Trait (tel. 91-83-16). **Caudebec-en-Caux** is a few kilometers beyond St.-Wandrille in the heart of the Parc de Brotonne, and also has a campsite. It is the center of a large network of long and short hiking trails through the forest and surrounding countryside. the **syndicat d'initiative** is located at the Mairie (tel. 96-11-12): open 10am-noon and 3-6pm in summer.

Dieppe

Dieppe is the seaside resort closest to Paris, and it serves as a major link to England via the Sealink ferry to Newhaven. It has become a popular holiday spot for French and British alike, and it is packed with vacationers throughout the summer. Try to avoid this overpriced, overtouristed city and stay elsewhere along the coast. Dieppe does, however, retain some of the grandeur which attracted colonies of illustrious Englishmen in the nineteenth century (such as Ruskin, Beardsley, and Oscar Wilde) to its shores.

The major attraction in Dieppe is the **beach** extending along the entire city front. It is a pebble beach, and the water is warm enough for swimming only in the height of summer. On the cliffs west of the city stands the fifteenth-century **Château,** now the civic museum, with its celebrated ivory collection, sampling of Impressionist paintings and permanent exhibit of George Braque's prints. Open daily 10am-noon and 2-6pm, closed Tues. in off-season. Admission 4F during special exhibits, otherwise, 2F.)

In August, 1942, an abortive Anglo-Canadian invasion in Dieppe claimed 1600 lives. The Canadian cemetery, located in Hautot-sur-Mer (a ten-minute walk from the Hostel), is an impressive, somber sight.

Practical Information

Several trains daily link Dieppe with Paris' Gare St.-Lazare (a two-hour trip). On Sundays, when a reduced round-trip fare is offered, the number of trains increases dramatically.

Syndicat d'Initiative: blvd. Général de Gaulle (tel. 84-11-77). From the train station, go left, then take a right through the grounds of the Hotel de Ville. Books rooms—a valuable service in this town—for 5F. Open Mon.-Sat. 9am-noon and 2-7pm, closed Sun.

Post Office: 2, blvd. Marechal Joffre. Open Mon.-Fri. 8am-7pm, Sat. 8am-noon.

Train Service: SNCF Information Bureau at the station (tel. 84-15-00). Also has currency exchange (Banks in Dieppe are open Sat. and closed Mon.).

Bus Service: Compagnie Normande d'Autobus (next to train station) connects the towns along the coast (tel. 84-21-97).

Police: quai Duquesne (tel. 84-87-32); **Hospital:** ave. Pasteur (tel. 84-20-75).

Accommodations

Unless you have a reservation, it will be nearly impossible to find a room here during the summer. Even the Hostel and campgrounds are likely to be filled. Try the centrally located **Hôtel au Grand Duquesne,** 15, place St. Jacques (tel. 84-21-51) which has singles and doubles for 55F. Breakfast 9.50F, and no showers. Or, **A Scottish Pub,** 12, rue St. Jacques (tel. 84-13-16), with singles 45-50F, and breakfast 12F.

Auberge de Jeunesse (IYHF), rue Louis-Fromager (tel. 84-85-73). A stopover for hordes of English schoolchildren. Take "Janval" bus opposite the syndicat on the blvd. General de Gaulle. 70 beds at 22.50F per night.

Camping: Camping du Pollet is a rugged 2-star site east of the city. **Camping Pre st. Nicholas,** route de Pourville (tel. 84-11-39); a two-star site open all year, 3km west of the city.

Food

Stay away from the direct vicinity of the Sealink disembarcation, and look for the local fish specialties: *sole dieppoise, harengs marinés, soupe de poisson,* and *marmite dieppoise,* a bouillabaisse based on cream. If preparing your own food, buy fish at the port center. There are supermarkets on rue Duquesne and on rue Gambetta (near the Hostel).

The Café Le Viking (corner of rue Gambetta and ave. Jean-Jaurès) provides filling meals for 23F. *La Mouette a Vèlo* (109 quai Henri IV) has a 35F menu, and couscous á la carte for 30F, in addition to some more expensive seafood (open evenings only). *La Molière* on the quai du Hakle also has a 35F menu, and main dishes 15-35F in much more pleasant surroundings.

Near Dieppe

The road from Dieppe to Le Havre passes through some of the most spectacular Norman countryside, balanced between the white cliffs along the coast and the green fertile lands of the interior. Hitching is easier on the inland D925, but the twisting coastal road provides stunning panoramas. Cycling is a good idea if you want to explore these villages, but the CNA (Compagnie Normande d'Autobus) bus service will shuttle you up and down the steep hills more easily. Be prepared to spend the night where you get off, because there is not likely to be another bus until the next day. No buses run on Sunday.

Next door to Dieppe, but inaccessible by bus or train, **Varengeville** is the site of the chateau de Miromesnil where Guy de Maupassant was born, and the **Parc Florale des Moutiers**, botanical gardens of unusual variety. One mile from Varengeville's main road is a beautiful twelfth-century Romanesque church, surrounded by a 13th-15th century maritime cemetery, and perched on the end of a rocky outcrop of coastal cliffs and commanding a sweeping view of the bay. Georges Braque, who designed the stained glass windows for the church to replace those destroyed in the war, is buried here. Of course, the main attraction is the **Manoir d'Ango**, a sixteenth century chateau (open daily July-Aug., 2:30-6:30pm, weekends only in off-season; admission an extortionary 20F, with no discounts), however the proprietors are strange enough (reports of tourists being bitten by their dogs abound) and the tour short enough, that you may do well to skip the chateau altogether.

Fécamp, two-thirds of the way to Le Havre from Dieppe, is an important deep sea fishing port and resort, famous for its massive eleventh century **Eglise de la Trinité.** The dimensions and harmony of the church are stunning; the nave is as long as that of Notre Dame de Paris, and the tower at the transept crossing rises some two hundred feet high. To appreciate this "book in stone", you can rent two cassettes (10 and 15F) at the Office de Tourisme. Fecamp is also the home of the celebrated Benedictine liqueur, distilled from the aromatic plants that grow on the cliffs. Guided tours of the factory, **Musée de la Benedictine,** 110, rue Alexander-le-Grand (tel. 28-00-06), last about thirty minutes and cost 10F, including a sample, 5F for 14-18-year-olds and over 65 (without tasting), free for those under 14. Open daily 9-11:30am and 2-5:45pm. For accommodations in Fecamp, try **Hôtel du Commerce,** 28 place Bigot (tel. 28-19-28), with rooms between 55 and 80F, or **Hôtel Moderne de la Gare,** 3, ave. Gambetta (tel. 28-04-04), with singles 45F, and doubles 60F. Fecamp has an **IYHF Hostel** above the town on rue du Commandant Rocquiny, a bit of an uphill climb from the station. Open July-Aug. only. **Camping Château de Reneville** (tel. 28-20-97) is a nice two-star site with hot water and a good view over the beach.

Etrétat, the next, much smaller, coastal resort, is famous for its two portals, the natural cliff arches of the **Falaise d'Amon** and the **Falaise d'Aval,** which frame the town's beach and harbor. A walk around the base of Falaise d'Aval (possible only at low tide) reveals that the whole cliff has been honeycombed with block houses and gun-emplacements, now covered with seaweed and barnacles. In town, the **Eglise Notre-Dame,** an eleventh-century Romanesque structure, has an attractive interior with a beautiful, light nave. The **syndicat d'initiative,** on the place de la Mairie (tel. 27-05-21), is open year round for help with touring and accommodations. Two possibilities are the **Hôtel l'Escale,** place Maréchal Foch (tel. 27-03-69), with rooms 60-105F, and the three-star **campground** on the rue Guy-de-Maupassant (tel. 27-07-67) open mid-March to mid-October.

Le Havre

Le Havre is France's largest transatlantic port. Most cruise ships from North America stop here, as do the car ferries from Rosslare in Ireland and Southampton or Portsmouth, England. However you approach, it is impossible to escape the glut of refineries, warehouses, and factories which line the city's docks.

Virtually bombed to dust during World War II, Le Havre has become a testing ground for much of France's modern architecture. Whether you like the broad avenues and functional design is purely a matter of taste, but some buildings do stand out: the monolithic **Hôtel de Ville** and **Eglise St.-Joseph** by August Perret, and the fascinating **Musée des Beaux-Arts André Malraux** on the blvd. John F. Kennedy (tel. 42-33-97). The latter contains an airy, well-displayed collection of the canvases of Ernest Boudin and the Norman Impressionists and many works by Dufy, Pissaro, Monet, Sisley, and others. Open daily except Tues., 10am-noon and 2-6pm. Admission 4F, students free.

Practical Information

> **Syndicat d'Initiative:** place de l'Hotel de Ville (tel. 21-22-88). Accommodations service. Open 9am-12:30pm and 2-7pm daily in summer except Sun., Mon.-Fri. rest of year.
>
> **American Express:** 57, quai Georges V (tel. 42-59-11). Open Mon.-Fri. 8:45-noon and 1:30-6pm, closed Sat.
>
> **Post Office:** rue Jules-Siegfried (tel. 42-31-87). Open Mon.-Fri. 8am-7pm, Sat. 8am-noon.
>
> **Port Information: Townsend-Thoresen Car Ferries,** quai de Southampton (tel. 26-57-26), Le Havre to Southampton and Portsmouth; **Normandy-Ferries,** rte, du Mole Central (tel. 26-57-26), Le Havre to Southampton, take bus #4 from Hôtel de Ville or the Train Station to stop "Abattoirs"; **Irish Continental Line Car Ferries,** same terminal as Normandy-Ferries (tel. 21-36-50), Le Havre to Rosslare.
>
> **Train Station:** Information (tel. 26-53-53).
>
> **Bus Information:** Office of Autobus du Havre, next to tourist office, place de l'Hôtel de Ville. Open Mon.-Sat. 7am-7pm, Sun. noon-7pm.
>
> **Police:** 30, place Jean-le-Brozec (tel. 25-22-55);
>
> **Emergency:** (tel. 17); **Hospital:** 55*bis,* rue Gustave Flaubert (tel. 22-81-23).
>
> **Telephone Code:** (35).

If you find yourself stuck in Le Havre, avoid the sleazy areas around the Station and the port. The **Hôtel Jeanne d'Arc,** 91, rue Emile-Zola (tel. 41-26-83), with singles at 49F, breakfast 9.50F, and the **Hôtel Dieppe,** with singles 49F and doubles 51-61F, breakfast 9.50F, showers 7F, one block over at 118, rue de Paris (tel. 41-22-78), are both conveniently located. On rue Louis-Brindeau, **Hôtel France** at #85 (tel. 41-79-96) and the **Hôtel Petit-Vatel** at #86 (tel. 41-72-07) offer singles for 55F, doubles from 65F. The closest thing to a hostel in Le Havre is the **Union Chrétienne de Jeunes Gens,** 153, blvd. de Strasbourg (tel. 42-47-86), which really is for French workers, but if they have space you can stay there. 30F, 35F with sheets, breakfast 6F. Meals in the cafeteria run between 20 and 25F. Closes at 10:30pm.

For inexpensive grub, try the **Maison des Jeunes,** porte Oceane Nord-ave. Foch, which offers cafeteria-style food for young people or **Au Moulin de la Galette,** 117, rue de Paris, with salty crèpes from 5F to 18F, and desert crèpes 5-15F. Menu at 30F. Open until 2am daily. Or go down the street to #101 and have mussels or other shellfish at **L'Armoricain** with their 33F menu.

Near Le Havre

From Honfleur to Trouville stretches the **Corniche Normande.** The fourteen kilometer road runs along a fairly steep hill, bordered by typically Norman hedges, rose gardens, and green pastures, and rolls down to the water's edge. (Hitching is dangerous here since the roads are extremely narrow and full of curves.) **Pennedepie** and **Criqueboeuf** are charming villages to explore, and the larger Villerville has a four-star campsite on a pebbly beach, **Camping des Graves** (tel. 87-21-41).

A few kilometers further down the road are **Deauville** and **Trouville**, twin playgrounds of the nineteenth century beautiful people. Somewhat worn by the years, the two towns retain their Second Empire elegance and are still the province of the bored and rich. In the summer they come alive when horse racing, casino gambling, and a thriving nightlife attract the denizens of Europe's *haute monde*. The budget traveler may feel out of place in these towns, but they are still worth a few hours of strolling and people-watching.

To the west of Deauville, the resorts are smaller and less pretentious. **Houlgate,** with its mile-long sandy beach and absence of gambling and nightclub facilities, is basically a family resort. To the east of the town, about an hour's walk along the beach, are the **Vaches Noires** cliffs, crumbling limestone hills which contain important fossil deposits of ancient crustaceans, recently the scene of scientific research. The cliffs can be reached only at low tide. Houlgate boasts many of the same activities (and the same prices) as the other towns. One exception to this is the **Hostellerie Normande,** 11, rue E. Deschanel (tel. 91-22-36), with sixteen rooms, singles from 45F, doubles from 65F (open Feb.-Nov.). Or try the nearby two-star **Camping Plage,** rue des Dunes (tel. 91-18-92); open April-Sept., hot showers.

Just across the river Dives is the lovely town of **Cabourg.** Another faded nineteenth-century resort, the town center has an impressive casino and a grand hotel facing the sea across the promenade Marcel Proust, so named because the author once stayed at Cabourg. The **syndicat d'initiative,** located in the Jardins du Casino (tel. 91-01-09) is open daily 9am-noon and 2-6pm. To camp in Cabourg, try three-star **Camping Plage,** ave. Charles de Gaulle (tel. 91-05-75), open April-Sept., or the smaller two-star **Oasis Camping,** Rte. Nationale 813 (tel. 91-10-62) or three-star **Le Vert Pré,** rte. de Caen (tel. 91-41-68). Bicycles can be rented at the Station, or at M. Delanoe, 21, ave. de la Mer.

Caen

In the twelfth century, Caen rivaled Paris in beauty, culture, and commercial prosperity. Ravaged by the Allied bombings in 1944, the capital of Lower Normandy has since been neatly rebuilt with a feeling for its history, so that William the Conqueror's favorite town retains a charm unmatched by other cities.

Caen served as the ducal seat of William the Conqueror from 1035 to 1087, and much of the town's history is tied to his reign. The red flag with two gold lions that flies above the chateau was the standard of the Dukes of Normandy, which the Plantagenet kings incorporated into the English flag. The people of Caen are also pleased to remind you that the very name "Plantagenet" derives from *planta genesta*, the yellow flower that grows in the nearby countryside. Geoffrey, the forebearer of Henry II, Richard the Lion-Hearted, and Bad King John, used to wear a sprig of this plant in his hat.

Smaller than Rouen, Caen is visibly a university town—political posters and graffiti cover all wall-space, and students crowd the many small cafes on both sides of the Chateau up the hill towards the campus. Recently, the students at Caen have gained a reputation for radicalism, allying themselves with the Communist party and the burgeoning anti-nuclear movement.

Practical Information

From the train station, turn right onto rue de la Gare which continues as ave. du 6 Juin, Caen's main artery. About 2km down is the town center. If you arrive by bus, the Gare Routière is one block over from rue St.-Pierre.

Office de Tourisme: place St.-Pierre (tel. 86-27-65) by the church. Open Mon.-Sat. 8:45am-7:30pm, Sun. 10am-noon and 3-7pm, 8:45-12-15 and 2-7pm in the winter. English-speaking staff. Also an office at the train station. Ask for regional information; they publish itineraries covering all of lower Normandy's "cheese-and-cider routes."

Post Office: place Gambetta. Open Mon.-Fri. 8am-7pm, Sat. 8am-noon.

Police: rue Jean Romain (tel. 86-08-34); **Hospital:** ave. Côte de Nacre (tel. 94-81-12).

Babysitting: call CROUS (94-73-37).

Bike Rental: Cycles Beth, 228, rue d'Auge (tel. 82-25-95), 25F per day.

Telephone Code: (31).

Accommodations

University Housing: CROUS, 23, ave. de Bruxelles (tel. 94-73-37), office closes at 4pm. 33F per night, including hot shower. No curfew, but a bit of a walk from town. No accommodations available Oct.-Jan. Breakfast about 5F at **Restaurant B,** east of track field. Buy a student's meal ticket and you can eat dinner there for 5F (at 7:30pm). To stay here you must have a valid student ID.

Hôtel Demolombe, 36, rue Demolombe (tel. 85-48-70), between the place St.-Pierre and the Abbaye-aux-Hommes. Low prices, proprietor likes students. Singles 42-45F, doubles 51-74F. Breakfast 9F. Showers 16F.

Hôtel St.-Jean, 20, rue des Martyrs (tel. 86-23-35), near place de la Résistance. Quiet location, clean and neat. Strict management. Singles 40F, doubles 60F. Breakfast 10F.

Hôtel Ma Normandie, 43*bis,* rue Ecuyère (tel. 76-13-53). Near the Abbaye-aux-Hommes. Nine rooms only. Doubles 45-68F. Breakfast 9F.

Hôtel de la Paix, 14, rue Neuve-St.-Jean (tel. 76-18-99). Very comfortable, pretty establishment with a friendly proprietor, who is very helpful with sightseeing advice. Singles 42F and 51F. Doubles from 51F. Obligatory breakfast 16.50F. Telephone in every room, showers.

Central Hôtel, 23, place Jean-Letellier (tel. 86-18-52). Near the Château in a secluded, shaded square. Modern and plush. Singles 53F, doubles 53-85F. Breakfast 10F.

Camping: Terrain Municipal, rte. de Louvigny (tel. 73-60-92). Hot showers. Open June-Sept.; take bus #13 (Louvigny).

Food

There are several inexpensive creperies and brasseries near the Château around the rue du Vaugeaux and ave. de la Libération. Fruit and vegetable markets take place every morning under the trees on place Courtonne.

Chez Pierrot, 28, rue Ecuyère. A friendly, neighborhood place. Very filling 4-course menu for 33F.

L'Auberge de l'Atre, 25, fue Ecuyère, 34.50F menu; serves *andouillette grillée* (grilled sausage), a popular regional dish.

Le Pelican, 56, rue d'Auge, near the Train Station. 38F *menu* in a very pleasant atmosphere.

La Petite Marmite, 43, rue des Jacobins. 38F *menu touristique.* 54F *menu* gives you the Caen specialties *soupe de poisson* (fish soup), moules marinières (mussles), and *tripes a la mode de Caen* (intestines).

Sights

Having experienced a period of great prosperity during the late eleventh century, Caen is now home to some of the finest Romanesque architecture in all of France. William the Conqueror's reign coincided with a new, positive attitude towards Christianity on the part of the Norman dukes: persecution was stopped, monasteries were re-opened, and new churches were built. Both of Caen's great abbeys were founded in 1066 by William and his bride Matilda.

The **Eglise St.-Etienne** of the **Abbaye-aux-Hommes** is breathtaking in its classic simplicity and grandeur. Note especially the alternating large and small arches and the elegant decoration at the gallery level. The west facade, with its soaring square towers, is remarkable for its symmetry and elegant carving. For a good view of the abbey, go up to the place St.-Martin. Guided tours are given daily every hour 9am-5pm (except at 1pm) and cost 4F. The smaller and less ornate **Eglise Abbatialle de la Trinité** of the **Abbaye-aux-Dames** has a Romanesque interior with two sixteenth-century towers. Particularly striking are the red stained glass windows in the east end, modern replacements for the original windows destroyed in World War II. Take note of the beautifully worked wood of the organ and the confessionals, and be sure to visit the crypt (enter through a low doorway in the south transept). Both abbey churches close their doors from noon-2pm.

In the center of town, the remains of William's **Château** provide a good view of the surroundings and a pleasant refuge from the city. Within the grounds, the modern **Musée des Beaux Arts** contains a few paintings by Rubens, Van Dyck, and Brueghel, as well as the outstanding *La Vierge à l'Enfant* by Van der Weyden. More interesting is the **Musée de Normandie** across the way, which details Norman peasant life through the centuries and such local crafts as lace-making and candle-making. Both museums are open daily excxept Tues., 10am-noon and 2-6pm Mar.-Oct.; till 5pm the rest of the year. Admission 3F, 5F for a combined ticket.

In the shadow of the château stands the striking **Eglise St.-Pierre.** Its exterior shows evidence of the evolution of the Gothic style from the thirteenth to the sixteenth centuries, and its famous bell tower rises majestically into the sky. The east end is notable for ornate Renaissance decoration, and it backs into Caen's main square, the **blvd. des Alliés.**

Caen boasts a number of bars and discos, many on the streets that wind up around the Chateau towards the University. In town, on the place St.-Pierre, the Taverne Flamande offers live jazz nightly after 9pm in a café setting. Concerts are listed in *La Saison Musicale* and include numerous performances by Caen's chamber orchestra. In the summer, the **Festival des Soirées de Normandie** has performances in churches and chateaux; ask at the syndicat for a complete listing. Student reductions available.

Bayeux

Bayeux is a quiet town frequently flooded by tourists in search of the famous tapestry. The residents take it all with Norman stoicism, however, and a trip to Bayeux can be an exhilarating experience.

The Tapestry (actually a linen embroidery) is exhibited in the former

Bishop's Palace across from the Cathedral at 6, rue Lambert-LeForestier. Commissioned by William the Conqueror's Queen Matilda, the tapestry illustrates the story of the defeat of England's King Harold. It's best to see it before the onslaught of tourists at noon; you'll be able to identify Harold, William, and Edward, and follow the story from court to battle. If you can't tell a long bow (Norman) from a crossbow (English), note that the English are depicted with moustaches and the Normans without. The main subjects occupy the center of the tapestry; above and below run ornamental borders with scenes from Aesop's fables, hunts, and finally the bodies of the slain. The museum is open daily 9am-7pm from June-Sept., 9am-noon and 2-6pm the rest of the year; admission 10F, students 5F.

Bayeux's magnificent **Cathedral**, for which the tapestry was originally commissioned, stands across the street. Untouched by World War II, it is a masterpiece of Norman decoration. Gothic spires top the Romanesque towers, and statues depicting religious figures loom above columns in the nave and over the frescoes in the crypt. The Cathedral is open daily 8am-noon and 2-7pm; the crypt closes at 6pm, and to visit it you must ask the sacristan. Also in Bayeux is the **Musée Baron Gerard** (included in the admission ticket to the tapestry) which houses a rather inconsequential collection, but does contain some nice work by David and some of his eager students, as well as a showcase of Bayeux lacework.

The **syndicat d'initiative,** 1, rue des Cuisiniers (tel. 92-16-26), is housed in a worn sixteenth-century wooden building. For the cost of a phone call, they will book you a room. They also operate a currency exchange. Open daily in July and Aug. 9am-7:30pm, and 9am-12:30pm and 2:30-7:30pm except Sun. the rest of the year.

Accommodations and Food

Auberge de Jeunesse (IYHF): rue des Cordeliers. 50 beds for 22.50F a night. Open July and Aug. only.

Family Home, 39, fue Général de Dais (tel. 92-15-22). Friendly proprietor and homey atmosphere. Arrange in advance to prepare your own meals in the large communal kitchen. 40F for a bed in a twin-bedded room (or a 50F single) includes shower and breakfast.

Centre d'Acceuil, chemin de Boulogne (tel. 92-08-19), has beds for 30F a night.

Foyer des Jeunes Travailleuses (women only), 46, ave. Conseil (tel. 92-07-85). A limited number of beds for 20F without sheets, 25F with. Breakfast 6F, cafeteria open for other meals.

Hôtel de la Tour, 31ter, rue Larcher (tel. 92-30-08). Over a brasserie, right by the Cathedral. Not very friendly. Singles and doubles 50-60F. Breakfast 10F.

Hôtel Notre-Dame, 44, rue des Cuisiniers (tel. 92-87-24). Singles start at 55F, doubles at 60F for one large bed. If you stay here as long as a week, you must take one meal (35F) here daily.

Camping: Municipal Camping, blvd. Eindhoven (tel. 92-80-43), within easy reach of the town center. Open March-Nov.

For good, simple food, try the **Crêperie,** 8, rue de la Juridiction; crêpes and whole wheat *galettes* for 9-13F each. **Champion,** a self-service restaurant on blvd. d'Eindhoven, has the cheapest food in town. **Ma Normandie,** near the Cathedral at 41, rue St.-Patrice, has a fine *menu* for 39F.

Near Bayeux

Three kilometers north of Bayeux on the D516 is Arromanches, the eastern-most of the D-Day invasion beaches. The British built Port Winston here in one day on June 6, 1944. Mammoth blocks of concrete were towed across the Channel at 1½ mph and sunk in a wide semi-circle around the beach; the harbor provided shelter while the Allies unloaded tanks and bulldozers. The Musée du Débarquement (tel. 22-34-31), right on the beach, houses mementoes and photographs of the British and Canadian landings. (Open daily 9am-noon and 2-7pm. A film show is included in the price (7F) of the badly-organized tour) If you're in Arromanches around anniversary time (early June), expect to be swamped by parties of visiting North American veterans.

Farther west is Omaha Beach, the focal point of the landing. The American cemetery at St.-Laurent, on the hills above the beach, is a sad memorial to the many who died. (More than six thousand of the approximately sixty thousand American soldiers who landed at Normandy were killed on the first day.) Juno Beach, the landing site of the Canadian forces, lies east of Arromanches. The Canadian cemetery is located at Bény-sur-Mer—Reviers, near Courseulles, and there are commemorative monuments at Bernières, Courseulles, and St.-Aubin. For further information, contact the Comité du Débarquement, place des Tribunaux, 14400 Bayeux (tel. 92-00-26). There is a fairly large two-star campsite at Arromanches, ave. de Verdun (tel. 22-36-78).

The Cotentin Peninsula

The road from Cherbourg to Coutances passes through the rugged Cotentin countryside and a handful of picturesque, historic towns. At the northern tip of the peninsula is Cherbourg, a major port which connects France to Wey-mouth, England (weekly) and to Rosslare, Ireland (every two days, covered by Eurail pass). For port information, contact Townsend-Thoresen Car Ferries at (tel. (32) 43-20-13) or Sealink at (tel. (32) 53-24-27). The Youth Hostel is near the Train Station at 109, rue de Paris, 21F a night.

Bricquebec and St.-Saveur-le-Vicomte are more typical of this area, com-posed of plain granite houses and Romanesque churches, with remains of medieval fortresses. Follow the coastal route down to Granville and you'll see some spectacular vistas.

In Lessay there is a fine Romanesque abbey, beautiful for both its architec-ture and its setting. Visit on Sunday to hear the Mass sung in Gregorian chant. Coutances, a cathedral town superbly placed on a hill southeast of Lessay, has long been the region's religious center. The Cathedral escaped wartime de-struction, and remains particularly striking when viewed from a distance. Note the multiplicity of small, pointed towers (twelve in all) tucked into the two main spires—a common feature of churches in the area. The interior is also typically Norman, with Romanesque piers and arches surmounted by a Gothic gallery and windows added two centuries later. The splendid lantern-towers can be climbed by making arrangements in advance with the sarcistan. Also worth seeing is the landscape garden, a fine example of French love for hor-ticulture; the intimate flower arrangements and the spiral hedge are memora-ble.

Granville is a charming seaside town built on a rocky promontory and ap-proached via a twisting road which winds down from the cliffs above the town. (Drive or hitch along the D971). Water cures are offered at the Hotel des Bains, and the narrow streets of the ville basse (lower city) are full of pleasant cafes. The ville haute (upper city) has preserved its fifteenth-century fortifications, and a walk around the ramparts provides fine views. Within the walls is the massive fifteenth-century **Eglise Notre-Dame**.

The **syndicat d'initiative** in Granville is across from the casino at 15, rue Georges Clémenceau (tel. 50-02-67). Ferry crossings from Granville to the nearby island of Jersey are 120F one way (160F for a round-trip excursion fare, 200F for three days). All departures are early in the morning. For information, contact Vedettes Armoricaines, 12, rue Clémenceau (tel. 50-77-45).

Southwest of Granville on the D973, **Avranches** sits happily atop a butte in a northern corner of the Mont. St.-Michel Bay. Benedictine monks from Avranches set out in the eighth century to build Mont St.-Michel, and on a clear day there is a superb view of the Mont from the **Jardin des Plantes** in the west end of the city. The **Musée de l'Avranchin** on place St.-Avrit houses the manuscripts and books saved when the abbey was sacked during the French Revolution. Open 10am-noon and 2-6pm; admission 5F and 2.50F (tel. (33) 56-00-22). The **syndicat d'initiative** is next to the bus station on rue General de Gaulle (tel. 58-00-22) and is open daily 10am-noon and 2-7:30pm.

Mont St.-Michel

No matter how many times you've seen it in pictures, it's hard not to be over-awed upon first glimpsing the Mont St.-Michel rising out of the water. Built painstakingly over several centuries on this tiny island (now connected by a causeway), the abbey buildings are an outstanding tribute to the monastic virtue of solitude. The Mont today is understandably the victim of unrivaled tourist invasions; try to get there in the morning, but the crowds are as inevitable as the Mont is memorable.

To get to Mont St.-Michel by train, you must change to a connecting bus in Pontorson. Unfortunately, your railpass is not valid for this ride, and the charge for the 9km journey is 25F round trip. (Don't bother to buy tickets for the tourist-trap museums which the bus driver sells after the journey.) The bus, with frequent service, may be your best bet, and hitching is difficult. You can also rent a bike at the Pontorson train station for a half-day (12F) or whole-day (18F) and bike the 9km—the road is straight and mostly flat farmland.

The **syndicat d'initiative** (tel. 60-14-30) is located behind the stone wall to the left (after passing through the Porte du Roi). It's open 9am-noon and 2-6pm (closed Sun.), and sells posters and books at lower prices than the commercial stores. The office also has money exchange and a schedule of tides (*Horaire des Marées*). Exchange rates at Mont St.-Michel are badly inflated.

Accommodations and Food

Unless you are thrilled by the idea of staying on the most touristed peninsula in the world, there is no reason to remain overnight on the Mont. If you're determined to stay, though, the **Hotel de la Croix Blanche** on rue Grande (tel. 60-14-04) has a few rooms for 55F. When you're hungry, the **Croix Blanche** has a reasonable 32F *menu* or omelettes à la carte for 18F, and you can sit on a terrace and gaze. The best idea, however, is to pack a picnic and eat in the abbey gardens near the top of the hill (a few flights below the entrance to the abbey, admission 3F).

To keep afloat financially, you should center your stay at drab Pontorson, or at one of the two **IYHF Hostels** in the area.

Pleine-Fourgères, about 4km from Pontorson on rue de la Gare, (tel. 56-15-62), 19F a night. Open July-Aug. only.

St. Malo, 37, ave. Père Umbricht, St. Malo (tel. 56-15-52). Huge, modern, and efficient, with facilities for volleyball and tennis. (For directions, see the St. Mâlo Accommodations section.) 12.50F a night; dinner 23.50F, breakfast 7F. Open all year.

In Pontorson:

Le Relais Clémenceau, 40, blvd. Clémenceau (tel. 60-10-96). One block from the station on the corner of rue Leconte de Lisle. Clean, modern rooms for 50F, doubles 58-120F. *Menu* 38F and 48F.

Hôtel le Mascaret, 8, rue Couesnon (tel. 60-10-69). Rooms from 53F for a single or a double.

Camping: Pont d'Orson, rue de la Victoire, right in Pontorson. This 1-star site is simple but adequate. 3F per person, showers free.

There are several cheap eateries along rue Couesnon in Pontorson, but the best is **Le Grillon,** a snack bar at 37, rue Couesnon, with crepes (8-16F), sandwiches, and a grill *menu.* **La Cave,** 37, rue de la Libération, is also a hotel with double rooms from 53-72F; breakfast 9.50F, shower 6F.

Sights

The origins of Mont St.-Michel lie in the eighth century when an oratory was built here by the Bishop of Avranches. This modest structure was expanded over the years with Romanesque and Gothic buildings on the top and sides of the rock, and fortifications around them. The **ville basse,** also fortified, grew up as the abbey's fame spread and visitors multiplied. Enter via the **Porte du Roi,** the only break in the outer walls, or the **Grand Rue,** a busy pedestrian street full of souvenir shops and restaurants. Although the crush is somewhat maddening, it may help you recreate the frenzied atmosphere of a medieval pilgrimage with merchants hawking holy relics. After climbing several flights of stairs, you will arrive at the abbey entrance. Admission is 9F, students 4.50F (half-price on Sundays). The abbey is open 9-11:30am and 1:30-6pm, and you can only enter the abbey if you're on a guided tour. With a tour (and no extra fee) you may follow the group through the lower halls of La Merveille and through the equally fascinating crypts. English-language tours (lasting about 45 minutes) Mon., Tues., and Wed. at 11am, 3pm, and 5pm. French-language tours leave every 15 minutes. More detailed tours with an emphasis on art history are available with a guide from the **Caisse Nationale des Monuments Historiques et des Sites** (ask at the Admission booth). These tours leave at 10am, 11am, 2pm, and 4pm, and cost 16.50F for adults, 10.50F for ages 18-25, 7F for those under 18 and over 65 (July and August only).

The church itself is a simple Romanesque structure with a Gothic cloister from the fifteenth century; the central crossing lies on the highest point of the island. After the peaceful cloister and refectory, you will wander down into the church foundations and the earlier structures dating back to the year 708 A.D. The tour then progresses through the three levels of **La Merveille,** the graceful thirteenth-century structure next to the church which houses all the abbey functions. If the tour is large enough, you'll have plenty of time to linger in the narrow passageways and wonder at the complexity of the abbey's construction.

After the tour, head down the ramparts and into the abbey garden for some superb views of Normandy (to the east) and Brittany (to the west). From here, you can also study the huge buttresses that climb the entire island to support the abbey—remember that every stone was brought here by boat and lifted by pulley. Take your time walking through the twisting streets of the ville basse as you return to the parking lot.

At high tide, the sandy beaches alongside the causeway are covered as the water rushes in at speeds of up to 15mph. To see this spectacle, you must be within the abbey fortifications a good hour beforehand. If you have parked your car on the beach, the attendants will tell you when it must be moved.

Brittany (Bretagne)

Brittany's saw-tooth coastline is defined by the cliffs, cool grottoes, and expanses of sandy beach sculpted by extreme tides. Beginning at **St.-Malo,** the coastal circuit leads from the vast luxurious beaches of the **Côte d'Emraude** westward past the rocky **Corniche Bretonne** and striking mauve granite promontories of the **Corniche de l'Armorique.**Continuing along the high headlands and sandy, pine-covered terrain of the harshly beautiful **Presqu'ile de Crozon,** you'll pass the thundering shore of **La Cornouaille,** where Celtic customs are kept alive, especially in the regional capital, Quimper.

Breton architecture is as somber as many of the bleak natural vistas. Buildings are hewn from the hard granite native to the region, a material impervious to devastating sea winds. Enclaves of roses and near-tropical vegetation flourish on the lee side of waved cliffs, sheltered from sea breezes and nourished by the temperate gulf stream. Forays into the heather-covered moors and farmlands of Brittany's interior, the **Argoat** (country of wood), are worthwhile. Take a leisurely trip inland and you'll be exposed to Breton culture undisturbed.

Unlike most of the French, the Bretons are a Celtic people who were driven across the channel during the Anglo-Saxon invasions of England in the fifth and sixth centuries. The Bretons are ethnically closest to the Welsh and Irish, and the relation is noticeable in modern Brittany. Bretons are virtually all fair-skinned, with red or dark hair, and the Breton language, still spoken in isolated rural areas, combines Romance and Celtic elements. The historic ties with Britain are particularly evident in the composition and style of the folk music and in the featured musical instrument, the *binou,* whose closest relative is the Scottish bagpipe. For Breton color, attend an annual village *pardon,* a popular festival held to honor the patron saint of the parish. The faithful, attired in traditional dress and bearing candles, gather and march behind other members of the congregation reverently carrying banners and religious icons. Afterwards, the solemnity gives way to revelry as the parish throws the biggest party of the year. The best-known *pardon* occurs near Vannes at **Ste. Anne d'Auray** in mid-July. Other extravagant *pardons* are held in mid-May at **Treguier,** Trinity Sunday at **Rumengol,** mid-August at **Perros-Guirec,** the last Sunday in August at **Ste.-Anne-la Palud** and late September at **Josselin.** These dates vary from year to year (usually, the *pardon* is held on the Sunday nearest the Saint's day), so contact a departmental tourist office or the syndicat d'initiative in one of the larger towns for more up-to-date information.

There is another modern, turbulent side to life in Brittany, too. Breton penchant for tradition and the slowly growing modernization of land and lifestyle cause friction whenever they rub too closely. The growth pains are especially acute because Brittany is not a wealthy province. Industrialization has come only recently and the traditional vocations of farming and fishing have become more and more difficult to pursue. This economic plight has in the past spurred on the move for Breton separatism; recently, however, more autonomy has been granted to local government under Mitterrand and the French government is beginning to support the preservation of Breton culture. In June, 1979, students were allowed to replace a section of the French language exam with Breton.

More discordant notes have disrupted the provincial scene, as Bretons try to preserve the natural beauty of their shores. In 1978, the tanker *Amoco Cadiz* ran aground, dumping thousands of tons of oil on the Côte de granite Rose in the western part of the peninsula. A huge volunteer force labored for months cleaning the beaches and the rocks. In 1980, another disaster struck as the tanker *Tanis* crushed off the Ile de Batz. Profoundly cynical of official efforts to regulate tanker traffic, the local volunteer force left the cleaning up to the army. Just as this crisis settled, huge crowds gathered in May 1980 at Plogoff in the southwest of Brittany to protest the planned construction of a nuclear facility there. Yet if the Bretons protest, they also cling to the jobs which the local nuclear submarine base provides.

Practical Information

Getting to Brittany is hardly a problem, but once you're there, getting around is a different matter. Trains leaving from Paris' Gare Montparnasse take three hours to reach Rennes. The Paris-Quimper connection averages a reasonably efficient 6 hours, but within Brittany, travel on public transportation can be an annoyance. By the look of the map, the train seems promising. Along the northern coast, the Paris-Brest trunk line has extensions to St.-Malo (from Dol), Dinard (from Dinan), Paimpol (from Guimgamp), Lannion (from Plouaret), and Roscoff (from Morlaix). In the south, the Quimper-Paris route has extensions to Camaret (from Chateaulin), Concarneau (from Rosporden), Quibéron (from Auray), and Le Croisic (from Pont Château or Savenay). But there are no direct train connections between these finger tips, and connections are often badly timed. To the railpass-toting traveler committed to the tracks, this may often mean a wait of a couple of hours in a train station, or a journey which seems to take you over the longest possible path between two points.

The multitude of private bus lines operating in Brittany are a mixed blessing. They do connect points the train lines miss, but their prices range from the slightly high to the blatantly outrageous (the 35 minute ride from Quibéron to Carnac is 22F round-trip). This leaves bicycling as the best alternative. The Youth Hostels in Rennes, Ninan, St.-Brieuc, Paimpol, Lannion, Morlaix, Lorient and Quimper rent bikes for 15F a day to IYHF members. St.-Brieve, Morlaix, Lorient, and Quimper also have reciprocal arrangements—you can rent a bike at one and drop it off at another. The train stations at Dinard, Roscoff, St.-Malo, and Vannes also rent bikes for 18F a day to IYHF members. The train stations at Roscoff, St. Malo, Vannes and Chateaulin also rent bikes for 25F a day, but require a 150F deposit. Again, you can drop your bike off at the SNCF station in another town. Pick up the brochure *Train et Velo* in any train station for details. Hitching can be slow on the small roads, but is usually reliable on the larger ones.

If you balk at crowds, beware from early to mid-July through to the end of August when the part of Paris that does not depart for the Côte d'Azur arrives in Brittany to fill the campgrounds and hotels. Accommodations are impossible to find and you will miss the true nature of the region under the tourist masses.

On the other hand, many of the *stations balnéaires*, the coastal resort towns like St. Malo, Quiberon, and Concarneau, will seem curiously ghostly and deserted if you come in June or other off-months. Many restaurants, cafés and hotels will still be hibernating and there will be practically no night-life (though of course you will have the beaches practically to yourself). In any case, the best strategy for visiting Brittany is to avoid the coastal life and glitter altogether. Try instead to spend some time on any of the fairly undespoiled islands off the coast, Bréhat, Batz, Belle Ile and Ouessant, especially where you will see the more traditional, rustic Breton life and the Breton life of the sea brought together, or head to the inland cities and towns starting with Quimper and explore places like Auray, Plóechmel, Pleyben, Carhaix and Quimperlé, where there are fewer tourists.

If you're in Paris and planning a visit to Brittany, collect information at **Maison de Bretagne**, 17 rue de l'Arrivée, 15*eme* (tel. 538-73-15 Metro Montparnasse-Bienvenue).

Rennes

A three-hour train ride from Paris, Rennes is the gateway to the Breton Peninsula as well as its administrative center. In 1720, a clumsy carpenter set fire to his workshop and then to half the city. Jacques Gabriel (the architect of the place de la Concorde in Paris) then rebuilt the town along the lines of the General Ulysses S. Grant school of architecture: imposing, austere, and very monotonous. Now primarily a university town, all told the city does not have much to offer the enthusiastic tourist. Rennes does, however, have excellent facilities to help you plan a *séjour* in Brittany. Probably the best strategy for a visit to Rennes would be to make it a brief, two to three hour stop (a hop off the train or bicycle) for information and a stretch and then move on to Dinan or St. Malo to the north, Nantes to the south, all of which are readily accessible by train in a few hours. Visit the **syndicat d'initiative** and the **Centre d'Information Jeunesse Bretagne** (make sure to ask for the booklet *Camping, caravaning, auberges de Jeunesse Bretagne*, which lists all of the youth hostels and just about all of the campgrounds in the entire department. Also addresses for further information within Brittany and without).

Practical Information

Rennes has large, helpful maps posted in all the major squares. Use the one on the place de la Gare to get you to the syndicat d'initiative—Rennes' most worthwhile attractions.

Syndicat d'Initiative: Pont de Nemours (tel. 79-01-98). Open Mon.-Sat. 9am-7:30pm, closed Sun. (In off-season, closed 12:30-2:00pm).

Centre d'Information Jeunesse Bretagne, in the Maison du Champ de Mars (first floor), 6, cours des Allies (tel. 79-28-55). Information on accommodations, hitching, possible (but unlikely) work, cultural events, cycling, and more for all of Brittany. Mon. 12noon-7pm, Tues.-Fri. 9am-7pm, Sat. 9am-12noon, 2pm-6pm, closed Sun. (During school vacations, July-Aug., open til 5pm, closed Sat. and Sun.)

Post Office: corner of rue d'Alma and rue Beaumont. Postal information (tel. 79-09-20). Open Mon.-Fri. 8am-7pm, Sat. 8am-noon. Closed Sundays and holidays.

Bus Station: blvd. Magenta (tel. 30-87-80). Services to St. Malo, Paimpont, Fougeres, Mont.-St.-Michel, Dinard, Nantes, Angers, St.-Nazaire, Le Croisic, Ploermel. Open 6am-8:30pm.

Train Station: For information (tel: 79-12-12) from 7:30am-7:30pm, and for reservations (tel. 30-45-96) from 8am-noon and 2-6pm, except Sun.

Student Travel Service, 7, place Hoche (in the CROUS building. tel. 36-46-11) open Mon.-Fri. 9:30-11:30am and 1:30-4pm, closed weekends. BIGE/Transalpino tickets and information.

Telephone Code: Ille et Vilaine (99).

Accommodations and Food

If you do end up staying in Rennes, the best of the less than attractive options is the IYHF **Auberge de Jeunesse,** 40 rue Montaigne (tel. 50-52-67), 22F per night, breakfast 7F. (From the station turn right and follow signs beginning at the ramp over tracks or take bus #1. Reception 8-10am and 5-11pm.) Among hotels, **Hôtel de la Guerche** (tel. 30-37-79), 29 Rue St. Helier not far from the station is the cheapest; singles and doubles 41-51F, breakfast included (ask at the syndicat for others).

As all over Brittany, crêperies are the cheapest places to eat, which is convenient since they sprout up everywhere. For a proper restaurant, try **Restaurant des Carnes,** 2 rue des Carnes with *menus* at 22 and 35F (off Blvd. de la Liberté, closed August).

In the way of sights, Rennes has two museums to offer, the **Musée de Bretagne** and the **Musée des Beaux Arts,** conveniently housed in one building on the quai Emile Zola four blocks from the syndicat (Admission 6F, 3F with student ID). Open daily 10am-noon, 2-6pm, closed Tues.). Both are good, small museums. Outdoors, wander the **Jardin du Thabur,** a pleasant 26-acre park formerly owned by the abbey of St. Mélaine. For cultural events including theatre festivals in November, consult the syndicat or the **Maison de la culture,** 1 rue St. Hélier (tel. 79-26-26).

St.-Malo

Geographically isolated and commercially prosperous, the original St.-Malo was an island once fortified in granite, aloof, proud, and fierce in its fight for independence. A free city in the thirteenth century, it refused to adopt either a Norman or a French identity in the fourteenth century, while holding out against English attacks from the sea. The city's motto amply sums up the Malouin attitude: "neither French nor Breton, I am a man from St.-Malo."

St.-Malo became noted as the town of *armateurs*—ship-builders and outfitters for commerce, fishing and privateering. Today's St.-Malo, with its modernized fishing facilities and new commercial port, is one of Brittany's largest cities. Old St.-Malo is now connected to land by an isthmus, and has grown together with its former neighboring communes to form one unit. **Paramé** and **Rotheneuf** lie to the east with long beachfront promenades, and **St.-Servan** to the south, a site dating back to Gallo-Roman times. Most recently razed by fire in 1944, when it was a particularly entrenched German stronghold, it has the rather stolid, inorganic feel of a city entirely rebuilt. But the industrial air does not pertain so much to the old city. Old St.-Malo too was largely destroyed during the war, but has been successfully rebuilt to recall the *corsaire* town it once was.

Practical Information

St.-Malo consists of the old walled city (called *intra muros*) and a complex of the former towns of St.-Servan, Paramé, and Rotheneuf. From the train station take ave. Louis-Martin to the syndicat d'initiative near the walls of the old city. Most of the inexpensive hotels and restaurants are within several blocks of the long beach which extends southeast of the old city to Paramé.

Syndicat d'Initiative: Port de Plaisance, near the entrance to the old city (tel. 56-64-48). Summer hours: Mon.-Sat. 8:30am-8pm, Sun. 9:30am-6pm. In Winter, lunch break closing. Ask for the city map and bus map if you're heading for the hostel or campsite.

Post Office: 1, blvd. de la Tour d'Aubergne (tel. 56-12-05). Open Mon.-Fri. 8am-7pm, Sat. 8am-12noon. If you want to receive mail at the post office in the old city (place des Frères Lammennais), it must be addressed "*Poste restante*, St.-Malo-*intra muros*." Hours at this second branch are: Mon.-Fri. 8am-12:30pm, 2-7pm, Sat. 8am-12noon.

Train Station: intersection of ave. Louis-Martin and blvd. de la République (tel. 56-08-18).

Bus Station: Bureau des Voyages, Esplanade St.-Vincent, next to syndicat. **Tourisme Verney** buses (tel. 40-82-67), **Courriers Breton** buses (tel. 56-79-09). City bus tickets are 4.80F apiece, 32F for a *carnet* of 10.

Student Tickets: BIGE/Transalpino tickets at **Agence Boutin** travel bureau, in the building facing the syndicat. Open Mon.-Fri. 9am-12noon, 2-6:30pm. Student tickets must be purchased at least 24 hours in advance (tel. 40-88-59).

Police: place des Frères Lamennais (tel. 56-14-30). Emergency, dial 17.

Hospital: Centre Hospitalier de St.-Malo, 2 Rue Laennec (tel. 56-23-71).

Bicycle and Mobylette Rental: Rouxel, 5 ave. Jean Jaurès (tel. 56-14-90), near train station.

Wind-Surfer Rental: *(Planches à voile)* **Franck Yachting,** 51 Rue de la cité (tel. 56-65-91) and **Technic Plongée,** 68 blvd. de Rochebonne (tel. 56-62-93). As with hanggliding, you haven't lived until . . .

Laundromat: 3 Rue Ernest Renan (near intersection with Blvd. de la République, two blocks from the station) open daily 7am-10pm.

Telephone Code: Ille et Villaine, 99.

Accommodations

Not surprisingly, St.-Malo is stuffed to the gills in summer, particularly in August, so reserve ahead or arrive early. Do not sleep on the beaches; even if the water is 350 yards away when you lie down, it will dash you against the wall within six hours.

Institution de St.-Malo, 2 rue du College, near the Cathédrale St.-Vincent in the old city (tel. 40-85-58) has dorm rooms available. Exact dates vary each year, so call first—approximately July 5-August 5, singles 25F, doubles 44F, breakfast 8F, free showers. Pension available at 70F per day.

Auberge de Jeunesse (IYHF) 37 Ave. du Pére Umbricht. A little too large and very popular. Unfortunately, groups take all the good two- to four-bedded rooms in summer, leaving the crowded, noisy annexes to the backpackers. Close to beach. Has tennis and volleyball facilities. The most attractive detail, however, is that it shares the compound and facilities with the **Foyer des Jeunes Travilleurs,** part of a national system of inexpensive lodgings for workers and *chomeurs* (the unemployed) under the age of 26. The Foyer has a common room with color TV and a wide selection of French magazines, but it is far more interesting just to hang around and talk to the residents, who are surprisingly forthcoming if you speak some French. With a little talking, you should be able to eat breakfast or dinner with the *jeunes travailleurs*. Prices at the hostel are 22F per person, generous breakfast 7F, dinner 20F, bike rental 18F. Reception 9-10am, 5-7pm, 8:15-10pm.

Hôtel Cézembre, 9 rue de la Pié-qui-Boit (tel. 40-94-63). A pleasant small hotel with reasonable prices for St.-Malo. rooms for one or two start at 67F, 75F with two beds, 87F for three people (2 beds), 150F three people and three beds. Breakfast 12F, shower 10F.

Hôtel Le Neptune, 21 rue de l'Industrie (tel. 56-82-15). On a drab side street parallel to the Chaussée du Sillon, close to the old City and one block from beach and promenade. Singles and doubles start at 65F, 25F for an extra bed in the room. Breakfast 11F, no showers.

"Maison Familiale": Madame Le Du, 15 rue de la Malouine (tel. 56-57-82) Offering hospitality more than accommodation, Madame Le Duc is a wonderful *citoyenne* of St.-Malo. Most of her children are grown-up, so she now fills the house with foreign guests. Call and she will probably invite you to dinner (she prefers to invite couples), and then she is equally likely to object to your paying. Do strenuously offer to. She is willing to put people up in a pinch, but it's not entirely convenient (nor is the house entirely clean). Kindness, rather than a thirst for profit motivates Madame Le Du, so try to protect her from her own hospitality. Madame Le Du speaks a little English and is fond of her connection with *Let's Go*.

Camping: The closest and most scenic campground is at the camping de la cité d'Alien near the Promenade de la Corniche in St. Servan. There are four campsites in the vicinity; inquire at the syndicat.

Food

As with accommodations, the cheaper restaurants are usually outside the walls of the old city. An outdoor market takes place on Monday, Thursday and Saturday at Rocabey (next to the post office) and in the old city on Tuesday and Friday.

La Goëllette, 3, rue de la Pié-qui-Boit, located within the walls with a good 41F menu.

Crêperie Chez Chantal, 2, place aux Herbes, near the old city post office. Good place for a snack, with the cheapest crêpes in the old town. *Beurre-sucre* crepe for 3.20F.

L'Hôtel du Sillon Restaurant, one of the first buildings on the left side of Chausée du Sillon. Beautiful dining room overlooking the beach. The 41F *menu* includes *moules marinieres* (marinated mussels), the *poisson du jour*, and dessert or cheese. Great place for a splurge.

Le Vauban, 7, blvd. de la République, near the train station. *Menu* for 29F includes *paté de campagne, limande meunière* (fish), and dessert or cheese.

Sights

The best way to see St.-Malo and enjoy its remarkable setting is to explore the *ramparts*. The fortifications themselves are not architecturally unified, but you'll have the old town at your feet on one side, and wonderful vistas of the sea on the other. Enter by the Porte St.-Vincent onto the lively place Chateaubriand. On your right, built into the ramparts is the **Museum of St.-**

Malo. Each floor presents a specific period of Malouin history with consummate taste. After inspecting the treasure chests, maps, and other pirate paraphernalia, climb to the turret for the highest public vantage point on this part of the emerald coast. Open daily 10:30am-5pm. Guided visits only; 4F, 2F with student ID. Closed Tues. Avoid the private wax-museum across from the Museum St.-Malo.

The Porte Saint-Thomas leads you up to the **Fort National,** a former prison, accessible only at low tide. Further along the ramparts, at the **Tour de Bidouane,** climb down to the beach and along the stone walkway to the islets **Petit Bé** and **Grand Bé,** sites of the unmarked tomb of the Romantic poet Chateaubriand, who requested to be buried there to hear the sound of the wind and the sea. Be sure you know the schedule of tides (*horaire des marées,* available at the syndicat) before you walk out there, otherwise you may have to admire both the view and the damp wind for some six hours before the tide recedes and you can get back.

The old town is largely a reconstruction, but you can see some old houses on rue Chateaubriand (#3 is where the poet was born), rue du Pelicot, and rue Saint-Vincent. The Gothic **Cathédrale de St. Vincent** has also been extensively restored—the twelfth century nave combined with the fiery, modern windows achieve a strange effect.

The **Musée International du Long Cours Cap-Hornier** at the Tour Solidor offers nautical history and has a good view onto the Rance estuary. Guided tours at 10:30 and 11am, 2pm, 2:30pm, 3:30pm, 4pm, 5pm, 5:30pm in the summer (fewer in winter). Admission 4F, students 2F.

Near St. Malo

St.-Malo makes a perfect base to explore the fascinating Emerald Coast. To the east lies **Cancale** (accessible by **Couriers Normands** bus service), which boasts the finest oyster beds in Brittany, and the scenic **Pointe de Grouin.** Further east you will find **Mont St. Michel.** With the dearth of cheap accomodations there, it makes an excellent daytrip from St. Malo. You can catch an early train to Pontorson (change at Dol) and then travel the remaining 9km to the Mont by bus, though the 25F bus fare is outrageous. The whole trip takes approximately two hours.

Dinard, a fifteen minute (18F roundtrip) boat ride from St.-Malo, is the Breton haven (or is it heaven?) for the Great Gatsby set. On its excellent beach, you can watch paddleboats, windsurfers, sailboats, and almost anything else you can think of. Be sure to walk around both the **Pointe du Moulinet** and the **Pointe des Etetés** to see the lovely mansions and more distant points along the Emerald Coast. Restaurants and hotels are expensive in Dinard, so make a daytrip of it.

Finally, several ferries operate between St.-Malo and the Channel Islands, and between St.-Malo and Portsmouth on the English mainland. The **Condor, Jaguar,** and **Emeraude** lines all have several sailings a day to Jersey during the summer for 126F one way, 164-230F roundtrip, with reductions for people 15-23 years old. You can catch Sealink connections there to Sark and Guernsey. Brittany ferries also run between St.-Malo and Portsmouth for 220F, deck class (it's cheaper to go from Calais or from Oostende in Belgium). For information and tickets, consult the Gare Maritime next to the syndicat d'initiative near the entrance to the old city.

Dinan

Dinan nostalgically prides itself on being the best preserved medieval city in Brittany. The *vielle ville* stands perched two hundred feet above the port at the Vallée Rance, which extends to Dinard, St.-Malo and the sea. After exploring the cobblestoned streets and the ornate fifteenth-century houses, hike along the numerous paths which branch out from the port. The small town atmosphere of this part of Brittany will provide a welcome contrast to the artificial touristed air of Dinard and St.-Malo.

Practical Information

Syndicat d'Initiative: 6, rue de l'Horloge (tel. 39-75-40).

Post Office: place Duclos, for information (tel. 39-25-07). Open Mon.-Fri., 8am-7pm, Sat. 8am-noon.

Train Station: place du 11 Novembre (tel. 39-22-39).

Bus Station: place Duclos (tel. 39-21-05).

Port Information: Vedettes Blanches et Vertes, Quai de la Rance (tel. 39-18-44).

Police: (tel. 39-03-02). Emergency: dial 17.

Hospital: Centre Medical, Rue Léonce Petit (tel. 39-04-02).

Telephone Code: 96.

Accommodations

Plentiful campsites and the friendly Youth Hostel compensate for the lack of cheap hotels in Dinan.

Auberge de Jeunesse (IYHF). Moulin de Meen, in the Vallée de la Fountaine des Eaux (tel. 39-10-83). When there are no bus loads of screaming kids, this is a wonderful hostel. Kitchen facilities, common room with fireplace, and an open and relaxed atmosphere. Breton music and culture here during the off-season. 22.50F a night, 7F for breakfast.

Hôtel Au Laurier Rose 6, Rue de la Poissonerie (tel. 39-11-75). Comfortable, dark old rooms right in the center of the old town, in an authentic old half-timbered building. Singles 35F, doubles 50F-65F, 85F for full pension. Breakfast 7.50F. Shower free.

Hôtel du Théâtre, rue Ste. Claire (tel. 39-06-91) has an equally good location in the old town, across from the syndicat. Singles and doubles 37F and 45F, triples 86F. Breakfast 10F. No shower, bath 10F.

Camping: Camping de la Hallerais (tel. 39-15-93) is a large campground 3km northeast of Dinan. From the port, follow the rue du Quai along the Rance and then follow the signs.

The **Crêperie des Artisans,** 6 rue du Petit Fort, offers *menus* at 28F for a four course dinner of *galettes* and crêpes. (Try the Rocquefort with fresh cream.) On the same street at #48, **La Kabylie** serves *couscous* for 32-47F, appetizers a la carte, for 7-10F. For regional specialties, try **Le Dauphin** at 11, rue Haute-Voie, which serves braised duck, grilled salmon, *pintadeau forestiére* (young hare) in their 38-48F menus.

Sights

Wandering down the **rue de l'Apport** and **place des Merciers** with their over-hanging second-floor stories (once meant to shelter cloth-vendors and beggars from bad weather) and soak up the medieval atmosphere of Dinan's streets. Go on a market day (Thurs. or Sat.) when the streets are crammed with lively stalls. On the rue de l'Horloge climb the tower for a splendid view in every direction of the surrounding area. Open daily 10am-noon, 2-6pm; admission 2F. The **syndicat d'initiative** is located in the ornate sixteenth century **Hotel de Keratry** on the same street. Around to the other side is the **Eglise St.-Sauver.** More of interest for its patchwork of architectural styles than anything else, it boasts an attractive Romanesque west portal and Gothic facade.

The chateau, where you can visit the tower, a dungeon and a folklore museum is on the **Promenade de la Duchesse Anne** (open daily except Tues. 9-12noon, 2-6pm (2-7pm in the summer). Nov.-Feb., closed mornings, open 2-5pm. Admission 3F.) The collection includes a variety of traditional regional costumes and local crafts. The **Promenade des Petits Fossées** extends along the foot of the castle and offers the most spectacular view of all.

The highlight of Dinan is really the **rue du Jerzual,** running from the place des Cordeliers to the walls of the old city. Along this precipitous street you will find several interesting handicraft workshops. Note particularly the artist sculpting delicate glass statuettes from molten glass rods. Craftsmen working on leather, wool, and pottery can also be found along the same street.

The boat trip to St.-Malo along the Rance River goes through a deep narrow valley with tiny ports chiseled into its steep, wooded banks. 2½ hours. 50F one way, 70F round trip, 30F and 40F for children to age 12. For information (tel. 39-18-14).

The Northern Coast

The Breton coast stretching from Dinan to Brest features some of the most spectacular scenery in France. The northern coast's three principal geographic divisions—the **Côte Emeraude,** the **Côte de Granite Rose,** and the **Ceinture Dorée**—all offer fascinating diversity, from rugged windswept points of rock to serene coves with sandy beaches. Youth Hostels are conveniently located near the most worthwhile site. They range in quality from the rugged tent-camp near Cap Fréhel to the well-equipped hostel of Paimpol.

Transportation will be your greatest problem along the Northern Coast. Local trains connect Paimpol, Lannion, and Roscoff to the Paris-Brest truck line, but not directly to each other. Hitching or cycling are the best alternatives because the most beautiful areas are also the most inaccessible. The Hostels of St.-Brieuc and Morlaix rent five-speed bicycles for 18F a day or 120F a week. Otherwise ask at any syndicat for information on rentals. For 3F you can buy the *Guide Touristique-Côtes-du-Nord* which has a list of all bike and car rental places in the region, plus a wealth of valuable information on outdoor activities.

The bus service of **C.A.T.** *(Compagnie Armoricaine de Transports)* is fairly good but expensive (Brieuc to Paimpol 29F). It centers in St. Brieuc (6, rue du Combat des Trente, tel. 33-36-60) with lines radiating to St.-Malo, Dinan, Dinard and to Rostrenen and Carhaix in the idyllic **Argoat** country of Brittany's interior. To the west, buses run to Paimpol and to Lannion; change at Lannion for buses to the coastal towns of the Côte de Granite Rose all the way to Morlaix.

Côte d'Emeraude. The Côte d'Emeraude between Dinard and St.-Brieuc is dotted with family-type resorts (Lancieux, St. Jacut are particularly pleasant) resting on sandy dunes at those spots where the craggy outcroppings of rock curve around to form small unprotected bays. **Quatre-Vaux** is full of grassy dunes or try the sands of **Pen-Guen**. **Camping de la Ferme de Pen-Guen** is just across the road overlooking the beach (tel. 41-92-18).

The **Pointe de St.-Cast** is worth a stop, and is only two kilometers outside the town of the same name. Jutting far out into the sea, green fields descend right to the water, and on a good day you can see St.-Malo and the whole craggy coast in between. On the side of the point away from town is **Camping de la Ferme et de la Fontaine**, La Ville Norme (tel. 41-92-67). At the **Office de Tourisme** in **St.-Cast** (tel. 41-81-52) open daily June 1-Sept. 30, ask for information on other campsites—hotels are prohibitively expensive. Also ask about boat trips to Cap Fréhel and Fort la Latte, to the west, just across the bay.

Most spectacular but least accessible for an overnight stay is the popular **Cap Fréhel**, which probably offers little sense of solitude during the summer, because of the number of daily visitors, but it is still beautiful. Fern, heather and tiny yellow and white flowers cover this windswept cape. A pioneer spirit prevails at the **Plévenon Youth Hostel**, 4km from the Cap. Very primitive, the Hostel is nothing more than a tent, a tap, and a toilet (the last a different hole every week). You can buy your food in Plévenon and cook it at the hostel (open July-August, about 13F per person. Call first at the Auberge at St. Brieuc (tel. (96) 61-29-33) to make sure it is open).

Don't bother coming to St.-Brieuc unless you plan to rent a bicycle. **The Youth Hostel** (tel. 61-91-87), 22.50F a night on rue Alphonse-Daudet, borders a pleasant rose garden, has cooking facilities, and a stock of seventy five-speed bicycles (18F per day). They also suggest the best biking routes for you to take. Consult the map near the station for directions to the Hostel. If you are not biking continue to Guimgamp, where you can catch a connecting train to Paimpol.

Paimpol marks the beginning of the Côte de Granite Rose, where there are fewer foreigners, and the locals are less used to tourists. Here the rocky coves are actually warmer than the long exposed beaches around St. Malo.

With its history as launching site for fishing expeditions to Newfoundland and to Iceland, Paimpol still retains the negligent swaggering air of a seafarer's town and remains attractive precisely because tourism is not its main industry. The giant fish market held every Tuesday and the clientele partaking at the numerous portside bars are evidence enough. Try **La Taverne** and **Le Pub**, both on rue des Islandais, off Quai Morand (open after 5pm).

For both bed and board, the **Youth Hostel** situated on the sprawling grounds of the Château Kerraoul, is the best deal. From the station, left on Avenue General de Gaulle, take a right at the first light, then a left at the next light. Keep straight until the Gendarmerie, then keep to your right and continue following the signs to "Kerraoul"—the Hostel is across the crossroads in a large park. 22.50F a night in 6-10 bedded dorm, breakfast 7F, dinner 21F including wine.

Other options in town include the **Hôtel Berthelot** at 1, rue de Port (tel. 20-88-66) which is clean and comfortable and has doubles for 53F, breakfast for 12F, shower for 7F, and the **Hôtel Gouriou** on the route de l'Arcouest (tel. 20-92-30) which is located in a solitary place on top of a hill, on the road between Ploubazlanec and Arcoest, with a friendly proprietor and attractive rooms: single 52F, double 55F, breakfast 12F. Campers should head for **"Le Rohou"** in Arcouest (tel. 20-92-68) and **"Les Mouettes"** (tel. 20-93-48) or at Ploubazlanec **"Les Hortensias"** right off the main road.

For meals in Paimpol, try **Café de la Place**, place du Martray—ham or steak with *frites* for 22F, fish soup for 18F, omelette 22F, with a view of the center of activities here. Or try the crêperie across the way; crêpes 8-20F.

While in the are a don't miss **Ile de Bréhat.** Pack a lunch, and hitch or take a bus from the Gare SNCF to Arcouest. This *pointe* has craggy red and black rocks and a solitary, wide expanse of rocky shoreline. Ferries leave every hour or so (consult schedule at bus station or at **Syndicat d'Initiative** in Paimpol, place de la République, open 9am-noon and 3-7pm during season only); the roundtrip is 15F, or 30F for a circuit of the island by sea. But you really should take time to debark and explore careless Bréhat—this incredibly pastoral, flowered little island is given an unreal air by the silence and surrounding moss-covered rocks at sea (they rise out of the muddy green seabed at low tide). The western and northern sides of the island are almost totally uninhabited and offer more wild dolmen-like rock outcroppings.

To the east of Paimpol, 5km along D786 through beautiful and somewhat wild Breton countryside is the enchanting old town of **Lézardrieux,** on the **abbaye de Beauport**—built at the end of the twelfth century—a good example of Norman style. Open daily in summer 9am-noon, and 3-7pm; entrance 4F.

Rent a bike (in Paimpol; avenue du Géneral Leclerc, 20F a day, 200F deposit) or catch a bus to Tréguier, an old bishopric with a cathedral, and the site on May 19 of a very popular *pardon* in honor of one of Brittany's favorite saints—St. Yves.

From Tréguier to Perros-Guirec along the coast is wild, sparsely inhabited country, but to get there you'll have to cycle or rent wheels. For accommodations you must be prepared to camp out in the open or to knock on doors; Breton farmers in this region are known for allowing people to camp on their grounds. The **pointe du Chateau** offers another jutting-out point—stop at the chapel of Saint-Gonéry in Plougresceant, and the chapel at the Port-Blanc, also the sight of a small, white-pebble beach.

Perros-Guirec. Further west, Perros-Guirec is a popular resort with a harbor and two well-protected, sandy beaches. There is a good view above the town on blvd. Clemenceau. Exiting north from the town by the N786 and turning left onto the rue de la Clarte will take you to the **Chapelle de Notre Dame de la Clarte** (sixteenth-century). Most spectacular is the cliff path called **Sentier des Douaniers,** 2½km long, which will take you to Pors Rolland in **Plouman'ach,** a very picturesque fishing resort. The **parc municipal** beyond Pors Rolland contains a row of untouched rocks, known as **Château Diable,** and the coves of **Pointe du Squewell.** Further on is the Pors Kamor lighthouse. From Perros you can take a three hour boat trip around the bird sanctuary on **Sept Iles,** a group of islands off the coast. Regular service in summer only, in June departures at 2pm, July and August, 9am and 2pm. Cost 45F. (For information, contact the **Perros-Guires Office du Tourisme,** Place Hotel de Ville, tel. 23-21-15 or vedettes blanches, 1 rue Emile le bac, tel. 23-22-47.)

The **Trébeurden IYHF Youth Hostel** (Auberge de Jeunesse du Toeno, Commune de Toeno, tel. 23-52-22) will put you in a better shorefront site than most hotels. The **Ceinture Dorée,** stretching from Trébeurden to Roscoff, is attractive for its milder climate and gentler, rolling landscape. **Morlaix,** dominated by a graceful, awe-inspiring viaduct (built in 1864), today retains row upon row of the corbelled "maisons à lanterne" dating from its heyday as a trading post. With its beautiful eighteenth- and nineteenth-century facades and narrow city canals, Morlaix is worth a short visit. Ask for the walking tour "Le circuit des Venelles" at the Pavillion du Tourisme, place des Otages (tel.62-14-94). The Morlaix **IYHF Youth Hostel,** 3, route de Paris (tel. (98) 88-13-63) is a dismal little place perched at the side of a busy road, but seems to be popular anyway (22.50F a night). From the train station, go straight down rue Giambetta and turn left down the stairs (rue Courte) which will take you into the center of town. Cross Place Emile Souvestre into rue Carnot (straight across) and turn right onto rue d'Aiguillon, cross the canal into the route de Paris. The hostel is up and around the curve, on the right side of the road. About a twenty minute walk.

Rising up out of the artichoke fields are the light-colored stone towers of **St.-Pol-de-Léon**—a charming old Breton town with a cathedral and an abbey. The cathedral is a very successful mélange of Romanesque and flamboyant Gothic. Both structures are imperfect but display distinct regional characteristics. Note especially the wood-carving of the chancels and alterpieces. At St.-Pol-de-Léon, you can stay at the **Hôtel-Restaurant** at 31, rue Cadiou (tel. 69-01-51) with singles for 48F, doubles 55F, 2 beds 48F. Two excellent places to eat are: **Crêperie Ty Korn, rue des** Minimes, on a side street off from the apse of the cathedral—for 8-11F, very crisp crêpes popular with the locals; and **Auberge la Pomme d'Api**, 49, rue Verderel—great seafood *menu* for 35F.

Nearby Roscoff is a bit more of a resort town, but it also provides a pleasant mix of small town and warm beach. Take in Roscoff from St. Pol or Morlaix (Both St. Pol and Roscoff are served by SNCF trains and buses from Marlaix, which are reasonably frequent in the summer.) From Roscoff, take the ferry to the beautiful **Ile de Batz** (ferries hourly in summer, 14F round trip. Call Roscoff's syndicat to be certain of departure times, which vary with local needs and whims). This small island has a quaint town, only a smattering of tourists, and great stretches of desolate coastline ideal for picnics or camping, with only the cows to disturb your bucolic bliss. It is one of the handful of islands immediately off the coast (along with Ouessant, Brehat, and Groix) where the traditional Breton farming and seagoing lives are still harmoniously combined. The island's **Youth Hostel** is presently in an agreeable state of disarray. The old buildings are being rebuilt to make the hostel a year round outfit (presently open April to December only), and in the meantime some of the accommodations are in tents (though kitchens and very pleasant common room facilities with a fireplace are finished in one of the buildings). Toilets and showers were makeshift in 1982 (pit and cold, respectively) but plumbing should be in by 1983. The Finistare departmental direction of the French hostels has great ambitions for the hostel here (permanent sailing school and organized trips): though work is coming slowly it is still a very good-natured place to stay. To reach it, take a right at the cafe near the pier and walk up the hill, following the signs. The stay is 22.50F a night, dinners (a bit meager) at 20F, breakfast 7F, (tel. 61-77-61). You can buy food in town, though prices will be better if you stop on the mainland. Or in July and August, try the **Crêperie Ty Yann,** with a very cheap *menu* of three crêpes, cider and coffee, conveniently located across the road, a stone's throw from the hostel. There are wonderfully secluded beaches near the hostel as well.

Brest is a large modern port with little to see. Its **IYHF Youth Hostel** on rue Gaston Ramon (tel. 45-07-60) has crowded rooms and inadequate showers. However, you will have to stop here if you want to go on to the fantastical **Ile d'Ouessant.** By virtue of its isolation and the rigors of its physical setting, Ouessant developed a Breton subculture found nowhere else (including elaborate ceremonies for men lost at sea and, traditionally, the right of women to ask a man for his hand in marriage). Much of the traditional life is still intact. Sheep and crucifixes dot the isolated landscape of this windswept, green-pastured island. Boats leave from the port de Commerce, 1er épéron in Brest, several times a day. Call the Service Maritime Departémental (tel. 80-24-68) for schedules (72F round trip) or inquire at the Pavillon de Tourisme, place de l'Hôtel de Ville (65F round trip). The boat crossings take 1½ hours.

The Crozon Peninsula

The rugged, cruciform Crozan Peninsula is Brittany at its finest. Dotted with small towns and modest resorts, it offers spectacular coastal scenery, sparkling beaches, and fine food, all at the calm pace of traditional Breton life. You may find the calm punctuated occasionally by anomolous military presence; recently a nuclear submarine base was installed on the Ile Longue (not actually an island and entirely closed off to prying, non-military eyes) at the northern tip of the peninsula across the bay from Brest. In the planning, the base caused almost as much uproar as the nuclear reactor in Plogoff, but in the end, as always, the locals were happy for the jobs it created. Many Bretons are also amused by the strategic setting of the base which, with the bottleneck strait at Brest, promises to keep the submarines in what amounts to a big bathtub. In any case, the base has apparently left this lovely peninsula undisturbed.

The **Pointe de Penhir** is one of the finest capeš in Brittany, with sheer granite cliffs and crashing waves. Climb out onto the rocks for a superb view of the isolated rock masses of the **Tas de Pois**. Amazingly, there is a grassy plain on the leeward side of the point which leads down to a sheltered beach.

Near the point is the lobster port of **Camaret**, with a long pier lined with cafes. The chapel of **Notre Dame de Roc'h-Amadour** sits at the end of the pier; Camaret's pardon is held here on the first Sunday in September. At the end of the pier, you'll find the seventeenth-century Château Vauban, which houses Camaret's **Musée de la Marine.** Just outside of Camaret are the giant Lagatiar **menhirs,** arranged in a Stonehenge-like circle. They are a staggering sight.

Less mystic but equally impressive is the resort of **Morgat**, with a fine beach framed by cliffs and caves, and palm trees, cacti, and lush tropical vegetation growing amid the pine groves.

To Crozon's north, the **Pointe des Espagnols** offers a superb view over Brest and the Plougastel Peninsula. At the **Pointe de Dinan,** you can cross the natural arch and look out at the Atlantic. When cycling around, turn off the main roads periodically to visit villages with poetic Celtic names like Croas-an-Doffen and Pen-ar-Menez.

Practical Information

It takes a bit of effort to reach Crozon or Morgat. Infrequent buses (railpasses valid) run from Châteaulin on the Brest-Quimper railway line; they tend to run in the early morning and late afternoon. The road passes through some fine countryside: to the north, the **Parc Regional de l'Armorique** to the south, several villages with the simple granite churches, houses, and calvaries for which Brittany has become renowned. The wind and hills, however, make this very difficult to cycle.

The best base for exploration of the coastal scenery is the town of **Camaret,** at the end of the SNCF busline. Camaret happily retains much of its small town charm, while combining the facilities of a major lobster-port with those of a *modest station balénaire*. The effect is a pleasant mixture of fishing port with coastal resort.

Syndicat d'Initiative: place Kleher (tel. 27-93-60). Two blocks from the SNCF station where buses stop. Walk to the water and take a left on the Quai Kléber. Open every day in summer, 9am-noon and 1-7pm.

Post Offiice: 2, rue de Verdun (tel. 27-92-51). From the place St. Thomas rue de la Mairie becomes rue de Verdun, 3 blocks.

Bus Station: Rue de la Gare, at quai Kléber.

Currency Exchange: Banque National de Paris, Quai 6. Toudouze (tel. 27-90-47).

Bicycle Rental: Mecamar on the quai near the Tour Vauban (tel. 27-95-29). 20F a day, 10F half day. No deposit required, but ID held instead.

Medical Emergency: (note: there is no hospital in Camaret proper) **Centre Medical,** Hôtel de Ville, Place Champ de Foire, Crozon (tel. 27-05-33).

Police: Gendarmerie, tel. 27-00-22 (Emergency dial 17).

Accommodations and Food

In Camaret there are two reasonably priced hotels. Both are on the Quai Styvel. The **Vauban** (tel. 27-91-36.; open Mar.-Oct.) has rooms for 65-86F and the **Hôtel du Styvel** (tel. 27-92-74; open April-Sept.) has rooms for 72-83F. The **Camping Municipal** (tel. 27-91-31) is relatively close to the center of town, in the Parc des sports. A more luxurious three-star site is available 5km away in Lambezen at the **Camping de Lambezen** (tel. 27-91-41). There are also six campgrounds in the Crozen-Morgat area including two three-star sites. Ask at the Crozon-Margat syndicat.

For restaurants, try **La Crêperie Rocamodour** on the quai Kléber or the **Restaurant à l'abri** on the rue de l'Abri du Marin above the quai Vauban.

If you are just interested in the beach and a small, attractive resort, you might want to stay in Morgat, though you will pay for the pleasant environs. The **Hôtel Les Grottes** (tel. 27-15-84), on the road between Crozon and Morgat, 102, blvd de la France-Libre (tel. 27-15-84, close to the Morgat **Syndicat Les Grotte** is pleasant, but a little expensive (90-120F per person for room, breakfast, and full dinner). For dinner in Morgat, **A la Grange de Toul-Boss,** on the place d'Ys seems to combine an antique shop, farm yard and restaurant. It is also a very reasonably priced crêperie (crêpes 6-10F).

To reach Morgat, take the SNCF bus to Crozan. From the station, take the rue de la Gare to the rue Alsace-Lorraine, and then turn left at the next major street, the blvd. de la France Libre, which becomes blvd. de la Plage. The Morgat syndicat is on the right, just before the beach. Open in the summer 9:30am.-12:30pm., 2-7pm., Sun. 10am.-noon; tel. 27-07-92. At the other times of the year, inquire at the Crozon syndicat, Place de l'Eglise (tel. 27-21-65) which is closed in the summer.

Quimper

Historically the capital of La Cornouaille, the oldest and most traditional region of Brittany, Quimper has managed both to grow and to retain the Breton flavor which you can hear in the accents, see in the homes, and smell in the patisseries. With a profusion of cheap hotels and restaurants, it makes a fine touring center for some of the superb surrounding countryside.

Quimper holds the most important regional folk festival, the **Festival de la Cornouaille,** during the third week in July. The festivities include concerts, ballets, cinema, parties, and plays in the Breton and French languages. All through the year, however, Quimper sports its Breton heritage proudly: many women wear the traditional dress in the marketplace; speaking Breton is a matter of prestige; and bookstores prominently exhibit Celtic books and records. If you know any Irish folk songs, you can make a fortune playing on the sidewalks here.

There are also French language summer courses given at five levels. For information on courses, contact Cours d'Eté de Quimper, Faculté des Lettres de Brest, B.P. 860, 29 279 Brest CEDEX (tel. 03-06-87). After June 30: Secrétariat, Cours d Eté, Residence Universitaire, rue de l'Universite, 29 000 Quimper (tel. 90-61-18).

Practical Information

Frequent trains from Paris make the six hour journey to Quimper.

Office de Tourisme: 3, rue du Roi-Gradlon, next to the cathedral (tel. 95-04-69). Tickets are available here for excursions by boat or by bus. The very helpful staff speaks English. Open weekdays and St. 9am-noon and 2-6pm, Sun. 9:30am-noon. In July and August, 8:30am-8pm continuously.

Post Office: Corner of blvd. de Kerguelen and rue de Juinville. Open Mon.-Fri. 8am-7pm, weekends 8am-noon.

Police: rue Th.-Le Hars (tel. 90-15-41); **Hospital:** Centre Hopitalier Laennec, 14, rue Y. Thepot (tel. 90-30-30).

Bus Station: Buses leave for the surrounding towns from the Gare Routière next to the train station, ave. de la Gare. There is another bus station (Compagnie Armoricaine de Transports, CAT) at 5, blvd. de Kerguelen, with departures for Morlaix, Concarneau, Châteaulin, Brest, St.-Brieuc, Pointe du Raz, and Douarmenez. CAT (tel. 95-02-36). Not all buses leave from the same place. Consult the syndicat for information on departures.

Airport: Air Inter flies to Paris and other cities from Quimper. For information, contact **Agence Bretagne Voyages** 20 rue du Parc (tel. 95-61-24).

Bike Rental: Locavelo 107, ave. de Ty-Bos (tel. 53-30-04). Also rents by the week.

Currency Exchange: Crédit Agricole, place Aléxandre Massey (also known as place de Brest) is open Saturday. Be careful of holidays though since banks will take a long weekend (Fri. noon-Tues. morning). The syndicat does not change money. The **Hôtel Moderne** opposite the train station might, but they have a limited supply of cash.

Accommodations and Food

Reservations for all hotels and campsites are necessary during the Festival de Carnouailles in the second half of July.

Auberge de Jeunesse (IYHF): 6, ave. des Oiseaux, Bois de l'Ancien Seminaire (tel. 55-41-67). A 25-minute walk from the train station. Turn right as you leave the station and follow the road over a bridge which crosses the river at an angle. Walk along the river and following (successively) blvd. de Kerguelen, rue de Parc and quai de l'Odet which (all the same road). Turn right on rue de Pont l'Abbé, and then follow the signs to the hostel. If you're too tired to walk take Bus #1 from the station to the *Lycée Chaptal* stop (in the direction of Penhars). The hostel offers clean but cramped quarters, and the wardens are relatively unfriendly. 22.50F a night, kitchen available.

Hôtel St. Mathieu, 18, rue St. Mathieu (tel. 55-37-20). Near the center of the old quarter, one and a half blocks from the church with the same name. Agreeable rooms, friendly management. Singles 60F. Optional breakfast 11F. Showers free.

Hôtel Brizeux, place St. Mathieu (tel. 55-28-68). Across from the church; quite popular—may be full. Singles 55F, doubles 65F, triples 85F. Shower 5F. Breakfast 12F. For places in July and August reserve in April.

Hôtel de France, on the blvd. Kerguelen (tel. 95-00-29), with rooms from 40-60F and the Hotel de Cornouaille, Rue Aristide Briand (tel. 90-05-05) with rooms from 45F-60F.

Hôtel Celtic: 13, rue de Douarnez (tel. 55-59-35). A block up from the church. Musty, large hotel with a few singles for 55-60F, doubles 60F, triples 65F. Shower 5F. Breakfast 12F.

Sights

The old quarter centers around the Cathédrale St.-Corentin, dedicated to Quimper's patron saint, one of the many Breton saints unrecognized by Rome. St.-Corentin was the spiritual advisor of good King Cradlon, who ruled La Cornouaille from Quimper in the sixth century. The cathedral was constructed over a period of 200 years, from the thirteenth to the fifteenth centuries. A statute of the king stands between the two distinctive spires of Norman inspiration, added in 1856. The cathedral was built in stages, and the fifteenth-century nave is situated several degrees askew of the choir built two centuries earlier. Although church officials claim that the architect did this on purpose—an unlikely occurance—nobody seems to have a good explanation. After studying this unique construction, look at some of the stained glass windows in the nave.

The cathedral garden provides a good vantage point for studying the elegant construction of the Gothic apse. From here, you can climb the old city ramparts for a good view of the cathedral and of the Odet river as it flows from Quimper. Also within the cathedral garden is the entrance to the **Musée Departmentale Breton.** Open daily in summer 10am-noon and 2 6pm, admission 4F, 2F with student ID and free on Sunday and Wednesday. It contains works by Carraci, Boucher, Fragonard, Corot and Boudin. It has a great collection of Flemish still-lifes, and also of paintings inspired by the Breton landscape, and a special room devoted to Quimper's native son, Max Jacob.

Quimper has an attractive old quarter with several restored houses; the **rue Kéréon,** with its sudden perspective of the cathedral, is especially fine. Follow the rue du Salle for a look at authentic Breton furniture and pottery displayed in shop windows, and browse in the bookshops and music stores to get an idea of current Breton culture. For another pleasant walk, follow the flower-lined banks of the Odet river and climb up **Mt. Frugy** (on the south side of the river beyond the bus station) for a superb view of the city.

If you want to see more Quimper pottery after your visit to the museum, there are two *faienceries* in Quimper open to visits: **Les Faienceries de Quimper H.B.Henriot** (visits 5F for adults, Mon-Fri., 9-11:30am, and 2-5:30pm; tel 90) just across from Notre-Dame de Locaris; and **Faienceries Keraluc,** which lies farther from the center of town but offers free tours (Route de Benodet, Mon-Fri 8-12, 2-6; tel 90-25-29).

Near Quimper

The Odet River winds for a delightful twenty kilometers from Quimper down to the Atlantic, through a lovely landscape of cliffs and woods. **Vedettes de l'Odet** will take you down the river and back for 50F (buy tickets at the syndicat), but you might prefer to cycle alongside it yourself. The route down the east bank via the D34 leads to the touristy resort of **Bénodet;** you're better off with the D20 and D144 which snake through tiny villages along the west bank and offer better views of the river. You can also rent a boat yourself from **Ty Lan** in Gouesnac'h (tel. 91-63-22); call in advance, as this is a bit out of town.

Less accessible is the rugged heartland of Brittany, **La Cornouaille,** so-named because its original inhabitants came from Cornwall in England (supposedly from King Arthur's court at Tintagel). Largely because of its isolation, the region has resisted change and retains its maritime and agricultural economy. **SNCF** has frequent buses to the port of Douarnenez, and **CAT** offers daytrips to various places. Biking is an arduous task here; you might prefer hitching and taking the local buses (inquire at the syndicat). In any case, don't expect to get around quickly in this region.

Douarnenez is a particularly active fishing port and fish-packing town. It's not spruced up for tourists, but it does offer a magnificent view of the bay and paradise for lovers of fresh seafood. The fishing boats come in at 11pm and the fish are auctioned off beginning at 6am. The big market takes place Monday and Friday and is quite a sight. The best place to eat in town is **La Cotriade** at 46, rue Anatole France. The food is excellent and the decor and solicitous service will amuse you.

The westernmost point of La Cornouaille and of all France is the **Pointe du Raz,** with truly awe-inspiring cliffs and waves. You might be struck with awe in a totally different way by the nuclear power plant presently under construction here. Anti-nuclear supporters may want to make a pilgrimage to the nearby village of **Plogoff.** This tiny community became celebrated in French anti-nuclear circles by disavowing all government support and declaring its "independence" for nearly three weeks to protest the construction.

The **Penmarch peninsula,** at the southern tip of La Cornouaille, also offers some superb coastal scenery dotted with tiny villages. Here the somewhat flatter terrain makes for easier cycling. C.A.T. runs buses to Audierne, and Pointe du Raz (about 46F one way for a 3hr trip).

Concarneau

Like St.-Malo to the north, Concarneau grew prominent both as a coastal fortress and as a port city, and today has become a heavily touristed summer resort. The **ville close,** or walled city, sits in the middle of the harbor, girdled by granite ramparts and connected to the rest of town by only a drawbridge. Though full of tourist shops and cafes, it still retains an intriguing atmosphere, especially in the evening.

To escape from the crowds or just to take a look around you can climb the castle ramparts for a fine view of the harbor (as usual, the visit to the ramparts is part of a tourist racket—2.30F a visit; closed at 8:30pm) You can avoid paying the admission fee by going to the end of the ville close where there is a part of the wall not under the control of the goungers. The **Musée de la Peche,** in the ville close has a large exhibit on the fishing industry, but you have to be a real fishing fanatic to want to pay the 10F admission.

The city's fish market is right across from the ville close, in front of the large warehouses on the port. Concarneau is France's tuna-fishing port, and between midnight and about 6am the quays come alive as fishermen unload their daily catch, and buyers bid for the fish. Try to catch the spectacle if you're out late or up early.

Concarneau's beaches are somewhat overrated, as the extensive tides deposit heaps of seaweed and muck on the rocks. The best beaches for swimming and picnicking are the **Plage Des Petits Sables Blancs** on the coast road to the west of town. Take the bus from avenue Pierre-Guéguin near the port to either of these beaches, or for Cabellou, the resort town on the other side of town. Concarneau's big local festival is called "Les Filets Bleus" and is held on the third Sunday in August.

Practical Information

Rail service to Concarneau has virtually ground to a halt, but the SNCF provides bus service (railpasses are good) from Rosporden, 13km to the north.

Syndicat d'Initiative; place Jean-Jaurès (tel. 97-01-44) is open daily 9am-noon and 2-6pm and in July and Aug. 9am-8pm. Information on boat trips and bike rentals available.

Bus Station: corner of ave. Pierre-Guéguin and quai Carnot, at parking lot of the port. *Transports Caoudal* (tel. 97-35-31) provides services to Pont-Aven and Quimperlé (7F to Pont-Aven, 3F for baggage).

Post Office: rue des Ecoles.

Bike Rentals: M. Trousset, 119, ave de la Gare (tel. 97-49-73) and farther from town, **Lacabellou,** on the beach at Cabellou (tel 97-41-03)

Sailboat Rentals: Locabato, 17, ave du Dr. Nicolas (tel 97-04-77).

Market: on place Jean-Jaurès, Mon. and Fri.

Telephone Code: 98

Accommodations and Food

Auberge de Jeunesse (IYHF), place de la Croix (tel. 97-03-47) is tucked behind the Marine Laboratory. Superb location by the beach, on a seawall. 22.50F, Breakfast 7F, dinner 20F. Has been very agreeable atmosphere with outstanding meals, but the directorshop is changing, so the character is not predictable for 1983. Still the cheapest place to stay in Corcorneau, though.

Hôtel de la Gare, 56, ave de la Gare, (tel. 94-04-23), unattractive, but as cheap as you'll find in Concarneau. Singles and doubles 50-60F. **Hôtel de Bretagne** across the street is about the same. Rooms 47-66F. Both are closed on Sunday, except in August (Bretagne is open only Easter-October, de la Gare all year.)

Hôtel des Ramparts, ville close (tel 97-10-15) A bit older, but the location makes up for it. In the heart of the most touristed area. Only eleven rooms, and popular, so reserve in advance. Singles and doubles, 55-75F. Breakfast 12F. (they will reserve by phone.)

Camping: Camping du Dorlett (tel. 97-16-44) is near plage des Sables Blancs; **Camping de Kersaux** (tel. 97-37-41), open May 1-Sept. 30, next to plage du Cabellou, about 2km out of town; **Camping rural de Lochrist** (tel. 97-25-95) rents tents, about 4km out of town. There are few other camping grounds in the area. Inquire at the syndicat.

Food is discouragingly expensive in Concarneau—a three-course seafood menu will cost you 40F. A simple, but good quality creperie is located on Avenue de la Gare at the corner of rue Vulcain. In the ville close **La Bagatelle-Breiz ar Moor** has omelettes for 20-25F and large salads for 22-30F, and is open til midnight. For buying your own food, there is a **Codec** on the place de la Maine and an open market in the main square.

Near Concarneau

Heading east toward **Quimperlé,** the countryside becomes colorfully massed with yellow genets. **Pont-Aven,** nestled sleepily in a lovely valley, was Gauguin's last residence before he left France for Tahiti; the **Musée** there houses his works, and those of painters he inspired. More worthwhile is the annual summer exhibition at the **Musée de l'Hotel de Ville** (open 10am-1pm and 2:30-7pm daily, admissions 7F, students 4F) and the **Chapelle de Trémalo** (16th c.) with its impressive crucifix that inspired Gauguin's famous "Yellow Christ." Seven kilometers away is a beautiful beach at **Raguenes.** You can camp right there, or closer to Pont-Aven, at the luxurious "Roz-Pin" (tel. 06-03-13), open May 1-Sept. 30. In Pont-Aven, a good place to eat is **La Bonne Auberge** at #40 on the street leading to the N873 out of town. It has a filling, home-style menu for 38F.

Quimperlé is an attractive hillside town which deserves a stop to see the **Église St.-Croix,** the finest example of Romanesque art in Brittany. Its floor plan is copied from the Holy Sepulchre at Jerusalem and is in the form of (square) Greek cross rather than the traditional rectangular Latin cross. The apse and vaults are exceptional. The **Hotel d'Europe** in Quimperlé is not far from the train station on a large square (tel. 96-00-02) and has comfortable rooms for 50F.

Outside Quimperlé, the forest of **Carnoet** protects the ruins of a Cistercian abbey from too many prying eyes. **Lorient,** on the coast to the south, was founded in the eighteenth century as the main post of the powerful French East India Company and remains a major port today, depending on fish rather than the spices and tea of yore. The city was a submarine shelter during World War II and was utterly destroyed. It now shows little trace of its colorful history. There is a superb new **IYHF Youth Hostel** located by the ocean, about 3km from the train station, at 41, rue Schoelcher (tel. (97) 37-11-65); take bus C. Lorient is also the base for exploration of the **Ile de Groix,** another of the small, spectacular Breton coastal islands. There is a youth hostel here open June through October; call the Lorient hostel for information. For boats to the island, inquire at the syndicat, Place Jules Ferry (tel. (97) 21-07-84)

Quiberon and Belle-Ile

The seaside resort of Quiberon is located at the tip of the Quiberon peninsula, which is joined to the mainland by a thin isthmus. A very popular holiday spot, the town is directly accessible by train from Paris during the summer only, with connections at Auray on the Paris-Quimper line. While most travelers come to Quiberon for a seaside vacation, many find only other vacationers. Come before July before the crowds pour in—you can cycle, hitch, or take a bus from the Auray train station.

Quiberon's major attractions are the **Plage de Port-Maria,** the rugged **Cote Sauvage** on the western side of the peninsula, and the spectacular **Belle-Ile,** which is easily accessible by ferry. Cycling provides an easy and popular means of getting around the area. In the summer, Quiberon becomes one of France's busiest harbors for sailing and pleasure boating. Obscured by all this hoopla, however, are the town's huge sardine fishing and canning industries; walk by the canneries for a very different look at life on Brittany's south coast.

Practical Information

Syndicat d'Initiative: 7, rue de Verdun (tel. 50-07-84). In July and August open Mon.-Sat. 9am-7pm, Sun. 10am-noon, 5-7pm. Grab a copy of their hefty, free tourist brochure—it's the only free thing you'll get in town.

Post Office: place de la Duchess-Anne. Open Mon.-Fri. 9am-noon and 2-5pm; 9am-7pm during the summer. Telephones outside P.T.T.

Police: ave. Général-de-Gaulle (tel. 50-07-39); Hospital at Auray-Hopital General le Pratel (tel. 24-15-51).

Bike Rentals: Cycl'omar, 17, place moche (tel. 50-26-00) near the Grand Plage. 27-35F depending upon the model. Bikes also available at the Youth Hostel for 18F per day.

Boat Rentals: Loc'haliguan, 16, rue des Courlis (tel. 50-25-03)

Accommodations and Food

As in all popular *stations balnéaires,* food and lodging are very expensive. Camping here makes especially good since some hotels require pension.

Auberge de Jeunesse (IYHF), 45, rue du Roch-Priol (tel. 50-15-54), 1.5km walk from the station (follow signs as you walk out of the station toward your left). A small, pleasant Hostel which is terribly overcrowded in the summer (though you should always be able to find a place in the tents or campground behind the hostel). Picnic tables and fireplace and a communal feeling. 22.50F per night. No breakfast. Showers available. Reservations available in late July and August.

Hôtel de l'Océan, 7, Quai de l'Océan (tel. 50-07-58) on the port. As the rule in Quiberan, a bit high. Four rooms for 58F, several others for 62F (1 or 2 people). Shower 7F, breakfast 10F. Full pension required in July and August. Pleasant proprietor. (Open Easter through October only).

Hôtel le Corsaire, rue de Port-Maria (tel. 50-15-05), right by the water. Behind the gaudy front, clean accommodations. A single for 50F, some doubles for 64F-75F, Breakfast 12F, full pension required in July and August. One stroke of generosity: a free shower in Quibéran.

Le Ker-Mor-Braz, 1 rue du Port Maria, facing port right in center (tel. 50-17-68). Nice family run place. Rooms 75-100F and in season demi-pension required (breakfast and either lunch or dinner). 95F per person per day. Shower 5F.

Au Bon Acceuil, quai de l'Océan (tel. 50-07-92). Rooms 65-70F, 90-100F with pension required in season. Lo, another free shower.

Camping: Most of the campsites are located on the east side of the peninsula where the beaches are broader and more spacious than the one in Quiberon proper. There are nine campgrounds in the area, but most are filled in summer. Try Camping du Goviro, blvd. du Goviro (tel. 50-13-54). Open Easter-Sept. 30.

Even the crêperies are overpriced here, so try to cook for yourself. In the morning, fishermen bring their catches to rue de Verdun and sell them right from the basket, or go to the quai de l'Ocean at any time of the day and see which of the canneries are open—many of the shops sell fish on a retail basis.

If you'd rather have your seafood cooked for you, the **Brasserie Chez Job** at the corner of quai de Belle-Ille and rue du Port-Maria offers simple dishes from 15-25F; the **Restaurant La Licorne** on the quai usually offers seafood as their *plat du jour* (15-34F).

Sights

The Côte Sauvage runs for 6km along the west side of the Quiberon Peninsula. Barren heaths with their isolated *menhirs* evoke a Celtic atmosphere, and the view over ragged cliffs and points is superb. Those pleasant little coves may lure you to swimming, but the coast is well-named for its savage tides and the signs marked *baignades interdites* (bathing forbidden) are there for a purpose: people have drowned in these treacherous waters.

There are frequent boat departures for **Belle-Ile** from Port-Maria in Quiberon. The trip takes less than a half-hour and costs 20F each way (no reductions), but the journey is well worth the expense. Its cliffs are magnificently high and the rocks off-shore have taken the most fantastic shapes. The green, yellow and purple of thick heather covers the most wild spots, and the fields of grass seem to converge simultaneously with the horizon and the sea. The best way to see the island is by bicycle. You can rent a bike from **Louis Banet,** (tel. 31-84-74).

One excellent route follows the D30 road to the spectacular **Grotte de L'Apothicaire** on the Côte Sauvage. Nestled in the rocks off the northwest corner of the island, the grotto got its name from the rows of cormorants' nests that used to be perched on the rocks in a line like a row of apothecary's brown bottles. Nearby, a craggy silver and pink point of mica and quartz offers a view of the various rocks and other points of the Côte Sauvage.

Other places of note on the island are the little fishing port of **Sauzon**, the **Pointe des Poulains** (site of the remains of Sarah Bernhardt's Chateau), the rough **Aiguilles de Port-Coton**, and the nearby **Plage de Port-Donnant** (off the D25), where waves crash onto the sandy beach between high, natural stone walls. (Note: The strength of the current here makes swimming extremely dangerous.) The island's main town, **Le Palais,** has a walled citadel which contains an interesting museum that is well-designed, but quite expensive (admission 10F, 5F with student ID). Further in toward the mainland, the village of **La-Trinite-sur-Mer** boasts one of the largest pleasure ports in France and a wonderful view across the Bay of Quiberon.

Near Quiberon

Northeast of the Quiberon peninsula lies some of the most superb country-side in Britanny, with great pine forests and open heaths. This is also one of the oldest settled parts of Brittany, and the *menhirs* and *dolmens* scattered throughout the area served as reminders of the ancient Breton ways.

Just a few kilometers east of **Plouharnel** (on the Aurey-Quiberon railway line) stand the great **Alignements du Menec** near **Carnac.** Here over a thousand *menhirs,* some over ten feet high, stretch for nearly a mile toward the horizon. Although it is unclear whether the *alignements* served as a religious sanctuary or as an astronomical guide, they remain a source of amazement over ten thousand years after their placement. Also at Carnac is the **St. Michel Tumulus,** a great burial chamber within an earthen mound. Although most of the decorations have been removed, you can tour the internal passageways with a flashlight. For more information on the various druidic sites, contact the **Syndicat** at Carnac Plage, 74 Avenue des Druides.

To visit the major sites at Carnac, you can ride a bicycle from either Auray or Quiberon (there is no train service to Carnac. There are also buses from both towns, though all of the three companies that serve the line charge exorbitantly for the 20 minute ride—11F each way. (The bus stop at Carnac Plage is conveniently located next door to the syndicat.) If you don't have a bicycle, you might want to rent one at Carnac plage. Agence ABC at 62 Avenue des Druides is a block away from the Syndicat (tel. 52-93-73). Their prices are reasonable, if you are fast on pedals; 9F for an hour on a one-speed, 11F on a 5-speed, 19F and 25F for a half-day, 27F and 35F for a full day.

If you are very serious about your pre-historic Celts, you can stay in any one of a dozen campgrounds around Carnac, including three on the *route des alignements* alone, a stone's throw away from the stones (inquire at the Syndicat for a list). Hotels in Carnac are outrageous. If you want to spend some time in the area exploring the sites in a little more comfort, many local families rent rooms. Inquire at the syndicat, but they may not be of much help, since this is an operation which cuts into the business of their sponsors among the hotels. You will probably have to wander around town a little, but the signs *chambres à louer* are everywhere. (Very near the alignements at the far end of the *route des alignements*—**M. and Mme. Le Leuch,** Kerlescan, Carnac (tel. 55-77-40) rent very attractive rooms for two people at about 50-60F. Showers included.

Because of the expense of hotels around Carnac-Plage (a town with aspirations to become a major resort, you may want to choose another base altogether for exploring the hundreds of megaliths around the area. A possible choice is **Auray** with several inexpensive hotels. The town has a picturesque medieval bridge spanning the Auray River and an old quarter that makes for a pleasant stroll. A few kilometers to the north is the village of **St.-Anne-d'Auray,** which holds one of the finest *pardons* in Brittany during the week in July. The **syndicat d'initiative** in Auray, at place de la République (tel. 24-09-75) will be glad to help with accommodations.

The **Auray River** meanders south from the town through gentle wooded terrain dotted by chateaux with superb vistas over the water. The river passes by several oyster-fishing villages and empties into the lovely Gulf of Morbihan, which is best toured from Vannes.

Vannes and the Gulf of Morbihan

Vannes was the seat of the Breton kings until they capitulated to the French in the sixteenth century, and it has traditionally been the center of the Morhan region, sometimes also known as the Vannetois. Although slummy on the outskirts, Vannes retains a charming old quarter within its old city walls, a fine cathedral, and many inexpensive hotels, making it a fine base for touring the Gulf of Morbihan.

Practical Information

Syndicat d'Initiative, 29, rue Thiers (tel. 47-24-34). Walk down the ave. Victor-Hugo from the train station. Open daily 9:15am-6pm (later in July and August). Information on the Morbihan region. In July and August, walking tours of Vannes start here daily at 10:30am and 3pm (1½ hours; 6F, 3F for those under 25).

Post Office: place de la Republique.

Bus Station: Compagnie des Transports Morbihanais (CTM), place de la Gare (tel. 47-21-64), has regular service to Sarneau, St. Gildas-de-Rhuys and Port-Navalo on the Presqu-ile de Rhuys, opposite Vannes, across the gulf. **Transports et Tourisme de l'Ouest (DROUIN),** rue du 116ᵉ R.I. (tel. 47-29-64), has service to Larmor-Baden.

Port Information: Vedettes Vertes (tel. 47-10-78) or (63-79-99).

Women's Center: Centre d'Information sur les droits des femmes, 12, rue Marechal Le Clerc (tel. 42-59-61). Open 3 hours a day, varies so call first.

Police: (tel. 47-19-20); **Hospital: Centre Hospitalier,** 1, place Docteur Grosse (tel. 54-22-42).

Telephone Code: (97).

Accommodations and Food

Hôtel le Relais Nantais, 38, rue Auguste-Briand (tel. 47-15-87). On a quiet street near the place Bir-Hakeim, which also has several inexpensive hotels and restaurants. From the station, follow the rue Clisson and take a left on the blvd. de la Paix until rue August-Briand. Clean accommodations. Rooms 45-70F, doubles 50-70F. Breakfast 10F, showers 8F. Very friendly proprietors.

Hôtel Le Duc, 4 place Bir-Hakeim (tel. 47-27-58). Fairly pleasant as well. Singles and doubles start at 45-80F. Stingy breakfast for 10F.

Hôtel Marée Bleue, 8, place Bir-Hakeim (tel. 47-24-29). A bit more expensive. Rooms from 64-75F and their restaurant offers a 3-course menu for 42F.

Hôtel de Verdun, 10, avenue de Verdun (tel. 47-21-23). 58-58F for one bed. Large spacious and modernized. Probably heading for a second star (and higher prices). Shower 10F. Breakfast 10F. Extra bed in room 35F.

Camping: Camping municipal de Conleau (tel. 63-13-88), 3km from town on a wooded site near beach. From Place Gambetta or rue Thiers follow rue du Port which borders the pleasure port. 6.50F per person.

There are several good grocery stores along the rue de la Fontaine, and the pastry sold at **Le Croissant d'Or,** place Henry IV, is warm from the oven and really exceptional. For light-eaters, **La Coupe** on rue Alexandre Le Pontois, opposite the ramparts, has 4 crêpe *menu* for 22F, salads 15-18F, omelettes 12-15F; a bargain. Similarly, **La Cave St.-Guenael** at the foot of the cathedral provides quick service and a three-crêpe *menu* for 29F. For more substantial fare, the Restaurant La Banjamine on rue des Halles has regional specialties, with *menus* at 40F and 50F.

Sights

Only one wall of the great **château** remains, but it makes an imposing sight when viewed from the nearby park. You can climb the fifteenth-century ramparts for a good view into the **old quarter** with its restored houses and narrow streets. The quarter winds around the **Cathédrale St.-Pierre,** providing some superb views of the Gothic buttresses and unmatched towers. From the cathedral, walk to the **Place des Lices** to see some finely detailed woodwork on houses of the fifteenth-and sixteenth-centuries. The **Musée Archéologique** there has a collection of artifacts from the megaliths at Carnac and other sites nearby (entrance 8F, students 4F, hours 9:30am-12noon, 2-6pm). The city of Vannes is also in the process of opening a new **Musee des Beaux Arts** around the corner on the rue des Halles in a scrupulously restored sixteenth century building open 10am-12:30pm, 3-6pm, entry 5F, students 2.50F. The collection should be fully installed by 1983.

The **Vedettes Vertes** boat service (tickets and information right on the quai: tel. 47-10-78) will take you around the gulf of Morbihan for 45-56F—the higher fares include trips up the Auray river to Le Bono and Auray. Your ticket allows you to get off at any stop and pick up a later boat. The largest island in the gulf, Ile-aux-Moines, is only 6km long and offers some superb pine groves right next to pleasant beaches. Be sure you make it to the other end of the island, where there are dolmens, beautiful heather moors, and deserted little roads. Bike rentals on the quai will cost you 20F (per half-day), but is well worth it. Breton life has changed little here; there are few cars, and fishing still provides the main source of income. The island's tiny town contains some very typical Morbihan thatched-roof cottages and the ever-present simple granite church. In the summer, the island becomes a family resort, but this quiet invasion does little to disturb the restful atmosphere.

The **Vedettes Vertes** by-pass the **Tumulus of Gavrinis,** an ancient burial mound 100 meters around, made of stone and covered with earthworks. An archaeological dig continues to explore the mounds and its artifacts estimated to be 7000 years old. To reach the tumulus, take a bus from Vannes to Larmor-Baden, and then take the boat to Gavrinis. (March 15-Sept. 15 only; 15 minute ride costs 6F.)

A stop at Port-Navalo will put you on the less-touristed **Presqu'ile de Rhuys.** There is a fine campground, practically at the tip of the peninsula. Across from the town of Port-Navalo, the village of **Locmariaquer** remains one of the prettiest spots in Brittany. Just beyond are the **Gran Menhir** and **Merchant's Table,** the broken remains of a very large *menhir* and a ritual tomb with rare remains of drawings. The Merchant's Table is composed of three huge "tables" suspended on points to form the galleries. Both the *Menhir* and the Table rank among Brittany's most important archaeological sites.

The less massive **Domen des Pierres-Plats,** a kilometer out of town in the opposite direction, is not half as spectacular as the beach here—good swimming and, on a good day, a wide view of the coast toward Quiberon and of Belle-Ile in the distance. You may want to spend the night at one of the several campsights on this breezy, mild land's end.

The formation of the Gulf makes for challenging and varied tides and for some of the strongest currents anywhere. These waters are treacherous for small sailboats, but if you are experienced, the waters of the eastern part of the gulf may be quite manageable. Inquire at the syndicate about sailing schools which can give you information and guidance. You can rent boats at **Vannes Nautic,** Pointe des Emigrés (63-20-17) at the Port of Vannes.

Nantes

Nantes is a large, engaging, and lively city with some identity problems. Superficially, it is perhaps the most Parisian city outside of Paris—wide boulevards separate warren-like *quartiers,* immaculate gardens, polished cafes, even an administrative division by "arrondissements." On the other hand, Nantes would like to be the cultural center of Brittany. But its economic role as a major port on the Loire estuary gives it an air far removed from the cottages of Marbihan. He the Breton culture seems something of a graft. The city's long history of wealthy shipping merchants ties it more closely to the gentle region of the **Loire-Atlantique** to the north and to the **Vendée**—scene of bloody fighting in 1975—to the south. Despite these differences, Nantes actively pursues Breton regionalism with several museum exhibits and a two-week festival in June called the **Quinzaine Celtique,** which attracts Celtic visitors of every nationality.

Until the fifteenth century, Nantes was very much a part of Brittany, as the great Ducs de Montfort, François I and II, ruled the duchy from its **Chateau.** But it was also in this city that Brittany was finally ceded to the French crown in 1532, ending its independence forever. In 1958, King Henry IV of France came here to sign the far-sighted **Edict of Nantes,** granting religious freedom and full political rights to the French Protestants, or Huguenots—a declaration that was later revoked amid great bloodshed. The following centuries were prosperous ones, and many of the city's elegant buildings date back to the eighteenth-century period of wealth and expansion.

Today, Nantes is a huge port and industrial center, as well as an important university town. Nearly all trains to Brittany from the south and east pass through Nantes, and there are frequent connections to Tours, Paris and Lyon.

Practical Information

Nantes spreads for miles on both sides of the Loire River centered around a forty-story skyscraper amusingly named the Tour Bretagne. The city's major axes are the **Cours John Kennedy,** which runs west from the train station, and the **Cours des 50 Otages,** which runs north to the tower.

Syndicat D'Initiative: Place du Change (tel. 47-04-51). Open Mon.-Sat. 9:30am-12:30pm and 1:30-7pm. They also distribute maps of the city bus system. The syndicat no longer handles tickets for the Quinzaine Cetique, but you can find them at the **Centre Culturel Breton,** 3, Rue Harrouys (tel. 47-17-86).

CROUS Travel: 14 Rue Santeuil (tel. 71-92-02). Information on student travel opportunities; also a BIGE/Transalpino ticket agency (discount rail fares for people under 26).

Main Post Office: place de Bretagne. Open weekdays 8am-7pm and Sat. 8am-noon.

Currency Exchange: Crédit Agricole, place du Commerce (tel. 71-54-85), is open Saturdays. Take escalators up from the street level to the bank entrance.

Train Station: Gare d'Orleans, 22, blvd. Stalingrad (tel. 50-50-50).

Bus Station: Champs de Mars (tel. 47-48-28). Most city buses stop at either cours Franklin Roosevelt or place de l'Ecluse to the north.

Police: (tel. 74-21-21); **Medical Emergency at Night:** (tel. 74-12-34).

Laundromat: 56, rue de Maréchal Joffre, 2 blocks from the Musee des Beaux-Arts. About 15F for wash and dry.

Women's Center: Centre d'information féminin et familial, 4, rue d'Argentre (tel. 48-13-83). Hours vary so call ahead.

Information for the Handicapped: Association des Paralysés de France, 11, rue du Maréchal Le Clerc. They will provide information and a guidebook on request.

Telephone Code: (40).

Accommodations

There are several inexpensive hotels in the student section of town west of the place Royale and on the rue du Maréchal Joffre near the Musée des Beaux-Arts.

Centre Jean Macé, 90, rue du Prefet Bonnefoy (tel. 74-55-74). Dormitory accommodations in single rooms, 30F per night, showers available. Breakfast 7F, dinner about 20F. Well located near sights; from the train station, turn right off the Cours John Kennedy onto rue Henri IV which becomes Rue Sully. The Centre is at the corner of Rue Sully and Rue du Prefet Bonnefoy on your right.

CROUS Service de Logement, 2, blvd. Guy Mollet (tel. 74-71-90). Open Mon.-Fri. 9am-5pm. Call first as they are a ways out of town. They are surprisingly unhelpful as CROUS people go, so you might try the résidences directly: **Residence Casterneau,** rue A.-Bauge (tel. 52-12-24), or **Residence Chanzy,** rue Chanzy (tel. 29-44-33). Both are on the city's outskirts, so ask for bus instructions.

Hôtel St. Daniel, 4, rue de Bouffey (tel. 47-41-25). Good location in the new pedestrian section. Friendly proprietor. Eight doubles for 50F, seven for 65F, shower 5F, breakfast 10F. Try to get a room looking over the pretty courtyard. (closed Sun. during the day noon-8pm).

Hôtel Strasbourg, 16 Rue de Strasbourg (tel. 47-54-47). A few blocks from the station on a busy street. Looks plain but the rooms are nice. Singles 43F, doubles 55-70F, Shower 5F, Breakfast 10F. The proprietress is really friendly, and she enjoys a chat.

Hôtel Armoric, 10 rue du Marais (tel. 47-49-08). Three blocks north of the syndicat. Several rooms for 39-48F without shower, 56F with. Friendly service. Next door at #12, try **Hôtel d'Orleans** (tel. 47-69-32) which has nicer rooms than next door, but the owners are extremely proper. Single room 40F; others 56F. Showers 11F. Breakfast 12F. Closed July 15-31.

Camping: Nantes' municipal campground is a four-star site with all the necessary features, 3km north of the city center on the D39 by the hippodrome (tel. 74-47-94).

Food

The locals are particularly proud of their two regional white wines, *Muscadet* and *Gros Plant*.

Self Croc-Pouce, 17, rue Pare. Undistinguished menu but good filling lunch for 30F.

Crêperie des Echevins, 1, rue des Echevins just off place du Bouffay (tel. 47-15-71). Much in vogue with the students of Nantes. Come early for a seat (doors open at 7pm). Plat du jour at 30F, but everyone comes for the house specialty, a super and filling crêpe called *pavê nantais*, 21-25F depending on filling. Vegetarian versions available. (closed Sun.)

La Brocherie, 13, rue Beauregard. Their specialty is brochettes; 35F *menu* includes wine but not dessert, and the desserts are too good to be missed.

La Poule au Pot, 8, rue J.-J. Rousseau, *menus* for 25 and 37F. Not far from place Graslin (closed Sat. eve. and Sun.).

Restaurant Le Doge, 2, rue du Bouffay. Good 40F *menu*. Closed Sat. eve.

Nantes has a number of districts crowded with restaurants of various descriptions and prices. Try the area roughly defined by Rue de la Baderie, Rue de la Juinerie and Rue Bouffay. For crêpes, especially look to the area around Rue Crebillon and Rue Contrescarpe.

Sights

Nantes' fifteenth-century **Chateau** presents an impressive front with its round towers and surrounding moat. Built by Francois II, it was the birthplace of Anne, Duchess of Brittany and queen to two successive kings of France. The Chateau now houses three museums, the best of which is the **Musée des Arts populaires et regionaux** which will give you an idea of the riches of Breton traditional culture. This may be the closest you can get to the true Breton traditions today, so those interested in the culture should look closely at the colorful regional costumes, the multitude of lace caps, and the fine carved oak furniture, especially the *lits clos*. Note how widely the lifestyles vary from region to region, even within Brittany.

The **Musée Tour de Fer-à-cheval** houses temporary exhibits, usually quite good, in a tower that has been splendidly converted to its new use. These exhibits are also often devoted to Breton subjects. The **Musée des Salorges** is a nautical museum which may be of interest only to seagoing fanatics. (The Chateau and museums are open daily 10am-6pm; closed Tues., except during the summer. Entry to the courtyard is free, but a ticket for the three museums costs 5F, 2.50F for students.)

Near the Chateau stands the **Cathédrale St.-Pierre,** which was badly damaged inside by a fire in 1972. Everything behind the transepts has been walled off for restoration. The exquisite exterior and main portal are marred only somewhat by two rather ungainly, modern towers. Inside, the white Vendée stone and the missing stained glass windows (destroyed in the fire) give the nave an astonishing aura of Gothic purity. The ornate tomb of Francois II rests in the south transept beneath a fine modern window.

Two blocks from the cathedral on the rue Clemenceau is Nantes' **Musée des Beaux-Arts.** Restoration of the museum building began in 1980 and is still underway, so only a fraction of the works are presently on display. The collection, which should be fully open in 1983, includes some fine paintings by de la Tour, Courbet, and Rubens. (Open daily except Tues. 9:15am-noon and 2-5pm, Sun. 11am-5pm; admission 5F, 2F for students.)

Other museums in Nantes include the **Musée Thomas Dobrée** (a private collection of art now owned by the state, with a library of rare books and manuscripts); the **Musée Archéologicque;** the **Muséum d'Histoire Naturelle,** and for the fanatic or a lark, the **Musée Jule Verne** (you guessed it, a *Nantias*). Entry to all is 5F, students 2.50F (for hours and addresses, see the booklet *Musées de la Loire Atlantique* at the syndicat.)

West of the Chateau, much of eighteenth-century Nantes retains its classical grandeur. The **Ile Feydeau,** between the allée Turenne and the allé Tuouin, was at one time an island where the wealthy sea merchants built their houses. Walk down the **rue Kervega** for the best view. Even more stately is the eighteenth-century **place Royale** and the **rue Crébillon** leading to the **place Graslin.** Off this street is the **Passage Pomimaraye,** a nineteenth-century gallery in iron and glass, executed with typical Victorian-era exuberance.

A major architectural sight overlooked, curiously, by all offices except the bus company, is Le Corbusier's **Cité Radieuse,** a place of pilgrimmage for Corbu-buffs embodying a unified conception of suburban life. Take bus 31 from the Commerce stop on the cours Franklin Roosevelt.

The students at **Nantes University** do their share for the Breton regionalist movement, but they seem largely intent on continuing the city's strong cosmopolitan tradition. There are some fine bookstores near the place St.-Pierre. University residences and centers are scattered piecemeal through the city, but the area north of the rue Crébillon seems to be most popular in the evening.

Atlantic Coast

Just one hundred kilometers south of the Loire, Aquitaine is a world apart from the staid chateaux country. The long, sandy coastline of the Vendee and Charente-Maritime has long been the home of prosperous port towns and is now a tourist area. Inland, the **Poitou** and the **Charente** present a colorful panorama of medieval hilltop towns, red-tiled roofs, and Romanesque churches. Blessed with a milder climate than any other part of France except the Mediterranean coast, this region presents an intriguing blend of north and south.

The rich archeological and architectural remains in the Aquitaine testify to a rich history. **Saintes** has a superb collection of Roman works as well as a ruined amphitheater, as this area was a major Roman center under the Empire. It was during the eleventh and twelfth centuries, however, that the region attained its greatest prosperity, and it is now a veritable treasure of Romanesque art.

France gained the independent duchy of Aquitaine when King Louis IX married the powerful heiress Eleanor, only to lose it a scant ten years later when she divorced him and wed the young Henry Plantagenet, the new King of England. Aquitaine, surely one of the finest and most contested dowries in history (including its great wine-producing capital Bordeaux) did not revert to the French until centuries later. By then, the English preference for claret (their name for red Bordeaux wine) was well established. In the eighteenth century, lucrative trade with the Canadian colonies brought unparalleled wealth to **La Rochelle** and other port cities. The ties with French Canada still remain: this area has been active in supporting Quebecois separation. Though the port industry remains important, tourism is now a major concern for the coastal towns, and the beaches and campgrounds are packed all summer long.

Transportation along the Atlantic Coast is quite good, with major train lines running to La Rochelle, Saintes, Poitiers, and Angoulême. Hitching and cycling are both good ways of seeing the countryside, and local tourist offices can advise you on rural accommodations. For a vacation of a different sort, inquire about traveling by boat down one of the region's main rivers, the Clain and the Charente.

An intriguing array of food awaits the visitor. Shellfish comes fresh from the coast, while *farci* (a stuffed meat dish), *canard* (duck), and *chabichou* (a rich goat cheese) are available inland. The most famous drink here is not wine but brandy from **Cognac.** You should also try *pineau*, a mixture of cognac and grape juice.

Poitiers

Poitiers' superb natural setting on a plateau encircled by the River Clain has made it a regional center for centuries. Recent archeological excavations have unearthed massive Bronze Age and Roman relics, establishing that the city was a major outpost of the Roman Empire. It was here, too, that Charles Martel turned back the Moorish invasions in 732, firmly establishing the borders of Carolingian territory.

171

From the tenth to the fifteenth century, Poitiers was ruled by the rich and powerful Counts of Poitou and Dukes of Aquitaine, while developing into a center of ecclesiastical learning. Many fine churches from this period still stand, and Poitiers is a tour-de-force of Romanesque art and architecture. In a sense, Poitiers seems unaffected by change, despite the more recent invasion of tourists.

Practical Information

Poitiers lies on a well-traveled rail line three hours from Paris, and trains run to Bordeaux and La Rochelle in under two hours. The train station lies at the bottom of the small pear-shaped plateau of Poitiers, where you will find most of the town's churches and amenities for the visitor. The walk up to the center of town is rather steep—start by following the stairs along the walls on blvd. Solferino. Otherwise, you can take the bus (5F roundtrip).

Syndicat d'Initiative, Hôtel de Ville (tel. 41-21-24). Open Mon.-Sat. 9am-noon and 2-7pm. Guided tours of the city at 10am, 5pm and 9pm (for groups only) during the summer. There is also a small but extremely helpful office in front of the train station. The office will find you a hotel room for a 5F fee.

Office Départemental du Tourisme: 11, rue Victor Hugo (tel. 41-58-22). Close to place dué Maréchal Leclerc. Very helpful in giving information on the town and the surrounding regions. Open. Mon.-Sat. 9am-noon; closed Sun.

Centres de Documentation et d'Animation de la Caisse Nationale des Monuments Historiques: 102, Grand Rue (tel. 41-20-93). Information on historic sites and Romanesque churches and monuments.

Centres Information Jeunesse: 64, rue Gambetta (tel. 88-64-37). Near the Hotel de Ville on the walking street. A gold mine of clues on places to stay, cultural activities, even a ride board for hitching. Open Mon.-Fri. 10am-7pm; Sat. till 6pm.

Post Office (PTT): rue des Ecossais (central bureau) and rue de la Marne. Telephones upstairs. Open Mon.-Fri. 8am-7pm; Sat. 8am-noon. Also at 5, rue Jacques de Grailly.

Train Station: At the base of the town on blvd. de Grand Cerf (tel. 58-22-88). Discount tickets for those under 26 available through OTU, 76, rue des Carmelites (tel. 41-71-47).

Bus Station: place Thezard, by the Parc de Blossac (tel. 41-14-20).

Police: 45, rue de la Marne (tel. 88-94-21), or Emergency (tel. 17).

Hospital: 15, rue de l'Hotel Dieu (tel. 88-20-10), or Emergency (tel. 18).

Medical Emergency: (tel. 88-33-34).

Currency Exchange: Credit Agricole, 18, rue Salvador Allende. Open until 6pm on Sat. and 7pm on Mon. Charges 10F commission to change cash, but provides a good exchange rate. Credit Lyonnais, rue Victor-Hugo, is also open Sat.

Bike Rental: at the train station and Cyclanun, 49, rue Arsene Orillard (tel. 88-13-25).

Laundromat: rue Faubourg de Pont-Neuf, across from the Hotel Lion d'Or.

Telephone Code: (49).

Accommodations

The cheaper hotels lie at the center of town.

Auberge de Jeunesse (IYHF), 3 "Belle-Jouanne," 17, rue de la Jeunesse (tel. 58-03-05), 3km from the station. Take bus #9 (the last bus leaves at 7:30pm). Avoid this dreadful youth hostel if at all possible. 22.50F per night; 7F for sheets; but sleeping bag is okay.

University Housing: July-Sept. only. Check with CROUS before 5pm. 76, rue des Carmelites (tel. 01-83-70). Housing available for 23F, not including breakfast, with student ID at residence Marie Curie (tel. 41-61-78). University restaurant at 21, rue Jean-Richard Block.

Hôtel du Plat d'Etain, rue du Plat d'Etain, off the place du Marechal-Leclerc (tel. 41-04-80). Behind the theater near the **Hôtel de Ville.** Clean, low-key, and old-fashioned. Singles 42F; doubles from 61F. Breakfast 11F or 13F with croissants. Closed last week in Aug.

Hôtel Jules-Ferry, 27, rue Jules-Ferry (tel. 41-23-55). Near the church of St. Hilaire on a quiet street. From the station, follow blvd. de Pont Achard for ten minutes to rue Jules-Ferry. Singles from 40F; doubles from 60F; breakfast 9F.

Hôtel du Lion d'Or, 28, Faubourg de Pont-Neuf (tel. 41-13-02). Take bus #1 from *centre ville,* direction Cité Université. Get off at the first stop after the Pont Neuf. Singles 42F; double beds 50F.

Hôtel le Carnot, 40, rue Carnot (41-23-69). On a commercial street, so plead for a room that faces the back. Four rooms at 42F; breakfast 10F. No showers. Looks as if it deserves its sleazy reputation. Also has a bar-restaurant on the ground floor, frequented by locals. The *à la carte* selections are good buys. *Menu* 30.50F and 38F, wine and service included.

Camping: The municipal campground, **Le Porteau** (tel. 41-44-88) is a hill 2km out of town. A mediocre place, in spite of the panorama. If you are put in the annex, don't use the horrible facilities there, but walk across the road to the caravanners' hot showers and clean bathrooms. Take the bus that stops across the street to the left of the station, in front of the *boulangerie.* **Camping St. Benoit** is on the Route de Passelourdin, 5km from Poitiers.

Food

Poitevin cuisine is a mixture of northern and southern styles. Try the *fromage de chèvre,* the local *andouillette* (spicy sausage), and, if you're up to it, the *anguilles* (eels). Baked goods are also superb, from the *brioche* and *clafoutis* to the local *macarons.* The cheapest place to shop is the basement of Printemps, but the indoor market at the place du Marche is more tempting. The outdoor market at the place du Marche on Tues., Thurs., and Sat. is a real spectacle—just about anything you could consider eating (and some you couldn't) is sold here, dead or alive.

Most hotel-bars in Poitiers offer five-course menus for around 35F, but on Sunday you'll find almost nothing open. Take your goods and picnic in the Parc de Blossac (open 7am-8pm).

Snack Notre-Dame, place Charles de Gaulle, just across from the Notre-Dame Cathedral. Tables outside filled with students. Small, but good food. No *menus,* but *plats* from 12-25F. Try the cherry tart.

Le Regal, 18, rue de la Regratterie. An uninspiring place, but its central location and 28F four-course, wine and service included, *menu* make it worthwhile. Closed Sun.

Café de la Plage, 68, rue de la Cathédrale. A good place to stop for one of many ice creams offered. More substantial fare on 33F menu, whose choices make a vegetarian meal possible. Fun atmosphere. Open till 10pm except Mon.; closed three weeks in August. Across the street, try the **crêperie Le Roy d'ys,** at 51, rue de la Cathédrale. *Galettes* 6-18F; crêpes 5-15F. Open daily, except Sun. and Mon., till midnight.

Le Croc Bio, 4, rue de la Chaine. In the University area (where else would you find purple walls in Poitiers?). Set "healthy" meals at 20F, but in this *restaurant associatif,* you may pay more if you can.

La Grande Muraille, rue des Veilles Boucheries. Chinese restaurant with filling 28.50F *menu,* and main dishes at 12-25F. Open till 10:30pm daily.

La Pacha 50, rue St.-Simplicien, serves Arabian specialties, such as *couscous,* for 19-32F, including extra-hot shrimp for 21F.

Restaurant Maxime, 4, rue Saint-Nicolas. The 42F *menu* is copious, with its house salad, beef, and ice cream; but if you want to splurge, go for the 52F *menu* which includes *crepes aux moules,* fish, cheese, and dessert. The owner of this restaurant is also the cook.

Sights

If you're a fan of Romanesque churches, Poitiers is an unparalleled delight. Most famous of the churches is **Notre-Dame-La-Grande,** a small jewel of Romanesque handicraft. The west facade, with its unique cone-shaped towers, contains a rich array of sculpture depicting Christ's salvation. The interior is one of the finest you'll ever see: gentle, diffused light illuminating the rare frescoes on the walls and the geometric patterns decorating the columns.

For a simpler elegance, visit the **Eglise St.-Hilaire** in the southern part of the city, the church where the 13-year-old Richard the Lion-Hearted was titled Count of Poitier. Walk around the exterior to take in the perfect symmetry of the radiating chapels and the dominance of horizontal lines in the perspective. Inside, note how the choir is raised above the crypt, a practice carried over from the early Christian churches. The narrow separation of columns from the side walls was a structural advance which would later lead to lighter, Gothic construction; here it creates a fascinating combination of barrel and groin vaults. The **Eglise Montierneuf,** in the north end of the city, has a plain Romanesque front hidden by trees, the same towers which seem to be de rigeur for Poitiers, and a simple barrel-vaulted interior. But if you walk around it on the blvd. Chassaigne, you'll get quite a surprise: an elegant, soaring apse supported by the lightest of flying buttresses.

Pointiers also contains the oldest existing Christian building in France, the **Baptistére St.-Jean,** dating from the seventh century. The octagonal font built into the floor dates from the fourth century, and recent diggings have uncovered the aqueducts used to bring water in and out. The original frescoes are barely visible in some of the chapels, and on the whole the durability of the stone-and-brick construction is quite remarkable. The Baptistery serves as a museum of Roman and early Christian decoration, with many carved sarcophagi and friezes. (Open Mon.-Sat. 10am-noon, and 2-6pm (5pm in winter); closed Wednesday, admission 4F.)

Next to the Baptistery is the **Musée Ste.-Croix** in a modern building built over an ancient abbey. This is a superbly designed museum containing innumerable relics from Poitiers' Bronze Age and Roman settlements as well as a fine collection of Dutch and Flemish paintings. (Open daily except Sat., 10-11:30am and 2-5:30pm; free entrance.)

For a glimpse at the Romanesque architect's non-ecclesiastical pursuits, visit the **Palais de Justice,** the former palace of the Dukes of Aquitaine. The vast twelfth-century timber-roofed King's Hall once echoed with the ballads of troubadours, plans of crusading knights, and the soft verse of Eleanor of Aquitaine's *Courts of Love.* You might want to make the walk across the Pont Neuf to see the **Hypogee Martyrium.** An interesting remnant from the ancient past, it is an underground chapel dating from the 17th century, where Christian martyrs were buried by the Romans.

In mid-April, Poitiers hosts **le Printemps Musical de Poitiers,** a festival with concerts, exhibits, and debates (tickets range from 15 to 35F). From July 20 through September 15, an **International Salon of Art and Poetry** is conducted. An eight-concert series **Rencountres Musicales de Poitiers** is held from October through June. For more information visit the tourist office of the **Maison des Jeunes et de la Culture,** 16, rue 37, rue Pierre de Coubertin (tel. 47-84-94).

Poitiers has several nightclubs, which charge 50F for the privilege of entering and having a drink. If you want to dance and are willing to pay the price, two places are popular with the young crowd: **18/25,** on rue des Essarts, or **La Grand' Goule,** 46, rue de Pigeon Blanc. If you are up for a little jazz, try **Le Tapis Vert** or **L'Arlequin,** place Montier Nieuf in the University area.

Near Poitiers

About 20km east of Poitiers lies the town of **Chauvigny** typical of the Vienne region with its medieval walls rising from a spectacular hilltop site. Inside the town's defenses stands the Romanesque **Eglise St.-Pierre,** notable for its intricate sculpture depicting episodes from the Bible. The **abbey of St. Savin-sur-Gartempe,** 10km to the east, displays a remarkable collection of frescoes even finer than those of Notre-Dame-la-Grande. There are three buses daily that go to St.-Savin via Chauvigny, or you can hitch along the N151. Chauvigny has a few inexpensive hotels and a three-star **campsite** at La Fontaine (tel. 46-31-94); 5F a person, and 3.50F a tent. Closes at 10pm. There is also a small one-star site at St.-Savin.

Halfway to Angoulême on the D1, the town of Civray boasts one of the finest Romanesque churches in France, the Eglise St.-Nicholas. The sculptural work on its classically ordered west facade is truly remarkable. A few buses leave daily from Poitiers.

La Rochelle

Once the coastal power of Aquitaine, La Rochelle profited from its position as a port city vital to both France and Britain. In the seventeenth century, the powerful and unscrupulous Richelieu, who saw the independent town as an obstacle to uniting France, convinced Louis XIII to beseige the town. After a large portion of the population had starved to death, La Rochelle finally surrendered. The city did not regain its former wealth until the twentieth century, when its white sand beaches and magnificent old buildings were rediscovered by vacationers. Its picturesque harbor is thronged with summertime visitors, and with frequent departures from nearby La Pallice for the beaches and campgrounds of **Ile de Ré,** it endures more backpacking students than just about any other city in France. Today La Rochelle, which used to boast that it had kept the English out of Aquitaine, welcomes them heartily.

Practical Information

La Rochelle is served by frequent train service from Paris, especially in summer, and the ride from Poitiers takes about 1½ hours. From the station, walk up the ave. General-de-Gaulle to the harbor. All the major attractions and accommodations are located between here and the place de Verdun.

Office de Tourisme: 10, rue Fleuriau (tel. 41-14-68). Includes a hotel booking service. Open Mon.-Sat. 9am-8pm in July-Aug.; otherwise, open Mon.-Sat. 9am-12:30pm and 2:30-6pm. Organizes walking tours of the city. Daily at 10am in summer.

Office Departmental du Tourisme de la Charente-Maritime: 11*bis*, rue des Augustins (tel. 41-43-33), next to the Maison Henri II. Open Mon.-Fri. 9am-noon and 2-5pm. Information on the area surrounding La Rochelle.

Post Office: place de l'Hôtel de Ville (tel. 41-35-50). Main office, with Poste Restante, is located on the blvd. Marechal-Joffre by the train station.

Police: 2, rue place de Verdun (tel. 41-22-24); **Emergency:** tel. 17; **Health Emergency** (tel. 41-31-31 or 18).

Train Station: blvd. Maréchal-Joffre (tel. 41-34-22).

Buses: Citram, 30, cours des Dames (tel. 41-04-07) runs buses to Saintes, Cognac, Angoulême, and points in between. Océcars, 44, cours des Dames (tel. 41-93-93) has routes going to the coastal towns.

Ferry Crossings: Ile de Ré ferries leave from La Rochelle-Pallice every twenty minutes in season. Information (tel. 42-61-48). Take bus #1 to La Pallice from the train station or place de Verdun.

Bike Rental: The Vélos Municipaux on the Quai Valin will lend (for free!) a bike for three hours. For four hours you pay 2F and 2F an hour after that. Open daily (except Sun. and Mon.) 9am-noon and 2:30-6pm. At the train station (18F a day) or Locasport Plage de la Concurrence, west of the harbor (18F a day). Here you can also rent windsurfers by the hour or the day (about 100F for the day). Moped rental: M. Salaun, 3, place de la Solette (tel. 41-66-33); also rents windsurfers.

Laundromats: rue de la Pepinière (open 7am-10pm), and on the rue St. Jean, near the Tour de la Lauterne.

Hitching Service: CDIJ, 14, rue des Gentilhommes (tel. 41-16-99), or 41-16-36). Call here also for babysitting.

Telephone Code: (46).

Accommodations

Hotels are expensive and generally filled. The best location for cheaper hotels is on the east side of the harbor from the train station to just above the place du Marché.

Centre International de Séjour, Auberge de Jeunesse (IYHF), ave. des Minimes (tel. 44-43-11), 2km from the station on the way to the Port de Minimes. Take bus #12 from the place de Verdun or follow the ave. de Colman left from the station, walk along the embankment, and follow signs along the Chemin de la Sole. Modern with restaurant-bar, cafeteria, and gameroom. 30F a night with Youth Hostel card, 34F without; includes breakfast and shower. Lunch and dinner 17.50F. Bicycle rentals available.

Hôtel le Perthus, 15, rue Gambetta (tel. 41-10-16). Simple and neat. Eight rooms from 45F; breakfast 10F. Just off the place du Marché. Closed in Oct.

Hôtel de la Paix, 14, rue Gargolleau (tel. 41-33-44). Also just off the place du Marché. Singles and doubles 65F, 70F with showers; showers 8.50F; breakfast 14F. Open 7am-10:30pm. Breakfast can be served outside.

Hôtel de Bordéaux, 45, rue St.-Nicholas (tel. 41-31-22). Off the quai Valin, five minutes from the train station. 22 rooms 55-100F. Breakfast 12F; showers 6F; baths 10F. Hotel being renovated by new management and is becoming very attractive, although the restaurant's prices are rising beyond budget range. Owner speaks English. Crowded.

Camping: Camping Municipal, blvd. A. Rondeau Port Neuf (tel. 34-81-20) is a two-star site with space for five hundred, surrounded by factories (take bus #6 to Port Neuf). There are two other two-star campsites in the immediate vicinity: one at Richelieu, plage d'Aytre (tel. 44-19-24) and the other at La Lizotiere (tel. 44-19-33).

Food

Every day until noon there is a market on place du Marché where you can get fresh fish, fruits, and vegetables. Otherwise, the harbor area is ringed with restaurants specializing in *les fruits de mer* (seafood). You can't beat the atmosphere in the restaurants around the place de la Chaine, but in all likelihood, you can't afford their prices either. The restaurants with better bargains are on the opposite side of the harbor and near the place du Marché.

La Solette, place Fourché. Light meals and snacks in a quiet square, 15-35F. Try grapefruit with shrimp for 15F.

Le Dauphin, 17, rue des Merciers. A cafeteria of slightly better than ordinary quality. Daily specials for 23F sometimes include seafood. Couscous 20-27F; grills 20F.

Restaurant des Canards, 2, rue des Canards. On a tiny street off the quai Valin. A good place for a local splurge; has a very simple 30F menu and a fish, meat, salad, cheese, and ice cream whopper for 50F. A la carte choices include *langoustines* (spiny lobster), 23F; *moules marinieres* (mussels in white wine, butter, and garlic sauce), 20F; and catch of the day, 22F.

Le Débit Parisien, 6, rue Thiers. Near the place du Marché. Popular local place, although low on atmosphere; has 35F menu.

If you want seafood, but restaurant prices prove too depressing, stroll down to the end of the cour des Dames to **Les Delices de la Mer,** where you can get take-out mussels and oysters for 10F or 12F and shrimp sandwiches for just 4F.

Sights

La Rochelle's famous towers guarding the port date from the late fourteenth century. Because of its defense system, the city became a thriving commercial center over the next two centuries, renowned for its wealthy bourgeoisie and immortalized in Alexandre Dumas' *The Three Musketeers.* John Calvin settled near here, and La Rochelle became an important Huguenot stronghold—this led to the city's brutal destruction at the hands of Cardinal Richelieu in the seventeenth century. It was not until the eighteenth century, when trade in sugar and Canadian furs emerged, that the region finally began to recover. The oldest tower, the **Tour St.-Nicolas,** is the least touristed of the three. It is also the most forbidding. Whenever the town was threatened, a chain was passed between here and the **Tour de la Chaine** to seal off the harbor; the chain rests alongside the Place de la Chaine now. The Tour de la Chaine today presents a rather hokey *son et lumière* show on La Rochelle during the Middle Ages. (Both open 10am-noon and 2-6:30pm. The Tour St.-Nicolas is closed on Tuesdays and the Tour de la Chaine is closed from Sept. to April. In the winter, St. Nicolas is open only in the afternoon and is closed on Tues. and Wed.)

A low rampart runs from the Tour de la Chaine to the **Tour de la Lanterne,** also known as the **Tour des Quatre Sergeants.** Rising more than 45 meters, it is topped by a flamboyant steeple. Originally part of the defense system, it was later used as a prison. The walls of many of the rooms show the carvings and signatures of its prisoners. The tower's nickname derives from its use as a prison for four sergeants who, in 1822, committed the capital crime of crying *"Vive la Republique"* during the Restoration Monarchy. From the top of the tower, you'll have a panoramic view of the city, and on clear days across to the Ile de Re. (Open same hours as the Tour St. Nicolas; admission 6F, 3F with student ID).

Beyond the picturesque harbor with its whitewashed town houses, lie La Rochelle's elegant arcaded streets, built during its eighteenth-century heyday. Walk underneath the fourteenth-century **Grosse Horloge** and up the rues du Palais land Chaudriér. On the rue Gargolleau is La Rochelle's **Musée des Beaux Arts,** with a rather undistinguished collection aside from the two landscapes by Corot and several works by the nineteenth-century painter, Eugène Fromentin, La Rochelle's native son. Open daily, except Tues. and Sun. morning, 10am-noon and 2-6pm, till 5pm in winter. Admission 3F, 1.50F with student ID; 5F and 2.50F during exhibitions. Nearby, the ornate **Renaissance Hotel de Ville,** has a lovely arcade gallery. Open Mon.-Fri. 9:30-11am and 2;30-5pm; only in the afternoon during the winter. Admission 3F for a guided tour. For oceanography buffs, La Rochelle has an **aquarium** south of the harbor off the ave. de Minimes, which is open daily 9am-7pm, Sun. 10am-7pm. Admission 11F; children 5.50F.

Near La Rochelle

The coastline near here offers one of Europe's longest sandy stretches. It is lined with commercialized resort towns like **Rochefort** which is expensive and overrun with tourists. **Les Sables d'Olonne,** north of La Rochelle, has a very good if crowded beach and a small **auberge de jeunesse,** Ecole des Chirons d'Olonne, with kitchen available, open July and August. Rochefort is served by trains from La Rochelle, and Les Sables d'Olonne by SNCF buses (railpasses valid) from Nantes. You might prefer to hitch or cycle along the coast, stopping in the smaller, less-touristed towns—don't expect rides from vacationers, though.

If you want to go to the beach, go to **Ile de Ré,** a fifteen-minute ferry ride from La Pallice of La Rochelle (10F round trip). The island has 60km of beach, two-thirds of it sandy, and plenty of campgrounds. It has become very popular with French youth, but the expanse of the sand prevents it from seeming too crowded. If you are down and out, this is a great place to be in the summer since you can scrounge oysters, clams, and mussels from the ocean, and the local crowds are real hell-raisers. The island rarely sleeps, and you can find people up and ready for a party at any time of the day or night. There are nightclubs scattered over the island, but be wary of these: they cost at least 30F and are generally not worth it. Better to stick to a midnight swim "a la francaise" or a clambake on the beach. There is a two-star camping site at Sainte-Marie on the Ile (tel. 30-22-47).

The **syndicat d'initiative** at the harbor (tel. 09-60-38) will provide you with a list of the dozens of campgrounds; there are several a 500-yard walk down the road to the right. The larger **Ile d'Oleron** has even more sandy beaches and an old castle besides. Connected to the mainland by a toll bridge (20F round trip), the island is also served by a busy port. Hotel rooms on both islands are priced out of sight.

Inland from La Rochelle is the **Marais Poitevin,** known as "Green Venice," a recovered expanse of marsh, drained by slow-moving canals and waterways. All is luxuriant green solitude interspersed with fields of brilliant sunflowers, stretching in from the coast nearly to Niort.

The **Saintonge** region southeast of Niort has numerous Romanesque remains—ruined abbeys and country churches can be found in the tiniest villages and hamlets. At Surgères, not far east of La Rochelle, is a well preserved twelfth-century church and feudal castle. There is a two-star municipal campground on rue de la Geres (tel. 05-18-01). In **Aulnay,** further along the D121, the **Eglise St.-Pierre** has a dazzling arrangement of sculpture and ornamentation.

Saintes

Saintes stretches peacefully along the banks of the glinting Charente River amidst flat expanses of fields that extend 30km to the sea on one side and 38km to Cognac on the other. Originally the Roman capital of southwest France, Saintes adopted Christianity in the third century, and spent much of its time after that fending off fire-bearing barbarians. The barbarians succeeded in leveling Saintes several times, and when in the eleventh century things calmed down a bit, the citizens of Saintes breathed a sigh of relief—and set about building churches. The Romanesque bulk of these buildings contrasts starkly with the fine Roman constructions, remaining as souvenirs of the town's early history.

The **Musée Archéologique** on the Esplanade André-Malraux next to the office de tourisme is an intriguing forest of Roman columns, friezes and cornices piled in two buildings and across a small square. Most of the works date from the demolition of the town's ramparts in the first three centuries of the common era, but the harmony of their element and the quality of workmanship is evident even today.

Across the street is the incongruous sight of a **Roman arch** rising between the street and the river. Originally erected in the first century on a bridge linking the two sides of town, an inscription is still visible along the top, dedicating it to Tiberius, Germanicus, and Drusus.

Most evocative of Saintes' Roman remains is the **Arènes Gallo-Romain,** a ruined amphitheater about a ten-minute walk away on the other side of the river. (Follow rue des Jacobins past the hospital.) The steep-sided ruin takes you by surprise, situated as it is in the midst of a residential area, where the ground abruptly sinks away and you'll find the steep-walled ivy-covered ruins giving way to a beautiful view of the Eglise St.-Eutrope. The tunnel entrance and several of the supporting arches still stand, and the structure, capable of holding a 20,000 person audience, is clearly a remarkable feat of engineering.

The nearby **Eglise St.-Eutrope** is one of the many churches built in the eleventh century on the pilgrimage routes to Santiago da Compostela in Spain. The interior has been marred by a rather weak Gothic alteration, but the crypt containing the tomb of St. Eutrope (entrance on the side of the bell tower) retains its air of purity and simplicity. Back across the river is the **Abbaye-aux-Dames,** one of the most beautiful of the many Romanesque churches in the region. The interior was redone with Angevin vaulting in the twelfth century, but the west facade and the Poitou-style central tower are particularly striking. The Abbaye is the site of a festival of ancient music in mid-July (tickets cost about 30F, with reductions for students). For information, contact CIRMAR, Boite Postale 214, 17104 Saintes (tel. 46/93-41-35), or inquire at the tourist office.

Practical Information

Office de Tourisme: Esplanade André-Malraux (tel. 74-23-82 or 74-25-99). On the right bank near the Triumphal Arch. A fifteen-minute walk from the train station. Walk left down ave. de la Marne and follow ave. Gambetta to the right until the river, then turn left. Open June-Sept. daily 9am-7pm; Sun. 10am-noon and 3-7pm. The rest of the year open daily 9am-noon and 2-6:30pm; closed Sun. and Sat. afternoon.

Post Office: 10, cours National (tel. 93-05-72). Near the bridge. Open Mon.-Fri. 8am-7pm; Sat. 8am-noon.

Train Station: ave. de la Marne (tel. 74-00-77). A ten-minute walk from the center of town; follow the ave. Gambetta towards the *centre ville*. Check here about cruises on the Charente. A day trip is 60F; one-half day 30F.

Bus Station: Autobus Aunis et Saintonge, 1, cours Reversaux (tel. 93-21-41) and at the SNCF station. Buses run frequently to Royan and the Ile de'Oleron, although it is much simpler to take the train.

Bike Rentals: Heline, 177, ave. Gambetta (tel. 93-43-38). The only commercial place that rents bicycles in Saintes; 22F for the day; 77F for a week; 300F returnable deposit, or passport. Closed Mon. and Sun.

Telephone Code: (46).

Accommodations and Food

Auberge de Jeunesse (IYHF), rue du Pont Amilion (tel. 93-14-92). Close to the center of town, a fifteen-minute walk from the train station down ave. Gambetta and to the left past the Abbaye-aux-Dames. Run by a friendly couple who keep the doors open 24 hours a day. Fully-equipped kitchen and a common room with ping-pong, 22.50F a night; 9F for a camping space in the large yard. You can also rent a bike here for 15F a day or 50F a week.

Hôtel des Voyageurs, 133, ave. Gambetta (tel. 93-23-01). Typical one-star place on the way to town from the station. Double beds 50F; two twin beds 52F, 75F with shower. Breakfast 10F; shower 9F; bath 10F. The restaurant is also worth trying out, with main dishes 16-33F.

Le Gambetta, 72, ave. Gambetta (tel. 93-02-85). A small place with only nine rooms, but it's inexpensive. Three rooms from 38-63F; breakfast 7.50F. Closed September and one week in February.

Camping: Camping Municipal, 6, route de Courbiac (tel. 93-08-00). A two-star site spreading over green fields along the banks of the Charente next to the municipal swimming pool—a healthy half-hour walk from the train station. Either follow

ave. Gambetta across the river and turn right on quai de l'Yser, or take the bus
from the train station and then walk. Open May 15-Oct. 15 7am-10pm.

The *marche* is a boisterous affair that takes place daily except Monday,
although the location changes frequently: Wed. and Sat. at the base of the
Cathedral; Thurs. and Sun. near the Abbaye-aux-Dames at Place St. Pallais;
and Fri. and Sat. on the cours Reversaux. The prices are low and the vendors
will let you sample their fat oysters and little shrimp if you're interested.
Escargots are the specialty here, cooked in garlic and parsley. The **Pension St.-
Michel** at 28, rue St. Michel is where the market people go to eat after their
morning's work, for its well-prepared dishes and family-style service, although
it is closed in the summer. At the **Crêperie Victor-Hugo,** you can choose from a
variety of sweet and savory crepes from 5F (closed Mon. and Tues.). **La
Plaisance** is a pleasant little place on 16, cours Reversaux, on the way to the
Arenes. Frequented by local people; menus at 33F and 60F. For a fine meal,
you should try **La Goul' Benaise** on the place Blair, which serves regional
specialties on 35F and 55F menus, including frog legs, roast beef in *pineau,*
and stuffed crab. The congenial proprietress cooks much of the fare herself
and enjoys chatting. A really special place.

Near Saintes

Royan, a half-hour train ride from Saintes, is the principal resort on the Cote
de Beaute. If you don't mind murky water and crowded shores, the five
beaches lining the Cote Sauvage, especially La Palmyre and La Courbre, are
nearly untouched and lovely; the bustling harbor and some of the buildings are
also worth seeing.

One of the most exciting modern buildings anywhere is Notre Dame de
Royan, designed by Guillaume Gillet and built from 1955 to 1958. Instead of
columns or piers to support the ceiling, internally strengthened walls were
used to support the ultra-thin (eight centimeters) ceiling. The design permits
every member of the congregation to see the main altar without obstruction.

The **Office Municipale du Tourisme** is located in a pavilion near the beach at
the end of the blvd. de la Grandiere, about fifteen minutes from the train
station. Cheap rooms are scarce, but try **Hotel Astoria,** 42, ave. Marechal-
Leclerc (tel. 05-06-99), one block from the station, which has nine doubles at
55F, extra beds for 30% supplements; breakfast for 8F; and showers for 7F. It
is open May through September. Only two blocks from the beach, there is a
three-star **campsite,** Clairefontaine, ave. Louise, at nearby Pontaillac.

Cognac

A short, half-hour ride from Saintes brings you to an alcohol-lovers' Mecca,
the city that has given its name to some of the most celebrated beverages in
history. Cognac sits proudly among carefully tended fields where strictly regulated soils bear white gold, the grapes which are used to distill another generation of cognac brandy. The city itself preserves a small-town atmosphere, but
within its confines stand the distilleries of Hennessy, Martell, Remy-Martin,
and every other well-known exporter of cognac. The very air reeks of the stuff,
but not the bars—85% of the local specialty is exported, and the residents stick
to less expensive wine or to *pineau,* a combination of cognac and grape juice,
aged at least three years and costing at least 35F per bottle in the shop. Pineau
comes in white or rosé, whereas cognac comes only in amber, the color gained
not from the grape but from the tannins of the Limousin oak casks used to age
it. No other wood will do, just as no other process is substituted for the

centuries-old double distillation. It would take a strong stomach to drink this new cognac: the aging and the blending of different vintages creates the soft and smoother drink. The older the cognac is, the smoother and sweeter it becomes, so there are various designations according to age: from VS (very special) or VSOP (very special old pale), which is at least eight years old, up to what is known as Paradise, which is at least fifty or more.

Cognac lies aging behind many a blank wall of the town, and on these walls live possibly the happiest organism in the world—a species of small black mushrooms that subsists exclusively on the vapors that escape from the pores of the wooden casks. (Think of them and weep.)

Practical Information

Office de Tourisme: place Francois 1er (tel. 82-10-71). Turn right from the train station and then take a right on rue Elisee Mousnier, and another on rue Bayard. Follow straight to the place Francois 9er. Here you can sign up for various guided tours and have them help you find a room for the price of a telephone call. Open Mon.-Sat. 9am-7pm in the summer and 9am-noon and 2-6pm in the winter.

Post Office (PTT): place Bayard (tel. 82-08-99). Closed Sun.

Train Station: Information (tel. 82-07-99).

Police: 14, rue Richard (tel. 32-11-01); **Medical Emergency:** Ambulance (tel. 82-15-61).

Bike Rentals: M. Demontier, 53, ave. Victor-Hugo. Open daily, except Sun. and Mon., 8am-noon and 2-7pm; closed in August.

Telephone Code: (45)

Accommodations

Cognac does not runneth over with hotels, but you won't have much trouble finding a room, as long as you don't arrive late at night.

Le Cheval Blanc, 7-9, place Bayard (tel. 82-09-55). A pleasant hotel across from the post office, and across as well from an excellent little restaurant. Singles 40F; doubles from 48F; breakfast 10F. Closed Sun.

La Residence, 25, ave. Victor Hugo (tel. 32-16-09). Another pleasant place not far from the center of town, with double beds for one or two at 51F and two-bedded rooms from 60F; breakfast 12F; showers free.

L'Auberge, 13, rue Plumejeau (32-08-70), with double beds for one or two at 50F; doubles from 60F; breakfast 12F.

Camping: Camping Municipal de Cognac (tel. 32-13-32). A several kilometer walk through the town and out into the *autoroute* (for a few hundred meters) will bring you to a charming campground right on the banks of the Charente, where you can fish or swim (3.70F a person a day, and 1.75F a tent; hot showers for 2.50F and clean bathrooms). From the tourist office, follow rue Henri-Fichon until it ends, then turn left. Walk out of Cognac and continue until you come to the river; the campground is just across the bridge. You can try hitchhiking, but don't expect quick results.

Drink and Food

To taste the stuff that made this town famous, you can go to the cognac houses, but there are other ways of getting your sips in. M. Christian Jamonneau stands behind the bar in **La Lieutenance,** a sixteenth-century house originally owned by the sister of François I and now the property of **Maison Prunier**. Here, at this last of the cognac *dégustations* houses, you can taste cognac, *pineau*, and various flavored liqueurs. When you've had enough and you can still see straight, go upstairs to see a mini-exhibit on the history of Cognac put together by the owner. La Lieutenance is located on Grande Rue du Cognac and is open until 7pm, but if there are people around, the place could stay open until 10pm.

The cheapest place actually to buy a bottle of cognac or *pineau* is in the basement of Prisunic, a supermarket on place Francois 1er. If you are a bit more picky, go to La Cognatheque, place de la Corderie (opposite the tourist office) and ask for some guidance. Three good and relatively inexpensive *pineaux* you might try are the rosés of Villard, Gombert, and especially Seguin.

If you'd rather eat than drink, there is a market every morning in the big building at Place d'Armes, where you'll find everything from oysters to grapes.

Le Sens Unique, 20, rue du 14-juillet (tel. 82-06-50) is a cozy little place with a barrel-shaped bar, where you can eat like crazy for 29F. Try the *langoustines* for an entree; the *coquilles de Charente* are snails, a specialty of the region.

Brasserie Alsacienne, place Francois 1er, has good 28F (wine included) and 35F *menus*.

Le Chantilly, 146, ave. Victor Hugo, is a truly "local" place with a simple restaurant-bar that serves four-course set *menus* for 35F, including the bottle(s) of wine on your table. Open every day for dinner.

Sights

The joy of visiting Cognac lies in making your way from one brand-name to the next. Tour the warehouses, listen to the films about the history of each house, and collect your nip bottles of golden brandy. **Hennessy,** in particular, is worth seeing since the tour is more informative and less propagandized than the others. The film has a little humor and you are treated to a (short) boat ride across the narrow Charente. Most of the *chais* are open to visitors Mon.-Fri. from 9-11am and 2-4:30pm. The tourist office will give you a complete list of hours. **Otard** and **Polignac** are open on Sunday during the summer.

When you tire of trudging through the fragrant warehouses, where it is said that 2,000,000 potential bottles of cognac evaporate through the pores of the barrels each year, venture out into the countryside where the actual distilling takes place. Only certain grapes are approved as ingredients for cognac, and the regions in which they can be grown are regulated just as stringently. Vineyards lie in concentric circles with Cognac as their center. The closer to Cognac the vineyard is, the higher its prestige. There are six vineyards (or "crus") from the aristocratic *Grande Champagne* to the *Bois Ordinaire*. Numerous small distilleries also operate in the region (as for example on the *routes* to Saintes or Angoulême), and in many you can have a look around and taste the cognac and *pineau* produced on the site. Unfortunately, these *chais* are spaced far enough apart to make a walking tour difficult; usually six kilometers at least. The closest *cru* is **Borderies,** four kilometers away, but you can sign up for a tour with the syndicat. **Herz,** in place Francois (tel. 32-42-42), rents cars for a steep 150F a day (plus 1.30F a kilometer).

Cognac has a few claims to fame besides drink. By the second half of the fourteenth century, the city was a bustling port, trafficking in wine and salt, and in 1448 a certain Charles d'Angoulême brought his new wife, Louise de Savoie, to stay for a while. Their son Francois was born in the chateau here—

the same Francois who later became King Francois I of France. A statue of Francois stands in the center of town, and the chateau in which he was born now serves as a museum as well as the *chais* of Baron Otard cognac. The tour of this house is thus more historical—and overdone—than others.

Cognac was also the birthplace of the postcard, and some of the earliest ones are on display at the Musee du Cognac (open daily, except Tues., 10am-noon and 2:30-6pm in summer).

Help is usually needed for the fall grape harvest *(vendanges)* which stretches from late October into November, making it France's last harvest of the year. Ask at the syndicat for details. You are better off with a smaller distiller, if possible; they will provide food, lodging, and a small income for your toil.

Angoulême

Like Poitiers, the old town of Angoulême is on a steep-walled plateau encircled by rivers. The city is most noted for its Romanesque **Cathédrale St.-Pierre** perched by the southern ramparts. The square campanile may make you think you're in Italy, but the facade is pure Aquitaine, with its distinctive towers and ornate decoration. The carvings were made in the twelfth century at the same time that the *Chanson de Roland* was set down, and the doorway and its flanking arches tumble about in scenes of earthly life of the Middle Ages—equestrian jousting and hunting parties. Above, the false tympanums depict a more religious scene, with Christ surrounded by the symbols of the four evangelists—the Ascension culminating in the Last Judgement.

From the Cathedral, start your way around the city's **ramparts** by following the blvd. Paul-Doumer. The views are superb, although urban sprawl makes up much of the tableau. Surrounding the ramparts at the western end, the **Jardin Vert** offers a pleasant spot for a picnic or a walk. Here, at the foot of the ramparts, Angoulême's **Animation Festival** in July and **Folk Festival** in August are held annually.

The north side of the ramparts borders on the oldest part of Angoulême, neglected for many years and still largely unchanged. This area centers around the **Eglise St.-Andre**, redone in a Gothic style but retaining the original Romanesque tower and entrance. Nearby, the **Hotel de Ville** offers a tour of the rooms where Marguerite of Valois was born. The **Musée Archéologique,** on the rue de Montmoreau, displays regional treasures from Gallo-Roman to recent centuries.

Practical Information

Angoulême is easily reached by train from Poitiers, Limoges, or Bordeaux, making it an easy day trip. Alternatively, because of relatively inexpensive accommodations, you can use it as a base for exploring the Charente countryside. From the station, walk up the ave. Gambetta to the center of town.

Bureau du Tourisme: Hotel de Ville (tel. 95-16-84 or 92-18-48). A regional office with itineraries on the surrounding countryside. The annex or **Pavillion du Tourisme** is located right in front of the train station, place de la Gare (tel. 92-27-57). Both are open Mon.-Sat. 9am-noon and 2-6pm, closed Sun.

Post Office and Telephone (PTT): Champ de Mars, open weekdays 8am-7pm, Sat. until noon, closed Sun. There is also a branch right outside the train station (tel. 92-23-11).

Train Station: SNCF, at the intersection of rue de la Grande and ave. Gambetta. Modern and comfortable.

Buses: STGA (tel. 92-44-43) and **Autobus Citram** (tel. 95-58-68), both on the place du Champ de Mars. Bus connections to the surrounding towns.

Bike Rental: M. Pelton, 5, rue des Arceaux (tel. 95-30-91).

Commissariat de Police: Champs de Mars (tel. 95-21-22); **Medical Emergency:** SAMU (tel. 92-92-92).

Laundromat: 3, rue Ludovic-Trarieux in Vieux Angoulême daily 7am-2am; and 11, rue St.-Roch. Open daily 7am-10pm.

Telephone Code: (45).

Accommodations

Auberge de Jeunesse (IYHF), on the Ile de Bourgines, next to the campsite (tel. 92-45-80). A very nice 90-bed Hostel in a modern building next to a stream and small woods, 2km from the train station. Free passes for the nearby town pool; canoe and bike rental. Meals and good kitchen available. 22.50F a night; breakfast 7F; sheets 8F, not necessary if you have a sleeping bag.

Hôtel du Faisan Dore, 41, rue de Geneve (tel. 92-01-60). Reasonably priced for a small hotel with modern decor. Singles and doubles from 50F, and breakfast 9F. Good location in the old town.

Hôtel La Bourse, place Gerard-Perot (tel. 92-06-42). Less than a ten-minute walk up the hill along the ave. Gambetta from the train station. A very comfortable, well-equipped hotel. Singles and doubles start from 45.50F or 65.70F with shower in room. Breakfast 12.50F, showers 6F. Closed first three weeks in September.

Hôtel La Crabe, 27, rue Kleber (tel. 95-51-80). A small quiet, but very nice place, a five-minute walk from the train station. Doubles 43.50F; breakfast 10F; showers 5F. A good restaurant as well, serving tasty and generous dishes (*menus* 33F).

Le Gaste, 381, rte. de Bordeaux (tel. 95-11-54) is a clean one-star with twenty-five rooms from 49F for a double bed, single or double; breakfast 9F. Unfortunately, it is a little way out of town, a healthy walk from the train station.

Camping: Camping Municipal is located 2km from the train station, not far from the Youth Hostel. Find the river, then follow it to the right until you come to the Pont de Bourgines. The ground is a little way past the bridge to the right. Bus #7 goes there from Place du Champs de Mars. Descend at St.-Antoine, right before the bridge. Otherwise, Camping des Alliers is several kilometers away on the rte. de Bordeaux.

Food

Several bistros and restaurants lie near the Hôtel de Ville, but the most charming places dot the streets of Vieux Angoulême. The covered market (les Halles) is two blocks down rue De Gaulle from the Hotel de Ville. It is much more reasonably priced than any store on the walking street, rue Marengo, except perhaps Prisunic at #31. For a minor splurge on regional specialties, try the boulangerie-salon du thé at 34, rue Marengo which sells *clafouti* for 3F and delectable chocolate *marguerites* and *duchesses*. The finest places for a picnic are by the ramparts or streams of the Jardin Vert and on the Youth Hostel grounds by the small dam.

La Petite Auberge, 50, rue de Geneve. A good dinner spot with menus at 30F and 40F. Closed Sun.

La Sicilia, rue Ludovic Trarieux, is in the old town and has a pleasant atmosphere. Pizzas run from 15F to 29F, and big salads 8-24F. Take out, too. Closed Tues, but open Sun. Open till midnight.

Kervenir Crêperie, 10, rue d'Aguesseau, offers a wide variety of crêpes for 7-20F and light specialties like salad Niçoise, 17F. Open till 1am Tues.-Sat.

Le Palma, 4, ramp D'Aguesseau. A pretty place with wall-size photos of the sea. Delicious *soupe de poisson* (fish soup). This place is not dirt cheap, but has good deals, nonetheless. Closed Sun.

Near Angoulême

At La Rochefoucauld are a sixteenth-century *donjon,* chapel and galleries. There is a *son-et-lumiere* at the chateau every evening during the summer, but check at Angoulême's **bureau du tourisme** before starting out. Only one bus each day goes to the town, so you might want to hitch along the N141. North from La Rochefoucauld is **Confolens,** a well-preserved medieval town, interesting to visit for its old houses and bridge, with frequent connections to Angouleme. The **tourist pavilion** at Confolens is located on the main road (tel. 84-00-77). Every August Confolens holds its **International Folk Festival.**

For accommodations in La Rochefoucauld try the **Hotel de France,** 13, Grand-Rue (tel. 20-02-29), with doubles from 53F and menus from 32F in the restaurant. The **Hotel de Vienne,** 4, rue de la Ferrandie in Confolens (tel. 84-09-24) has rooms from 45F. La Rochefoucauld has a two-star municipal **campsite,** as does Confolens (tel. (45) 84-01-97).

Bordeaux

An industrial center and busy shipping port, Bordeaux city center, with its eighteenth-century architecture and crowded pedestrian alleys sliced by the Garonne River, offers considerable big-city charm. An important wine capital, Bordeaux serves as an excellent base for visits to the nearby vineyards and popular seaside resorts.

Bordeaux was joined to England for three hundred years. When Eleanor of Aquitaine married Henry Plantagenet in the twelfth century, she brought on an alliance with England which upset the balance of power and led to three centuries of strife between the English and the French. As part of the British empire, Bordeaux experienced its greatest period of prosperity, and it was at this time that the production of wine became economically important. Today, Bordeaux remains one of the largest and most-famed wine-producing centers in France.

There are three main families of red Bordeaux wine: Medocs and Graves; Saint-Emilions, Pomerol, and Fronsac; Bordeaux and Côtes de Bordeaux. All of these are named after the region from which they come except Graves, which, despite its solemn sound, is named for the small pebbles that are found in the soil on which these vines are grown. The white wines are a different story: there are two types of these, the dry (sold in a white bottle) and the *liquoreux* (in a green one), each made by a different process. The former are harvested and fermented like most wines, but the latter, such as the Sauternes, gain their qualities from "the noble rot", a microscopic mushroom that attacks the over-ripe grape.

If you want more information on this fascinating subject, contact the **Conseil Interprofessional du Vin de Bordeaux (CIVB),** 1, Cours de XXX Juillet, 33075

Bordeaux (tel. (56) 52-82-82). The **Vinothèque,** next to the office de tourisme, has knowledgeable salespeople, and wines of all prices, from bottles of *"petit vin"* at 7F up to the aristocrats costing thousands. And if you want to sample the stuff without leaving the gates of the city, the **Hotel des Vins,** rue Abée de l'Épée, just beyond place Gambetta, has free wine-tasting.

One of the most interesting things to do is to visit the *chateaux* where the wines are made (buy a bottle or two while you are there). On your own, take Bus "N" to **Chateau Haut-Briand,** where you will find free tours and tasting. Or else make your way to **St.-Emilion** about 35km east of Bordeaux by car or bus (leaving from the Gare Citram, 23.50F one way). A small village with medieval, ecclesiastical remains, St.-Emilion looks out over hillside vineyards where some of the world's greatest wines are produced. It also offers some good wine at inexpensive prices and free wine-tasting. For tours and visits to the caves in St.-Emilion, ask at the **syndicat d'initiative,** Doyenne de St.-Emilion (tel. 24-72-03). North of Bordeaux in the Pauillac commune, the wine museum at **Chateau Mouton-Rothschild** provides a vicarious thrill, but visits are made by arrangement only (tel. 59-22-22). If you want to cover more ground in less time, the syndicat d'initiative runs bus tours of the wine country from May 15-Oct. 16—a different tour for each day of the week (except holidays). The price of 40F, 30F with student ID, includes three wine samplings.

Practical Information

The train station which serves interregional (non-local) runs, **Gare St.-Jean** lies a couple of kilometers south of the center of town. Go east three blocks to the river, then north along the quai, past porte de la Monnaie, porte des Salinieres, and porte Cailhau, until you reach the great open spaces of the Esplanades des Quinconces. Just off the esplanade are the **syndicat d'initiative,** Maison du Vin and Grand Théâtre. The rue Sainte-Catherine is part pedestrian street, and it connects the **place de la Victoire** with the other main square, the **place de la Comedie.**

Syndicat d'Initiative: 12, cours du 30 Juillet (tel. 44-28-41). Large office, always crowded and rather impersonal. Provides information about accommodations, restaurants, tours and entertainment; be sure to get their map of the city. Open June through August Mon.-Fri. 9am-7pm, Sat. 9am-6pm, Sun. 9am-2pm, rest of the year. Currency exchange Sat. and Sun. 9am-noon and 2-6pm. They offer tours of the city, as well as interesting afternoon bus tours (30-50F for students) of the nearby vineyards. Take bus #8 from the train station.

Centre d'Information Jeunesse d'Aquitaine: 5, rue Dufour-Dubergier (tel. 48-55-50), supplies all the warmth and personal attention that the syndicat lacks. Has reams of information about campgrounds, Youth Hostels, and activities in the region. The staff is attuned to needs of students, especially for eating and entertainment. **Allostop Voyages** (pre-arranged rides to wherever you want to go) is also located here; open Mon.-Fri. 3-7pm. In July and Aug. also look into the **CIJ-Pass,** a 10F youthpass sold here and at the syndicat, entitling the holder to all sorts of discounts on transportation, accommodations, and services. Open Mon.-Fri. 8:30-7pm.

CROUS: Cours Aristide-Briand (tel. 92-75-30 or 92-92-65) offers information on university dorms, whose price hovers around 25F per night.

Central Post Office (PTT): 52, rue Georges-Bonnac. Information (tel. 96-83-41) open Mon.-Fri. 8am-7pm. Sat. 8am-noon. Poste Restante same hours, but mail can also be picked up at telephone exchange. Sun. 9-11am. Telephones and telegrams both open Mon.-Sat. 8am-10pm.

Regional Buses: Gare Aubus Citram, 14, rue Fondaudege (tel. 81-18-18).

Wheels: Mobylette Roques, 19, allées de Tourny (tel. 52-07-71) rents mobylettes (30F/day) and bicycles (20F/day). 200F deposit.

Hitching: For Bayonne, Biarritz: take bus "G" to its terminus on the N10. For Toulouse: take "B" or "L". For Perigueux: takes bus 4bis or try **Allostop Voyages** (see Centre d'Information Jeunesse d'Aquitaine).

Police: Rue Casteja (tel. 90-92-75).

U.S. Consulate: 4, rue Esprit des Lois (tel. 52-65-95). Open Mon.-Fri. 9am-noon and 2-4:30pm.

Harvest Work: For information on grape-picking, contact the Employment Office, Terrace du Front Medoc (tel. 90-92-92). Also check with Centre d'Information Jeunesse.

Laundromat: Try the one at 32, rue des Augustins, near cours de la Marne, between place de la Victoire and the lycee Montaigne. Open 7am-10pm "365 days of the year."

Telephone Code: (56).

Accommodations

Bordeaux has countless cheap hotels, especially around the train station and around the Esplanade, but go early, since hotels begin to fill up by mid-afternoon.

Auberge de Jeunesse (IYHF), Foyer Barbey, 22 cours Barbey (tel. 91-59-51). Close to the station, and south off cours de la Marne. Huge (230 beds); not too appealing, but clean good bathrooms and good cooking facilities. Hostel card not required, but 10am-6pm lock-out and 11pm curfew are both strictly enforced. Nightly fee without hostel card 21F, with 19F; breakfast 5F; sheet 4F, but sleeping bags okay without sheet.

Maison des Etudiantes, 50, rue Ligier (tel. 96-48-30) is probably the best deal in town and is the only Cité Universitaire housing open in the summer. A nicely run foyer with single rooms for 25F, but just for women, with student ID. Showers free; good location. From the train station, follow cours de la Marne all the way up to the point where it turns into cours de la Liberation. Rue Ligier is to the right off the main drag. Open all night, all year.

Hôtel-Bar de Poissy, 210, cours de la Marne (tel. 91-55-91) near train station. All rooms have cabinet de toilette (bidet and sink) and free use of showers. Singles from 40F; doubles from 55F; breakfast 8F. Closed in August.

Hôtel La Boëtie, 4, rue de la Boetie (tel. 81-76-68), is one of the more inexpensive one-stars you'll find around, with 55F singles and doubles; doubles with shower 70F; shower 8F. No breakfast.

Hôtel San Michel, 32, rue Charles Domercy (tel. 91-96-40) is a small place of only 12 rooms. In a street with several other one-stars. Closed in August.

Camping: There are no campgrounds in the city itself, but four lie in the immediate vicinity. Camping Pichey is located at 108, rue Henri-Vigneau in Merignac (tel. 47-13-72). Camping Bellegrave, ave. du Docteur-Narcam in Pessac (tel. 45-50-68), is a one-star site with space for 150. Camping les Gravieres at Villenave d'Orgnon (tel. 87-00-36), is a two-star site in a forest by the river, with space for 200. All four are surrounded by countryside and are open all year.

Food

Known in France as *"la region de Bien Boire et de Bien Manger"* (the region of fine drinking and dining), Bordeaux offers a variety of specialty restaurants. Along with the celebrated wine, you'll find fat oysters, *confits* of duck and goose, and mushrooms that approach the truffle in quality. The area around place General-Carrail, especially along the rue des Augustines, has some moderately priced establishments.

Bar les Quinconces, corner of Alles d'Orleans and quai Maréchal-Liautey, three blocks from the syndicat d'initiative, has a great four-course *menu* with wine for 28F and excellent *cafe au lait* at 4F.

Oniriaz, rue de Guienne, beside the Marché Victor-Hugo. Feast on giant salads and desserts (each costs about 15F). Closed August. Or try the nearby **Nara,** 10, rue Guienne, a macrobiotic restaurant and store. Also closed in August.

Crêperie St. Pierre, 5, place St. Pierre, in the old, newly renovated section of town. Specializes in light fare, crêpes and galettes, 8-18F. Salads 15-18F. Closed Mon. and Sun. evening.

Le Jardin, 15, rue Montbazon, right across from the side museum entrance. This place verges on the elegant. 30, 50, and 90F *menus*. If you're hungry and it's Sunday, the one decent place to buy food is an anonymous epicerie on the rue de la Rousselle.

La Basque, 13, rue du quai Bourgeois, is a local place which serves a four-course 40F *menu* (service and wine included) of Basque specialties. Main dishes mostly 20-35F, including many seafood plates. Closed Sun. and Mon.

La Lyre, 9, quai Richelieu, is one of the few affordable seafood restaurants around. Serves shellfish, *bouillabaisse, lamproie* (a regional specialty), and anything having anything remotely to do with the ocean, but it'll cost you 50F to try these delicacies. Closed Wed.

There are two university cafeterias (Resto U) in the downtown area: the **Central,** 42, rue Sauteyron, just off the place de la Victoire, and the **BEC,** 38, rue de Cursol, near the city hall (lunch 11:30am-1pm; dinner 6:30-8pm). Tickets for both locations are sold to French students in advance, ten at a time, at the Central from 9am-1pm (5F each). Foreign students can also buy them there, but at the unsubsidized price of 11F each, so you are much better off waiting outside one of the restaurants during a meal and buying a ticket from one of the local students. (Closed in summer.)

If you are around the Esplanade de Quimconces and feel in the mood for a few fresh oysters, go to **Huitres Brunet,** rue de Conde (closed in August).

Sights

Bordeaux's showpiece is its **Grand Théâtre,** whose vestibule and grand staircase influenced Garnier's Opéra in Paris. Though the building is lavish, performances are reasonably priced (operas cost 15 to 55F; other performances 20 to 60F), and students get 50% off except on opening night. The regular season runs October 5 through July 1.

The **Cathédrale St.-Andre** in the place Hotel de Ville is the most highly decorated building in town. Built in late eighteenth-century Gothic style, it is replete with flying buttresses, intricate stonework, and fanciful twin towers. The **Jardin Publique** was vandalized during the Revolution and subsequently used as a target range by the army; but from 1856 on, it was gradually renovated and redesigned in the English style. Today it is a lovely 25 acres of green in the center of Bordeaux, complete with a swim boat and botanical gardens. Museums are scattered throughout the town, but the two most important ones are both just behind the Mairie. The Musée des Beaux-Arts has a fine collection of French art, including works by Delacroix, Corot, Renoir, and Matisse. Open daily except Tuesday, 10am-noon and 2-6pm in summer, closes 5pm in winter; admission 3.20F, 2.20F with student ID, free on Wed. and Sun. The Musée d'Aquitaine has a collection of archeological treasures from the area, including the 2,000 year-old *Vénus à la Corne*. Open 2-7pm except Tuesday and Sunday; admission 2.50F, 1.50F with student ID. The museum also oversees archeological sites throughout the city, and you might want to visit some of these. (Ask at the tourist office for details.) Bordeaux is making a great effort to restore the city around the place du Parlement and you may be interested in a walking tour through some of these lovely eighteenth- and seventeenth-century streets. Tours leave daily at 10am from the tourist office (12F; two hours).

Bordeaux holds a musical festival in May, and during the summer there are concerts of all kinds (20F) at the Palais des Sports on cours Victor-Hugo, and comedies (35-45F) at the Theatre Femina on rue de Grassi. Information (tel. 90-91-60, extension or *"poste"* 1259) is in the Grand Théâtre (open 9am-noon and 2-6pm, Mon.-Fri. in summer; Tues.-Sat. in winter.

Near Bordeaux

To the southeast of the city, in the direction of Leognan, lies the beautiful 13th-century Chateau de la Brede (open daily except Tuesday, 9:30-11:30am and 2:30-5:30pm), home of the great philosopher Montesquieu (1689-1755).

On the coast lies Arcachon, long a popular seaside excursion from Bordeaux. The beach, a sandy stretch on a gulf just back from the sea, is crowded but beautiful. Try some excellent Arcachon oysters with a bottle of Graves. The syndicat d'initiative, place Roosevelt (tel. 83-01-69) is open daily 9am-1pm and 2-7pm. You can get information on hotels and restaurants here. In town there is a three-star municipal campground open Apr.-Oct. (tel. 83-24-15), and an IYHF Youth Hostel lies across the bay at Cap Ferret (tel. 60-64-62), open only in July and August. Miles of clean beaches and pine forests stretch southward from Arcachon. The huge dunes at Pyla-sur-Mer, 117 meters above sea level, are the largest in France. These resulted from a successful forestation project begun in 1788 by the engineer Bremontier.

The Dordogne

The small villages, medieval churches, and chateaux of the Dordogne lie between the Massif Central and the sun-baked Midi, nestled amidst rugged forests, mountains, and cliffs. Much of the area's charm results from its concealed isolation. Many of the buildings seem to be forgotten or cast away in the middle of the wilderness. Castle tops rise suddenly from the woods; church steeples—even an entire town such as Rocamadour—appear abruptly, carved out of a cliffside.

Only recently discovered by international tourists, this wooded and fertile region was the haunt of prehistoric man some thirty-five thousand years ago.

The grottoes and caves south of **Périgueux** have relinquished many of the traces of prehistoric man: flint and stone implements, carvings, and the incomparable paintings of horses and bison. The most famous of these, at **Lascaux,** are permanently closed to non-scientists to prevent further deterioration of the Cro-Magnon wall paintings, but others, near **Les Eyzies,** are still open and can transport you back through time.

You can strike your own balance with the ancient and the wild by sampling some of the region's age-old culinary specialties. The most celebrated of these are the expensive but delectable *truffes* (truffles); but *foie gras, confit d'oie,* and *confit de canard* (goose or duck, prepared in goose fat) are also renowned. All of these can be sampled in restaurants or purchased from *traiteurs*.

While the Dordogne's secretive towns are besieged by tourists in summer, the countryside remains pristine and reserved, and it's not hard to find villages that have escaped almost everyone's notice. All the main towns are linked by bus and train, yet the services are neither frequent nor convenient. In July and August, tourist buses travel from the larger cities through the valley, and to more remote spots such as Les Eyzies and Rocamadour. Périqueux, the region's capital, makes a good touring base for the Dordogne and is well-situated for trains to Les Eyzies and buses to Sarlat. Hitching can be a problem on the perilous gradients and bends of the small roads, but hiking and cycling are excellent ways to familiarize yourself with the area. The Dordogne also offers many *Sentiers de Grand Randonée,* clearly-marked, long-distance footpaths that form an extensive network through such cities as Limoges, Les Eyzies, Sarlat, Souillac, and Cahors. For help with itineraries or all kinds of information on the Dordogne, write the **syndicat d'initiative,** ave. de l'Aquitaine, Périgueux, 24000, Dordogne, France.

Périgueux

While Périgueux lacks the dramatic attractions of other towns in the region, it can be a welcome relief from the tourist-packed hot spots of the area and a good base for further explorations. The unique Cathédrale St. Front, with its domes and Greek coupolas, give the town a Mediterannean casualness, and the narrow shop-lined streets of the *vielle ville* and lingering twilights over the river make Périgueux an agreeable town in its own right.

Practical Information

Syndicat d'Initiative: 1, avé. de l'Aquitaine (tel. 53-10-63). Open summer Tues.-Sat. 8:30am-noon and 1-8pm: Mon. 9am-noon, 2-7pm; Sun. 9am-noon. Not very friendly, but efficient. From late June-Sept. they run three guided tours of the town for 10F each (in English on request).

Centre d'Information Jeunesse: 1, ave. de l'Aquitaine (tel. 53-52-81). Next to the syndicat, with tons of information on concerts, excursions, and other youth activities. Open Tues.-Sun. 2:30-6:30pm. Wed. and Sat. 9am-noon (closed Mon., and also Sat. in Aug.).

Office Départmental du Tourisme: 16, rue President Wilson (tel. 53-44-35). Abundant information on the Dordogne region and organized bus tours in summer to Les Eyzies, Sarlat, and several Bastide towns (tours 50-60F; some in English). Open Mon.-Sat. 9am-6:30pm in summer; closed Sun.

Post Office: ave. de l'Aquitaine (tel. 53-60-82) near the syndicat. Open Mon.-Fri. 8am-7pm, Sat. 8am-noon. Sun. 9-11am. Telephones available.

Transalpino tickets: Le Temps d'I Voyage. 11 cours Fenelon. Open daily 9am-noon and 2:30-7pm; closed Sun., and Mon. mornings.

Police (tel. 08-17-67). **Medical Emergency:** ave. de Paris (tel. 69-84-63).

Bike Rental: Au Tour de France, 96 ave. du Maréchal Juin (tel. 53-41-91). 25F for one day, 40F for two, with 100F deposit. For a racing bike, 35F, 50F, and 150F respectively. Also try **V. Huot Sports,** 41*bis,* cours Saint-Georges (tel. 53-31-56).

Car Rental: The most resonable rates are available at **Europcar,** 14, rue Dénis-Papin, right across from the station, with a special weekend rate (Fri. evening—Mon. morning) of 285F, unlimited mileage, You wouldn't want to bring a car to the already jammed streets of Les Eyzies or Rocamacour, but driving is a good way to see the *bastides* and smaller towns.

Train Station: rue Dénis-Papin (tel. 08-29-61). Direct, swift trains to Les Eyzies, Bordeaux, and Paris. To reach the center of town, turn right outside the station and bear left on rue des Mobiles-de-Coulmiers/Président-Wilson.

Bus Station: place Francheville (tel. 08-76-00). Modern and near the town center. Buses to Limoges, Bordeaux, and Brantôme; **Laribière Cars** (tel. 08-05-15) go to Sarlat and Les Eyzies from the station.

Telephone Code: (53).

Accommodations

Many hotel owners here close on Sunday, and others close up in August and go on vacation themselves. Opposite the train station you'll find clusters of glum hotels—three one-star look-alikes flanked by a zero star and a two star. All the one-stars offer singles for around 48F and doubles for 65F. (None accepts reservations.) The **Hôtel Terminus,** 20 rue Dénis-Papin and the **Hôtel du Midi** (tel. 53-41-06) next door are run by the same overworked family. They offer clean, pleasant rooms on a noisy street. Singles 48F, doubles 55F; and a good 38F menu. The **Hôtel des Voyageurs** at #22 offers no-frills accommodations with doubles from 45F. The **Hôtel de Quatre Chemins** (no telephone), on rue Maréchal Juin has singles in an old, wood-paneled house for 35F; but there is a curfew of sorts, since the owner insists on locking the door early at night.

To get away from the station, try the **Hôtel Lion d'Or** at 17, cours Fenelon (tel. 53-21-52) about fifteen minutes from the station near the center of town, with singles for 45F and doubles for 50F; breakfast 10F. Or try rue Eguillerie on the pedestrian section itself. The **Hôtel de L'Universe** at #3 (tel. 53-34-79) has rooms for 50-80F (often full) and the **Café de La Paix** at #12 (tel. 53-22-55) has a few at about the same prices and offers a large five-course meal for 35F.

The closest campground to the city lies 1.5km away—**Boulazac,** Barnabé-Plage (tel. 53-41-45), a two-star site on the river, with canoe rentals. Open all year. Take the city bus, destination Cité Belaire, from the cours Montaigne. **Lesperat,** camping-de L'Isle (tel. 53-57-75) is a three-star site, 3km from town on the route de Brive. Open summer only. Some farms in the region offer rooms or campgrounds. Get information from the syndicat d'initiative.

Food

The bustling outdoor daily market in the place du Coderc and the sprawling market on Wednesday and Saturday around the cathedral offer fresh produce and local delicacies. There are several *traiteurs* and *charcuteries* with delicious salads and specialties along the rue Limogeanne, and you can gather up your finds and dine among the Roman ruins of the Jardin Galo-Romain.

Lou Chabrol, 22 rue Eguillerie, is a friendly and elegant restaurant, and it offers good samples of the famous Perigord cuisine. The delicious, five-course at 50F *menu* is the only affordable option. Try the fricassée ris de veau (beef sweet-bread).

La Crêperie, rue Limogeanne. A cozy, friendly atmosphere with inexpensive if not wonderful food. Pizzas 12-17F, crêpes 5-15F, and ice-cream concoctions 10F. Great staff. Closed Mon. afternoons and Sun.

Lou Campagnard, 2 rue Lammary, a block down from the fancy shops of the rue Limogeanne, this cozy restaurant is full of regulars and serves a simple and filling meal for 28F, wine included.

Pizzeria Les Coupoles, place Daumesnil, across from the cathedral, has large pizzas from 12F and fresh pasta from 10F. Closed Sun. and Mon.

Phoebus, 11 rue Notre Dame, is a casual bar-restaurant frequented by young people. It offers a 30F menu, snacks, and large salads from 14F, and a wide selection of foreign beers, 5-16F.

Sights

Quite a few Gallo-Roman remains have been preserved over Périgueux's two-thousand-year history, including the **Tour de Vésone** which marks the center of the ancient city. The Roman **Arènes** is buried except for the stairwells and traces of the vomitorium (the arena exit) and is now encircled by a restful park. Périgueux can be spotted from miles away, marked by the white domes and four-story belfry of its **Cathédrale St.-Front.** The town's centerpiece is more remarkable for its shape than for its elegance. Built in the form of a Greek cross with great domes and cupolas, the Cathedral has retained a few elements of the original eleventh-century edifice, which was almost completely destroyed by fire in 1120. The western facade dates from this earlier period and does not harmonize with the rest of the building which has been transformed by restorations through the centuries. Free guided tours of the church are offered every day from 9am-noon and 3-5pm. For 10F you can visit the Cloisters and climb the dome.

The old quarter of Périgueux is full of narrow streets and fifteenth-century houses well-worth exploring. In late afternoon, the markets begin to close, and the dusty squares fill up with lively games of bowls. On the Allées de Tourny, the **Musée du Périgord** has exhibits on the region's prehistoric heritage. Skeletons and Stone Age implements are the most interesting part of the museum's collection, although artifacts from the town's Roman past, including some attractive mosaics, are also on display. (Open 10am-noon and 2-5pm; admission 2F). Excavations of Roman remains continue in Périgueux, and the **Villa de Pompéus** in the south of the city is quite interesting. The **Eglise St.-Etienne-de-la-Cité,** between the bus station and the Arènes, has been destroyed and rebuilt on several occasions during its troubled history. It remains an incomplete, but impressive, illustration of native Romanesque style.

You can kill your appetite by visiting the **Champion Foie Gras Factory** (pâté factory) at Château de St. Laurent-sur-Manoire on RN89, four miles out of town (tel. 53-69-00), and receive a guided tour around the *foie gras* production line (where part of the "production" process includes the cruel force-feeding of ducks).

On summer evenings, be sure to find out what's playing at **La Caverne,** 3, port de Graule off ave. Desmounil—a dim, vibrant dive that offers nightly concerts from July-Sept., featuring everything from jazz to regional music. It's best to buy tickets (30F) in advance between 3-6pm. Open Tues.-Sat. 9pm-2am.

Near Périgueux

Fifteen miles north of Périgueux lies **Brantôme**, a beautiful village which André Maurois called a "dream world." Still relatively unspoiled, the town is surrounded by a bend of the River Dronne, and all its buildings are quiveringly reflected in the water below. The architectural highlights include the **Pavillon Renaissance**, and a Romanesque abbey with cloisters and a splendid eleventh-century belltower.

The rest of the abbey buildings are now occupied by the town hall and by the **Musée Fernand-Desmoulin**, named after a local painter, which exhibits both his works and some prehistoric artifacts discovered around the town. (Open daily June 15-Sept. 15, 10am-noon and 2-6pm.) The town is also known for its weird sculpture in the **Grotte de Dernier Judgement**. But Brantôme's real beauty rests in its pastoral setting: one glance takes in the stone bridge, weeping willows, and a weir on the river—all perfect for a lazy afternoon or roadside picnic. The regular commuter buses leaving from the Gare Routière, place Francheville in Périgueux, also provide access to some interesting spots, such as **Lake Chambon** and **Villars**, where there is a cave with extensive stalactite formations (open July 15-Sept. 15 10-11:30am and 2-6:30pm). **Chancelade** has the remains of an abbey and a museum of religious art. Short bus rides make many castles accessible: at **Exicideuil**, the last ruins of a twelfth-century chateau compare with the fortified medieval castle at **Bourdeilles**, which also has a furnished Renaissance section. Most of the castles in the area disguise themselves as fortresses. By contrast, the seventeenth-century château at **Hautefort** is closer to the decorous pleasure domes of the Loire.

South of Périgueux, between Bergerac and Agen, are the **bastide towns**, about twenty-five small feudal fortress towns. Half were built by the English and half by the French in the thirteenth century, when both countries claimed sovereignty over the area. Yet the *bastides* share a common design—they are all composed with rows of rectangular blocks cut at right angles by narrow streets, and surrounded by squared ramparts. Many of these towns retain their churches, ancient houses, and much of their fortifications—**Monpazier** in particular and also **Lalinde, Villeneuve, Villeréal**, and **Puylaroque**. All are nearby and with a car or bike you can visit several in a day. Otherwise, take the weekly bus tour organized by the Périgueux tourist office (60F) which covers several of the more interesting *bastides*.

Les Eyzies

At the junction of the Vézère and Beaune rivers lies **Lez Eyzies-de-Tayac**, a small village framed by sheer chalk cliffs in which prehistoric man once carved out shelters. Since the discovery of the cave paintings and drawings at the turn of the century and the subsequent discoveries of the tools and weapons of Cro-Magnon man, Les Eyzies has become a center of archeological evacuation. Exit Cro-Magnon man stage left; enter modern archeologist and tourist stage right. Don't be deterred by tourist-packed streets and long waits for tickets—a look at these lingering symbols from the pre-historic past can be a unique and startling experience.

If you plan to visit, you must come as early in the day as possible (the 7:45am train from Périgueux arrives shortly before 8am; round trip 48F). From the train station, turn right and walk down the village's only street one kilometer to the center of town and another kilometer on the D47 to the legendary **Grottes de Font de Gaume**. These are the only caves of their kind in the world still open to the public. Inside you will find silhouetted drawings of horses, deer, and bison—very faint, but still a cause for wonder. The authorities protect the cave very carefully. Only twenty people are admitted at a time in small, closely monitored groups and at half-hour intervals daily during peak season. Admission 10F; 5F for those aged 18-25 and on Sunday. Because of these restrictions, and because many of the limited tickets are bought in advance by tour groups, the road to the Grottes is paved with hard-luck stories. If you're truly anxious to visit the caves, come here first thing in the morning. In midsummer, if you arrive by 8am, you'll probably get a ticket for an afternoon visit. The doors open at 9am, and you can return ten minutes before the forty-five-minute tour begins. Each group is led by an enthusiastic guide armed with a flashlight and a wealth of information. The Grottes are open May-Sept. 9-11am, 2-5pm; Oct.-Apr. 10-11am, 2-3pm; closed Tues. throughout the year.

While the Grottes display prehistoric paintings, its counterpart down the road, the **Grotte des Combarelles,** reveals dazzling prehistoric carvings. To get there, continue 2km past the Grottes de Font de Gaume. Visitors are admitted in groups of ten; the slightly rambling tour lasts thirty minutes and leaves at fifteen-minute intervals. Tickets are available at 8:30am for morning tours, 12:45pm for afternoon tours, and go quickly. Admission 9F, 4.50F students and Sundays; same hours as the Grottes de Font de Gaume.

Back in the town itself, the **Musée National de Préhistoire** exhibits a vast collection of artifacts, together with explanatory notes, photographs, and vivid reconstructions. There is even a small sample of cave drawings and carvings on display for those who don't make it into the caves, and in front of the towering museum a towering sculpture of a Cro-Magnon man looms over the valley. Open daily except Tues. 9:30am-noon and 2-6pm Mar.-Nov.; closing at 5pm Dec.-Feb. Admission 6F, 4F for students and on Sun.

Les Eyzies is linked to Agen and Périgueux by infrequent trains, to Sarlat and Souillac by weekly tourist buses. If you're waiting in the station with time to spare, walk two minutes to the left of the station to the somber, eleventh-century **Eglise de Tayac.**

Practical Information

Syndicat d'Initiative, place de la Marie, five minutes from the station (tel. 06-97-05), is very helpful. They provide an excellent list of caves in the area and advise you how to get limited tickets. In summer, they run tours through the museum and to far-flung places in the area. They also have information on area canoe rentals and horse trails. Open Mon.-Sat. 9am-noon and 2-6pm.

Post Office: Down the street from the syndicat. Open Mon.-Fri. 9am-noon and 2-5pm; Sat. 9am-noon.

Bike Rental: Bikes are available at the train station for 15F a half-day, 20F per day (150F deposit), or at the syndicat d'initiative for 25F a day; 40F for a ten-speed. Biking is an especially good idea here, since many caves lie 10km away, and the countryside is especially beautiful.

Telephone Code: (53).

Accommodations and Food

Hotels in Les Eyzies are relatively few and expensive; most require at least *demi-pension* (you pay for bed, breakfast, and dinner). Some rooms are available in private homes. In general, Les Eyzies isn't a good place to stay unless you reserve far in advance or camp.

Hôtel du Périgord (tel. 06-97-26) has thirteen rooms and a garden. Rooms 50F, *demi-pension* 66-113F; *pension* 103-150F. Open Mar. 15-Oct. 15.

Hôtel des Roches (tel. 06-96-59) has twenty smart, two-star rooms with a spacious garden. *Demi-pension* 97-130F; *pension* 102-134F. Open Mar. 15-Oct. 15.

Hôtel de France (tel. 06-97-23). All rooms have baths or showers. *Demi-pension* 90-130F, *pension* 135F. Open Apr.-Nov. 11.

Camping

The area is ideal for camping and there's usually plenty of room. **La Rivière** (tel. 06-97-14) is just out of town on the route de Périgueux. Take a left at the fork of the train station and continue just past the river. Cold showers, but cheap meals at the snack bar and canoe rentals on the river. 15F a night for two people and a tent. **L'Etang Joli, La Combe,** on route du Bugue (tel. 06-96-62) is 6km from Les Eyzies, with a restaurant and grocery store. There are more sites within 10km of town, as well as several farms on which you can camp. Ask at the syndicat for details.

Most hotels offer meals which are expensive and well prepared. The **Café de la Marie** serves inexpensive snacks and the **Auberge du Musée,** opposite the museum, serves a large and filling menu for 40F. A more imaginative option is to explore the **Halle Paysanne des Eyzies.** Located 500m outside of town on the route du Bugue, this rural shopping mall is full of tempting local produce on the ground floor (free samples available) and arts and crafts upstairs. A small market along the town's major street also offers plenty of food on Monday mornings.

Near Les Eyzies

The hills around Les Eyzies are pock-marked with caves, oddities, and rock formations, and as you travel northwest from the village along D47 you'll run across a series of roadside attractions. Most interesting of these is the **Grotte du Grand Roc,** which lies half-way up the chalk cliffs and which offers a splendid view of the Vérzère Valley (from the mouth of the cave). It has no cave paintings but contains some interesting stalactites and stalagmites. Open daily in July and Aug. 9am-6:30pm; otherwise daily 9am-noon, 2-6pm; closed Dec.-Mar. Admission 12F for the twenty-five-minute tour. Next to the Grand Roc, the **Laugerie-Basse** (open daily Feb. 15-Nov. 15, 9am-noon, 2-6pm; admission 6F) and the **Laugerie-Haute** (open daily except Tues., Apr.-Sept. 9am-noon, 2-6pm; admission 5F, 2.50F for students and on Sun.) display interesting cross-sections of accumulated layers of ground containing human remains and showing various epochs of habitation in the caves. Serious devotees of prehistory will not want to miss the **Abri du Cap-Blanc,** a collection of sculptures six kilometers from Les Eyzies (open July-Aug, 10am-noon, 2-6pm; closed Tues. and Fri. afternoons; admission 6F), and the **Grotte de la Mouthe** (open all year Tues.-Sun. 10am-noon and 2-5pm; admission 7F).

Sarlat

Until 1962, Sarlat was merely the quiet capital city of **Périgord Noir,** a town distinguished from the rest of Périgord only by its rock formations. But then the citizens of Sarlat began thinking hard, and working still harder, and in 1965—presto, Sarlat was a quaint, handsomely-recreated medieval community and an irresistible tourist trap. The stone of the renovated old quarter has been returned to its former glow. Small merchant shops have been reestablished and buildings here wear plaques stating the date of their construction. Visitors come in droves, and Sarlat can seem like one enormous gift shop. To experience the very real charms of these finely sculpted fifteenth-century hotels and half-timbered shops, wander during the early morning or late evening hours when tourists are fewest and the atmosphere is purest.

The *vielle ville* is neatly bisected by a modern commercial thoroughfare, the rue de la Republique, known locally as "la Traverse." To the east lies the sixteenth-century **Cathédrale St.-Sacerdos,** which gracefully combines both Romanesque and Gothic elements. Be sure to walk through the **cour du cloître,** where you can best see the progression of styles which begins with the twelfth-century tower of the facade. Around the back and up the hill, you'll find an area much less crowded and more intriguing. Look also for the **Bishop's Palace** and the **Maison de la Boétie,** where Etienne de la Boétie, a companion of Montaigne, was born. Built in the sixteenth century, the Maison's pointed gable and highly decorated windows exemplify the Italian Renaissance style.

Around the protected medieval city are narrow streets, unexpected passageways, ancient *Hôtels,* and lively merchants' stalls. On Saturdays, the whole town becomes one sprawling and colorful emporium, as the stalls of the weekly market mingle with craftsmen selling everything from sweetmeats to live trout. in July and August, there are also lots of arts and crafts exhibitions hidden away in churches and alleyways, and in mid-July Sarlat stages a month-long festival of musical and theatrical events (those held in the central place de la Liberté cost 30-70F; others cost 40F, with frequent student reductions).

Practical Information

Office de Tourisme, place de la Liberté (59-27-67), a busy but helpful office housed in the sixteenth-century Hôtel de Maleville. Offers comprehensive information on excursions, camping, bike tours, suggestions about walks and hikes, a room-finding service, and money exchange when banks are closed. Interesting daily tours leave from here and last an hour (8F). Open Mon-Sat. 9am-noon and 2-6pm; in July and Aug. open till 7pm and Sundays 10am-noon and 4-6pm.

Post Office: place du 14 Juillet (tel. 59-12-81). Open Mon.-Fri. 8am-noon, 2-7pm; Sat. 8am-noon. Telephones here too.

Train Station: ave. de la Gare, route de Souillac. To get to the center of town, walk downhill along the ave. de la Gare, turn right on ave. Thiers, and continue straight. For information call 59-00-21. To get to Sarlat from Périgueux or Les Eyzies, change trains at Le Buisson.

Buses: SNCF buses (rail passes valid) linking Sarlat to Souillac and small local villages, leave from outside the train station and place Pasteur, between the station and the *vieille ville.* During summer months excursion buses leave daily for Rocamadour, Les Eyzies, the *bastide* towns and elsewhere. You should reserve a place a day ahead at the tourist office. Tickets 50-70F.

Bicycles: Au Velo Dingo, 6, rue Fenelon. 25F. a half-day, 35F a day, 150F a week; deposit 100F. Identification required. Closed Sunday, but you can rent a bike from Sat. night to Mon. morning. Rentals also available at the station for 15F a half-day; 20F a day; deposit 150F.

Emergencies: Police (tel. 59-05-17); **Medical:** rue Jean-Le-Claire (tel. 59-00-72).

Telephone Code: (53).

Accommodations and Food

The best bet in Sarlat is the **Youth Hostel,** since most hotels are expensive and geared for at least *demi-pension.* In the summer, reservations are highly recommended for any hotels in the area. The tourist office keeps track of every available room in Sarlat and can also find you a room in a local home.

Auberge de Jeunesse (IYHF): 15*bis*, ave. de Selves, route de Périgueux (tel. 59-47-59) offers particularly spartan accommodations, but this is offset by a homey atmosphere and kindly director. 19F a night; sheets 7F; and bicycles rented for 15F a day. Kitchen available. Twenty minutes from the station, but only five minutes from the *vielle ville*. Follow rue de la République out of the old quarter and continue down ave. Gambetta. At the fork, turn left down ave. de Selves. No curfew. Open June-Sept.

Hôtel Marcel, 8, ave. de Selves (tel. 59-21-98), opposite the Youth Hostel. The cheapest rooms in town—rooms with a double bed 45F, other doubles start at 60F. Breakfast 12F, and a good 37F *menu*.

Hôtel du Commerce, 8, rue Louis-Mie (tel. 59-33-31) is only three minutes from the medieval quarter off ave. Gambetta. Small and cozy; rooms 50-65F.

Hôtel du Lion d'Or, 48, ave. Gambetta (tel. 49-00-83), just outside the *vieille ville,* has some rooms for 60F. Reserve well ahead.

Camping: Three large sites are within easy reach of Sarlat. The closest is **Les Perières** (tel. 59-05-84), half a mile out on the D47 road with space for 270 tents. It has its own swimming pool, tennis courts, game room, library, and bar, and rates are comparatively high. Slightly farther away (1½ miles) is **Les Accacias** (tel. 59-29-30) at La Canéda. Slightly less expensive, offering hot water and food. **Rivaux** is north of Sarlat (1½ miles) on D47 off of D6 (tel. 59-04-41), with hot showers.

There are plenty of attractive and inexpensive restaurants in the old city. The best deal is the **Restaurant Le Commerce** (different from the hotel) on rue Albéric Gabuet, which offers outdoor seating in a quiet square and a four-course meal for 29F. **Le Grain de Sel,** 3 rue la Boétie, has tables in a pleasant alley and a light meal for 32F. For local Périgord specialties, try the expensive, but very good **La Tour du Guet** on rue Rousset, west of the rue de la Républic, which has a huge *menu* for 43F. **La Crêperie du Presidial** is a quiet alternative to the busier spots of the *vieille ville,* serving meal crêpes for 7-14F and dessert crêpes for 5-17F, in an ancient timbered house. Open late during summer evenings. Follow the rue Salamandie from the Hôtel de Ville and turn right at the end by the Presidial.

Near Sarlat

Unless you have a car or bicycle, traveling here can be difficult unless you're willing to take one of the four buses which start running in July. But regular commuter buses do run between Sarlat and some nearby attractions. SNCF buses leave three times daily from place Pasteur and take about twenty minutes to reach Le Buisson. These buses can take you to **Beynac,** a village on the banks of the Dordogne. Here the austere castle perched on a hilltop presides over an entire region of fortress-topped hills. The wonderful view from the top includes the castles of Marqueyssac, Castelnaud, and Fayrac. An interesting Romanesque church in nearby **Carsac** (three buses daily; destination Souillac; fifteen-minute trip) merits a visit. Buses leave from the station and from the place Pasteur in Sarlat. For the walker, the syndicat has a booklet, *Les Chemins du Périgord,* discussing interesting hikes in the area.

Souillac

Souillac lies farther east along the Dordogne Valley, and it is a great relief from its more sensational neighbors. This quiet, medieval town grew up around a Benedictine abbey. Almost completely destroyed during the Hundred Years' War, and again in the sixteenth century, the Abbey was rebuilt in the eighteenth century. Its buildings have housed the town's administrative offices since the Revolution. Though it has witnessed plenty of destruction, the **Eglise Abbatiale** remains not only intact, but pleasantly light and spacious. The Romanesque east end of this pillarless building is particularly striking when viewed from the place de L'Abbaye. The church is crowned by three domed couplas, similar to the Byzantine-Romanesque cathedrals of Périgueux and Cahors. Most intriguing of all is the inner west wall of the church, with its carved figures of Joseph and Isaiah, and a bas-relief above the door depicting devils and fantastical monsters devouring each other. These were originally intended for the church's facade, but were moved after the facade was destroyed during the Wars of Religion. To the east of the Abbey rises the former belltower of the **Eglise St.-Martin.** The church was destroyed by the Huguenots in 1572, and the belltower, badly damaged, was left standing on its own.

Souillac is located in some of the most beautiful countryside of the Dordogne, and it is a good starting point for camping, biking, canoeing, and hiking expeditions, as well as for the usual excursions to Les Eyzies, Sarlat, and Rocamadour. Many good swimming sites along the Dordogne are an easy bike-ride away, and the 20km ride to Rocamadour, via Lacaue, is both scenic and relatively easy. In mid-July, Souillac hosts a modest, three-day **jazz festival.** Tickets are 40-45F for individual concerts, 80F for three days of events.

Practical Information

Syndicat d'Initiative: blvd. Louis-Jean Malvy (tel. 37-81-56). Helpful information on the town and its activities, as well as on excursions and hiking. Accommodations service. Open June-Sept., Mon.-Sat. 9am-noon and 2-7pm; Sun. 10am-noon; otherwise Mon.-Sat. 2-5pm.

Post Office: near the syndicat on blvd. Louis-Jean Malvy (tel. 37-78-21). Open Mon.-Fri. 8am-7pm; Sat. 8am-noon.

Train Station: A small station on the Paris-Toulouse line. To reach the city center, walk two kilometers down the hill on ave. Jean-Jaures bearing left; turn right on ave. Général-de-Gaulle at the bottom. To reach Rocamadour, take the SNCF bus from the station to St. Denis-prés-Martel (a half-hour ride costing 20F; rail pass good) and from there wait for the train to Rocamadour station. In Rocamadour you'll still have a 5km walk. Souillac is a regular stop on the train between Paris, Cahors, and Toulouse.

Buses: SNCF buses for Sarlat leave from outside the train station and from the Square Chapin, downtown, six times daily. Summer excursions to Les Eyzies, Rocamadour, Sarlat, and nearby caves cost from 60-75F; tickets and departures from the syndicat.

Bike Rental;: Au Velo Dingo, 10, rue de la Halle. 25F for a halfday; 150F a week; 100F deposit. Identification required. Ten-speed rentals more expensive. At the station: 15F a half-day; 20F a day; 150F deposit.

Canoe Rentals: Available from **Safaraid** at the camping de Lanzac on the river. 23F an hour, 95F a day or 440F for four days. Canoes can be dropped off at six points along the Dordogne and there are buses to bring you back to Souillac.

Police: (tel. 37-78-17); **Medical Emergency:** (tel. 32-78-17).

Telephone Code: (65).

Accommodations and Food

Hotels in town do not cater to the summer tourist invasion, and it can be difficult to find rooms in high season. The **Auberge du Puits** on place du Puits (tel. 37-80-32) is an attractive hotel with a few doubles at 50-60F; breakfast 10F. There is a reasonably-priced restaurant downstairs with a 34F *menu* (closed Nov.-Dec.). The **Hôtel du Beffroi** on place St.-Martin (tel. 37-80-33) is a tiny hotel-cafe nestled behind the Hôtel de Ville with five rooms at 30-100F. Campers should head for **Les Ondines** (tel. 37-86-44) on the banks of the Dordogne; or **Lanzac,** a quieter, less crowded site on the other side of the river next to the Pont de Lanzac, with canoe rentals available.

Most of Souillac's hotels offer sizeable *menus* for 35F. The restaurant of the **Hôtel du Beffroi,** on the place St.-Martin and called **Chez Jeanette** by loyal locals, offers the best deal around, with delicious *menus* at 26F and 35F. The **Hôtel de France** at 64, blvd. Louis-Jean Malvy offers a great four-course *menu* for 33F, while the **Grand Hôtel,** near the syndicat, has a 35F *menu* and a pleasant garden setting. Several *charcuteries* and food stores line blvd. Louis-Jean Malvy, and a large market is held Monday and Wednesday mornings at the place l'Halle. The first and third Friday of every month brings the Farmers' Fair to town, and booths selling nuts, herbs, and flowers, honey, live trout, and duckling spring up around the streets of Souillac.

Near Souillac

Traveling southeast on the D43 through the highly scenic Dordogne valley, you will come to a breathtaking view of the **Château de Belcastel,** clinging tenaciously to an outcrop of rock above the town of Lacave. Although the Château itself is not open to the public, you can wander freely around the terrace and chapel beside it and enjoy the striking panorama as you approach town. In Lacave itself, the petrified **Grottes de Lacave** offers one-hour guided tours (17F) complete with elevator and electric train through "twelve fairyland halls." These caves also feature stalactites, mirages, and some prehistoric remains. Open from Apr.-Oct. 8am-noon, 2-6pm; in Aug. 8am-7pm. For information call 37-87-03. Excursions to Lacave are available from Rocamadour and Souillac.

Rocamadour

Rocamadour proudly announces itself as the *"deuxième site de France"* (the second-best tourist attraction in France—the first is officially Mont. St. Michel). All of this town has been built into the side of a sheer cliff face. Its miraculous setting is perfectly suitable, as Rocamadour has long been renowned for its marvels, miracles, and revelations. Along with Rome, Jerusalem, and Santiago de Compostella, Rocamadour is one of the major pilgrimage sites in the Western world. Kings and popes flocked here, and pilgrims were convinced that a city defying gravity must be obeying some higher laws.

Rocamadour has been blanketed in myths and legends ever since a mysteriously preserved body was unearthed near the Chapel of the Virgin. Some maintained that it belonged to a local hermit who came to live out his life on the rock, while others were convinced that it belonged to Zaccheus, one of Jesus' followers. Some were sure that the name of the town meant "the Rock of St. Amadour," while others believe that it was derived from *roc amator* (lover of the rock). Whatever the explanations, Rocamadour is a strikingly beautiful cliff village. It is still the site of an annual pilgrimage (the week of September 8) and a Mecca for camera-toting tourists.

To reach Rocamadour, most visitors drive or take tourist excursion buses, but the town is accessible by train from Brive-la-Gaillarde (or from Souillac, take the SNCF bus to St. Denis-près-Martel to get on the same train line). To reach the town from the train station, you must walk 5km along a winding country road (hitching isn't easy because the passing cars are stuffed with tourists), but it's a pleasant trek through quiet fields and farmlands. It takes about forty minutes. When you come to the intersection near the camping area and the Hospitalier (you should leave your car here), take the pedestrian route through the Porte de L'Hôpital down toward the city—it affords the most stunning approach and the best view of the craggy town.

The only thing harder than getting to Rocamadour is getting lost once you're there—the town has only one curling, crowded street running parallel to the rockface between the river and the sky and defended at either end by two of the town's eight thirteenth-century fortified gates. Ascending steeply beside this street is the **Escalier des Pèlerins,** a staircase with 216 steps which pilgrims still climb on their knees in penance. The staircase leads to the **Cité Religieuse,** consisting of a fortified **Evêché** (bishop's palace) which stands before the **Basilique St.-Sauveur,** a massive eleventh-century edifice. Nearby stand the **Chapelle Miraculeuse,** where countless generations of pilgrims have come to offer thanks for miracles and salvation, and the **Chapelle St.-Michelle** with a beautiful fresco of the annunciation. Above the door of the Chapelle Miraculeuse is an antique sword plunged into the stone and reputed to be the legendary sword of Roland. Dotted around the churches are free exhibitions, crypts open only to those on guided tours, and a **Musée Tresor** containing items related to the sanctuaries (open daily April-Oct. 9am-noon, 2-6pm; admission 5F).

Still higher up—accessible by the zigzagging pathways through the trees—is the **Château,** first built in the fourteenth century to protect the pilgrims below and now inhabited by the chaplains of Rocamadour. The only reason for climbing up is the exceptional view of the valley and the town that the ramparts afford. Open Apr.-Oct. 9am-noon and 2-7pm; in Aug. 9am-7pm. Admission 3F. You can take an elevator (5F up, 7.20F return), but it only takes you to the mid-point, the Cité Religieuse). Try and see Rocamadour early in the morning when you will have it almost to yourself, or late at night when the sheer rock face is beautifully lit up against the stars.

Practical Information

Rocamadour has two **syndicats d'initiative:** one at the Hospitalier, on the road from the train station; the other, central one, in the Hôtel de Ville on the only street (tel. 33-62-59). The central office is open Easter-Sept. 10am-noon and 3-6pm, except Mondays; in July and Aug. both offices are open daily 10am-noon and 3-8pm. Both sell useful brochures and have a room-finding service. Rocamadour has no banks, but you can change money at the central syndicat. Since Rocamadour is a small town, it is much better suited for day trips than for longer stays. Inexpensive rooms are hard to find. In July and August you can call 33-62-80 for hotel reservations, and the syndicats can usually find a room if there are any left. It may be worth trying the tiny **Hôtel du Touriste** (tel. 33-62-33) with six rooms at 50-60F and a terrace overlooking the valley. Also try the **Café du Globe** (tel. 33-63-18) with similar prices. The **Hôtel Terminus** (tel. 33-62-14) offers one-star rooms for 60-126F, and the **Hôtel Lion d'Or** (tel. 33-62-04) has singles for 43F and doubles for 50F. The **Hôtel**

Belvédère (tel. 33-63-25) is 1 km above the town and commands a wonderful view. Rooms cost 72-115F. Reserve in advance for all these hotels.
There are several campgrounds nearby, and some campers set themselves up in nearby open fields. **Camping Lafajadou** (tel. 33-63-57) on a plateau just below town, has a snack bar and usually plenty of room. **Relais du Campeur** (tel. 33-63-28) above Rocamadour at the Hospitalier, is better equipped, with hot showers and a food store, but it lacks the proximity and view of the other campgrounds.

Food in Rocamadour is not particularly cheap or well prepared, but several less-expensive restaurants offer *menus* for 38F and have terraces overlooking the Alzou Canyon. One of the better restaurants is **Chez Anne Marie**, with a decent 38F *menu*, quick service, and a terrace lined with medieval flower pots. Crêpes and sandwiches are sold all along the street, and there is one small *épicerie*. During the summer (the only time Rocamadour really functions) there are concerts regularly in the Basilique.

Fifteen kilometers from Rocamadour and ten kilometers from the train station is the **Gouffre de Padirac**, which contains some of the most remarkable and enchanting natural formations of any cave in Dordorgne. The hour-and-a-half tour brings you down steps and elevators and along an underground river by boat to progressively larger and more impressive chambers. Padirac is open daily Easter-Oct. from 9am-noon and 2-6pm, and from 8am-7pm in Aug. (tel. 33-64-56 for information). There are a couple of hotels and a campground, but Padirac makes a better daytrip by bike or car. Excursions to Padirac leave twice a week from Rocamadour (35F) and there are excursions, including both Rocamadour and Padirac, from Sarlat and Souillac (60F).

Cahors

South of the Dordogne Valley lies Cahors, the quiet and attractive ancient capital of Quercy. Green hills surround Cahors, and the waters of the river Lot enclose and reflect this lovely town. The most remarkable structure of the town is the **Pont Valentré**, a fortified bridge whose elegant towers and arches once welcomed pilgrims and repelled invaders. The bridge, constructed in the fourteenth century, is known as the **Pont du Diable** because legend has it that the architect bargained with—and tricked—the devil in order to construct it. To revenge himself after failing to obtain the architect's soul, the devil repeatedly toppled the central tower, and when a nineteenth-century architect replaced the tower he added a sculpture of the devil trying to push the tower over.

Cahors has several fifteenth-century hotels in the *vielle ville* surrounding the **Cathédrale St.-Etienne**, particularly the **Maison de Roaldès**. Like the church at Souillac, the cathedral is built around three domed coupolas, but the imposing facade gives it more the air of a fortress. The beautifully sculptured portal of the north facade represents Christ's ascension. The interior is constantly under restoration, and the white arches of the nave are mostly covered, but you can still see the contrasting Gothic arches and rose windows of the choir. To the right of the choir you can enter the **Cloister,** a badly damaged but beautiful example of flamboyant gothic, which provides a good view over the domes of the cathedrale. The **chapelle musée**, next to the cloister is worth the 3F admission to see the weirdly realistic fresco of the Last Judgment painted on its arches. The cathedrale and museum are open everyday 9am-noon and 2-6pm. In mid-July, Cahors hosts a brief **Festival de Blues**, with tickets 40F for each concert. If you want to paddle along the Lot, the syndicat has a lot of canoe routes and rentals.

Practical Information

Syndicat d'Initiative: place Aristide Briand (tel. 35-09-56). Offers bundles of information on area camping, canoeing, and a book of suggested routes for hiking and bicycling as well as a guide to exploring regional wines. Tours of the *vielle ville* leave here twice daily in summer and cost 6F. Open 8:30am-noon and 2-6:30pm, except Sun.

Post Office: rue Wilson, between the Pont Valentre and the syndicat. Open Mon.-Fri. 8am-7pm; Sat. 8am-noon.

Train Station: A small station on the Paris-Toulouse line, forty-five minutes from Souillac. To reach the center of town, turn right from the station on ave. Jean-Jaurès and turn left at rue Wilson, a ten-minute walk.

Buses: Leave from in front of the station to Souillac, Sarlat, and Toulouse. Limited excursions are organized by **Voyages Belmon**, 2 blvd. Gambetta (tel. 35-59-30).

Bike Rental: Combes, 117 blvd. Gambetta (tel. 35-06-73).

Telephone Code: (65).

Accommodations and Food

Cahors doesn't cater to the usual crowds of invading tourists, and a hotel room can be hard to find in August. The **Foyer des Jeunes Travalleurs**, rue Frédéric Suisse (tel. 35-55-36) often has places in summer; or try **Mon Auberge**, 261, rue Jean-Jaurès, a few blocks from the station, which offers doubles (with slightly lumpy beds) for 50F and a good *menu* for 38F, including a well-stocked salad bar. By the cathedral, the **Hôtel de la Paix**, place Galdemar, is a large hotel with singles for 40F and doubles for 50-65F.

The **camping municipal** (tel. 35-04-64) lies five minutes from the syndicat. Follow rue Gambetta across the Pont Louis Philippe, and it's right on the river bank. Open all year. The large Cahors market is held on Wednesday and Saturday mornings in front of the cathedral, or you can buy groceries at the Monoprix by the syndicat.

Marie Colline, 3, rue St. Pierre, is a vegetarian restaurant on a quiet alley off of rue Foch. It serves good soups, souffles, salads for 12F, and 18F for plat du jour. Closed Monday and Tuesday, **Le Palais**, 12, Gambetta has simple omelettes for 14F, large salads for 20F, and a garnished plat du jour for 28F. For dessert, try the extravagant ice cream treats and rich chocolate cakes at **Le Chantilly**, 69, rue Gambetta. You can try the well-known red wine of Cahors in local restaurants or wine stores; or else get a list of vineyards from the syndicat and visit the local *caves*.

The Languedoc

The Languedoc has never been very comfortable with Parisian rule, and it's easy to see why: this is a hardy, southern land, and its people are as much Spanish as French in looks, accent, and tastes. Since the region fell under French domination after the thirteenth-century Albigensian War, policies set in the northern capital have often disrupted local craft traditions, leading to poverty and resistance. The area has clung with proud aloofness to its socialist tradition, and the newspapers on the stands today—*L'Humanité, La Dépêche du Midi*—are the direct descendants of nineteenth-century journals founded by Jean Jaurès and other famous socialist leaders.

Southwestern regionalism continues, centered around the ancient *langue d'oc*. Banned by French leaders in the sixteenth century, the language has undergone a renaissance and is becoming officially recognized. High school students may now take one of their university qualifying exams in *langue d'oc*, although there are still stories of children being forced to wear dunce-caps for speaking in their native tongue. The justifiable claim remains that the southwest is not getting its fair slice of the French governmental pie, and political resistance continues to be almost a way of life.

Despite its gruff political exterior, the Languedoc is a land of beauty and history. The rugged hills yield sweet fruit and wines, and a strong Mediterranean influence throughout the Middle Ages has created styles of art and architecture completely different from those in the north. In this region you'll find some of France's finest museums.

Toulouse has been for centuries the political and cultural center of the Languedoc, and it remains a good base for touring the nearby cities: **Auch,** capital of Gascony, a mysterious land lost in the past, renowned for fine cuisine and fiery drink, *Armagnac;* **Castres,** birthplace of Jean Jaurès and home of the Goya Museum; and **Albi,** with its giant basilica and childhood home of Toulouse-Lautrec. Further south is **Carcassonne,** the double-walled medieval city restored by Viollet-le-Duc, and **Perpignan,** capital of the once-Spanish province of Roussillon. Amongst these cities the terrain varies considerably and is united only by a rugged, unspoiled beauty.

Transportation in the region will take you dependably to the major cities and not much farther. Robert Louis Stevenson explored the area on a donkey, but you should avoid the pain in the ass. The hilly countryside makes cycling difficult and the sparse traffic reduces hitching possibilities, but it is relatively easy to explore both the city and country areas by foot. The people of the Southwest are generous and helpful, and the region is one of the least expensive in France.

Be adventurous in sampling southwestern cuisine, and it will reward your pallet without breaking your budget. The most popular local dish is *cassoulet*, a mixture of white beans, pork and goose, and other stews abound. *Roquefort* and *St. Nectaire* are tangy, fermented cheeses, and all sorts of luscious fruits come from the Garonne Valley. Don't forget to wash it down with a glass of one of the sweet, full-bodied red wines of Languedoc-Roussillon.

Toulouse

Toulousains know their city as *"la ville rose,"* which aptly describes both its architecture and its politics. Largely constructed out of brick, Toulouse glows pink in the morning, red in the heat of the midday sun, and mauve as night begins to fall. Of the city's 400,000 inhabitants, 150,000 are students, and they have not failed to make their mark on the city, most noticeably in the political sphere. Toulouse is the capital of a political region known as *le midi rouge,* and this city has traditionally voted for left-wing candidates. A more conservative streak has recently emerged in 1971, when Toulouse elected its first non-socialist mayor since the turn of the century—but tinges of red are still apparent everywhere, as the graffiti all around the city boldly declaims.

In many ways, the city's radical leanings represent a statement of opposition to strong central rule from Paris, both culturally and economically. After becoming a major commercial center for the Roman Empire and then the capital of the Visigoth kingdom in the fifth century, Toulouse entered into an era of cultural splendor in the ninth century only to be crushed by the French kings in the thirteenth century (after the Albigensian War). Slowly the *langue d'oc* faded until the Edict of Villers-Cotterets in 1539 legally imposed the northern *langue d'oeil* upon the reluctant region. Today, *langue d'oc* has been revived by the traditional *Occitan* societies and has become a major element of Toulousain separatism.

In the last half-century, Toulouse had developed a reputation for poverty, partly owing to governmental neglect and partly owing to a huge influx of immigrants: Spaniards in the 1930s, Jews from Central Europe in the 1940s, and Maghrebs since the 1950s. You'll even see a sizable Asian population here, which is rare in other parts of France. The poverty has not been entirely overcome, and it is in parts unnerving, but the city has made great progress in the last decade. Along with its vast student population, this cultural diversity paradoxically gives Toulouse a vitality and a solidarity which other French cities often lack.

The center of France's aero-space industry (local hero Ste.-Exupéry used to fly from here to Africa), Toulouse is a major transportation center for the southwest, but those who come here simply to change trains are missing some of the finest religious art and architecture in France. The **Basilique St.-Sernin** is a brick-and-stone Romanesque marvel, **les Jacobins** is a striking example of the *gothique du midi*, and the **Musée des Augustins**, set in a former convent, houses a superb collection of religious sculpture. Other fine churches and elegant Renaissance hotels line the narrow streets of the city.

Practical Information

Toulouse sprawls widely on both sides of the Garonne valley, but the museums, churches of interest, and important sights are located within a compact section in the center of the town near the place Wilson and the place du Capitôle. From the train station, walk down the broad allées Jean-Jaurès to the place Wilson and turn right on rue Lafayette to reach the syndicat.

Syndicat d'Initiative: Donjon du Capitôle, rue Lafayette (tel. 23-32-00), in the little park behind the Capitôle. Brisk and efficient office. Free accommodations service, English-speaking. Runs excursions (45-50F) to places of interest nearby. You can change money here on Saturdays, 2-5pm when banks are closed, and buy tickets for local buses and trains. Open July 1-Sept. 15, daily 9am-7pm; closed Sun. the rest of the year.

Post Office: 9, rue Lafayette, opposite the syndicat. Open Mon.-Fri. 8am-7pm, Sat. 8am-noon.

Train Station: blvd. Pierre-Sémard (tel. 62-50-50 for information). Trains run regularly to Paris, Bordeaux, and elsewhere.

Bus Station: 68, blvd. Pierre-Sémard (tel. 48-71-84), next to the train station. Connections to Albi, Castres, Carcassonne, Moissac, and other cities of the region. For information (tel. 23-11-02).

Hitching: For Carcassonne: take bus #2 to RN113. For Paris: take bus #10 to start. For Auch, Bayonne: take bus #64 to RN124. For Albi: take bus #16 or 19.

Police: (tel. 23-11-22). Medical Emergencies: (tel. 49-33-33).

Women's Center: Claire Maison, 43, rue Jean de Pins (tel. 42-03-72).

Laundromat: rue Héliot, near the station. Also at 20, rue Cujas; open 7am-9pm daily.

Telephone Code: (61).

Accommodations

There are plenty of inexpensive hotels near the train station; try rue Caffarelli, off allées Jean-Jaurès. The area is quite sleazy, though, and the *concierges* tend to be suspicious or even hostile. (Be sure to find out about curfew regulations.) Numerous hotels are also scattered around the stylish shops in the center of town.

Auberge de Jeunesse Villa des Rosiers (IYHF), 125, ave. Jean-Rieux (tel. 80-49-93), Mediocre Hostel quite far from the center, with slightly dirty conditions. Take bus #22 (direction Côte Pavée) from the train station. A Hostel card is required, and a fine of 3.50F per day is added if you forget to pack up before 9:30am. 20F per night, sheets 8F. Breakfast 7F.

University Housing: In the **Cité Universitaire Daniel Foucher,** by the Parc des Sports on an island in the Garonne. Take bus #26 from place Jeanne d'Arc to the final stop by the Casino Supermarket; follow the allée H.-Seller across the bridge and turn right to the dormitories. Very lively in the summertime, and plenty of rooms available; 16F per night. Or try **Foyer Sonacotra,** 118 ave. de Fronton (tel. 47-62-58); or **Foyer San Francisco,** 92, route d'Espagne (tel. 40-29-28). Call beforehand in either case. The syndicat has a list of private homes and hostels that will accommodate women.

Hôtel Splendid, 13, rue Caffarelli (tel. 62-43-02). By far the friendliest and most wholesome place around. Rooms are clean and very quiet; there are a couple of singles at the top of the building for 40F. Otherwise, doubles 60F. Breakfast 10F, no showers except in rooms. Closed July. Down the street at #15, try **Hotel Régence** (tel. 62-74-26) which has a single for 35F, doubles 39F. Breakfast 7.50F, showers 8F.

Hôtel St.-Antoine, 21, rue Saint-Antoine (tel. 21-40-66), just off place Wilson. Rooms are large and clean. The tattooed owner and his bulldog ask 45-50F for a room with a double bed. Breakfast 12F, showers 8F.

Hôtel Grand Balcon, 8, rue Romiguieres (tel. 21-48-08). A large, 60-room, two-star hotel with a few very small cheaper rooms. Well-located, about 15 minutes from the station. Friendly proprietor, nice lobby and reception. Singles 38-54F, doubles 54-68F. Breakfast 11F.

Nouvel Hôtel, 13, rue du Taur (tel. 21-13-93) has just changed management and was entirely redone two years ago. All rooms have double beds and run 50-90F. Breakfast 10F, showers 10F.

Camping: there are excellent campgrounds outside the city: **Pont de Rupe,** ave. des Etats-Unis (RN20 south), chemin du Pont de Rupe (tel. 70-07-35), is the municipal site; reachable on bus P. **Les Violettes,** on RN113 after Castanet (Deyme) (tel. 73-51-46), is a four-star extravaganza; and **La Bouriette** is a two-star site at St.-Martin-du-Touch along the RN124, at 201, chemin de Tournefeuille (tel. 49-19-20).

Food

Largely because of its student and immigrant populations, Toulouse is crowded with inexpensive and interesting restaurants of all varieties. There are outdoor markets in the various squares which can equip you for picnics in the luxuriant Jardin Royal or Jardin des Plantes. Many budget restaurants are located off the Place du Capitôle.

Auberge Louis XIII, 1*bis,* rue Tripière. Tucked away in a quiet street off the pedestrian rue. St.-Rome. Entry through a lovely tangled garden. A student hang-out. *Menu* at 27F. Open noon-2pm and 7-9:45pm; closed Aug.

La Table Ronde, 59, rue Pargaminières. Beautiful place with a pleasant atmo-sphere. Often plays are performed here at night. *Menu* 40F, main dishes 17-45, and a lunch-time *menu* for 28F. Service charge 13%; the house wine is good and inexpensive.

Au Coq Hardi, 6, rue Jules-Chalande off St.-Rome. Popular with students, tradi-tional family-style meals. *Menu* 26F, four-course meal 45F. Closed Sat. night and Sun. The **Restaurant de la Corde** at #4 features an intriguing approach through a courtyard and up a winding staircase, as well as a 37F *menu;* closed Sun. and in Aug.

Crêpe Joyeuse, 20, place Victor-Hugo. Crêpes Lolita, crêpes Love Story, (etc. 5-13F), *steak haché* (14-16F). Closed Sat. lunch, Sun., and in Aug. **La Crêperie,** 39, rue St.-Rome, is in an ancient cave and stays open till dawn; closed Mon.

Le Tunis, 85, rue Pargaminières, two blocks off place du Capitôle. Tunisian specialties 22F, *couscous,* 20-45F, service 10%. The **Sidi Bousaid** at #9, rue des Lois, serves similar food at slightly lower prices. They also have Algerian and Moroccan wines, but the decor is nothing special, and you may find yourself the only non-Algerian here.

Le Pharaon, 18, rue Pharaon. In a former abbey. The atmosphere is medieval, yet very funky. Theater or music at night and helpful bulletin boards. A student hang-out. Lunch *menu* 26F. Dishes 24-30F. Closed August.

Les Filatiers, 42, rue des Filatiers. On a pedestrian road which is a continuation of rue St.-Rome. Take a table outside and watch the passersby as you enjoy your 23.50F menu.

Sights

Start your ecclesiastical tour of Toulouse with the majestic **Basilique St.-Sernin,** possibly the grandest Romanesque church in France. The oldest part of the church, the brick west facade, is deceptively dull. Inside you'll find an elegantly proportioned, low-roofed church with long transepts and five rounded chapels, all surmounted by a five-story octagonal tower which be-came the symbol of Toulousain power. Note especially the **Porte Miégeville** by the north transept, with a panoply of sculpture by twelfth-century masters whose expression and movement is very close to Gothic, and demonstrates how advanced the local artists already were. While looking at the interior of St.-Sernin, bear in mind that the arcaded gallery level (above the side aisles) was used to accommodate the thousands of pilgrims who would stop here on their way to Santiago de Compostela in Spain. The massive supporting piers lead to a wealth of sculpted and painted decoration on the upper levels, most apparent in the bays of the nave near the choir. The ambulatory, choir, and chapels are still closed for renovation, but they should be reopened by the end of this year. There are very useful guided tours of the Basilica daily at 3pm in the summer.

Just down the rue de Taur is the **Eglise Notre-Dame-du-Taur,** originally known as St.-Sernin-du-Taur after St. Saturnain, the first Toulousain priest, who was martyred in 250 A.D. by being dragged through the city by bulls *(taureaux)*—hence the name *du Taur*. His name was corrupted over the years to St. Sernin, and his remains were long ago moved to the crypt of the Basilica. The church itself is an oddly short Gothic structure with a line of supporting columns down the middle, but the stained-glass windows are a very fine subdued blue. Step across the street for a view of the defense tower above the frieze on the west facade.

If the Basilique St.-Sernin is one of the finest examples of a southern Romanesque church, **Les Jacobins,** on the rue Lakanal, holds that honor for southern Gothic, or the *gothique du Midi*. (The name of the church derives not from the radicals of the French Revolution, but from a monastic order founded some eight centuries earlier.) The exterior is plain brick with thin buttresses, but the interior is majestic and lively. A row of thin columns divides the single nave into two unequal aisles; amber colonettes run up the columns and from the light vaults while creating a beautiful multi-color effect against the light stone. On the column closest to the curved east end, the ceiling pattern looks like an enormous spider. Note how the tall stained-glass windows (actually a twentieth century addition) seem to shine red on one side of the nave and blue on the other.

For 1F, you can enter (from the northwest end of the church) the cloister, *salle capitulaire* and chapel of St.-Antonin. The **cloister** is again representative of the region with its red-tiled roof supported by wooden beams sloping down to the courtyard. The thin supporting double columns stand at right angles to the frieze and give an interesting effect of airiness. Take your time to enjoy the restfulness of the cloister and to appreciate (from the far side) the fine view of the octagonal tower. The **chapel** is a Gothic addition notable for its decorated plaques over the intersection of the vaults. The *salle capitulaire* repeats the decor of the main church with its many colors and thin columns; weekly piano concerts are held here on summer evenings with tickets from 25F available at the syndicat. The church is open daily 10am-noon and 2:30-6:30pm; closed Sunday mornings.

The **Musée des Augustins** (entry on rue Metz off the rue Alsace-Lorraine) houses an unsurpassed collection of Romanesque and Gothic sculpture, mostly from Toulousain churches. Situated in a former Augustin convent that closely resembles Les Jacobins, this extremely elegant museum of brick and glass has probably the finest collection of Romanesque capitals anywhere— note especially the fifteen gargoyles (some winged) from another former abbey, Les Cordeliers, which burned to the ground in the nineteenth century and was largely pillaged. Drainage water flowed down the troughs of the gargoyles' backs and out their gaping mouths. Also superb is the collection of statues of Apostles from the local church La Daurade. The museum is open daily except Tues., 10am-noon and 2-6pm, Wed. 2-10pm; admission 7F. The **Musée de Vieux Toulouse,** on rue de Moy, is open June-Sept., daily except Sun., 3-6pm, Wed. 2:30-5:30pm (admission 5F).

Toulouse's secular buildings are also worthy of attention. In the seventeenth century, the pastel-blue dye produced in Toulouse lost out to the indigo coming from the Indies, and Toulouse lapsed into decline. Before that, however, Toulouse was a prosperous city, and every dye merchant built his own mansion *(hôtel particulier)*. Over fifty of these have survived, and many have recently been restored from their state of neglect. Perhaps the finest is the **Hôtel d'Assezat,** in the place d'Assezat, rue de Metz, which has a lovely courtyard (imagine it without the grime) where the bright color of brick contrasts with the almost white stone. Other hotels are scattered throughout the city, but you can do just as well by walking the narrow streets of old Toulouse (bounded by the rue Pargaminières, the rue de Metz, the rue d'Alsace-Lorraine, and the Garonne) and ducking into the courtyards of the various buildings—invariably they are elegant brick constructions with pleasant gardens. One interesting exception is the **Hôtel de Pierre,** rue de la Dalbade, an imposing grey stone building in the Neoclassical style.

Toulouse has a most interesting **Monument aux Morts,** dating from the end of World War I, at the intersection of rue de Metz and blvd. Lazare Carnot. Instead of glorifying one heroic soldier, a panel on the interior of the arch portrays the confused and helpless throng being herded to its destruction. Most of the city's green space is concentrated in the area south of here. You couldn't find a calmer or healthier park than the **Jardin des Plantes,** or the more formal **Jardin Royal** across the street. Both are shady havens with plenty of benches and even a few drinking fountains. For bicyclists seeking a bit of greenery, the **Grand Rond** unrolls into the allée Paul-Sabatier, which takes you to the Canal du Midi.

During the summer (July 1-Sept. 15), the syndicat organizes excellent tours of the city (12F). Tours around the historical monuments begin Mon.-Fri. at 9:30am; visits to Les Jacobins begin Mon.-Fri. at 3pm; walking tours of the city start Sat. and Sun. at 3pm.

Despite its abundance of students, Toulouse is often quite subdued at night. Most buses stop running by 10pm, and the ones that do continue double their fares. There are plenty of clubs, discos, and cafe-theaters, however, in the area around rue St.-Rome and rue d'Alsace-Lorraine; though many are private, others charge about 20F for non-members. For film fanatics, there are over a dozen cinemas clustered around the place Wilson, with three specializing in serious, artistic films. The syndicat can provide you with a list of *ciné-clubs* and information on summer concerts held in the Cathedral, cloisters, and churches (tickets 20-50F). If you just want to take in the nighttime air, seek out a cafe in the smaller squares of old Toulouse. The favorite student bar is **Le Toulouse-Lautrec** on rue Pargaminières, and **Le Cafe Belger** on 25, blvd. de Strasbourg offers more than a hundred kinds of beer. Bear in mind, though, that the popular cafes around place Wilson and blvd. de Strasbourg charge twice as much as smaller places half a block away in less action-packed neighborhoods.

Auch

Auch, pronounced to rhyme with "gauche", is the center of the ancient duchy of **Gascony,** a gnarled and forested region which never fully shed its medieval cloak. Hidden away in the rolling foothills north of Tarbes, Gascony seems to have been forgotten by time and by Paris. Auch is the commercial center for the sparsely settled countryside, and is the only city in the area.

Auch occupies a superb hilltop site, and presents fourteenth-century **Tour d'Armagnac,** a former prison, and the craggy **Cathédrale Ste.-Marie.** The river **Gers** divides the city into two sections known as the Lower and Upper Towns. From the train station is the Lower Town, turn left down the ave. de la Gare, and then turn right down rue Voltaire. Follow this street as it changes name and crosses the river to the Upper Town. Turn left on blvd. Sadi-Carnot, and walk along the river until you come to the **escalier monumental,** a formidable staircase which seems to lead towards the heavens. In the middle stands a statue of the most famous of Louis XIV's musketeers, d'Artagnan, who was born near Auch in 1615, and later immortalized by Alexander Dumas and Hollywood alike.

The Cathedral, on the square at the top of the staircase, is an elegant piece of flamboyant Gothic constructed in the late fifteenth and early sixteenth centuries. The west facade and square towers, in classical style, were added a century later, but with such care and elegance that they harmonize perfectly with the rest of the structure. Note how gently the pointed arches seem to emerge from the supporting columns; also notice the unique flat-arched design of the triforium level (in between the lower arches and upper windows), another Renaissance touch.

The masterworks of the Cathedral are the ornately carved choir stalls, made of oak soaked in the Gers for thirty years, then dried and carved by unknown local craftsmen who doubled as monks. There are more than fifteen hundred figures in all: the large upper figures (labeled) depict biblical characters, the lower ones mythological beings, and the scenes on the short stairways depict the life of Christ. The altarpiece dates from the Renaissance, but hardly seems out of place. (Admission to the choir is 2F.)

The creator of the fourteen stained glass windows of the apsidal chapels is better known: Arnaut de Moles, a local sixteenth century painter. The vivid combination of colors is most striking, and closer study reveals a deep expression of emotion in the figures—this is flamboyant Gothic at its ornamental best. Admission to the Cathedral's treasure is free, but you have to ask to see it. Try to convince your guide to take you up the winding stairs for a view of the Cathedral from above; while you're at it, ask him to take you for a walk on the roof of the Cathedral. The Cathedral is open daily 7:30am-noon and 2-7pm; the choir is open 8am-noon and 2-6pm; 9am-noon and 2-5:30pm in the winter.

The **Maison de Gascogne,** on rue Gambetta, is a mall in which regional crafts and specialties (largely culinary and alcoholic) are exhibited and sold during July and August (open 9:30am-12:30pm and 3-7:45pm). You can sample, for free, baked goods such as the flaky *croustade,* practically dripping with sugar, and the fiery *armagnac,* the Gascon answer to Cognac, somewhat sweeter and rather more herbal. By making the entire tour of the lower level, you should be able to get about eight free tastes of *armagnac* and *floc d'Armagnac,* the local version of *pineau.* Upstairs, from July to September, there are exhibitions of regional art, and each one of the twenty local towns occupies a small booth in which it seeks to seduce tourists. The **Musée des Jacobins,** on rue Charras, has, among a collection of regional arts and crafts, a selection of rare furniture from Auch, all set in a former convent. Open Tues.-Sun. 9am-noon and 2-5pm; admission 5F, students 2.50F.

To drink in Auch's timelessness most fully, walk through the narrow hillside streets surrounding the Cathedral. From the place Salinis, follow the narrow road which leads under the medieval **Porte d'Arton** to the **pousterles,** homicidally steep and narrow ancient stairways—watch your step going down. Walk back to the Gers for a pleasant picnic on the banks of the river.

Practical Information

Syndicat d'Initiative: place de la République, opposite the Cathedral (tel. 05-22-89). Open daily 9am-noon and 2-6pm; closed Mon. Free sporadic tours (usually on summer Saturdays) of the Cathedral in the morning, and of the museum in the afternoon.

Post Office: rue Gambetta. Open Mon.-Fri. 8am-7pm, Sat. 8am-noon. Telephones here too.

Train Station: ave. de la Gare. Information, reservations, and tickets open daily 5:15am-7pm. There are five trains daily to and from Toulouse (1½ hours, 28F). For more distant destinations (such as Montauban or Lannemezan) you must make bus connections just outside the station.

Police: (tel. 05-24-11). **Medical Emergencies:** ave. des Pyrénées (tel. 05-11-10).

Telephone Code: (62).

SAMU: (tel. 05-33-33). Ambulance.

Accommodations and Food

Most of the hotels cluster on the ave. de la Marne near the place de Verdun, just three minutes from the train station.

Foyer des Jeunes Travailleurs, Grand-Garros (tel. 05-34-80). From the station, walk left on the ave. de la Gare, right on route de Pessan, and left on the rue Augusta. Singles for 35F. Call before making the 20-minute walk from the station.

Hôtel de la Gare, ave. de la Gare (tel. 05-23-81). Turn right on leaving the station. A little decrepit, with communal washbasins in the corridor. Singles 37F, doubles 45F. Closed Sat. and Sun.

Hôtel de Paris, ave. de la Marne (tel. 05-01-23). Larger, more expensive, but plush. Singles from 48F, doubles from 58F. Restaurant downstairs offers menus from 37F. The **Hôtel la Marne** across the street has 40F singles, doubles at 60-70F, with optional *pension* (includes wine). Their menus start at 35F.

Camping: Île St.-Martin: (tel. 05-00-22) A three-star site by the river, amidst trees, about 2km from the town. Cross the river, turn left, and follow this course. Near the Maison des Jeunes et de la Culture.

Looking for budget food in Auch is like searching for costume jewelry in Tiffany's; you might as well resign yourself to paying a little more than usual and, perhaps, getting a very good gourmet meal. Try some of the specialties of the region: *cêpes* (mushroom puffballs), *poules-au-pot* (chicken), *tourins à l'ail* or *à l'oignon* (garlic or onion soup), *garbures* (a tripe dish), *palombes* (ring-doves), *confits* (conserves—of goose, etc.), *maigrets* (the lean parts of the duck), and *patis gascon* (apple or plum cake). Alternatively, you can sample some of the cheaper pates at the *charcuteries* and some of the local melons and prunes at local fruit vendors. On Thursdays, the Lower Town operates an open market on ave. Hoche until 3pm. The Upper Town holds their own market Saturdays until 6pm, right beside the place de la Liberation in front of the Cathedral.

Les Trois Mousquetaires, 5, rue Espagne, off place de la République. Menu at 40F (excluding service and wine). *Couscous* for 40F.

Chez Bébé, 1, place Betclar, off rue Lamartine near the Cathedral. An archetypal French restaurant filled with appreciative locals. The four-course menu at 34F offers several regional specialties.

Galerie Poisson d'Or, 24, rue Daumesnil, opposite the museum. Serving tea and cakes only, this combined gallery, children's library, and tea-shop has a large, unkempt room where children can play at being Cezanne. Open Tues.-Sat. 2-8pm.

Restaurant "Le 54": place Puits-de-Mothe, around the corner from the museum. Hamburgers, crêpes, and omelettes (6-15F). Outdoor tables.

Restaurant Le Rimbaud: 7, rue des Grazes. Has a 38F menu. Try the *specialitees gasconnes* (23-60F).

Albi

From afar, Albi is a city of red-tiled roofs on the banks of the Tarn, dominated by its two monotonously red-bricked giants: the **Palais de la Berbie** and the **Basilique St.-Cécile.** Those who enter these two monoliths will find explosions of luminous color; the former contains the **Musée Toulouse-Lautrec,** and the latter has an interior covered with enchanting decorative work. Other treasures are scattered around the weaving lanes of the old quarter at the foot of the Cathedral, in the medieval and Renaissance buildings where artisans still practice hard trades and soft sells.

Practical Information

Syndicat d'Initiative: 19, place Ste.-Cécile (tel. 54-22-30). Changes money on Mondays, when all local banks are closed. Also has a blackboard listing hotel vacancies. Open in July and Aug., daily 9am-7pm, rest of year daily except Sun., 9amnoon and 2-6pm.

Post Office: place du Vigan (tel. 54-17-85). Open Mon.-Fri. 8am-7pm, Sat. 8amnoon.

Bus Station: Place Jean-Jaurès.

Train Station: At the end of ave. Maréchal-Joffre (tel. 54-05-63). Open daily 5:30am-10:30pm. About ten trains daily make the hour-long trip to and from Toulouse. To reach the center of town, follow the ave. Maréchal-Joffre and the ave. de Gaulle.

Police: (tel. 54-12-95). **Medical Emergencies:** Centre Hospitalier, rue de la Berchere (tel. 54-25-87).

Telephone Code: (63).

Accommodations

Albi attracts droves of tourists, so its few hotels fill up very quickly and have little incentive to go out of their way to be friendly. Reserve well in advance if you wish to stay here, or commute from more accommodating Toulouse.

Maison des Jeunes et de la Culture, 13, rue de la République (tel. 54-20-67). Provides hostel-like lodging, with lock-outs, without curfew, and open to all. 14F a night including shower, breakfast 7F and other meals 18F. Overflows with activities and bulletin boards, though the setting is rather gloomy. Open 7am-4pm, with evening check-in at 8pm.

Hôtel la Regence, 27, ave. Maréchal-Joffre (tel. 54-01-42). One block from the station. A little expensive, but worth the difference. Good, large, well-ventilated rooms. The proprietor is unusually friendly. A room with double bed costs 37-75F, breakfast 10F.

Hôtel Lyonnais, 6, rue Docteur-Camboulives (tel. 54-05-48). On the place Vigan, the main square. Rooms with double bed 45F for one, 65F for two. Breakfast 10F, showers 8F. Reserve well in advance.

Hôtel du Marché Couvert, 52, rue Emile-Grand (tel. 54-04-90). In the middle of the marketplace, only a block away from the Palais and Cathedral. Quiet, ordinary rooms. Singles 45F, doubles 60F including shared showers. Breakfast 10F. Closed Nov.-April. A similar zero-star hotel, located in the midst of Vieil Alby, is the **St. Clair,** rue St.-Clair (tel. 54-25-66), with rooms from 42-60F, showers 6F.

Camping: The **Parc de Caussels** is a 300-place site, located 2km east of Albi on the D99. Hot showers available, swimming pool nearby. 25F per pair.

Food

Albi lends its own unique flavor to some of the typically hearty dishes of this region: *cassoulet, pâtés,* and *tripes.* If you try the bon-bon known as "la Brique du Vieil Alby," you'll find out why. Remember that a typical Albigensian stew should be washed down by the local *Gaillac* red wine. You might want to explore the large indoor market on place St.-Julien, and picnic in the appealing Parc Rochegude.

Auberge St. Loup, 26, rue de Castelviel, behind the Cathedral. Local specialties served in a medieval inn with intimate atmosphere. *Menu* 40F, entrees 8-33F. Those especially brave might want to try the *gras double* (made with sheep intestines)

Le Vieil Alby, 25, rue Toulouse-Lautrec, in the old quarter. *Menus* for 35F and 48F. If you're feeling rich, try the *cassoulet,* 45F. Closed Sun.

Restaurant Couronne, 77, rue Croix Verte, off the lices Georges-Pompidous. Less expensive than the restaurants in the tourist area. Simple, unpretentious family cooking, and the 25F *menu* includes wine (but not service). Closed Sat. night and Sun.

La Tartine, 17 place de l'Archevêché, opposite the cathedral and museum. Specializes in tea, salads, and desserts. Try the filling *salade tartine* (9F), or the *pêche sorbet.* Perfect for a light lunch in the sunshine.

Sights

Albi is a place of pilgrimage for those interested in Henri Toulouse-Lautrec, aloof chronicler of Paris and beloved son of Albi. Born to an aristocratic family, Toulouse-Lautrec turned poster-painting into an art form and created storms of controversy with his unique interpretation of form and color, his low-life subjects, and his often savage view of French life. Until his early death at the age of 37 in 1901, he remained apart from the Impressionist circle and far from the public's taste—for this reason, the collection of works gathered by the artist's assiduous mother and housed in the **Musée Toulouse-Lautrec** is the best anywhere. It contains all 31 posters and nearly 600 sketches and rough drafts. It's interesting to see that as the drafts grew less rough, their visions grew more so, becoming grimmer and uglier as the artist reworked them. The museum wisely starts with a room devoted to pictures of the artist by himself and by those who knew him; you need only see this squat, sadly comic figure to understand the source of Toulouse-Lautrec's remoteness and bitterness. An aristocratic midget who was exiled to the sidelines of Parisian society, his paintings portray the melancholy languor of Gay Paris. Upstairs is a fine collection of art by Lautrec's contemporaries, showing the magnitude of his influence on French painting; and every summer the museum also features an extensive special exhibition (in 1980, of Impressionist paintings from Chicago, in 1981 of the works of Miro). The museum is situated within the **Palais de la Berbie,** which also contains a chapel and a few archeological exhibits. While in the museum, be sure to walk out onto one of the balconies, which claim dazzling views over all the walls, bridges, and gardens of Albi. (The museum is open July-Sept., 9am-noon and 2-6pm; in winter open 10am-noon and 2-5pm and closed Tues. Admission 10F, students 5F; there are guided tours for 4F). Devoted fans of Toulouse-Lautrec can visit the artist's birthplace, the

Maison Natale de Toulouse-Lautrec, in Vieil Alby (open 9am-noon and 3-7pm in summer only; admission a steep 10F, 8F for students).

Next to the Musée Toulouse-Lautrec is the imposing **Basilique Ste.-Cécile,** presiding heavily over the entire town. Built in 1282 after the victorious crusades against the heretical Cathars in the Albigensian War, the Basilica was designed to serve as a fortress as well. The exterior features huge defense towers rising some five hundred feet above the Tarn and virtually solid walls unbroken by windows of any size. The interior is a perfect example of the *gothique du midi,* a design which recalls the classical style of church-building and suggests the strong Italian influence in the area. This is also apparent in the rich decoration of walls, ceilings, and arches, which were painted by Italian artists and embellished by the carvings of Burgundian sculptors in the early sixteenth century. In the summer, lighted and guided tours of the Basilica take place at 9pm (6F; regular guided tours leave regularly and cost 5F). The vast organ, the largest in France, was finally restored in May 1981, and you can occasionally hear performances on it.

The loveliest sight in the area, however, is **L'Eglise** and **Le Cloître St.-Salvy.** Strangely ignored by visitors, the church has an orthodox grandeur softened by the radiant violet light of its stained glass windows. The cloisters outside reflect a similar balance between dusty stonework and glorious floral colors, and are equally peaceful.

A pathway next to the entrance to the Cathedral leads to the narrow pedestrian streets of **Vieil Albi,** where several craftsmen exhibit their trades and wares in a somewhat touristy atmosphere. The prices are steep, but you can always just watch or look at the timber-framed houses. For a different picture of working Albi, cross the Tarn—here in the working-class section, the town retains its old flavor from years of neglect.

Albi entertains a number of festivals and celebrations during the summer. The **Feu de la St.-Jean** on June 24th kicks off the season with dances and a giant log fire, and the **Festival du Théâtre** takes place during the first two weeks of July. By far the most important occasions are the six-day **Festival International du Film Amateur 9-5mm,** with a busy agenda of screenings and banquets during the first week of August (tickets free at the tourist office); and the **Festival de Musique,** a fine series of concerts, operas, ballets, and even flamenco guitar recitals. Concerts are most often held in the beautiful and intimate courtyard of the Palais, or in the Cathedral (tickets cost 30-100F and are usually sold out in advance). The Bureau de Festival is set up just inside the gates of the Palais for ticket sale from July 6-August 5 (tel. 54-97-88; open daily 10am-noon and 3-6pm). Even if you miss Albi at its most festive, there are often small exhibitions and free concerts all around town.

Near Albi

About a kilometer away from Albi on the route to Cordes is the **Verrerie Ouviére,** 146, ave. Dembourg, one of the most famous socialist monuments in France. Here Jean Jaurès, in his finest hour in 1896, led the striking glass-workers of Carmaux, 17km to the north, in the construction of their own cooperative factory. Last-minute financing from two syndicalist groups and a large donation from Mme. Dembourg, an Albi resident sympathetic to the workers' cause, made the dream possible. Today the Verrerie Ouvrière has a thriving business, a new plant, and still plows back an unusually large share of benefits to its employees. There is a small **museum** documenting the strike and the history of bottle-making and a superb statue of Jaurès by the entrance. You can visit the factory; though fully automated and much changed since 1896, it will show you why Jaurès called glassworking "a small journey into hell every day." The workers all live in the neighborhood, since the machine run 24 hours without stopping and the workers come in for irregular eight hour shifts. The museum's hours are equally irregular, and it caters primarily to groups. Call before coming (tel. 60-67-70); it's quite likely that they'll be glad to let you see it.

Continuing down the road another 15km, you'll come to the little walled medieval city of Cordes. Buses leave Albi at 7:45am and 5pm from the bus station (Place Jean-Jaurès, tel. 56-00-12). There is one one-star hotel in town and a campsite nearby: *Camping le Moulin de Julien* (tel. 56-01-42), 1km out of town on the road to Gaillac.

Albi is perched at the western tip of the **Vallée du Tarn,** a large, outstretched district of cliffs, forests, and quiet little towns. **Le Château du Bose** is in a forest 45km from Albi (open from Easter to All Saints' Day), and is the place where Toulouse-Lautrec spent a happy childhood. At the other, eastern end of the Valée is **Millau,** gateway to one of France's most overwhelming natural wonders, the **Gorges du Tarn.** The region is accessible only by excursion buses, cars, or bicycles. Experienced equestrians can follow a trail that leads for several days through the heart of the Vallée, while novices can rent horses by the hour. Local artists offer intensive two-week courses in detailed craftmanship (contact the syndicat in Albi for details).

Castres

Castres is most famous for its native son, the famous socialist leader Jean-Jaurès. Leaping into prominence in 1896 as leader of the striking glass-workers of Carmaux, Jaurès vociferously joined other socialists, notable Emile Zola, in defending Captain Dreyfus, and you can see a copy of *J'Accuse*, Zola's open letter to the President of the Republic affirming Dreyfus' innocence. After the turn of the century, Jaurès fought a losing battle against rising militarism in France, and sought in vain to avert war by organizing an agreement between the French and German working-classes. In 1914, his position as a beleagured Gandhi-like martyr was sealed when he was assassinated in a Parisian cafe. His funeral attracted greater numbers than almost any other in French history, and his name is given to a prominent street in nearly every city in France.

Practical Information

Syndicat d'Initiative: place Alsace-Lorraine, across from the Jardin (tel. 59-92-44). A friendly place which distributes tasty sweets for free. Full of information on the National Park nearby, its mountains, lakes, and suggested itineraries. Open 9am-noon and 2-7pm; closed Sun. and Mon. morning in summer, also closed Mon. afternoon the rest of the year. May move to a new location in summer '83.

Post Office: blvd. Alphonese-Jain, near the syndicat (tel. 59-28-54). Open Mon.-Fri. 8am-7pm, Sat. 8am-noon. Telephones here too.

Train Station: ave. Albert 1er (tel. 59-22-00). Six trains daily make the hour's journey from Toulouse. To get to the center of town, follow ave. Albert 1er to the left and continue until the fork when you turn right down blvd. Henri-Sizaire to the Jardin de l'Evêrché.

Bus Station: place Soult (tel. 35-37-31). Buses run regularly to Toulouse, Carcassonne, and Albi.

Banks: All local banks are closed on Mondays, and there are no alternatives for changing money.

Police: (tel. 59-49-86). **Medical Emergencies:** blvd. Maréchal-Foch (tel. 59-24-00).

Telephone Code: (63).

Accommodations and Food

The least expensive hotels are located opposite the train station. Try the Regina (tel. 59-21-61), 38.50F for one person, 50F for two; with shower 45F and 55F. Carcasses at 3, rue Auque (tel. 59-04-97) is even less expensive, but you'll have to do without a shower (30F per person and 5F for breakfast). If you wish to sleep in a chateau surrounded by 27 acres of land, contact M. and Mme Piquot, Parisot 81110 St.-Avit (tel. 50-30-57). The castle has fourteen rooms and is run by an English lady (90F complete *pension;* all meals are vegetarian, but in the off-season meat is cooked on request). Minimum stay is six nights and there are no shower facilities, but you can always go for a swim. The chateau lies 20km east of Castres, on the road from Soual to Dourgne.

Hôtel Splendid, 17, rue Victor-Hugo (tel. 59-30-42), in the middle of town. Well-maintained. A room with a double bed 45-70F; breakfast 10F, communal shower 6F. Closed Sun.

Hôtel du Perigord, 22, rue Emile-Zola (tel. 59-04-74). One block away from Hotel Splendid. Large, unusually fine rooms, most of which have two beds. Singles 45F, doubles 55F. Restaurant downstairs offers 35F, 50F menus.

Camping: Municipal, two stars, 140 places, ave. de Roquecourbe (tel. 59-56-49). Near the center of town, by the side of the river.

A large market convenes every morning till about 12:30pm on the place Jean-Jaurès. Your best bet is to buy food here and picnic in the shady Jardin de l'Evêché. Try the local *roquefort* and *bleu* cheese (both very sharp) and the milder *brousse,* also the tangy goat's cheese.

For eating out, try rue d'Empare (plenty of good restaurants with menus for 45F, or the rue Malpas. **Le Languedoc,** on the route de Toulouse near the station, has *menus* from 28F. For a lighter meal, try **Les Sarrasines,** 34, rue Villgoudou. Enjoy some crêpes (6-18F) and salads (7-16F) in a decor of lavender and lace.

Sights

Castres' two greatest monuments display a consistent theme; one commemorates a pacifist, while the other exposes the atrocities of war. The first is the **Musée Jaurès,** packed with pamphlets, trenchant political cartoons, old photographs, and faded newspaper articles that catch all the flavor of Jaurès' spirited, often bitter rhetoric, and reveals as much about turn-of-the-century France as about the Socialist pacifist himself. Nevertheless, from the collection of his school reports to his postcards, his bed, and endless drawings of his arresting bearded face, Jaurès' remarkable life is movingly displayed.

Next door is the **Musée Goya,** which boasts a splendid collection of Spanish paintings from the early Catalonian and Aragonese masters to a portrait of Philip IV by a student of Velazquez. But the museum's claim to fame is its bevy of Goyas. These span a period of over fifty years, and include a disarming self-portrait, in which Goya wears a benign and bemused Ben Franklin gaze, as well as *La Junte des Philippines,* his largest canvas. *Les Désastres de la Guerre* portrays the pathos and horror of the Napoleonic Wars, while the forty etchings of *Tauromachie* focus starkly on moments of terrible violence during bullfights—their cumulative effect is savage. Most interesting of all, perhaps, are the *Caprices,* nightmarish drawings of fiends prettying themselves and corrupting one another; the horror of these depictions, as Baudelaire remarked lies in the fact that the grotesque monsters are unmistakably human. Both museums are in Castres' Hôtel de Ville, or **Palais de l'Evêché,** which stands at the head of the beautiful and impeccably manicured **Jardin de l'Evêché,** designed by Le Notre before he was commissioned for Versailles. (Open daily 9am-noon and 2-6pm; opens Sun. at 10am in July and Aug; closes 5pm and on Mondays in off-season. Admission 5F, students 3F.)

Castres was once a major textile center, and from the **Quai des Jacobines** you can get a fine view of the medieval merchants' houses across the River Agout. Here lived the tanners, dyers, and spinners; the wooden galleries were used for drying, while the arched entryways opening into the river allowed for easy shipment. Today there is little of the industry left in Castres, and the dilapidated houses are undergoing extensive renovation.

Castres hosts a two-week **Recontres Internationales de la Guitare** starting the second full week of July. There are courses, workshops, and lectures during the daytime, and public concerts at night. Instructors include virtuosos like John Williams and the repertoire ranges from flamenco to jazz and classical guitar to Japanese koto, making it well worth attending. Concert tickets are 60F, 50F for students. For information on attending the Master Classes, write in May to **Service Animation,** Maire de Castres, 81108 Castres (tel. 59-12-43 or 59-62-63). Castres also stages smaller festivals of Occitan culture (in June), Bach (September), and French music (October).

Around Castres there are many important granite quarries, and the **Sidobre,** only 15km away, is famous for its weird, irregular rocks, in particular the wobbly Roc de l'Oie. This makes a good day-trip by bike, or by hitching along ave. de Sidobre. Sidobre is at the northwest corner of a large National Park, the **Parc Natural Regional du Haut Languedoc,** which is seldom visited but is starkly beautiful, full of lakes, and well-prepared for campers and hikers. On its western edge are the rugged **Montaignes Noires.** The most convenient base for visiting these is **Mazamet** (syndicat tel: 61-37-07), a town with several restaurants and hotels, accessible in 25 minutes by train or thumb from Castres.

Carcassonne

The **Cité de Carcassonne** is a thirteenth-century Disneyland: a double-walled, fortified city with towers and turrets rising from a steeply-walled plateau in the Garonne Valley. It is one of the most famous architectural follies in all of Europe. An agglomeration of fortifications from Roman times to the thirteenth century, Carcassonne fell into disrepair after the Wars of Religion, and had been so thoroughly pillaged by villagers seeking material to build their own houses that little more than a few crumbling walls remained. In 1844, Viollet-le-Duc, the famous architect and chief of the newly-created government section of historic monuments, decided to restore the ancient fortress. If Viollet's grandiose visions were not matched by his attention to historical detail, he nevertheless created a living and popular museum of medieval urbanism.

The Cité is perched above the *ville basse*, the ordinary town of modern Carcassonne, nicknamed, inscrutably, "La Pucelle du Languedoc" (the Virgin of Languedoc). Most shops, offices, and hotels—as well as the train station—are situated down in the regular town; to get to the Cité, you'll have to walk about 3km along steep streets. From the station, follow ave. Jean-Jaurès to the left, turn left at square Gambetta (a central park), and continue over the bridge

Pont-Neuf. Once on the other side, just follow the signs until you reach the citadel Cité.

Syndicat d'Initiative: blvd. Camille-Pelleton, place Gambetta (tel. 25-07-04). Follow ave. Jean-Jaurès from the train station. Open Mon.-Sat. 9am-noon and 2-6:30pm, to 8pm in summer; Sun. 10am-noon. You can change money here when the banks are closed. The syndicat has two annexes: one at **port du Canal** near the station (open July 1-Sept. 15, daily 8:30am-noon and 4:30-6:30pm); the other in a magical grotto in the **porte Narbonnaise,** to your right as you enter the Cité (open July and Aug., daily 9am-8pm, Sept. 9am-noon and 2-7pm; tel. 25-68-81).

Post Office: rue Jean-Bringer. Open Mon.-Fri. 8am-7pm, Sat. 8am-noon. Telephones here too. There is also a post office in the Cité, off rue de Vicomte Trencavel, open Mon.-Fri. 9am-noon and 2-6pm.

Bus Station: Blvd. de Varsovie (tel. 25-12-74).

Train Station: Behind Jardin A. Chenier (47-50-50). Carcassonne is a major train stop between Toulouse (45 minutes away) and points east.

Bike Rental Bourrouñet, 12*bis,* rue Auguste-Comte (tel. 25-66-64).

Police: (tel. 25-19-01). **Medical Emergencies:** route de St.-Hilarie, D342 (tel. 25-60-30).

Telephone Code: (68).

Accommodations

The Youth Hostel is located (miraculously) in the very middle of the Cité, yet its 10pm curfew prevents you from enjoying the Cité after nightfall. If the Hostel is full, you'll have to find a hotel in the Ville Basse—the ones in the Cité are exorbitantly expensive.

Auberge de Jeunesse (IYHF), rue du Vicomte Trencavel (tel. 25-51-60), within the walls of the Cité. Bed and breakfast 26.50F, sheets 6F. Some kitchen facilities, but not enough—you'll have to rely on the rather expensive food stores nearby. Often full, Hostel card required. Open 7:30am-10am and 6-10pm.

Camping: Stade Albert-Domec (tel. 25-11-77), on the Aude and Canal du Midi, with 500 places. Or try the three-star **Les Larandières-Pennautier,** less well-located (tel. 25-41-66).

Hôtel St. Joseph at 81, rue de la Liberté (tel. 25-10-94) is just five minutes from the station in the midst of Carcassonne's entertainment district, and offers clean, large, well-maintained rooms and a friendly management; no singles, double beds 40-50F, rooms with two beds 60-70F, breakfast 8F, showers 5F.

Hôtel Bonnafous, rue de la Liberte #40 (tel. 25-01-45), a bit shabby and small, but makes up in friendliness and information. The owner is an expert on ancient Mediterranean peoples and will talk about it for hours. He'll speak to you in English, but you'll have to speak French. Rates are set in dollars: $7, 8, 12 and 13 for 1, 2, 3, or 4 people respectively. Showers are 9F, breakfast 8F.

Hôtel Trivoli, same street at #37, is also small, but amiable. Singles 49F, doubles 58F, and breakfast 10F.

The **Astoria,** 18, rue Tourtel (tel. 25-31-38) is near the station and doesn't charge for an extra person in the room; or try **Le Cathare,** 53, rue Jean-Bringer (tel. 25-65-92) in the middle of town. The **M. J. C. Centre International de Séjour** is a *foyer* at 91, rue Aimé-Roman (tel. 25-86-68) that sometimes has rooms available for 21F a night, 60F *pension*.

Food

The restaurants within the fortress-like Cité are varied and inexpensive. Most serve the regional specialty, *cassoulet* (a stew of white beans, pork, goose, duck, and sausage). The ingredients vary, but every good *cassoulet,* so they say, is followed by violent gastric reactions the following morning. For provisions, try the market in place Carnot (known as "place aux Herbes") on Saturday mornings.

There are many restaurants in the Cité along Cras Mayrevieille with menus under 30F (not including service). In the Ville Basse, there are inexpensive restaurants all around the blvd. Omer-Sarraut; and **Le Splendid,** rue Courtejaire (end of the street past the theatre), offers a 24F menu that includes wine, service, and three courses. Or try:

> **L'Ostal des Troubadours,** 5, rue Viollet-le-Duc in the Cité. An absolute delight: the rooms are full of colored streamers and lights. The atmosphere is very warm and the food is excellent value for the money, especially when accompanied by the nightly music. *Menus* at 24 and 39F (excluding service). Open daily 11:30am-4pm and 6pm-3am.

> **Le Vieux Four,** rue St.-Louis in the Cité. Same management as L'Ostal, and an almost identical *menu* (with *menus* 26F and 39F excluding service), but the food and service come across as a poor imitation. Next door, try **Le Comte Roger,** where you can still have *cassoulet* and two other courses for under 35F. Closed Mon.

Sights

Occupying a strategic position on the road between Toulouse and the Mediterranean, the original fortifications at Carcassonne date back to the Roman Empire in the first century and the Visigoths in the fifth century. The idea of a double-walled fortress came from the defense-works first seen by the French in Palestine during the Crusades, and double-walled fortresses were employed by the Toulousain Raymond Counts during the Albigensian Wars against the northern French leaders. Withstanding sieges against the forces of Charlemagne and Simon de Montfort, the city's military importance later lapsed, and it was neglected until Viollet-le-Duc arrived to save it.

You can spot the different epochs of construction by walking through the grassy *lices* (formerly used for jousting tournaments) between the two sets of walls. The bottom layers of the inner wall, with their rather haphazard arrangement of brick and stone, date from the earliest period, which the odd-shaped towers with rounded fronts and flat backs date from the Visigothic era. The upper layers of thicker, flatter stones and the taller towers date from the thirteenth century, as does the entire outer wall of fortification. In various places you can spot the crumbled remains of a former tower; were it not for Viollet-le-Duc, all of Carcassonne would look like this. Viollet was a master of medieval engineering. The intricate arrangement of wooden beams supporting the turrets, for example, or the massive arches and buttresses. The blue slate roofs used for the towers of the inner ring of fortresses are so out of place amid the red-tiled roofs of the Midi that local authorities have recently embarked on a scheme to re-roof using local materials.

Entrance to the *lices* and outer walls is free, but to visit the thirteenth-century **château Comtal** and the inner towers you will have to take the guided tour from the château gates within the city. Tours (conducted only in French) leave regularly from 9-11am, 2-5pm, and at 9pm, last an hour, and can be about as exciting as watching the grass grow. Admission 9F, 5F for those 17-25years of age with ID, and on Sundays. The château has had a checkered history since its construction in the twelfth century by Philip the Bold. It has served as an armory and barracks for several regimes, including that of Napoleon.

At the other end of the Cité, take a look at the apse of the **Basilique St.-Nazaire** which has beautiful stained glass windows and is generally considered the finest in southern France. The nave is done in a very simple and pure Romanesque style, which is enhanced by the lightness of the choir and windows. The tower represents another Viollet goof—he restored it with crenellations in a Visigoth style that clashes badly with the charm of the rest of the structure. Finally, walk through the narrow streets of Carcassonne which, despite their touristy nature, exude an atmosphere of medieval times. About a thousand people live here year-round in a sort of thirteenth-century time warp.

There is nothing of outstanding interest in the Ville Basse. The best thing about the **Musée des Beaux-Arts,** rue de Verdun, is that it's free. An uninspiring collection of middling to totally obscure paintings is displayed in two levels of galleries that might come in handy if it's raining hard and you're waiting for the Youth Hostel to open. (Museum open 9-11:45am and 2-6pm, closed Sundays.)

Around the blvd. Omer-Sarrant nightly unfolds a world as rough and urgent as the Cité is unreal and aloof—bars, bowling alleys, and pinball parlors are packed full, and the air maintains a defiant indifference towards the touristed Cité.

Carcassonne stages a small **Festival** during July, with concerts in some of the more picturesque churches and monuments; for information, contact the **Théâtre Municipal** (tel. 25-33-13).

Near Carcassone

From Carcassonne to Perpignan, the road (unfortunately, not the train) leads through the starkly beautiful region known as **Les Corbières,** past ruined chateaux sitting atop multicolored limestone cliffs. This hot, dry region is sparsely populated and rather forbidding for the traveler (especially the hitch-hiker), but those who venture out will be happily rewarded. For those who wish to stay in the area, it is more practical to try **Lezignan,** the main city in the region, 35km from Carcassonne, where there is a lavish camping center, "La Pinède," only a few hundred yards from the center of town. The finest chateau is the **château de Peyrepertuse** on the D14, actually two ruined thirteenth-century castles in a magnificent hilltop setting. The **Fort de Salse,** 16km north of Perpignan on the flat coastland, is daunting for its massive brick walls and Spanish towers. Smaller but no less impressive chateaux dot this once heavily-contested land, and in many small towns you can visit the *caves* where the region's celebrated wines are painstakingly prepared.

Perpignan

Seedier than a watermelon, and considerably less refreshing, this southern-most town in France is crowded with innumerable beggars and much poverty. Perpignan, in short, has little grace or glamour, but it does offer authenticity and striking images. When there's entertainment in the streets, it's likely to be local people of all ages joining hands in a folk dance that celebrates the community and its traditions.

Perpignan has only belonged to France since 1659, when it was acquired from Spain under the "Traité des Pyrénées," and it is still defiantly more

Catalan than French—at once more fiery and more relaxed than cities to the north. Midway between the Mediterranean and the Pyrénées, Perpignan's strategic location was always its main asset, reaching a peak between 1276 and 1344 when the city served as the royal residence of the Kings of Majorca. The **Palais des Rois de Majorque** is still the city's most impressive sight (now that it has been restored). Its main attractions are the immense arcaded courtyard, its two superimposed chapels, and the splendid Salle de Majorque. The **citadel,** however, was converted for use as an arsenal in the last century, and is only now being restored; its forbidding walls surround the Palace, and the gates are open daily except Tuesday, 9am-noon and 2-6pm.

Worth seeing if only for its enchanting setting is **La Case Païral,** a museum of Catalan culture and folklore, with exhibits on local music, dress, dance, agriculture, and religion. It is housed in **Le Castillet,** another impressive brick castle which offers a fine view of the city if you manage to climb all the steps to the top. (Open Mon.-Sat. 9am-noon and 2-6pm, also Sun. July-Sept. Admission 2F, students 1F.)

The **syndicat d'initiative** is in the Palais Consulaire on quai Maréchal, and will help you find accommodations without charge and provide you with information on the Roussillon countryside (tel. 34-29-49). From the train station, follow ave. de Gaulle to *centre ville,* cross the canal and turn right of quai de Lattre de Tassigny. Although Perpignan is not a pleasant city to stay in, it does have a lively Youth Hostel, **La Pépinière (IYHF),** on ave. de Grande Bretagne (tel. 34-63-32), with spartan kitchen facilities and an amiable management (30F a night including breakfast; you must be out by 9am, closed 10am-6pm and curfew 11:30pm). A block from the syndicat, the **Maison Européenne de la Jeunesse** at 32, rue Maréchal-Foch (tel. 34-39-96) offers similar accommodations for 25F a night. (Reception area open Tues.-Sun. 2-7pm, July 15-Aug. 18; 4-7pm Aug. 19-Sept. 14; 5-7pm Sept. 15-Sept. 30. Negotiable 12:30am curfew.) Campers can stake their claim at **Relais Santouge,** 95, route de Prades (tel. 54-64-68), a two-star site; or at **La Garrigole,** rue Maurice-Levy (tel. 54-66-10), a smaller, one-star site.

Perpignan does not boast outstanding restaurants. Try the student places around place de la Loge; the nicest is **Cafe de la Bourse.** The rue Grande la Monnaie has a variety of restaurants, and the cafes on blvd. Clemenceau offer inexpensive menus from 25-30F. The wholesale foodmarket, not far from the city center, also serves as a major starting-point for inter-city trucks—a good spot from which to hitch towards Spain or towards Toulouse.

Near Perpignan

Buses depart frequently from the promenade de Platanes in Perpignan for the 13km trip to **Canet-Plage** (syndicat. tel. 80-35-88; 11 campsites), a popular resort on the lovely Mediterranean coast. You are better off going there for the day than looking for a hotel room or campsite. Further south along the coast are two other resorts, *St.-Cyprien* (syndicat tel. 21-01-33; 8 campsites) and **Argeles sur Mer** (syndicat tel. 81-15-85; 59—count'em—campsites.) In **Thuir,** you can visit the **Chocolaterie Cantalon** (tel. 85-11-22), daily from 2:30-5pm and see an accompanying film.

South of Argélès the Pyrénées come right to the shore, creating magnificent coastal scenery and giving the region its name **Côte Rocheuse** (rocky coast). At **Collioure,** 27km from Perpignan (syndicat tel. 82-15-47; two campsites), three beaches are squeezed in amongst the cliffs, the lovely town, and a giant Spanish-style chateau. The Côte Rocheuse is not accessible by train but there are buses from Perpignan.

If you're in the mood for mountains, head west from Perpignan along the River Tet into the **Conflent,** a beautiful region in the often-overlooked **Pyrénées-Orientales.** Traveling southwest towards the half-French, half-Spanish land of **Andorra,** you will pass jagged peaks and lush forests. The syndicat in Perpignan can provide you with all the necessary information; the GR 10, if you are walking, leads west from Collioure past the nine thousand foot **Pic de Canigou** towards the Haut-Pyrénées.

Montpellier

Montpellier is the regional capital of Languedoc-Roussillon. More importantly, it's a venerable university town, and one which stands close enough to the beach to keep its students in a state of exquisite torture through spring exams. During the summer, thousands of foreign students flock here to learn French painlessly at the university by the sea (four-six week programs, write to C.E.R.A.V.U.M. 11, rue St. Louis, 34000 Montpellier). In the last decade the town has boomed; and some quarters have become very modern while others have deteriorated considerably, but the city is struggling to preserve its rich architectual heritage. The newly restored pedestrian zone and the abundance of seventeenth and eighteenth-century mansions are charming and gracious as ever. Montpellier itself is a good transportation base from which to explore the south of France.

Practical Information

The place de la Comédie is the hub of activity, a combination of sleek modern buildings, eighteenth-century hotels, and wide open spaces which comes magically alive at night. To get there from the train station, follow rue Maquelone (it's a five minute walk).

Bureau Municipal du Tourisme: place de la Comédie (tel. 60-76-90). Information on Montpellier and the beach towns nearby. Hotel booking service and change on summer weekends. Open July and Aug. Mon.-Sat. 9am-6pm, Sun. 9am-1pm. Rest of the year 9am-6pm, closed Sunday. Another office in train station (tel. 92-90-03)

Post Office: place Rondelet (tel. 92-48-00). Open Mon.-Fri. 8am-7pm, Sat. till noon. Telephones: daily 7am-9pm (Sun. 7:30am-9pm) at telephone annex at post office on place Aristide-Briand (near prefecture).

Train Station: place Auguste-Gilibert; information (tel. 58-56-80). Numes 30 minutes away by train, Beziers one hour.

Bus Station: Gare Routière, rue du Grand St.-Jean (tel. 92-01-43) right next to the train station. Buses to Aigue-Mortes, Palavas, la Grande-Motte, etc.

Discount Rail Tickets: BIGE/Transalpino agent at **Vovac,** 6, rue Aristide-Briand (tel. 60-50-98), behind prefecture. Open Mon.-Fri. 9am-12:30pm and 2-6:30pm.

Bike Rental: Le Velo, 6, rue des Ecoles Laiques, at the end of rue Aiguillerie (tel. 66-05-59).

Telephone Code: (67).

Accommodations

In summer university housing is available for short and longer stays. Information at CROUS, 2, rue Monteil (tel. 63-53-93); open Mon.-Fri., 10am-9pm. There are plenty of hotels concentrated around the streets along blvd. Victor-

Hugo and around the train station. The tourist office will also find rooms free of charge.

Centre Internationale des Jeunes, impasse de la Petite-Corraterie (tel. 79-61-66) A hostel-like center with dormitory accommodations and an early curfew. Ten minutes from the place de la Comédie near the blvd. Louis Blanc.

Hôtel Majestic, 4, rue du Cheval Blanc (tel. 66-26-85) three blocks down rue des Etuves from the tourist office. Narrow rooms up a narrow stairway, six singles for 35F, six doubles for 45F.

Hôtel Plantade, 10, rue Plantade (tel. 92-61-45). A block west of blvd. Ledru-Rollin; only twelve doubles, but quite reasonable, 50-67F. Breakfast 8.50F.

Hôtel Fauvettes, 8, rue Bonnard (tel. 63-17-60). The street runs right next to the Jardin des Plantes, and the hotel, in echo, has its own little garden. Rooms from 45-70F. Breakfast 9F.

Camping: Le Montaubéron, route de Maugio (tel. 65-40-60) is a three-star site 2km from the train station. Take bus #15, direction route de Maugion, from the station or place de la Comédie. There are four sites at nearby **Palais-les-Flots,** six at **Lattes.**

Food

Ask the townsfolk about Montpellier's specialties, and they'll mention *beurre de Montpellier,* a butter mixed with garlic and spices which makes bread eating a gourmet experience. You can buy it in charcuteries or in the morning street market held daily around the prefecture.

Crêperie Cris et Dan, 11, rue Jacques-Coeur, off place de la Comédie. Serves delicious crêpes with numerous fillings in a lovely stone room which once served as a wine cave. Come here anytime for a snack, except between 7:30-10pm, when supper is served and there is a two crêpe minimum per person. Across the street at #20, try **L'Auberge Inn,** a vegetarian restaurant with a 38F *menu.* You can eat more cheaply à la carte. The chef manages to incorporate specialties of the region into his dishes. Closed Sun.

Le Provençal, 18, rue de Petit St.-Jean. An excellent and popular restaurant serving regional food. Very small so come early. *Menu* for 25F or 38F *menu* includes wine.

Au Vollier Nommé Désir, 10, rue de College Vergier, near the Centre des Jeunes. Seafood specialties, changing art exhibitions on the walls. They have a *menu* for 38F. Try *chomloi* for dessert—if you like marble cake, hot fudge, raisins, rum and whipped cream, you'll like this.

The university restaurants are open during the term: 11:30am-2pm and 6:30-8pm (check at CROUS, 2, rue Montreil, to see which are open in summer). The food is not gourmet, but it's edible. (It's hard to get a student meal ticket in this town, though). University restaurants are **Arceaux,** rue Gustave; **Boutonnet,** rue Emile-Duployé; **Triolet,** place Eugène-Bastillon; and **Vert-Blois,** ave. de Vert-Bois, route de Mende.

Sights

The seventeenth-century Promenade de Peyrou in the upper part of town terminates in a large **Triumphal Arch,** erected in 1691 to honor Louis XIV. A

GETTING THERE IS HALF THE FUN

Mail this card and receive a free packet of material:

-Flight information to Europe
-International Student I.D. Card Application
-Eurail and Britrail Pass Application
-International Youth Hostel Card Application
-European car rental information
-Travel guide list
-Accommodation voucher information

HSA TRAVEL SHOWS YOU HOW

———————————— FOLD HERE AND FASTEN ————————————

Name ————————————————
Address ————————————————
————————————————

FIRST CLASS
PERMIT NO. 34979
BOSTON, MASS.

Business Reply Mail
No postage stamp necessary if mailed in the United States

Postage will be paid by:

Let's Go Travel Guides
Harvard Student Agencies, Inc.
Thayer Hall B
Harvard University
Cambridge, MA 02138

READER SERVICE CARD

Help Us To Get To Know You

In order to suit your travel needs better with each edition, it helps us to know a little about you.

1. Occupation: student non-student affiliate other   2. Age: 15-18 19-22 23-26 27-30 31-35 36-40 41-65 65 and above

3. Season in which you will begin travel: spring summer fall winter

4. Length of stay in Europe: 2 wks. or less 2-4 wks. 1-2 mos. 2-6 mos.

5. Will you travel: alone with one friend with two or more friends with family with tour group

6. Primary reason for travel: study work pleasure

7. Plan to spend in Europe (exclusive of transatlantic travel): $400-800 $800-1200 $1200-1600 $1600-2000 $2000-2800 over $2800

8. Mode of transportation to Europe: charter flight standby flight budget flight APEX flight · other commercial flight

9. From which city will you leave the U.S.?: Boston Chicago Dallas L.A. Miami NY Other

10. Please circle all modes of transportation you plan to use within Europe.Please underline the primary one: rented car purchased car bus train bicycle motorcycle hitching caravan

11. Please circle all modes of accomodations you will be using. Underline the primary one: campgrounds university hostels friends · hotels other

12. Will you carry: backpack suitcase other

13. What prompted you to buy Let's Go! ?: recommendation of a friend use of previous Let's Go! saw it in a bookstore an ad in   a review or article in

14. Will you use a travel agent to help plan your trip? yes no

15. Please circle the countries you plan to visit. Underline your first destination: Austria Belgium Bulgaria Czechoslovakia Denmark East Germany Finland France Great Britain Greece Hungary Iceland Ireland Israel Italy Luxemborg Morocco Netherlands Northern Ireland Norway Poland Portugal Romania Scotland Spain Sweden Switzerland Turkey USSR West Germany Yugosolavia

16. What kinds of information in the Let's Go!:volume did you find most helpful? (please rank according to importance): transportation accomodations prices eating orientation and background sights other(please specify)

17. Is there any information that you would like included in future volumes, or have you any suggestions for improving Let's Go!: volumes?

18. Compared to other sources of information that you consulted, would you say that this Let's Go!: volume was: indispensable excellent good adequate poor

Name _____

Address _____

City _____ State ___ Zip ____

please do not use this card after Feb. 1, 84   LGE monumental **Equestrian Statue** of the Sun King stands midway along the promenade leading toward the **Château d'Eau,** the arched terminus of the exquisitely preserved aqueduct which supplied the city with water. Stroll here in the evening when the arch and pool are illuminated and there is recorded Baroque music.

The **Musée Fabre,** 13, rue Montpellieret near the tree-lined esplanade, has a fine collection of paintings second only to Lille in the provinces. Open 9am-noon and 2-5:30pm, closed Monday, admission free. The Collection Xavier-Atger, at the Faculté de Médecine, rue de l'Ecole-de-Médecine, is housed in the library next to the cathedral. The collection contains works by several Renaissance and Baroque masters, among many others of interest. Open Mon.-Fri. 10am-noon and 2-7pm, Saturday morning; closed August and Sunday; admission free.

The **Quartier Aiguillerie** and the **Quartier du Cannau** make interesting walks through the narrow, twisting streets of the old town. The **Cathédrale St.-Pierre** flanks the somber medieval quarter. Just across the blvd. Henri IV is the peaceful **Jardin des Plantes.** The rue de l'Université is lined with intriguing bookstores and snackshops. At night, carouse among the cinemas, cafes, glittering fountains and wandering musicians of the place de la Comédie. During the month of July, the **Théâtre Municipal,** place de la Comédie, hosts a **Dance Festival** of performances, workshops and films. The theatre offers drama and concerts year-round; call (tel. 66-31-11) for information. Throughout the year, the **Café Doyen,** 13, rue du Grand-St.-Jean, has folk music, jazz, and theatre starting at 9pm, closed Sundays.

The Mediterranean coast around Montpellier is breaking out in a rash of new resorts. **Le Grau de Roi** remains a pleasant village, but **La Grande-Motte, Carnon, Palavas** and other coastal towns have a disturbing, unfinished feeling about them. To the west of Montpellier along the Cap d'Agde are long, unspoiled beaches with pine groves reaching nearly to the water. The cathedral in Agde, with its crenellated roof, resembles a castle from a distance. Buses leave Montpellier regularly for these towns. Northwest of Montpellier, the spectacular **Gorges de l'Herault** stretch for thirty miles along the Herault river, running parallel to highway D4 and close to St. Guilhem-le-Desert, which has interesting ruins of an abbey, castles, and fortifications.

The Pyrénées

Still fighting for status as France's premier mountain range, the Pyrénées remain more accessible and less touristed than the Alps, their slightly taller rivals. Aside from Lourdes and the ski resorts in winter, the Pyrénées are free from crowds which makes them a better alternative for hardy explorers.

The Pyrénées were most probably created by the shifting of the Iberian Peninsula, a process which even today accounts for continued avalanches and rockslides and also for the process of overthrusting (the placement of one rock layer over another, softer layer) which gives the peaks their jagged profile. The most prominent valleys in the region are filled with multi-colored granite, and the most famous, the **Cirque de Gavarnie,** is a massive granite face. Their unique arrangement, steeply sided valleys (once totally glaciated) leading south to the great ridge, allows even the inexperienced climber the chance to scurry above magnificent vistas or snow-capped peaks, high mountain valleys, and waterfalls.

A varied landscape and the wide range of rare wildlife are proof that one area has thus far escaped ever-encroaching civilization. Climb high enough and you are likely to see the famous *ibards*, or mountain antelopes; since the creation of the **Parc National des Pyrénées** in 1967 (one of only five in France), their once-menaced population has doubled. The Pyrénées shelter the last colonies of brown bears, eagles, and vultures in France, species still in danger of extinction. Cows and sheep graze at heights of nearly eight thousand feet, and lovely mountain flowers grace the valleys.

The towns of **Lourdes** and **Tarbes** are most useful for the access they provide to the mountain region; from here you can choose the smaller **Cauterets, Luz,** or **Gavarnie** as a base. If you're coming from Spain, you can come via Jaca over the Somport or Portalet passes, or through the principality of Andorra and west on the D618.

Once you are in the mountains, accommodations are not expensive: there are the refuges of the Club Alpin Français (CAF; either guarded or unguarded) along major trails, shepherds' cabins often available in the summer, and campgrounds of the Comité de Sentiers de Grande Randonnée. The **Grande Randonnée No. 10,** or GR10, runs across the length of the Pyrénées, past its finest scenery. If you plan to follow any part of this, pick up the guide GR10 in a bookstore (38F)—it has good trail direction and up-to-date listings of refuges along the route. Also essential is one of the detailed purple 1:25,000 maps (30F) of the Parc National—there are four for the entire region.

Hiking

Exercise caution. Trails may be well traveled but you'll still be hours away from emergency services in town. Take care to keep your feet dry, cool, and blister-free. Sprinkle them liberally with powder, wear double layers of socks (cotton and wool) under light but sturdy-soled boots (vibram is good material). Your daypack should be light, too—keep it down to the bare essentials: map, army knife, trail food, a sweater, a change of socks, and a poncho. Travel with a companion if possible, leave a copy of your itinerary with the local CAP or police station, and check the local weather report before you leave. Inexperienced hikers should familiarize themselves with their trail and their gear before heading out. On a first trip, it might be worth joining a guided hike. Contact the Club Alpin Français for details. (**Beware:** storms often channel up the valleys with amazing swiftness.)

Whether or not you do hit the trail, you will have the chance to sample the mild *fromage des Pyrénées* (or *fromage du pays*), made either from cow's or sheep's milk. When you stop in a village, try to sample some of the fine Béarn cuisine: duck and goose pâté, fresh fish, and their superb rose wine. Your greatest memory of the Pyrénées, though, may be the Béarnaise people themselves who, half-French and half-Spanish, tend to be as expansive and hospitable as the region they inhabit.

Pau

Pau is a city of gardens, set against the backdrop of the Pyrénées. The sixteenth-century capital of the independent country of Béarn, Pau was the seat of a thriving court—King Henri IV was born in the Chateau here. He never forgot his native city, and its glory grew as his son became king and conquered Béarn for France.

In the nineteenth century, this hillside town became popular as a winter vacation paradise for the English well-to-do. But when Queen Victoria decided to take her 1889 winter holiday in Biarritz, Pau slipped out of the international limelight. The remnants of the town's glory days are still here: the Chateau, the boulevards, and the extensive resort facilities created for the English colony. Unfortunately, prices have become equally regal, and Pau is no longer the reasonable resort it once was.

Today, Pau makes a good base camp for forays into the mountains, although access is somewhat limited. For a trip into the mountains, SNCF buses link Pau to **Laruns**, just north of the Park. From here you can catch a local bus, hike or hitch to **Gabas**, a good departure point with camping and a CAF (Club Alpin Français) refuge. Some of the finest sights in the Pyrénées are accessible from Pau; the **Col d'Aubisque**, the **Pic du Midi d'Ossau** (10,100 feet), and the **Lac d'Artouste** (all with CAF refuges nearby).

Practical Information

Office Municipal du Tourisme: In the Hotel de Ville, place Royale (tel. 27-27-08). Information on the Pyrénées region with a separate hiking/camping desk. Open daily in summer 9am-12:30pm and 2-7pm. Mon.-Sat. 8:45am-12:30pm and 2-6:15pm in winter.

Student Tourist Office: AGEP, 8, place Clemenceau (tel. 27-94-93). The room-finding service for long stays in Pau can get you a place for as little as 10F a night. Open Mon.-Fri. 10am-noon and 2;30-5:30pm.

Comité Departemental du Tourisme des Pyrénées-Atlantiques: Parlement de Navarre, rue Henri IV (tel. 27-06-03). Information on trips into the Pyrénées.

Post Office: corner of cour Bosquet and rue Gambetta, off place Clemenceau (tel. 27-76-89). Open Mon.-Fri. 8am-7pm, Sat. 8am-noon. Closed Sun., except Poste Restante, open 8-11am and telecommunications open 8am-noon. An additional telecommunications office is at 2, ave Université.

Train Station: At the base of the hill dominated by the Chateau. An uphill walk to the center of town, but once you've climbed the hill everything is conveniently close. Every five minutes, daily 7am-10pm, a free *funiculaire* across the street from the station climbs to the blvd. des Pyrénées. Train information (tel. 27-59-42) is open Mon.-Sat. 9am-noon and 2-6:30pm, but a small reception bureau, also in the station (phone connected automatically when information is closed), gives limited information service 24 hours a day.

Bus Station: Courriers des Basses-Pyrénées, 34, rue Michel-Hounaud (tel. 30-01-79). City buses depart from the place Clemenceau (3.50F).

Police: Rue O'Quin (tel. 27-94-06); **Medical Services:** Croix Rouge (Red Cross), 9, rue Louis Barthou (tel. 27-78-42); **Hospital:** 10, cours Bosquet (tel. 27-89-89).

Telephone Code: (59).

Accommodations

University Housing available July-Sept. Residence Gaston Febus, ave. Poplawski (tel. 02-73-35, reception in building D), rents out dorm rooms for only 15F (hot showers included) with student ID. Take bus #4 or 4*ter*. CROUS is located at 68, rue Montpensier (tel. 32-56-47) Swimming pool nearby.

Hôtel Bernard, 7, rue de Foix, a block from the syndicat (tel. 27-40-28). In the heart of town; very small interior. Singles 40F doubles 44F. Breakfast 9F, showers 8F.

Hôtel de la Pomme d'Or, 11, rue Maréchal-Foch (tel. 27-78-48). On a main boulevard, but the hotel has a courtyard that blots out the bustle, and heavy curtains in rooms looking onto the street do the same. Doubles 65-70F, 100F with showers. Breakfast 10F.

Hôtel le Béarn, 5, rue Maréchal-Joffre (tel. 27-52-50). Rooms with double bed 50-70F, showers 5F, breakfast 11F. Windows look onto dead-end street. Well kept.

Hôtel Vinet, 10, rue Valéry-Meunier (tel. 27-47-51). Off the rue Maréchal-Foch. A bit more expensive, but very pleasant and located on a quiet street. Some rooms 50-65F, double beds with showers 100F. Breakfast 12F.

Camping: There are several camping sites in the outskirts. **Camping le Terrier** (tel. 32-81-82), on the D501 in Lescar, is a three-star site open year round. Equally pleasant and only 2km away in Gelos is the **Camping Base de Plein Air** (tel. 27-01-71), pleasantly situated by the river, with all necessary services, open May-September.

Food

For inexpensive fare, try the rue Léon-Dura, and other streets leading up to the university. The **Cafeteria le Kamok** at 4, rue Joffre and 20, rue Foch offers pizza (8.50F), quiche (9F) and other quick snacks, but you may want to splurge in Pau. The region that brought you Béarnaise sauce has many other specialties to offer: salmon, pike, goose *(oie)* and duck *(canard)* pâté, and the three-course menu featuring *crudité* (a cold vegetable platter including baby asparagus and eggs béarnaise). **Chez Olive** at 9, rue du Château, offers *poulet basquaise* (chicken in a hot pepper sauce) and menus for 35F and 55F (closed Friday). **Chez Nanou,** at 5, rue de Parlement (practically across the street) also offers good menus from 40F.

Sights

On a clear day, you can see almost the whole range of the Pyrénées from the Blvd. des Pyrénées. Plaques identifying the various mountain peaks are riveted onto the iron railing that extends along the walkway. The view stretches some 80km over the vineyards and hills to the jagged, bold heights of the Pyrénées. Immediately below the walkway is an exceptionally beautiful French garden, and adjoining the boulevard, at the extreme eastern end, is the **Parc Beaumont,** a large English garden.

The **Château,** a rambling structure with six square towers, occupies the highest point in Pau, overlooking the river. Built by the viscounts of Béarn in the twelfth century, the Castle owes its fame to the Kings of Navarre. King Henri IV, who was born here, was cradled in the giant tortoise shell still housed here. The Château also holds more than fifty Gobelins tapestries. Open in summer 9:30-11:45am and 2-5:45pm, till 5pm in winter; admission 7F, 3.50F with student ID. Entrance to the **Musée Béarnais,** on the third floor, with exhibits of local traditions and arts, is an extra 2F.

The **Musée des Beaux-Arts,** rue Mathieu-Lalanne, has a small but interesting collection of paintings, including a few works by El Greco, Ribera, Zurbarán, and Rubens. The prize of the collection is a Degas, *The Cotton Bureau at New Orleans.* Note the painting by Brueghel of Velours (second son of Brueghel the Elder), so different in style from his famous father. Also, compare Velasquez's *Infante Marie Anne d'Autriche* with the modern takeoffs hung next to it. (Open daily except Tuesday, 10am-noon and 2-6pm; admission free.)

Lourdes

A town of just over 18,000, Lourdes is swamped each year by four-and-a-half million pilgrims. Sick and crippled people have often spent their life's savings to be bathed in the "miraculous" healing waters here.

Since the Apparitions in 1858 of the Virgin to Bernadette Sibirous, a young girl of the town, the miracle of Lourdes has been debased into a pre-packaged tourist industry. As the site of one of the most recent miracles recognized by the Church, the town is second only to Paris in its concentration of tourists. Enormous special trains, buses, and charter flights from all over Europe and the world bring entire parishes at a time to the sacred site. The souvenir stands are loaded with thousands of Virgin-shaped water-bottles, kitsch paintings, plastic rosary beads, and dashboard crucifixes. The trinkets, bought by millions of crippled and diseased people as religious trophies, capitalize on desperate hope.

Yet, at the Basilique Pius X and the Cave of the Apparitions, the resounding hymns of mass pierce the carnival atmosphere. Here, at least, faith seems less distorted, less hollow. Healing and miracles aside, Lourdes provides a fine base for an excursion into the Hautes Pyrénées. Accommodations are inexpensive, and the SNCF runs buses to Pierrefitte (railpasses valid) with connections to the best touring and skiing centers: Cauterets, Luz-St.-Sauveur, and Gavarnie (railpasses not valid). You should have no trouble hitching to these places as well.

Practical Information

Municipal Tourist Office: place Champ Commun (tel. 94-15-64). Open Mon.-Sat. 9am-12:30pm and 1:30-7pm Sun. mornings in summer.

Accueil des Jeunes: on the esplanade leading up the Basilica. Help with accommodations for youth (tel. 94-34-54).

Post Office: PTT and long-distance telephone, corner of rue de Langelle and chaussée Maransin. Open Mon.-Fri. 8am-7pm; Sat. 8am-12pm.

Train Station: ave. de la Gare (tel. 94-35-36). Lourdes receives frequent train service between Bayonne and Toulouse, as well as direct service (eight hours) from Paris. In the summer, there are over a dozen trains daily from Paris. Pyrénées buses leave from the train station and the square/parking lot below the tourist office.

American Express Agent: Office Catholique de Voyages 14, chaussée du Bourg. Open Mon.-Fri. 9am-noon and 2-7pm, Sat. 9am-noon.

Police: 7, rue Baron-Duprat (tel. 94-02-08); **Medical Help:** 2, ave. Marqui (tel. 94-78-78); **First Aid:** (tel. (59) 27-15-15) throughout Béarn region.

Telephone Code: (62).

Accommodations and Food

Just about every house in Lourdes serves as store, restaurant, and hotel, so you should have no trouble finding lodging. In fact, there are so many hotels here that residents have started putting up signs on their doors saying "This is not a hotel" to keep out unwelcome intruders. Lourdes has about 160 one-star hotels: most are not too expensive and are comfortable. As a rule, the higher-priced hotels are nearer the grotto. There are three lower-priced alternatives:

Centre des Rencontres "Pax Christi": 4, route de la Forét (tel. 94-00-66). A five-minute walk up the road behind the Basilica. Hostel-like accommodations for 20F a night, including breakfast and shower. Sheet rental 9F. Avoid the meals.

Camp des Jeunes, Ferme Milhas, chemin des Carrieres Peyramale (tel. 94-03-95). A ten-minute walk uphill out of town. 12F a night for dorm accommodations, 8F in your own tent—for both you need a sleeping bag. Kitchen and food store available, but you must provide your own utensils. They will encourage you to participate in evening services and "community" activities.

Auberge de Jeunesse, quai de l'Adour (tel. 93-31-59). Across the street from the Salle des Sports. About 2km from the station: walk down the ave. Bertrand-Barère to the place de Verdum (syndicat is here), turn left on the rue Maréchal-Foch, and turn right when you reach the river. The warden and friends are ardent mountain lovers and will help you with hiking itineraries. Clean with good kitchen; lock-out until 6:30pm; 20F per night.

Again, shop around the hotels, which are not overly expensive. You can get a decent, if not exciting, four-course meal for about 40F at most places.

Sights

The objective of every visit to Lourdes is the **Cave of the Apparitions,** where Bernadette had the visions that transformed the town. Shortly after the miracle, the Basilica was built on this site, and has ministered to the needs of pilgrims ever since. The massive structure is actually made up of three superimposed churches. The modern **Basilique Pius X,** near the grotto, is a concrete monstrosity that looks like a cross between Madison Square Garden and a parking garage—fortunately most of it is underground. It can accommodate up to twenty thousand people at one time. In addition to the basilicas, Lourdes also contains a **castle-fortress** (accessible by elevator). Perched on a hill in the center of town, its museum documents Pyrénéen folklore and mountain geography (open in summer every day 9-11am and 2-6pm, closed at 5pm in winter; admission 10F).

The **Musée de Cire,** 87, rue de la Grotte (open daily 9am-noon and 1:30-7pm, 8-10pm in July and August; admission 14F) immodestly proclaims itself to be the best and biggest religious wax museum in the world, and it very well may be so. After all, how many religious wax museums are there?

If you want to get away from the crowds, cross over the Gave de Pau and wander along some of the steep streets of Lourdes, or else walk alongside the river away from the Basilica. You'll find some lovely scenery here, in the limestone foothills of the Pyrénées; the **Lac de Lourdes,** 3km west of town off the N640 (10F round trip bus fare from tourist office), is a pleasant if over-touristed spot where you can go riding or rent a rowboat and bask on the crystal lake.

Cauterets

Set three thousand feet up in a breathtaking valley on the edge of the **Parc National des Pyrénées Occidentales,** Cauterets is probably the best place to go if you want to establish one base while touring and taking in some of the Pyrénean scenery. The town itself, like several others in the region, became renowned for its bath cures in the late nineteenth century and hence has some elegant Victorian hotels and a train station offering SNCF bus service to Lourdes via Pierrefitte (16F).

Although heavily touristed, Cauterets retains the tranquility of a mountain town. In the winter, some of the best skiing in the region is just a gondola, chairlift and t-bar ride away. Long, silky white runs drop hundreds of meters vertically, while cross-country ski-trails lead into the heart of the National Park past Alpine refuges and spectacular vistas.

Practical Information

Municipal Tourist Office, place Clémenceau (tel. 92-50-27). Information center by day (Mon.-Sat. 9am-noon, 2-7pm, Sun. 10am-noon) but office for guided hiking tours in the evenings (6-7pm).

Post Office: rue de Belfort (tel. 92-54-00). Open Mon.-Fri. 9am-noon and 2-6pm, and Sat. 8am noon. Telephones.

Regie municipal des sport de montagne: (tel. 97-51-58); **Park National,** place de la gare (tel. 92-52-56) offers hiking trips, nature films and a Pyrénean flora and fauna exhibit. Open daily 9am-noon and 5-7pm.

Accommodations and Food

For accommodations in Cauterets, stay at the **Centre Jean Beigbeder,** ave. du Docteur-Domer (tel. 92-52-95). From the SNCF station, walk up the hill along the path that leads in front of the gondola station; continue past the tennis courts and turn left. 12F per night in large, 14-bed tents; or you can pitch you own tent (6F), 4F for showers, 4F a day to use the excellent kitchen facilities. Run by a friendly couple who know all the local hiking trails. (Open mid-June to mid-September only. If full, try the **Hôtel Le Téléphérique,** 36, rue Richelieu (tel. 92-53-80) with singles for 50F and doubles for 67F. There are also plenty of campgrounds near Cauterets and in the winter several dorm-like accommodations for skiers are open.

Your best bet for low-cost dining is to eat pizza or crêpes, and the **Crêperie Patisserie Salon de Thé** on 8, rue Richelieu offers both. (Pizzas 17-19F, crepes 5-13F and delicious dark *galettes* for 5-13F.)

Near Cauterets

If you want to do some hiking, pick up one of the purple 1:25,000 maps of the Parc National des Pyrénées (30F); for the Cauterets region use #2—Balaïtous. The GR10 passes through Cauterets and continues to Luz-St.-Sauveur by two different paths; the easier one crosses the plateau of Lisey while the other, more popular and breathtakingly beautiful, leads past the **Lac de Gaube,** glaciated fields of the Vignemale eleven thousand feet up, Gavarnie and the village of Gedre. This is definitely the place for serious climbers. Other easily accessible routes lead to the **Lac d'Estom** and the **Lac d'Ilheou** via the gondola from town. There the refuge R. Ritter (open June 15-September 30) makes a fine base camp for hiking circuits. Use the GR10 as your departure point to **Lac Noir** and the **Pontou des Sahucs.**

Gavarnie is a picture-perfect mountain village set in the **massif du Marboré.** In the winter its ski slopes are less packed than those of nearby resorts, and during the rest of the year its spectacular scenery draws adventurers from all France. A horseback ride away—there are over 400 mounts in Gavarnie— you'll find **Brèche de Roland,** 2800 meters above sea level, and the famous **Cirque de Gavarnie;** a short walk will take you into the Parc National, down to the pretty town of **Geidre** or to the foot of the two mile high mountain range. The **syndicat d'initiative** in Geidre (tel. 92-48-26) will help you plan your hiking itinerary.

Après-ski or après-hiking activities are generally limited to drinking binges by the hearth or disco-hopping. **Chistera Disco,** rue Richelieu in Cauterets, is open weekend evenings (free admission).

The Basque Region (Pays Basque)

Many believe that the Basque way of life is fast receding in the coastal towns under a swarm of beach chairs, sun hats, and tourists, and when you see the crowded beaches at **Biarritz** and the less crowded ones at **Anglet,** you may agree. Nonetheless, these cities and the charming **St.-Jean-de-Luz,** further south, remain enticing for their superb coastal scenery and ocean swimming, and the Basque presence gives them an atmosphere different from other resorts. Just a few kilometers inland, **Bayonne** is a hustling commercial center and home of the **Musée Basque,** housing a fine collection of artifacts relating to Basque culture.

The French Basques, although less militant than their Spanish brethren, are equally nationalistic. They believe that *Euzkadi* (the Basque word for the Basque country) is one nation, even if now divided between France and Spain. Unlike the industrialized Spanish *Pais Basco,* which was linguistically liberated after the death of Franco, the Pays Basque must watch its language slowly disappear. The economy has been suffering a dramatic recession and much of the population is emigrating to the big cities further north and to the coast. The Basques blame the French government for ignoring their particular concerns. Several nationalistic political parties were started in the 1960s, but while they initially met with moderate success, most lost popular support due to alleged connection with the ETA (the militarist Spanish Basque Liberation Front); and although the comparatively inactive French Basques may identify more with France than *Euzkadi,* they do harbor their militant cousins from French police investigations and threatened Spanish extradition.

The Basques are best known as a mountain people, and you should make the effort to visit the smaller towns in the Pyrénean foothills, where lifestyle and language remain intact. Accessible by train from Bayonne, **St.-Jean-Pied-de-Port** is popular, yet still maintains its indigenous charm. Bus services usually pick up where trains leave off, and in spite of the political unrest, hitchhiking and cycling are still the best modes of transportation.

The Pays Basque is not a gentle region, and its people are not wealthy—note the simplicity of the timber-framed houses and of the farm equipment. The Basques are a rugged people of surprising fortitude: the regional sport, *pelote* (known as *jai-alai* in the United States), is a fast-paced game in which a hard ball is hurled at a front wall by means of a *chistera,* or appendage, laced to the wrist. Try to get to a *fronton* (arena) for a *pelote* match to appreciate the quickness and skill of the local players. (Tickets to the world cup matches in St.-Jean-de-Luz which are played all summer, start from 22F).

Underneath this rugged exterior, however, the Basques are a fun-loving people, most evident in late July and early August, when every town holds a *fête,* for several days of drinking and dancing. The most famous festival occurs in Bayonne during the last week in July. Basque cuisine is also something of a treat, and it is not expensive. The succulent Bayonne ham is renowned throughout France, and good Basque fish stew closely rivals *bouillabaise.* Less well known are the region's wines. Once a major wine-producing region, the Pays Basque is now making a comeback, and some of the local reds can be quite a treat.

Bayonne

Bayonne plays its role as the political and cultural center of the Pays Basque with overwhelming spirit. On market days, the narrow streets and quays of the city are filled to bursting with an animation that is uniquely Basque. This activity reaches its frenzied apogee on the six days following the last Wednesday in August, when Bayonne hosts its renowned festival, replete with concerts, dances, bullfights, and fireworks.

Bayonne's regional importance stems from its location at the confluence of the Adour and the Nive rivers, and has been a major port, military base, and industrial center ever since the twelfth century. Chocolate first came to France through its port, and the arsenals of Bayonne are given credit for inventing the bayonnet in the eighteenth century. Today, with its twin-towered Gothic Cathedral dominating one side of town, and its massive citadel guarding the other, Bayonne is a delightful walking city.

Practical Information

Bayonne is trisected by the confluence of the broad Adour and its tributary, the Nive. Across the Pont St.-Espirit from the train station, wedged between the merging rivers, is Petit Bayonne. Here you'll find the Musées Basque and Bonnat, the Chateau Neuf, and the Arsenal d'Artillerie, along with a few inexpensive hotels and superb restaurants. Five smaller bridges connect to Grand Bayonne on the west bank of the Nive. Spread below the central Cathédrale Sainte-Marie are the chic pedestrian malls and the Chateau-Vieux.

Syndicat d'Initiative: place de la Liberté, Grand Bayonne (tel. 59-31-31). Under the arcade on the side facing the river, same building as the Hotel de Ville and Théâtre Municipal. (Open in summer Mon.-Fri. 9am-noon and 2-7pm, and Sat. 9am-noon.)

Post Office: rue Jules-Labat, Grand Bayonne. Open Mon.-Fri. 8am-7pm, Sat. 8am-noon.

Police: rue Jacques Laffitte (tel. 25-77-00).

Hospital: rue Jacques Loeb (tel. 63-50-50).

SNCF Train Station: off the Place République (tel. 55-50-50).

Telephone Code: (59).

Accommodations

Decent hotels are neither abundant nor cheap in Bayonne. Most are clustered around the train station, but there are a few small hotels in Petit Bayonne around the rue Pannecau and around the place Paul Bert. Camping de la Chêneraie on the RN117 (tel. 55-01-31), 3km away in St. Frederic, may be your best bet. Open March 15-October 15; 7.50F per person, 17F more for car, tent and use of the heated pool.

Hôtel des Basques, 4, rue des Lisses, Petit Bayonne (tel. 59-08-02). Right off place Paul-Bert, near Eglise St.-André, facing Caserne du Chateau Neuf: a short walk from the train station. Singles and doubles 48-55F; showers 8F.

Hôtel du Midi, opposite the train station, just before rue Ursule (tel. 55-02-68). Friendly owners, excellent rooms for the price. Room with double bed 52F, 58F with private shower. Closed Oct. 15-Nov. 15.

Hôtel du Moulin, 12, rue Ste.-Catherine (tel. 55-13-29). Two blocks from the station, this is a small hotel in a quieter location. Simple but clean: singles 48F, and doubles 68F with a pleasant little bar downstairs.

Hôtel Monbar, 24, rue Pannecau (tel. 59-26-80). Typical small hotel in Petit Bayonne with simple accommodations; doubles with showers, 72F.

Food

Food in Bayonne is good and less expensive once you get away from the train station. The streets of Petit Bayonne are filled with small restaurants and cafes offering *menus* for under 37F, so walk around and take your choice. Sardines and anchovies are always fresh and unlike anything you've had from a can; Basque fish stew is a spicy treat. The *charcuteries* hold their own, too, with *carci* (stuffed pork) and zesty salads of all types. Your best best, economically speaking, is the municipal market right on the Nive on the Grand side by the Pannecau bridge.

Bar des Amis, rue Cordeliers, Petit Bayonne. For 38F you'll be stuffed to the gills with a tureen of soup, bread, appetizers (including an entire fresh trout), duck, roasted veal or beef, salad, and dessert and coffee to boot. Lone diners are obliged to sit by the kitchen where they can contemplate the baguette guillotine.

Restaurant Irintzina, 9, rue Marengo, Petit Bayonne. Good food, *menu* at 30F. Closed Sun.

Restaurant Dacquois, 48, rue d'Espagne, Grand Bayonne. Regional specialties served to a local clientele; *menu* at 30F.

Restaurant Euzkiduna, 61, rue Pannecau. Small restaurant decked out in copper pots and checkered blue tablecloths serving regional dishes from 24-50F. *Moules* (mussels) at 24F, *pâté de la maison* at 28F, and chicken *à la basquois* at 34F.

Sights

The **Cathédrale Notre-Dame** seems a little out-of-place in this Basque city, but it is still very striking. Built in a northern Gothic style in the thirteenth century, its golden stone and twin spires weren't added until the nineteenth century. The narrow nave was built in the purest Gothic style, and is remarkable for its soaring vaults, stained glass windows and graceful lines. The **sacristy** contains a few paintings and interesting carved stone portals (ask the guard for the key). A nearby door before the right transept leads into the **cloister** with its fine arched passageways.

Bayonne is blessed with two of the finest museums in this part of France: the **Musée Basque,** corner of quai des Corsaires and rue Marengo, by Pont Marengo, has fine exhibits concerning every aspect of Basque life: costumes, furniture, fishing boats, and a room devoted to *pelote*. On the bottom level, note the unique rounded cruciform Basque tombstones, a primitive shape that reappears in the decorative arts as well as in the front wall of *pelote* arenas, or *frontons*. The museum tries to evoke the mystery and hardiness unique to the Basque character. Open July through September 9:30am-12:30pm and 2:30-6:30pm; admission 4F, 2F with student ID; closed Sundays and holidays. The library downstairs contains over 10,000 volumes, including just about everything published concerning the Basques, and is open to the public during museum hours Monday through Friday.

Bayonne's fine arts museum, the **Musée Bonnat,** 5, rue Jacques Lafitte in Petit Bayonne, has reopened after extensive renovation. Bonnat, a native of Bayonne, was a celebrated nineteenth-century painter who bequeathed his extensive collection to the city and even directed the construction of the museum. Rich in the works of Delacroix, Dégas, Antoine Barye, and Rubens, several rooms exhibit the works of Bonnat himself; it is interesting to compare his grandiose, classical style with the major schools of French nineteenth-century painting. The bottom floor contains Bonnat's archeological collection and a massive treasury of drawings on rotating exhibit. Open daily except Tuesday 10am-noon and 4-8pm in summer, 1pm-7pm in winter. Fridays open til 10pm. Admission 5F.

Anglet

Where Bayonne is frenetic and Biarritz pretentious, Anglet is peaceful and suburban. Five kilometers from Bayonne and three from Biarritz, it is really an extension of both. Yet Anglet is fast becoming a resort in its own right. The 4km of fine, sandy beaches have the highest concentration of lifeguards anywhere on the coast; **Chambre d'Amour** is one beach renowned for its surfiing, and along the beach is a 370-acre pine forest with recreational facilities and hiking paths.

The few hotels in Anglet require full *pension* and tend to be expensive, but the superb modern **Auberge de Jeunesse (IYHF)** on the route des Vignes (tel. 63-86-49) makes Anglet the best spot to stay in the region. There are two methods of getting there, but neither one is very easy. From the Biarritz Hotel de Ville, take one of the six daily orange line buses to the Total Gas Station at the corner of the blvd. des Plages and allée de Fontaine Laborde, and then follow the signs. Or, if you're coming from Bayonne, take the blue line (buses every twelve minutes) from Bayonne Hotel de Ville to Cinq Cantons, right at the **syndicat d'initiative** (tel. 03-77-01) and PTT. Located in a beautiful wooded spot, the Hostel is clean, relatively new, and large (95 beds). You can stay indoors or camp outside; breakfast is compulsory, and lunch and dinner are offered during the summer. Since it is very popular with surfers, the Hostel is often full in the summer, and you might want to make reservations or arrive an hour before opening to secure a place, rather than sleeping on a cot in a tent (23.50F) provided by the Hostel. The snack bar offers quick fare at decent prices (cheeseburgers 12F, ¼ liter of beer, 10F).

You may want to sign up in advance for the surfing program, ten days of lessons (sessions held from June 21 to Sept. 8) for about 1,200F including tuition, room and board. You must be at least sixteen years old and a good swimmer. Write to the Centre National FUAJ 6, rue Mesnil, 75116 Paris, for their *Vacances-Activités en France* booklet.

Three of Anglet's campgrounds are two-star sites: **Chambre d'Amour,** route de Bouney (tel. 03-71-66), has eight hundred places and is open April through September; **Barre de l'Adour,** 130, ave. de l'Adour (tel. 63-16-16), has six hundred places and is open Easter through September 30; **Fontaine Laborde,** ave. de Fontaine-Laborde (tel. 03-89-67), has three hundred places and is open Easter through September. All are well-situated and fully equipped.

Biarritz

Biar-"ritz", although geared for the jet-set, is still accessible to the budget traveler (unless you develop a taste for the casinos), and its pounding surf is one of the most striking natural wonders in Europe. Biarritz is regaining the turn-of-the-century glory it lost during the transformations brought on the city by the aristocratic "grand tour," surfers, and the mass tourism boom. The town where Napoleon III and Queen Victoria and her retinue summered has now acquired Californian surf shops and visitors of all ages.

Once again, Biarritz's major sites are its people *en grande promenade*. And they have returned with good reason, tempted by the warm and sandy beach, set beneath a line of cliffs topped by a pair of grand casinos.

A walk on the flower-strewn promenade, by the surf and the casinos, is obligatory. Basque song and dance troupes often stage performances in the gardens and the Hotel du Palais, which was built as the summer residence for Napoleon III and Eugenie of Montijo. The **Musée de la Mer** on the Esplanade du Rocher de la Vierge is open Mon.-Sat. in summer, 9am-7pm and Sun. 10am-noon and 2-6pm. The **Exposition de Modèles Anciens** (antique car show) at 13, avenue Reine Victoria, is open daily in summer from 10:30am-1:30pm and 3:30pm-midnight; admission 2F. These sights won't keep you away from the casinos very long, but they're worth a try.

Practical Information

Syndicat d'Initiative: In the square d'Ixelles, at the corner of ave. Joseph-Petit and rue Louis-Barthou (tel. 24-20-24). The mayor closed down the local student information center two years ago, calling it a "breeding-ground for communism," but at least the syndicat is very helpful and attuned to the needs of all. Open Mon.-Sat. in summer 9am-7:30pm and Sun. 10am-12:30pm.

Post Office: rue de la Poste. Open in summer Mon.-Fri 9am-7pm and Sat. 9-11:45am.

Train Station: The downtown station has closed down and now all trains go through Biarritz-la Negresse (tel. 23-58-95) 3km out of town, with regular shuttle bus service to town.

Police: ave. Joseph-Petit (tel. 24-68-24); Medical Emergency: (tel. 24-41-83).

Telephone Code: (59).

Accommodations

The cheaper hotels, also those more likely to have vacancies, are generally up the hill from the beach near the train station. Everything is booked up for July and August, so reserve in advance, plan to camp, or stay in Anglet and commute.

Hôtel Barnetche, 5*bis*, rue Floquet (tel. 24-22-25). Rooms are 55-61F including breakfast. Open summer only.

Hôtel Dufan, 18, rue Jean Bart (tel. 24-14-45), primarily for long-term stays, has five or six doubles for 58F. Showers 6F, breakfast 8F. *Pension complet* 70F. These fill up even faster than rooms in the rest of Biarritz, so try early. (Closed Sat.)

Hôtel Alga Hesi, rue de l'Imprimerie (tel. 24-50-14). In a charming part of town, a five minute walk from the beach and town center. Rooms 50-80F for 2 or 3 persons. If full, try the cheaper but less inviting Chalet Reine next door which has doubles for 65F. Showers 6F, breakfast 9F (closed Oct.-May).

Camping: In Biarritz itself there are three sites, but the whole coast is full of campgrounds (there are over a dozen in St.-Jean-de-Luz). In Biarritz, the Municipal on ave. Kennedy, quartier de la Négresse (no phone), is the least expensive, but Splendid (tel. 23-01-20) and Biarritz (tel. 23-00-12), both on the rue d'Harcet, are closer to the beach.

Food

Hôtel Dufau, 18, rue Jean-Bart. Even if you don't stay here, you can sample their excellent *beignet de cervelle fimancière*. *Menus* at 29, 38, and 49F.

Las Vegas Self-Service, 21, ave. Edouard VII. Dishes 6-18F including an assortment of regional specialities. Try the *saumon froid* (18F) or a *salade* (17F), and top off your meal with *gâteau basque*, a Basque cake (5.50F).

La Pizzeria, 20, ave. Edouard VII. Pizzas 19-25F and other specialities (spaghetti bolognese for 18F and desserts for 12F). A fancy place with tablecloths, candles, and a fireplace.

St.-Jean-de-Luz

Biarritz and Anglet don't have a monopoly on fine beaches in the area—some of the most spectacular scenery can be found further south along the Côte Basque. Frequent trains running to the Spanish border stop at Bayonne, Biarritz, and then at the smaller towns to the south; take advantage of this for planning day-trips down the Basque coast, as accommodations there tend to be expensive. Superb beaches await you at **Guethery** and **Hendaye,** and St.-Jean-de-Luz offers a perfect scallop-shaped bay, where bright blue tuna trawlers ply the waters and the Pyrénées serve as a backdrop. St.-Jean-de-Luz has preserved its Basque character better than Biarritz in the face of the tourist onslaught.

The summer season abounds with festivals, bullfights, concerts, grand *chistera,* and the world cup of Cesta Punta. Tickets to the lightning-fast *Pelote Basque* start at 22F, and matches are played most Tuesday and Friday nights throughout the summer and well into September. The principal backdrop for the buzz of activity is, of course, the beach and the pleasant walkway alongside it, but the town itself is also quite pretty. Louis XIV was married to Maria Theresa of Spain in the **Eglise St.-Jean Baptiste,** one of the finest examples of Basque architecture. Its plain exterior conceals a brightly decorated nave with three galleries traditionally reserved for men. The women sit below under a wooden barrel vault. The bachelor sun king once stayed in the **Maison Louis XIV** on Place Louis XIV. Redone in seventeenth-century style, the house is open to the public from June 8 to September 22 daily except Sun. morning, from 10am-12:30pm and 3-7pm; admission 6F.

Practical Information

Syndicat d'Initiative: place Foch (tel. 26-03-16; follow ave. de Verdun from the station) will give you maps and city events information, and provides an accommodations booking service. Open Mon.-Sat. 10am-12:30pm and 2-7pm, Sun. 10am-noon.

Post Office: blvd. Victor-Hugo (tel. 26-01-95). From July 1 to Sept. 30 open Mon.-Fri. 8am-7pm and Sat. 8am-noon.

American Express Agent: Socoa Voyages, 31, blvd. Thiers (tel. 26-06-27). Open Mon.-Sat. 9am-12:30pm and 2:30-6:30pm.

Train Station: ave. de Verdun (tel. 26-02-08). Bike rental next door.

Police: rue de la Corderie (tel. 26-08-47).

Banks: open on Sat. until noon, but closed Mon. Occasional afternoon banking hours.

Market Day: Tuesday and Friday mornings on the blvd. Victor-Hugo.

Telephone Code: (59).

Accommodations and Food

Hotels fill up rapidly in the summer, so you might want to reserve in advance. If you're stuck for a room, the **Centre UCPA** (tel. 26-18-17) in nearby Ciboure may have space.

> **Restaurant Hotel Elisabeth,** ave. Labrouche, a block from the station. The best deal at 58F.

> **Hotel Chiquito,** 10, rue Deluc (tel. 26-42-68). Doubles 70-90F, with sink and bidet. Breakfast included. Near the Casino (a rather dumpy roulette, boule and blackjack joint).

> **Hôtel Eskualduna** (tel. 26-00-55) has simple singles and pleasant doubles for 95F. Showers 10F.

> **Hôtel Chez Loulouche,** 4, rue Deluc (tel. 26-08-72). Beachfront location shows up in the price, 139F for a double, which mercifully includes breakfast.

> **Hôtel Restaurant de Verdun:** across from the train station. Singles are 45-60F and doubles go for 80F.

> **Camping:** There are twelve sites in St.-Jean-de-Luz proper, eleven more within 13km, most of them with three stars, and their combined capacity is in the thousands. Incredibly, most are filled, but the syndicats in Biarritz and St.-Jean-de-Luz will find you a free camping spot where possible. **Camping International** (tel. 26-30-32), **Camping Chibaou Berria** (tel. 26-11-94), and **Camping de la Ferme** (tel. 26-27-83) are all in the Quartier Erromardie north of downtown.

Basque and Spanish specialties are the rule, but prices are steep. There are plenty of shops on the blvd. Victor-Hugo and the rue Gambetta where you can buy your own fare and do it yourself. Try *pâté de canard* (duck pate; 9F a jar) on a *baguette* with slices of tomato. The **Restaurant Ramuntcho,** 24, rue Garat, has a wonderful *menu* for 35F including two dishes and dessert. A steaming heap of mussels can be washed down with an unorthodox red wine, Corbières (10.50F a half-bottle).

St.-Jean-Pied-de-Port

The heart of the Basque culture rests in the small mountain villages nestled in the Pyrénées, and you should travel here if you want to get a better view of some of the region's spectacular scenery. The survival of the Basque way of life is largely a result of the region's inaccessibility. Villages tend to lie in isolated mountain valleys with few connections to the outside.

An ancient capital of the inland Pays Basque, **St.-Jean-Pied-de-Port** lies in a beautiful mountain valley, flanking what was once the most popular pilgrimage route to Santiago da Compostela in Spain. In recent years it has become somewhat touristed, and for a good reason—it is one of the prettiest bases in the area.

The ancient **haute ville,** framed by the **Porte d'Espagne** and the **Porte St.-Jacques,** consists of one narrow street bordered by houses made from the dark red stone of the region. Alongside the Nive is the **Eglise Notre-Dame-du-Pont,** a simple church which doubles as fortress (note the machicolated tower outside). At the top of the rue d'Espagne is the path up to the massive **citadel,** which is closed to the public, but walk around the former moat for a fine panorama of the valley.

Practical Information

Syndicat d'Initiative: 14, place Charles-de-Gaulle, (tel. 37-03-57). Open 9am-12:30pm and 2-7pm Mon.-Sat.; in winter 9am-12pm and 3-6:30pm, Sun. 10am-12:30pm. Located right in the center of town (main square) and has walking and hiking itineraries for sale.

Train Station: Ave. Renaud (tel. 37-02-00). Regular train service to Bayonne.

Post Office: rue de la Post. Open Mon.-Fri. 9am-12pm and 2-6pm, Sat. 9am-12pm.

Police: rue d'Vgange, (tel. 37-03-36).

Hospital: Fondation Luro, Ispoure, (tel. 37-00-55). For taxi-ambulance (tel. 37-05-70 or 37-05-00).

Telephone Code: (59).

Accommodations and Food

The least expensive hotels lie on the outskirts of town. Try **Le Bon Accueil,** a short walk from the Porte d'Espagne on the D918 (tel. 37-00-48), with eight rooms for 40F and meals from 28F. The syndicat d'initiative will help with accommodations and has an accommodations board outside when closed.

If they have room, **La Vieille Auberge** offers the best deal in town. 50F gets you a double with dark wooden cabinets, a small terrace with a view, and a shower. *Petit déjeuner* 9F and *menus* for 37 and 40F. **Hôtel Itzalpea,** place du Tringuer (tel. 37-03-66), has very plain rooms. For a double 60F, showers 5F, and breakfast 8F. Around the block from the tourist office and through the ancient city walls, **Hôtel Ramutcho** (tel. 37-03-91) has good rooms with pleasant views, 64-80F; showers 5F, breakfasts 11F.

You can also rent rooms in private homes for 70-80F and up. Get a list in the tourist office. St.-Jean-Pied-de-Port boasts a nice **municipal campground** on the Nive riverbank and a pelota's throw from the municipal fronton (5.50F per person, 3.50F per tent).

St. Jean is a good place to sample some Basque specialties. **Restaurant Hillion,** place du Tringuer (across from the tourist office) has a 25F *menu* that includes *crudité, poulet basquaise,* and *gâteau basque.* **Bar Restaurant Americain** is run by American immigrants who offer a 35F *menu.*

Sights

In the summertime, St.-Jean-Pied-de-Port abounds with activity. There are dances and concerts every other night, and a different kind of *pelote* almost every day at the fronton. Tickets cost 15-20F, but you can easily watch a match from the fence. Jai-alai fans should not miss the **Musée de la Pelote Basque** (2F). Books available in the tourist office map out one- to six-hour excursions in the surrounding mountains and villages. One interesting route leads from St.-Jean-de-Luz to the spa town of **Cambo-les-Bains** through the pretty villages of **Ascain, Sare,** and **Ainhoa.** A single train line follows the River Nive past Cambo through some superb mountain scenery to St.-Jean-Pied-de-Port.

St.-Jean is also part of the grand footpath from Paris to Santiago de Compostela. Each weekend one of the region's villages has festivals which include public dancing (until as late as 3am) on Saturday and Sunday evenings and a public meal consisting of mutton and beans on Tuesday.

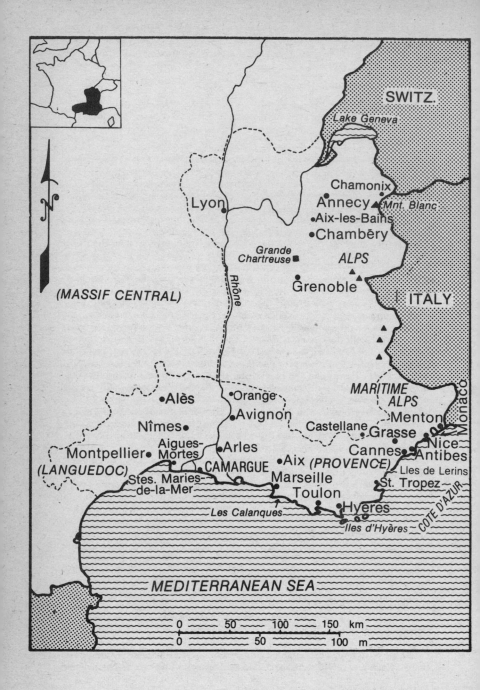

Provence

In this favored province of the Romans, the hills are colored with lavender, mimosa, and grapevines, and the air is fragrant with the *herbes de provence*—thyme, rosemary and sage—that grow wild over the hills. The vibrant, almost magical quality of the region inspired countless medieval troubadours in their musical verses of courtly love. Van Gogh came to Provence in search of "another light . . . a more limpid sky," and he spent years struggling to capture the almost frighteningly blue sky. If the same sky covers all of Provence, the landscape varies, with mountains in the east, haunting rock formations along the Delta, and gentle hills and rocky cliffs in the **Vaucluse**.

With their impressive Roman remains, **Orange** and **Arles** sit near the Rhone as it heads for the Mediterranean. **Avignon** was famous as the seat of the papacy in the later Middle Ages, and it is now best known for its summer arts festival. Roman **Nîmes** and elegant **Aix-en-Provence** stand at the tips of the Provençal triangle formed at the mouth of the Rhône, gateways to the unspoiled Languedoc on one side and the pampered Côte d'Azur on the other. The dreamy marshland of the **Camargue** and the long beaches of the southern coast can offer respite from crowds who descend upon Provence in search of its summer music and arts festivals.

The people of Provence are proud of their Roman origins, and they consider themselves more aware of their emotions than their northern countrymen. The shaded promenades, fountains and endless glasses of *pastis* at sidewalk cafes encourage a slower, more relaxed pace of life. Though the nineteenth-century poet Frederic Mistral is still a great hero here, the *provençal* dialect he attempted to revive is heard less and less, as many Provençal customs disappear or become festivalized.

Ever since Julius Caesar exalted the Provençal wines in his *Commentaries*, the region has been exporting wines. Try in particular the *Côtes du Rhône* and the *Châteauneuf du Pape*. The temperate climate also encourages fruits and vegetables to flourish here—melons, asparagus, rice from the Camargue, olives, garlic, and other herbs abound. Sample dishes like *ratatouille* (a rich blend of eggplant, zucchini, and tomatoes), *bouillabaisse* (a thick and usually expensive fish stew), and *pistou* (a delicate vegetable soup with just a touch of basil). Also try *l'aïoli*, a mayonnaise-like sauce, made from olive oil and a mild garlic, and served with hors d'oevres, vegetables, and fish soup.

Rail and bus connections between major Provençal cities are excellent. Bicycle rentals are available at the train stations in Aix, Arles, Avignon and Nîmes. If hitching during the summer, note that the vacationers are not likely to pick you up. Finally, always call ahead for room reservations or else arrive early in the day if you plan to visit a town during festival time, and be prepared for higher prices.

Orange

Orange is a sleepy, ancient town with tangled, narrow streets surrounding its main attraction, the best-preserved **Roman Theater** in France. Most of the theater's surrounding benches have been reconstructed (again providing their original discomfort), but the magnificent stage wall, with its presiding statue of the Emperor Augustus, has remained largely intact. Open daily 9am-noon and 2-5pm in Oct.-March; till 6:30pm April-Sept. Admission 10F, 8F students, includes the adjoining **Musée Lapidaire.** Under Roman rule the residence for legionnaires in Gaul, the city eventually came under the control of the House of Orange-Nassau, the present-day ruling family of the Netherlands. When the Protestant stronghold of Orange was returned to France, Louis XIV had the chateau and the town fortifications razed to the ground as a precaution, leaving only the grand wall of the Theater, which he then praised as "the finest wall in my kingdom."

The **Arc de Triomphe,** the imposing structure standing on the ancient "via Agrippa" which connected Arles to Lyon, testifies more to the vanity and power of Rome than to any particular triumph. However, the elaborately portrayed battle scenes on the north facade commemorate one of Caesar's victories in 49 B.C. Take a walk up the hill of St. Eutrope for a view over the rooftops of Orange and out into the Vaucluse stretching away in the distance. This beautiful area between the Rhone and Durance rivers abounds in delicious-smelling fields of lavender and spices, and small villages are perched amongst these rocky hills. Southwest of Orange lies Châteauneuf-du-Pape, where the strong, rich, red wine is produced. There are **Youth Hostels** at Saignon (tel. 74-39-34), Fountaine de Vaucluse (tel. 20-31-65) and Séguret (tel. 36-93-31) and campgrounds are scattered over the region. For a free walking map, visit the **office de tourisme** in Orange, located in the Park on cours Aristide-Briand (tel. 34-70-88 open summer 8am-6pm daily, except Sun. till 1pm. In the off season closed 2pm-4pm and Sundays.) Another summer branch occupies a kiosk across from the Roman Theater. You can rent bikes from **Hertz,** 13, blvd. Daladier (tel. 34-00-34) for 35F a day.

The town of Orange comes alive on weekends from mid-July to early August, when the theater performs its ancient function and becomes the setting for a series of celebrated opera and chorale productions. Information about performances is available from the **Maison du Théâtre,** places des Frères-Mounet, 84100 Orange (tel. 34-15-52 and 34-24-24). Ticket prices range from 60-300F for opera, 40-220F for concerts.

Orange's few inexpensive hotels fill up fast on festival nights. On a quiet square near the forum are **Hôtel St. Florent,** 4, rue du Mazeau (tel. 34-18-53), with singles at 50F, doubles at 65F, and **Au Père Tranquille,** 8, place aux Herbes (tel. 34-09-23) with 45F singles, doubles 60F, and breakfast for 10F. Two blocks over toward cours Briand is **Hôtel Fréau,** 3, rue Ancienne College (tel. 34-06-26), with clean and simple rooms for 48F. The train station lies about ten minutes from the center of town, but if you don't feel like moving, you can stay at **Hôtel de la Gare** (tel. 34-00-23), which has doubles with showers for 63F, triples 105F. To reach the **Camping Municipal St.-Eutrope** campsite (tel. 34-09-22), you will have to take a strenuous up-hill hike, but a soothing swimming pool is next door. Open March 15-Sept. 30; two people and a tent 7F.

Restaurants are expensive in Orange, but take advantage of the Thursday morning market held at the place Clemenceau, or stock up at the Prisunic Grocery store. From any cafe you can order a *Pan Bagna,* the traditional sandwich of the midi. The best cafes are at the Place aux Herbes and by the Hotel de Ville. Two moderately-priced restaurants with good provençal food are **Le Yalca,** rue de Tourre, and **Le Becfin,** 14, rue Weber, both with 45F *menus. Berlingots carpentras* are a popular candy from a nearby town. Buses to Vaison-la-Romaine leave 5 times a day from the station and from the cours

Pourtoules. Banks in Orange close on Saturday and Sunday, so don't spend your last centime on the opera.

Vaison-la-Romaine

A bustling town at the foot of **Mont Ventoux** (1912 meters), Vaison-la-Romaine is actually two towns. The picturesque medieval quarter sits high on a hill, protected by the remaining shell of its twelfth-century fortress, while on the other side of the river **Ouveze,** still connected by the 200-year old Roman bridge is the Gallo-Roman town, which contains some of the most important and visited ruins in France.

Despite its name, the rich Roman heritage of this town was ignored until priests began excavations in 1910. These excavations continue slowly today. What was once a lettuce patch is now the uncovered and reconstructed **Roman Theater,** not as well-preserved as the theater at Orange, but a rival for drawing festival crowds. From mid-July to mid-August Vaison hosts jazz, dance, opera, and drama in the acoustically perfect antique theater. Ticket prices are cheaper (40-120F), crowds are smaller, and events occur more often than at Orange. Every four years in early August (next in 1983), Vaison holds its famous **Choralie,** which brings together several hundred chorale groups from all over the world. Tickets for this are hard to come by, since there is barely enough room for the chorale groups, but music resonates throughout the town and there are informal concerts on street corners. For festival information and reservations, write to Bureau du Festival, 84110 Vaison-la-Romaine, or stop by the festival office, place Sautel (tel. 36-24-79).

The Roman ruins which are open to the public are the **Quartier de Puymin** and **Quartier de la Villasse;** both contain the foundations of wealthy Roman houses, with their elaborate baths and gardens and remarkably preserved mosaics. Scheduled summer tours provide the best way to see these fascinating ruins and the adjoining museum. An enthusiastic tour guide and a little imagination will help bring the ruins back to their former glory (8F). Tours, in French only, leave from the office de tourisme, ave. de Gaulle (tel. 36-02-11). Open 9am-7pm every day from mid-July-Sept.; 9am-noon and 2-5pm from Oct.-March; and from 9am-6pm the rest of the year. By the Quarter Villasse is the **Cathédrale Notre Dame,** a potpourri of styles and eras, and the more interesting, adjoining eleventh-century **Cloître,** with its still visible capitals and unique, double-faced gothic cross (8F student *forfait* will get you into all the monuments; hours same as tourist office).

A five-minute walk uphill from the ruins will take you to the narrow, winding streets and gardens of the feudal quarter. The whole community once moved here for protection against highwaymen and religious wars, but the original Roman village was eventually reclaimed. Climb up to the abandoned fortress for a fine view of the vineyard-covered Ventoux area.

In 1483, Pope Sixtus II gave Vaison the right to hold a weekly market, and Vaison exercises that right every Tuesday morning. The lively market is a sensual delight, filling the whole town center with sweet smelling herbs and inexpensive fruits, vegetables, clothes and pottery. There are no trains to Vaison, but buses run five times a day to and from Orange (11F) and also from Avignon. Hotels are scarce and expensive, but there is a good **Camping Municipal** (tel. 36-00-78; open March-Oct.) about 1km down ave. César Geoffray, or try the **Centre Cultural à Cour Joie** (tel. 36-00-78) next door. The **Auberge des Plantanes,** 12, place Susauze (tel. 36-02-16), off the place Monfort, has small, neat singles for 48F and a good 30F *menu* downstairs. Eight km from Vaison, on the route to Orange, in the beautiful, sun-scorched village of **Se-**

guret, is an exceptional **youth hostel** (tel. 36-93-31), 25F a night with breakfast, home-cooked dinners 23F. Open June 15-Sept. 15. The only disadvantage to this charming hostel lies in its night-time inaccessibility; the last bus from Vaison leaves at 4pm. The tourist office has walking maps of the area, and you can rent a bike from Monsieur Derey on cours Tauligan. Break up your promenades by visiting the area wine *caves,* which offer samples of the fine rosés of the Ventoux, and the strong red wines of Gigondas.

Avignon

Like the rest of Provence, Avignon took most of its inspiration from Italy—not from the Romans but from their successors, the medieval papacy. In the fourteenth century, when a feud broke out between the King of France and the Vatican, Avignon suddenly found itself the seat of the papacy (the so-called "second Babylonian captivity"). Although the seven French popes maintained their stronghold here for less than a century—Gregory XI transferred the seat back to Rome in 1377—they had enough time to build the immense **Palais des Papes,** and to transform Avignon into a somber, overwhelming network of battlements, towers, and chapels guarding the Rhone.

Avignon is sternly circumscribed by a circle of rugged city walls built to keep out highwaymen, but not even stone walls can hold back the crowds who descend for the tumultuous **Festival** from early July to early August, when the town overflows with plays, musicians, films, and young people from all over Europe. Prices of hotels and restaurants increase at this time, and unless you plan ahead, you may have to join the crowds sleeping on the streets and riverbanks.

Practical Information

Avignon's main axis is the **rue de la République,** which extends from the train station to the center of town. As you walk along it you'll pass all the essential points: the station, the city wall, post office, tourist office and Festival center, banks, cinemas, place de l'Horloge, and the Palais des Papes, with its adjoining Cathedral and gardens.

Office de Tourisme, 41, cours Jean-Juarès (tel. 82-65-11) about 3 blocks from the station. Pick up the fine brochure on Avignon (in English) for 3F, the bus schedule, and a list of foyers and cheap restaurants. Open daily in July and Aug. 9am-8pm, otherwise 9am-6pm; closed Sun. Guided tours of the city are given from July-Sept. daily except Sun.; 10F, 5F students. The Accueil located across from the station at the left turret of the porte de la République will help find accommodations (open late nights: 7pm-2am.)

Reserving Accommodations: The syndicat runs a service that will book a room for 2F (tel. 82-02-03) but they won't accept reservations in advance. During the Festival, all bargain rooms vanish quickly, so arrive early. There's also a **Centre de Réservation** outside the station, on the left as you exit (tel. 86-65-08 or 86-67-84; open daily 9:45am-noon and 2-6:30pm), where you can also change money on weekends and holidays.

Festival: Box office at the tourist office (tel. 86-24-43), open 10:30am-12:30pm and 2:30-6:30pm daily after June 15. After 5pm, no tickets are sold for same-day performances, but you can often procure a ticket by lining up an hour before the performance. Most tickets cost 40-60F. For any "off" events, you can buy tickets at the door (30-40F) or contact the "off" bureau, Conservatoire de Musique, opposite Palais des Papes, open daily 11am-12:30pm and 3:30-6:30pm. A kiosk in the place de l'Horloge has festival information and a schedule of free street performances. For Festival information tel. 86-24-43, 9:30am-12:30pm and 3:30-6:30pm from June 15 till the festival, 8am-10pm during the festival. Or write after June 15th (at least a week in advance) to Bureau du Festival, BP 92, 84006 Avignon Cedex, with payment enclosed.

Post Office: Ave. du Président-Kennedy (tel. 82-99-40). Right behind the walls across from the train station. Open Mon.-Fri. 8am-7pm, Sat. and Sun. 8am-noon. Telephones upstairs. Also a post office in Place Pie, same hours, with Poste Restante (specify which office on letters) and shorter telephone lines.

Train Station. Porte de la République (tel. 82-50-50). Twenty trains a day travel to and from Paris. Arles is only 20 minutes away. Central information desk open 9am-noon and 2-7pm. Bike rentals are available at the station, 20F a day with 150F deposit.

Bus Station: Some excursion buses leave from outside the train station (tel. 86-36-75). Open Easter-Sept., 8:15-11:30am and 2-6pm. Normal intercity buses leave at the Porte St.-Michel; turn right from the station and the buses are on the left about a block away. Schedules are posted there, or ask at the train information desk.

Police: (tel. 86-41-41). **Medical Emergency:** Hôpital Durance, Chemin du Lavarin (tel. 89-91-31).

Telephone Code: (90).

Accommodations

Hotels in Avignon become outrageously expensive during the Festival and the handful of cheaper ones are reserved long in advance. A single will run at least 65F. Several organizations open up inexpensive dormitory accommodations during the festival. Get a list from the tourist office (there's no youth hostel), or try some of the following alternatives:

Pax Christi, rue Buffon (tel. 85-13-34). An exceptionally warm and relaxed place, organized by a Christian charity and run by a group of young, good-natured volunteers. 15 minutes from the town center in an interesting area. 42F for dorm bed, breadfast, and dinner. Additional 3F membership fee. Showers free. Curfew 2am. Open only during the festival. No reservations.

Foyer Bagatelle, Ile de la Barthelasse, across the river in the camping compound (tel. 86-30-39). 16F a night, breakfast 9F. **Foyer YMCA,** 7bis, chemin de la Justice (tel. 25-46-20), bed and breakfast 23-48F. **Foyer des Jeunes Contadines,** 75, rue Vernet (tel. 86-10-52), women only; located near the center of town. Singles 35F, rooms with 2 or 3 beds 25F. Breakfast 5F. **Association Jeunesse Accueil,** le Candau de Bellevue, Rte. de Nimes, Les Angles (tel. 25-00-49). Leave Avignon by the Porte de l'Ouille, cross the Pont Daladier—the first bridge to the left of the Pont St.-Benezet—and follow the Ancienne Route de Nîmes. Tent accommodation, 7F per night; breakfast 6F, meals 20F, cold meals 10F (open July and August only). **CEMEA** organizes week-long stays at different centers in Avignon, 100F a day, *pension complet*. An artsy, chic crowd which includes many festival workers. Reservations should be made in advance through their main office, 76, blvd. de la Villette, 75019 Paris, but you may be able to get in at the start of a session. Festival office at 8, rue Frédéric Mistral (tel. 86-49-72). **CROUS,** 39, ave. G. Permamos in Paris (tel. 329-12-43) also organizes week-long stays during the Festival.

Le Saint-Paul, 10, rue Dorée (tel. 82-33-06). Great location—take a left off rue de la République down rue Mignard. Pleasant and convenient. Singles 59F, doubles 79F, includes breakfast. Showers 7F.

Hôtel Pacific, 7, rue Agricol-Perdiquier (tel. 82-43-36). One block before the syndicat. A well-kept hotel with comfortable rooms. No singles, doubles 60-75F, breakfast 12F, showers 6F. On the same street, the **Parc** at #18 (tel. 82-71-55) is slightly more expensive, and the **Splendid** at #17 (tel. 86-14-46) has a few rooms for 60F.

Le St.-Pierre, 4, rue Banasterie (tel. 82-47-18). Provides the basics, but little more. On a quiet street. Singles 45F, doubles 70F.

Le Phocéen, 2, rue Campane, is faded but cheap; 2 singles at 30F, 10 doubles at 40F, 3 triples at 70F. The required breakfast is 10F. Always booked up during the festival.

Excelsior, 2, rue Petite Calade (tel. 86-22-96). A bit worn, but generally comfortable, with a pleasant terrace. One single at 68F, doubles 90-130F, breakfast included.

Camping: Bagatelle (tel. 86-30-39) and **TCF Municipale** (tel. 82-63-50) are two immense campgrounds across the river on the Ile de la Barthelasse. Hot showers, cafeteria, quiet green setting, and a view of the Palais.

If you want to call in advance, try the **Angleterre,** 29, blvd. Raspail (tel. 86-34-31), with singles for 75F. The **Savoy,** 17, rue de la République (tel. 86-46-82) is a huge and plush two-star hotel on the main drag, with rooms for 60-70F, breakfast included. **Le Paris-Nice,** 38, cours Jean-Jaurès opposite the syndicat (tel. 82-03-21) is another central, two-star hotel with some rooms at 60F.

As a last resort, you can try sleeping on the banks of the river or in front of the train station. The police won't bother you, but guard your valuables carefully. (Another alternative is to sleep here during the day and spend your nights romping at the Festival.)

Food

Cafe-restaurants overflow the place de l'Horloge. Meals are overpriced here, so wander off to dinner and return for coffee when puppeteers, strolling musicians, and clowns compete to entertain you. The **parc le Rocher des Doms,** overlooking the Rhône, is a nice picnic spot and has an outdoor cafe by the flowery pond. (You can get good provisions from the large indoor market at **Les Halles,** daily except Monday, or the supermarket in the Nouvelle Galeries on rue de la Républic).

Ask at the tourist office for the list of restaurants with 30F meals, or wander past the off-beat restaurants along **rue des Liefs** and **rue Philonarde** in the immigrant quarter. Avignon specialties are the côtes-du-Rhône wines, melons, honey from lavender, and the strong *liqueur de Poire*.

Le Pain Bis, 6, rue Armand-de-Pontmarin, very relaxed and refreshing. At noon they serve sandwiches, cold plates, and drinks under an archway in a quiet, narrow street (10-25F). In the evening, they offer a good vegetarian *menu* for 35F, and occasionally have live music. Closed Sunday.

Crêperie du Cloître, 9, place des Chataignes, behind the Palais des Papes in a quiet, cloistered square. Simple buttered crêpes to extravagant dessert crêpes (6-18F), 3-crêpe *menu* 26F and exotic teas. The strawberry tea is strange and sweet. Open noon-2pm and 9pm till late. Around the corner **La Bergerie,** 3, rue Banastière, has more substantial fare and provençal specialties; 5-course, 45F *menu*. Try the delicious *gratin de moule provençal*.

Les Pieds dans le Plat, 48, rue des Lices is a chic, Parisian-style café-restaurant with great salads and fancy hamburger plates (17-19F) and inexpensive drinks and desserts. Or try **l'Ecuelle** at #28, which has a more traditional *menu* at 35F.

Le Brasserie Centenaire, 21, place Pie, has the best situated terrace in this popular square; 18F garnished plat du jour, 26F *menu.* A block down, off rue Thiers, is **La Pignotte,** 4, rue d'Amphoux, with a tiny dining room and an enormous menu selection. Good pizza and pasta from 15F. **Le Noctambule,** 22, rue du Chapeau Rouge, is a dimly-lit, artsy bar for late-nighters, with crêpes and beer.

Sights

The vast, brooding mass of the **Palais des Papes** has no peer anywhere. Windowless and forbidding, it has the demeanor of a hostile fortress rather than a residence, and its function as a barracks during the Revolution still seems more appropriate than its modern use as a showplace for Picasso exhibitions and theatrical spectacles. The exterior, a facade of recessed arches, towers, and slender spires, provides a different impression from every vantage point. Look for the Renaissance graffiti in the **Chapelle St.-Martial.** The interior, which you have to visit in a crowded, guided tour group, is notable for the dimensions of its halls and the frescoes decorating the chapels. Not all depict religious and biblical scenes; some of the chambers are covered with vibrant frescoes of the hunt. Summer tours (in French only) last 75 minutes and cost 20F (students 10F). Adjacent to the Palace is the **Cathédrale Notre Dame des Doms,** a rather heavy, Romanesque church with a richly decorated interior which provides a cool respite from summer heat. Built in the twelfth century, it has been considerably restored and rebuilt since. Built under two of the Avignon popes (one of whom is now ornately entombed unde the cathedral, 2F visit). The Cathedral's fortifications retain most of the towers and battlements of their original construction.

At the far end of the place du Palais is the austere **Petit Palais,** which once housed cardinals and now houses a fine collection of Italian primitive and Renaissance paintings. Admission is 6F for students, but for 8F you can take the guided tour which leaves once daily, and then wander around on your own.

From the lovely park **le Rocher des Doms** (open daily 7:30am-9pm) you can see the twelfth-century **Pont St. Benezet,** which ends abruptly half-way across the Rhône. Only four of the original 22 arches remain. This is the "Pont d'Avignon" of the nursery rhyme, and legend has it that the bridge was constructed on the advice of a shepherd boy, St. Benezet, who was told by visiting angels to build a bridge across the Rhône.

Visible across the river is Villeneuve-lez-Avignon, its hillside dominated by the **Fort St.-André,** a fine, feudal castle with terraced gardens. When Avignon belonged to Italy, France began at Villeneuve. If you cross to the fort, you can enjoy a respite from the crowd and also a clearer perspective of Avignon, whose Palais from a distance resembles a crumbling deity. Closed at midday and on Tuesdays, the **Tour de Philippe la Bel,** a fourteenth-century fortification, still stands where the Pont St.-Benezet used to end. Also worth a look are the ruins of the **Chartreuse du Val de Benediction,** founded during the popes' Avignon residency.

Finally, don't miss the **Musée Calvet,** 65, rue Joseph-Vernet. Housing an impressive collection of paintings, from Breughel canvases through those of David, Dufy, and Vasarely, the museum also has the usual exhibits of Paleolithic molars and grinning skulls. Open daily 9am-noon and 2-6pm, closed Tuesday; admission 10F, students 5F.

Entertainment

The **Festival d'Avignon** is a riot of activities, a non-stop explosion of plays, films, dance, mime, and everything else from Gregorian chants to an all night reading of the *Odyssey*. There is hardly a cloister, church, or basement without some play or event, or an archway without a sitarist or puppeteer. The official Festival has twelve different venues, most impressively the courtyard of the Palais and the municipal theater; events start between 9:30 and 11pm. The "Off" fringe festival has at least 35 different locations. For film fanatics, the **Utopia** and **Cinevox** each show 25 films a day (admission 14F). There are also exhibitions, video shows and concerts galore. If you happen to be here on Bastille day (July 14), the festivities are intensified by fireworks and dancing in the streets.

Avignon calms down considerably during the rest of the year, but if you can not be here during the Festival, all is not lost. The **Théâtre Municipal** on place de l'Horloge (tel. 82-23-44) offers regular productions of opera, drama, and classical concerts. The box office is open daily 11am-6pm (tickets 20-100F, student discounts available). The **Conseil Culturel**, 8*bis*, rue de Mons (tel. 82-67-08) has information on jazz clubs and theater groups in operation all year round.

Near Avignon

Since many of Avignon's neighboring towns are closely and often dra-matically set on rocky hills, it's worth hopping from city to village and back again, or take advantage of abundant camping (ask for a list of campgrounds at any tourist office). Early morning excursion buses in summer descend to the beaches of **Saintes Maries-de-la-Mer** and return in the evening. **Carpentras** preserves a small triumphal arch and a magnificently decorated fifteenth-century synagogue, the oldest in France. From mid-July to mid-August the town hosts a festival of opera, ballet, and drama in its open-air theater. Write or call the Hôtel de Ville after July 1 (tel. 63-15-45). **Gordes,** which houses a permanent Vasarely exhibition in the Renaissance chateau (open daily except Tues., 10am-noon and 2-6pm), is a picturesque town cut into hillside. Nearby is the twelfth-century Cistercian **Abbaye de Senanque** (syndicat tel. 72-05-65). Châteauneuf-du-Pape is the home of world famous vineyards and a ruined castle, and it hosts several classical concerts at the end of July (for information call the syndicat, tel. 39-71-08).

The tiny, luxuriant village of **Fontaine-de-Vaucluse,** where the poet Petrarch lived for sixteen years after meeting Laura in a church in Avignon, is also the site of one of the largest springs in the world. In spring, water gushes out of a funnel-shaped cave at the base of a cliff to form the cascading river Sorgue, which then flows into a smooth Roman canal. The source is impressive even in summer and fall, when the water-level drops and you can descend down into the cave. Forget about hotels in this heavily-touristed town, but there is a **municipal camping** sight open June thru mid-Sept. (tel. 20-32-38) just outside of town. The **Youth Hostel** (tel. 20-31-65), a fifteen minute walk from town, also allows camping year round. The **syndicat d'initiative** (tel. 20-32-22) is open Easter thru Oct. 15.

Arles

Arles is a town with an international flavor. The main sights in Arles are Roman; its most famous resident (Van Gogh) was Dutch and its meals and entertainment have a Spanish touch. The sunbaked city offers summer dances and concerts in its **Antique Theater** and bullfights in the **roman Arena.** If the restorations of these monuments seem a bit whimsical, they at least evoke the spirit of this "Little Rome of Gaul," where Emperor Constantine kept his second capital. Arles' status as a religious center during the middle ages is recalled by the **Eglise et Cloître St.-Trophime.** Beaches and intriguing marshland of the Carmargue are only a half-hour away.

Practical Information

Office de Tourisme: (tel. 92-29-35), a modern office by the esplanade at the corner of blvd de Lices and rue Jean-Jaurès, next to the Post Office. They'll find you a room for the price of the phone call. Ask for their free brochure on Arles and the region. Open Mon.-Sat. 9am-12:30pm and 2-7pm, Sun. 9am-1pm. Nov.-April it closes at 6pm and on Sundays. The **Bureau du Festival** and box office are at 35, place de la République (tel. 96-47-00), next to the Eglise St.-Trophime.

Bus Information: For all excursions to such places as Les Baux, consult **Les Cars Verts de Provence,** 16, blvd. Georges-Clemenceau (tel. 96-27-64 or 96-35-02) or **Arles Voyages** next door (tel. 96-88-73). Buses from here go as far as Morocco (every Tuesday). Regular buses travel to Nîmes, Salin-de-Giraud, Port.-St.-Louis-du-Rhône, and Stes.-Maries-de-la-Mer (21F each way) several times each day, leaving from the train station off place Lamartine or the Station Bar on blvd. des Lices.

Bike Rentals: At the train station or Ets Mountuori, rue de 4 Septèmbre.

Hitching: To hitch north to Les Baux, follow ave. Lamartine 2km out towards Avignon to D17. For the Carmargue, cross the Rhône and take the ave. de la Carmargue, or for Nîmes keep following N113.

Launderette: **Washmatic,** rue Jouvène. Open 8:30am-12:15pm and 2:30-7pm. Closed Mon. mornings.

Telephone Code: (90).

Accommodations

Hotels are relatively numerous and clustered around the **place Voltaire** and **place du Forum.** In July and August, you should arrive early to be sure to get a room.

Auberge de Jeunesse (IYHF), ave. Maréchal-Foch (tel. 96-18-25). About a 20 min. walk from the station, though only 5 min. from the main drag. If you arrive by train, follow ave. Talbot to ave. Emile-Combes, then follow the arrows at the large intersection at the end of this avenue. Clean and modern but near railroad tracks and a little expensive. 36F per day including breakfast. Meals 27F; showers free. Often booked up by groups, so come early. Open June-Oct., 7:30-10am and 5-11pm. Next-door you'll find the municipal swimming pool (5F); open 10am-8pm, closed Mon.

Hôtel Moderne, 12, place du Forum (tel. 96-08-21). Located by the best cafe spot in town, 15 minutes from the station. Clean and sunny. Twelve rooms between 42-60F. Breakfast 9F, showers 5F. Reservations advised for July and August. Closes at 11pm, so ask for a key.

Hôtel du Trident, 9, rue de la Liberté (tel. 96-00-60), right off the place du Forum. With its original paintings and even a piano in one of the rooms, this hotel still resembles the fashionable home it used to be. You can bring food and eat on the terrace or hang out in the drawing room. In the attic is a 40F single and 50F double; other doubles from 56F to 75F, and one six-person room with shower, 169F. Breakfast 10F, showers 8F. The front door is kept locked, so you must ring to enter.

Hôtel Mistral, 16, rue Docteur-Fanton, (tel. 96-12-64), off the place Forum, has faintly decrepit rooms, but you can't beat the prices or location; singles 25F, doubles 40-50F, showers 3F, breakfast 9F. Another faded bargain is the nearby **Pizzeria-Hôtel de Studio,** 6, rue Réattu (tel. 96-33-26) by the musée Réattu with clean, adequate rooms. Doubles for 35F, 70F with two beds and a shower. Breakfast 10F, showers 10F.

Hôtel de France, place Lamartine (tel. 96-01-24). Looks out on a rather bleak square, but conveniently next to the station. Rooms are modern, well-equipped, and neat. Most large rooms for one or two people 56F. Breakfast 13F, showers 9F. Or try the **Terminus Van Gogh** next door (tel. 96-12-32), a pleasant place decorated with Van Gogh prints. Singles 47-58F, breakfast 7F, showers 6F.

Camping: There are several sites in this area but none are in walking distance. The closest is **Camping City,** 67, rte. de Crau (tel. 93-08-86). **Camping Sauvage** (tenting or lighter) is permitted free of charge on the **plage d'Arles,** Salin de Giraud (unfortunately 50km from Arles) and on the routes to Cray and Tarascon. Inquire at the syndicat.

Food

Arles is full of colorful restaurants which are surprisingly inexpensive. A busy open market is held Wednesday and Saturday mornings along the blvd. Combes.

Lou Gardian, rue du 4 Septèmbre. An excellent, family-run place serving provençal specialties. Try the deliciously spiced *cuisses de grenouilles provençal* (frog legs). The food is served in large tureens and elegant pots, and the portions are large. *Menus* at 29F, 40F and 65F are all bargains and include both wine and service, though you'll have to tolerate the Muzak. Closed Sunday. Crowds pour in as soon as the doors open at 7pm, so make reservations or come late.

Le Galoubet, 18, rue de Docteur-Fanton, near the place de Forum. There are several restaurants on this street, but Le Galoubet is by far the best. Simple decor, but excellent cuisine and refreshingly fast service. *Menus* at 27F and 32F including wine. If the food grabs you, ask about a room upstairs (45F; *demi-pension* 72F). Try the pistachio ice cream.

Le Poisson Banane, rue du Forum. Enter from rue de Barreme opposite Hôtel du Trident. Any place that takes its name from a J. D. Salinger story is off to a good start. Run by young people, the atmosphere is warm and welcoming. Shady, vine-covered terrace. Great for late-night indulgences. *Menu* 30F, elaborate desserts from 14F. Try the banana mousse. Closed Wed. and from Nov.-Feb.

Le Criquet, 21, rue porte-de-Laure. A tiny place near the arena with a self-congratulatory air. A decent 30F *menu* features provençal specialities and includes wine. Try their simpler version of *bouillabaisse,* or the *lapin en sauce provençal* (rabbit). Arrive early for the noon day sitting. Two evening sittings at 6:45pm and 8:15pm. It's best to reserve a table on summer evenings.

The best cafes for relaxed sunning and sipping are on the **place de Forum,** where everyone seems to know everyone else; or the **place Voltaire,** strung merrily with colored lights on summer evenings. Those on the busy blvd. des

Lices are crowded and noisy, though the **Maison de la Bière,** opposite the
syndicat, offers beer from around the world at 9F a draw.

Sights

The elliptical **Arena,** one of the largest remaining amphitheaters in France
(holding up to 26,000 bodies), dates from Augustan times. In the eighth century
it was converted into a fortified stronghold, of which three of the four towers
still stand. The top of the amphitheater commands a fine view of the Rhône,
the Camargue, and the plains of the surrounding area. Today, the arena has
been restored to its original purpose of bloody entertainment; bullfights take
place here from Easter to October. The **Antique Theater** nearby retains the
plan, if little of the elevation, of the original Augustan construction. Of the
original stage wall, only two admirable marble columns remain, though they
are sufficient to give an eerie effect to the drama and dance spectacles given
here in the summer. The **Jardin d'Eté,** also in the area, is a pleasant place to
have lunch, but don't even consider sitting on the well-surveyed lawns. The
elegant **Cloister** of the **Church St.-Trophime** and its adjoining chambers are a
worthwhile visit. Notice the simple twelfth-century arches which join them.
The intricately carved pillars and capitals are remarkably intact, especially
along the north galleries. On your way out, take a look at the carved front
portal of Christ in Judgement on the Church St.-Trophime.

Also of interest are the **Thermes Constantin,** ruins of Roman baths constructed in alternating layers of brick and stone, and the **Musée Réattu,** an
exciting, craftily-organized showpiece. An intricate series of inter-connected
rooms is filled with statues, paintings of the Camargue by Henri Rousseau, and
exhibitions of photography and contemporary art. There are two rooms devoted to the classical painter Réattu, but the museum is proudest of the 56
drawings tossed off by Picasso in 1971 and donated by the painter to a city he
often visited and greatly admired. The **Musée d'Art Chrétien** is one of the
richest in the world for early Christian sarcophagi. Many of the more interesting ones come from the Alyscamps, originally an ancient Roman burial ground
and consecrated for Christian use by St.-Trophime. In the Middle Ages, this
cemetery enjoyed such celebrity that bodies were brought to it from great
distances, and Dante referred to it in his *Inferno.* Under the museum are four
extensive galleries dating back to the Romans.

All of the above sights are open 8:30am-12:20pm and 2-6:50pm daily in
summer. Individual admission is 2-5F, with no student discounts. If you plan
to visit most of them, buy a *billet globale* which entitles you to visit all for 16F
(12F for students). The syndicat organizes guided tours in the summer of the
Cloister and Alyscamps (daily except Sun, 3-5F) and on specific topics such as
"Tracing the steps of Vincent Van Gogh."

The **Musée Arlatan,** curiously by-passed by most tourists, houses an extraordinary folk museum, with everything from a stuffed bull to kitchen utensils.
The museum strives to preserve the Provençal traditions which are fast disap-
pearing: the attendants are clothed in regional dress, the signs are in Provençal
dialect, and the exhibits suggest true pride in the Provençal heritage. Open
daily April-Sept. 9am-noon and 2-6pm, closes March at 5pm and in Oct.-Feb.
at 4pm; admission 3F, students 1.50F.

Like most Provençal cities, Arles holds a **Festival** during July and August as
well as an impressive series of international photography exhibitions and
workshops. Every year, on the last Sunday of April, the ancient Confrèrie des
Gardians (the Carmague version of cowboys) gather in the Arena for the **Fête
des Gardians,** a traditional but tame version of a rodeo. On July 2nd and 4th

bonfires are lit in the streets and natives parade in traditional Arlesian costume.

Near Arles

Eighteen miles from Arles is **Les Baux,** a mountain village cut into the rock and overlooking a wild and desolate valley. Once the home of the most powerful counts of Provence, the almost impregnable city held 6000 inhabitants and controlled 79 other towns. In 1632, the castle and its defenses were destroyed by Louis XIII as he criss-crossed the south wiping out Protestant resistance. Only a small portion of the town remains inhabited, and its venerable stone buildings and streets overflow with souvenier shops and busloads of tourists. To avoid the clutter and crowd, walk through the **Porte Eyguires,** once the sole entrance to the town, to the valley below, or walk up to the **Ville Morte** (6F admission), which dominates most of the hill. These medieval remnants merge into the mountainside, the ruined chateau juts starkly into the landscape, and the whole scene gives a sense of a previous, unconnected, and abandoned civilization. From the top of the chateau, you'll get an extraordinary view of the **Val d'Enfer,** and to the south one can see Arles, the Camargue and (on clear days) the sea. It is said that the parched, brutal Val d'Enfer may have inspired Dante's otherworldly imaginings. Les Baux gives its name to bauxite (the chief source of aluminum), but tourism seems to be the main enterprise nowadays. You probably wouldn't want to spend the night here, but if you're stuck, try the one-star **Mas de la Fontaine** (tel. 97-34-13) down below the parking lot. If possible, visit the nearby son-et-lumière show, set in deep caves, called the **Cathédrale d'Image** (continuous shows from 1-6pm; admission 20F, 16F for students; open Easter-Nov.) Buses leave Arles from blvd. Clemenceau, (16F one way).

Four kilometers down the road to Les Baux is the **Abbey of Montmajour,** whose tower, church, and cloisters are worth a visit. From Les Baux, it's a short trip to St.-Remy, site of two interesting Roman monuments. The **Triumphal Arch** is considerably damaged, but what remains contains fine sculpture and ornamentation. Close by is a pyramidal mausoleum with bas-reliefs and sculpted figures. The birthplace of the prophet Nostradamus, **St.-Rémy** also hosts a **Jazz Festival** in late July (stay, if necessary, in **Hôtel de la Caume,** quartier de la Galine; (tel. 92-09-40). Ten minutes away by train on the line to Nîmes, a remarkable, sprawling castle dominates the banks of the Rhône at **Tarascon,** and there's a **Youth Hostel** at 31, blvd. Gambetta, (tel. 91-04-08, open March 15-Oct. 15).

The Camargue

The Camargue is Provence's shadow, its darker, stranger side, unpeopled and untamed. While Provence is hilly and vivid, the Camargue is an endlessly flat and desolate stretch of marshland.

The Camargue seems almost a world apart, with its famous white, wild horses galloping freely across the plains. Extraordinary birds, such as the pink flamingoes, land here on their migratory paths. Many of the area's inhabitants are either gypsies or gardians—rugged cowboys with wide-brimmed hats and tight jeans. Around the tall grass and small pools a cold wind from the north, the *mistral,* whips and howls for days on end.

The area has remained unspoiled because much of it is a protected national park. A small protective zone is accessible to tourists without a permit, but entry into the **Reserve Naturelle Zoologique et Botanique de la Camargue,** one of Europe's most celebrated natural sanctuaries, is limited to scientists or researchers. If you're affiliated with a university, though, any letter from an authority might get you in. In either case, you must first write to the Preserve Office, 2, rue Honoré-Nicolas, Arles.

The area's most famous sights are off-limits, but if you wish to visit anyway, the best of the options are to go by car, or to rent a bike in Arles and follow the D36 to the **Salin-de-Giraud**; it's also possible to rent a bike in **Les Ste.-Maries-de-la-Mer.** Many people enjoy riding the local horses, which have short necks, powerful limbs, and luxuriant manes, but you must generally follow the fairly limited routes set out by a guide. The syndicat in Les. Stes.-Maries will give you a list of all the horse rentals in the area (100F for a half-day, 160F for a full day). It is possible to take a jeep tour of the wild, but these are quite expensive. Although trains don't run in the area, there are buses from Arles to Les Stes. Maries five times a day. The trip takes just under an hour and costs 21F each way; buses leave from outside the station and the Station Bar, blvd. des Lices in Arles, and outside the Arena in Les Stes.-Maries. Tour buses also leave from blvd. Clemenceau in Arles, and from outside the train station in Avignon (tel. 86-36-75).

Les Saintes-Maries-de-la-Mer

The main settlement in the Camargue proper, Les Saintes-Maries is a bright little place sunning itself lazily by the sea. The town is said to have originated when the three Marys, accompanied by the risen Lazarus and their Egyptian servant Sarah, fled their homeland and settled here. Sarah is now the patron saint of the gypsies and on May 24-25 each year (also a smaller version in mid-October) the **Pilgrimage of the Gypsies** is held here. Nomadic people assemble from all over Europe and carry Sarah's statue, amid flowers and fanfare, down from the church to the sea.

Despite its saintly origin, people comes to Les Stes.-Maries to swim, sun-bathe, and windsurf (windsurf rentals available on the beach below the arena, 40F an hour, 25F ½ hour). The beaches in town are usually packed, but if you walk out past the camping, you'll have 25km of beach and dunes to explore. Topless bathing is common, and there is a nude beach 3km out of town. There are several walking and bicycle trails which cut through the natural reserve. The suspicious-looking church-fortress is open daily 10am-noon and 2-7pm; the Statue of Sarah is in the crypt, haloed by candles. You can climb onto the terrace for 5F. A series of Camargue-style bullfights (done without killing the bull) occur on summer evenings in the arena.

While walking through the streets of Les Stes.-Maries, you might be confronted by gypsies grabbing you and pinning medallions onto your shirt. Don't be intimidated, and refuse to pay them. They'll finally curse you and give up.

Practical Information

Syndicat d'Initiative: 5, ave. Van Gogh, next to the arena (tel. 97-82-55). Open daily 9am-noon and 2-7pm. You can change money at the booth next door. Open Mon.-Sat. 9am-1pm and 3:30-6:30pm.

Post Office: ave. Gambetta. Open Mon.-Fri. 8am-7pm, Sat. 8am-noon.

Bike Rental: Hôtel Méditerranée, rue Frédéric-Mistral; or **Force 5,** ave. d'Arles. 40F per day, 70F for two days, special rates for longer periods. Force 5 also rents windsurfing equipment at 150F per day.

Telephone Code: (90).

Accommodations and Food

By far the best way to spend the night here is to camp. Camping on the beaches is now forbidden, although some still sack out on the sand. There are two large, crowded camping grounds right by the ocean and 5 minutes from the center of town. **La Brise** (tel. 97-84-67) is large, open all year, and accepts reservations; 20F for 1 person and a tent. **Le Large** (tel. 97-87-26) next door is much smaller with cold showers; 14F a night, open July-Sept. **Le Clos du Rhône,** 2km on the other side of town is a much quieter three-star site on the banks of the petit Rhône, 18F a night. There is a **Youth Hostel** 10km along the route to Arles at Pioch Badet (tel. 97-91-72), a regular bus stop between Stes.-Maries and Arles.

You'll have trouble finding any hotel rooms for less than 90F, except at the **Bellevue,** rue de l'Etang (tel. 97-81-47), a quiet hotel in a calm area which offers a few rooms for 60F (breakfast 10F). Or stay at **Hôtel de la Plage,** ave. de la République (tel. 97-84-77), which is scruffy but centrally located, and which offers rooms for 50-90F.

Get your provisions at the **Economica,** 12, ave. Victor Hugo, or at the market on the place des Gitaines. All the restaurants in town are expensive and not particularly good. The best bargains are the self-service cafeterias: the **Self-Service** on ave. Van-Gogh, or the Palais de la Bière, 11 G.-Leroy, with good snacks and the best jukebox in town. Many restaurants along rue Frédéric Mistral offer two crêpes and a dessert at lunch time for around 30F, or try the *charcuteries* along rue Victor Hugo.

Aix-en-Provence

Nestled at the base of Monte Ste.-Victoire is Aix (pronounced "Ecks"), a tranquil city of opulent fountains and stately hotels that preserves the dignity it enjoyed five centuries ago as the capital of Provence under the beneficent rule of King René. "Le Bon roi" fostered literature, the arts, and *joi de vivre* (he is said to have introduced Muscatel grapes to Provence). His influence is still felt throughout the town; you can pay your respects at the fountain in the center of town which depicts the good king with vine in hand.

Although the people of Aix are equally proud of local painter Cezanne, the closest you'll get to one of his paintings here are the indifferent doodles of his kept in the **Musée Granet.** The *atelier* (studio) in which he painted during the last few years of his life was restored by American patrons.

Aix's grandest flourish is the **cours Mirabeau,** a wide promenade that sweeps through the center of town, linking the station and syndicat in the west with the churches and the university in the east. On one side of the boulevard are cafes and a few small shops; on the other are some of the best preserved hotel facades in France, with carved doorways and wrought-iron balconies. The streets to the north of the cours Mirabeau are, by contrast, random and winding, and you will arrive in open squares, or fountains will appear where you least expect.

Every summer, Aix hosts a **Music Festival** that is characteristically plush; while Avignon's events are easy-going and casual, concerts in Aix are refined and expensive, with ushers in tuxedos. Numerous others, though, plug into the Festival less grandly—electric guitars and amplifiers pop up, painters sell their water-colors, and Aztec pipes mingle with xylophones and conch shells in and around the cours Mirabeau.

Practical Information

Though close to the other towns in Provence, Aix is not very well connected to them by train. From many cities—such as Arles—you must travel via Marseille (2 hours total). The center of Aix is small enough to explore on foot. From the train station it's a 5-minute walk down ave. Victor Hugo to the place du Général de Gaulle, referred to as "La Rotonde". The cours Mirabeau begins here.

Office de Tourisme: place du Général de Gaulle, a lackadaisical office providing tours of the city daily except Sunday during the summer; tours leave at 10am, 4pm, 9pm, and Wed. and Sat. at 3pm off-season (12F, students 6F). Also an off-hours currency exchange here.

Bureau du Festival: A desk in the Palais de l'Ancien Archevêché (tel. 23-11-20; or 23-37-81 for information throughout the year). Reserve tickets by mail or phone before July 1. Bureau open Feb.-June, 9am-1pm and 2-6pm; thereafter 10am-1pm and 3-7pm. The green booth in the courtyard outside sells tickets during the Festival from 9am-1pm and 3-7pm.

Post Office: 2, rue Lapierre (tel. 27-68-00). Across "La Rotonde" from the tourist office. Open Mon.-Fri. 8am-7pm, Sat. 8am-noon.

Train Station: off rue Gustavo Desplace at the end of rue Victor Hugo (tel. 26-12-50). Several trains daily to Marseille. **Bus Station:** rue Lapierre, behind the Post Office (tel. 27-17-91). Daily buses to Avignon, Marseille, the Alps, and the Riviera.

Student Travel: BIGE/Transalpino tickets at **European Student Travel Center,** 3, rue Lieautaud (tel. 27-93-83).

Bike Rental: At the train station, 12F for a half-day, 20F per full day plus a 150F deposit. Or try **Fanfan,** 10, place de la Marie (tel. 27-29-83).

Police: (tel. 26-04-81). **Medical Emergencies:** Centre Hôpitalier, chemin des Tamaris (tel. 23-98-00).

Women's Center: Information Femmes, 8, rue Pierre et Marie Curie (tel. 23-47-36).

English Bookstore: Paradox, 2, rue Reine-Jeanne (tel. 26-47-99).

Laundromat: Off la Rotonde on the corner of rue Bernadines and rue de la Fontaine. Also, near the University at 60, rue Boulegan (closed Aug.). And **Le Laver,** on rue Aumone Vieille, is a laundromat with character and couches.

Hitching: The autoroute A8 swings right through Aix, but hitching can be tricky. You're better off waiting for the long haul rather than taking a short ride and being dropped off on the higway. For Avignon, follow blvd. de la Républic till it becomes A8. For Nice, follow cours Gambetta.

Telephone Code: (42).

Accommodations

Inexpensive hotels in the center of town are hard to find; during the Festival it is virtually impossible—either arrive early or make reservations.

Auberge de Jeunesse (IYHF) quartier du Jas Bouffan, ave. Marcel-Pagnol (tel. 20-15-99), near Fondation Vasarely. A 20-minute walk from the center of town; take bus 8 or 10 from La Rotonde (last bus 8:15pm). A relatively new hostel in a neighborhood of high-rises. Bed and breakfast 30F, dinner 25F, sheets 8F. Cooking facilities available. Curfew 10pm.

CROUS, Cité Universitaire, cité des Gazelles, ave. Jules-Ferry (tel. 26-33-75, ext. 96). Out of the center of town. During July-Sept. the university opens up its rooms for short or long stays. Singles, 28F a night for students, 43F for non-students or those over age 30. Breakfast 7F, meals 18F. Minimum stay of two nights. Or call the **Foyer Hôtel Sonacotra,** 16, chemin du Petit Barthelemy (tel. 64-20-87). Women can try **Les Abeilles,** ave. du Maréchal (tel. 59-25-75) or the **Foyer Etudiantes Saintes Maries,** 1, rue du Bon Pasteur (tel. 21-05-08).

Hôtel du Casino, 38, rue Victor-Leydet (tel. 26-06-88). A short walk from the cours. A large old hotel in the old town which has retained vestiges of its former elegance—there's even some stained glass. Some rooms are quite nice, but ask to see your room before you pay for it. Singles 50F and up, doubles 75F and up, breakfast 10F, showers 8F. Reservations requested.

Hôtel Trianon, 13, rue Maréchal-Joffre (tel. 26-35-57). Probably one of the best places in town. Well-located on a relatively tranquil street, about 15 minutes from the station. The rooms are clean and the prices reasonable. Singles 55F, doubles 65F, 80F with shower. No breakfast. Showers 7F.

Pax Hôtel, 29, rue Espariat (tel. 26-29-79). Near the cours on a noisy street, but the rooms are reasonable. Singles 42F and up, doubles 53F-100F, no breakfast, showers free.

Camping: All campsites lie outside of town. **Chanteclerc,** val St. André on the route de Nice (tel. 26-08-27) is a four-star campground charging 30F per night for a person and tent, and **Ste. Victoire,** 13, Beaurecueil (tel. 28-91-31) is 14F a night.

Food

Specialties of Provence include fresh vegetables and seafood, sometimes under the garlicky sauce of the south known as *aïoli*. Aix is the greatest center in France for prepared almonds used in cakes and cookies. Pass up the best known of the confections, *calisson* (a small almond iced cookie, expensive and mediocre), and go instead to one of the *patisseries* or *salons du thé* along the rue d'Italie and ask for *frangipan*, a delicious and buttery hot pastry.

The cafes on the cours Mirabeau serve good, dependable meals—but they're more suited to people-watching and sipping coffee than to dining. For a meal, look instead for the eccentric and colorful little places tucked away on the back streets which cater to Aix's student population. For provisions, try the fish, vegetable, and flea market in the **Palais de Justice** in the place de Verdun on Tues., Thurs., and Sat. mornings. If you're desperate and low on cash you can eat at the fast-food cafeteria **Fluch,** next to the syndicat.

La Pomme di Pin, 26, rue Aumone Vielle, is the kind of French restaurant you dream of finding. Set off from the crowds in the quiet place Ramus, it is small (seven tables), intimate, and friendly. The windows are covered with witty, puckish comments from the manager assuring you that salt and pepper come free of charge. Plat du jour 27F, *menu* 40F. Closed at lunch, opens at 8pm.

Chez Patrick, at the corner of rue Marsallais and rue Verrerie, has good food and quick service. *Menu* 32F, omelette 8F, salade niçoise 15F, dining on the terrace.

La Laitue, 3, rue Gibelin, near the Musée du Viel Aux, offers full-meal salads for 20-25F—everything from leek to dandelions. It doubles as a milk bar, serving shakes, ice creams, and teas.

Hacienda, 7, rue Merindol. The food is much better than the location. Quick service and a 27F plat du jour; 31F *menu,* wine included.

Restaurant Universitaire, ave. Jules Ferry, is the university cafeteria with nearly digestible food. Pinch a meal ticket off a resident student (5.60F) or pay the passage rate of 18F. There are other student cafeterias on ave. Gaston-Berger, traverse de Coques, and 2, cours des Arts et Metier. In summer contact CROUS to see which of the three is open.

Sights

If you can rouse yourself from the cushioned, wicker cafe chairs (not a simple feat), Aix does have some small museums of note. The **Musée des Tapisseries** has a small, but fine collection of Beauvais tapestries from seventeenth and eighteenth centuries. True to the tradition of the Beauvais tapestry factory, the scenes are pastoral and literary rather than mythical or historical. The back room of the museum often has contemporary weavings as well as a collection of looms from various eras. Open daily, except Tues., 10am-noon and 2-5pm; 2-6pm in summer. Admission 5F, students 3F. The **Musée Granet** has a striking collection of Roman sculptures intermingled with Egyptian mummies; it also houses a large number of Dutch and classical paintings. Open daily 10am-7pm; admission 10F, students 5F.

The **Musée du Viel Aix** is an eccentric collection of exhibits on local life history and popular customs. Some parts look just like a packrat went wild, but others are highly informative. See the sections on the "Jeux de Fête-Dieu," a sort of town pageant-tournament-puppet show invented by King René to bolster the traditions of chivalry, which he felt were threatened by the invention of powder weapons. There is a printed English guide to the exhibits, available at the entrance. Open daily except Monday 10am to noon and 2-5pm, 6pm in summer; closed February. Admission 5F.

The **Cathédrale St.-Sauveur** is an architectural melange of additions and carvings from eleventh-century Romanesque to late flamboyant Gothic. The main attractions are beautiful sixteenth-century carved panels of the main portal, which are in perfect condition, thanks to their protecting wooden shutters. The interior's claim to fame is the **triptych of the Burning Bush,** which shows King René and his Queen in odd juxtaposition with the Virgin and Child and the burning bush of Moses. This work is also usually closed away, but for a small tip, the guard will show it and the front panels to you, a complementary lecture included. Also take a look at the baptisery, which dates from the fourth century and is strangely incorporated into the rest of the church. Adjoining the church is the delicate thirteenth-century **Cloître St.-Sauveur,** which has a wooden roof over the galleries instead of the usual heavy arches. During the Festival, mass is held every Sunday at 10:30am, and visitors are welcome to sing with the choir (choruses are in five languages), but show up at 10am. **Bibliothèque Méjanes,** located in the Hôtel de Ville, houses an impressive collection of illuminated manuscripts and often displays works of contemporary artists. Open 10am-noon and 2-6pm; closed Sun., Mon., and Fri. morning. For more arcane interest, the **Fondation St.-John Perse** has all the materials you'd want or need to explore the world of this knotty modern poet. Open 10am-noon and 2-6pm; closed Fri.

A perfect response to the haughtiness of Aix is the stunning **Fondation Vasarely,** outside the town on ave. Marcel-Pagnol, Jas-de-Bouffan (near the Hostel; catch bus #8 from La Rotonde, and follow it to the end of the line). The building itself, with its enormous and defiant pattern of black and white circles, is well-suited to display Vasarely's gigantic and vibrant op-art murals—hypnotic experiments with color and shape that reach from the floor to the dome high above. The rooms are hexagonal, there are mirrors all around, and you can imagine the wowing result. This impressive collection is open daily except Tues., 10am-5pm (admission 10F, 5F for those under age 20). After all that visual stimulation, you can relax in the park outside, one of the quietest spots in Aix.

Cézanne's **Atelier** is a short uphill walk out of town at 9, ave. Paul-Cézanne. It remains much as he left it in 1906, with his easel, a smock, and an unfinished canvas. The room in a rather sentimental touch, also displays a fresh still life assortment of oranges and apples. There are some Cézannes here, but they remain under cover, and the attendant is reluctant to remove the wraps. Unless you are a true Cézanne devotee, you may find the content not worth the 8F regular admission, 4F with student ID, though there is a fine view of the orange-roofed houses in the village from the *atelier*. Open daily 10am-noon, 2-5pm, closed Tuesdays; July-Sept. closes at 6pm.

To appreciate the setting in which Cézanne painted, a better alternative is to walk along D17, now called the **route de Cézanne**, which leads toward Mte. Ste-Victoire. The scenery may have a déjà-vu quality to it; Cézanne often set up his easel to paint along this route. The road runs by the quarry and to the hamlet of **Le Tholonet** where you can pause for refreshment before heading back to town.

For Picasso devotees who are willing to hitch or rent a mobylette, the modern master is buried in **Vauvenarges**, just 10 miles east of Aix. You can see the nineteenth-century chateau where Picasso lived. Visitors are not allowed entrance, but his sculptures are on display in the park.

Entertainment

Aix is famous for its **International Music Festival,** held from mid-July through early August. It draws first-rate musicians and renowned orchestras from around the world. Tickets run high, seats are scarce, and student discounts are rare. In 1982, the program featured opera in the **Théâtre de l'Archevêché** (tickets 100-350F), concerts in the **Cathédrale** and **Cloître St.-Louis,** 60, blvd. Carnot (tickets 70-140F), and recitals by advanced music students at the **Cloître St.-Sauveur,** (*Une heure avec* . . . tickets 40F).

Strictly speaking, the Festival begins and ends with these concerts, but in practice everyone else takes the opportunity to celebrate. There are numerous exhibitions all over town, and lots of improvised youth activities—strange dances around the fountains, all-night rock concerts or reggae performances. Wander around at night and follow your ears.

Although Aix's primary source of entertainment is the never-ending parade on the cours, there are excellent jazz clubs frequented by a lively, appreciative crowd. Addresses change year to year, so check the posters on the streets or inquire at the syndicat. The cinema **Studio 24,** 24, cour Sextius (tel. 27-63-32), is run by an endearing fellow who shows his own favorite films; during the summer there are six or seven films each day.

Nîmes

Nîmes, like Rome, was built with Roman labor on seven hills. Two thousand years later, it still competes with Arles for the title "la Rome Française." The emblematic enchained alligator, visible throughout the city, symbolizes Augustus' victory in Egypt over Mark Antony and Cleopatra. The immediate result of this victory was the gift of Nîmes.

Nîmes is a modern town with wide boulevards and a busy commercial section, but her Renaissance quarters and Roman monuments are still displayed to their best advantage. Most prominent of these is the **Roman Arena**, host of traditional summer bullfights, and a prestigious jazz festival.

Practical Information

Office de Tourisme: 6, rue Auguste (tel. 67-29-11) across from the Maison Carrée; from the train station follow ave. Feucheres to the arena, then walk five blocks up ave. Victor-Hugo. Information on bus and train excursions to the Pont du Gard, the Camargue, and nearby towns. In July and August daily guided tours of Nîmes leave from here, 5F. Also exhaustive festival information. Open July-Aug., Mon.-Fri, 8am-7pm, Sat. 8am-noon and 2pm-6pm, Sun. 10am-noon. Shorter hours off-season. Will change money on weekends, though at a less favorable rate than those offered at banks. For a recorded French announcement of the week's events, call tel. 67-86-86.

Comité Départemental du Tourisme du Gard: 3, place des Arènes (tel. 21-02-51 or 21-08-11). Information on sights and facilities in the region. Same hours as syndicat, but closed on Sat. afternoons and Sun.

Train Station: at the end of ave. Feucheres (tel. 67-27-46). Twenty minutes by train to either Arles or Montpellier. Also trains and SNCF buses (Eurailpass valid) to the beaches at Porte Camargue and Le Grau du Roi, one hour away. **BIGE/Transalpino tickets** on sale at the Tourisme SNCF office at the station. Also, the station is the only place in town with **bike rentals.**

Post Office: blvd. de la Bruxelles. Near the Arena, at the opposite end of ave. Feucheres from the station; also an office on blvd. Gambetta. Open Mon.-Fri. 8am-7pm, Sat. 8am-noon.

Laundromat: 4, place de la Cathédrale, or on top of Les Halles on rue des Halles, or else 22, rue Porte France, behind the church St. Paul.

Telephone Code: (66).

Accommodations

Inexpensive hotels are in very short supply. The tourist office will find you a room for free. Most hotels are scattered around the Arena or around place G. Peri.

Auberge de Jeunesse (IYHF), Chemin de la Cigale (tel. 23-25-04). A 3.5km walk from the train station, and buses don't run after 8pm. Take bus #6 from the train station to the Cigale stop, and then walk uphill. (To walk the whole thing, go past the jardin and up the Ales highway; the last uphill stretch is marked.) Seventy-eight beds and camping space available. Beds 22.50F a night, obligatory 7.50F breakfast in July and August, 6.50 for a sheet. The Hostel is pleasant and informal with a nice garden. Kitchen facilities available. Lock-out 10am-6pm. The office closes at 10pm but there is no curfew.

Hôtel de Paris, 31, rue de la Sérvie, right across from the train station (tel. 67-35-46). This slightly faded hotel has eight double rooms from 43-48F, and quadruples from 71-88F. Breakfast 10F, showers 8F.

Hôtel La Couronne, square de la Couronne (tel. 67-51-73). In the center of town, a two-minute walk from the Arena. Adequate, comfortable rooms. Singles 48F, doubles 52-130F. Breakfast 10F, showers 8F. Restaurant downstairs, with 35F *menu.*

La Dauphine, 26, rue Dorée (tel. 67-33-75). A pleasant, cozy hotel on a quiet street. Singles 45F, doubles 80F, breakfast 10F.

Hôtel Némausa, 4, ave. Feucheres (tel. 67-44-12), between the station and Arena. Large, spacious, and friendly, this is reputedly an old hangout of Georges Sand and Chopin. Doubles and triples 58-70F; large rooms for four, five and six people 110-140F. Breakfast 10F, showers 8F. Reservations advisable in summer, or show up early in the morning.

The two-star **Hôtel Amphithéâtre,** 4, rue des Arènes (tel. 67-28-51), has a few rooms for 43F, or try the nearby **Hôtel de France,** 4, blvd. des Arènes (tel. 67-23-05) with 60F doubles.

Camping: The new three-star **Camping La Bastide** on route de Générac (tel. 38-09-21) lies about 4.5km from the train station; 35F a night for 2 people and tent. **Transports Gardois** has a few daily buses to the campground leaving from the St. Paul Church. The last leaves around 6pm. Otherwise, **Le Camargue,** at Margueritis, route de Poux, (tel. 26-40-95) is about 15km away.

Food

Nîmes has specialties that you won't find in other parts of the region. *Brandade de Morue* is a delicious blend of pureed fish with olive oil and spices. *Tapenade d'olives,* a paste of olives and anchovies and *herbes de provence,* is used on *canapes* for hors d'oevres. For dessert, try *croquants villarets,* dry cookies flavored with almonds, and especially favored by the people of Nîmes.

Le Cigalon, 11, rue Sigalon, has provençal fish specialties and a 30F *menu.*

Chez Albert-Restaurant du Théâtre, 4, rue Racine. Near the Maison Carrée, a block from blvd. Victor Hugo towards the fontaine. A 30F lunch *menu* in a pleasant, dimly lit dining room.

Les Hirondelles, 13, rue Bigot. A generous 32F *menu* with wine and service included. A lively family atmosphere. Closed Saturday. Or around the corner try the popular **Le Pesqualuna,** 15, rue Porte de France, with a 42F *menu,* reservations suggested for the evening meal. Closed Tuesday.

L'Escargot, 10, rue Fresque. The tacky appearance belies what's inside—some very good food. A 27F *menu* and *paella* 38F.

Pizzeria Cerutti, 25, rue de l'Horloge behind the Maison Carrée. For night-owls, this place is open until 3am. Pizzas and pasta from 28F.

Sights

Although distributed throughout the entire city, all of the antique monuments in Nîmes lie within easy walking distance of one another; a required 10F ticket admits you to all of them (available at any of the monuments). The **Maison Carée** (Square House) is unique in its proportions—actually rectangular, its length (26.50 meters) is almost exactly twice its width (13.50 meters). Built in the first century B.C., it was dedicated to the adopted sons of the Emperor Augustus. The portico of this Roman temple is in the Greek style, with fluted Corinthian columns and exquisite decorations; it was Thomas Jefferson's inspiration in designing the Virginia state capital at Richmond, and thereby influenced much of American classical architecture. Inside is the **Museum of Antiquities** with the statues of Venus of Nîmes and Apollo with a Quiver, and some Roman mosaics. Open 9am-noon, 2-5pm, until 7pm in summer.

The **Roman Amphitheatre** is a classic; although smaller than the one in Arles, it is preserved almost intact. Bullfights are held here (20-60F) April through September, alternating with classical and jazz concerts.

A short walk along the Canal de la Fontaine brings you to the **Jardin de la Fontaine**, an eighteenth-century melange of fountains, pools, and stairways. The ruins of the Roman Temple of Diana were uncovered during the construction of the garden, and they were incorporated into the design of the whole by the architect Mareschal. A military man, Mareschal was much criticized by his townsfolk, who said that his masterpiece looked more like a soldier's parade ground than an ornament for the city. Take a look and decide for yourself. Then climb to the top of the nearby Roman **Tour Magne** for an admirable view of Nîmes and the countryside. The tower is open 9-11.50am and 2-6:30pm; the garden is open till 11pm in summer.

Ancient history addicts will want to see the **Castellum**, the remains of the "plumbing" system that distributed water from the Eure to the different parts of the city. The only relic of this kind in the world, the basin has ten small holes used to divert water into five different canals which led to every quarter of the village.

Less pragmatic, but equally intriguing, the **Cathédrale St.-Castor** has a capacious but short Romanesque nave and exquisite wrought iron fencing. Note the elaborate sculptures on the balcony of the facade depicting old testament scenes from the Garden of Eden to the drunkeness of Noah. The **Eglise St.-Paul**, bypassed by most tourists, has a polychromed apse with vibrant, geometrically patterend columns and a splendid fresco of Christ Pantocrator.

Entertainment

The Arena is the site of an annual **International Jazz Festival** in mid-July. In past years, this festival featured such artists as Dizzy Gillespie, May Roach and Chic Corea. Tickets are 50F each, 280F for the series, and reservations can be made through the **Jazz Club**, 45, rue Flamade, 3000 Nîmes (tel. 21-34-02). There are various concerts throughout the city, including ones at the Temple of Diana (during **Nîmes en Fête** from early July to early August). The **Café-Théâtre le Titoit de Titus,** 6, rue Titus, off the canal, sponsors innovative drama, comedy, and concerts throughout the year. Closed July and August. **Le Cabaret,** blvd. Gambetta, has soothing jazz on the terrace on Fridays, Saturdays and Sundays year-round. No cover charge. Also worth a mention is **Le Semaphore,** 25a rue Porte de France, a block over from blvd. Victor Hugo (tel. 67-88-04). This excellent cinema mounts a great summer festival during all of July with 14F films. They also have occasional concerts and talks with filmmakers.

Near Nîmes

A 20km drive toward Avignon brings you to the **Pont du Gard,** a three-tiered Roman aqueduct that still spans the River Gard. Built two thousand years ago without mortar or cement, this astonishing feat of engineering stands sixty meters high and 325 meters long. Don't just stand and gape—walk the length of it. There are several cafes along the road to the aqueduct and a campground on the banks of the river. Take the **Courriers du Midi** bus from the **place de la Couronne,** with about eight departures daily during the summer (15.50F one way; tel. 84-96-86 for information).

A tourist-office sponsored bus tour to Pond du Gard and **Uzes,** site of the unique Romanesque **Tour Fenestrelle,** runs July-Sept., Tuesday and Sunday.

(Tour prices range from 37-85F.) To find out about excursions to the Camargue, Cevennes, and other areas, contact the syndicat d'initiative.

The environs of Nîmes offer some amazing natural wonders. When the Alps and the Pyrénnés were created, the limestone of the Mediterranean was driven against the solid bulk of the Massif Central and fashioned into great pleats and grooves. Over the millenia, water and time have etched out great jeweled caverns and underground lakes. (Ask at the Nîmes Tourist Office for details about trains and hikes in these regions.)

Most accessible from Nîmes is the wild terrain of the Camargue area west of the Petit-Rhône. **Aigues-Mortes,** the city of the "dead waters," is set in the midst of gray swamps and gloomy lagoons. It is a walled and melancholy town that has remained intact since the reign of Louis XI. From the **Tour de Constance,** you can walk along the mile-long ramparts which enclose the town (5F).

SNCF trains and buses (Eurailpass valid) leave Nîmes frequently for Aigues-Mortes and the nearby beaches at **Porte Camargue** and **Grau du Roi.**

Grapes have been grown on the hills of the Gard region since Roman times, but today the "wines of the Midi" are spoken of with a condescending laugh. The friendly winemakers will welcome you into their caves so you can judge for yourself. The Nîmes Tourist Office will give you information on the various wines grown in the region and a map with the caves marked on it.

To the northwest of Nîmes is the **Parc National des Cevennes,** a beautiful preserve of magnificent forests, low mountains, and spectacular gorges and caves. **Alès** makes a good starting point for camping or hiking tours. Many of these areas are accessible by train or bus; information is available at the office de tourisme (tel. 52-24-86) in Alès. In the park there are information centers at Florac and Genolhac. There is also a daily train from Arles to Paris, "Le Cevenol," which passes through this spectacular countryside.

Côte d'Azur

Paradises are made to be lost, and the seductive loveliness of the Riviera has almost been its undoing, as shrewd developers have turned its beauty to profit and its pleasures into big business. Today the area is as crammed with low-budget tourists as with high-handed millionaires, Graham Greene has recently launched a public crusade against the organized crime and pervasive corruption of Nice; and many Frenchmen disparage the coast as a shameless European Miami Beach, a shadow of its former self.

Yet the Côte d'Azur remains irresistible, an uncommonly beautiful garden of delights that is ravishing even when ravished. Its colors alone are spectacular: dazzlingly white villas rim a startlingly blue sea, while silvered olive trees shelter roses and mimosa. By day the beaches encourage sunning and swimming *au naturel,* while at night the many clubs and casinos offer pleasures of a more sophisticated sort.

Art and artists, like Nature, have long favored the area. Here are some of the world's most stylish and sumptuous museums of modern art—here, too, linger images of F. Scott Fitzgerald and Cole Porter at **Cap d'Antibes;** of Picasso, Renoir, and Matisse, sketching in the luminous foothills around **Nice.** Even today the Côte is the cherished playground of writers and of those most celebrated of contemporary artists, the movie stars, who flock to bathe and sun themselves at **Cannes** or **Cap Ferrat.**

A brief list of the festivals along the Riviera suggests something of the careless opulence and dream-like air of the area. There is the **Film Festival** in Cannes each May, **Carnival** in Nice each February, the **Monte Carlo Rally** in January and the **Grand Prix** in May, an **International Bridge Tournament** in Antibes, as well as tennis championships and **Jazz Festivals** around the coast in summer.

But don't let the immodest material and natural wealth of the Côte intimidate you—you can explore the Riviera fully and cheaply without difficulty. It's best to stay in one of the larger, less expensive cities (Nice in particular) and make day-trips to quieter beaches and smaller coastal retreats. The entire Côte d'Azur section between St. Raphael and **Menton** is conveniently compressed, with buses and trains running very frequently, quickly, and inexpensively between all towns, large and small. (Both lines follow the coastline, so always choose a window seat, if you can.) For example, Nice lies only 20 minutes from Monaco, 30 minutes from Antibes, and 40 minutes from Cannes. Trains for the Coast leave the Gare de Lyon in Paris every hour during the summer, and the trip takes 7-10 hours.

Groups might also consider renting a car to explore the spectacular coast—firms will often waive the 500F deposit if you flash them a credit card. Mopeds rent for about 60F a day (with a 300F deposit). Try to deal only with the bigger firms in large cities, as those in small towns tend to rent mopeds in dangerously bad shape. (Be sure to wear a helmet.) Hitching is easy between smaller towns, but fairly bleak along the main autoroute. Finally, you should surrender to bodily indulgences while on the Riviera. Try such regional specialties as *bouillabaisse*, a hearty fish soup, *salade niçoise, soupe au pistou*, made with vegetable and basil, or other dishes incorporating such local products as herbs, garlic, and olive oil. After your meal, indulge your James Bond fantasies, provided you follow the advice of Bond's creator, Ian Fleming: "Do not approach casinos with timidity or reverence. They are simply fruit-machines tended by bank clerks and mechanics."

Beaches

Familiarize yourself with the Côte's offerings before you stalk the perfect tan. If you've come just for the sun, try to arrive in early June or in September, when the warm air and water aren't obscured by fashionable hordes of beached lemmings. In the summer, optimal swimming tends to be during the two-hour period before the 8pm sunset. Always bring a towel; even the sand beaches are a bit rocky, so you'll want something to sit on. Nearly all the beaches are topless, and some are as bottomless as the Lord's pockets, so you can pursue your uniform St. Tropez tan without turning red from embarrassment (or harrassment).

Ironically, the largest towns have the worst beaches. **Marseille** has no beach to speak of; while the beaches at **Nice** are pebbly, at **Cannes** private, and at **Monte Carlo** remote. Seek out the quieter beaches between towns: **Cap Martin**, between Monaco and Menton, is slightly rocky, but offers good swimming and few crowds; **Cap d'Ail**—and, to a lesser extent, Eze-sur-Mer—between Nice and Monaco, is famous for its sheltered beauty. West of Nice, **Antibes** and **Juan-les-Pins** both offer long, white-sanded *plages* with clear water and fine swimming; and around the *calanques* (mini-fjords), accessible only by moped, the privacy of the beaches is rarely enforced. Among the finest of sandy beaches stretch between St. Raphael and St. Tropez, but those near the latter town are now as celebrated for their exclusiveness as for their attractiveness. Since almost all of the towns on the Côte lie along one local rail line, it may be worthwhile hopping in and out at small stations to see what you can find.

Many travelers end up sleeping where they lay their towels during the day. A number of beaches provide showers, toilets, and even towels for a small fee (5-10F). Accommodations are extremely tight in high season, with youth hostels, *relais,* and hotels often booked months in advance. If you do sleep on the beach, avoid all drugs and be courteous; the police will often demand identification, but rarely ask you to move on. It is neither possible nor safe to spend the night on the beaches at Nice, Cannes, and Juan-les-Pins. Wherever you are, be sure to guard your valuables closely.

Marseille

Contrary to rumor and Bogart movies, Marseille is not teeming with thieves, spies, and white slave traders, nor are its docks lined with drunken sailors and ladies of the night. But Marseille is a large city with a clamorous port—full of nomads, tattooed young men, and North African people and customs—and the Marseillais are notorious in France for their jovial bawdiness, rough accents, and skillful swearing. Thus Marseille is the black sheep of the Riviera, a city charged with color and commotion, offering a rugged history and a ragged vitality in contrast to the glamour, gloss, and pretention of its more sophisticated sisters.

Orientation

The center of town is the Vieux Port, which is flanked by two impregnable fortresses and guarded on surrounding hills by the city's old quarters. Running straight out of the port is Marseille's main artery, **La Canebière,** a turbulent, crowded thoroughfare affectionately known to English sailors as "Can 'o Beer." And between La Canebière and the station are the narrow, dusty streets of the North African quarter, where you can hear shrill Moroccan music all around you, and see ladies in exotic African gowns, and visit shops with embroidered caftans billowing in their doorways. As bespangled merchants lay their wares out on the street each day, the **Cours Belsunce** is transformed into a cacophonous African bargain bazaar. (You will face rip-offs here as well as bargains. Remember, for example, to be firm in your refusal to pay the men who will, unsolicited, take a photo of you and then demand 15F in payment.)

As you leave the station, turn left and descend the majestic steps before you. Continue straight down the blvd. d'Athènes until you arrive at La Canebière—and the Tourist Office and Port—on your right. The streets leading off blvd. d'Athènes constitute the North African section of the city.

Office Municipal de Tourisme: 4, La Canebière (tel. 54-91-11) near the Vieux Port. English spoken; information on boats, festivals, and youth activities. You can reserve hotels here free. Sight-seeing tours leave daily at 9:30am. Open Mon.-Sun. 9am-7pm in summer, till 6:30pm and closed Sundays in winter. In July and August, additional offices operate at the station, in the Vieux Port, and on the beach.

Post Office: Hôtel des Postes, on corner of rue Colbert and rue Barbusse (tel. 91-19-10). Closed from noon-2pm Mon.-Sat. and all day Sunday. 24-hour telephone and telegraph service available. At night, enter via 2, rue Petre.

Train Station: Gare St. Charles. Information (tel. 95-92-12), open daily from 8am-8pm. The nearby *bureau d'accueil* (reception desk) is always open. Information office open 8am-8pm. Trains leave regularly for Arles and Nice. There is also an information and reservation service at the tourist office (tel. 33-76-87).

Discount Rail Tickets: BIGE, Transalpino tickets available at **Vovac**, 8, rue Bailli-de-Suffren (tel. 54-31-30), at the corner of quai des Belges in the Vieux Port. Open Mon.-Fri. 9:30am-12:30pm, 2:30-6:30pm, Sat. 9:30am-1pm. Also at **Voyages Was-teels**, 87, La Canebière (tel. 50-89-12) and **Tourisme SNCF**, 7, blvd. Garibaldi.

Airport: Aeroport de Marignane (tel. (42) 89-90-10) for information. Flights to Corsica (273F) and elsewhere. Buses for the airport leave from the front of the Gare St. Charles every half hour from 7am-8pm and 80 minutes before each scheduled take-off between 8pm and 7am. The Air France office at place de Gaulle (tel. 54-92-92) is open Mon.-Fri. 9am-12:30pm and 2:30-7pm.

Boats: For information on boats to Corsica or North Africa, go to SNCM, 61, blvd. des Dames (tel. 91-92-20). Boats to Corsica from Marseille or Toulon cost 156F second-class. In mid-summer, you can get fourth-class seats for 122F; out of season (in the Blue Period), those under 22 or traveling in pairs can get discounts. All boats leave from Gare Maritime de la Joliette.

Port Information Office: place de la Joliette (tel. 52-70-72) provides the names of liners in port and those liner owners who will allow visits on board.

Currency Exchange: At the train station, open daily 8am-noon, 2-5:30pm. **Change de la Bourse**, place du Général de Gaulle, off La Canebière, open Mon.-Sat. 8:30am-noon and 2-7pm. Or try **Changes Voyages**, 39, La Canebière.

U.S. Consulate: 9, rue Armény (tel. 54-92-00). Open Mon.-Fri. 10:30am-noon and 1:30-3:30pm.

Canadian Consulate: 24, ave. du Prado (tel. 37-19-37). Open Mon.-Fri. 8:30am-4:30pm.

Police: Tel. 91-90-40; at night, 37-19-20.

Telephone Code: (91).

Accommodations

The larger hotels in Marseille tend to be oriented toward businessmen on expense accounts, while some of the smaller ones are devoted to seamy business transactions of their own. Hotels near the Opera tend to specialize in hourly rates. In many places, the prices posted are misleading—the least expensive rooms are often unavailable or non-existent.

Both hostels lie far from the center of town. If you are fearless or desperate, the cheapest and least popular hotels are in the **North African quarter** along rue des Dominicaines or rue Bernard du Bois. Unrecognized by the Tourist Office, these are dingy, dirty, and dangerous—but they may save you at midnight when all other accommodations are full, and they charge only 35F a night. Women should avoid them at all cost. Otherwise, try any of the places that line the station on the **blvd. Maurice Bourdet** and **place des Marseillaises,** or the more central two-stars on **rue Breteuil.**

Auberge de Jeunesse (IYHF): Bois-Luzy, ave. de Bois-Luzy (tel. 49-06-18). Located on a hill with a view of the *calanques* and the sea. Relaxed atmosphere, cooking facilities, and hot showers. The rooms and office close 10am-5pm, but the common rooms stay open during the day. Take bus #8 or #6 from cours Joseph-Thierry. There is a second Hostel at **Bonneveine** at 47, ave J.-Vidal (tel. 73-21-81). Very large, but often filled with school groups. Cooking facilities. Dinner 20F. Both hostels charge about 20F per night.

Hôtel Beanlieu, 1, place des Marseillaises (tel. 39-70-59). A little more expensive than its neighbors, but a lot more polite and respectable. Small, clean, modern rooms. Singles 55F, doubles 85-110F. Breakfast 10F, shower 10F.

The Grenoble, nearby at #5 (tel. 39-19-07), charges 45F for a single, 65F with shower, and 8.50F for breakfast. The Riviera and Little Palace, around the corner on blvd. d'Athènes are slightly cheaper.

Hôtel de France, 1, blvd. Maurice-Bourdet (tel. 39-18-82). also near the station; noisy, but clean. Rooms 42-50F; with shower, 62F. Breakfast 9.50F. Similar deals can be found along the street.

Hôtel Breteuil, 27, rue Breteuil (tel. 33-24-20). Large, clean rooms with telephones and a helpful management. Twenty minutes walking distance away from the station, but still centrally located. Singles 55-110F, doubles 75-140F. Breakfast 9F, meals 33F, showers 6F. The Ste. Anne, at #23 (tel. 33-13-21), is similar, charging 55-100F for rooms, 9F for breakfast.

Camping: Marseille's campsites are away from the urban pollution, to the south of the central city near the Parc Borely, a large, densely-wooded park with an English garden. The best sites are Les Vagues, 52, ave. de Bonneveine (tel. 73-04-88) not far from the sea, and Mazargues, 5, ave. de-Lattre-de-Tassigny (tel. 40-09-88). The Auberge de Jeunesse de Bois-Luzy allows camping in tents as well.

Food

Marseille is the celebrated home of *bouillabaisse,* a fish stew cooked with wine, saffron, and a touch of cayenne pepper which makes a meal in itself. Lobsters and mussels are often included among the mélange of fresh, local seafood. For the real thing you can expect to pay about 100F for two. Michel-Brasserie des Catalans, 6, rue Catalans, has some of the best *bouillabaisse* in Marseilles. (The tab, 220F and up, will terminally mangle your wallet.)

The restaurants on the quai de Rive Neuve in the Vieux Port all serve their own versions of the famous stew, but some have a reputation among French travelers for making customers violently ill. If you want to try your hand at your own fish concoction (and prepare it at the Hostel), the fishermen sell their wares direct from the boat each morning on the quai des Belges at the base of La Canebière. Come early for the best quality and the most colorful scene.

Along the blvd. d'Athènes, most cafés offer *menus* for 30F, and there are some very good *couscous* restaurants near rue longue des Capucins (this is a rough area, however, and unaccompanied women should definitely steer clear of it). Other options include the Brasserie le Français, 46, cours Belsunce, with a 38F *menu,* Chez Soi, 5, rue Papère, with a filling 35-50F *menu.* Chez Tino, across the street, offers a greasy three-course *menu* for 30F, including wine and service, and Pizzeria Pytheas, rue Pytheas, has a 24F bargain *menu.*

Sights

The Parc du Pharo, at the mouth of the Vieu Port, contains a castle built by Napoleon III with excellent views of the harbor and the city. The nineteenth-century Basilique de Notre Dame de la Garde crowned with a gilded Virgin and lined with multi-colored marble is rather ugly, but the main attraction is the view from the top, which takes in the Pomèques and Ratonneau Islands, Château d'If, the city, and its surrounding mountains. On August 15, the church is the object of a local pilgrimage celebrating the Assumption of the Virgin Mary. Notre Dame is open from 6am-5pm, depending on the season. To get there, take bus route #60, or follow rue Breteuil and turn right down blvd. Vauban.

North of the port, on ave. Robert-Schumann, is the **Ancienne Cathédrale de la Major,** which has a Romanesque altar reliquary of 1122, a delicate ceramic relief by Luca Della Robbia, and a fifteenth-century altar dedicated to Lazarus. Here you'll also find the tomb of a Bishop Xavier of Belsune who unselfishly devoted himself to the suffering Marseillais during a catastrophic eighteenth-century plague.

The gaudy **Palais Longchamp** (at the eastern end of the blvd. Longchamp) was built in the late nineteenth century and contains both a water tower at its center and the diverse **Musée des Beaux-Arts.** The museum is particularly strong in Provençal painting, especially Valerie Bernard's morbid and banal symbolic pieces, but also exhibits paintings of Marseille's early history and devotes one entire room to Antoine Daumier (1808-1879), a native of Marseille. A renowned engraver and sculptor, he often depicted everyday scenes and common people in quite a satirical fashion. The museum also displays works by Ingres, David, and Rubens *(The Wild Boar Hunt),* as well as some early cubist landscapes by Raoul Dufy (1877-1953). Open 10am-noon and 2-6pm; closed Wednesday morning and Tuesday. Admission 4F, free with student ID and on Sunday morning.

Try to see at least one of Marseille's many small specialized museums. **Musée Contini,** 19, rue Grignan, contains primarily Provençal ceramics, but also has changing contemporary art exhibitions. The house, an old seventeenth-century mansion with an elegant courtyard, is worth the visit. Open 10am-noon, 2:15-6:30pm, closed Tuesdays; admission 5F, free with student ID and on Sundays. Ship lovers might visit **Musée de la Marine,** opposite the Tourist Office (open 10am-noon, 2:30-7pm; admission free). **Musée Grobet-Ladabie,** 140, blvd. Longchamp, is also in a lovely mansion and displays musical instruments, some medieval sculpture, tapestries, Flemish paintings, and even a few Corot landscapes. **Musée du Vieux-Marseille,** Maison Diamantée, rue de la Prison, is an historic museum which features *santons;* tiny clay figures characteristic of the Provençal region, and maritime history displays and maps.

To see the working side of Marseille, visit the liners in the bay by applying to the Port Information Office (see the Orientation section). Bring your passport or identity papers and be sure to tip the crewman who takes you around.

Motorboats run from the quai des Belges to the Chateau d'If (18F round trip; the trip takes 15 minutes each way), which was immortalized by Alexandre Dumas in *The Count of Monte Cristo.* The tour guides are willing to play along and will point out the hole through which the Count escaped. The fortress was originally designed to defend Marseille, but was later changed into a prison which confined Mirabeau and many Huguenots. Boats will also take you to the Ile de Frioul, a large, park-like island, and in summer, to Cassis.

Along the blvd. Michelet (en route to the *calanques)* is Le Corbusier's **Cité Radieuse,** designed in the early 1950's. It embodies many of the architect's theories on modern, efficient, moderately-priced housing and, with its 2000 citizens, aspires to be a united city-within-a-city.

Between Marseille and St. Tropez

It is especially worthwhile on the overcrowded Côte d'Azur to abandon well-known and well-traveled places and to seek out more private discoveries. **Cassis** is a perfect example of this principle. Only 23km (and as many minutes by train) from Marseille, this idle, rich, and beguiling little town basks in the quiet and careless beauty which once distinguished the Riviera. Immaculate white villas are clumped around the hills above Cassis, while the town itself—a network of winding staircases, slender alleyways, and gardens thick with flowers—rests beside a bright port and the deep blue sea.

You can enter the town's **Post Office** (open Mon.-Fri. 9am-noon, 2:30-5:30pm; Sat. 9am-noon) by way of a sumptuous garden. In the same compact square, you can visit a museum and a charming *syndicat* (open daily 8:30-noon, 2:30-6pm; tel. 01-71-17) that greets you with wood-chimes, helpful advice, and inspired English. Right behind the place Pierre Baragnan is a small, casual **beach** (where waiters bring you drinks as you sunbathe). If you find it too crowded, follow the walled pathway around the rocky cliffs and you'll come upon a silent bay, a deserted beach, and countless coves.

Cassis is reached by a 35-minute walk from the station—a blessing in disguise, since the distance helps keep the crowds at bay. Once at Cassis, there's little to do but relax and enjoy yourself. The *syndicat* can furnish information on snorkeling, windsurfing, and water-skiing. If you want to see the sunny, rock-encircled inlets known as *les calanques,* you can take a forty-five minute walk or hire one of the boats in the port (20-30F for trips of 45 or 90 minutes; Moby Dick II, on blvd. Jean-Jaurès (tel. 01-73-04) offers a student rate of 15F). **En Vau** has the highest cliffs, **Port Pin** offers a small, tree-studded beach, and **Port Miou's** rocks are covered with blooming heather. If you're really taken with the *calanques,* you can visit some more from Marseille by taking a long hike south along the coast or by taking bus #21 to the end of the line.

But Cassis is not picture-perfect. You have to pay for the idyll, and everything here is prohibitively expensive; a two-star hotel, for example, will set you back 132F. The only feasible way to linger is to stay at **Camping Les Cigales** (tel. 01-07-34), ten minutes from the town and near the ocean, or to take the 10km walk along route B559 towards Marseille to **Youth Hostel La Fontasse** (tel. 01-02-72). Those who have lived to tell the tale report that the Hostel—like much in Cassis—rewards those who take the trouble to find it. Bear in mind, however, that there are no showers, water is collected in cisterns, toilets are primitive, and you must carry up your own food.

If you must eat in Cassis (an expensive indulgence!), try Le **Frincole,** 5, rue Pasteur, just behind the port, which offers pizza for 18-20F.

Toulon

If you want a base on the western fringe of the Riviera and have ruled out Marseille, try **Toulon,** a large city less interesting, less visited, and consequently less expensive than its neighbors along the coast. The city does have its seedy side, with slightly more than its share of sleazy red-light districts and dozing drunks. Nevertheless, the overall atmosphere is more that of a modest seaside resort than a sailor's port or a tycoon's hideaway. Toulon boasts small, but relatively isolated beaches, reached by taking bus #3 to Mourillon. Best of all is the huge, boisterous fruit and vegetable market that overflows Cours Lafayette from 6am-1pm each day, and the bustling **Fish Market** behind the Hôtel de Ville. On a sunless day—there are allegedly only 73 of them each year on the Riviera—you can always visit the **Naval Museum,** quai Stalingrad (open 10am-noon and 1:30-6:30pm, closed Tuesday; admission 8F, 4F with student ID), which is full of old models and replicas of ancient seafaring vessels. For a splendid view of the coast and the city, you can take a *téléphérique* (cable car) up **Mt. Faron** for 17F. Open daily 10am-noon, 2:15-7pm, closed Monday morning; take bus #40.

From late May to early July, Toulon hosts an international **music festival,** which attracts such renowned groups as the Beaux Arts Trio, as well as a wide range of non-classical music. Tickets run from 15-45F; you can buy them from a special office at the *syndicat d'initiative* (open 9am-noon, 2:30-6:30pm; tel. 24-03-81).

The **syndicat** itself, at 8, ave. Colbert (tel. 22-08-22), can supply you with helpful advice and assistance in finding a room (open Mon.-Sat. 8:30am-noon, 2-6:30pm; in July and August, 8am-8pm, and Sun. 9am-noon). To get there, turn left on leaving the station and proceed down blvd. de Tesse until you come to ave. Colbert.

Rue. Jean-Jaurès, in the midst of the pedestrian area, about 20 minutes from the station, is the best place to start your hotel-hunt. **Hôtel de Provence,** at #53 (tel. 93-19-00) is small and friendly, and it offers many singles between 42 and 69F. Breakfast is 10.50F. The **Lux Naval,** at #52 (tel. 92-97-46), has rooms from 40-75F, with breakfast 12F. **Lutetia,** at #69 (tel. 93-07-75), charges similar prices, and **Le Bristol,** at #67 (tel. 92-73-79), offers full *pension* for 90F. **Hôtel du Théâtre,** 8, rue de l'Humilité (tel. 92-70-81), has fifteen rooms with telephones in a friendly atmosphere for 42.50F, 53.50F with shower. Breakfast 8.50F. Women can try the **Foyer de la Jeunesse,** 12, place des Armes (tel. 93-05-55) for 25F per night, which also has a self-service cafeteria with some of the lowest prices in town.

For restaurants, look around the Old Port—but remember that those on the waterfront charge for the view—or along the rue de Domet. You can camp at **La Garde,** 6km away in Beauregard, Quartier Ste.-Marguerite (tel. 20-56-35).

Near Toulon

The islands off the coast near Toulon make venturing to Toulon worthwhile. They are known as the **Iles d'Hyères,** or the "Golden Isles," a reference to the color of the sun's reflection off the mica rock. Reaching these treasured isles can be expensive, but few regret the trip. In July and August, boats along the quai Stalingrad in Toulon will take you from Toulon to **Porquerolles** (about 50F for the 1½ hour round trip); a two-hour trip will also stop at the **Ile du Levant** and **Port-Cros.** Throughout the year, you can visit the latter two from Hyères Port, reached by infrequent trains, or by a 20F, forty-minute bus ride from Toulon. Boats leave at 9:30am and return at 8pm. Boats for Porquerolles leave from **La Tour Fondue,** reached by traveling to Hyères as described above and then taking bus #66 for forty-five minutes; the boat trip costs 21F in winter, 30F in summer. In July and August, you can visit all three islands from La Tour Fondue, trips leaving at 9:30am and returning at 5:45-6:45pm daily, except Sunday.

Porquerolles Island is the largest of the group, with sandy beaches, pine trees, and purple heather. The island has become fashionable, but don't let the villas deter you. The lighthouse, which offers a fantastic panoramic view of the entire island, should be your main target. **Ile du Levant** is the home of one of Europe's most famous nudist colonies, **Héliopolis,** which is rather ironic since monks originally settled the island. The island also has massive, jutting cliffs, long *calanques,* and lush vegetation. **Port-Cros** is the least cultivated of the islands, and is hilly, rugged, and peaceful. The natural springs nourish greenery and flowers, and the entire island is awash with color—it is often referred to as the "Island of Eden." Although it is a wildlife reserve, it is privately owned and camping is unfortunately prohibited. The "Solitude Walk" is well worth the trek and is precisely that, unless you come on a weekend in peak season. The hike to **Port-Man** is longer but well worth the effort.

If you find yourself in Hyères, savor the carefully-coiffured elegance of this oldest of Riviera resorts. The **syndicat d'initiative** in Hyères, jardin Denis, place Clemenceaux (tel. 65-18-55; open Mon.-Sat. 9am-noon, 2-6pm), will provide lists of campgrounds and hotels. There are fine beaches and well-equipped campgrounds around **La Carte** on the **Glens Peninsula**.

East of Toulon is **Cap Brun**, which has peaceful little coves and smaller crowns. The beaches at **Les Sablettes** (10.50F round trip by bus, 8.50F by boat from Toulon) are often densely packed, but it is a good, long stretch of sand and ocean. **Bandol** (on the railway line) has served as a refuge for many literary figures—including Bertolt Brecht and Thomas Mann—and is the area's leading resort. It has a long expanse of beach, but its beauty is marred by housing projects. Bandol's other claim to fame is as the greatest tennis center in Europe; the syndicat can provide information, should you yearn to hit a few.

St. Tropez

St. Tropez is preceded—and exceeded—by its risqué reputation. The media are forever transmitting images of wealth and beauty exposing themselves on the beaches, of celebrity-studded streets, and of decadent high-living. Some of the images reflect the truth. St. Tropez does have plenty of trendy restaurants and arty shops, and styles do run the gamut from outlandish to outrageous.

But remember Edward Lear's description of St. Tropez decades ago: "Bosh!" St. Tropez happens to be a pleasant, surprisingly tranquil little port, but it is in fact no more attractive than many other Riviera resorts, and you should think very carefully before taking the considerable trouble—and spending the sizable fee—to visit a place whose only unique feature is its name. Importantly, St. Tropez lies well off of the rail-line, so you will have to take a bus from St. Raphael (the trip takes an hour and costs 30.50F each way for those with luggage, 28F for those without. Buses leave about once an hour between 7am and 8pm. You can also take buses from Toulon, for 37.80F, or Hyères, for 30.10F.) Moreover, the famous beaches are all 3-8 km. away from the center of town. The **plage de Pampelonne** (8km away) has the most sand, the **plage de Tahiti** the most wealth, and the **plage des Salins** (3km) the most public space. To get to them, you must either rely on the infrequent Sodetrav buses (two each day to Salins, three to Pampelonne), or rent some wheels (from Louis Mas, 7, rue Joseph Quaranta (tel. 97-00-60), who charges 31F a day for a bicycle, plus 200F deposit and an identity card, 39-44F for a moped, plus 300F deposit, and 50-70F for a motor-bike, plus 500F deposit. He is open Mon.-Fri. 8am-noon, 2-6pm). Otherwise, you'll have to be content with **Les Cannoubieres,** a smaller, quieter beach close to the town. You needn't worry about being underdressed at any of these beaches, but be prepared to have your body critically inspected by all.

Within St. Tropez itself, the most attractive showpiece is the **port,** where barely-clad locals gather to see and be seen. To get there, bear left when you leave the bus and continue left at each fork in the road until you reach the sea. It is also well worth strolling around the picturesque village, and climbing up the **Citadel** to enjoy a panoramic view of the entire gulf. The **Annonciade Museum,** rue de la Nouvelle Poste, houses paintings by such modern artists as Signac, Matisse, and Rouault (open 10am-noon and 3-7pm, closed Tuesday. Admission 8F).

St. Tropez holds a major festival, or *bravade,* each year on May 16-18 to honor its patron saint—a Christian martyr beheaded by Nero whose body was set adrift, only to land in this town which to this day takes good care of its bodies.

The **syndicat** on the quai Jean-Jaurès (tel. 97-41-21; open Mon.-Sat. 9am-7pm, Sun. 10am-1pm, with shorter hours in winter), can give you information on sports and can help you find a room, possibly in a private home. The only inexpensive hotel is **Les Chimères,** bord de la mer (tel. 97-02-40), just outside town, which offers some rooms for as little as 56F, breakfast included. Camping is by far the cheapest alternative, though you may need reservations. **La Croix du Sud,** rte. de Pampelonne (tel. 79-80-84) is a four-star site, open Easter-September; **Les Tournels,** rte. du Phare de Camarat (tel. 79-81-38) is open all year. If you're stuck, try sleeping on the Plage des Salins. Many restaurants here are quite reasonable. **L'Abricot** on quai F.Mistral serves inexpensive snacks; **Grenadine,** rue de la Citadelle, offers quiche, salad, and desserts; and **Mario,** 7, rue de la Miséricorde, offers French and Italian entrées in an attractive setting for 20-35F.

There are three IYHF Hostels on the Côte, although they're hard to reach. Always call ahead before setting forth. Though near the sea the Hostel **Le Trayas/Théoule-sur-Mer,** rte. de la Veronese (tel. 44-14-34) is a 2km bus ride from the Le Trayas station. The Hostel at **Fréjus,** 37km from St. Tropez, domaine de Bellevue, rte. de Cannes (tel. 40-21-85) is a long walk from the Fréjus station. **La Garde Freinet** (tel. 43-60-05: closed mid-Dec. to Jan. as well as Sat. nights) is a small hostel, but try it in a pinch. Get off the train at Les Arcs (15km from St. Tropez).

Between St. Tropez and Cannes

When the glitter and crowds become intolerable, head to one of the nearby hill towns, such as **Grimaud,** with its shady lotus trees, an old fortress and an eleventh-century barrel-vaulted church. **Port Grimaud** is a widely publicized picture town, modeled after an idealized Italian fishing village. To some it is a pastel paradise, to others a modern fake.

Nearby **St. Maxime** is another popular tourist center with a sandy beach. (The **syndicat** is at Promenade Simon-Lorière (tel. 96-19-24).) **Les Issambères** and **St. Aygulf** also lie beside the sea. You pass through these seductive sites on the bus from St. Raphael, which hugs the shore as it winds towards St. Tropez. Any of them might prove equally appealing and unpeopled.

St. Raphael itself, and **Frejus,** ten minutes away by bus, are also worth seeing. If you're waiting for a bus for St. Tropez (they leave outside St. Raphael station), spend your time at St. Raphael's own modest beach. (To get there, take a two-minute walk straight ahead.) The spacious **syndicat,** place de la Gare (just opposite the station), can provide useful assistance and suggestions for camping from 8:30am-noon and 2-7pm.

The **Corniche d'Esterel,** the *massif* (rock mass) between St. Raphael and La Napoule, offers the most spectacular scenery on the Côte. Red rocks are splattered with the rich green of olive trees and the brilliant yellow of mimosa blossoms. Forming a series of inlets *(calanques),* the rocks plunge abruptly into the jet blue of the Mediterranean Sea. You can catch only a glimpse from the train or bus, since most tracks pass through dynamited tunnels; the best way to see the Esterel is to rent a mini-bike in Cannes.

The village of **La Napoule** offers a peculiarly droll museum, set in a medieval chateau, which houses the bizarre works of American sculptor, Henry Clews. His art features a grotesque menagerie of scorpions, lizards, and gnomes (admission 6F, students 4F). La Napoule is between St. Raphael and Cannes on the train line.

Cannes

Cannes is the costliest and showiest jewel in the Riviera's collection, sparkling with opulent villas, 14F lemonades, and streets that look like a series of

New Yorker ads. Yet the plebian traveler can still do reasonably well here once ensconced on Cannes' public, shady beach.

The heart of the town is the **Promenade de la Croisette,** a long and lavish boulevard that runs beside the sea. On one side of the road are palatial luxury hotels; on the other, beaches whose every square inch is private, owned by the hotels, studded with parasols, and peopled by spoilt refugees from a Harold Robbins novel (no coincidence, perhaps, as Mr. Robbins lives here). Palm trees stand in the middle of La Croisette, which is bordered by exclusive ports and spotless gardens, and where men wash the parking meters early each morning.

Don't despair, though. If you walk far enough westward down La Croisette (and it is a very attractive walk), you will come to a small block of public beach. There are other public beaches past Port Canto and past Palm Beach (on place Franklin Roosevelt)—the one near Palm Beach offers lessons in windsurfing. Remember, though, that the chairs along the main Promenade are not thoughtfully provided for weary back-packers; you have to pay 1.50F to collapse here. And beware of thieves at all times.

Apart from perfecting your tan, there's little to do here except window-shop. Venture along the winding alleyways past rue St. Antoine, or visit the Lord's Tower.

Every May, 350 films are unrolled, unreeled, and unveiled at the famous **International Film Festival,** as directors, actors, producers, and star-gazers gather around the Palais des Festivals. All you can do is stand outside and gape; screenings are restricted to members of the profession. Throughout the summer, festivities are always going on and fireworks going off in Cannes.

When you leave the station, walk straight ahead. You will quickly cross the rue d'Antibes, Cannes' major shopping street, and as quickly arrive at La Croisette.

Practical Information

Syndicat d'Initiative: Offices at the station (tel. 99-19-17) and at 50, La Croisette (tel. 39-24-53 or 39-94-41). The former is open daily 9am-1pm, 2-7pm in winter, and 8am-9pm in July and August. The latter closes on Sundays out of season and at 8pm in summer. The office staff is very helpful; they will make hotel reservations free of charge, and they can tell you about renting cars or bikes. For everything from parachuting to jai alai, ask for their Sports/Loisirs brochure. English spoken.

American Express: 8, rue des Belges (tel. 38-15-87). Open Mon.-Fri. 9am-noon and 2-6:15pm (money exchange until 5:30pm), Sat. 9am-noon. For currency exchange, you can also try **Office Provençal,** 17, rue Maréchal-Foch (tel. 39-34-37), open daily 9am-noon, 2-7pm, closed Sundays out of season.

Post Office: Main Post Office, Bivouac Napoléon. For late-night phone calls, enter at rue Notre Dame. A smaller branch is on rue Reine Astrid (near Palm Beach), open Mon.-Fri. 8am-noon, 2-5pm.

Train Station: SNCF, Information (tel. 99-33-00).

Discount Rail Tickets: BIGE/Transalpino tickets on sale at the Tourisme SNCF office in the Station (tel 39-20-20). Open Mon.-Sat. 9am-12:30pm and 2-6:30pm.

Bus Station: Quai St.-Pierre (tel. 39-31-37). Buses depart for Mougins, Juan-les-Pins, and Grasse every 45 minutes in summer. Buses also leave for Grasse (11F each way) right outside the Train Station.

OMJASE (Municipal Youth Office): 2, quai St.-Pierre (tel. 38-21-16). Information on scuba-diving, wind-surfing lessons, etc.

Hospital: Pierre Nouveau, 13, ave. des Broussailles (tel. 45-44-00).

Police: 38-38-74.

Accommodations

Although most Cannes hotels have more stars than you can afford, there are, surprisingly, many good bargains—all well-maintained, centrally located just off the rue d'Antibes, and close to the beach. Be sure to book ahead.

Hôtel de Bourgogne, 13, rue du 24 Août (tel. 38-36-73). Near the station on a street with several other hotels. Rooms are basic but clean. Singles 50 60F, doubles 83F with showers, breakfast 11F.

Hôtel des Allées, 6, rue Emile Négrin (tel. 39-53-90). Small but clean rooms. Singles 54F, doubles 78F, optional breakfast 11F.

Hôtel Nationale, 8, rue de Maréchal-Joffre (tel. 39-91-92). Bare, basic rooms, and a spirit of restrained elegance. Ideal location. Singles 50F, doubles 65-75F; breakfast 10F, showers 7F.

Hôtel Chanteclair, 12, rue Forville (tel. 39-68-88). Fifteen minute walk from the Station, off the beaten track. Set in a courtyard. Gruff, but manageable. Singles 45F, doubles 79F; showers 6F. Breakfast optional at 10F.

Camping: Le Grand Saule, blvd. de la Frayere in nearby Ranquin (tel. 47-07-05) packs them in like sardines. For more breathing space, try the campgrounds around Mandelieu which offer twelve sites. **Camping Les Pruniers,** la Pinède, on the N559 (tel. 38-99-23) isn't gorgeous, but you'll get in.

Food and Entertainment

The elegant sidewalk cafes on La Croisette, Cannes' center of conspicuous consumption, are very expensive. But elsewhere, try:

Les Glycines, 32, blvd. d'Alsace, on the other side of the railroad tracks (just behind the station), serves a plentiful 25F menu in a restful garden from 11:30am-1pm and 6:30-7:30pm. After 8pm, the *menu* is 35F. A real find. You can also stay here (well-kept rooms start at 64F, and a double with full *pension* costs only 120F), though the passing trains may keep you up at night.

Casino Supermarket and Cafeteria, 55, blvd. d'Alsace, is certainly a bargain. A featureless cafeteria sells entrees with vegetables for 16-20F, and a plate of spaghetti (if you're really broke) for 10.30F. Provisions sold downstairs. Open daily 11am-10pm.

Pierrot, located fifty yards away from Casino Supermarket on blvd. d'Alsace, is a vegetarian restaurant that's slightly more expensive (*menu* 45F, *plat du jour* 33F), but unusual and stylish.

Chez Mamichette, 11, rue St. Antoine. A cozy, cheerful Savoyard restaurant that is perfect for a splurge. Try the *fondue Savoyarde* (33F) or the *menu* at 45F. Closed Sunday.

Pizza Firouzeh, Port Canto. Who cares about the food! Its splendid view overlooks the entire stretch of ocean, and its prices are reasonable. Pizza 18-28F, sandwiches 10F, shish kabob 35F. Good for a snack. Open 11am-midnight.

Discos and cabarets are plentiful in Cannes, but it'll cost you a night's lodgings to get in. Stay all night to get your money's worth.

Whiskey à Go Go, 115, ave. de Lérins. Facing the beach, popular with the 18-21 aged crowd. (The branch in Juan-les-Pins is better.) Open from 10pm on; admission 50F. **Playgirl,** just opposite, costs 55F.

Between Cannes and Nice

The **Iles de Lerins** are off the coast of Cannes, just a short boat trip from the port. Owned by a Cistercian order of monks, the smaller **St.-Honorat** still has an active monastery; its quiet pine forests provide a welcome change from fast-paced Cannes. **Ile St.-Marguerite,** also pleasantly forested, is better known for its **Fort.** This was the home of the Man in the Iron Mask, well known to Dumas fans. Ten boats leave daily from the harbor at Cannes in summer, and five in winter. Cannes-Ste.-Marguerite takes 15 minutes and costs 14.40F; Cannes-St.-Honorat 30 minutes and 18F. For the Son-et-Lumière shows on the islands (daily at 9pm from June through September), 25F will buy both a return trip and a ticket to the show.

Mougins, set on a hill only 8km from Cannes, is one of the most peaceful towns on the coast. Picasso came here to find inspiration among the rambling hills of olive trees and the gentle streams and valleys. Walk through the streets of this old fortified town, and climb to the top of the monastery tower for an unrivalled view of the coastline. Buses leave from Cannes' Gare Routière (Quai St.-Pierre) every hour during the day.

Grasse, in the hills outside Cannes, is the perfume capital of the world, and the *parfumiers* offer free guided tours around their factories. Grasse may be fragrant, but there's not much to see; visit the town if you seek fresh air, but don't go just to take the tours. The guides show you how to make scents in a mechanical, blasé manner that strips the process of all its romance. The **Fragonard Parfumerie** is the largest factory (open daily 8:30am-6:30pm). Next door is a **Museum of Perfumery** at 20, blvd. Fragonard, which displays bottles, vases, and the history of the industry from ancient times. The *syndicat* is at 6, place de la Foux (tel. 36-03-56). Buses leave Cannes regularly on the 45-minute trip to Grasse (11F each way).

Most towns on the Riviera stay up late, but no place is as hopping as **Juan-les-Pins.** Boutiques remain open until midnight, cafés until 2am, and night clubs until 4 or 5am. Your best bet might be to leave your pack at the Station, stay at a club till 5am, and then stake out a spot to sleep on the beach at dawn. Alternatively, the nearby **Relais International de la Jeunesse,** blvd. de la Garoupe (tel. 61-34-40), is set amongst the villas and pines of the Cap d'Antibes. (It's open June to September; 24F for bed and breakfast, a good dinner for 20F.) Take a bus from the Antibes train station, direction Eden Roc, or walk (forty minutes). From Juan-les-Pins station it's a thirty-minute walk.

Unless it is July or August, you might find a reasonable room in Juan-les-Pins. The **Tourist Office** at 51, blvd. Guillemont (tel. 61-04-98) will provide hotel lists but will not make reservations (open daily except Sun., 9am-noon, 2-6pm). Otherwise, try **Hotel des Fleurs,** 3, ave. Admiral Courbet (tel. 61-05-25), with doubles from 64F (closed Jan.-March 15), or **Hotel Trinanon,** 14, ave. de l'Esterel (tel. 61-01-98), with doubles from 65F.

Also near Cap D'Antibes, the affluent resort where ailing Americans practice gossipy dissipation in Fitzgerald's *Tender is the Night* (the celebrated Hotel du Cap charges 880F for a double), is **Antibes** itself, a busy, glossy resort by the sea, where everything seems to exist on a small scale. Antibes boasts numerous artists and posh galleries, but its prize possession is undoubtedly the **Musée Picasso,** place du Chateau (open daily, except Tuesday, 10am-noon and 3-6pm; admission 10F, students 5F, free on Wednesday). The museum is itself a stunning work of art, set in a modern chateau, perched on a cliff beside the sea, where Picasso lived and worked in 1946. Its cool, white walls, narrow archways, and windows opening onto the sea dazzle with their elegance; its holdings are equally brilliant. On the first two floors are a garden with sculptures, and several small rooms furnished with drawings, paintings, and ceramics by Picasso (who characteristically discovered pottery in Vallauris and promptly dashed off 2,000 plates in a year), as well as striking photos of the artist, a cigarette always in hand. The top floor features his atelier and paintings by younger contemporaries. The collection is distinguished by its whimsical *jeux d'esprits;* its holdings are more mischievous and less twisted than Picasso's earlier works. For accommodations in Antibes, check with the **Tourist Office** at 12, place de Gaulle (tel. 33-95-64), open Mon.-Sat. 9am-noon and 2-6pm. Keep an eye out for Graham Greene, who lives on nearby ave. Pasteur.

Vallauris has always been known as the pottery capital of France. Picasso was fascinated by the town's ceramics and came here to work shortly after World War II. Most of the stores sell mass-produced, low-quality ware, but the **Galerie Madoura** does sell high-quality reproductions (at 1500F a plate, though, you might just want to look; open Mon.-Fri. 9:30am-12:30pm, 2:30-6pm). This summer Vallauris hosts its biannual exhibition of ceramics and modern art from over thirty countries. To get to this world's fair of pottery, take the train to Golfe-Juan and then take the bus or walk the 2km to Vallauris.

Biot, east of Antibes, is the home of the **Musée National Fernand Léger.** Housed here are large canvases of Leger's cubist, geometric renditions of mechanized modern life; even his human figures seem to be composed from bolts and tubes. Open daily in summer 10am-noon and 2:30-6:30pm, till 5pm in winter; closed Tues.; admission 8F, students 4F. Take the bus from Antibes, as the train stop is a good 3km from the museum.

Nice

Flavored, but not tyrannized, by its tourist industry, Nice is a down-to-earth, accommodating city that serves as an excellent base for Riviera explorations. It has all the accoutrements of a Riviera town—casinos, museums, a long beach, a casual affluence, even a playboy mayor—but it lacks the affected aloofness of its neighbors. Furthermore, Nice is blessed with all the conveniences of a big city—reasonable prices, good public transportation within the town and to all points on the Coast, and a population accustomed to visitors. Ian Fleming once called Nice an "exciting jungle for the venturesome and for those with shallow pockets." The description is as apt as ever.

The majestic **Promenade des Anglais** (appropriately enough, the grandest street in this often-English-speaking town) sweeps along the coast, but the beach which it chaperones is not one of the town's greatest assets. It is thin, crowded, and entirely pebbled. You may want to find a room in Nice and then travel elsewhere for your swimming and sunbathing.

Nice sustains a natural sparkle and energy that more poised and resplendent Riviera towns often lack. The pedestrian zone west of the **place Masséna** swarms with boutiques, busy restaurants, and tourists of all races and tongues. The **Vieille Ville,** tucked untidily into the southeastern pocket of Nice, is also limited to pedestrians, but is as different as can be. As you wander around the area's tiny, twisted streets, you'll be jostled from scruffy, pungent Third-

World markets to chic Continental shops, now surrounded by Arabic, now by heavily-accented French. You'll also find prices considerably lower than in the more manicured areas, so this is a perfect area for purchasing provisions. Finally, don't neglect the superb museums in Nice, most of them hidden amidst attractive houses in the city's restful suburbs.

Arrive in Nice early in the day during the summer, or else you'll almost certainly be forced to join the hordes of visitors who sleep outside the train station. Since it is so convenient, Nice is annually infested by students, and the station moonlights as one of the largest American college dormitories on the Continent.

Practical Information

Bureaux d'Information/Accueil de France: ave. Thiers (tel. 87-07-07), at the train station. English spoken. After 10am, they will book you a room (you pay 10F, and 4F will be deducted from your hotel bill). They will also give you information on car rentals, and on every activity from flying to scuba-diving. Ask for a large map if you want to find your way around the Vieille Ville. The *syndicat* has other offices around town, including one at 5, ave. Gustave V (tel. 87-60-60). Both are highly efficient, and open daily July-Sept. 15 from 8:30am-8pm. Out of season Mon.-Sat. 8:45am-12:30pm, 2-6pm.

Telephone Information: 24-hour "What's On In Nice" (tel. 85-65-83). For information on leisure activities in summer and sports in winter, tel. 87-63-99.

Centre d'Information Jeunesse: Esplanade des Victoires (tel. 80-93-93) will tell you all about sailing and other youth activities.

American Express: 11, promenade des Anglais (tel. 87-29-82). Open Mon.-Fri. 9am-noon and 2-6:30pm (financial services close at 5pm), Sat. 9am-noon (May-Oct.). Be prepared for long lines.

Currency Exchange: when AmEx is closed, try **Or Charrière,** 10, rue de France. Open Mon.-Fri. 9am-7pm, Sat.-Sun. 9am-noon, 2-7pm.

Post Office: 23, ave. Thiers near the train station. For longer hours, go to place Wilson. Open Mon.-Sat. 8am-10pm, Sun. 8am-7pm. Both places have Poste Restante, so ask your correspondents to specify one or the other.

Train Station: ave. Thiers. Regular departures for all stations along the coast, as well as for Italy and Northern France. You can also take showers here (10.30F) use dressing rooms (3F), and rent towels (3F) from Mon.-Fri. 9am-8pm, weekends 8am-8pm. A bathroom is open all night from 9pm-8am. All the facilities are unusually clean.

Central Bus Station: Gare Routière, promenade du Paillion (tel. 85-61-81), off ave. Jean-Jaurès across from the Old Town. Autoroute buses to Monaco and Cannes. Frequent departures to smaller towns around Nice.

BIGE/Transalpino tickets: Available at **CROUS,** 18, ave. des Fleurs (tel. 96-85-43), open Mon.-Sat. 8:45am-12:15pm, 1:30-5:15pm; also at **Vovac,** 6 bis, rue de Russie (tel. 88-95-95), open Mon.-Sat. 9:30am-12:15pm, 2:30-6:30pm. It costs 550F to Paris, 315F to Munich, 494F to Madrid, and 744F to Casablanca with these tickets, available to everyone under 26.

Boat Service to Corsica: Buy tickets at **SNCM,** 3, ave. Gustav V. (perpendicular to the promenade des Anglais; tel. 89-89-89). Open Mon.-Fri. 8:30am-noon, 2-6pm, and Sat. 8am-noon. Boats leave from the quai du Commerce (take bus #1 or #2 from ave. Jean Médécin or walk). A 2nd-class ticket costs 143F. In mid-summer, there are also 4th-class tickets for 112F; out of season (in the Blue Period) there are 30% discounts for those under 22 and special deals for couples. Allow 7-10 hours for the crossings (there are 2-3 a day in summer, none or one otherwise).

Moped Rental: Loca 2 Roues, 29, rue Gounod (tel. 87-20-07). Bikes are in good shape. 30F a day, plus 200F deposit for a bike; 60F plus 500F for a moped; 80-200F plus 1000F deposit for a motor-bike. Open Mon.-Sat. 8am-noon, 2-6pm.

English Bookstore: The Riviera Bookshop, 10, rue Chauvain (open daily 9:30am-12:30pm, 2-6pm; closed Sun. and Mon. morning) is extremely friendly and full, and even has a few second-hand copies. The **English Bookshop** on 4, rue de Congress (open Mon.-Fri. 9:30am-12:30pm, 2-7pm; Sat. 10am-12:30pm, 2-7pm) is larger, plusher, but much less helpful.

Laundromat: 27, blvd. Raimbaldi. 10F wash, 1.50F for drying. Detergent 2F. Open Mon.-Sat. 8am-7:30pm.

SOS Medical Service: (tel. 83-01-01); **All-night Pharmacy:** 7, rue Masséna (open 7:30pm-8:30am, tel. 87-78-94); **Crisis Line:** (tel. 87-48-74).

Police Emergency: 17

Telephone Code: (93)

Accommodations

During July and August, it is difficult to get a room in Nice (especially a single). It is tricky the rest of the time, too, since you should arrive by 9am, and yet some places don't know what rooms are available until 10am (most do not accept reservations). However, there is a web of hotels just outside the station and not far from the beach—all are pleasant, fairly inexpensive, and accustomed to English-speaking guests. The area near the tracks in Nice is friendly, respectable, and crowded with interesting hotels and restaurants. If the ones we list are all full, try others in the same area. Otherwise, you can always try the Vieille Ville, thirty minutes from the station, where rooms are often less expensive.

Auberge de Jeunesse (IYHF), rte. Forestiere du Mont Alban (tel. 93-23-64). Take bus #14 (4.50F) from blvd. Jean-Jaurès. A small Hostel (64 beds). Bed and breakfast for 26.50F, shower included. Lockout 10am-6pm; 10pm curfew. Proprietor is very nasty when hostel is full (June-Sept.).

Relais International de la Jeunesse, ave. Scuderi la Cimicz (tel. 81-27-63). Take bus #15 from place Massena (4.50F). Set in an old villa, a large, unofficial hostel with a swimming pool in back (3.50F). Run by students, terribly inefficient. Luggage must be kept only in a common storage room. 24.50F for bed and breakfast. May be allowed to stay only 1-2 nights when large groups take over.

Hôtel des Orangers, 10bis, ave. Durante (tel. 87-51-41). Three-minute walk from the station, with well-lit airy rooms. Recently renovated, rooms are spotless and well-equipped (with kitchenette and refrigerator). 45F per person, with shower. No singles.

Hôtel Darcy, 28, rue d'Angleterre (tel. 88-67-06). 3 minutes from the Station. Extremely kind management. Rooms are dark, cramped, and somewhat noisy, but the congenial warmth and inexpensiveness of the place more than compensate. 1:30am curfew. Singles 47F, doubles 78F, triples 120F (all including breakfast). Breakfast 8F, showers 6F, towels 2F.

Hôtel de la Gare, 35, rue d'Angleterre (tel. 88-75-07), has a helpful owner, but can be unreliable and unfriendly. Singles 43F, spacious doubles 74F, with breakfast 10F, showers 6F.

Novelty, 26, rue d'Angleterre (tel. 87-51-73) is pleasant enough. Singles 40F, doubles 57-77F, breakfast 9F.

Hôtel Belle Meunière, 21, ave. Durante (tel. 88-66-15), near the station. Clean, bright rooms and a hospitable manager. Singles 51F, doubles 67F; multi-bedded rooms available. Breakfast included, served in a sunny outdoor garden. Breakfast 10.50F, showers 8F. Off-season rates negotiable (closed Dec.-Jan.).

Hôtel d'Orsay, 20, rue d'Alsace-Lorraine (tel. 88-45-02) is more expensive—singles 55F, doubles 100F, breakfast 10F—but is cozy and clean.

Hôtel St.-François, 3, rue St.-François (tel. 85-88-69), in the Vieille Ville. Hard to find, and about thirty minutes from the Station, but set in the bustling little streets of the Old City. Next to the morning fish market. Singles 45F, doubles 65F, shower 10F, optional breakfast 10F.

Hôtel Interlaken, 26 ave. Durante (tel. 88-30-15). Not the quaintest of hotels but big (45 rooms) and across from the Station. Somewhat noisy. Serves meals downstairs. Singles 52-68F, doubles 52-68F, triples 88.50F. Breakfast 10.50F. At least 100F for rooms with shower.

Hôtel des Mimosas, 26, rue de la Buffa (tel. 88-05-59), is about fifteen minutes from the Station and five from the beach. Away from the American-filled area, and therefore cheaper. Singles 35-45F, doubles 45-55F, breakfast 9F. The **Mignon** (tel. 88-07-43) in the same building has similar prices.

Food

Seafood restaurants in Nice have become prohibitively expensive, but alternatives abound. For lunch, skip the restaurants and prepare a picnic instead. The fruit market just to the east of place Masséna is bustling every morning, as is the fish market in place St.-François which resumes in the afternoons. The Old City is full of bakeries and cheese shops. Try to avoid eating a meal at cloned and overpriced tourist places on the rue Masséna. They are most appropriate for people-watching, so enjoy the view with a drink or a dessert in hand, and save the big eating for other places.

In the Old City, restaurants may serve *couscous* (a North African dish of steamed cracked wheat cooked with meat and vegetables) or *paella* (a Spanish mixture of saffron rice, chicken, and seafood). Few restaurants open before 7pm, but most stay open late.

Near the Station:

Le Saëtone, 8, rue d'Alsace-Lorraine. An engaging, cosy, and very authentic restaurant, frequented by discerning locals and specializing in traditional local dishes—the kind of unspoilt place you dream about, but for the racy American muzak. Try the *soupe au pistou* and *tarte aux poires*. Since it's small, it fills up quickly. *Menus* for 25 and 31F. Closed Wednesday.

The Café d'Angleterre, around the corner on ave. d'Angleterre, is similar, if a little brighter and more impersonal. Reserve in advance. *Menus* 32 and 36F.

La Raclette, 10, rue de la Buffa. Its namesake, a melted-cheese and potato concoction, takes a long time to prepare, but its worth it (and huge) at 20F.

La Paillote, 29, rue Assalit. Edible Vietnamese food in an exotic decor (the bill is presented in a lacquered box). A refreshing change from familiar French fare. *Menu* at 32F. Similar Vietnamese restaurants abound—especially in this area. Try the **Escale à Saigon,** 6, rue St.-Siagre.

In the Old City:

Casa Julio, at the Porte Fausse, corner rue St.-Vincent and rue Gallo. A zesty combination of Spanish and Provençale cuisine. *Menus* at 32.50 and 45F. The *paëlla* (38F) is fragrant and filling. Closed Wed., Thurs., and at 10pm every other night.

Le Saf Saf, 1, rue Ste.-Claire. A Tunisian restaurant with *couscous* for 30-45F. Try the *couscous saf saf* (45F) and a bottle of Algerian wine (15F for a half-liter).

CROUS, 18, ave. des Fleurs, distributes the addresses of student cafeterias. Buy a ticket from a student (4.80F) and sneak in. During the summer, the cafeteria at the **Residence Universitaire** in Montebello (near the Musée Matisse) is a good place for an inexpensive meal.

Sights

The most confirmed museum-haters will have a hard time resisting the smooth, modern museums around Nice. Visiting them also allows you to glimpse the leisurely and luxurious residential areas that rest in the hills outside the center of town.

Among the best is the **Musée Matisse** (take bus #15, 4.50F, to ave. des Arènes-de-Cimiez). Housed in a villa overlooking the ruins of a Roman bath complex, the collection spans Matisse's career, from the Impressionist-inspired oils of the 1890s to the simpler line drawings of the 1950s. Matisse's sculpture—poorly represented in the U.S.—is also exhibited, as are his studies for the famous chapel at Vence. (Open 10am-noon, 2:30-6:30pm in summer, 10am-noon, 2-5pm otherwise. Closed Sun. mornings and Mon. Admission free.) While in the area, visit the **Franciscan Monastery** nearby, and wander around its beautiful gardens.

Also on the route of bus #15 (or a healthy walk from your hotel) is the **Musée National Marc Chagall,** ave. du Docteur Menard. Like most Côte d'Azur museums, this is a strikingly elegant, modern building that makes radiant use of glass, space, and light. The highlight of the collection is a set of seventeen oil paintings depicting Old Testament themes. Replete with the usual Chagall menagerie of flying and upside-down figures, the paintings render familiar scenes (like Noah's Arc or Jacob's dream) in a strikingly original form. The *Song of Songs* bridal series is especially intriguing. The noiseless gardens outside are thick with lavender and rosemary; cap off your visit with a refreshing *café au lait* or *orange givré* in the museum's outdoor cafe. The museum is open July-Sept., 10am-7pm; Oct.-June, 10am-12:30pm and 2-5:30pm. Closed Tuesdays. Admission 8F, 4F for students and on Sundays.

The **Musée des Beaux-Arts Jules Cheret,** 33, ave. Baumettes, is an absolute must for lovers of the grotesque. Among the artists whose works are displayed here is Gustav Albert Mossa (1883-1971), an undeservedly unknown Niçoise painter. His best works employ expressionist techniques to depict classical themes; the resulting symbolism is frighteningly bizarre. Open daily except Mon.; 10am-noon, 2-6pm June-Sept., closing 5pm otherwise. Admission free.

In town, visit the **Musée Masséna,** housed in an elegant villa at 35, promenade des Anglais. It is furnished and decorated in the Napoleonic style of the

First Empire, and upstairs are canvases by Renoir (who lived nearby), Duffy, and Sisley. (Open 10am-noon and 2-5pm. Closed Mon. Admission free.) The **Musée International de Malacologie,** 3, cours Saleya, has 15,000 shells.

If you've had your fill of Gothic and Romanesque churches, take a look at the **Eglise Russe,** 17, blvd. Tsavevich (a five-minute walk from the train station). Before the Revolution, Nice was a favorite resort for wealthy Russians; built between 1903-12, the church is very Russian in form, dominated by six onion domes. Their typically Niçois tiles, however, give the building a hybrid feeling. Entrance costs 5F. No shorts or sleeveless shirts are allowed inside the Church, which is open daily 9am-noon and 2:30-8pm in summer, 9:30am-noon, 2:30-5pm in winter.

Nice has many parks and public gardens, the largest of which is the **Jardin Albert 1er.** Located where the promenade des Anglais meets the quai des Etats-Unis, it offers a quiet, shady refuge with benches, fountains, and leafy nooks. Be sure to look at the ornate, eighteenth-century Triton fountain. Jardin Albert also contains a bandstand where evening concerts are frequently performed.

The ruins of a chateau rest on the hills above the Old Town. Climb the stairs as medieval pilgrims did, or take the lift. As a reward for the climb, you'll come upon a park with exotic pines and unusual cacti, as well as a view of the port and the Bay of Angels.

Entertainment

Most of Nice's bars along the waterfront cater to the middle-aged, piano-bar set, and charge accordingly. Bars around the place Masséna lean toward the jukebox sort, but the cafés in the Old City tend to be more reasonable.

The **Semaine des Spectacles,** published every Wednesday (2F), carries entertainment listings for the entire Côte. In mid-July, the **Jazz Parade** draws some of the most commercially successful jazz musicians from the U.S. Mainstream music plays simultaneously from three stages for seven hours at 50F a shot (35F in advance).

Between Nice and Monaco

Nice is ideally suited for day-trips, either to the big cities on each side of it, or to smaller villages on or overlooking the coast. You can either leap on and off the train to Monaco, visiting the small towns en route, or take buses circumscribing the towns of St.-Paul-de-Vence and Vence. Buses leave the Gare Routière about every hour from 7am to 7pm. The last return bus leaves Vence at 6:40pm, so don't spend an evening there unless you won't mind hitching back. Special loop tickets are available which allow you to get on and off the buses all day (tickets 20F).

If you decide to see **Vence** and **St.-Paul-de-Vence,** there are two buildings well worth a visit. The first is the **Fondation Maeght,** in St.-Paul, a half-mile walk from the center of town. The museum, designed by Sert, is actually part park, with fountains, wading pools, and split-level terraces. Works of Miro, Picasso, Calder, and Chagall are presented with such understanding and love that these abstract pieces seem natural in their garden setting. Indoors there are rotating exhibitions usually devoted to a single artist. (Open daily 10am-12:30pm, 3-7pm. Admission 15F, students 10F.) St.-Paul itself is among the best preserved hill towns in France. Walk along the ramparts, virtually unchanged since the sixteenth century, for a panoramic view of the hills and valleys of the Alpes-Maritimes. The village has become an artists' colony, and ateliers, galleries, and expensive boutiques fill the lower floors of the houses.

Restaurants are also over-priced in St. Paul, so go on to Vence instead where food is cheaper.

The second building is Vence's **Rosary Chapel,** 1.5km from the bus stop. The chapel's tiny interior was designed by Matisse, who considered it his masterpiece. Two of the walls are dominated by green, gold, and blue stained-glass windows; light from the windows bathes the interior in color showing the internal harmony of Matisse's creation to be as powerful as it is unusual. (Open May-Sept., Tues. and Thurs. 10-11:30am and 2:30-5:30pm; Mon., Wed., Fri. and Sat. 4-5pm; Sun. 4:30-5:30pm. Open Tues. and Thurs. only in off-season. Admission free.)

Another full and varied day-trip from Nice would include **Villefranche-sur-Mer, St.-Jean-Cap-Ferrat,** and **Beaulieu-sur-Mer.** Villefranche and Beaulieu are on the rail line between Nice and Monaco, and there are buses connecting both of them with Cap Ferrat, current haunt of the Beautiful People. If you sleep here, look in at the **Fondation Ephrussi de Rothschild,** a pink Italianate villa housing much fine French art. The huge garden complex is even more impressive.

Villefranche-sur-Mer is a fairly important port which has attracted many artists to its narrow streets and pastel houses, including Aldous Huxley and Katherine Mansfield. Climb up to the **rue Obscure,** one of the most peculiar streets in France, with its small cramped houses totally sheltered from the elements. Jean Cocteau decorated the fourteenth-century **Chapel of St.-Pierre,** with boldly executed scenes of the Apostles and the Camargue gypsies of Stes.-Maries-de-la-Mer. The chapel is open from 9am-noon and 2:30-7pm in summer, 2-4:30pm in winter, and 9am-noon, 2-6pm the rest of the year. Closed Thurs. Admission 4F.

You might also get out at **Eze-sur-Mer.** A little road, Les Chemins de Pins, leads away from the Station, through an alleyway, to a secluded beach. On the other side of the tracks, a steep road leads all the way up the precipitous hillside to the famous village of **Eze,** perched upon a cliff. (The walk takes about an hour.) It was from this lofty pinnacle that Nietzsche surveyed the world and composed *Beyond Good and Evil.*

The finest beach east of Antibes is unquestionably at **Cap d'Ail.** From the Station walk down the stairs, under the tracks and turn right. You'll find small rocky coves to the east—perfect for sunning, but dangerous for swimming. A half-kilometer walk to the west reveals the sheltered beach of Cap d'Ail. A bit pebbly, the beach is enclosed by cliffs, so swimming is safe here. The **Relais International de la Jeunesse,** blvd. de la Mer, Cap d'Ail (tel. 78-18-58) is on the way to the beach. Situated right on the sea, it's an old villa in an exclusive neighborhood, with a young, friendly management. There's a midnight curfew, so you can't stay here if you want to gamble the night away at the casino. Bed and breakfast 24F; dinner 20F. After three days you are expected to take dinner, but in summer longer stays are discouraged. (Open March 15 through October 1, but check beforehand.)

Monaco/Monte-Carlo

The Monaco of legend glitters with majestic wealth and playboy glamor, its streets graced with royalty and its casino crowded with debonair spies. In reality, Monaco—likened by Chekhov to "a luxurious water-closet"—is a concrete mess, clogged with unsightly high-rises and gaudy new hotels. The ugliest town on the Riviera, it is also the edgiest; many claim that it is a harsh police state, and that, having won an American princess, Prince Ranier is steadily developing (or degrading) the town so as to seduce American business. (Princess Grace, the former Grace Kelly of American films, died in a tragic accident here in 1982.) Monaco increasingly resembles a sister of Atlantic City—and although you'll glimpse many Ferraris here, expect to find the casinos thick with penniless students and lusterless leisure suits.

There's no good reason for spending any time in beachless Monaco, but there's no reason not to wander over one evening to sample its once-elegant pleasures. From the station, bear left; on your right you will see a strenuous but lovely walk to the **Palace**, the **Museum of Oceanography**, and the narrow streets of Monaco-Ville, which command regal views of the sea. To the left is **La Condamine**, the pretty port which leads to the racier, more elegant, and more commercial heart of Monte Carlo. Both areas lie about twenty-five minutes away from the Station.

Among events in Monaco, the **International Festival of Arts** is held periodically from December through April, and there is a gala **Fireworks Festival** on the last Tuesday in July and the first two Tuesdays in August. Evening concerts are held in the Cour d'Honneur of the Prince's Palace, with tickets running from 20 to 100F. Program information is available from the Tourist Office. In late May, the **Grand Prix** automobile race roars to its finish through the winding streets of Monaco. The drama and excitement lie as much in the dynamics of the crowd as in the race itself.

Practical Information

Office National de Tourisme: 2, blvd, des Moulins (tel. 30-87-01). Near the Casino. A plush, modern office that will make hotel bookings free of charge, but might suggest the more expensive alternatives. Open Mon.-Sat. 9am-7pm, Sun. 10am-noon. From June 15-Sept. 1, there is also a booth at the station, and you can always call the main office from a special phone at the station. (Bring your passport here, and they will endorse it with a "Principauté de Monaco" stamp.)

American Express: 35, blvd. Princesse Charlotte (tel. 30-96-52). Open Mon.-Fri. 9am-noon and 2-5:30pm, Sat. 9am-noon.

Post Office: Square Beaumarchais, Monte-Carlo. Monaco issues its own stamps, but unless you mail the postcards here you'll have to start a collection. Open Mon.-Sat. 8am-7pm, Sun. 8am-noon. There is another office in place de la Visitation, Monaco-Ville.

Train Station: ave. Prince Pierre. Trains make the twenty-minute trip from Nice regularly. Returning trains are less frequent. Information open Mon.-Sat. 8am-noon, 2-6:45pm, Sun. 8am-noon, 2-6pm.

Local Buses: These connect the entire town and, given all its steep hills and staircases, you may want to use them. Tickets cost 4.50F.

Long Distance Bus Service: All buses leave from the port. To Nice, along the Lower Corniche, from 6am-9pm; stops at Cap d'Ail, Eze-sur-Mer, Beaulieu-sur-Mer, Villefranche-sur-Mer. Along the Middle Corniche, from 6:50am-7pm, to 8pm weekends, stopping at Cap d'Ail, Eze-Village, Col de Villefranche. To Menton along the sea, stopping at Roquebrune-Cap-Martin, from 6am-9pm. To La Turbie and on to Italy. Buses every 30-60 minutes depending on the route. Buses tend to be very slow.

Current Activities: tel. 50-07-51.

Bike Rental: Auto-Motof Garage, 7, rue de la Colle, near the station (tel. 30-24-61)

Hospital: ave. Pasteur (tel. 50-48-55).

Police: Emergencies (tel. 17); otherwise (tel. 30-42-46).

Telephone Code: (93).

Accommodations and Food

"I had decided to get out at Monaco," wrote Evelyn Waugh, "because, I was told, the hotels were cheaper. . . ." No longer. Monaco offers neither convenient nor inexpensive places to stay. Furthermore, hotels here don't display their prices, many are on holiday in June, and all serve expensive breakfasts. Still, there are some acceptable budget accommodations:

Hôtel de la Poste, 5, rue des Oliviers (tel. 30-70-56). A good location on a narrow street near the beach and Casino. One of the best budget deals in town, and therefore booked months in advance. Singles 62F, doubles 83F including breakfast. No showers. Serves a good dinner for 33F.

Hôtel Cosmopolite, 4, rue de la Turbie (tel. 30-16-95). Very near the train station. Nothing to rave about, but clean rooms. Singles 66F, doubles 87F, including breakfast. Showers 6F. The Hôtel de France, at #6 (tel. 30-24-64), is nicely decorated. It has a few rooms for 52F and 68F; the others are over 100F. Breakfast 13.50F, showers 7F.

Camping: There are no campgrounds in Monaco, but there are two sites between Roquebrune and Cap Martin, on the N7 heading to Italy. Camping de Banastron (tel. 35-74-58) is on the sea, but has only eighty campsites; open April-Oct. Toracca, ave. Général-Leclerc (tel. 35-62-55) is a three-star site with 120 places and a restaurant. Fleur de Mai, route de Gorgio (on D23) is the largest with two hundred spots.

The best places to eat are amidst the touristed snack-bars and souvenir shops of Monaco-Ville, where the food is undistinguished, but inexpensive. Try L'Estragon, 6, rue Emile de Loth, with menu at 30F, cheap pizza, and cheerful outdoor seating, or L'Aurore, 8, rue Princesse Marie de Lorraine, with a 33F menu.

Near the station, you might try Restaurant de la Roya, 21, rue de la Turbie, which serves paella and a variety of seafood specialties. It's a homey place, with parakeets to serenade you as you dine. Menu at 33F, plat du jour 28F, served only until 9pm. Closed Monday. Chez Cinto, at #19, is a family-run restaurant which attracts local workers with its unpretentious and nourishing fare. Menus at 38F and 45F.

Sights

The Casino is an extravagant folly, worth visiting even if you're not a gambler. Surrounded by gardens and overlooking the coast, the old Casino building was designed by Charles Garnier, and resembles his Paris Opera House. The interior is an example of late-nineteenth-century rococo at its best, with red velvet curtains, gold and crystal chandeliers, and gilded ceilings, even though it has, in Ian Fleming's words, "the drabness of a Strauss operetta played in modern dress." Here Mata Hari once shot a Russian spy, and here an English couple once won 30 million francs in a week. Nowadays, the rooms teem with incongruous back-packers and tourists. The slot machines open at 10am, the salle américaine (for blackjack and craps) opens at 3pm, but the hard-core veterans arrive after 10pm. Admission to the main room—or "kitchen"—is free (you must be over 21), but it costs 20F to enter the Salons Privés, where French games like chemin de fer and trente quarante begin daily at 3pm.

The Casino also houses the sumptuous theater that was the sometime stage for Sarah Berndardt and the long-time home of Diaghelev's **Ballets-Russes.** You can only visit by attending a ballet or opera performance; tickets are expensive, but here at least you are guaranteed a return for your money.

For a taste of Monaco's new and democratic vulgarity, you can also visit the **Loew's American-style Casino,** as gaudy and brash as the older Casino is elegant. Like a Vegas palace, this place has a haphazardly mythical theme (there are large Tarot-like cards on the wall) and a joyless, garish air. Admission is free.

Monaco-Ville is full of stately "sights." At 11:55am each day, you can see the Changing of the Guard outside the **Prince's Palace,** a ritual which, given the size of the Principality, resembles a Marx Brothers' parody. Skip the uninteresting State Apartments and the Musee du Palais, along with their combined 18F fee.

You can have a much better time at the excellent **Oceanographic Museum,** directed by Jacques Cousteau, but you'll have to fish for 27F (students 13.50F) to get in. The Museum is open daily in summer 9am-7pm, and opens at 9:30am from Oct. to June. The **Jardin Exotique,** with its outstanding cactus collection, provides sweeping views of the coast as well as grottoes with stalagmites and stalactites. (Open May-Sept. 9am-7pm, otherwise 9am-noon, 2-6pm. Admission 17F, 11F with student ID.)

Menton

After the fast and corrupting pace of Monte Carlo, nearby Menton will seem tranquil and refreshing. This is a health spa favored as a retirement colony, where families flock for safe vacationing and where the natives speak a dialect that mixes both French and Italian and can be understood by neither nationality. Menton has its own **casino** (open Mon.-Thurs. 4pm-3am, Fri.-Sun. 4pm-4am), but its prize possession is the **Jean Cocteau Museum.** Although best known for his brilliant work in film and fiction, Cocteau was skilled in all the plastic arts. The museum, located in a seventeenth-century stronghold, houses a representative collection of his work rarely displayed elsewhere. (Open daily except Tues., 9am-noon, 2-6pm. Admission 3F, students 1.50F.)

One block from the Train Station is Menton's **covered market.** Choose from a selection of quail, rabbit, goat, horse, cheeses, fruits, and pâtês, all laid out in loving profusion. The **Youth Hostel** is located in the campground **Plateau St. Michel** (tel. 35-93-14). It is a twenty-minute walk from the station up a winding cascade of steps—the view alone, however, is worth the excursion. (Hostel fee is 26.50 per night with breakfast and shower.) The campground, at 13F for two people and a tent, is a convenient alternative. For other accommodations and a list of campgrounds, try the **syndicat d'initiative** in the Palais de l'Europe, ave. Boyer (tel. 57-57-00), which will book rooms.

The road leading out of town to the north will bring you to **L'Annonciade,** a Capuchin monastery and peaceful retreat located 2km from Menton. **Gorbio** (7km from Menton) is a medieval town surrounded by olive groves and ruins of an ancient castle which faces the ocean. **Cap Martin,** to the west, offers quiet beaches along the rocky coast. For the best lookout at Castellar (8km from Menton), stop at the **Café des Alpes,** where the high mountains cascade down to the aquamarine sea.

Corsica

> *They (the Corsicans) told me that in their country I should be treated with the greatest hospitality, but if I attempted to debauch any of their women, I might expect instant death.*
> —James Boswell

If the French call Corsica l'Ile de Beauté, they also describe it as *sauvage*. For Corsica is like an attractive shrew who won't be tamed; there is no denying the island's wild profusion of natural beauty, but you must be willing to struggle and to compromise in order to enjoy it. If you are a creature of comfort, consider skipping this island; hotels are much less common and more expensive than on the mainland, and public transportation is almost nonexistent. But if you want to get away from it all (including conveniences and other Americans), or if you're an ardent camper or an adventurous lover of the outdoors, then this is the place to go. Expect to be stretched, scratched, and exasperated—and you may find something precious.

Corsica's heartland features thickly-forested islands, divided by creeks and covered with vineyards, grazing sheep, and *maquis* (underbrush). Around them winds a jagged, rocky coastline, blessed with dazzlingly clear water and long, sandy beaches. The air, too, is amazingly clear, and is bathed almost year-round by brilliant (often scorching) sunshine.

If Corsica is physically the Riviera's country cousin—more rugged and less touched—socially, it is entirely unrelated. Underdevelopment has been the island's curse as well as its saving grace. Where the Côte d'Azur is cultivated and opulent, Corsica is culturally barren and desperately poor.

For most people, the island's history begins and ends with Napoleon—the native son who, as Emperor of France, did little to improve the conditions of his birthplace—but the island knew an earlier history of colonialism. First a Greek and later a Roman and a Pisan colony, Corsica became a Genoese protectorate in the thirteenth century. Enjoying only a brief period of independence from 1755 to 1769, the island has since been under French rule.

The Corsicans themselves are a stubbornly insular people. They shrug off all connections to France, and while most Corsicans speak French, they much prefer their own language, which is similar to Italian. Their fierce independence sometimes takes on a more militant form; on almost every wall in every town, you can see scrawled slogans ordering the French to go home, evidence that the separatist issue still burns strong.

Practical Information

Try to visit Corsica before June 14, the day marking the beginning of "high season" in the tourist trade. Services grow more frequent between then and Sept. 15, but prices soar.

Once you're in Corsica, collecting pamphlets is worth your time and trouble. A single brochure lists all of Corsica's hotels, another lists all its camping sites, and still another contains all useful addresses and telephone numbers, including the places to contact for horseback-riding, hiking, sailing, and other sports. You can also find the train schedule for the entire island on a single piece of paper. Any Corsican *syndicat* will give you these brochures free of charge.

Getting There and Getting Around

Air France and **Air Inter** fly to Bastia and Ajaccio on Corsica from Paris (435F one way), and from Nice or Marseille (225-270F). Flying in from the Riviera, then, is not much more expensive than sailing second-class, especially if you can get a 25% youth discount. Air France's office is in Bastia (6. ave. Ejile-Sari; tel. 31-27-74) and Air Inter's are in Calvi (quai Landry; tel. 65-01-38) and Bastia (9, blvd. Général-de-Gaulle; tel. 31-44-74).

The **Société Nationale Maritime Corse Mediteranée (SNMC)** operates car ferries from Marseille, Toulon, and Nice, docking at Bastia, Calvi, and l'Ile Rousse in the north, and Ajaccio and Propriano in the west. Allow 6½-11½ hours for the crossing (the crossing from Nice to Bastia is the shortest, that from Marseille to Bastia the longest). There are about six trips each day in summer, three otherwise. From Marseille or Toulon, a second-class ticket costs 156F, from Nice 143F; in summer, fourth-class tickets are available for 122F and 112F respectively. Out of season, in the Blue Period, there are 30% discounts for those under 22, and other similar reductions. InterRail card holders are given a 33% discount. Crossings from Corsica to Italy are shorter and a little less expensive. Bastia-Leghorn takes 4½ hours, Bastia-Genoa takes 7. Fares from Bastia vary from 89-146F in low season to 136-170F in high season. From Calvi, fares are 120-152F, depending on the season. Tirrenia ferries also travel three times daily from Bonifacio to Santa Teresa in Sardinia (30F, one hour), and once to La Maddalena (35F, 2½ hours).

Once on the island, those traveling in a group might consider renting a car. This costs about 90-140F per day, plus 1-1.60F per kilometer, and insurance of 12-23.50F. You can also rent a mini-bus for 245F and 2.45F per kilometer. Check with different firms to discover individual offers. Mobilettes rent for 50F a day from **Solvet,** which has offices in Bastia (6. ave. Sari; tel. 31-31-80), Ajaccio (rue J. B. Maglioli; tel. 21-20-20), and Corte (ave. de la Poretta; tel. 46-02-03). The roads in Corsica are very primitive, so be careful while driving—especially on the mountain roads, where you're safest going at a cow's pace.

(The bus from Ajaccio to Bonifacio, for example, takes over 4 hours to cover 90 miles!) Gas is cheaper than in France, but carry some extra with you, since gas-stations are few and far between. If you do run out of gas, call the local *Brigade de Gendarmerie.*

Public transport is slow and infrequent. Two trains a day run from Ajaccio, via Corte, to Ponte Leccia and from Ponte Leccia to Bastia or Calvi. Fares are high, and the rattly, cramped, Disneyland-like trains are extremely slow. Bastia-Calvi (93km) takes 3 hours, and Bonifacio isn't even on the train-line. All trains, moreover, are run by the private Corsican Railways; no passes are valid except Inter-Rail (50% off). Buses are no more frequent than the trains and no less expensive, but they are slightly more comprehensive and more comfortable (some even show videotaped movies). Hitching, which is slow, but possible, may be your best bet.

Aooommodatlons and Food

Hotels on Corsica are rare, and those that exist are expensive. Yet even with their high prices, most hotels fill up by early morning during high season. Camping, however, is possible almost anywhere. There are dozens of campgrounds, and all the beaches are open to campers as well. To camp in the mountain forests legitimately, you should obtain permission from **La Compagnie des Eaux et Forets** at 4, blvd. Marcaggi in Ajaccio. Beware of fires, as the *maquis* is highly flammable.

Corsican cuisine, like the land, is unsophisticated and striking. Seafood is excellent along the coast; try *calamar* (squid), *langouste* (lobster), *gambas* (prawns), or *moules* (mussels). In fall and winter you can order *nacres* (pink-shelled mollusks) and *ursens* (sea urchins). Other delicacies include *pâté de merle* (blackbird pâté)—a cruel killing but a native prize—spicy pork sausages, and excellent cheeses; *brebis* (made from sheep's milk) and *chèvre* (made from goat's milk) keep without refrigeration, so you can buy large quantities.

Corsican wines are excellent and as inexpensive here as on the mainland (8-10F a bottle). *Mascat* is a sweet wine especially worth tasting. Finally, there are several potent *eaux de vie* available, flavored with Corsican berries. The unofficial national drink, however, is *pastis,* a wickedly strong brew made from anis and drunk at all hours.

Bastia

Bleak, busy, and industrialized, Bastia is Corsica's least characteristic city, but it is also the island's largest port, so your boat may well deposit you here. If you get stuck here waiting for a ferry, you can visit the old port, from which you can climb to the fifteenth-century **Governor's Palace** and there visit the **Musée Ethnographe Corse** (open daily in summer, 9am-noon and 3-6pm, in winter Mon.-Sat. 9am-noon, 2-5pm; admission 2F). In the main city, the place St.-Nicholas is the center of all local activity.

From Bastia, you can explore the string of fishing villages and quiet inlets of **Cap Corse,** a thirty-mile peninsula north of the city which points toward France. The road around the cape passes sheltered coves and high, forest-covered mountains. Sprinkled among the hills are olive groves, lime trees, and old fortified towns which mark the period of Genoese rule. During high-season, buses travel each day along the *corniche* around the Cap from Bastia to **St. Florent,** a new beach resort that can be skipped in good conscience. Only limited accommodations are available, but you could try **La Pecheur** (tel. 35-60-14) in **Centuri,** a tiny, unspoiled port near the tip of the peninsula.

Practical Information

Sydicat d'Initiative: 35, blvd. Paoli (tel. 71-02-04) Information on the entire island and bus schedules for touring the Cap Corse (open daily 9am-noon and 2-5pm).

Tourist Office: place St.-Nicholas (tel. 31-00-89). Tourist information and guided tours for Bastia only. Open Mon.-Fri. 8:30am-noon and 2-6pm; till 4pm Sat. in summer.

Post Office: ave. Maréchal-Sebastiani. Open Mon.-Fri. 8am-7pm, Sat. 8am-noon, Sun. 8am-11am. Telephones available.

Train Station: place de la Gare, just off ave. Maréchal-Sebastiani (tel. 32-60-06). Corsica's most modern station, but still very quiet and empty. Trains to Calvi take 3 hours and cost 51F.

Airport: Bastia-Poretta, 20km away (tel. 36-03-52). The bus from here into town takes 30 minutes and costs 20F.

Buses: Bastias, 40, cours Paoli, runs buses to Calvi once a day (taking 3½ hours, costing 34.10F, and passing Ile Rousse en route). **Kallistour,** 3, Residence Ornano, runs tours around Cap Corse (5 hours, 60F). Other firms along ave. Maréchal-Sebastiani go to Porte Vecchio, Corte, or Ajaccio twice a day.

Boats: SNCM, Hôtel de la Chambre de Commerce (tel. 31-36-63), runs boats to France. Open daily 8-11:15am, 2-5:30pm.

Sogedis, 5, bis rue Chanoine-Leschi (tel. 31-18-69) runs a variety of boats to Italy, and even to Elba. Open daily 9am-noon, 2-6pm.

Auto and Motorbike Rental: The following are all within a block of each other by the port: **Solvet,** 6, ave. Sari (tel. 31-31-80); **Mattei,** 5-7, rue Chanoine-Leschi (tel. 31-57-23); **Avis,** 2, rue Notre Dame de Lourdes (tel. 31-25-84); **Hertz,** square St.-Victor (tel. 31-14-24).

Police Station: 31-26-17.

Hospital: Blvd. de Toga (tel. 31-28-27).

Telephone Code: (95).

Accommodations and Food

Stay in town only if you're so exhausted from the ferry ride that you can't move on. There are several cheap hotels near the port or near the train station, but most are dingy. Ask at the tourist office for a list or try **Hôtel de l'Univers,** 2, ave. Maréchal-Sebastiani (tel. 31-03-38), a large hotel with adequate if unexciting rooms, five minutes from the port or station (singles 55F, doubles 65F, rooms with two beds 70F). The **Hôtel des Voyageurs** at #9 (tel. 31-61-03) offers various doubles for 60-80F. **Camping Casanove** (tel. 37-02-18) lies 4km north of Bastia, but is a small and ill-equipped site (4F per person). The tourist office can direct you to other campgrounds.

Chez Gino at 11, ave. Sari is an absurdly cheap restaurant; pizzas cost 10F, huge ice-cream concoctions cost 10F, and for 30F, you can eat like a king. Neither the food nor the decor is special, but the service is bouyant and the clientele (mostly families) is unpretentious and wholesome. In more elegant quarters, **Restaurant Jack,** at 18, rue César-Campinchi, serves a sustaining fish *menu* for 38F. Otherwise, try your luck with the many places that dot the seaside between and including the New Port and the Old.

Côte Orientale

From Bastia to Porto-Vecchio stretches the island's only relatively flat road, which closely follows the Côte Orientale (Corsica's east coast). Although you won't find spectacular scenery here, the island's longest fine-sand beaches line the shore. Inland, along the **Plaine Orientale**, the land is heavily cultivated with grapevines and fruit trees or thick with *maquis*. **Moriani Plage,** a beach 39km south of Bastia, has several campgrounds; the 8km long, sand beach near **Ghisonaccia** (the trip's half-way point) is another perfect camping spot.

A small town 70km from Bastia, **Porto-Vecchio** is a pleasant place to spend a few hours. Still imprisoned by its sixteenth-century Genoese walls, the streets are winding and narrow, and the thirty-foot-thick walls have been hollowed out for use as homes, stores, and restaurants. From the **Porte Genoise** (formerly the city's main gateway), there is a panoramic view of the port and the inlet of the Tyrrhenian Sea on which Porto-Vecchio lies. The **Plage de Palombaggia,** 9km to the south, is a picture-postcard beach with a crescent of fine sand shaded by parasol-like pine trees. Seven km to the north of Porto-Vecchio, the **Plage de Golfo-Di-Sogno** is surrounded by well-equipped campsites. In the town itself, the **Hôtel le Mistral** on rue Jean-Nicoli offers comfortable singles from 45F and doubles from 60F. For the best meal in town try **La Mariniere** (follow the road from Porte Genoise to the harbor), which serves a four-course 40F meal that includes a scrumptious *soupe de poisson.* The **syndicat d'initiative** on rue Maréchal-Juin (tel. 70-09-58) is open Mon.-Sat. 9am-noon and 2-6pm.

Bonifacio

Clinging limpet-like to the rocks above the sea, Bonifacio was once designed to keep intruders out; now it welcomes them in by the score. Bonifacio's high point, in every sense of the word, is its **Citadel,** which commands a majestic view over the straits to Sardinia, 13km away. From this great height, you can see why Bonifacio was founded as a fortress (the French Foreign Legion still sets up camp here). And although the climate is wearing away parts of the town, you will notice that virtually every house still has a steep staircase whose lowest flight can be raised like a mini-drawbridge in case of invasion.

Tours of the old city leave from the **syndicat d'initiative,** 20, rue Longue (tel. 73-03-48), four times daily (office open Mon.-Sat. 9am-noon and 2-6pm). Given in French and Italian only, the tour costs 6F and includes the **Genoese Bastion** and the **Eglise St.-Dominique,** both presently under renovation. The town also has a "Napoleon slept here" house which you can by-pass without regrets. From the port below you can take a sea excursion to the now-deserted islands of **Lavezzi** and **Cavello.** The view of Bonifacio jutting proudly out on a limestone promontory makes the adventure (20F round trip) worthwhile.

Bonifacio is another Corsican town where you won't find a free room much past noon in the summer. The hotels and restaurants are all clustered around the port below the city, and none have much color or character. The **Hôtel des Etrangers,** ave. Sylvere Bohn (tel. 73-01-09) has singles from 60F and doubles with showers from 80F. The **Hôtel des Voyageurs,** quai Comparetti (tel. 73-00-46) has doubles for 70-90F; if it's full, try **La Pergola** (tel. 73-00-80) next door. There are three campgrounds within the region. **Campo di Liccia** (tel. 159) on the N198 is one of the best-equipped and is open June to September. The syndicat d'initiative will provide you with more information. For dining out, try **La Rascasse,** on the quai Comparetti, which has a 45F *menu,* or the amiable **La Suita Rocca** nearby.

Bonifacio is very hard to reach. Since it does not lie on the train route, you must either take the 8F, forty-minute bus ride from Porto Vecchio, or settle for a four-hour odyssey from Ajaccio, which will deposit you in town long after the last hotel has put up its *complet* sign. It is much easier to leave town; **Tirrenia** runs boats to Sardinia—three times each day to Santa Teresa (30F, 1 hour), once to La Maddalena (35F, 2¼ hours). Just follow the quai Comperetti to its end and buy your tickets shortly before departure time. The Tirrenia office (tel. 73-00-96) is open daily 9-10am, 12:30-2pm, and 3:45-5pm.

The road northwest to Ajaccio crawls through mountains and intermittently affords stunning glimpses of the sea far in the distance. **Sartène** (on N196) is a town built on granite, surrounded with megalithic stones and fantastically-shaped rock faces. Like Bonifacio, the town sponsors an extremely unusual Good Friday Procession, the *Catenacciu,* featuring a red-hooded Christ bearing a heavy wooden cross and dragging a long chain with his leg. He walks through the candlelit streets of the old town in a reenactment of the Calvary drama. The **syndicat** is on cours Saraneli (tel. 77-05-37).

You can continue to **Propriano,** a popular summer resort set on the Valinco gulf, with its busy fishing village and sandy beaches. The **syndicat** here is at 2, ave. Napoléon (tel. 76-01-49). After leaving town, the road continues to twist and wind all the way to Ajaccio, Corsica's capital.

Ajaccio

Though symbolically the most important city in Corsica, Ajaccio still has the feeling of a small town—the fact that the fish market and the tourist office share the same building reflects this provincial atmosphere. Ajaccio is known primarily as the birthplace of Napoleon. Half the streets are named after one Bonaparte or another, and the whole town goes wild on his birthday, August 15. If you cherish the Little Emperor as much as his hometown does, you can visit the house in which he was born (just off the rue Bonaparte, for devotees only; open 9am-noon and 2-6pm, closed Sun. noon-Tues. 2pm; admission 6F, students 3F). Next to the syndicat is the **Salon Napoléonien,** which features lots of busts, portraits, and a bronze death-mask (open daily in summer 9am-noon, 2:30-5:30pm; in winter Mon.-Sat. 9am-noon, 2-5pm; admission 2F). On rue Fesch, 6F (students 3F) will admit you to **Napoleon's tomb.** Better than all these is the **Musée Fesch,** next door on rue Fesch, which houses an excellent collection of Italian primitives and Renaissance paintings. (but it may be closed for renovation). All things considered, then, you may want to spend the entire day at the uncrowded, sandy beach, found along blvd. Lantivy.

Southwest of Ajaccio, at the mouth of the Gulf, are the **Iles Sanguinaires,** whose dramatic grottoes can rescue you from the single-minded intensity of Ajaccio. Many private entrepreneurs offer excursions by boat from the harbor for about 25F per person. Alternatively, you can take a bus to the mouth of the Gulf and view the Iles from the mainland (take the bus marked "Parata" for 4.50F from the place de Gaulle). The Genoese **watchtower** here is in better condition than most, so be sure to take a careful look at its engineering. For those who want to get off the shore and walk up into the mountains, the tourist office's brochure *Promenades autour d'Ajaccio* maps out some rugged, scenic hikes in the area.

Off the road leading south from Ajaccio is the archeological site of **Filitosa.** Recently uncovered, huge stone monoliths carved with human faces stare mutely and aristocratically out to sea amidst an otherwise wild landscape (ask the syndicat d'initiative for directions).

Practical Information

Syndicat d'Initiative: Hôtel de Ville, ave. Serafini (tel. 21-40-87). Next to the Port, if you sail from France. In addition to information on Ajaccio, you can pick up a list of campsites and a schedule of bus excursions. Open Mon.-Fri. 9am-noon and 2-6pm. Closed Sat. afternoon and Sun.

Post Office: Cours Napoléon (tel. 21-13-60). Open weekdays 8am-7pm, Sat. 8am-noon. Telephones downstairs.

Airport: Campo dell'Oro, 7km away. Bus into town costs 9F.

Train Station: ave. Jean-Jerome Levie (tel. 23-11-03). Trains run twice a day to Corte (36F, 2½ hours), and, via Ponte Leccia, to Calvi (78F and 5 hours).

Buses: A variety of firms provide an equal variety of routes to Calvi, Corte, and other towns. Ollandini, 4, rue J. R. Marcaggi, runs to various towns, including Corte (33F and 2 hours). Their office in place de Gaulle runs buses to Bonifacio (56F and 4 hours).

SNCM: Quai L'Herminier. Boats to France. Open 8-11:45am, 2-6pm.

Car Rental: Avis, 3, place de Gaulle (tel. 21-01-86); Hertz, 8, cours Grandval (tel. 21-70-94). Or try a smaller firm like Balesi, 4, rue Emmanuel Arène (tel. 21-08-11).

Bike Rental: Location 2 Roues, 21, blvd. D. Paoli (tel. 23-23-25). Bikes 35F, mopeds 65F, motorbikes 150F.

Police Emergencies: (17). Police Station: (21-88-26).

Hospital: ave Impératrice-Eugénie (tel. 21-15-10).

Telephone Code: (95).

Accommodations and Food

Expect to pay as much for a mediocre hotel here as you would for a plush one elsewhere.

Hôtel Columba, 2, ave. de Paris (tel. 21-12-66). A small and pleasant hotel with reasonably large and sunny rooms. Gracious and helpful owners. The best deal in town. A couple of singles, 63F; doubles 95F. Multiple accommodations available. No breakfast; showers extra. Reserve ahead if possible.

Bélvédere Hotel, 4, rue Henri-Dunant (tel. 21-07-26). Walk up the flight of stairs at the corner of rue de Sergent Casalonga and rue Maréchal-Ornano. A large, old hotel surrounded by a lovely garden with a view of the mountains and the sea. Singles 55F, doubles 77-98F. Breakfast 9F, showers 5F. Reservations recommended.

Hôtel de la Poste, 3, rue Ottavy (tel. 21-02-15). Centrally-located, behind the post office. Much less dingy than it looks from outside; rooms are large and clean, if a little dark, and the proprietors are eager to please. Singles 50F; doubles with one bed 80-90F; breakfast 10F. On the next street is the **Centre Hôtel,** 4, rue Lorenzo-Vero (tel. 21-30-01), a one-star annex to a two-star hotel, with similar prices to the Poste.

Chez Pardi at 60, rue Fesch, is frequented by locals and has a fine restaurant upstairs that serves Corsican specialties. Its *menu* costs 38-50F. **U Fucono** at the foot of rue Général-Campi near the place de Gaulle also serves well-prepared local dishes in an equally snug setting. The 30F *menu* includes wine. Get there early—by 8pm all the tables are full. **Da'Mamma,** passage de la Guignette, an alleyway between cours Napoléon and rue Fesch (follow the Scotch House signs), is a very pleasant, leisurely restaurant serving well-cooked, very large meals. *Menu* 35F. The morning market on blvd. du Roi Jerome, behind the syndicat will provide with you a bountiful picnic lunch. After dinner, the cafes along the port allow you to gaze at the fishing boats and watch the passers-by.

Ajaccio to Calvi

Perhaps the most heart-stopping of all Corsica's stretches of road leads from Ajaccio northwards to Porto, sweeping past beaches and small resorts, then ascending steeply through wooded gorges and huge mountains. After **Tiuccia,** which is notable for its ruined castle, there is a series of small, shady crescent beaches that remain uncrowded even in summer. **Cargese,** at the end of the gulf of Sagone, is a small Greek Orthodox community. The Greek mass still echoes in the **Eglise Greque** every Sunday, and the traditional chants, incense, and candlelight contribute to an unearthly, haunting beauty. If you want to stay over here, try the **Hôtel de France** (tel. 26-41-07), which offers large rooms with showers (singles 65F, doubles 80F).

Piana on the beginning of the **Gulf of Porto** is the gem of Corsica, with sheer, jutting cliffs of rose-colored granite, fragrant eucalyptus trees, and sandy beaches. Pleasant for a stopover, the **Hotel la Continental** (tel. 26-12-02) offers the best deal in town (singles 55F, doubles 70F). Between Piana and Porto, the road goes through the area called the **Calanques of Piana.** Here the scenery is more spectacular than ever—huge red mountains plunge into little bays filled with emerald and black water. The final turn of the road brings you to the Gulf of Porto, a breathtakingly beautiful vista. **Porto** itself, however, has nothing to offer unless you are a camper. There is a lovely site right on the beach; if you prefer, stretch out on the hilltop by the ruins of the Genoese tower and avoid the town's overpriced hotels and restaurants.

The final 75km from Porto to Calvi is one of the most dangerous stretches of road around, but unfortunately there is no alternative route. The trip takes three and a half hours by bus and is almost impossible to hitch, since the road is so lightly traveled.

Calvi

Calvi is a distillation of all that is loveliest in Corsica—a languorous town outstretched beside the blue sea, with snow on the mountains behind its bright port and long, white beaches. But beware; Calvi knows how to use its beauty for a profit, and it is already a chic resort with prices that will make your eyebrows rise and your heart sink.

Within the walls of the fortified part of town are silent, winding streets and the **Oratoire St.-Antoine,** a fifteenth-century building now a museum of ancient and medieval religious art. But perhaps the best reason for strolling around is to watch the waves below.

The **syndicat d'initiative,** place de la Gare (tel. 65-05-87) next to the station, will provide maps, hotel lists, and information on trains and excursions (open Mon.-Sat. 9am-noon and 3-6pm). Across the street is the **post office,** and behind the syndicat is the **public telephone office,** which is open for self-dialed long-distance calls from noon to 10pm. The station (trains are 3 hours, 43F from Corte; 5 hours and 78F from Ajaccio) closes at 7:30pm, so make sure that you don't leave your baggage there. If you fly in, you'll have to take a 30F taxi to cover the 7 km into town; if you wish to sail out, SNCM, quai Adolphe-Landry (tel. 65-10-38), will take you to mainland France, and **Sogedis**, Port de Commerce (tel. 65-10-84), to Italy. Buses scatter around the island, and **Bastias**, opposite the station, will rent you bikes.

Accommodations in Calvi are extremely tight, and equally anti-social. Proprietors will cheerfully inform you that their hotels have been booked for a year, or else will charitably offer you left-over rooms at prices higher than in St. Tropez. **Hôtel Belvédère**, place Christophe-Colombe (tel. 65-01-25), offers a few singles for 95F and doubles for 110-135F. Avoid the draconian old lady there. The **Hôtel du Centre** on rue Alsace-Lorraine (tel. 65-02-01) has fairly dull rooms, but they're cheaper than most others in Calvi. Singles 110F, doubles 130F with showers. Luckily, campsites abound, so ask at the syndicat d'initiative for the nearest ones. Of the many similar restaurants around the port and sinuous streets, **Restaurant du Roi de la Bouillabaisse** lives up to its name—portions are large, and there is a good 35F *menu*. And after a perilous drive, you can always nibble on a Rocky Road from **Baskin-Robbins** on rue Alsace-Lorraine. One of the few towns on Corsica with nightclubs and discos, Calvi caters to its younger tourists.

Ile Rousse is one of Corsica's oldest resorts, serving a primarily middle-aged clientele. This stretch is one of the most heavily touristed on the island, luring crowds with its white-powder sand beaches and calm, shallow water. Boats travel from here to the Côte d'Azur; buy tickets from **SNCM** at ave. Aolizi (tel. 60-09-56). A train runs along the coast between Calvi and Ile Rousse ten times daily in summer, five times daily off season (9.50F). Several campsites lie along the route—just hop off the train when you see the beach or campsite that suits your fancy.

One such site is **Algajola** (7.50F from Calvi on the same train), which demonstrates how a village can grow up inside and around a ruined fortress, using the walls for barriers. If you want to stop here, try the **Hôtel l'Esquinade** (tel. 60-70-19) at the edge of town (doubles 90F, triples 110F with shower). The beach here is as crowded as those on the Riviera, but lacks all the excitement, so there's really no reason to bother with it. If you do stay here, the **syndicat d'initiative** (rue Joseph-Caliji; tel. 60-04-35) has a list of pensions that are cheaper than the town's hotels, which is lucky, since the hotels make even the beaches seem empty by comparison.

Three kilometers out of Calvi (toward the airport) is the vineyard **Clos Landry**. Here you can visit the wine *cave* and sample the latest vintage year. In September, the cave is open daily while the wine is being made, otherwise call ahead (tel. 65-04-25) to find out when you can visit.

Corte

Corte is a sleepy little town with a single main street, huddled defensively against a mountainside. It is the largest Corsican town not on the coast, and for this reason (as well as for its impregnable location) was made the capital of the embattled eighteenth-century Corsican Republic. Now, however, there is little to do or see here; Corte is a pleasant, highly picturesque base for excursions, but nothing more.

There is no syndicat here, but the reception desk at the **Hôtel de la Paix**, place du Duc de Padoue (tel. 46-06-72) can furnish some assistance. The best place to stay is the **Hôtel de la Poste** across the street from the Post Office, on ave. Baron Mariani (tel. 46-01-37), where friendly proprietors will offer you a large room with shower and breakfast for 85F. If it's full, try the **Hôtel du**

Nord, 22, cours Paoli (tel. 46-00-08), where 80-110F will get you a comfortable double with shower. (Try to get a room that doesn't overlook the cours Paoli, however.) Since there are only four hotels in Corte, check in early in the day or not at all. The **Chez Julien,** 24, cours Paoli, serves Corsican specialties, *couscous,* and fresh fish, as well as a 35F *menu;* the food is unremarkable, but the service is gracious and sometimes especially indulgent towards Americans.

While in Corte, the best thing to do is leave: walk up to the **Citadel,** perhaps, for a view across the inland peaks, or take one of the two daily trains (2½ hours to Calvi, 1½ to Bastia; the station lies 1km from town, and it affords a striking view of snow-capped peaks behind the irregularly tilted town), or one of the two daily buses (to Ajaccio for 36F, or Bastia for 30F) run by **Ollandini** from the Brasserie Majestic de l'Université (opposite the Uniroyal station on cours Paoli).

Southwest of Corte, a tiny road stretches 15km through the **Gorges de la Restonica.** The scenery here is reminiscent of a rocky American national park, and it's more sparsely populated than the rest of the island. A crystal clear trout-filled stream, its banks lined with fig trees, poplars, and chestnut trees, cascades down the mountainsides. Camping here is excellent and is permitted just about anywhere. As the road climbs above 5000 feet, it is lined with gnarled pines and offers vistas of snowy peaks. Follow the course of the river on foot up to the **Lac de Milo,** a snow-fed beauty at almost 6000 feet, surrounded by mountains that reach up to 8000 feet. Wear good hiking shoes if you're tempted by the heights.

East of Corte lies the **Castagniccia,** a low, hilly region filled with chestnut trees (chestnut flour was once the staple of the Corsican diet). This virtually untoured region gives you a strong sense of what life in Corsica has been like for the last three hundred years.

The road southeast from Corte (N200) will take you to the **Etang de Diana** on the coast. The water here is calm and abnormally salty like the Dead Sea. Continue south through the level, fertile plain of **Solenzara,** which was once a malaria breeding region and is now filled with green meadows and meandering rivers.

The Alps

Dorothy Parker called them "beautiful, but dumb," and it is true that neither the modern cities nor the timeless snowy peaks of the Alps have much human history to relate. But for those tired of courtly intrigues and wars of religion and those willing to sacrifice depth for beauty, this highest, most startling, and most spectacular of Europe's landscapes can provide relief and exhilaration. From whichever direction you arrive, suddenly the mountains are there, without warning. **Mont Blanc** crowns the Alps, but more gentle terrain will meet you first as you travel through the surrounding Pre-Alps, particularly the scenic verdure of the **Chartreuse Valley** and the more rugged beauty of the **Vercors** range.

Train lines efficiently link the Alps' main cities to France, Italy, and Switzerland, and a through bus system serves even its most remote villages. (This is fortunate, since hitching on back roads can leave you stranded between points.) Once you step down from your train, bus, or car and have laced up your walking shoes, you usually have nowhere to go but up. Flowery meadows, icy lakes, and magnificent panoramic views give ready returns to the most experienced or amateur hiker alike. Serious climbers recommend the **Topo-guides** (hiking maps), but local syndicats will often provide free trail guides, and trails are clearly marked by red arrows painted on rocks and trees. Sophisticated climbing gear is available for rent, but it will be less expensive in the main cities than in the mountain resorts. Before you hike, be sure to consult **Club Alpin Français** or the **Compagnie des Guides** for warnings and suggestions. The area is well-endowed with campgrounds and youth hostels; ski resorts, like Chamonix, often have chalet-dormitories where you can sleep for 20-30F a night, and the Club Alpin maintains mountain refuges (28F a night for non-members). Unofficial camping, though often illegal, is quite common and quite easy, but if it seems possible that you are on private property, try to get permission before setting up camp.

Food here has a Swiss twist. Try the *fondue savoyard* (melted cheese with white wine, served with bread) or *raclette* (fondue served with bread, potatoes, and meat). *Gratin dauphinois* is a delicious local dish made from potatoes baked in cream and spices. The area boasts excellent ham, trout from the cold mountain streams, and *eaux de vie,* liqueur distilled from every kind of fruit. The famous local cheeses include *tomme de Savoie, St. Marcellin* (half goat's milk), and the sweet and creamy *Reblochon;* the best regional wines are the *Roussettes.* For sweets, indulge in the *gâteau de Savoi* (a sponge cake), the *roseaux d'Annecy* (chocolate-covered liquers)*,* the *chartreuse* liqueur, and the potent *framboise,* made from local raspberries. In July and August, you can find tiny wild strawberries growing beside the mountain roads, and in September, hikers search for blueberries along the lower mountain trails.

Grenoble

Most of the ancient town of Grenoble lies buried under the clean lines of contemporary buildings, and somehow even the surrounding and imposing peaks add to the thorough modernity of this mountain metropolis. The people of Grenoble, most of whom have moved here in the past 40 years, take great pride in their city's role as the industrial, cultural, and sports capital of the Alps. Grenoble's university is one of France's largest (25,000 students) and most cosmopolitan (it hosts many of the main American exchange programs)— and its lively presence makes itself felt in the city's numerous cafes, shaggy radicals, fascinating bookshops, and serious politics. The result is an uncommonly young and dynamic city, but Grenoble also has many of the problems which often accompany sprawling factories and suburbs, including a high crime rate. Grenoble is well-situated for trips into the mountains, but don't make this city your only alpine stop.

Practical Information

Grenoble is arranged around a complicated network of bus routes. Services begin at around 6am, but stop completely by 9pm (8:30pm on Sundays). Buses run two to three times hourly (once on Sundays) and a regular ticket costs 3.50F; you can buy a *carnet* (a set of ten tickets) for 20F from the Maison du Tourisme, their kiosk outside the train station (open Mon.-Fri. 7am-7pm, Sat. 9am-noon and 3-7pm), or at Grande Place. Transfers are free if made within the hour.

Maison du Tourisme: 14, rue de la République (tel. 54-34-36). If you don't want to take the 15-minute walk from the station, take bus #12. A bright, efficient office in the center of town. Information on mountain excursions, guides, hotels, the local transportation system, and currency exchange. Open Mon.-Sat. 9am-6:30pm; closed 12:30-1:30pm on Sat.

Club Alpin Français: 32, ave. Félix-Viallet (tel. 87-03-73). This group runs a series of mountain refuges which cost 28F per night for non-members. Pick up a list. Advice on climbing, routes, etc. Open Tues.-Fri. 4-7:45pm, Sat. 9-11:30am.

Climbing Equipment: Rentals available at La Randonnée, 13, rue Montorge (tel. 54-31-81).

Post Office: blvd. Maréchal-Lyautey (tel. 54-81-54). Open Mon.-Fri. 8am-7pm, Sat. 8am-noon. Also a branch office next to the tourist office, and one in the Grande Place (open same hours).

Train Station: place de la Gare (tel. 42-60-27). There are regular trains to Lyon, Paris, Geneva, and Chamonix. Also an information office in the station (open daily 8am-7:30pm).

Bus Station: Gare Routière, place de la Gare (tel. 87-34-26), next to the train station. Extensive daily service includes major ski resorts, the Chartreuse Valley, Vercors, and summer excursions.

Dauphine Information Jeunesse: 1, passage du Palais de Justice, Jardin de Ville (tel. 54-70-38). Has a free ride-board service. Open Mon.-Fri., and Sun., 11am-7pm. July and Aug. 1pm-6pm (same days).

Centre d'Information Féminine (Women's Center): Jardin de Ville (tel. 44-28-59). Open Mon.-Fri. 10am-12:30pm and 1:30-6:30pm.

Student Travel/BIGE: Wasteels, 50, ave. Alsace-Lorraine (tel. 47-34-54).

Bike Rental: Musto, 70, ave. Jean Perrot (tel. 54-24-22).

English-Language Bookstore: Arthaud, 23, Grand rue. The second floor has a fair selection of English paperbacks at reasonable prices (17-35F). A student card will get you a 10% reduction. Or **Just Books,** 2, rue de la Paix, is cozy and perfect for browsing.

Laundromat: Sellsa Service, 65, place St.-Bruno. Open 7am-8pm.

Police: (tel. 47-47-47); **Medical Emergencies:** Centre Hospitalier Régional de Grenoble (tel. 42-81-21). Near the Olympic Village and southwards, Hôpital Sud (tel. 09-80-50). For emergencies, (tel. 42-42-42).

Telephone Code: (76).

Accommodations

Grenoble has a few inexpensive hotels, but the alternatives—hostels, *foyers,* and camping—are clean and well-equipped. Most are quite a distance from the center of town, however, so you'll have to put up with the high bus fares and the early stopping times (9pm).

Auberge de Jeunesse (IYHF), ave. du Grésivaudan, Echirolles (tel. 09-33-52). About 4km out of town, but take bus #8 or tram #1 to La Quinzaine and you're right there. A modern building with a garden, library, music room, cooking facilities, TV, and evening volleyball. 4-6 in each room; 22.50 per night. Breakfast 6F. Closed 10am-5:30pm, but not strictly enforced. Midnight curfew.

Hôtel de la Poste, 25, rue de la Poste (tel. 46-67-25). A bleak and dilapidated zero-star, but centrally located and very inexpensive. Singles 35F, doubles 50F.

Hôtel Université, 7, rue D. Rochereau, off rue Alsace-Lorraine (tel. 46-10-31). Clean, dreary rooms for 45-55F. Breakfast 10F.

Hôtel Bellevue, 1, rue de Belgrade (tel. 46-69-34). A cozy, well-maintained hotel near the *téléphérique,* and overlooking the River Isère and the mysterious old town on the other side. Some rooms are 42F and 58F, most are costlier. Breakfast 10F, showers 6F. Less expensive, but in a less charming location, is the **Randon,** 26, rue Maréchal-Randon (tel. 42-00-42) with singles for 40-45F and breakfast 10F.

Foyers. Grenoble has a large number of *foyers,* primarily for students and young workers. Most cost 25-35F for a functional modern single. Get a complete list from the Maison du Tourisme and call first to make sure there's room for short-term visitors.

Olympic Village, 10, place Pierre-Gaspard (tel. 09-00-20). Often full. Take bus #15 to the Arlequin stop.

Foyer les Ecrins, 36, rue Christophe-Turc (tel. 09-40-74). Looks like a run-down college dorm from the outside, but the rooms are pleasant enough. Restaurant, TV rooms, and cafeteria. 280 singles at 35F per night. Meals 25F, free showers. Walk, or catch bus #15 or 18 from the station to the center of town, then bus #13 from rue de Belgrade, which lets you off right outside. Or take bus #15 from the station to Carrefour Viallex, and walk around the corner.

For university housing, contact **CROUS,** 5 rue d'Arsonval (tel. 87-07-62), near the station, which is best for long-term stays. Or try:

L'ALEJT, Domaine Universitaire, St.-Martin-d'Hères (tel. 54-24-81). On the campus, and limited to ages 17-25. From the station, take bus #22 to Domaine Universitaire. Closed in August.

La Houille Blanche, 57, ave. du Grand Châtelet (tel. 54-56-01). Bus #15 or 18 to place de Verdun, then #10 or 6 to Grand Châtelet. Students only.

Foyer de l'Etudiante, 1, rue du Vieux Temple (tel. 42-00-84). Women only. Accommodations are clean, if unexciting. Very well situated, near Notre Dame and the river. There are also women's *foyers* at (tel. 42-42-49), (tel. 44-11-80), (tel. 44-25-31), (tel. 42-36-20), (tel. 42-40-85), and (tel. 09-29-63), but many only take long-term visitors. Men should try (tel. 44-32-51) for a fairly central, all-male *foyer.*

Camping: Camping Municipal "Bachelard," rue Albert-Reynier, off cours de la Libération, surprisingly close to town (tel. 96-19-87). Take bus #1 or 8 and get off just before the elevated highway.

Food

Some of the best deals in town lie in the gigantic **supermarket** near the Youth Hostel (tram #1 or bus #8) with its extensive *charcuterie* and a wide assortment of food. The cafeteria next door offers meals for about 25F. Intriguing restaurants run by immigrants and also charging only 25F line the narrow streets around **rue Chenoise** and **rue St. Laurent,** across the river. Be sure to try the tarts and chocolates made with the local *noix de Grenoble* (walnuts).

Le Galocher, 48, rue St. Laurent. A delightful vegetarian restaurant that makes a very refreshing change from the usual French fare. Pleasant service and wonderfully filling food. Lunch menu 30F, huge four- to five-course dinners for 35-41F.

Try their onion tarts and passion fruit tea (a big pot for 5F). Open noon-1:30pm and 7-9:30pm, closed Sunday and in August. Down the street is **La Grillerie** at #32, which has *couscous* and a no-frills *menu* for 25F. Or try **La Porte Pot** at #73.

La Baleine Crêperie, 20, rue Chenoise. This colorfully painted cafe is in a lively neighborhood and offers delicious, inexpensive snacks and crêpes. For extravagant ice cream dishes, try the **Belle Hélène**, place de Gardes, next to the Jardin de Ville. The namesake *poire belle hélène* is especially good (17F).

Le Cantilène, 11, rue Beyle-Stendahl. A small restaurant near the post office, with hand-painted windows, dark wood tables; light and airy. The food is typically French, but the servings are small. Menu 30F. Closed Sun.

Le Tonneau de Diogene, 6, place Notre Dame, offers inexpensive snacks and a vivacious student crowd. Quiche, omelettes, salads (9-13F), *gratin dauphinois* (8F), and a delicious chocolate mousse (9F). Closed Sun. If you can't handle the cafe scene here or on place Grenette, try the artsy **Café l'Absinthe** in place Vaucanson. Guinness on tap, 11F. Closed Sun.

For a change from the routine, visit **Le Saigon**, 16, rue Docteur-Mazet, which serves Chinese and Vietnamese food (35F menu, closed Tues.). More exotic and slightly more expensive is **Le Vietnam** at 25, rue Doctuer-Mazet (40F menu, closed Mon.).

Sights

Grenoble boasts a futuristic bubble of a cable-car (**Téléphérique de la Bastille**) that leaves every two minutes from the quai St.-Stéphane-Jay (9am-midnight, Tues. starting at 11am) and whisks you up to the imposing **Bastille** in three minutes flat (9F one way, 15F round trip). From the top, you can enjoy a sweeping view of the city and the surrounding *cirque* (circle) of mountains, which are especially dramatic at sunset. From here, you can climb up the mountain walls (well-marked and of varying difficulty); the less ambitious can climb downward through an intricate series of winding paths, tunnels, caves, and bridges, which lead through the **Parc Guy-Pape** or the **Jardin des Dauphines**. Stop off for a drink on the outdoor terrace before reentering the urban bustle. Pathways are open every day 8:30am-midnight, Tuesday 11am-midnight.

The riverbank, whose eighteenth-century houses are now filled with students and Italian immigrants, is the most attractive and romantically Parisian section of Grenoble. Next to the formal, manicured **Jardin de Ville** is the elaborate Renaissance **Palais de Justice**, which you can visit only on Saturday (ring for the concierge). The **Musée de Peinture et de Sculpture**, place Verdun, displays an excellent, moderately-sized collection of works by Baroque and modern masters, as well as some flashy avant-garde sculpture. Open daily except Tuesday 1-7pm; admission free. The Alps were a stronghold of the Resistance, and history buffs should make a point of visiting the **Musée de la Résistance**, 14, rue J. J. Rousseau, open Mon. and Wed. 3-6pm, Sat. until 7pm. Admission is free. If it's a rainy day, stop in at the **Musée Dauphinois**, rue Maurice-Gignoux, definitely one of the most stylish and well-organized collections of the popular folk art of the region. Museum hours are 10am-noon and 2-6pm every day but Tuesday.

The town is proud of the modern sculptures gracing its streets. The most famous of these is the Calder stabile (stationary, unlike the mobile), just in front of the train station. Much of southern Grenoble is a case study in geometrical architecture and urban planning. The **Olympic Village**, novel in 1968, now seems a bit frayed; further south, the **Grand Place** is a gargantuan shopping-mall whose walls are covered with defiant and bizarre murals.

Near Grenoble

The monks of the **Monastery of the Grande Chartreuse** sought to produce the "Elixir of Long Life" but came up instead with the celebrated Chartreuse liqueurs. The Monastery's architecture is the prototype for the "charterhouse style" which has influenced communal institutions and hermitages around the world. Built in 1084 by St. Bruno, it was destroyed twice—once during the Revolution and again by the Germans in 1940. You cannot visit the Monastery, but there is an excellent view of it from **Correrie**, about 1.2km from the main road. The **Museum** in Correrie presents a faithful depiction of the monk's daily routine (open May-Sept. 9am-noon and 2-6:30pm, shorter hours off-season and on Sun.; admission 7F).

The charming resort town of **St. Pierre de Chartreuse** lies 2km away, scenically situated in the Chartreuse Valley and surrounded by wooded pathways. The 15km route near St. Laurent du Pont passes through some of the most picturesque countryside in the Alps (this path is now considered a national monument).

Grenoble is the gateway to some of the Alps' most renowned ski resorts: **Alpe d'Huez** (*syndicat d'initiative* tel. 80-35-41), **Chamrousse** (*syndicat* tel. 97-02-65), and **Les Deux Alpes** (*syndicat* tel. 80-52-23). A ski-lift ticket in these top resorts will cost about 80F, while medium-height resorts like St. Pierre de Chartreuse or **Lans en Vercors** (*syndicat* tel. 95-42-62) sell lift tickets for about 45F. During the summer, these resorts serve hikers, bikers, and sun-seekers. There is also limited summer skiing in Les Deux Alpes and Alpes d'Huez. There are **Youth Hostels** in Alpe d'Huez (tel. 80-37-37, open Dec.-April, July-Aug.) and Chamrousse (tel. 97-04-23). For information on ski conditions, call (tel. 858-33-33).

To the east lie the Hautes-Alpes, with Briançon at their center. You can get here through the **Val d'Isère** over the Iseran pass, from the North, or by the scenic **route des Grandes Alpes.** The famous **Tour de France** bicycle race passes through the N6 nearby, a spectacular road but steep and grueling if you're thinking of cycling on your own.

Chambéry

Set among hills covered with raspberries and strawberries, Chambéry serves as a quiet and very pleasant retreat from the bustle of the larger Alpine resorts. Apart from the handsome and arcaded pedestrian zone of the old city, Chambéry's main attraction is its **Château,** for centuries the seat of the dukes of Savoy. (Don't bother to visit the attached Musée de l'Histoire Naturelle.) On your way back, walk down the rue de Boigne, which leads from the Chateau to the remarkable **Sites des Eléphants** statue.

Chambéry has three worthwhile museums to offer. The **Musée des Beaux Arts,** place du Palais de Justice, houses one of the finest collections of Italian painting in France, including Uccello's *Portrait de Jeune Homme* and Titian's *Jeux d'Enfants*. Open daily except Tues., 10am-noon and 2-6pm, closes at 4:30pm in off-season. The **Musée Savoisien** has some delightful primitives as well as a complete history of the region. Open daily 10am-noon and 2-6pm. The **Musée des Charmettes,** a 2km walk out of town, is the house where Rousseau lived with Mme. de Warens. The interior has been reconstructed, and now displays items of interest from Rousseau's life. Open daily except

Tues., 10am-noon and 2-6pm; Oct.-March open daily 2-4:30pm, and Wed. and Sun. 11am-noon. Admission 5F, students 2.50F.

Gardens abound in Chambéry—the **Jardins du Verney**, the **Clos Savoiroux,** with its statue of Rousseau, the **Parc des Loisirs de Buisson Rond,** are just a few of the available spots for a secluded picnic. Summer theater continues throughout the season, and there is a small Folklore Festival in mid-July, as well as occasional impromptu jazz festivals.

Practical Information

Office du Tourisme: place Monge (tel. 33-42-47). Open daily 9am-noon and 2-7pm in summer, till 6pm off-season. Ask for a free copy of *15 Jours à Chambéry*, a bimonthly list of activities, restaurants, and services. In the summer the syndicat runs daily tours of the Château, the old town, and the city by night (5-10F, students 4-5F).

Centre d'Information Jeunesse: 9, rue de la République (tel. 70-48-58). Sells Transalpino and other tickets, provides all information on hostels and *foyers,* and sometimes has information on jobs, digs, etc. Open Tues.-Thurs. and Sat. 9am-noon and 2-4:30pm.

Train Station: Gare SNCF, place de la R. Sommeillers (tel. 62-00-73). Trains run frequently to Grenoble, Annecy, and Aix-les-Bains.

Bus Station: Gare Routière, place de la Gare (tel. 69-92-10). Regional buses to Annecy, Chamboix, and Aix-les-Bains, and excursions to the Grande Chartreuse (50F), Chamonix (80F), and the Vercors (80F).

Post Office and Telephones: square Paul-Vidal. Open Mon.-Fri. 8am-7pm, Sat. 8am-noon.

Bike Rental: D. Brouard, 28, ave. de Turin (tel. 70-13-54). 30F per day plus deposit.

Laundromat: place Mouge. Open 7am-10pm daily.

Telephone Code: (79).

Accommodations and Food

Chambéry has few hotels, but many of them are pleasant, inexpensive, and rarely full.

Auberge de Jeunesse "Le Châtelard" (IYHF), Le Châtelard-en-Bauges (tel. 63-84-44). In front of the syndicat d'initiative in Le Vieux Bourg, reachable by bus from Chambéry. Thirty-six beds, 22.50F per night.

Maison des Jeunes et de la Culture, 311 Faubourg-Montmélian (tel. 33-43-46). 28F per night, sheets 10F.

Central Hotel, 9, rue Rochereau (tel. 33-63-35). As well-situated as the name suggests, with large and well-kept rooms. Singles 30-33F (with bidét), doubles 42F. Breakfast 10F, showers 6F.

Hôtel Savoyard, 35, place Monge (tel. 33-36-55). A small, cozy hotel. Singles 50F, doubles 55-60F. Attached to the hotel is an excellent restaurant with polite service and fine food, menu at 35F. Closed Sun. in off-season.

Hôtel de la Banche, place Hotel de Ville (tel. 33-15-62). Small, but in excellent location. Try to get one of the rooms with timbered balconies. Singles 53F, doubles 75-80F. Breakfast 10F.

The **Cafeteria Flunch** on rue des Ducs has *plats du jour* from 13F. Wander down the place St. Leger or the adjacent rue Croix d'Or, and you'll find many pizzerias and creperies. The **Café de l'Horloge** boasts 180 different kinds of beer and plenty of friendly spirit. The **Café Pourquois Pas,** 11, rue de la République, is a non-profit, young people's club with good music, inexpensive drinks, and a friendly atmosphere. Open nightly from 8pm, membership 10F a year or 5F a night.

Near Chambéry: Aix-les-Bains

On sedate **Lac du Bourget,** the largest lake in France, lies Aix-les-Bains, renowned for its thermal baths. The elegant town center stands in sharp contrast to the lively, crowded lakeside. The **Musée Faure** has a beautiful Impressionist room with canvases by Sisley, Pissarro, Renoir, Cezanne, plus two rooms of Rodin sculpture and watercolors. Open daily except Tues., 10am-noon and 2-6pm in summer, till 4pm and closed Wed. in winter. Campgrounds, swimming areas, and boat rentals along the lake are plentiful, though you may prefer to continue on to the Lac d'Annecy. If you decide to stay here, the **syndicat d'initiative** (at the end of the ave. de Gaulle; tel. 35-05-92) will give you information on hotels and rooms. Try the **Hôtel les Deux Savoies,** 12, ave. du Grand-Port (tel. 35-14-86), which has the cheapest rooms. The **Camping Municipal Sierroz** (tel. 61-21-43) is large and conveniently located across from the lake. A large market fills the place Clemenceau every Wed. and Sat., and there is a Prisunic supermarket on rue de Genève.

If you stay overnight, you can make the classic morning excursion to the **Abbaye d'Hautecombe.** This nineteenth-century lakeside abbey admits the public to its Sunday Mass, still sung in Gregorian chant. Throughout the year, boats depart from the Grand-Pont, Aix, at 8:30am, 10am, 2:45pm, and 3:45pm (daily in summer) for the abbey. A round-trip ticket costs 21F. Aix hosts a **chamber music festival,** which usually takes place in July—ask at the syndicat for information. The little town of **Revard,** a 20-minute bus ride from Aix, has extensive cross-country skiing in winter.

Annecy

On the northern tip of the beautiful Lac d'Annecy, the town of Annecy exudes the flavor of a popular vacation spot, so you might as well admit that you're on the beaten track and then enjoy the town's considerable charms. At times, Annecy has the spoiled, jaded prettiness of a French mountain resort, but with its lakeside walks, intricate passageways, and canals bright with flower-boxes, it is undeniably attractive.

Practical Information

Maison du Tourisme, Bonlieu, at place de la Libération (tel. 45 00 33). On the main floor of a huge, modern complex by the lake. Information on mountain climbing, hiking, hotels, campgrounds, and rural lodgings (including farms that rent out tent space). Open 9am-noon and 2-8pm in summer, Sun. and holidays 9am-noon. Tours of Annecy leave from here twice daily, July-Sept.; students 10F. Ask for *Le Mois à Annecy,* a free monthly booklet listing events of all kinds, excursions, nearby walks, and train and bus schedules.

Club Alpin Français: Corner of ave. du Parmelan and rue de Mortillet (tel. 57-02-22). Open Tues.-Sat. 7:45am-12:15pm and 3-7:15pm, and until 8:30pm on Fri. (hours variable).

Post Office: 5, rue des Giliéres (tel 45-10-19). Open Mon.-Fri. 8am-7pm, Sat. 8am-noon. Telephones on the first floor.

Train Station: (tel. 51-34-08). Frequent trains daily to Grenoble (2 hours), Chambéry (45 minutes), and to St. Gervais and Chamonix (1½-2 hours).

Bus Station: Gare Routière (tel. 45-08-12), next to the train station. Voyages Corlard, 3, rue de l'Industrie, across the street, organizes one-day excursions to Geneva, Chamonix, Turin, and elsewhere. Regular buses connect towns around the lake.

Bike Rental: Loca Sports, 37, ave. de Loverchy (tel. 45-44-33), or at the train station.

Police: rue des Marquisats (tel. 45-21-61). **Medical Emergencies:** Hôpital, 1, ave. Trésum (tel. 52-81-21).

Telephone Code: (50).

Accommodations

Annecy is an extremely popular resort, especially in the summer. As soon as visitors begin to arrive, local hotels shoot up their prices, so camping or hosteling may prove to be the best idea.

Auberge de Jeunesse "La Grande Jeanne" (IYHF), route de Semnoz (tel. 45-33-19), about 4km uphill from the station. Follow the signs from the tourist office or try hitching to avoid this 45-minute uphill walk. 22.50F per person; breakfast 7F, and decent meals 23F. Cooking facilities available. The office is open 8-10am and 5-10pm. No curfew.

Maison des Jeunes et de la Culture, 52, rue des Marquisats (tel. 45-08-80). Very comfortable and pleasantly located near the lake. The best deal in town (if there's space); 30F a night, 4 beds to a room. Breakfast 6.50F, meals 24.50F. It's best to reserve in advance.

Maison de la Jeune Fille, ave. du Rhone (tel. 45-34-81), not far from the station. Clean, but somewhat drab accommodations for women; minimum stay usually a week. No curfew but there are other tiresome rules.

Hôtel des Alpes, 12, rue de la Poste (tel. 45-04-56). Centrally located and comfortable. Small and likely to be full, so call ahead. Singles or a couple 51-58F, doubles 57-64F; breakfast 9F.

Hôtel du Château, 16, rampe du Château (tel. 45-27-66), near the Château in the old town. A clean place in a quiet, unusual setting. Two singles at 47F, others at 50F; doubles from 51-95F. Breakfast 11F, showers 7F.

Clématites, 19, rue Vaugelas (tel. 45-17-86). Five minutes from the train station, up several flights of stairs. This hotel looks and smells old, but it's inexpensive, and many rooms have terraces. Rooms 50F and up.

If you don't mind the inconvenience, walk along the **ave. de Cran** on the north side of the station for about ten minutes, and you'll find several quieter and less crowded hotels than those in the center. Try the **Savoyard,** 41, ave. de Cran (tel. 57-08-08), with doubles for 61F; or **La Pargola,** at 20, rue Fabien-Callond (tel. 57-30-11), singles 60F, doubles 75F; or **Le Lauriers** at #10 (tel. 57-25-46), with rooms from 70F.

Camping: There are dozens of campgrounds around the lake. **Le Belvedère,** route de Semnoz (tel. 45-48-30) is run by the city and packed from Easter through mid-Oct. The food store sells staples at reasonable prices.

Food

Markets, *charcuteries,* and the inviting lakeside may convince you to forget about restaurants and think about picnics instead. The **Jacques Pauvert Traiteur,** 4, rue Grenette, sells crab salad, *ratatouille,* and stuffed grape leaves (all expensive, but you can order just 100g of each). On Tuesday, Friday, and Sunday mornings, there are street markets around the place Ste.-Claire, and on Saturday mornings along blvd. Taine; the nearby Prisunic, rue du Lac, has a well-stocked supermarket. But if you can't resist having a leisurely meal on a terrace overlooking a canal or pedestrian walkway, here are a few suggestions:

Au Bord du Thious, place St.-Francois-de-Sales, on the canal near the Palais d'Ile, has delicious crepes, cider, and sundry ice cream delights. Lunch-time crêpe *menu* for 28F. Try *fermière* (made with eggs and country gruyère), a liqueur crêpe, or an exotically-flavored *sorbet.* Opens at noon for lunch and 5pm for dinner; closed Monday.

Restaurant des Vieilles Prisons, 5, rue Perrière, overlooking the Thious. Garnished plates start at 20F, a good *menu* at 35F.

Le Revil, 8, rue Notre Dame, up a narrow stairway to an elegant dining room. The 45F *menu* is excellent (try the *gratin dauphinois*).

Le Crocodine, place Ste.-Claire. A trendy young place with flashy ferns and glass. Plat du jour 28F, *fondue savoyarde* for 2.56F.

Sights

Annecy has plenty of churches, photogenic canals, a quirky old town, a *Palais de l'Ile* jutting out on a tiny island in the midst of the river, and a Château with an indifferent museum inside (open 10am-noon and 2-6pm, closed Tues.; admission 5F, students 2.50F). But the city's claim to fame is surely its lake.

Enjoy **Lac d'Annecy** by jumping in for a swim; you can take a dip almost anywhere along the shoreline and at any hour. Then lounge on the grass nearby in any of the public gardens, or wander away from Annecy along the shore. Various boats cruise the entire lake, charging 38F for the 2-hour trip. Some will take you to the touristy but scenic **Téléphérique de Mont-Veyrier** for a view of the lake and the Alps (38F, boat and téléphérique 60F). If you want to explore on your own, the lakeside is full of boat rentals, but they're not cheap (2- and 5-person pedal-boat 25F and 35F per hour; rowboats 20F per hour; and wind surfboards 31F per hour).

It may be worthwhile to visit one of the smaller cities around the lake. Within a 10km bus ride of Annecy are **Veyrier, Sevrier, St.-Joriez,** and **Menthon St.-Bernard,** each with its own hotels, campgrounds, and excursions. The upper part of the shore is ringed by mountains and dotted with châteaux.

Every year in mid-July, Annecy holds the **Festival de la Vieille Ville,** a dazzling—if crowded—week long celebration featuring concerts of all kinds, plays, films, circuses, and innumerable street performers. Nearly all events are free. On **Bastille Day** (July 14), fireworks are released in lavish quantities high above the lake. The **Fête du Lac,** with illuminated *embarcations* (floating floats) and fireworks, is held on the first Saturday of August. Prices range from 15-90F, depending where you sit on the shoreline. Each year, the boats are

decorated according to a certain theme; past themes have included "Famous
Lovers" and "Beyond the Planet Earth."

In winter, hotel prices drop, and Annecy becomes a quiet base from which
to ski in the Savoie. The nearest ski resort is **La Clusaz**, reached by a 25-minute
bus ride (19F).

Near Annecy

The impressive **Gorges du Fier**, six miles from Annecy (take the train to
Lovagny, direction Aix-les-Bains) is a roaring torrent that cuts through cliffs
and crashes spectacularly over rocks in the river below. Open Easter to mid-
Oct.; one hour walk, 10F. In the same town, you'll find the gorgeous fourth-
century **Château de Montrottier**. The tower offers a superb view of Mont
Blanc, and the castle is filled with Asian costumes, armour, and pottery. The
required but informative tour lasts about an hour and costs 11F, 8F for students. Open Easter to Oct.

To take one of the many lovely walks around Annecy, stop by the tourist
office to pick up a list and detailed information. **La Forêt du Cret du Maure**
(near the Youth Hostel) is peaceful, flowered, and fragrant. From **Talloires**,
eight miles from Annecy on the lake, you can walk to **La Cascade D'Angon** (1
hour) or the **Hermitage de St.-Germain** (about 45 minutes), a small pilgrimage
village with a beautiful Alpine garden.

For lovely green upland country, mountain villages, and Alpine pastures,
head for some of the nearby towns. **La Clusaz** has a small IYHF Hostel, Chalet
"Marcoret," in an idyllic setting on route du Col de Croix-Fry (23F per night;
tel. 02-41-73). **Morzine**, a popular winter and summer resort, also has an IYHF
Hostel (23F per night; tel. 79-14-86). Morzine is famous for its winter skiing,
but in summer it is crowded with hikers and climbers. You can visit **Lac de
Montriond**, a sparkling mountain lake at an altitude of 3,490 feet. Nearby
Avoiraz, accessible only by cable car from Morzine, is a chic resort *sans*
automobiles. **Flaine**, a relatively new resort, is often dubbed the "intellectual's
ski resort." It is mostly avant-garde pretension, with its films and galleries, but
the skiing in winter is very good.

There are many gardens and national parks in the Alps, but the two best are
in the Savoie region. The Botanical and Alpine Garden in the center of **Sa-
moens** has waterfalls, small ponds, and terraces decorating its eight acres of
exotic and Alpine plants. (Open daily, 8am-noon and 1:30-7pm; admission
free.) The **Parc National de la Vanoise** is situated between the Arc and Isère
valleys in one of the wildest parts of the Alps. Fishing for the superb trout is
permitted and the region lends itself to mountaineering and hiking.

There are numerous mountain refuges among the meadows and lakes, as
well as an **IYHF Youth Hostel** in Lanslebourg (tel. (79) 05-90-96) and many
hotels in Lanslevillars. To enter the Park, take a train from Chambéry to
Modane, and you'll land within a two-hour hike of the first refuge, or you can
hitch along route N6 to Lanslebourg.

Chamonix

While the **Mont Blanc massif** may lack the green countryside and postcard
charm of the smaller Alps, it more than compensates with the sheer immensity
of its snow-covered peaks. Even the overgrown and overglorified resort, with
its spiderweb of trains, cogs, and téléphériques to whisk you from mountaintop to mountaintop, can hardly detract from the grandeur of the Alps at their
most spectacular. Crowds flock here in winter to enjoy some of the best ski

conditions in the world, and in summer, they come to walk, hike, or climb. If you can find a place to stay and get past the cablecar lines, there is plenty of mountain here for everyone.

The approach by train prepares you gradually for the splendor of the mountains. At **St. Gervais** you change from an express train to a little red mountain cog. Sit on the right for the best view as the train makes its way through the town of **Servoz,** with its gorges, and heads up to Chamonix. The views of the peaks get more spectacular with every turn as the train draws closer and closer to Mont Blanc, the highest peak in Europe. After Chamonix, there is one more stop—the pretty little hamlet of **Vallorcine**—before the SNCF line (and Eurailpass validity) runs out.

Chamonix includes both the central town and the complex of villages nearby, scattered between forests and mountains. **Les Bossons, Les Praz,** and **Les Pèlerins** are all easily reached by foot or by bus, and other sights are within half an hour by train or bus (ask the tourist office for details). Remember that directions and locations are often expressed in altitude—Chamonix is at 1035 meters, and everything else is up the mountain.

Practical Information

Office du Tourisme: place de l'Eglise (tel. 53-00-24). Modern center offering extensive information on hotels, camping, and climbing, as well as morning and evening weather forecasts. Also a bureau de change in the same complex (open weekdays noon-2pm and 6-8pm, weekends 9am-8pm) and a travel agent (open 9am-noon and 2-6:30pm). Office also sells a hiking map for 10F, and will give information on ski conditions. Ask for their bimonthly guide to events in Chamonix. Open daily in summer 8am-8pm, in winter daily 8:30am-12:30pm and 2-7pm.

Office de Haute Montagne: In the place de l'Eglise, opposite the tourist office (tel. 53-22-08). Provides detailed information on hiking and climbing. Also organizes daily hikes and gives climbing lessons. Downstairs is the **Compagnie des Guides** (tel. 53-00-88) which has ski instructors, a climbing school, guided hiking, insurance, and ski excursions. Also get information here on hostels and huts in the mountains, especially in the Aiguille region; most cost 28F or 14F for members of the Club Alpin Français. Open daily 9am-noon and 3-7pm.

Club Alpin Français: ave. Michel-Croz (tel. 53-16-03). Information on mountain refuges, route conditions, etc., and a message board in the window (buy, sell, rendezvous, rides). Open 9:30am-noon and 3-7:30pm, Wed. 4-7:30pm; closed Sun.

Mountain Rescue: P.G.H.M. Secours en Montagne: place du Mont Blanc (tel. 53-16-89). Accident victims or "their heirs" are responsible for all rescue expenses, although there is a cheap accident insurance available (ask here or at the Club Alpin Français).

Bike Rental: Av Grand Bi, route du Bouchet, 27F per day.

Post Office: place Jaques-Balmat (tel. 53-15-90). Open July-Aug., Mon.-Fri. 8am-7pm, Sat. 8am-noon; closed Sun. Long-distance telephone calls can be made here.

Medical Emergencies: Hôpital de Chamonix, rue Vallot (tel. 53-04-74).

Laundromat: Lav'matic, 40 impasse Prime-vère; or Self-Laverne, 282, rue du Dr.-Paccard.

Telephone Code: (50).

Accommodations

Though a tiny area, Chamonix has plenty of hotels, chalets, and hostels. Most hotels require you to take *pension* (bed and three meals daily), and prices are uniformly steep. Chalets with dormitory accommodations are definitely your best bet. If you prefer a hotel, the cheapest are in neighboring villages, or try the **Bluets,** rue du Lyret (tel. 53-02-57), at 40F for a small room; the **Valaisanne,** ave. Ravenal le Rouge (tel. 53-17-98), at 52F; or **Phalenes,** rte. des Pecles (tel. 53-12-25), at 90F for *demi-pension* (breakfast and dinner included).

Auberge de Jeunesse (IYHF), Les Pèlerins (tel. 53-14-52). Take the bus from place de l'Eglise (direction Les Houches, 4F) or walk twenty minutes from the Aiguille *téléphérique* station on route des Pèlerins. If you come by train, get off at Les Pèlerins, one stop before Chamonix/Mont Blanc, then cross the river and walk uphill, cross the highway and follow the signs. You can leave your baggage off in one of the common rooms—the office opens at 5:30pm. Literally a barracks, but TV, hot showers, and a spectacular view compensate. Guided group tours in summer and winter. Free 25% discount on cable cars, 23F a night with Hostel card, 27F without. Breakfast (optional), 6.50F, dinner 24F. Closed Oct. and Nov.

Le Weekend, 193, Bois du Bouchet (tel. 53-19-16). Turn right at Club Alpin Français and follow Bois du Bouchet. After a ten-minute walk from the station. A small restaurant-chalet with the best prices in town. The owners are friendly, the quarters cramped but coed. 18F for a dormitory bed in a small attic room, and the strangest stairs you've ever seen. Optional breakfast 10.50F, showers 4.50F. Open only in summer. Restaurant offers Swiss fondue at 25F and inexpensive snacks.

Chalet Le Chamoniard (tel. 53-14-09), off the main road to the right, near the Bois du Bouchet. Lots of space, inside and out, only ten minutes from the center of town. Charming owners, pleasant dorm rooms (4-6 in a room); 25F per night, sheets 5F, optional breakfast 10F.

La Montagne (tel. 53-11-60), off the Bois du Bouchet, a twenty-minute walk from the station. A very clean, large chalet in a quiet forest clearing. 20F per person to sleep on modern wooden planks. Free showers; no smoking. Lights out 10:30pm, curfew 11pm.

Refuge des Amis de la Montagne, 54, chemin de la Cascade (tel. 53-17-83). Centrally located, but spartan dorm rooms, 22F per night. Free hot showers. No breakfast. If you want to eat out, try one of the many nearby restaurants with snack menus at 30F.

Chalet Ski Station, 6, route des Moussoux (tel. 53-20-25), to the left of the *téléphérique* of Brévant. Well located. Basic dorm set-up. 25% discount on Brévant *téléphérique.* 25F per night, sheet rental 4F. Showers 5F. Kitchen facilities available.

In neighboring villages, try **Refuge Le Moulin** in Argentière (tel. 54-05-37), 25F for a bed and 10F for breakfast. In Les Houches, **Taconnaz** (tel. 54-43-28) charges 20F for bed, 10F for breakfast, open in summer only; **Le Prarion** (tel. 78-31-56) charges 31F for a bed; and **Notre-Dame des Neiges** (tel. 54-40-58) charges 90F *pension* (three meals included). *La Flegère* in Les Praz (tel. 53-06-13) has 100 dormitory beds at 26F a night, open in summer only.

Camping: A complete list is available at the office du tourisme. The closest to Chamonix is **Les Rosières** in Les Praz (tel. 53-10-42), 3km and a 25-minute walk away; or **Les Drus** in Les Bois (tel. 53-18-05); also 3km away. Or try **Les Deux Glaciers** (tel. 53-15-84), on the road to Annecy, in Les Bossons, or one of the other sites along this road. In Les Pèlerins, there is a site not far from the Youth Hostel. Since all the campgrounds sit 1000 meters above sea level, be prepared for cool Alpine evenings.

Food

Chamonix is definitely not a place to eat cheaply or well. The going price for *menus* is 45F, and service is rarely included in the quoted prices. Avoid the restaurants at the top of the *téléphériques*, which charge enormous prices for forgettable meals. The **Supermarché Payot Pertin,** 117, rue Vallot (open Sunday morning) is a massive supermarket where you can stock up for your Alpine outings, while the **Traiteur,** in quai d'Arve (open 8-11:30am and 3-7:30pm) offers everything from *paëlla* to *salade niçoise.*

Brasserie Nationale, 3, rue Dr. Paccard, next to the post office, is the unofficial home of many serious climbers. During the day, offers good food, with *menus* at 40F and 50F and swiss fondue at 27.50F. Becomes a lively bar at night. For another pleasant—and quieter—bar, go around the corner to the **Alpenstok,** place de Saussure.

Self-Service, rte. du Bouchet, has large cafeteria-style meals for about 30F.

La Taverne de Chamouny, ave. de Michael-Croz. The *menus* are expénsive, the fondue at 29F is delicious and filling. Omelettes 11-14F. A nice terrace to spend long evenings on.

La Potinière, rue du Dr. Paccard, opposite the post office, has the most creative ice cream in town. Try the "Mont Blanc," the "Auguille de Midi," or the "Tunnel." Delightfully caloric. 15-23F a go. *Menu* 39F, fondue 23F. A nice place for a breakfast in the sun and for watching the crowds go by.

Sights

Don't get this close to spectacular Mont Blanc only to stop in Chamonix. The best way to get into the mountains is to hike. Chamonix is an intricate web of climbs and walks, well sign-posted and remarkably varied. Wander along almost any road, and you'll soon come to a path affording views of the mountains, Alpine flowers, or stretches of woods. Hikers can buy the 10F map of the mountains, describing various trails from the Club Alpin or the tourist office; even if you're not in terrific shape, you can try one of the less strenuous "Promenades à Pied" on the back of the map, which take 1-3 hours round trip. Serious climbers can buy the expensive but useful Topoguide or Carte Touristique at local bookstores.

If you want to skip the more prosaic mountain bases, invest in train and téléphérique tickets so that you won't miss the many walks which begin in the mountains. One of the most spectacular of these is the walk to **Lac Blanc,** a gemlike, turquoise mountain lake surrounded by needling, snow-covered peaks. Walk 25 minutes down the Bois du Bouchet, hitch, or take a bus (4F) to Les Praz, and then take the **La Flégère téléphérique** (16F one way, 23F round trip). From here, hike upward for almost two hours past the Alpine violets, daisies, and buttercups to the blue lake, which is often still covered with ice in July. Don't forget to pack a lunch—even though Alpine catering will follow you to these heights, the prices at the lakeside refuge are exorbitant. Other less-demanding hikes last about 1½ hours and take you through the **Petit Balcon Nord** (depart from Tours) or the berry-lined **Petit Balcon Sud** (depart from Argentière). **Les Posettes** is an excellent three-hour hike from Buet. Or, more casually, walk past the téléphérique Brévent to the nearby village of **Moussoux,** or follow the Bois du Bouchet to the sleepy little town of **Les Praz.**

Don't leave Chamonix without trying one of the *téléphériques*—though their prices are as steep as their trajectories, they're quite an experience. The most popular is the **Aiguille du Midi** (*aiguille* means needle), the highest, most spectacular cable-car in the world. Cars leave regularly from the station in South Chamonix, but go as early as you can, as crowds and clouds usually gather by mid-afternoon. The simplest trip takes you to Plan de l'Aiguille (19F one way, 27F round trip), but most people go a stage further to the Aiguille du Midi (45F one way, 70F return) right through the clouds. The crowds in the cars might be suffocating, and the long lines depressing, yet almost no one is disappointed. Spend some time at the top, and enjoy a spectacular view of Mont Blanc. From here, you can continue to a third stage, in Italy (75F one way, 120F return; take your passport), and if you've got money to burn, you can continue on to the Italian Val d'Aosta. No matter how far you go, dress warmly and be prepared for long waits to catch your cable-car back down the mountain. (Always allow 2½-3½ hours for the trip. You can get 25% discounts for this *téléphérique* from the Youth Hostel).

If you want to hang on to your money, a much cheaper though less dazzling alternative is the **Téléphérique Brévent** (24F one way, 36F return; discount coupons available at Youth Hostel), which affords a splendid view of the entire Mont Blanc range across the valley. You can cut the cost by walking down—it's not too difficult but you ought to wear sturdy shoes. From here, you can walk to La Flégère (about three hours), with a panoramic view of the face of the Mont Blanc chain.

One of the strangest popular sights in Chamonix is the **Mer de Glace,** a vast glacier that moves thirty meters every year. Special cogs operate from next to the main train station (8am-6:30pm in summer; 20F one way, 31F return), or take the one-hour hike. There you can also visit La Grotte de Glace, a rather touristy cave full of sculpture carved from ice, with amusing, imaginatively shaped designs (including a grand piano and a sofa set); admission 5F.

Chamonix offers little for the non-hiker in summer. Biking in the relatively flat Chamonix valley is a pleasant way to get around (see Practical Information for bike rentals). The swimming pool and indoor ice-skating rink both cost 14F. Chamonix has sunny but very limited summer skiing. In winter, ski lift tickets cost between 70F and 85F a day. If your feet are sore, visit the **Musée Alpin,** salle de le Résidance, off ave. Michael Croz, open daily 2-7pm, on rainy days also open 10am-noon; admission 8F. Bus excursions leave daily from the front of the tourist office and the train station for Geneva, Val d'Aosta, Venice, and elsewhere.

Massif Central

Covering a huge area in the center of France, the Massif Central has been cut off from both commercial routes and historical events for centuries, and industry and tourism have only recently made inroads into this mountainous region. The mountains were formed by relatively recent volcanoes, and if they lack the spectacular crags of the Alps and Pyrenees, they have a haunting mysteriousness all their own. Over the millenia, forests and vegetation have partially covered the slopes, and once-boiling craters have evolved into clear blue lakes. Isolated villages and farms are scattered over hillsides and river-banks. Numerous feudal châteaux were left virtually untouched and unembellished by the Renaissance, and the solid religious architecture was built to last for centuries.

Auvergne, at the heart of the area, contains some of the most beautiful and unspoiled countryside in France. The mainstay of the economy is still the strongly independent farmer, and the region remains one of the poorest in France. The population has declined steadily since the beginning of the century as inhabitants move to industrialized cities, some to Clermont-Ferrand, but most to Paris. Those who remain are fiercely proud of their region and culture, and they are still willing to welcome an appreciative stranger. In late summer, small villages continue to hold their traditional *fêtes patronales* which climax in the famous *bourrée* dance, accompanied by the *cabrette,* a type of bagpipe. Major towns are few and far between in the southeastern corner. **Le Puy,** with its beautiful cathedral, has long been an important religious site. Hot springs still flow in **Mont Doré, Vichy,** and other towns; each spring reputedly heals a different malady. *Curistes* descend from all over the world to drink, gargle, and bathe their troubles away. The establishment of the **Parc Naturel Régional des Volcans d'Auvergne** in 1967 was a measure designed to preserve the area's unique beauty, and hikers and canoers will find abundant routes from Clermont-Ferrand to Aurillac. For information, write to 28, rue St. Esprit 63000 Clermont-Ferrand (or tel. (73) 92-42-42). On the northern outskirts of the Massif Central are **Bourges** in the farmland of Berry, and **Limoges,** capital of porcelain, set among the terraced pastures and waterways of the Limousin. Typical dishes include *la potée,* a stew cooked for hours and containing just about everything, and *tripoux d'Aurillac,* mutton wrapped in intestines. The Massif boasts a great variety of cheeses; try *Cantal, St. Nectaire* and *Bleu d'Auvergne.*

Train connections in the Massif Central can be relatively difficult. Trains wind slowly through the scenic countryside and stop frequently; it may take several connections and stopovers to get to a remote village. Either stick to the major lines which branch out from Clermont or resign yourself to the beautiful views and leisurely pace of provincial trains. Hitching can also be complicated, since major towns are not always connected by major roads, but with a good map and a little patience, you can usually get short rides from locals. Biking is a good way to get around restricted valleys and the gentler terrain of Limousin and Berry, but the steep winding roads of the central Auvergne don't lend themselves to long trips.

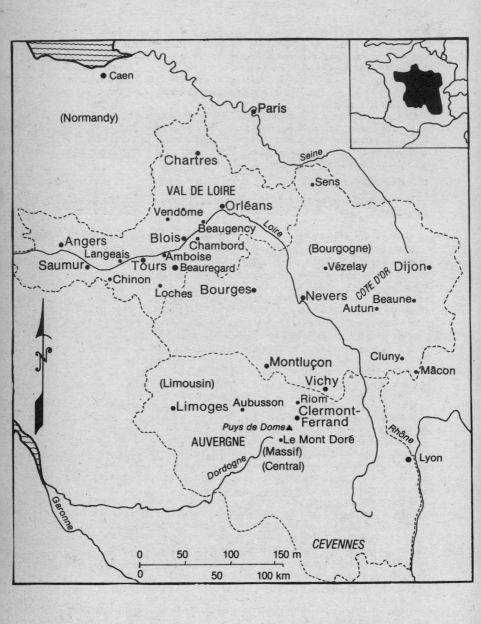

Caen

(Normandy)

Paris

Chartres

Seine

VAL DE LOIRE

Sens

Vendôme

Orléans

Beaugency

Loire

Angers

Blois

Chambord

(Bourgogne)

Langeais

Amboise

Vézelay

Dijon

Saumur

Tours

Beauregard

CÔTE D'OR

Chinon

Loches

Bourges

Nevers

Beaune

Autun

Montluçon

Cluny

Vichy

Mâcon

(Limousin)

Riom

Limoges

Aubusson

Clermont-
Ferrand

Puys de Dome

Rhône

AUVERGNE

Le Mont Doré

(Massif)

Lyon

Dordogne

(Central)

Garonne

CEVENNES

| 0 | 50 | 100 | 150 m |

| 0 | 50 | 100 km |

Le Puy

Le Puy occupies one of the most extraordinary sites in France. In the hollow bowl of gentle mountains, three jutting needles of volcanic rock tower over the red-brick roofs of the city, one balancing the eleventh-century **Chapelle St.- Michel d'Aiguilhe**, another the enormous crimson statue of **Notre Dame de France**. The narrow cobblestone streets are trimmed in dark volcanic rock and mount steeply to the magnificent, romanesque **Cathédrale Notre Dame**, still an important pilgrimage site.

On the southeastern edge of the Massif Central, Le Puy is relatively difficult to reach. Trains run regularly from St. Ettiene and Lyon, but north from Clermont-Ferrand or south from Nimes you must change at the tiny town of St. Georges d'Aubrac to a small train which usually leaves after every major arrival and takes about an hour to get to Le Puy.

Practical Information

The tourist office, most hotels, cinemas and businesses lie along the place de Breuil and blvd. St. Louis. The Cathedral and *vielle ville* are uphill from these.

Office de Tourisme: place du Breuil, (tel. 09-38-41) open 9am-noon and 2-7pm Mon.-Sat., 9am-noon Sun. Very friendly and helpful. Offers a list of hiking trails (10F), two two-hour guided visits to the town daily (10F), and summer excursions to Chaise-Dieu, St. Flour, Lac Bouchet, and area châteaux (35-80F).

Post Office, ave de la Dentelle.

Train Station: place Maréchal Leclerc (tel. 02-50-50), five minutes from the place du Breuil, follow ave. Dupuy left, then turn left at the square. Infrequent buses to local towns leave from the far (southwest) corner of place Michelet.

Laundromat: 12, rue Chéverie; open 9am-10:30pm, closed Sun.

Telephone Code: (71).

Accommodations and Food

Most hotels cluster around place Brueil, and they can fill up quickly during summer days. The **Hôtel Michelet,** place Michelet (tel. 09-02-74), has pleasant rooms from 50-68F, and **Hôtel du Veau d'Or** has twelve adequate doubles for 40F. The **Grand Hôtel Lafayette,** in a quiet courtyard off blvd. St. Louis (tel. 09-32-85), with an air of faded grandeur, offers singles for 43-48F, doubles from 58F. The two-star **Camping Municipal Bouthezard,** chemin Rodéric (tel. 09-55-09), is a thirty-minute walk from the train station. In July and August, it also provides space in large tents for 15F.

Restaurants can be very expensive here, but a market is held every morning (except Sunday) at the place du Marché Couvert, and on Saturday mornings farmers bring cheeses and live chickens and rabbits to place du Plot. **Restaurant Bresson,** rue des Cordelières has a good 29F *menu,* and the **Self du Breuil,** behind the tourist office, is a cafeteria with garnished plates starting at 12F. After dinner, try sipping *verveine* in the local bars, a strong liquer made from a local herb.

Sights

A long procession of streets and steps leads dramatically up to the facade of the curious **Cathédrale Notre Dame.** One of the most exciting Romanesque churches in the Auvergne, it is also one of the most unusual. The Cathedral was built with a strong Byzantine twist, as is demonstrated by its oriental arches and alternating light and dark volcanic stones. The lace-covered statue on the altar replaces the original twelfth-century wooden Black Virgin, which was the goal of many pilgrimages until it perished in flames during the Revolution. The paneled sacristy behind the altar has the air of a souvenir shop, but it actually contains the beautifully penned eighth-century bible of Theodulphe, (the personal bible of Charlemagne's great bishop) and a fourteenth-century copper and gold head of Christ. Notice the large sculptured horses, lions, and deer on the outside church wall between the sacristy and cloister. Separate from the church is the **St. Jean Baptistry** with its intriguing medieval religious artifacts, including a fourteenth-century reliquary which is supposed to contain, among other things, bones of saints, blood-soaked pieces of martyrs' clothes, and a piece of straw from the crib of Jesus. Admission 4F; open daily 9am-noon and 2-6pm. The **cloister** which adjoins the cathedral is solid and bright, with red tiles on byzantine arches. The intricate freize of hilarious faces and mythical animals is barely visible under the edge of the roof. Open 9am-noon and 2-6pm; admission 4F students. From here you can climb up the **rocher Corneille** for a tremendous view of the surrounding area, or climb even farther, up inside the cramped statue of the Virgin and child, for a view from Mary's halo. Open 9am-8pm in summer; admission 4F. On the edge of town, you'll find the eleventh-century oriental **Chapelle St.-Michel d'Aiguilhe,** which crowns a narrow, eight-meter needle of volcanic rock. Open in summer 9am-noon and 2-7pm; admission 3F.

For centuries, Le Puy has been known for its *dentelles,* and in certain shops you can still see aged women painstakingly weaving the delicate lace. The **Musée Crozatier** has a rich collection of hand-woven lace dating from the sixteenth century, in addition to a room of paintings and Gallo-Roman artifacts. The museum is located in the garden Vinay and is open summers every day but Tuesday 10am-noon and 2-6pm; shorter winter hours. Admission 5.50F, 2.50 students. The important **Fête de la Vierge Noire** takes place every August 15, and the whole town celebrates and dances as the statue of Mary is taken from the church altar and paraded through the streets.

A five kilometer walk from Le Puy, the **forteresse de Polignac** once housed the most powerful family in the area, and the ruins and site still make an interesting visit (follow blvd. St. Louis past the bridge to N102). Fifty kilometers north is the ancient mountain town of **La Chaise-Dieu,** best known for its Gothic abbey and festival of French Music, held at the end of August, beginning of Sept. (Get information from the préfecture at Le Puy; (tel. 02-35-10). Buses leave three times daily to La Chaise-Dieu from the place Michelet in Le Puy.

Clermont-Ferrand

Home of the Michelin tire empire, Clermont-Ferrand gives testimony to the Auvergne's strongly felt need to industrialize. If industry and urban sprawl thrill you, come here to visit the factories. Otherwise, stop in the city to spend a little time with the thriving student population and then head out to the lovely and more worthwhile countryside.

Major train lines from Paris and Lyon pass through the Clermont-Ferrand and continue on to Nimes, Beziers, and Toulouse. There are trains up to the mountain resorts of Mont Doré and La Bourbole, and a slow, three-hour train to Aurillac passes along the edge of the enchanting and mysterious **Park des Volcans,** passing ruined châteaux and stopping frequently at anonymous and picturesque villages. Buses in Clermont-Ferrand will take you just about anywhere in the large city for 3.80F (or buy a *carnet* of 10F tickets for 23F at the

TCRC office, 7 place Jaude). City buses #2 and #4 go from the train station to the center of town, place Jaude, and bus #2 continues on to the tourist office, where you can ask for a bus route map.

Practical Information

Office de Tourisme: There are three offices in Clermont-Ferrand. The main office is at 69, blvd. Gergovia (tel. 93-30-20; open summer, Mon.-Sat. 8am-8pm, Sun. 9am-noon and 2-6pm; winter, Mon.-Sat. 8:30am-6:30pm). This branch is well stocked with brochures and information on the area. From the train station, turn left on ave. de l'Union Soviétique and follow it around to ave. des Paulines, where you turn right and continue until this street turns into blvd. Gergovia, or else take bus #2 from the train station. The annexes on place de Jaude and rue de la Rolade at Montferrand are open only from June 15-Sept. 15, daily except Sun. and holidays, 9am-noon and 2-6pm.

Centre d'Information Jeunesse Auvergne, 8, place de Regensburg (tel. 35-10-10) provides information on youth activities and possible lodging in student dorms during the summer. Also information on hiking and canoeing.

Central Post Office: rue M. Busset, near the prefecture, open Mon.-Fri. 8am-7pm, Sat. 8am-noon.

Train Station: ave. de l'Union Soviétique (tel. 92-93-03). A currency exchange is open all week long in summer.

Bus Station: blvd. Gergovia, next to the office de tourisme (tel. 93-13-61 for information).

Chamina, 5, rue Pierre-le-Venerable (tel. 92-82-60). An extremely helpful organization which will give you maps and help plan hiking and climbing trips in the Massif Central; open Mon.-Fri., 10am-5pm.

Bike and Moped Rental: Mazeyrat, blvd. Gergovia (tel. 91-44-74).

Police: (tel. 91-61-95). **Medical Emergency:** (tel. 27-33-33).

Telephone Code: (73).

Accommodations

Clermont has a good number of inexpensive hotels clustered around the train station and a few near the center of town. The **Centre d'Information Jeunesse** (tel. 35-10-10) will help you find summer student housing or a place in one of several foyers. The best of these foyers are the mixed **Foyer International de Jeunes "Home-Done",** 12, place de Regensburg (tel. 93-07-82; take bus #18 from place Jaude) or for women, the **Résidence Philippe-Lebon,** 28, blvd. Côte-Blatin (tel. 91-79-09). To the right of the train station, the **Auberge de Jeunesse (IYHF),** 55, ave. de l'URSS **(tel. 92-26-39) is rude and ratty with a tiny kitchen, but convenient and cheap: 22.50F.** The **Grande Vitesse,** 33, ave. de l'URSS (tel. 92-38-74) has twelve comfortable rooms at 40F, and the nearby **Bellevue,** #1, and **Petite Vitesse** each have rooms from 45F. Around the corner the **Hôtel Provence,** 23, rue Jeanne d'Arc (tel. 91-62-57) has small, adequate rooms for 33-36F a night. In the center of town by place Jaude, the **Hôtel de Louvre,** 11, rue Perret (tel. 37-05-70) has nice, bright singles for 43-45F and doubles for 50-80F. Also in a perfect location is the nearby **Hôtel le Savoy,** rue de la Préfecture (tel. 36-27-22) with doubles for 50-60F.

Food

Clermont has lots of ethnic and student-type restaurants which you can find along rue Lamartine by place Jaude and around the cathedral. You can often find the area's specialty, *la potée* (a heavy soup of meat and vegetables), and meals always end with the local cheeses, *bleu d'Auvergne, St. Nectaire,* and *Cantal.* A large market is held every morning except Sunday and Monday in the place St. Pierre below the cathedral, with good buys on fruit and cheese.

Le Montaigut: 16, rue de la Préfecture has good Spanish-style cooking in its airy, first floor dining room; plat du jour 18F, 35F *menu* and paëlla for 40F.

Le Bougnat, 29, rue des Chaussetiers, has a contrived auvergnate atmosphere, but it's a good place to try traditional local cuisine. 42F *menu,* try the *tripes à l'Auvergnate* (intestines) or *la potée.*

La Bouffe de Tunis, 8, rue St.-Adjustor, by the place Jaude, has mid-eastern dishes from 24F including couscous and shish kebab, and Tunisian pastries for 6F. Classier than most Arab restaurants, but still lively; open till 12:30am.

Au Pied de Cochon, 4, rue Lamartine. This popular place has a 27F *menu* served elbow-to-elbow at communal tables. If you've got what it takes, try the house speciality, *pied de Cochon*—pigs' feet (20F).

Le Brisadois, 39, ave. Charras by the train station has a generous, four-course meal for 30F.

Sights

The center of the city is the lively **place Jaude,** built around a dramatic statue of the Auvergne chieftan Vercingétorix, hero of Gaul's resistance to the occupying Romans. Pass over the cathedral and walk on to the Renaissance **Fountaine d'Amboise,** delicately carved in dark volcanic rock. From here you can follow rue du Port to the beautiful **Basilique de Notre Dame-du-Port,** a heavy, twelfth-century church built in the pure Auvergnat Romanesque style. The badly damaged south tympan is unusually laid out, but walk around back to see the most beautiful part of the exterior, the harmonious geometric layers of arches around the gallery. The columns are also well-preserved, and the well-lit capitals of the choir are the finest part of the interior. The spacious crypt, easily reached by steps on either side of the altar, echoes the outline of the chancel.

For an interesting contrast, visit the Gothic **Cathédrale Notre Dame,** built only a century later than the basilique but after a revolution in architectural technique. Its slender spires (constructed of the sooty, velvety volcanic stone brought from nearby Volvic) form lovely silhouettes against the sky. The strong, light stone allows for unusually thin columns in the light, graceful interior. For a splendid view over the city and west to the Puy-de-Pome, climb the steep, winding steps of the tower over the Northern transcept (2.50F).

Clermont-Ferrand was once two distinct cities: the episcopal city of Clermont, and Montferrand, founded in the twelfth century by the Ducs d'Auvergne to rival the power of their neighbor. The two were merged in the eighteenth century. **Le Vieux Montferrand,** to the northeast of the city center, is presently being restored and has a few buildings of historical interest (take bus #7 from place Jaude). Walk up the rue Jules Guesde, past the **Hotel Fontfreyde** and the **Hotel de Lignat;** continue up the hill to the thirteenth-century **Notre Dame de Prosperité.** This is another edifice built out of volcanic stone; it stands on the site of the long-demolished chateau of the Auvergne dukes. (Walking tours of both Vieux Montferrand and Vieux Clermont begin at the office de tourisme).

Back in the center of town, several museums offer shelter on a rainy day: the **Musée du Ranquet,** 1, petite rue St.-Pierre, off the rue des Gras, has exhibits of

Auvergnat art and history; the **Musée Bargoin**, 45, rue Baillainvilliers, has archeology exhibits and painting galleries; the **Musée Lecoq**, 15, rue Bardou, is a natural history museum. This latter stands next to the **Jardin Publique**, a great place for a picnic with its lakes, lawns, and even a small zoo. All museums are free and open from 10am-noon and 2-5pm; closed on Mondays.

Nightlife

A large student population keeps Clermont dynamic throughout the year. **Thoren's** is a plush bar at 16, place Jaude with drinks and a good music system. **Le Clown**, on ave. Anatole France behind the train station, is a pleasant bar run by a jazz enthusiast which occasionally offers late night improvised jazz. The **Drop Club** on blvd. Trudaine has an open piano bar where you can play or listen; or try **1513** in a beautiful ancient courtyard, at 3, rue des Chaussetiers, a crêperie which hosts young local artists every Friday night. Open 7pm-1am, Sun. 4:30pm-1am. The **Cinema Rio**, 178, rue Sous-les-Vignes, hosts festivals and classics but lies far out past Montferrand (take bus #15).

Near Clermont-Ferrand

Le Parc Naturel Régional des Volcans d'Auvergne was founded in 1967 to save the unspoiled natural scenery of the area from industrial development and to promote the traditions of cottage industry and agriculture. Under this program, historical monuments in the park, including the medieval castles built from the volcanic lava and churches in the local Romanesque style, have been restored; and geological and botanical research projects to study the formation and composition of the volcanoes have been established.

Hiking paths have been marked through the most picturesque parts of the region and are catalogued in a booklet available from tourist offices which gives detailed and descriptive itineraries for the exploration of the park. The protected area includes three main sections: the Monts Dore, the Monts du Cantal, and the Monts Domes, the last most clearly presenting the profiles of extinct volcanoes. Try swimming in a chilly but profoundly clear crater lake—the cold heart of a now extinguished volcano.

The highest point of the volcanic domes is the **Puy-de Dome** (1465 meters) a massive, flat-topped peak to the west of Clermont-Ferrand, nearly always visible from the center of town. A toll road winds its way to the top, and tour buses leave daily from Clermont and area towns (inquire at the tourist office). If you're up for a long walk, take city bus #14 from Clermont to Royat, then follow the Col de Ceyssat for about 6km until you reach the sentier de Muletiers, a Roman footpath, which will lead you to the top in about an hour. The panoramic view from this summit is magnificent, extending over an eighth of France when the weather is clear. Two small towns set among the most beautiful of the Monts Dorés are **Orcival** and **St.-Nectaire**, both with magnificent, Romanesque churches. Each is served by occasional buses from Clermont and excursion buses from nearby Mont Doré.

Le Mont Doré

The rarified climate and warm mineral springs have long established this highest town of the Massif Central as a center for rheumatic and respiratory ailments. But if there are plenty of *curistes* in summer, there are also hikers who come to climb the highest point of the Massif Central, the **Puy de Sancy** (1886 meters) which rises above the village, and in winter Mont Doré is completely transformed into a ski resort. Trains run regularly from Clermont-Ferrand.

The **office de tourisme** is on ave. Général-Leclerc (tel. 81-18-88). It will help you plan hiking routes and change money on weekends, but to get help finding a room you have to call the **Centre de Reservation Hotelière** (tel. 81-13-23). Most hotels usually require *pension* (3 meals) but in summer you can escape to the three two-star campgrounds close-by. The large **municipal camping** site (tel. 65-21-60) lies right across from the train station, and it is usually packed. **La Plage Verte** (tel. 65-04-30), 2km from the station, is a small site on the route de la Tour d'Auvergne, with hot showers and a splendid view. **Camping de la Cascade** is 3km away on the route de Besse (tel. 65-06-23). The **Auberge de Jeunesse (IYHF)** occupies a comfortable chalet about 3km away on the route de Sancy (22.50F per night, tel. 65-03-53). Buses run from Sancy to Mont Doré every hour and hostel-dwellers can use them for free.

Near Mont Doré

Excursions from Mont Doré to various sights of interest, including the Puy de Dome, are offered by the **Cars Bellaigue** company on the place des Moulins (tel. 65-22-55), and prices vary between 37 and 95F for a full-day trip. But if you can walk at all, you will want to do so here, because a minimum of effort will reward you with sights you can't see from a bus. Ascend, either by foot or by funicular, to the **Salon du Capucin,** and from there take the wooded path (thirty minutes) to the strange rock shaped like a monk in prayer. From the summit, you'll have a good view of the Mont Doré and the Limousin country-side beneath. Or take the 25-minute walk to the **Grand Cascade,** on the route de Besse, and stand beneath the falling water under the projecting rocks. For something a bit more strenuous, follow the well-marked path to the summit of the **Puy du Sancy;** the two-hour hike will take you past the source of the Dordogne and offer you lovely views over the Massif Central. Then wander along the *chemin de crêtes* to see the remains of relatively young volcanoes (about 1½ hours to descend). Eight kilometers north of Mont Doré, the filled crater **Lac de Guery** offers sailing, swimming, and fishing.

La Bourboule, another mountain resort, is built on either side of the Dordogne River. Its most attractive feature, apart from its beautiful natural setting, is the extensive **Parc Fenestre,** located south of the Grands Thermes building. There are many good hikes in the surrounding area, and the **syndicat d'initiative** on the quai de l'Hotel de Ville will help you plan your itinerary.

Riom

In the 17th century, Riom and Clermont were great commercial and cultural rivals. Riom soon yielded its status as a great metropolis, but this ancient city, which preserved many of its ornate hotels and half-timbered houses from periods of past glory, may have won in the long run. Where there were once ramparts, a wide circular boulevard now circumscribes most of the *vielle ville*. The **syndicat d'initiative** at 16, rue du Commerce (tel. 38-22-38) will provide you with an annotated walking tour of the town's sixteenth-century *hotels particuliers*. The **Maison des Consuls** on the rue de l'Hôtel de Ville and the beautiful courtyard and sculptured stairway of the **Hôtel Guimoneau,** at 7, rue de l'Horloge, are the most impressive (walk through the arch into the court-yard to see the latter).

Riom's real claim to fame is the celebrated fourteenth-century statue of the Madonna and child, called the **Vierge à l'Oiseau.** The statute once stood over the central entrance of the Gothic **Eglise Notre Dame du Marthuret,** but it was moved inside to the first chapel on the right to keep it from weathering. The expressive statue displays an interesting contrast to the somber Auvergne Romanesque statues of the Virgin.

The **Ste. Chapelle** of the solemn **Palais de Justice** is an exquisite little place with tall stained glass windows that cover more space than the walls in between; visits are given by the concierge every day at 11am, 3pm, 4pm and 5pm.

Also worth a visit is the **Musée Régional Folklorique d'Auvergne,** near the Palais de Justice on the rue Delille. It houses a good collection of local arts and crafts, costumes, and musical instruments peculiar to the Auvergne (open 10am-noon and 2-5:30pm, closed Mon. and Tues.; admission 4F). Accommodations are not a great problem, and several cheap hotels are clustered together near the blvd. Dessaix in the southeast quadrant of the town. Of these, the largest is **Hotel des Sports,** opposite the post office at the southern extremity of the rue du Commerce (tel. 38-00-59), offering clean, basic accommodations. The road is busy and traffic makes the front rooms noisy, so ask for a room at the back if possible. The market in Riom is held Saturday mornings on the rue de Commerce.

There is a fine three-star campground, **Clos de Balenède** (tel. 86-02-47), with full facilities including washing machines, located at the entrance to Chatel Guyon, a pleasant resort town 5km from Riom. An infrequent SNCF bus runs between Chatel-Guyon and the Riom train station (ask for a time table at either station. Railpasses valid). You can rent bikes in Chatel-Guyon, at **Bec,** 65, ave. de Belgique (tel. 86-04-50).

Vichy

The name Vichy usually conjures up two phenomena: Vichy water and Vichy government. Both were designed as "cures," but nowadays the visitor is inundated by the first and led to believe that the second never existed. The years from 1940 to 1944, when Vichy was the seat of the German-backed Petain government, have been virtually eradicated from the town's visible history. The **Hotel du Parc,** which housed the puppet government, has been converted into a block of offices and apartments. The **syndicat d'initiative** is on the ground floor here and there are no identifying marks of any sort to commemorate the building's appearance in the spotlight of history.

Nowadays, the first thing to strike a visitor to Vichy is the advanced age of a large proportion of its inhabitants. These are the *curistes,* the silver-haired of *le tout Paris* who descend on Vichy in great numbers every summer to "take the water," and spend their days strolling around the town's parks and gardens. Everything here is aimed at this rather specialized clientele: the cinemas show Maurice Chevalier movies, the theaters stage sentimental operettas, and the restaurants serve light meals suitable for delicate digestions.

Everything here is slow, quiet, and dignified, like the world of a rich nursing home where everything is done to ensure the comfort of the inmates. The neatly trimmed public gardens are full of notices forbidding radios, picnics, ball-games, or any other disturbances of *l'ordre publique*. Streets in the center of town are lined with jewelers, perfume dealers, and expensive clothing shops, and anything so common as a bakery or a food store is relegated to the nether quarters.

The only time when dignity is threatened is in the morning, when the *curistes* pile into the **Parc des Sources,** the **Grand Etablissement Thermal,** and the **Etablissement Caillou** to get their prescribed daily dose of the water. In the glass and white-cast-iron **Hall des Sources,** you can sit amidst palm trees and observe the spectacle. A drink of water for yourself will cost 5.40F a glass, but one sip will probably be enough to put you off altogether; the water is quite warm, pungent, and reeks of sulphur. North of the Park are baths built by Louis XVI by request of his nieces.

Up the ave. Thermale is the **Maison du Missionaire,** where missionaries stay while taking the cure. It houses a strange collection of mementoes from missions in the former French colonies and other exotic places: paintings of missionaries on camel-back and lion-back, photographs of missionaries subsequently killed by disgruntled natives, model ships, stuffed animals, crafts and artifacts of Asian and African cultures (open 3-6:30pm, closed Monday).

There is, however, a sliver of the young life in Vichy. Across the river the **Maison des Jeunes** shows films and sponsors activities throughout the year, and the nearby **Centre Omnisport** coordinates tennis courts, gymnasiums and kayaking on the river (for information call tel. 32-04-68). There are no windsurf rentals along the river, but you can buy a 150F *forfait* from the **base municipale** by the Quai d'Allier, which allows you a month's use of city wind-surfing equipment, sailboats, tennis courts, swimming pools, and canoe-kayaks. There is an outdoor swimming pool and a beach (no swimming allowed at the beach) across the river by the campground and Youth Hostel.

Practical Information

Office de Tourisme: 19, rue du Parc (tel. 98-71-94). A sleek office with overstuffed couches and reams of information on the city, the waters, and the region, including excursions. Gives change on the weekend and will help you find a room for free. Open Mon.-Sat. 9am-noon and 2-8pm, Sun. and holidays 9am-noon and 2:30-7pm. A summer annex is open at the train station until 10pm.

Post Office: place Charles-de-Gaulle. Open Mon.-Fri. 8am-7pm, Sat. 8am-noon.

Train Station: at the base of the rue de Paris. For information (tel. 31-50-50).

Moped and Bike Rental: Cycles Gayet, 8, rue Source de l'Hôpital (tel. 32-12-37); Cycles Marchand, 13-15, Allée Mesdames (tel. 98-67-46 or 31-87-10). The train station also rents bikes.

Accommodations

Vichy is full of hotels, but most of them cater to the *curistes* and are open only during the months of the rigidly defined season (May through October). In the summer, it is worth booking ahead. The roads off the rue de Paris, which leads from the train station to the Parc des Sources, are lined with hotels. Prices rise the further west you go.

Auberge de Jeunesse (IYHF), 63, rue du Stade, Bellerive (tel. 32-25-14). Across the Allier River by the Pont de Bellerive. Open April-Oct. 19F per night. For this or for the campgrounds take bus #3 from the train station and get off right after the bridge. Cross the street and follow the road along the river for a 15-minute walk. Office open 8am-10pm.

Centre International de Séjour, across the river in the Maison des Jeunes complex (tel. 32-04-68). 23F for a single room plus 9F for sheets, breakfast 8F, meals 23F. Open all year but usually booked up completely in July and August.

Hôtel Sédania, 3, rue Bulot (tel. 98-54-89). Turn left out of the train station, right on rue Neuve, then left. A really cheap place, but very small and often full. Out of the center of town and off the main thoroughfare, it has its own garden. Singles at 22F, seven doubles at 30F. Breakfast 8.50F; one shower down the hall (3F).

Hôtel de la Concorde, 6, rue Président-Wilson (tel. 98-32-63). On the east side of the Parc des Sources. The main attraction of the hotel is its exclusive location on the very chic rue Président-Wilson overlooking the Parc des Sources; this is the only reasonable deal in a row of luxury hotels. Inside the hotel is comfortable, with an elevator and TV room. Singles from 45F, doubles 60-100F. Reservations recommended in season. Breakfast is an extra 8.50F. Open May 1-Sept. 30.

Hôtel Barcelone, 20 rue de Paris (tel. 98-22-57). A classy deal with a few singles for 35F and doubles for 45F. Full *pension* from 85F Carpets, elevators, and very kind proprietors. Often full.

Camping: Les Acacias au Bord du Lac (tel. 32-36-22), a four-star site, open March-Oct., is the closest site; a few hundred meters further is **Beau-Rivage** (tel. 32-26-85) another four-star site, open May-Sept., and so on down the line. Or you can try the less expensive one-star **Camping Municipal** site on the same road (tel. 32-30-11), open all year.

Food

Most restaurants in Vichy are associated with hotels, and their meals cater to the guests who are there to treat digestive complaints. They offer lighter and simpler meals than usual, and consequently the prices are lighter as well; if you've a small appetite and have been yearning to eat in a real live elegant restaurant, this is the place where such extravagance is most affordable. For buying your own food, there's a large covered market every morning but Monday at place du Grand Marché.

Le Bungalow sur le Lac, 1, quai d'Allier, a pleasant terrace between the garden and lake, which serves a good *menu* for 36F (service not included). Open May to Sept.

Le Chantilly, 90, rue de Paris, often recommended by locals. *Menus* for 38F and elaborate desserts with lots of *chantilly* (whipped cream).

Le Rossini, 6, blvd. du Sichon, is an expensive restaurant that makes itself affordable by serving a 38F *menu*. A good place for a splurge.

Le Foch Hôtel, 8, rue M. Foch, has a classy self-service cafeteria with most main courses between 15-23F. In their adjacent dining room they have a good 38F *menu.*

Le Bébé Rose, 8, rue Rauy Breton, off rue Clemenceau, is a popular hangout, with old American film posters and weird paintings on the wall. Serves inexpensive omelettes, salads, and sandwiches and plays great jazz and rock and roll; occasional live music and theater. Open daily noon-1am, Tues. 7pm-1am.

At night, **Le Grillon** on rue de Paris is a late night restaurant popular with young people. Otherwise the **Bar Brasserie Dupont** on rue Georges-Clemenceau is the place to come at night to spot the rarely-seen youth in the city. In winter the city is reclaimed by the many students who attend the local professional and technical colleges. Cinemas change their selections and clubs change their tunes. Try the nightclub **Le Boléro,** passage de la Comédie (45F for entrance and a drink), or the **St. James,** 34, blvd. Gambetta, which plays harder rock.

Near Vichy

Three kilometers east of Vichy is the town of **Cusset,** boasting a grand collection of fifteenth- and sixteenth-century houses on the rue St.-Arloing.

The syndicat d'initiative in either Vichy or Cusset (rue St.-Arloing: tel. 31-39-41) can provide you with a very clear and nicely drawn map of this area, carefully documenting the important houses and courtyards. There is also a **campsite** outside Cusset at the end of the rue de Montbenton.

The area around Vichy has many interesting Romanesque churches. To the north are **Bessay-sur-Allier, Toulon-sur-Allier,** and, of particular note, **Moulins.** Rich in Bourbonais history, Moulins has a **chateau des ducs** and an old quarter with half-timbered houses, in addition to its most famous *Triptique du Maitre de Moulins,* belonging to the treasury of the Gothic **Cathédrale Notre-Dame.** The treasury also has another tryptich attributed to the Flemish painter Joos van Cleves. There is also a museum of history and folklore on the rue des Orfèvres. To the south of Vichy, **Ennezat's** church has a pure Auvergnat Romanesque nave and a Gothic choir. All of these towns and villages are within easy day-trip distance of Vichy, and they are served by the bus line **CFIT,** with departures from the Gare Routière, place Charles de Gaulle, Vichy. All except Ennezat are also train lines.

Bourges

Bourges was the capital of France for fifteen years between 1422 and 1437, when the English Angevins and Burgundians shaved Charles VII's power, until only the center of his kingdom remained loyal to him. These were days of Charles' legendary struggle against England and the martyrdom of Joan of Arc. The impressive hotels and the medieval streets built in this era still exist in the more mundane capital of Berry.

The city's medieval magnificence is eloquently expressed in its **Cathedral,** visible from miles away in the Berry countryside. The gentle rolling farmland around Bourges is dotted with interesting seigneurial châteaux, some still notably inhabited. Less renowned than their royal counterparts on the Loire, the Bourges châteaux are also less crowded. The syndicat d'initiative can give you a list of their chateaux with access roads, opening hours, and descriptions in English. Bourges is on a major train route between Orléans and the Loire Valley to the north and Montluçon and the Massif Central to the south.

Practical Information

Office de Tourisme: 14, place Etienne-Dolet by the Cathedral (tel. 24-75-33), a twenty minute walk from the train station, follow ave Jean-Jarès to rue Mayenne. Offers an accommodations service (3F), and gives change on Sun. and Mon. Open Mon.-Sat. 9am-noon and 2-6:30pm, July through Sept. 15 open daily 9am-8pm. Walking tours of the city leave from here daily, 9F, students 5F.

Post Office: rue Moyenne, open Mon.-Fri. 8am-7pm and Sat. 8am-noon.

Train Station: place Général-Leclerc. For information (tel. 24-16-14). A few châteaux, Culan and Ainey-le-Vieil, can be reached by train.

Bus Station: Gare Routière, rue du Champs de Faire (tel. 24-36-42); connections to the surrounding towns are very infrequent and difficult.

Banks are closed Mondays except for **Crédit Agricole,** 69 rue d'Auron.

Police: 10, rue Michel-de-Bourges (tel. 24-19-26).

Medical Emergency: (tel. 70-70-70).

Car Rental: Europcars, 29, ave. Jean-Juarès (tel. 24-02-94), about 100F a day for a Renault 4.

Hitching: For Lyons, the Alps, and the Midi, take rue Jean-Baffier (bus #3 for the N153). For Tours and Orléans, try the ave. d'Orléans at the corner of the ave. des Près de Roi (N76). For Paris, ave. de Général de Gaulle (N140).

Laundromat: 68, rue d'Auron.

Telephone Code: (48).

Accommodations

Hotels in Bourges are rather scarce and rather expensive, and you might want to let the tourist offices find you a room (3F) rather than looking on your own.

Auberge de Jeunesse (IYHF), 22, rue Henri-Sellier (tel. 24-58-09). Across from a park, in a wooded site overlooking a stream. Modern and better than average Hostel. Kitchen facilities and meals available. 22.50F per night, no breakfast served. Closed Sat. 10am-6pm Sun. and closed daily 10am-4pm. 10pm curfew. Open all year.

Hôtel de la Nation, 24, place de la Nation (tel. 24-24-96). Central and comfortable enough for the price; rooms for 49-59F, breakfast 12F. Closed Sunday.

Hôtel Le Select, 30, rue Moyenne. Near the Cathédral, small doubles 42F, on a loud street that quiets down at night.

L'Idéal Hôtel, 12, place du GI Lederc (tel. 24-08-59) across from the train station; doubles for 53-91F. Might be ideal if it weren't so far from town and closed in August.

Camping: Camping Municipal is at 26, blvd. de l'Industrie, several kms. across town near the Youth Hostel. Follow ave. J.-Laudier across from the station to place Planchat (ignore the name changes), then take rue des Arènes and walk around to the left of the park. The first left is rue Henri-Selliers; turn right at the end of this street and you're finally there. The large campground itself is great for a municipal; the water is hot and the manager is very helpful.

Food

Restaurants can be very expensive, and you might have to spend 40 or 50F to try the local cuisine. A local specialty is *poulet en barbouille*, chicken roasted in the local red wine. The best-known local cheese is *chavignol*, which you can buy at the huge farmer's market held Saturday mornings at the place de la Nation. Ask at any charcuterie for the local *galette de pommes de terre*, a flat potato cake usually served hot.

Le Mangoire, rue des Hemeretts, recommended by locals, serves good food at low prices.

Restocrèpe "Aux Pachades", 66 rue Mirebeau, a lively place with good food and a 20F and 44F *menu*. Closed Sunday and Monday.

Piq' Assiette, rue Jaques Coeur. A 42F *menu* in a chic, chrome setting; occasional live music.

Le Mekhong, 8, place GI Leclerc, across from the train station, has a Chinese lunch *menu* for 35F.

Cafeteria, Maison de la Culture, place Andre-Malraux; 30F *menu*.

Au Senat, 8, rue de la Poissonière, is a real splurge, but serves good regional specialties; 53F *menu*.

Sights

The **Cathédrale St.-Etienne,** one of France's most beautiful monuments, is a spectacular Gothic accomplishment, visible for miles around. The five elaborately-sculpted portals of the thirteenth-century facade are symmetrically arranged and lend a charmingly unique touch to the Gothic structure. The center portal is considered a Gothic masterpiece, representing very realistically the *Last Judgment* in the tympanum. The life of the patron, St. Etienne, is the theme for the neighboring portal. In the center of the facade is a rose-window, ten meters in diameter. The five portals open to a high nave with double flanking side-aisles. The interior of the Cathedral gives a false impression of delicacy, with its exceptionally tall nave supported by narrow piers with narrow pillars surrounding the central column. Although many parts of the Cathedral have been destroyed and restored, the beautiful stained glass windows of 1215-1225 remain remarkably well-preserved. Come on a sunny day and watch the windows glow from gold to blue. Of the fifteen windows, a few of the more interesting ones are the first medallioned window on the north side (on the left as you face the altar) showing the story of Lazarus and the Last Judgment. The stories of the church martyrs are perhaps a little less familiar, but they are told on particularly fine and clear windows. Also, notice the two bright tapestries just to the left of the south door which represent St. Etienne performing miracles.

If you have time, visit the **crypt** (also known as the Underground Church), with twelve large windows providing a source of light. Not much remains in the crypt except for a white marble figure of the Duke of Berry and a few fragments from earlier devastations. The Cathedral is open 8am-noon and 2-7pm daily, and the crypt is closed Tuesday and Wednesday. Behind the Cathedral lie the beautiful gardens of the Hotel de Ville, with their profusion of flowers and cool, reed-grown ponds.

The **Palais Jacques-Coeur,** built by the powerful and talented minister of finance of Charles VII, is one of the most sumptuous urban buildings of the late Middle Ages, every bit as extravagant as the chateaux of the Loire and more accessible. An interesting contrast is achieved between the fortified west face with its towers and plain walls, and the much more delicate decoration of the east face. If you look at the base of the octagonal staircase tower, you can still see the inscription of Jacques Coeur's motto—*"A vaillans coeurs, riens impossible"* ("To the bold in heart, nothing is impossible"). The inside of the Palace is both luxurious and practical, with many interesting fifteenth-century household devices. (From April to October, the Palace is open 9-11:15am and 2-5:15pm; admission is 5F, discount with student card.) If you are interested in the **Cujas Museum,** collection of prehistoric and Gallo-Roman remains housed in an elegant sixteenth-century hotel, and the **Natural History Museum,** which includes a collection of 14,000 stuffed birds, you can buy a pass entitling you to see the Palais and the two museums (10F; student discount with ID). Also worth a visit is the luxurious Renaissance **Hôtel Lallemont** on rue Bourbonnoux, built by a rich fifteenth-century merchant. Two guided tours leave in the morning and three leave after 2pm. Closed Tuesday. Admission 5F.

There is one week at the beginning of April when Bourges picks up at night—the **Festival Printemps de Bourges** brings rock, folk and jazz groups, as well as large crowds of young people, down on the town for eight days of partying (dates are April 2-10 in 1983). The music is good, the atmosphere informal, and some of the concerts are free (most tickets are 30-50F). For information contact **Maison de la Culture,** place Entrée-Malraux, Bourges (tel. 20-13-84).

Châteaux of the Route Jacques-Coeur

The châteaux along the Route Jacques-Coeur hardly compare to the grandest châteaux of the Loire, but they are nonetheless impressive. A visit here is likely to be much more personal, as many of these old residences are still inhabited and all are situated in quiet little towns. None of the châteaux are more than 90 kilometers from Bourges, and the tourist office has helpful leaflets on each of them, complete with explicit maps, photographs, and English descriptions. **Culan** is a chateau 69km south of Bourges, captured by Philip Augustus in 1188 and rebuilt extensively in the thirteenth and fifteenth centuries. This castle, gracefully perched atop a steep crag, is furnished with fifteenth-century chests, Renaissance furniture, and fifteenth- and sixteenth-century tapestries and paintings. A few miles north of Culan is **Ainay-le-Vieil**, also known as the Little Carcassone, because of its octagonally shaped Romanesque towers. Most impressive is the beautifully carved facade of the Italian Renaissance manor. Inside are a fantastically carved fireplace and lovely polychromed ceilings. 35km south of Bourges is the château **Meillant**, set in a lovely park with a pond. This early Renaissance château was built by Charles I d'Amboise, and represents both medieval and flamboyant Gothic elements influenced by the Renaissance. At **Noirlac**, not far from Meillant, is a beautiful abbey and an important example of medieval monastic architecture. Other interesting châteaux in the area include **Menton-Salon, Jussy-Champagne, La Verrerie**, and **Boucard**. All except Noirlac charge 12F admission, 7F for students. Unfortunately, in spite of the close proximity of all these châteaux, the only way to see many of them is by car or patient hitching. Local buses stop at every little village and seldom make return trips the same day, and the Bourges tourist office no longer conducts excursions. Ainay-le-Vieil, however, is a stop on the train between Bourges and Montluçon, and Culan is on the Châteauroux-Montluçon line.

Limoges

Limoges and the province of Limousin mark the outskirts of the Massif Central. Around Limoges, terraced hillsides produce the celebrated cattle and dairy products of the Limousin and the Correze. Although this large, pleasant city is not overly interesting, it is a useful jumping-off point for trips to some of the least crowded and most beautiful countryside in France.

Limoges is famous for its porcelain and enamels. The **Musée National de Ceramique Adrien-Dubouché**, on the avenue St.-Surin, houses the largest collection of porcelain in the world, with exhibits ranging from Delft *faience* to English Wedgewood. It also provides an intriguing view of the changing domestic tastes of the wealthy in the displays of dinner services of Napoleon I, Ulysses S. Grant, Elizabeth II, and the late Shah of Iran. Open daily except Tues. 10am-noon and 1:30-5pm; admission 8F, 4F on Sundays. For a look at the production process, visit a gallery and porcelain workshop; **Porcelaines P. Pastaud**, 36, rue Jules Norriac and **Emaux C. Fauré**, 41, rue des Tanneries (close to the syndicat d'initiative) give tours to visitors. Workshops closed Sat. and Sun. On weekdays you can visit a factory, **Porcelain Ribes**, 40, ave. Hautes Places; open 9am-noon and 2-6pm. It is *not*, however, cheaper to buy porcelain in Limoges than elsewhere, although the selection is enormous. A few shops in town sell seconds *(porcelaines déclassés)* for an affordable price; try the shop at 12, blvd. Victor Hugo.

For enamels, the **Musée Municipal de Limoges** has an excellent exhibit of the town's own products, which date from the twelfth to the twentieth century. The most striking are the modern ones, but the most subtle belong to the fifteenth century. Every July and August there is an interesting international exhibition of enamel art work in the Lycée Guy Lussac beside the tourist office.

From the neatly trimmed **Jardin de l'Evêché,** there is a good view of the Cathédrale St. Etienne and its bell tower. This latter was built onto a Romanesque tower (no longer visible because of the supporting stonework added at a later date), and was originally intended to be separate from the main edifice when it was begun in 1273. At the end of the nineteenth century, however, a narthex was added to the Cathedral and linked up with the campanile. Work on the Cathedral continued from the twelfth to the nineteenth century, the chancel being finished in the early 1300s and the nave still incomplete by the end of the fifteenth century. Despite the interruptions, the Cathedral nonetheless appears as a unified Gothic whole. Of particular note is the facade of the north end of the transcept, a good example of the flamboyant style, with a striking, flame-like motif in the tympanum, and a fine rose window.

Limoges' old quarter, called **La Boucherie,** is a district of narrow streets and medieval houses where the town's butchers have lived and worked since the tenth century. **St. Avrelian,** the chapel they built to the patron saint of butchers, sits in the middle of the quarter.

Accommodations

The **syndicat d'Initiative** on blvd. des Fleurus, by place Wilson (tel. 34-46-87), will help you find a room for the price of the necessary phone calls and can also provide information on the surrounding countryside. Open in summer, Mon.-Sat. 9am-8pm and Sun. 9am-noon. The nearby **Centre d'Information Jeunesse,** 3, rue Jules-Guesde (tel. 77-53-53) has information on student housing and activities. Otherwise, **CROUS** on rue Alexis-Carrel (tel. 01-46-12) can find you a place in dorm rooms during the summer if you have a student ID. The **Auberge de Jeunesse (IYHF) Foyer des Jeunes Travailleuses,** 20, rue Encombe-Vineuse, by place Carnot (tel. 77-63-97), is fifteen minutes from the center of town, but is has nice single rooms for 30-50F, 33F for non-members. From the train station, follow ave. Général Leclerc to place Carnot, then turn left on rue Chenieux and down a block.

While in Limoges, try some of the many regional specialties, including *bréjaude* (a soup with bacon), *boudin* (a sausage often prepared with chestnuts), *gâteau de pomme de terre* and *clafoutis* (a pudding pastry made with unpitted black cherries and sold in patisseries and restaurants). To buy your own food, go to the open market held Tuesday through Saturday morning at the place de la Motte. At the far end of the adjacent covered market, **Les Halles,** you can sit at long tables with workers and students and get a good four-course meal for 28F, 21F if you have a student ID, every day except Sunday (lunch only). **Le Glacier** and **Le Paris** are two good brasseries on the place Denis Dussoubs which serve large mixed salads for 14F and garnished plates for around 18F. A block down at 18 rue Montmailler, **La Sancerre** has a good 32F *menu,* or try **Le Creusois** at #21, with specialties from the nearby department Creuse. The **Crêperie de la Cour,** place du Temple, is in a beautiful, half-timbered courtyard off rue de Temple, with dessert and meal crêpes for 10-13F. They play great recorded jazz and stay open till midnight; closed Monday. **Le Bayou,** 19, rue de Temple, is a night club with character, cheap drinks, good music, and occasional live jazz and rock. You can also eat at the university restaurants on the rue Alexis-Carrel, 16F, or else try bumming a ticket from a local student (5.60F).

The Limousin Countryside

The wooded valeys, ancient chateaux, navigable rivers, and numerous lakes of the Limousin countryside have much to offer those who can get out onto the roads by car or bicycle. For those who can't, train and bus service can be infrequent or non-existent, and hitchhiking on the rural roads can be slow or impossible. If you're not pressed for time, your hitchhiking may turn into a hike, but your efforts will be rewarded by shady roads which curve around green hills and brooks. A tent will give you a measure of security, for campgrounds are never far away, and they are almost always well situated. Ask at the Limoges tourist office for lists of the area campgrounds, châteaux, and canoeable lakes and rivers.

One excellent excursion for hikers is the 13km walk to the impressive, Romanesque abbey church at the village of **Solignac**. This huge, domed church in the Perigord style was built in the twelfth century and has interesting carved stone bas-reliefs outside and wooden misericords inside in the choir. To get there, walk out of Limoges on the ave. Baudin and hitch out the N21 to L'Aiguille, where the D46 crosses the Vienne River. Cross the bridge and then try hitching back along D32 on the other side to Solignac. If you want to keep walking after you've seen Solignac, take the half-hour walk up to the ruins of the twelfth-century **Château de Chalusset,** which sit on a cliff overlooking Solignac and the **Valley of the Briance.**

Other curiosities in the area are reached easily only by car or bike. St. **Léonard-de-Nablait** is an ancient town overlooking the valley of the Vienne river. Its twelfth-century Romanesque church has a particularly beautiful arched and columned bell tower. **Coussac-Bonneval, Montbrun,** and **Brie** are only three of the unexpected feudal castles you can discover in the countryside.

Aubusson, on D941 between Limoges and Clermont-Ferrand (or take the train from Limoges and change at Beussot), advertises itself as *"la Capitale de la Tapisserie"* (tapestries have been woven here since the eighth century). Influenced by Flemish weavers in the fourteenth century and reaching its height in the late sixteenth century, the local art began to lose its originality from the seventeenth century onwards, when it became merely a means of reproducing famous paintings. In our time, there has been a certain revival in Aubusson tapestry under the influence of the celebrated Jean Lurcat. Today, the town's workshops restore tapestries of the past and create new works of art based on the designs of contemporary artists (their Vasarely tapestries are truly striking).

The town is full of private galleries displaying examples of the indigenous craft, and it is possible to look without buying (given the prices, the latter is impossible anyway). The **Maison Corneille,** off the Grand'-rue (also known as the **Maison du Vieux Tapissier**), has a reconstruction of a weaver's studio, some old tapestries, and a collection of documents from the town's past. Open July-Sept., 9am-noon and 2-6pm; admission 5F. The **Hôtel de Ville** has a varied assortment of ancient and modern tapestries as well as a weaving demonstration. Open June 15 through Sept., 9:30-noon and 2-6pm; admission 8F. The town's greatest pride is the recently completed **Centre Jean Lurcat** on the ave. des Lissiers, five minutes from the *vielle ville* and across the river.

The center houses a museum of contemporary tapestries (which display the influence of Lurcat) as well as an annual tapestry exhibition covering some period of the city's history. The streets of the old town are pleasant to walk through, and from the **place de l'Eglise** or the ruined chateau there is a good aerial view of the town's blue slate roofs, turreted old houses, and stone bridge over the River Creuse. On the cliffs surrounding the town there are hiking trails with good panoramas. Twenty kilometers south of Aubusson is the **Lac de Vassivière,** surrounded by campgrounds and with abundant swimming, canoeing, sailing, and windsurfing. Obtain details from the **syndicat d'Initiative** in Aubusson, rue Vielle (in the pedestrian zone; tel. 66-32-12), which also has information on area excursions.

Aurillac

Aurillac is the capital of the Cantal, and it stands beside some of the most beautiful mountains in the Massif Central. A bright and agreeable town in itself, with a well-preserved *vieille ville* and narrow, winding streets that spread from the green valley up the sides of the surrounding hills, Aurillac is the only transportation center in a huge and lovely area, providing a good base (or starting point) for excursions into the extraordinary southwestern Auvergne.

The train station lies at the end of the ave. de la République, five minutes from the **office de tourisme,** which sits at the southeast corner of the park in the center of town. Open in summer 8am-10pm, Sun. 10am-noon and 6-10pm; shorter hours off-season. This very friendly office will give you lots of information on the area, help you find a room, or start you on a recorded (25F) or annotated (free) tour of the city. From the square, follow rue Delzons past the Palais de Justice to walk up to the Château St. Etienne. All that remains of the original thirteenth-century fortress is a dingy tower which offers a free view over the city and valley. In the renovated chateau next door, the **Maison des Volcans** is an extensive and very well-presented exhibit on the area volcanos and the physionomy øf the Auvergne. Open in summer 10am-noon and 2-7pm daily, except Sun. morning.

Accommodations and Food

The **Foyer de Jeunes Travailleurs,** rue de Tivoli (tel. 63-56-94) has beds available in summer for 15F, or try the **Hôtel de Paris,** 3, place Sémard, by the train station (tel. 48-03-39), which has comfortable singles 37-43F, doubles 48-53F, and a good 32F *menu.* **Le Palais,** 2, rue Beauclair, by the Palais du Justice (tel. 48-24-86) has rooms from 45F and a 29F *menu.* The three-star **camping L'Ombrade** is just past the town center on ave. Veyre (tel. 42-28-87).

Aurillac is known for its typical Auvergnate cuisine, and this may be a good place to try the traditional heavy cooking. Try the *tripaux d'Avrillac* (mutton folded in pieces of intestine), *truffado d'Aurillac,* made from potatoes and spices, and the local cheeses, *cabecon* (made from goat milk) and *cantal.* **L'Auberge,** 18, ave. Gambetta, is popular with locals and has a generous four-course *menu* for 30F. Or splurge at **La Reine Margot,** rue Guy de Veyre, which serves local specialties in an elegant setting, 42F (service not included). The **Milk Bar,** ave. Gambetta across from the park, is a good place for snacks or hanging out, with sandwiches 4.50F and omelettes 6F. A large market thrives every Wednesday and Saturday mornings at the place de l'Hôtel de Ville. Once a month (usually the third Wednesday), a huge fair fills up the streets and farmers come in from around the area to sell, shop, and socialize. You can rent a bicycle from **Malgouzou,** 22, rue Guy de Veyre (tel. 48-31-73), or else at the Vic-sur-Cère train station.

The Cantal Countryside

The surrounding volcanic mountains of the Cantal are older and greener than the Monts Dome to the northeast. Slow trains wind past feudal châteaux

and similarly ancient farmhouses (called *burons*), and the whole area creates a
unique sense of mystery and poverty-induced timelessness that you won't find
elsewhere in France. If you're looking for beautiful countryside and quiet old
villages, you can hardly go wrong by getting off at random train or bus stops,
but the tourist office at Aurillac will give you printed descriptions of towns and
lists of campgrounds and hotels, and will even book a room in neighboring
towns for free. Towns that don't lie along the major train lines from Aurillac
are served by very infrequent buses and (in summer) by excursion buses
organized by the tourist office. Hitching on the unfrequented rural roads can
be sporadic. Tourists will pass you by, and locals will carry you only short
distances.

By sticking to the train line between Aurillac and Clermont-Ferrand (about
six trains a day make this three-hour trip), you can cover a lovely stretch of
countryside. Five minutes by train from Aurillac, the feudal **château de Pesteils**
sits over the tiny village of Polminhac. Beside the fourteenth-century towers,
the seventeenth-century wing has finely-painted ceilings and furniture and
Aubusson tapestries from the period. The next train stop is at **Vic-sur-Cère,** a
popular summer resort in a beautiful valley by the river Cère, with an interesting Romanesque church and several paths up into the surrounding mountains.
The valley is a good place for cycling and you can rent a bike from the Vic-sur-
Cère train station. Both towns have large campgrounds, but if you camp,
prepare for chilly evenings. **Le Lioran** is the major ski resort in the Cantal and
in summer, ski trails become hiking trails. There are no campgrounds or cheap
hotels here, but it is only a half-hour train ride to Aurillac.

An hour and a half north by train from Aurillac is **Bort-les-Orgues.** Though
unattractive, this resort town is a good place from which to start hikes along
the beautiful valley of the Dordogne River and the nearby **Lac du Barrage de
Bort.** There are several cheap hotels in Bort, a **youth hostel** 25km away at Ussel
(tel. (55) 96-13-17), and numerous campgrounds surrounding the lake. Get a list
from the **syndicat,** place Marmontel (tel. 96-02-49) and ask for a guide to water
sports and rentals on the lake. Six kilometers from Bort is the **château du Val,**
which once overlooked the sleepy Dordogne, but with the construction of the
dam at Bort was magically transformed into a Gothic castle dramatically surrounded by a lake. The solid, rustic interior makes an interesting visit, but it is
the exterior, dominated by four large towers, and the setting which make it
worth the walk. Follow N122 north for five kilometers out of Bort, then turn
left on the well-marked road down to the lake. The busy roads are a pain to
walk along, so try to hitch a ride.

Salers is a very touristed but nonetheless very beautiful old town with most
of its medieval buildings intact. Set on a plateau overlooking the Marronne
Valley and below the magnificent **Puy Mary** (1787 meters), Salers is only 40km
from Aurillac, but is almost impossible to reach without a car. A bus leaves
Aurillac one morning a week, and in summer you can take excursion buses
from the Aurillac tourist office on Mondays and Fridays (50F).

St. Flour, on the eastern edge of the Cantal, sits high on the flat table of a
mountain and also maintains much of its medieval character. To get there from
Aurillac or Clermont-Ferrand, switch to a train or SNCF bus (railpass good) at
Neussargues, for the half-hour trip to St. Flour. If you catch the bus, be sure to
get off at the large square, Allée Pompidou, or you will end up at the train
station where you will face a difficult climb back up to the *haute ville.* The
ancient houses of the old city are built around the severe Gothic **Cathédral St.-
Pierre,** which towers over the vallée du Lander like a fortress. The interior of
the cathedral is similarly austere, with graceful lines, a cavernous nave, and a
strikingly beautiful fifteenth-century wooden crucifix called "le Bon Dieu

Noir." The **Musée de la Haute Auvergne** in the Hôtel de Ville has several rooms representing Auvergnate folklore, and a few rooms devoted entirely to the traditional Auvergne instrument, the *cabrette* (which is similar to a bagpipe, but more melodic and less annoying). The **Musée Douet** is housed next to the cathedral in the **Ancienne Maison Consulaire,** and it contains several richly-furnished rooms, ancient arms, and various paintings and sculptures. Both museums open every day 9am-noon and 2-7pm in July and Aug; Musée de la Haute Auvergne open throughout the year, except weekends. Admission for each is 2F for students. **La Sanfloraine** is a youth hostel and cultural center, ave. de Besserett in the *haute ville* (tel. 60-13-60), which has dormitory rooms for 20F (office open 5-10pm). **Camping des Orgues** is a three-star site in the *haute ville* (tel. 60-14-41) with free hot showers, 10F for one person and a tent; and **Camping de L'Ander** is in the *basse ville*, route de Vendèze (tel. 60-14-41), 7F plus 3F for a hot shower.

The Loire Valley

In many ways, a trip through the Loire Valley is a journey through French history. Scattered and majestic châteaux (castles), some of the most beautiful in Europe, recall the time when the Loire was the playground of the Valois kings. Verdant fields, quiet villages, and narrow cobblestone streets all contribute to the Loire's reputation as an ancient and peaceful valley. In recent years, however, industry has made its mark on the region. This is especially apparent in the larger cities—Angers, Tours, and Orleans—and in the roadside areas between; two nuclear power plants and several industrial complexes now stand near the banks of the Loire. Those towns which have not been industrialized rely for their livelihood on the tourists who flock to the most famous and accessible of the chateaux.

It is difficult to penetrate the carefully maintained facade which the Loire creates for its visitors, but the true beauty of the region lies in the less-renowned châteaux, the smaller villages, and the rarely-traveled roads.

After days of gaping at serene and stately châteaux, it is often easy to forget the tumultuous history of the valley in which they stand. The Norman invasions of the tenth century brought great abbeys and ducal fiefs to the Loire. Several of these were connected to the English Plantagenet kings; Henry II of England, for example, was a descendent of the ducs d'Anjou. Henry and his sons, most notably Richard the Lion-Hearted, spent many years here fighting the French crown, and the oldest fortresses at Chinon and Beaugency bear testament to the wars of this period. In 1204, the French monarch Philip Augustus took Angers from King John of England, and soon most of the area had passed into French hands. But the English were to return during the Hundred Years' War. Several of the châteaux, such as Angers and Saumur, date from this period of Anglo-French struggle. It was here in 1429 that Joan of Arc made her famous journey, meeting the young Charles VII at Chinon and marching on Orléans to lift the eight-month siege.

After this period of war and strife, the Loire was consolidated under the Renaissance French monarchy through coercions and marriage alliances, a process which culminated in 1492 in the marriage of Charles VIII and Anne of Brittany at Langeais. United France entered a period of unparalleled prosperity under the Valois kings. Fortresses were transformed into country residences of the nobility; they sprouted rounded towers and pointed turrets, and were adorned by works of the great Italian masters and filled with an opulence previously unknown in France. Some of the finest chateaux, notably Blois and Chambord, were built at this time. This was also the period of royal intrigues, court scandals, and infamous mistresses—the construction of two superb châteaux, Azay-le-Rideau and Chenonceau, was directed by a lady's hand.

Within a hundred years, the era of splendor dissolved into one of religious conflict. Amboise and Blois witnessed particularly bloody dissension, which culminated in the French Revolution. During World War II, the strategically located Loire valley was the scene of further conflict, and while the French and the Germans fought for control of the region, the strength of many châteaux was again put to the test.

Châteaux

In the last century, the châteaux have been renovated, some of them in period style, and many have been opened to the public. The reasons to visit the châteaux vary: **Azay-le-Rideau, Chaumont,** and **Cheverny** are notable for their interiors, the castle at Angers for its tapestries, and many others, especially **Chenenceau, Chambord, Chinon,** and **Villandry,** for their setting or exteriors. Most require their visitors to take a guided tour, which costs 8-12F (usually half-price with student ID, sometimes half-price to anyone under 25 years of age). Although the majority of tours are given in French, most châteaux provide a written English translation, which covers the basics.

The gateways up to the valley include Chartres, if you're coming from Paris, and Bourges, if you're entering from Burgundy. Both towns flank the châteaux country with their magnificent Gothic cathedrals. Once in the Loire, there are a variety of options for transportation. Trains provide convenient service to the major cities and towns, from which you can take tour buses, bikes, or mopeds to the outlying villages and châteaux. The regular bus services are usually infrequent and indirect. You will need at least five or six days to see the major chateaux if you travel by train—longer for hitchhikers and cyclists. (Keep in mind that a group of four renting a car together can beat tour bus prices.) Cycling is a great way to see the Loire, as the distances between châteaux are easily manageable, the terrain is mostly flat, and campgrounds are abundant. Travel at a relaxed pace; you'll be seeing plenty if you visit one or two châteaux a day. Hitching is generally hard work, but the many tourists driving from one château to another make it viable and somewhat easier than elsewhere in France. Nonetheless, you can still count on getting only short rides and doing a lot of waiting.

By train, the chateau country spreads out from the three larger cities: from **Angers** in the west, to central **Tours,** to **Orléans** in the east. Many of the major châteaux are accessible from these cities, but smaller, more attractive bases lie between them. **Saumur** and **Chinon** fall between Angers and Tours; **Amboise, Blois,** and **Beaugency** are located between Tours and Orleans. Though some of these towns have their own chateaux, many of the outstanding castles sit handsomely in the countryside or in small villages, and they often lie within a pleasant day's trip from the cities and towns.

As one would expect from so fertile a region, food in the Loire Valley is a real treat. Regional specialties include *rilletes* (a cold meat paste), *fromage de chèvre* (goat cheese), and the creamy, sweet *Port Salut* cheese, and freshwater fish, especially salmon, trout, and pike, are an important part of the cuisine. The Loire is perhaps more famous, however, for its light white wines and champagnes: Touraine, Montlouis, Vouvray, and the drier Chinon and Saumur—nearly every town has a local wine worth sampling. If you're traveling on rural roads, look out for signs marked *"cave/dégustation,"* which point to sources of free samples.

Orléans

Orléans' central location makes it a good base for exploring the upper part of the Loire countryside (known as the Loiret), but this town offers little else to its visitors. Badly damaged by bombing in 1940, Orléans today is a thriving commercial center which, unlike the rest of the Loire, is oblivious to culture-seeking tourists: it ignores the waterfront, which other cities make efforts to cultivate, and its distilleries make vinegar instead of wine.

Joan of Arc, France's other great Virgin, is honored here for her great feat of lifting the eight-month English siege from the town. The great lady of the Loire is depicted in the stained glass of nearly all of Orleans' cathedrals, and each spring, the town marks Joan's victory with a massive celebration (May 7th and 8th). The **Cathédrale de Ste.-Croix,** the city's showpiece (rue Jeanne d'Arc, open daily 8am-noon and 2-7pm), has a Joan of Arc chapel, with monuments and a series of stained glass windows in the nave depicting events from her life. The interior of the Cathedral is otherwise notable only for its cavernous size. Badly damaged by the Huguenots in 1568, it was rebuilt in the Gothic style; its towers, reminiscent of the cathedral in Strasbourg, and the imposing west front date from the eighteenth century.

A day's walk will take you through most of Orlean's sights, and a quick walk around the town will reveal a number of its Renaissance buildings. The **Hôtel Cabu** now houses the **Musée Historique,** containing beautiful Gallo-Roman bronzes from rich archeological finds in the area (open daily except Tues., 10am-noon and 2-5pm). The **Hôtel Groslot,** across the street from the Cathedral, is a beautifully simple building dating from 1500. The **Musée des Beaux Arts** is being transferred to a new building and won't reopen until 1984.

The most blissful spot in Orléans actually lies 6km south of the city. Situated next to the city university and the new high-rise city of **Orléans-la-Source,** the **Parc Floral** exhibits thousands of species of plants in superb arrangements. The park surrounds the source of the Loiret river, and the river itself creates a picturesque setting as it flows through the village of Olivet, a few kilometers to the west. (The Parc Floral is open daily 9am-6pm, 2-5pm December to March; admission 8F, students 4F. Take bus S to get there.) More adventurous hikers may wish to talk to the extensive **Forêt d'Orléans,** which stretches many miles north of the town. The syndicat d'initiative has a pamphlet and map with recommended routes.

Practical Information

The train station is located directly north of place du Martroi in the center of town, at the end of the rue de la République. Local and regional buses leave from outside the train station in the place Albert. Rue Jeanne d'Arc runs east from place Martroi right to the steps of the Cathedral.

Office de Tourisme: Next to the train station, place Albert (tel. 53-05-95). Open Mon.-Sat. 9am-12:15pm and 2-7pm (to 7:30pm in July-Aug.). A map with accommodations listings is located to the left of the syndicat.

Student Travel Information: 1, rue d'Illiers, at place Martroi (tel. 53-29-37). Transalpino tickets, train fares, etc.

Post Office: place du Général-de-Gaulle (tel. 53-49-53). Open Mon.-Fri. 8am-7pm, Sat. and Sun. 8am-noon.

Money Exchange: All banks in Orléans are closed Mondays except Credit Agricole, to the left of the station, rue Emile-Zola (tel. 54-05-50).

Bike Rental: at the train station, 20F per day plus 150F deposit.

Laundromat: Lavomatique, 106-108, rue du Faubourg Bannier, around the corner from Hotel Suzy.

Telephone Code: (38)

Accommodations

Auberge de Jeunesse, 14, rue Faubourg Madeleine (tel. 62-45-75). On west side of town 50 beds, kitchen facilities. Lockout 9:30am-5:30pm; doors close 10:30pm. Take bus B (direction Paul-Bert) from front of train station.

CROUS, 17, ave. Dauphine (tel. 66-28-81). On the south side of the Loire (La Source). Open late June-Sept. for 32F a night. To reach the University, take bus S from the train station.

Hotel Suzy, 80, rue de la Gare (tel. 53-61-60). In the north of town; from the station take ave. de Paris to rue de la Gare. Spotlessly clean. Very pleasant proprietor will help you with alternative accommodations if hotel is full. Rooms 47-58F. Breakfast 8.50F, showers in top-price rooms, otherwise shower 5F.

Hotel Le Touring, 142, blvd. de Chateaudun (tel. 53-10-51). Northwest of town. A little further out and a little quieter. Rooms from 45-75F, but most rooms are around 55F.

Hotel Charles Sanglier, 8, rue Charles-Sanglier (tel. 53-38-50). On a side street off the rue de Bourgogne. Very small, clean hotel. Singles and doubles 45-63F, showers 4F. The office is upstairs.

There are also some reasonably-priced hotels nearby on the rue du Faubourg Bannier just off the place Gambetta.

Camping: The municipal campsite of Orléans is closed. Check with the syndicat or choose from the following nearby sites: **St.-Jean-de-la-Ruelle,** rue de la Roche, a 2-star site (tel. 89-39-39) or **La Chapelle-St.-Mesmin,** rue des Grèves (tel. 43-60-46), municipal campsite of the château. Take bus BM for both sites.

Food

The local cheese is *frimault cendré,* a savory relative of *camembert,* and the local wine is *Gris Meunier.* Try any local shop or the Monoprix supermarket at 4, place République. There are several medium-priced restaurants serving varied cuisine along the rue de Bourgogne, a pleasant pedestrian street.

Le Bourgogne, 118, rue de Bourgogne. A cross between Tudor style and the back of a van. Popular, especially at lunch-time. Good 32F menu with wine; Bass ale on tap.

Vielle Dalle Indigne, 2, rue d'Alibert, by the river. A non-profit "alternative" restaurant and hangout, with occasional live music and good food for about 30F a meal. Membership costs 1F extra per meal. Open noon to 11pm. Closed Mondays and in August.

Hammamet, 158, rue du Bourgogne. *Couscous* in many varieties from 19-45F. Opens at 7pm.

Dany Grill, 22, rue Général-Sarrail. This restaurant is cluttered with bric-à-brac, and the rather eccentric proprietor has lined the rafters with coffee cups. At 50F, a worthwhile splurge. On a small side street in a residential area north of place Gambetta. Take rue Murlins to Chateaudun and bring a map. Open Tues.-Sat. 8pm-midnight.

Near Orléans

With its graceful vaulted bridge and twelfth-century towers, the small town of **Beaugency** remains a gentle evocation of the middle ages. During the Hundred Years' War, Beaugency fell four times to the English and was again badly damaged during the sixteenth century Wars of Religion.

The **château Dunois,** not very interesting in itself, houses an appealing **Museé de l'Orléans,** containing exhibits of local lacework, costumes, furniture, and childrens' games. Open 9am-noon and 2-6pm. Admission 5F.

Walk down the rue de l'Eveché and turn onto rue Ravelin to get a feeling for medieval Beaugency. On the place Dunois, the twelfth-century **Eglise Notre-Dame** is worth admiring for its gently sloping Romanesque perspective. Don't let the Gothic vaults in the nave fool you—they were added later, replacing those destroyed in the 1567 fire lit by the Huguenots.

The **syndicat d'initiative** at 88, place du Martroi (tel. 44-54-42) is open daily (except Wed. and Sun.) 10am-6pm, with information on the surrounding region and the bike rentals to get you there. There's an **Auberge de Jeunesse (IYHF)** 2 km out of town at 152, rte. de Châteaudun, in an old schoolhouse (tel. 44-61-31). For other accommodations, the **Relais des Templier,** 68, rue du Pont (tel. 44-53-78), offers comfortable doubles for 45-80F, and the **Hôtel/Bar de la Gare,** 6, rue de la Gare (tel. 44-54-04), offers cheaper, less elegant rooms for 40F.

Just over the bridge from town there is a campground with swimming, showers, and a restaurant. An open market is held daily on the place du Martroi. Beaugency lies only ten minutes away from Orléans by train and several trains stop in Beaugency each day as they travel between Orléans and Tours. The station lies north of the place du Martroi on the far side of the rue Nationale.

About 40km southeast of Orléans stands **St. Benoit-sur-Loire,** an ancient Benedictine monastery and basilica. This cloistered church provides a lovely diversion for those growing tired of château tours. The open porch tower, with scenes from the Book of Revelations depicted on its columns, is one of the purest examples of Romanesque architecture in France. The tower and trancept were built in the eleventh century and joined by the nave in the thirteenth. The result is a surprisingly subtle and harmonious passage from Roman to early Gothic architecture. The **Hôtel de la Madeleine** has rooms from 48F and a 42F menu. The **Camp du S.I.** (tel. 35-23-93) lies 4km away near the medieval château in Sully. The camp is closed in winter.

Three kilometers from St. Benoit sits the tiny Carolingian church of **Germiqny-des-Prés,** founded in 806 by Théodulfe, Bishop of Orléans and friend to Charlemagne. The church is considered to be the oldest in France. Ring the bell, and the curator will guide you through the largely reconstructed church. Buses to Germiqny and St. Benoit leave from the gare routière in Orléans (get a schedule from the syndicat). To hitch, take the N152 going east from Orleans to the D60.

South from Chartres on the route to the Loire is **Châteaudun,** the castle of the Dunois who was known as the Bastard of Orléans, Joan of Arc's most constant companion in the fighting against the English. Dominating the valley, the fortress walls merge with sheer cliffs, presenting an imposing and impregnable front. The ornamental chapel facade and Renaissance staircase relieve the severity of the original fortress. (Open daily except Tues., 9:30-11:45am and 2-6pm, shorter hours in winter; admission 6F.) The **syndicat d'initiative**, 3, rue Toufaire (tel. 45-22-46), shares a building with an **Ornithological Museum** housing a unique collection of stuffed birds, crammed together in great display cases—big birds, little birds, birds of paradise, ordinary birds, hawks, vultures, and even a few lifeless minerals which didn't need to be stuffed. There's a small, simple **Auberge de Jeunesse (IYHF)**, ave. des Martineaux (open mid-March through Sept. 30, kitchen available). The municipal· campground, **Moulin à Tan** a two-star site, lies 2km from town on rue de Chollet (tel. 45-05-34) (open mid-March to mid-Oct.) To hitch from Orléans, head northwest on D955. .

Vendome, a small Loiret city, can be reached after a short drive through gently rolling farmland. The abbey-church of **La Trinité** has a stunning facade, built in the 16th-century by Jean de Beauce, the architect of the north tower of the cathedral at Chartres. Walk up the hill to the ruined **château** which was dismantled by Henry IV in 1589. The fragments of the defending walls and half-standing towers enclose a lovely garden and terrace with a delightful view of the church and countryside. (Open Tues.-Sun. 9am-noon and 2-6pm; admission 5F, students 3F.) The **Office de Tourisme,** place St.-Martin (tel. 77-05-07) is at the base of the ramp leading to the castle on the banks of the Loire. **Camping Municipal des Grands Prés,** rue Geoffrey-Martel (tel. 77-00-27) is a large, three-star site (with a swimming pool), pleasantly situated on the river just outside of town. Buses to Vendome leave daily from Blois. To hitch, take D957 out of Blois.

Blois

The old town of Blois, with its winding, hilly streets and pedestrian walkways, retains much of its ancient charm. Tremendously soothing, the town even smells sweetly of the chocolate made in the nearby Poulain factory. Because Blois is so comfortable, you may see more tourists here than locals, but the town's château, old quarter, and proximity to the chateau in the Loiret-Cher region may convince you to join the throng of visitors.

The **château de Blois** is a record of royal ambitions, not all of them successful. Walk around the surrounding streets and terraces to appreciate fully the contrasting architectural styles. You can either take the guided tour (in English or French, with frequent departures) or walk through on your own. Start with the François I wing, fronted by a grand, ornamental staircase, with several rooms furnished in a fine Renaissance style. In 1588, the Catholic Henri, Duc de Guise, was assassinated here in an attempt to eliminate opposition to the Protestant King Henri III, who, in turn, felt the knife's blade eight months later. The basement of the wing houses a Musée Archeologique, with funerary urns and other artifacts from the Loire region.   ·

Continue into the **Salle des Etats,** the only part of the château (along with one tower) surviving from the thirteenth century. Three of the tapestries were woven from a cartoon drawn by Rubens. The fifteenth-century Louis XII wing next door houses a small **Musée des Beaux Arts** upstairs and a **Musée d'Art Religieux** below. (The château is open daily 9am-6:30pm, shorter hours off-season; admission 10F, students 6F, museum admissions included.) There is an overpriced, uninformative, and histrionic *son et lumière* show every evening in French and later in English (admission a steep 13F, ask at the syndicat d'initiative for times.)

South of the château, the **Eglise St.-Nicholas** has a fine, broad ambulatory with radiating chapels that is typical of the late Romanesque period. The

Gothic nave was added more than a century later. A pleasant garden leads from the church to the river through what was once the cloister of a Benedictine abbey. Blois' **Cathédrale St.-Louis** is a seventeenth-century reconstruction of a Gothic church. It stands just north of the old quarter with its half-timbered houses and its ancient archways and courtyards.

If you don't feel like château-hopping, you might want to indulge in a tour of the **Poulain chocolate factory** which lies to the west of town on ave. Gambetta. (Tours given Mon.-Thurs. at 8:45am, 10am, 1:30pm, and 2:45pm. The 2F admission also buys a small taste of chocolate.)

Practical Information

Blois is a major stop on the railway line between Tours and Orléans. The station is a five-minute walk from the château down ave. Jean-Laigret.

Office du Tourisme, 3, ave. Jean-Laigret (tel. 74-06-49). In a lovely Gothic pavilion. They will find you a room free of charge, and will also change money. They have information on bus tours of many of the châteaux around Blois. Open daily 9am-noon and 2-6pm, (9am-7pm in summer), Sun. 10am-1pm and 4-7pm.

Post Office: rue Gallois, near place Victor-Hugo in front of the chateau. Open Mon.-Fri. 8am-7pm, Sat. 8am-noon.

Bus Station: Autocars STD, 6, place Victor-Hugo (tel. 78-15-68). Trips to many châteaux.

Bicycle Rental: 3, rue Henri-Drussy (tel. 78-02-64), or the train station.

Police: rue de Jehan-de-Saveuse (tel. 74-00-89). In emergency dial (17). **Hospital:** Mall Pierre Charlot (tel. 78-00-82).

Telephone Code: (54).

Le Foulerie, 50, rue Foulerie. A nice, if expensive bar. Drinks 15-35F. Live music and 15F cover on Thurs., Fri., and Sat.

La Scala, 8, rue des Minimes. Italian specialties and pizza from 16F.

L'Orangerie, 41, rue St. Lubin, behind the château. An attractive, fairly expensive gay bar which is also open to straights. In a neighborhood with many restaurants.

Le Montesa, 3, rue du Puits Châtel, below the cathedral, in a 12th century vaulted basement. Menus from 40-70F.

Le Yannick, 19, rue Ponts Chartrains, across the river. A popular nightclub and restaurant. Opens at 9pm.

One attractive way to spend an evening is to go to the **place de la Résistance** by the river, choose your sidewalk café carefully, and then sit and watch the locals watch the tourists.

Châteaux Near Blois

Some fine châteaux lie in the wooded region south of Blois, but they remain fairly inaccessible by public transportation. Chaumont is about 2km away from Onzain on the opposite side of the river, served by infrequent trains and two buses daily from Blois which stop in Chaumont-sur-Loire. There are guided tours to Chambord and Cheverny from Blois for 46F, leaving Mon., Wed., and Fri. from mid-June to Mid-September (daily during July and August; for information, check the Office de Tourisme). The châteaux are all within bicycling range of Blois, and the bicycle trails are beautiful and largely flat.

Chambord is undoubtedly the largest and most extravagant of the châteaux on the Loire, so if you can see only one château, you might want to make it this one. A remarkable architectural undertaking, its mélange of dormers, turrets, and arcades seems a bit haphazard, yet a definite harmony of design magically appears when you view the château from afar. Chambord was built by François I for his frequent hunting trips to the nearby forests, and it is the work of an unknown Italian architect imported by the King (some think Leonardo da Vinci played a major role in its construction). The river Cosson was diverted to improve the setting, and visitors approach the château on a magnificent tree-lined avenue. Inside the château is an enormous double-helix staircase, designed so that one person can ascend and another descend simultaneously without seeing one another. Recently restored and refurnished with fine tapestries and portraits, the royal apartments only hint at the decadent court life under François and his successors, which culminated in the destruction of most of the original furnishings during the Revolution. Here Molière first staged many of his plays for Louis XIV.

Chambord is open daily 9:30am-noon and 2-6pm (closed Tues. from April-June). Admission 9F, students 5F. Take the guided tour in French or explore the château on your own. The expansive outlying grounds comprise the **Domaine de Chambord,** a beautiful wooded area and wildlife preserve inhabited by deer and wild boar. Information on walks in the area is available from the Office de Tourisme in Blois. A small **Auberge de Jeunesse (IYHF)** sits nearby in Montlivault at the intersection of the N751 and the N84 (open only July-Sept.), and there is a campsite at **Bracieux** on the rte. de Chambord (tel. 46-41-84). To bike or hitch take the D956 south from Blois to the D33, which goes right to the château.

Located only 9km south of Blois, **Beauregard** is a smaller, less-touristed château which conjures up the aura of sixteenth- and seventeenth-century French royalty. Although difficult to reach by public transportation (the only bus runs infrequently and stops several kilometers away), Beauregard makes a good day trip by bike. Hitching is also a good possibility; head south on the D956. Beauregard is much simpler than some of François I's hunting lodges, but it holds its own with its more extravagant neighbors. Most notable is the upstairs gallery, the largest portrait gallery in all of Europe, with over three hundred and fifty portraits of men and women from 1328 to 1643. The tour guide gives an amusing run-down of European history, pointing out bloodlines between the royalty and using the portraits and a flashlight as his props. (Open 9:30am-noon and 2-6:30pm; closes 5pm off-season. Admission 10F, students 5F.)

Cheverny, a stately home built in the seventeenth century, is remarkable for its original furnishings (although its architecture is not very interesting). Owned by the same family for three hundred years, Cheverny preserves a sumptuous and dignified interior seldom found in the Loire châteaux. The obligatory tour (in French) leads somewhat quickly through chambers with painted ceilings, portraits, antique furniture, and tapestries (notably a Gobelin of the *Abduction of Helen*). On the grounds is a compound housing purebred bloodhounds and a sad display of some two thousand antlers in the trophy room. The park around the château, with its formal gardens, is also very attractive, but an electrified fence ensures that the tourists see nothing without paying the 12F admission fee (6F for students). The château is open 9am-noon and 2:15-6:30pm (shorter hours off-season).

The two-star **Cour-Cheverny campsite** is very close to the town center (tel. 79-95-63). There is a **syndicat d'initiative** right in town (open Mon.-Sat. 3-7pm, 10am-noon on weekends as well). To hitch, go south from Blois on the D765. (Bikers will want to take a less direct and trafficked route.)

Perhaps the most underrated of all the chateaus in the area, **Chaumont-sur-Loire** stands as a good reminder that chateaux were first built to defend rather than entertain. A compact feudal fortress, its towers, battlement, and small drawbridge command the valley below. Interesting leaded glass patterns with Escheresque designs line the rooms, and unlike many châteaux in the area, the furniture is authentic to Chaumont. The château is best known for its luxurious stables *(écuries);* you'll be astonished to learn how well the horses were fed. Catherine de Medici lived here with her astrologer until the death of her husband, Henri II. She then forced Henri's mistress, Diane de Poitiers, to vacate the more desirable château of Chenonceau in exchange for Chaumont—Diane de Poitiers didn't do too badly. The château and écuries are open daily except Tues., 9:30-11:45am and 2-6pm, with shorter hours in winter. Chaumont-sur-Loire lies beside the river, southwest from Blois along the D751.

Amboise

Midway between Blois and Tours is the small town of **Amboise,** situated in some of the Loire's finest countryside. With its château perched high over a picturesque old quarter and stone bridge, Amboise is an exquisitely peaceful place to spend a day.

The **château d'Amboise** was begun by Charles VIII in 1492 and was built in a luxurious, highly decorated style influenced by the Italian Renaissance. After Charles' death in 1498, the chateau was completed by Louis XII and François I, who brought in Leonardo da Vinci to help. The remaining castle is actually only one wall of the original rectangular set of fortifications, as three of the walls were demolished at the beginning of the nineteenth century. This portion, the **Logis du Roi,** is lavishly furnished in a late Gothic style with fine tapestries. Together with the **Chapelle St.-Hubert,** where Leonardo da Vinci's bones have been reburied, it comprises the bulk of the guided tour. Best of all, however, is the **Tour des Minimes,** a giant five-story ramp for bringing horses and carriages into the château, replete with central ventilation. (The chateau is open daily 9am-noon and 2-7pm, till 6pm in winter. Admission 12F, students 5F.) There is also an extravagant Renaissance fête, involving a cast of hundreds, on scheduled evenings in July and August (admission 30F, students 25F).

From the château, walk alongside the cliffs on the rue Victor Hugo among centuries-old houses hollowed out of the hill and still inhabited today. Half a kilometer down the road is the **Clos Lucé,** the gracious manor where Leonardo da Vinci, under the patronage of François I, spent the last years of his life. The generally unsatisfying museum displays some fine furnishings and tapestries, but most highly touted are three rooms of models based on the master's drawings. The helicopter, bridges, machine guns, and artillery are fascinating; the models, unfortunately, don't measure up to da Vinci's visionary plans. Aside from a few copies of his more famous paintings, there isn't much in the house which really reflects da Vinci's character. The various gardens behind the house give a fine view of the château and chapel. (Admission a steep 14F, students 8F.)

Amboise is served by frequent trains betwen Tours and Orléans. The station is about one kilometer away from the château on the other side of the river (tel. 57-03-89); bike rentals for 20F per day, or 28F at the Shell gas station across from the syndicat d'initiative.

The **syndicat d'initiative,** on quai Général-de-Gaulle (tel. 57-09-28), is open daily 9am-noon and 2-6pm (9am-7pm in July and August; closed Sun. in winter). The post office is down the street (open Mon.-Fri. 8am-noon and 2-

6:45pm, Sat. 8am-noon.) Banks are closed Saturday afternoon and all day Sunday. There is a market next to the syndicat d'initiative on Fri. and Sat. mornings.

Accommodations and Food

Maison de Jeune, Ile d'Or (tel. 57-06-28). Well-situated on an island in the Loire, near camping and swimming facilities. Not an official hostel and usually booked by groups in July and August. Open 3-10:30pm all year. 22F per night.

Hôtel le Chaptal, rue Chaptal (tel. 57-14-46). In the town center, but on the expensive side. Drab rooms; singles 40-80F, doubles 80-130F. The large family restaurant has menus for 35F.

Hôtel à la Tour, 32, rue Victor-Hugo (tel. 57-25-04), right across from the chateau. Only six rooms above a bar, but a good price at 40-65F. Breakfast 12F.

Hôtel Platanes, rte. de Nazelles (tel. 57-08-60), in a drab neighborhood behind the train station. Rooms 40-50F; menu 35F, with regional specialties.

Camping: The best place to stay in Amboise is the superb site on the Ille d'Or (tel. 57-23-37). Showers and hot water. Fills up early during the summer.

Chez Roger, 7, rue de Général-Foy is open Mon.-Fri. for lunch only, and has an excellent cafeteria-style, fixed menu for 25F. For lighter fare, try **La Crêperie/Pizzeria Anne de Bretagne,** rue de Château, or **l'Epicerie,** 18, rue Victor-Hugo, which is open till 11pm.

Near Amboise

Chenonceau is perhaps the most appealing of the châteaux in the Loire: the architecture is interesting, the splendid setting spans the river Cher and is replete with formal gardens, and the interior contains many of the original furnishings. This is one château where you don't have to take a guided tour; pick up a pamphlet in the language of your choice and wander on your own. The crowds may be somewhat daunting, but the crush is handled well. The gallery even has piped-in Renaissance music. Begun in 1513, the palace was conceived from the outset as a private mansion rather than as a fortified castle. Be sure to see the well-preserved wooden ceiling, dating from 1521, in the small library on the first floor. The gallery over the Cher was built at Catherine's order; it served as a military hospital during the First World War, and as a passageway from occupied France during the Second. In the chapel on the ground floor, look for graffiti carved on the stone walk by the Scots guards protecting their Queen. The château is open daily 9am-7pm; admission 12F, students 6F. There is a *son-et-lumière* performance every night from June-Sept. at 10pm; admission 16F, students 8F.

Two trains run daily to Chenonceaux from Tours, but at inconvenient times. Your best bet may be hitching from Amboise (only 11km south on the D81) or from Tours (on the N76). For accommodations, try **Civray-de-Touraine,** 2km away on the route to Tours (tel. 29-92-18) or **Chez Madeleine Badier,** a little further on the route to Tours (tel. 29-92-48). Both hotels have rooms for 35F and inexpensive restaurants. For eating in Chenonceaux itself, try **Le Gâteau Breton** (tel. 29-90-14), with offerings à la carte and menus from 19F. Their *far breton* is a real treat. The tiny campsite in Chenonceaux is located just a few streets left of the entrance to the château. Camping is also available in nearby **Civray,** about 1km away (tel. 29-92-13).

Loches, 40km south of Tours, is a small and pleasant town on the Indre

River, with the remains of its once-royal château rising above the plain. (You might consider taking one of the frequent buses there for about 20F, as trains are few and far between.) The château was captured by Richard the Lion-Hearted in 1295, used as a prison for the next hundred years, and inhabited by Louis XI's mistress, Agnes Sorel, in the fifteenth century. The dungeons in which famous prisoners were confined and tortured in dangling cages were constructed during Louis XI's reign. The château is open 9am-noon and 2-7pm; admission 8F, students 5F. Also within the walls of the *cité medievale* is the twelfth-century Eglise St.-Ours, with its intriguing Romanesque doorway and the Gothic Angevin vaulting in the nave and porch. Other remains of medieval buildings are the **donjon** (the keep), the **tour ronde**, and the ramparts of the old town. The **Camping Municipal** is a beautiful two-star site with an indoor swimming pool. Open late March through September; 3.40F per person per night and 3.50F per tent. Take the N143 south, then follow rte. de Châteauroux to the stade Général-Leclerc. Ask the *syndicat* about walking tours in the lush, ruin-seeded countryside at the Pavillon du Tourisme, Place de la Marne (tel. (47) 59-07-98).

Tours

In an area where buildings are judged by their extravagance and towns by their preservation of ancient charm, Tours gets left in the dust of its urban sprawl. Despite its pretty squares and a smattering of Renaissance houses, it is neither attractive nor especially endearing.

Yet as a base for exploring the Loire by public transport, Tours may be the best place to stay. It has plentiful cheap accommodations, and many of the nicest chateaux are within 60km in the surrounding Touraine countryside. Just outside the city are some of the finest wine-growing areas in the Loire, such as **Vouvray** and **Montlouis**. Near the modern development of **Joué-les-Tours**, though, lies one of France's largest fields of nuclear missile silos. It's not open to visitors, but you should know that the modern era, too, has left its mark on the lovely Val du Loire.

Practical Information

The train station and regional bus station are in the place Maréchal-Leclerc, as are the office de tourisme and many restaurants and hotels. Several blocks north lies the older section; on its crowded streets you'll find the majority of the sights.

Office de Tourisme: place Maréchal-Leclerc (tel. 05-58-08). Open Mon.-Sat. 9am-12:30pm and 2-9pm, Sun. 10am-12:30pm and 4-9pm; in winter open Mon.-Fri. until 7:30pm. After hours, information on the town and hotels can be obtained for 1F from a vending machine outside the office. The office will book accommodations as well as bus tours of the chateaux. You can rent a tape-recorded walking-tour guide of the city in English for 30F (with 100F deposit, lasts 2½ hours).

Post Office: 1, blvd. Béranger (tel. 64-14-15). Open Mon.-Fri. 8am-7pm, Sat. until noon.

Train Station: 3, rue Edouard-Vaillant (tel. 05-38-01), Passenger information (tel. 61-46-46). Many long-distance trains to and from Tours require you to change at nearby St.-Pierre-des-Corps, so check the schedule carefully.

Bus Station: place Maréchal-Leclerc (tel. 05-03-49). Many excursions to chateaux, often at forbidding prices. Local routes can sometimes be just as good. Open Mon.-Sat. 8:30am-noon and 1:30-6:30pm.

Bike and Moped Rental: Bikes can be rented at the train station (tel. 05-38-01). Or try **M. Barat,** 28, rue Nericault Destouches (tel. 20-89-17), or **Au Col du Cygne,** 46, rue du Docteur-Fournier (tel. 05-06-05) which require a 200F deposit.

Laundromat: 102, rue du Commerce. Open daily 7am-9:30pm.

Medical Emergency: All-night doctors and pharmacy information (tel. 05-66-60). For emergency help call SAMU (tel. 28 15 15) or (tel. 18).

Open Market: blvd. Beranger, every Wed. and Sat. An extensive array of flowers and other beautiful, non-essential goods.

Telephone Code: (47).

Accommodations

Inexpensive rooms are plentiful in Tours, especially around the train station and off the ave. Grammont. For your safety, you are better off the further you get from the station. Many inexpensive hotels line the rue Blaise-Pascal, rue E.-Vaillant, and rue B.-Palissy (try #4a).

Auberge de Jeunesse (IYHF), parc de Grandmont (tel. 28-15-87). Basic, clean hostel 3km from the station, next to the University. Take bus #5 or 10 south to Ronsard (last bus leaves about 8pm). 22.50F per night. Lock-out 9am-5pm.

CROUS, parc de Grandmont (tel. 05-17-55). Take bus #1 to Parc Sud (last bus leaves at 8:30pm). Rooms available July-Sept. for 30F a night at the University. You must appear in person at Batiment A, 9am-1pm and 2-5pm. With the steep price, you're better off in a hotel, unless you want to sample the student life. You must obtain tickets in advance in order to eat in cafeteria (10.50F for foreign students, 5F for French students).

Le Foyer, 16, rue Bernard-Palissy, across the blvd. Heurteloup from the tourist office and straight down rue Bernard-Palissy. For men 16-25 years only; 30F per night in 3-bed rooms. Get there before 8pm and have proof of your age. Cafeteria serves main dishes 16F, *menu* 20F. Breakfast 5F.

Hôtel Bretagne, 8, rue Blaise-Pascal (tel. 05-41-43). The best of several cheap hotels lining the street. Singles and doubles at 60F include required breakfast; doubles and triples at 70F do not. Showers 8F, breakfast 10F. Unusually cheery management.

Hôtel le Comté, 51, rue Auguste-Comté (tel. 05-53-16). To the right and behind the station. One of the nicer, cleaner hotels in the area, but fills up quickly. Double-bedded rooms 51F, two double beds without shower 102F. Showers 8.50F, breakfast 10.50F.

Mon Hôtel, 40, rue de la Préfecture (tel. 05-67-53). The cleanliness and added touches of this small hotel make it a particularly good deal. Singles and doubles 50 and 55F, triples 75 and 85F. Showers 9F, breakfast 12F.

Olympic Hotel, 74, rue Bernard-Palissy (05-10-17). Plain, clean rooms; the beds sag a bit. Friendly management. Singles 48F; double beds 58F, 85F with shower. Breakfast 11.50.

Hôtel Vendome, 24, rue Roger-Salengro (tel. 64-33-54). One block off ave. Grammont. Well run and pleasant. One single for 40F, several doubles for 58F. Breakfast 11F.

Camping. There are dozens of campgrounds within a 20-mile radius, most near chateaux and along the Loire. Pick up a list from the bureau de tourisme. **Camping Tours-Ste.-Radegonde,** on the N152, is the closest to the city.

Food

The Touraine region is famous for its food and wine, but there are no bargains here. Try some of the local fish, especially salmon or trout, with one of the light white wines from Chinon, Montlouis, Vouvray, or Touraine. The charcuteries offer fine *rillettes* (a light version of pâté) and *andouillettes* (a chewy sausage made from intestines that you might find hard to stomach).

La Renaissance, 62, rue Colbert, lives up to its name with rejuvenating *menus* at 31, 45, and 70F. Service included, but beverages are extra. Nicely decorated, subdued atmosphere: a good place to splurge. Closed Mon.

L'Escabeau Crêperie, 23, rue de la Monnaie. Off the place Plumereau in the old quarter. Pleasant atmosphere; popular for late evening desserts. An à la carte meal including whole wheat *gallettes* runs about 32F, including service and drink.

Foyer des Jeunes Travailleurs, 16, rue B.-Palissy. Rooms are only for male working students, but anyone with a student ID can eat in the mostly male cafeteria. 16F buys you a main dish from noon-1:15pm; 20F gets the full meal from 7:20-8pm.

Self, 12, rue Edouard Vaillant, next to the station, offers unexciting meals from 9.50-22F and a main dish with drink for 14.10F. Open 11:30am-2pm and 6:30-10pm; closed Mon.

20 Tartes, on the rue Nationale right next to the museums, has a fine variety of quiche and pizza at 5F a slice.

Sights

Though the old quarter was seriously damaged during World War II, several buildings in the rue Briconnet and the rue du Change area have been preserved. Renaissance houses, some open to the public, dot the area. (Pick up an annotated plan from the office de tourisme.) The **Hotel Goüin** at 25, rue du Commerce, is one of the finest examples of a Renaissance facade, but don't bother paying to see the archeological collection inside. Flanking the rue des Halles, the **Tour de l'Horloge** and the **Tour de Charlemagne** are remaining fragments of the eleventh-century Basilique St.-Martin, a huge Romanesque masterpiece which stood on the pilgrimage route to Spain. (Enter at 3, rue Descartes.) The **Nouvelle Basilique St.-Martin,** a turn-of-the-century church of Byzantine inspiration, overlaps the foundation of the old structure, allowing the tomb of St.-Martin to remain unmarred. Some of the roads north of the church are lined by fifteenth-century half-timbered houses and graced with decorative details. Much of this area is now being restored, so be prepared to put up with a little dust and dirt. Also, the old quarter, especially the west port, is not safe at night.

To the east stands the **Cathédrale St.-Gatien,** begun in the thirteenth century and strongly influenced by the cathedral at Chartres. This is most evident in the beautiful choir and apse with their light, soaring arches and tall windows done in the rich "Chartres blue." The cloister, which still bears traces of Romanesque and Roman structures once on the site, contains marvelous sculptural detail and a replica of the grand stairway at Blois, but it is best for the superb view it gives of the thin flying buttresses supporting the nave. Closes at 8pm in summer, 5:30pm in winter; also closed noon-2pm. Admission 5F, 2.50F for students.

A short walk down the rue Jules-Simon, the **Musée des Beaux Arts** is housed in the former episcopal palace at 18, place François-Sicard. The collection includes works from the Italian Renaissance, several by Delacroix and a Rembrandt. The museum's lovely courtyard and gardens make a nice retreat from the rest of town. Museum open 9am-noon and 2-6pm; admission 5F, students 2.50F. The gardens are open Fri.-Sun. on summer mornings. More interesting is the unique **Musée de Compagnonnage**, 8, rue Nationale, Cloître St.-Julien, which displays an extraordinary array of pre-industrial artisan craftworks, including a chocolate violin. These trade emblems illustrate the posted quotation of Paul Valery: "The hand is the equal and rival of thought." (Opening hours and admission same as Beaux Arts, but closed Tuesday.) Next door, the **Musée des Vins de Touraine** occupies an ancient wine cellar, but you won't get any free samples for your 3F entry fee (1.50F for students).

Châteaux Near Tours

Something interesting lies in every direction from Tours, and sights can be reached by bike, moped, buses, or thumb. Although more expensive, a car rented by four people can beat many of the tour bus prices. These regional bus tours are the surest but most regimented way to see surrounding sights; many leave daily outside the train station. Hitching may be tough, but for about 4F you can take bus #5 or 10 out of town to the south near N751.

And don't let the proliferation of châteaux overshadow the many possibilities for *dégustation* (wine-tasting): the caves of **Vouvray** and **Montlouis** are within 10km of Tours.

Built in the 1530s, **Villandry** is most remarkable for its fantastic formal gardens. These were reconstructed according to the original plans when the castle was restored at the beginning of the present century, and they consist of three terraces of neatly trimmed and shaped shrubbery and flowers. Most interesting of these is the intermediate terrace which has knee-high hedges arranged in various patterns: a Maltese Cross, a Croix de Lorraine, and a charming reproduction of the **Carte du Tendre** with its four types of love (tender, courtly, passionate, and flighty). The castle itself is, by comparison, much less interesting. The tallest part of the building is the twelfth-century **donjon**, and the rest of the building is in the sixteenth-century Renaissance style. Admission is 12F, students 8F, for the gardens and a tour of the interior; 10F, students 7F, for the gardens alone. Open daily from 9am-6pm (gardens stay open till 7pm).

Ussé, with its pointed towers, white turrets, and chimneys, is the setting which inspired the story of *Sleeping Beauty*. Surrounded by the thick woods of the Forêt de Chinon, the fifteenth-century château rises above terraced gardens and the Indre River. The buildings which have survived represent only the east wing of the original plan, as the north wing was demolished in the seventeenth century. The tour of the interior, most notable for the gallery of Flemish tapestries, is somewhat limited since the Count of Blacas is still in residence from June-Oct. The château's private ownership may also help to explain the high admission price of 16.50F, 9.50F with a student ID. After the tour, don't miss the walk up to the watchtower and if you have time, see the exhibit of 18th and 19th century French costume. The château is open daily mid-March through September, 9am-noon and 2-7pm (2-6pm rest of year).

Azay-le-Rideau is a capricious Renaissance château, built expressly to the whims of the wife of a grand financier of François I. Built on piles on the Indre River, the turreted white stone, blue-roofed palace is gracefully approached by a narrow, shaded path. Beautifully proportioned, and surrounded by a moat and flower gardens, Azay-le-Rideau is straight out of a picture book, showing the influence of the Italian Renaissance in the open loggia on the court and the parallel staircases. The imitation battlements and crenelations were never put to the test, and the history of the palace is, on the whole, peaceful. The mandatory tour is quite unpleasant when crowded, so go early, especially in high season. Open daily except Tues., 9am-noon and 2-5pm; admission 10F, students 5F (students 7-18 years old 2F). There is a *son-et-lumière* perform-ance every evening. Performance time changes during the summer, so check at the Tours tourist office. The tourist office sells combination bus and admission fee tickets from Tours for 53F.

Trains to Chinon from Tours stop at Azay-le-Rideau, and with a little effort the two châteaux can be combined into a day trip. Azay-le-Rideau is a hefty 2km walk from the station, down the road to the left into the center of town. The **syndicat d'initiative** at 26, rue Gambetta (tel. 43-34-40) is open daily except Sun., 9am-12:30pm and 1-7pm, and will help with accommodations. The **Camping Parc du Sabot** (tel. 43-32-72), is a large municipal site on the banks of the Indre, just across from the chateau. (Open April-October). There is a bicycle exchange rental at **M. Depire**, 13, ave. Carmot (tel. 43-30-94).

Langeais, feudal and forbidding, was one of the last medieval fortresses built for defense. Constructed from 1465-69 for Louis XI, Langeais occupied a key position guarding the route from Brittany. Brittany's union to the crown was celebrated at Langeais in 1491 with the marriage of Charles VIII of France and Anne of Brittany. The château's interior was meticulously restored at the beginning of this century, and it is filled with some very fine Gothic furnish-ings. The tour is somewhat amusing, as the guide merely stands and points while a recorded tape gives the speech, but it includes a walk along the upper fortifications whose stone slabs, when drawn back, open holes for hurling the proverbial boiling oil, pitch, and stones at attackers. In the small chateau courtyard stand the ruins of the original eleventh-century fortress. The chateau is open daily 9am-noon and 2-5pm; admission 11F students 5.50.)

Several trains daily between Nantes and Tours stop at Langeais, but the Château is a hefty 10km jaunt from the station. Langeais is a small town with little in the way of indoor accommodations, but there is a **municipal campground** on the N152, open June 15-Sept. 15 (tel. 96-85-80). You can rent bicycles from **M. Vincent,** Station Touraine-Anjou (tel. 55-81-17).

Chinon

This is one town which affords a good sense of the texture and pace of life in the Loire valley outside of the châteaux. Though it doesn't have many inex-pensive accommodations, Chinon offers a restful atmosphere, striking château ruins, and good hostel and camping facilities. Birthplace of the great sixteenth-century writer, François Rabelais, Chinon's **old quarter** is a delightful maze of alleyways, chimneys, and medieval timber-framed houses, some with fine sculptural detail.

Perched splendidly on a cliff next to the old route to Tours, the **château de Chinon** is meant for those who want to wander leisurely through majestic ruins, letting their imaginations recreate the past. The château was never destroyed, but merely fell into ruin through neglect under Cardinal Richelieu and later under Napoleon. It was originally built by Henry II of England to protect his holdings in France, and when he died, his body was taken to Fontevraud. Chinon was successfully held for England by Richard the Lion-Hearted; when King John (Lackland) later lost it to King Philip of France after an eight-month siege in 1205, the château passed into French hands.

There were three parts of this eminently defensible château: the main **château de Milieu,** the **château du Coudray** to the west, and the **Fort St.-Georges** to the east. The last no longer exists; it once stood on the hill next to the present day entrance. An optional guided tour leads through the **Logis**

Royaux, partially reconstructed since 1970. The *logis* contains some medieval tapestry and sculpture and a helpful geneology for those who confuse their Valois and Capetians. The ruined great hall contains a plaque marking the site where Joan of Arc prophetically recognized Charles VII, then the beleagured Dauphin of France, in 1429. A month later, she set out on the campaign that freed Orléans and eventually installed Charles as king.

After the tour, you are free to wander around and take in the impressive fortifications. Note the king's secret entrance, a narrow staircase leading into the *logis* from the ravine separating the châteaux. The only other entrance was through the fifteenth century **Tour de l'Horloge,** which now houses a **Musée Jeanne d'Arc.** The museum is not very interesting, but the views from the tower windows are pleasant. The château is open daily except Wed., 9am-noon and 2-5:30pm, daily 9am-7pm in the summer. Admission is 8F, students 5F. There is a *son et lumière* performance nightly at about 10:30pm in the summer (the time changes with the date), which costs 10F.

The town's three churches, **St.-Maurice, St.-Etienne,** and **St.-Mexme** are in bad repair, and, apart from their setting, don't have much to offer. The **Musée du Vieux Chinon,** on the rue Voltaire, has a collection of local pottery (open 10am-noon and 3-7pm, admission 5F, students 3F). The **Cave Plouzeau,** 94, rue Voltaire (tel. 93-16-34), conducts tours and offers you some of their superb Chinon white wine from 10am-12:30pm and 2-7pm, for 5F admission. Closed Monday. You may also want to visit the kitschy but entertaining **Musée Animé de Vin,** at 12, rue Voltaire, which illustrates the wine-making process with "automatons" who lace their speech with Rabelais quotes, in English and in French. Free tasting included in the 8F entrance fee. There is a large, all-day market held every Thursday in the Place Hôtel de Ville. And on the first or second weekend of every summer month, Chinon holds a *marché médiéval* with crafts and beer under the trees. Ask at the Tourist Office for details. A ticket for various activities cost 15F.

Practical Information

There are four trains daily from Tours to Chinon. From the station, walk up ave. du Docteur-Labaussière to place Jeanne d'Arc and continue along the river to the center of town.

Office de Tourisme: place de l'Hotel de Ville (tel. 93-17-85). Provides information on the town, chateaux, accommodations, and local *caves* (wine cellars) and also changes money on Sat. and Sun. Open Mon.-Sat. 9am-12:30pm and 2-7pm, Sun. 10am-12:30pm.

Post Office: 10, quai Jeanne d'Arc. Open Mon.-Fri. 8am-noon and 2-6pm, Sat. 8am-noon.

Bike Rental: Some bikes are available from the tourist office (15F a day, 50F deposit) or from the train station (16F a day, plus deposit).

Police: (tel. 93-04-05); in an emergency tel. 17).

Telephone Code: (47).

Accommodations and Food

Auberge de Jeunesse: rue Descartes (tel. 93-21-37). Near the train station, across from the park by the river. Kitchen facilities. Open 8:30-11am and 5-10pm. 17F, no sheets necessary.

Hôtel Diderot: 7, rue Diderot (tel. 93-18-87). A large house with a courtyard is half home, half hotel with fourteen bedrooms. Singles 60F, doubles 75F. Breakfast 12.50F.

Camping: Right across the river at Ilc-Auger, off the RN749 (tel. 93-08-35). Very nice sites in an excellent location. Almost worth a visit for its beautiful view of the chateau on moonlit night. Open all year.

Restaurant Marceau, 24, rue Marceau, has four-course *menus* for 32.50F and up.

Pizzeria La Grappa, 50, rue Voltaire. Meals à la carte for under 20F; entrees 12-18F, pizza 18-24F. Closed Mon. and Tues. afternoon.

Saumur

Immortalized in Balzac's novel *Eugenie Grandet,* Saumur still bears traces of the provincial hole where Eugenie watched life go by. The vines which made old Grandet rich still provide the town's main source of income (along with mushrooms), but industry has gained a foothold in the suburbs. The **château,** constructed at the end of the fourteenth century, served as a fortified bastion during the Hundred Years' War. It became one of the Duke Rene's favorite residences in the fifteenth century and it was he who added the hospitable living quarters. This transition reversed during the Wars of Religion, when the defenses were strengthened by the Protestant governor of the town. The chateau's strength as a fortress was again demonstrated in 1940 when the members of Saumur's cavalry school used this strategic Loire position to check the German forces.

The chateau now houses the **Musée des Arts Decoratifs,** with a fine collection of medieval painting and sculpture, fifteenth- and sixteenth-century tapestries, and *faïence,* French pottery. (The upstairs **Musée du Cheval** should be of interest to equitation enthusiasts.) A mandatory guided tour blitzes through both museums in an hour, locking doors behind it, but the amiable guides will let you return afterwards if you want to see a bit more in detail. A climb to the **Tour de Guet** offers a magnificent view of the region. The chateau and museums are open daily 9am-7pm and 8:30-10:30pm in July and August, 9am-noon and 2-6pm off-season. Admission 8F, students 5F. Saumur's tradition as an equestrian center goes back to its establishment as the royal training ground for the cavalry in 1763. The French cavalry still train here, though in 1943 the school was enlarged to house "modern cavalry," or artillery.

Practical Information

Saumur is served frequently by trains between Nantes and Tours. From the modern train station, go right across the bridge to the Ile d'Offard, and continue across the old Pont Cessart to the city center.

Syndicat d'Initiative: 25, rue Beaurepaire (tel. 51-03-06). From the Pont Cessart, walk down the rue d'Orléans for two blocks and take a right on the rue Beaurepaire. They will phone free for accommodations within Saumur change money for free, and supply information on chateaux tours and vineyards in the area. (The Maison du Vin is in the same building.) Open 9am-8pm Mon.-Sat., Sun. 10:30am-12:30pm and 3-7pm in summer; shorter hours off-season.

Post Office: place Dupetit-Thouars, at the end of rue Portail Louis. Open Mon.-Fri. 9am-7pm, Sat. 9am-noon.

Bus Station: quai Carnot, two blocks to the right of the Pont Cessart as you enter town.

Bike Rental: Brison, on the corner of rue Dacier and rue d'Orleans. 18.50 a day with a 50F deposit.

Police: rue Montesquieu, just after the Hotel de Ville (tel. 51-04-32).

Hospital, rue Seigneur (tel. 51-25-24).

Market Days: Wed. and Sat., along the rue Molière and daily on the ave. de Gaulle. For especially fresh produce, try Les Halles (covered market) by the Eglise St. Pierre.

Telephone Code: (41).

Accommodations

Auberge de Jeunesse (IYHF), Ile d'Offard (tel. 50-45-00). Pleasant location on the end of the island next to the campground. Bike rental, kitchen facilities, and breakfast available. Open 7:30-10am and 5-10pm. 29.50F, including breakfast. You can get information here about canoe and kayak trips along the Loire to Nantes.

Central Hôtel, 23, rue Daille (tel. 51-05-78), is in the town center, not far from the main thoroughfare. Reasonable clean and quiet; the back rooms open only to the courtyard. Singles 53-58.50F, doubles from 58.50F; breakfast 10.50F, showers 8F. During the summer, they open an annex which gives them a total of forty rooms, so you should be able to find something here.

Hôtel de Bretagne, 55, rue St.-Nicholas (tel. 51-26-38). A small, centrally located place with rooms for 48F. Breakfast 10F.

Hôtel de Volney, 1, rue Volney (tel. 51-25-41). Across the street from the post office. Rooms without showers 62-125F. The wallpaper is pretty, but this is no real bargain. Breakfast 13.50F, showers 6F.

Camping: Next to the Youth Hostel, in a lovely spot on the Ile d'Offard. Showers available; shopping, swimming, and bar nearby. Open all year. 4.50F per tent, 5.50F per person.

Food

Saumur is the home of a fine white wine and champagne of the same name. The *caves* are just outside town; ask the syndicat about tours and *dégustations*.

Auberge St.-Pierre, place St.-Pierre. Two blocks from the Hotel de Ville. Fine menus at 27, 44, and 70F in an old house that looks onto the church.

Le Quichenotte, 41, rue Fourrier. A crêperie hidden away on the other side of the place St.-Pierre, with imaginative combinations at low prices, and a fixed *menu* for 29F.

Le Pullman, 52, rue d'Orleans. To remind you of those long-distance journeys, made to look like a train car; the booths are complete with overhead racks for your luggage. Specializing in fish dishes, with *menus* for 33 (without a fish course), 45, and 65F.

Near Saumur

The **Abbey of Fontevraud** was the celebrated monastic center of royalty and nobility from its founding in the eleventh century until the Revolution. More than half of the governing abbesses were of royal blood. The guided tour leads through the cupola-capped abbey church with the remains of the tombs of the

Plantagenets: Henry II, and Eleanor of Aquitaine, Richard the Lion-Hearted, and Isabelle of Angouleme, the wife of King John of England. The original tombs were destroyed during the Revolution; afterwards the British government repeatedly but unsuccessfully sought the transfer of the royal remains to Westminster. The Plantagenets, the French government maintains, were Dukes of Anjou first and kings of England second.

The church itself is a superb Romanesque structure of typical grace, with two cloisters alongside. As elaborate as the tombs and church is the enormous octagonal towered kitchen, the twenty-chimneyed **Evraud Tower.** The abbey is open daily except Tues., 9am-noon and 2-6:30pm, 10am-noon and 2-4pm in winter. Admission 7F, 3.50F Sunday and holidays, and 3F for students. There are three buses daily from Saumur to Fontevraud (about 20km); there are also buses from Saumur and Chinon to Montsoreau (4km away). Concerts and plays are held in the abbey throughout the summer; check at a nearby syndicat if you're interested.

A day trip to the countryside would allow you to view the local wine and mushroom *caves*. Most are located 3km west of Saumur on the D751 in St.-Hilaire.-St.-Florent; pick up a list at the syndicat. Most *caves* are open Mon.-Sat. 9-11:30am and 2-5:30pm.

A bit further along the D751, the **Musée du Champignon** provides tours through some of the *caves* where mushrooms are grown. Originally mined for stone to build the nearby chateaux, the *caves* now grow 70% of France's mushrooms. Open daily from mid-March to mid-November, 10am-noon and 2-6pm.

Angers

Once the center of a grand duchy with a flourishing culture, Angers retains only its chateau and its cathedral as reminders of this illustrious past. The city serves as the western gateway to the chateau region, and, like that area, it sports a long history of kings, queens, and battles. One of Angers' native sons, Henry Plantagenet, became Henry II of England in 1154 and founded the great Plantagenet line. Until the end of the fifteenth century, the ducs d'Anjou controlled a vast territory with Angers as their base, despite resistance from both the French and English crowns.

Angers is a major stop on the Paris-Tours-Nantes railway line. Although a large city, its major sights are fairly close to each other, between the station and the river Maine. The blvd. Maréchal-Foch leads to the Hotel de Ville and the main shopping area.

Practical Information

Office de Tourisme: Opposite the train station (tel. 87-72-50). Open Mon.-Sat. 9am-8pm; shorter hours in winter. Another office is located across from the chateau. Sponsors bus tours to the Anjou countryside and various chateaux. Accommodations service 2.50F. The map available from the vending machine outside the office (for 1F) is more useful for locating accommodations than the free one provided by the office. Open Mon.-Sat. 9am-7pm, Sun. 10am-7pm; shorter hours in winter.

Post Office: rue Franklin-Roosevelt (tel. 88-24-00). Near the Cathedral.

Bus Station: rue Plantagenet (tel. 88-59-25). Local bus information: to the right of the theater (in the same building) at the place du Ralliement.

Bike Rental: Cycles Lejeune, M. Thibaudeau, 33, rue Plantagenet (tel. 87-62-45).

Laundromat: Lavo Service, place Romaine. Open daily 7am-8pm.

Market Day: Open air market every Sat. on blvd. Bessonneau and place Louis Imbach.

Telephone Code: (41).

Accommodations and Food

Try the older section of town, between the place du Ralliement and place Molière. As you approach place Molière, the hotels get cheaper and the neighborhood more interesting, but seedier.

La Coupe d'Or, 5, rue de la Gare (tel. 88 45 02). Small, clean rooms, with a nice proprietor. One of the best deals near the train station. Most rooms for 48F, 63F with shower. Breakfast 10.50F. Some rooms in annex 2 blocks east.

A La Tour, 66, rue Baudrière (tel. 88-71-72). Closed Sun. Pleasant, simple rooms with a good, inexpensive cafe/restaurant below. Doubles 48-55F, 70F for a double with shower.

Hôtel Continental: 12-14, rue Louis de Romain, near the Cathedral (tel. 88-63-80). Dark and drab, but clean. 44F for a single, 50F for a double. Doubles with showers 63F. Showers 8F, breakfast 9F.

Camping: Parc de la Haye (tel. 48-35-08). An excellent municipal campsite, 4km outside the city. (Take bus #3 to Val d'Or.) 12F for two people and a tent. Showers available.

There are several good crêperies on the place Pilori near the Hôtel de Ville. Around the station, try **La Petite Marmite,** 22*ter,* rue Denis-Papin, which has regional specialties on a 26.50F *menu.* Also near the station on the rue de la Gare is a **self-service** place, with main dishes for 9-24F. **La Treille,** at 12, rue Montault, place St. Croix, has a fine 34.50F *menu* and several tempting vegetarian plates from 24-30F. Closed Sunday. **Les Gavottes,** on the corner of rue des Poiliers and rue du Mail, has *menus* at 24.50 and 30F and crêpes for 10-24F. Finally, **La Comédie Fast-Food,** 44, rue St. Laud, serves palatable food in a chic setting until 2am every day but Monday. Quiche costs 7F and hamburgers on brioche 8F.

Sights

The splendid **château** was built by the dukes of Angers at the beginning of the thirteenth century. It narrowly escaped destruction during the Wars of Religion when Henry III ordered its demolition but died before his plans were carried out. The walls are well preserved and present a bleak, uncompromising prospect to any potential attacker. From the river, the château is protected by the sheer cliffs on which it is built, and to the south its deep moat and seventeen formidable towers are equally daunting. (The moat is now drained and contains formal gardens and tame deer.) Most of the buildings on the inside were constructed during the fifteenth-century reign of Anjou's last and greatest duke, René le Bon, who not only commanded an empire that included Sicily, Piedmont, and Lorraine, but found the time to write several romances and volumes of poetry. An exhibition of his work is housed in the small Gothic chapel.

Angers' most famous attraction, the **Tapestries of the Apocalypse,** are displayed in a modern exhibition hall within the château. Woven in 1375-1380 by Nicolas Bataille for Duke François I of Anjou, over seventy pieces of this stitched representation of the Gospel according to St. John remain. It is remarkable for both the consistency of the figures and the flamboyant depiction of multi-headed lions and serpents. The tape-recorded tour (4F) is quite long-winded and takes 45 minutes, so you might consider buying the book on the tapestries instead (for 21F, available at the entrance). Also in the château is the **Logis du Governeur,** containing a fine collection of sixteenth- and seventeenth-century tapestries; guided tours leave every twenty minutes between 9:30-11:30am and 2-6:30pm. After all the tapestries, take a walk around the ramparts to discover why this château was never captured. The château of Angers is open 9:30am-noon and 2-6pm; 9am-7pm from July 1 through mid-September. Admission is 7F, 3.50F on Sundays and for students at all times.

Angers' prominent **Cathédrale St.-Maurice** has a twelfth-century nave remarkable for its unique Angevin vaulting, an elegant four-part arrangement which seems to merge the best of Gothic loftiness and Romanesque simplicity. Unfortunately, it is difficult to get a good view of the Cathedral from the surrounding streets. Go to the montée St.-Maurice (steps leading down to the river Maine) or to one of the towers of the chateau for the best views.

Don't miss the chance for a free *dégustation* at the **Maison du Vin de l'Anjou,** across the street from the château at 5bis, place Kennedy. The people here will let you sample some of the excellent regional wines (which are available at reasonable prices), and they will provide information on the many nearby *caves.* Open 9am-1pm and 2:30-6:30pm, closed Tuesdays.

Burgundy (Bourgogne)

Two hours south of Paris, Burgundy is rich in wine, traditional French cooking and religious architecture. When the power of the church was at its peak in the twelfth and thirteenth centuries, the abbeys and cathedrals which perch atop the province's hills and mountains inspired monastic architecture throughout much of France.

The court of the powerful Dukes of Burgundy reached the apex of its power in the fourteenth and fifteenth centuries. Ruling in the style of kings, they encouraged a flourishing artistic circle and supported the finest Flemish painters of the age. In 1420, Philippe the Good of Burgundy allied with England against Charles VII and took much of France with him. Not until 1477 did the duchy finally pass into the hands of the crown and come under the protection of Louis XI.

Vineyards cover the slopes of the limestone hills of Burgundy and the world's most expensive wines are produced from the grapes grown along its **Côte d'Or,** which stretches from **Dijon** south to **Sentenay.** Delicate white chablis wines are produced in the Auxerre region north of Dijon, and the light-bodied beaujolais wines are made in the southermost area between **Macon** and **Lyon.** Of all France's vineyards, those of Burgundy are most at the mercy of inclement weather. Forty million bottles are produced per year in Burgundy alone, 70% of which is exported to 145 countries. You can taste free samples at the *caves* in **Beaune** and many other villages along the *route de vin.* (Look for signs advertising *dégustation.*) Burgundy's renowned cuisine is centered upon its wine-based sauces. Culinary specialties include *boeuf bourgignon, escargots, coq au vin,* Dijon *moutardes* (made with white wine instead of vinegar), and *kir,* a beverage concocted with white wine (usually Aligote) and *crème de cassis* (blackcurrant syrup).

Grape harvesting is hard work, but if you're around in September and October and want to make some money, workers are almost always needed and the traditional grape *vendange* often borders on the festive. Local **syndicats d'initiative** will have details on grape-picking opportunities. You can also contact the following agencies: **Centre Régional des Jeunes Agriculteurs**, 42, rue de Mulhouse, Dijon (tel. 30-84-96) and **Agence Nationale pour les Emploi**, 6, blvd. St.-Jacques, Beaune (tel. 22-16-72). If these places refuse to help you because you lack a work permit, try going right to the vineyards themselves. You would be wise to make arrangements at least a week before the harvest begins.

But Burgundy harbors far more than vineyards. Here, the ambitious traveler will find beautiful, sparsely-populated countryside almost everywhere he goes. To the north and west lie the rolling pastures and rivers of the **Yonne** and **Nievre** regions, and wild mountains, forests, and lakes dominate the geographic center of Burgundy, the **Morvan.** Excellent free tourist literature is available from most syndicats d'initiative. Two good brochures are *Bourgogne Romane,* a guide to Romanesque churches in the region, and *Vignes et Vins de Bourgogne* (both also available in English).

From mid-July to mid-August, Burgundy hosts **Musique en Bourgogne,** with classical and early music concerts performed in the cathedrals and churches of Sens, Beaune, Vézelay, Tournus, and other towns. Pick up a copy of the schedule at any syndicat. You should buy your ticket a month in advance at the syndicat of the town where the concert takes place; seats range from 30-60F, all seats 20F with student ID. The **Festival des nuits de Bourgogne** takes place from mid-July to August and includes concerts in the châteaux at Fontenay, Bussy-Rabutin, Clos de Vougeot, and elsewhere. For details, contact the **Hôtel Chambellan** in Dijon, 34, rue des Forges (tel. 32-75-35).

Hotels are no cheaper in Burgundy than elsewhere, but camping is especially beautiful here. Sites are often nestled at the feet of spectacular mountains. The region's windy, hilly roads will strain the thighs of all but the veteran cyclist. Make sure to check altitude points on a map (*Michelin's* are particularly good) so that you know what to expect.

Dijon

From Charles the Bald, Charlemagne's grandson, to Charles the Bold, last Grand Duke of the Occident, Dijon was ruled by lords as colorful as the brightly-patterned tile roofs of Burgundy. In the fourteenth and fifteenth centuries the Dukes of Burgundy turned this duchy into a shimmering center of European art—and a powerful nexus of bureaucracy and justice. Enjoy the stateliness and pomp of an age when the mayor, magistrate, and marquis one-upped each other with the splendor of their *hôtels* (urban chateaux).

Today Dijon remains the wealthy cultural and commercial center of Burgundy. Its compact and well-restored **vieille ville** lends itself to aimless wandering and watching, and its prominent university keeps the ancient city young. The university also helps sustain the city's international flavor by running a very good language program for foreign students during the summer (4,6, and 8 weeks long). For information, contact CROUS, 3, rue Docteur-Maret (tel. 82-36-26).

Practical Information

If you plan to use the city buses a lot or to stay in the Youth Hostel, consider buying a 7-day **bus pass** at STRD, place Grangier. It costs 9.50F and is a good deal where the regular per-trip fare is 3.40F—not good during evening rush hour.

Office de Tourisme: place Darcy (tel. 43-42-12). A five-minute walk from the train station down the ave. Maréchal-Foch. Also an accommodations service for 5.50F and a money exchange. Open April-Oct., Mon.-Sat. 9am-noon and 2-9pm, other months until 6pm, and Sun. 10am-noon and 2-7pm. From July-Sept, 30 guided walking tours leave from here daily at 4pm (1½ hours; 8F, students 5F).

Centre d'Information Jeunesse de Bourgogne (CIJB): 22, rue Audra (tel. 30-35-56). Friendly organization which offers information on festivals, cheap restaurants, hitching, etc. Open Mon.-Fri. 8:30am-12:30pm and 1:30-7pm Sat. 9am-noon during the academic year.

Post Office: place Grangier (tel. 43-81-00) Open Mon.-Fri. 8am-7pm. Sat. and Sun. 8am-noon. Poste Restante only open until 11am on weekends.

Train Station: SNCF at the end of ave. Maréchal-Foch (tel. 43-47-12). About 2½ hours to Paris. For discount BIGE tickets, walk up one block from the station to **Agence Wasteels** at 16, ave. Maréchal-Foch (tel. 05-65-34), open daily 9am-7pm, Sat. till 6pm.

Bus Station: Next to the train station (tel. 43-58-97). Open for tickets 6am-8pm. Schedules are posted on windows, or ask at the station for information. Buy tickets when boarding the bus. Daily routes to Beaune, Avallon, and Autun.

Bicycle Rental: Motoconfort, 3, place Notre Dame (tel. 30-91-52); **Stand 51,** blvd. Foch (tel. 43-54-67). Both 30F per day, cheaper by the week.

Hitching: For Paris; via Sens, take the ave. Albert 1er for the south, ave. Jean-Jaures (the N74 for Chalon). The hitching is often very bad; forget it if you're in a hurry.

Laundromats: 36, rue Guillaume Tell, just above the train station; or rue J. J. Rousseau, off the place de la République. About 7F for washers, 4F for dryers.

Police: (tel. 41-81-05); **Medical Emergency;** Hôpital Général (tel. 41-81-41).

Telephone Code: (80).

Accommodations

Reasonably priced hotels often fill up fast, so plan on getting a place early or on using the accommodations service at the tourist office. In Dijon, you pay by the room, not by the person, and most rooms are large enough for two people.

Auberge de Jeunesse (IYHF), Centre de Rencontres Internationales, 1, blvd. Champollion (tel. 71-32-12). 4km ride from the station. Take bus #5 from the "Bar Bleu" in place Grangier toward Epirey to the end of the line (see above note about bus passes). Large, modern establishment often overrun with buses; 22.50F a night, fills up fast in July and August, so call ahead. Breakfast 7F, dinner 17F in cafeteria. No cooking facilities, but a grocery store across the street.

Foyer International d'Etudiants, ave, Maréchal-Lecler (tel. 71-51-01). Really the best deal in town. Take bus #4, direction Grezille. Get off at Parc des Sports. Sleek and shiny. Rooms 33F without breakfast. Cafeteria meals for 13F: breakfast 5F. Open July-Sept.

Hôtel du Théâtre, 3, rue des Bons Enfants (tel. 32-54-72). Centrally located on a quiet sidestreet. Rooms from 40-69F per night. Singles and doubles. Optional breakfast 11F. Reception in back of courtyard.

Hôtel Confort, 12, rue Jules-Mercier (tel. 30-37-47). On an alley off of rue de la Liberte. Large, almost luxurious doubles for 42F. Well-hidden, so may have space when other places are full.

Hôtel du Miroir, 7, rue Bossuet (tel. 30-54-81). Central but quiet, located down an alley and upstairs. Clean rooms (55-70F) and friendly management. Breakfast 11F.

Hôtel du Sauvage, 64, rue Monge (tel. 41-31-21). Near the church St.-Jean. An impressive courtyard leads to this briskly-run, decorous hotel. Rooms with breakfast are 63F for one person, 73F for two.

Hôtel Monge, 20, rue Monge (tel. 30-55-41). Well-located, homey, kind proprietress. Rooms 63F, 89F with shower. Breakfast 10.30F.

Camping: Camping Municipal du Lac, blvd. Kir and ave. Albert 1er (tel. 43-54-72). On a small lake, about 2km from town, behind the train station and past the Natural History Museum. Clean facilities, but usually crammed in summer, so stake out your site early. **Camping l'Orée du Bois,** rte. d'Etuales, Darois (tel. 31-60-22), is 9km out of town, a two-star campground open June 1-Sept. 15.

Food

Dijon has been known as a gastromonic paradise since the Gallo-Roman era. A Burgundy meal will be less expensive in a smaller town, but you might splurge once or twice here and make up the difference by picnicking, since the markets offer genuine bargains. Every Tuesday, Friday, and Saturday morning, stalls loaded with produce and bric-à-brac cluster at the intersection of rue Quentin and rue de la Liberté. Go late, when the venders have to cut prices to get rid of their produce. There is also a large supermarket in the basement of the **Nouvelles Galleries** on rue de la Liberté. The **Jardin de l'Arquebuse** and the park by the place Darcy are convenient picnic spots. For fancy gift jars of mustard at very reasonable prices, visit the **Maille** store, 32, rue de la Liberté (open Mon.-Sat. 9-11:45am and 12:45-7pm), which has been making mustard since 1777 and has an exhibit of antique jars.

Student Restaurant: Maret, 3, rue du Docteur-Maret, right off place Darcy, is the most central. With a student ID you can buy 12F meal tickets next door at the CROUS office. You can also try to buy a 5.60F meal ticket from a Dijon student. Closed July and August.

Moulin à Vent, 8, place Françoise-Rudé, near the ducal palace and open market, located in a half-timbered house with a cafe below. Very generous *menus* at 38F and 55F. Serves excellent *boeuf bourgignon.*

Au Bec Fin, 47, rue Jeannin. *Menu* at 40F changes daily and includes house and regional specialties.

Restaurants des Docks, 11, rue Albert 1er, on the road toward the campsite. The French equivalent of a truck stop, serving unembellished meals for 28F.

Brasserie du Théâtre, place du Théâtre. Popular and reasonable, with dining *à la belle étoile* (outside on the terrasse) 37F.

Taverne St.-Jean, 15, rue Monge. This classy place rewards you for spending a few more francs. Only a light *menu* at 45F, but a very good one at 58F. Closed Wed.

Le Vinarium, 23, place Bossuet, by the St.-Jean church, in a 13th century crypt. A gourmet splurge at 65F. Regional cuisine and *boeuf bourgignon.*

Sights

The imposing **Palais des Ducs de Bourgogne** is interesting only for its towers and the enormous kitchen which once produced Burgundy's finest cuisine. The **Tour Philippe Le Bon** is open daily 9:30-11:30am and 2:30-5:30pm; admission is 4F for a fun climb to the top. The **Musée des Beaux-Arts,** occupying a modern part of the Palace, has a wonderful collection of paintings from all periods. The medieval ties to Flanders and Burgundy are represented by an exceptional group of Flemish primitives. The museum's collection also includes painting by Carucci, Veronese, Titian, and French artists from Mignard to Manet (open daily 9am-noon and 2-6pm, closed Tues.; admission 3F, free on Sun. or with student ID).

From the Palais, walk along the rue des Forges and the neighboring streets for a look at the nobles' grand residences (the tourist office has a list of the flashiest homes). Be sure to look at the courtyard of #34, the **hôtel Chambellan;** the calm exterior gives no indication of the extravagant Gothic courtyard, with its harmonious balconies and stairways. If you enjoy strolling down the medieval streets, then don't miss the rue de la Chouette and the rue Verrerie (the grooved center of the pavement was the sewage conduit in the seventeenth century). Note the different styles of *eschauguettes* (watch towers) protruding from the corners of the Renaissance houses. Nearby, the seventeenth-century **Church of Notre Dame** was built in Burgundian Gothic style; its facade is a gargoyle extravaganza, each creature affecting a different pose or expression. Above the right tower sits the pride of Dijon, the **horloge à Jacquemart,** the clock and bell brought by Philippe the Hardy in 1382 after his victory over the Flemish. Originally, a single statue hammered the bell each hour, but in 1610 the lonely male statue was given a spouse, then a son to strike the half-hour, and finally, in 1881, a daughter to announce the quarter hour.

The **Cathédrale St.-Benigne,** also built in the 13th century, is a sombre example of the pure Burgundy Gothic style. It was built as a monastic church, and beneath it lies the sixth-century **Crypte of St. Benigne.** Next door is the **Musée Archéologique,** 5, rue Docteur-Maret. Formerly an abbey, the museum itself is an ancient building, and it houses a fine collection of Gallo-Roman and medieval artifacts. Open daily 9am-noon and 2-6pm, closed Tuesday; admission 5F, free with student ID.

Across the place de la Libération is the **Musée Magnin,** 4, rue des Bons Enfants, a sumptuous documentary of seventeenth-century living. Though paintings by Poussin, David, and many others hang on the walls, the museum is more interesting for the elegance of its period furnishings. Open same hours as the Musée Archéologique; admission 5F, free on Sunday.

Throughout June, Dijon plays host to many of the world's best symphony orchestras and chamber groups as part of *un été musical* (a musical summer). From mid-June to mid-August, **Estivade** presents dance, music, and theater in the streets. Dijon devotes a week in mid-September to the traditional **Fête des Vignes** and the **Festival International de Folklore,** which culminates in a colorful parade through the town. **Grenier de Bourgogne** organizes free jazz and entertainment in the park by place Darcy throughout the summer. The **office de tourisme** place Darcy, keeps a bulletin board where schedules of current events and upcoming festivals are posted. If your French is good enough, investigate the shows at the **Nouveau Théâtre de Bourgogne,** located at Théâtre du Parvis St. Jean, place Bossuet. The box office opens at 5pm and there are productions throughout the year.

Beaune

Beaune is a proud and prosperous town which for centuries has existed for the sole purpose of winemaking. The precious surrounding vineyards make incursions into the city itself, and even Beaune's churches are decorated with clusters of sculptured grapes. From the informative **Musée du Vin** (open daily 9-11am and 2-5pm, in the Hôtel des Ducs de Bourgogne) to the unique **Hôtel-Dieu**, a visit here is an education in Burgundy's lore. Try to visit one of the numerous *caves*, many of which occupy intriguing, labyrinth-like cellars, and most of which offer free samples. The oldest *caves* are the **Caves du Bourgogne** in the ninth-century crypt of the former Eglise St.-Martin. The **Maison Calvet,** 6, blvd. Perpreuil, whose cobwebbed *caves* are 3km long, gives tours and a slide show which explain both the manufacturing and the storage processes. Samples are free and of good quality. Closed Monday. The **Caves des Cordeliers,** next to the Hôtel-Dieu, features a tour and sampling *du tonneau* (from the keg). The schmaltzy tour offered by **Maison Patriarch Père et Fils** leads past astonishing numbers of dusty, aging bottles lying thousands deep along 9km of tunnels. Fortunately, the tour omits most of the tunnels and culminates in an energetic, if short, tasting session. Admission 15F, 12F with student ID; proceeds go to charity. The **Marché aux Vins,** by the Hôtel-Dieu, is the most pretigious of the Beaune *caves*. For 20F you are given a glass and one hour (no tour) to sample from 37 of Burgundy's finest wines. On most tours, the best wines come last, so save your most discerning moments for *les grands crus* (the great labels).

When you emerge from subterranean Beaune, you can go to the beautiful park de la Bouzaise beyond the city ramparts and lie down for a while. The **Hôtel-Dieu,** a landmark of Burgundy architecture, was constructed as a refuge for the poor by Nicholas Rolin, Chancellor of Burgundy and a most effective tax collector. Louis XI reportedly remarked that it was only fitting for Rolin to build a hospital for the poor, since he was responsible for the poverty of so many of them. The colorful courtyard roof illustrates the political ties this region once had to Flanders. The 20-minute guided visit ends with a brief glance at Roger Van der Weyden's *Last Judgement*. Open 9am-7pm, Tues. and Oct.-May open 9am-noon and 2-6pm; admission 7F for students.

The **Basilique Collegiale Notre Dame** is also worth a visit. It houses fifteenth-century Flemish tapestries depicting the life of the Virgin Mary and a venerated twelfth-century carved wooden Virgin. Built in the style of Cluny, the twelfth-century church looks like a miniature replica of Autun cathedral. In the second chapel on the left, you can also see an astonishingly realistic fifteenth-century fresco of the resurrection of Lazarus.

In July and August, a hot-air balloon just outside of Beaune gives tours of the area, but prices are sky-high too (250F for half an hour). Inquire at the tourist office.

Practical Information

Office de Tourisme: across from the Hôtel-Dieu (tel. 22-24-51). A money exchange and accommodations service, they will also provide lists of the *caves* in the region which offer tours. Open daily 9am-10pm in summer, till 8pm in spring and fall, till 7pm in winter. From July through Sept., walking tours led by professional guides start here daily.

Post Office: rue de la Poste. Open Mon.-Fri. 8am-7pm, Sat. 8am-noon.

Train Station: ave. du 8 Septembre (tel. 22-13-13). Follow this avenue straight into the center of town. Beaune is a frequent stop between Dijon and Lyon.

Buses: leave from the corner of rue Maufoux and blvd. Bretonnière for Dijon, Chalon-sur-Saône, Autun, and points of interest in the Beaune area. Bus schedules are posted at the Office de Tourisme.

Bike Rentals: Monsieur Douillot, 18 Faubourg St. Nicolas (tel. 22-36-37). Closed Sunday.

Laundromat: 24, Faubourg St. Nicolas. 7F wash, 4F dry. Open daily 7am-8:30pm.

Police: rue de l'Hôtel de Ville (tel. 02-36-37).

Telephone Code: (80).

Accommodations and Food

Finding a room is extremely difficult if you haven't planned ahead. With Dijon only a 20-minute ride away, however, you can always base yourself there instead. In Chalon-sur-Saône, a 20-minute train ride south, there is a large, modern **IYHF Youth Hostel** on the banks of the Saône, with a swimming pool and sailing club next door (tel. (85) 46-62-77).

Hôtel St. Nicolas, 69, Faubourg St. Nicolas (tel. 22-18-30), only a few minutes from the center of town. Lively and comfortable, with rooms from 45F. Breakfast 12F. Reservations recommended.

Hôtel Rousseau, 11, place Madeleine (tel. 22-13-59) is located in a pleasant square close to the center of town. The proprietor has seventeen rooms—singles 45F, doubles 55-65F, but he strongly advises reservations at least a month in advance during the summer. Breakfast 11F.

Hôtel de France, 35, ave. du 8 Septembre (tel. 22-19-99), facing the train station. May have a room when others don't. Rooms from 70F. Closed Wed.

Camping: Camping Municipal (tel. 22-03-91) is just five hundred meters from the town center. Come early in the day as it is often full in summer. Follow the route du Faubourg St.-Nicolas; **Camping Municipal de la Grappe d'Or** (tel. 21-22-48) is 10km south in Mersault, open March 1-Oct. 15.

Most of the restaurants in Beaune are not geared to a student traveler's budget, but the supermarket **SUMA,** rue d'Alsace, is a good place to buy food, and a large market operates on Saturday mornings at place Carnot, offering good *patisserie* (pastries) and candy as well as vegetables, fruit, and clothing. The **Bistrot du Marché,** 12, place Carnot, offers a generous regional *menu* for 35F. **Maxime,** at place Madelaine, has a decent 45F *menu* and pleasant outdoor seating. Next door the **Pizza Silvio,** rue d'Alsace, has a good 28F pizza *menu*.

Côte d'Or

Ever since the Roman invasion brought wine-making to Burgundy, the Côte d'Or has produced some of the world's most notable wines. Charlemagne kept his personal vineyard at Aloxe-Cortone, and Louis XIV fondly enjoyed his Nuits-St.-Georges on doctor's orders.

The region is a thin strip of ground which runs 60km from Dijon in the north to Santenay south of Beaune, and is roughly divided by route N74 into the great wines to the west and the lesser wines to the east. Ask at the tourist offices in Beaune and Dijon for lists of *caves historiques* in the area, and if you have transportation of your own, go visit these vineyards and wine chateaux. In October, the whole vine-covered valley turns a brilliant red and gold—this, as well as its monetary value, is what gives the valley its name. There are also local buses which leave often from Dijon and make frequent stops along the N74. The bus schedule reads like a wine menu.

Nuits-St.-Georges and **Vosne-Romanée** are particularly charming towns and good places to try local wines. The notable **château de Gevry-Chambertin** and the **château d'André-Corton,** with its bright Flemish roof (5km north of Beaume) both dominate sleepy villages; their wine *caves* are renowned for their size and quality. The magical **château du Clos de Vougeot,** home of the most celebrated wine fraternity, **la Confrérie des Chevaliers du Tastevins,** sits in the middle of the most expensive plot of vineyard in Burgundy. Unfortunately, wine-tasting is not permitted here, but the tour of the castle, winepress, and the *confrérie* is interesting. Open every day 9-11:30am and 2-5:30pm, admission 5F. Also worth a visit are the **château de Meursault,** with a 20F tour and wine-tasting, and the **château de Rochepot,** remarkable for its seductive hilltop setting and its interiors, as well as the nearby twelfth-century Roman church. Both lie about 10km southwest of Beaune.

Another good bet is the **Circuit du Côté Illuminé.** This 2½ hour guided bus tour through vineyards, chateaux, and *caves* leaves about 9:30am (time changes through the summer) from the Dijon and Beaune tourist offices. The cost is 55F, though student reductions are available. Leaves Dijon every evening except Sun., July-Oct. 15, and from Beaune every Tues., Thurs., and Sat., July-Sept. 15.

Sens

Named for an ancient Celtic people, the Senoni, Sens was one of the first great Gallic towns to come to power. For the centuries that the city was the ecclesiastical center of France, even the bishops of Paris answered to the archbishops of Sens. Only one hour from Paris, this town serves as a pleasant stop during train rides to or from Dijon.

The **Cathédrale St.-Etienne** is celebrated as France's first authentically Gothic cathedral and it reputedly was the model for England's Canterbury Cathedral. Note particularly the stained glass windows on the north side of the ambulatory which depict scenes from the life of St. Thomas à Becket and the Mausoleum of the Dauphin (son of Louis XV) and Dauphine in the Chapel of St. Colomba. Climb the staircase by the vestry to visit one of France's richest cathedral treasuries. The collection contains the liturgical vestments of two of Canterbury's renowned archbishops, St. Thomas and Edward of Abingdon (open 10am-noon and 2-5pm, closed Tuesday and during Sunday services). The **syndicat d'initiative,** place Jean-Jaurès, will supply you with maps, historical commentaries, and accommodations information. Walk straight down the ave. Vauban from the station, cross over the river, and follow the signs (twenty minute walk). The Cathedral is two blocks from the syndicat.

Nevers

At the junction of the Loire and the Allier rivers, Nevers and the Nievre region more closely resemble the gentle farmland and forests of neighboring Berry than the Morvan or the vineyards of Burgundy. Nevers is a fairly large but relaxed city, dotted in summer with lush, flowering parks. In the **Cathédrale-St.-Cyr et Ste.-Juliette,** you can gaze at a melange of architectural styles developed between the tenth and sixteenth centuries. The rare mixture is exemplified by the cathedral's two chapels at the front of the nave; one, to the west, is in a sombre Roman style, while the other, to the east, is flamboyantly Gothic. The **Palais Ducal** is a beautiful example of Renaissance architecture, and it offers a majestic view of the Loire river. The town is also known for its fine ceramics, some of which reside in the **Musée de Faïences** as well as in several stores. The **syndicat d'initiative,** place Jean-Jaurès, will locate vacant rooms and provides summer tours of the city and its monuments. Ask for their brochure on the Nievre countryside if you're interested in hiking, fishing, camping, or cycling. Open Mon.-Sat. 9am-noon and 2-7pm. Bike rental at the train station.

Two inexpensive hotels close to the train station are the **Hôtel le Tourbillon,** 100, Faubourg de Mouesse (tel. 61-10-66) with doubles from 48F, and **Hôtel de la Gare,** 44, ave. Général-de-Gaulle (tel. 57-06-59), with doubles for 45F. This hotel also has a reasonable *menu* for 35F, but you should probably wait to eat in style at l'**Etable,** on rue du 13*ème* de ligne, which has *menus* at 35F and 55F. The **Camping Municipal** is across the river by a swimming pool (tel. 57-56-95) and open year-round. Trains from the Loire valley and the Massif Central pass through Nevers to Dijon, Lyon, and Paris.

Vézelay

Perched high atop a hill overlooking patches of lush green forest, mountains, and pastures is the tiny town of Vézelay. This town is famous for its **Basilique de la Madeleine,** which supposedly houses the bones of St. Mary Magdalene. Though the authenticity of the relics have been challenged, the basilica has the honor of being considered the finest of Romanesque architecture in France. The twelfth-century transept and chancel, added to the original ninth-century structure, rank among the best expressions of the then-emerging Gothic style. You can spend hours examining the fascinating and often amusing figures on the capitals of the columns and on the inner tympanum depicting the enthroned figure of Christ in the narthex (entrance porch) of the church. The outside portal is a poor modern replacement of that destroyed during the Revolution. A **museum** above the chapter room contains sculpture removed from the church and gives a good idea of what the nineteenth-century restoration of the building must have involved. Climb the tortuous, narrow staircase of the tower (2F) for a wonderful view of the entire town and surrounding hills, including the spot behind the Basilica where St. Bernard launched the second Crusade in 1146 and Richard the Lion-Hearted gathered his armies before leaving for the Holy Land.

The town was an important pilgrimage site during the Middle Ages, but when the authenticity of Mary Magdalene's bones (housed in the crypt) was challenged, Vézelay lost a great deal of its former popularity. Now a backwater, Vézelay has remained basically unchanged since its days as a religious center, except that modern-day pilgrims tend to be French weekenders on their way to the nearby Morvan. The **syndicat d'initiative,** place du Champ de Foire (tel. 33-23-69), is open July 1-Sept., 11am-12:30pm and 3:30-7pm. In the off-season, bring your questions to the **Mairie,** rue St. Pierre (tel. 33-24-62).

Inexpensive accommodations are available at the **Centre Pax Christi,** rue des Ecoles (tel. 33-26-73) in the center of town. It's a little run-down, but the people are very friendly, and it has a superb view. Bed and breakfast cost 19F plus 3F for a membership card; lunch 21F, dinner 19F. Open continuously from July to the beginning of September, but also often open for groups and individuals during other months. The **Auberge de Jeunesse (IYHF),** 1km from town on the route de l'Etang (tel. 33-24-18), is on a peaceful, rural site, with kitchen facilities. 22.50F per night (lock-out from noon to 6pm) and adjacent camping, both open at Easter and June to Sept. It's easiest to travel to Vézelay from Paris or Dijon—change at Laroche for the train to Avallon, (or take the Dijon bus to Avallon) and take a bus from there. If you get off the train at Servizelles, which is the closer station, you're in for a 10km walk—there's no bus service. People are more willing to pick up hitchhikers here than in the wine districts, but traffic is sparse and rides will be short. Also, there is no currency exchange in Vézelay, so plan to have enough cash to last until you leave.

Semur-en-Auxois, Avallon, and the Morvan

Semur-en-Auxois is a forgotten, fortified town which sits among the beautiful rolling hills of the agricultural Auxois. The sights are limited to the elegant, thirteenth-century **Eglise Notre Dame** and the four towers which buttress Semur, but in this seductive medieval town, every narrow street, moss-covered building, and red-tiled roof is a sight in itself. To get the full effect of this hilltop fortress, walk down to the Pont Pinard and follow the Armaçon river around the village to the **Pont Joly**. From here you can see above the huge granite **Tour de l'Orle d'Or,** remnant of the dismantled chateau, which in spite of walls 5 meters thick is cracked in one long slice almost from base to summit. For the opposite view of the valley, climb the tower to the top of Semur (ask the *concierge*). Along rue Buffon lie the oldest houses and the largest number of shops. Semur also has an eclectic **museum,** rue J. J. Colenot, containing important manuscripts and rooms devoted to painting, archeology, and natural history. The hours are arbitrary, so ask at the Mairie if you want to see it.

The **syndicat d'initiative,** place Gustave-Gaveau (tel. 97.05.96), is open throughout the year except in June. The **Hôtel des Gourmets,** 4, rue Varenne (tel. 97-09-41), has the cheapest rooms in town (40F), which overlook a beautiful courtyard. If you stay here, you must also eat dinner in their very fine restaurant, where you can eat an omlette for as little as 12F, or indulge in the daily regional *menu* for 45F. The **Auberge du Donjon,** next door at rue Févret, has a meagre *menu* at 27F and a reasonable one at 35F. The Semur market on Thurs. and Sat. mornings has good buys on local cheese and fruit.

A **camping** site lies 3km south of Semur on the pretty **Lac du Pont,** and is open year round. The town's large lake has a beach, and in July and August you can ski, sail, or wind-surf here (though windsurfing costs 50F an hour). The **Hôtel du Lac** (tel. 97-11-11) has rooms for 60-120F and a restaurant. Close to Semur is the lovely twelfth-century abbey at **Abbaye de Fontenay.** Semur is an easy train stop between Paris and Dijon; get off the train at Les Laumes and step onto the awaiting Semur-bound bus. Banks are closed on Sunday and Monday.

High on a granite mountain, the old city of **Avallon** sits proudly on its medieval ramparts. Like several other large towns in the Morvan, Avallon has succumbed to economic necessity and industrialized, but its encircling walls, ancient homes, and choice location above the scenic Vallée du Cousin preserve Avallon's pre-industrial charm.

Walk along the ramparts and towers, following the ruelle des Remparts, and you'll see little indication that the town has changed since the fifteenth century. The best view of the city and valley is from the opposite side of the ravine in the extensive **Parc des Chaumes.** Before you take the big climb to the park, you can pack a lunch at the huge **Maximarché** on rue des Ecoles, by the train station, or at the covered market held on Saturday mornings by place du Général de Gaulle. The **Collegiale St. Lazare** retains portions of its eleventh-century construction, most notably its two Roman portals, and architecturally, it retains continuity with the Cluny style of Roman religious architecture in Burgundy.

Camping Municipal de Sous-Roche lies 2km away; walk along route de Lourmes and then climb back to the picturesque, clean, and quiet site. **Chez Mimile,** rue des Odebert, by the Terreaux Promenade, has nice, small rooms for 35F and a 25F *menu*. On the other side of the promenade, **Family Hotel** has functional doubles for 45F. Restaurants are no great bargain here, so you may want to try any of the three well-stocked *charcuteries* along the Grand rue Aristade Briand.

At the north edge of the huge **Parc naturel du Morvan,** Avallon is a good starting point for excursions into the beautiful rivers, mountains, and lakes of this region. For information on horseback riding, canoeing, sailing, and sight-seeing, ask at the Avallon **syndicat d'initiative,** place Vauban, for the several brochures about the park. Bikes are available for rent at the train station, place de la Gare, and at Garage Renault, rte. de Paris, but be forewarned that cyclists in the Morvan must contend with narrow roads and high altitudes. Check altitude points on a map (Michelin's are good) so you won't be unpleasantly surprised. Buses from Avallon leave regularly to Vézelay, Semur, and Dijon, and trains run infrequently to Laroche to the north (connection to Paris) and Autun to the south.

Autun

Autun lies in a beautiful valley southwest of Dijon, surrounded by the rolling hills of the Morvan countryside. The setting as well as the Roman ruins and outstanding cathedral attract visitors to the city.

Autun's Roman ruins testify to the importance of *Augustodonum*, as this city was called when it was founded by Augustus around 10 B.C. The route de Chalon leads to the remains of the enormous **Roman Theater.** Do as the Romans did and picnic on the spacious ledge seats. On the way to the campsite, you pass the **Porte d'Arroux,** which offers a superb view of the **Temple of Janus.** The most impressive views, however, are those captured from the campground itself or from the town center at place du Champ de Mars.

The intricately carved capitals in the **Cathédrale St.-Lazare** are reminiscent of those at the basilica in Vezelay, which was also constructed between 1120 and 1140. The magnificent tympanum of the Last Judgement over the central portal as well as many of the capitals are the work of an Autun native, Gislebertus. In the **salle capitulaire,** you can get an eye-level view of some of the church's displaced capitals. Climb the **bell tower** to the left of the altar for a truly outstanding view, and if you want to combine aural memories with visual ones, climb the tower as the bells ring the hour.

Just down the street is the **Musée Rolin,** installed in a fifteenth-century hotel belonging to Chancellor Nicholas Rolin. Even if you don't have time to inspect the well laid-out Gallo-Roman exhibit and the mosaic seahorses, at least get a good look at Gislebertus' *Eve*. This carving captures the moment before the fall in a uniquely poignant way. (Open 9:30am-noon and 2:30-7pm, Sun. until 5pm, 4pm during the off-season; admission 5F, 2.50F with student ID.)

The helpful **Office de Tourisme,** 3, ave. Charles de Gaulle (tel. 52-20-34), locates vacant rooms and cashes foreign currency and travelers checks when the banks are closed. It also has a well-stocked supply of brochures on the city and the area. Open Sun.-Fri. 9am-noon and 2-7pm, Sat. 9am-noon; closed Sundays Oct.-June.

As usual, the least expensive accommodations are located near the train station. **Hôtel du Commerce,** 20, ave de la République (tel. 52-17-90), has top quality doubles for 45F, but noise from cars and trains may bother you during the night. Across the street at #18 is the almost identical **Hôtel de France** (tel. 52-14-00) with rooms for 46f. Two blocks west of the train station, the **Hôtel le Petit Paris**, Faubourg St.-Andoche (tel. 52-11-92), has five quiet and comfortable rooms for 36F each, but the retired owner won't take new tenants on weekends and closes the hotel altogether in August; the hotel restaurant has a 26.50F *menu*. Centrally located **Hôtel le Grand Café Jaune**, 19*bis* rue de L. de Tassigny (tel. 52-27-66), also has only five rooms, but try anyway; light, airy doubles cost 60F. The three-star campsite, **Camping Municipal du Pont d'Arroux**, 1.5km from town (tel. 52-09-35), warrants at least a two-day stay. You can swim and fish in the river, and there is a restaurant and food store open April through September.

Autun might be the place for a nice Burgundian meal, since the prices are lower and the restaurants seem less touristed than those in other towns in the region, but you should still visit the large market operating Wednesday and Friday mornings in the place du Champ de Mars. **Le Meunier**, at 3, rue Jeannin, offers gracious dining and generous portions, with a *menu* at 45F (closed Mon. and in February). The **Auberge de la Bourgogone**, at 39, Champs de Mars, is a family restaurant serving regional specialties; 35F *menu* or try their *boeuf bourguignon* for 43F. Just outside of town, behind the Porte St. Andre, is the deceptive-looking **Chalet Blue**, on rue St. Pantaleon, run by one of France's award-winning chefs; highly recommended *menus* from 35F; closed in June.

On the edge of town on ave. du 2*eme* Dragon, you will find a small lake surrounded by swimming, tennis, and riding facilities. Autun stands at the southeastern corner of the **Parc naturel du Morvan**. Twenty-four kilometers from Autun, **mont Beuvray** and **St. Leger-sous-Beuvray** offer panoramic views, but as neither buses or trains travel there from Autun, you'll have to work to earn your glimpse of the spectacular scenery. The huge **Lac de Setton**, about 40km north, has extensive camping, sailing, and skiing in a superb setting. Bike rentals for excursions into the countryside are available at the train station or at **Magasin Cardinal**, rue de Paris.

To get to Autun, there are trains from Avallon and from Chagny on the Dijon-Lyon line, but you must change at Montchanin or Etang. A half hour bus ride from the Autun train station will bring you to the TGV train at Le Creusot for a two-hour train to Paris or a 45-minute ride to Lyon. Autun also has three buses daily to and from Chalon-sur-Saône and Beaune-Dijon. To hitch, take N74 3km outside of Beaune to D973.

Young people's choirs from all over Europe come to Autun at the end of July to participate in a two-week long festival, **Musique en Morvan**. There are concerts throughout the summer taking place at the chateau of Arnay-le-Duc and at the church of Saulieu, both nearby. The office de tourisme has a complete listing.

Tournus

Situated midway between Chalon-sur-Saône and Mâcon on the Saône River, Tournus straddles the border of two very distinct Burgundian *pays* (regions)—to the east lie the flat plains of Bresse, crisscrossed by gently undulating rivers and lakes; and to the west lies the more hilly, vine-covered *Tournugeios*, dotted with hundreds of Romanesque churches. Tournus offers not only a magnificent church and monastery, but also two local museums and an array of characteristic, ramshackle houses lining the peaceful, green banks of the Saône.

inspiring buildings in Burgundy. The Romans constructed a *castrum* here, providing stores and lodgings on Agrippa's Way for the Roman legions, and early Christians founded one of the first monasteries in France here and dedicated it to St. Valérien, who was martyred in 179 A.D. when he came to preach on the hill which became Tournus. The second monastery was founded as a place of refuge by the monks of Noirmoutier, who had fled the Norman invasion. The narthex and nave, finished in the early eleventh century, are among the earliest examples of the emerging Romanesque style. Miraculously, the Abbey at Tournus survived troubles with the lordship of Burgundian dukes, the sixteenth-century wars of religion.

Practical Information

For extensive touring, you'll need a car. Rentals are available in Chalon-sur-Saône or in Tournus at Garage Renault on RN6 (tel. 51-07-05). To hitch north or south, RN6 runs right through Tournus. The road headed towards Cluny (D56) is lightly traveled and thus offers few prospects for hitchhikers.

Office de Tourisme: place Carnot (tel. 51-13-10). Their brochure includes excellent information on the surrounding area. Open March 15-Oct. 31 only, daily 9am-noon and 2-6pm. Makes change on Sun. and Mon. and will help you find accommodations.

Post Office: rue du Puits des Sept Fontaines (tel. 51-15-16).

Train Station: ave. Gambetta (tel. 51-07-30). Tournus makes an easy day-trip from Beaune, Chalon, or Mâcon.

Bus Station: Buses leave to Chalon and Mâcon from quai de Verdun and from the train station. Information and schedules at Café du Centre, 6, quai de Verdun (tel. 51-09-69).

Accommodations and Food

La Petite Auberge, 48, place Lacretelle (tel. 51-06-85). Singles 40F, doubles 50F. Small, somewhat squeezed—you have to walk through the kitchen and family living quarters to climb up to your room. Restaurant-grill downstairs serves omelettes and *steak frites* at reasonable prices. 35F *menu*.

Hotel de la Madeleine, rue Désiré-Mathivet (tel. 51-05-83). 50F a room, 70F with shower. Rooms in back offer a narrow passageway view onto the quai and Saône River. Reservations recommended for July and August.

Camping: Le Pas Fleury (tel. 51-16-58). Follow ave. Général-Leclerc or ave. du 23 janvier out of town to the N6 (direction—Lyon) and turn left. The campground is at the river's edge behind the track field.

For a light meal, **Crêpàtout** at 2, rue Jean-Jaurès offers crêpe menus for either 16F or 25F (closed Fri.); the **Restaurant L'Abbaye** at 12, rue Léon-Godin serves an excellent selection of Bourguignon specialties and a four-course menu 41F (closed Thurs., open evenings only). Restaurant Gras, 2, rue Fenelon, serves Bresse specialties and a 34F menu.

Sights

The **Abbatiale St.-Philibert** is notable for the austerity of its monumental facade, and for its huge, unadorned columns. The narthex is the oldest surviving part of the structure (early tenth century), while the transversal barrel vaults of the nave are particular to Tournus and quite different from more standard Romanesque patterns. The transept and chancel are of a later Burgundian style. As you come out of the church, take the stairs to your left up to the second story of the narthex **(Chapelle Supérieure St.-Michel)** which was used for defensive purposes as well as for accommodating pilgrims. Turn left as you come down the stairs to find the cellar, study room, and capitulary hall of the monks. Returning to the street, you will find the refectory next door and the **Eglise St.-Valérien** further on (both now used as exhibition spaces). On the other side of the cloister, behind the abbatiale on rue A. Thibaudet, you'll find the excellent **Musée Bourguignon,** Perrin de Puycousin (open April-Oct. daily except Tues. 9am-noon, 2-6pm; 3F, students 2F), where you'll be guided rather quickly through rooms furnished in the style of the eighteenth-century Bourguignon period and containing furniture, period costumes, utensils, textiles, ironwork, and old prints of the principal architectural sights in the region. The **Musée Greuze** is interesting mainly for its Romanesque sculptured capitals recovered from the Tournus region. It is located on rue du Collège (open April 1-Nov. 1, 9:30am-noon and 2-6pm, closed Tues.; admission 4F, 3F students). Take time to walk to the Saône—cross the bridge and you'll be in the countryside—or else walk along the quai and enjoy its eccentric eighteenth-century facades.

Cluny

Although Cluny was an influential spiritual center during the Middle Ages, only the ruins of the glorious and ancient Abbey remain as a reminder of Cluny's former beauty. Between 1798 and 1823, the Abbey church was systematically dismantled by a mason tradesman who used the stone to build many of Cluny's present-day houses. Today, the only thing left to see is the south part of the transept, but it will give you an idea of the majestic dimensions of the original building. A small Burgundian village with very narrow, winding streets, Cluny is a refreshing change from the larger cities. To get to Cluny, take the train to Chalon-sur-Saône or to Mâcon, and then take the SNCF bus (free with railpass) through the beautiful beaujolais countryside. The road wanders past farms, forests, and gentle valleys on its way to the serene little town that spawned an architectural tidal wave.

Practical Information

Syndicat d'Initiative, 6, rue Mercière (tel. 59-05-34), changes money when banks are closed and will help you find accommodations or map out bicycle trips and other excursions. Open daily in summer 10am-noon and 1:30-7pm.

Post Office: rue de la Post, by the syndicat. Open Mon.-Fri. 8am-7pm.

SNCF Buses: leave several times a day to Mâcon and Chalon from the Pont de la Levée on D980. Ask for a schedule at the syndicat.

Police: on rte. de Mâcon (tel. 59-07-32).

Telephone Code: (89).

Accommodations and Food

Centre de Rencontre, 13, place Champ Foire, in an old house surrounded by fruit trees, this inexpensive and comfortable hostel is owned by an inveterate traveler who is often out of town. It's worth asking at the syndicat to see if the center is open. Bring a warm sleeping bag. Kitchen and hot showers available.

Hôtel du Commerce, 8, place du Commerce (tel. 59-03-09), is well-located and comfortable, with rooms from 40-65F.

Hôtel du Cheval Blanc (tel. 59-01-13) and **Hôtel Les Marroniers** (tel. 59-07-95) on rue de la Gare have small but basic rooms for 45F.

Camping Municipal de St. Vital, is a three-star site 500 meters from town on rue des Griottons, open June-Sept. Adjacent is a very nice swimming pool (open July and August) and a horse-riding center (40F an hour) open year-round.

The town market is only open Saturday mornings, place du Marché, but there is a large **Intermarché** supermarket just above town on D152. **Patisserie au Success,** 38, place du Commerce, is a family tea salon offering every kind of bonbon, brioche, and ice cream imaginable at reasonable prices. The **Restaurant le Nord-Est,** next to the Abbey, has a popular cafe and a good 30F *menu* upstairs.

Sights

Headquarters of the Benedictine order with its two thousand dependent abbeys, Cluny became the immensely wealthy intellectual capital of Europe during the height of its power in the twelfth century. When the abbey was brought under the dominion of the King of France in the fifteenth century, its power began to erode with the ensuing decadence and religious wars. With opulence also came the relaxation of monastic discipline. It was comfortable and serenely thriving Cluny which incited the twelfth-century mystic Bernard of Clairvaux to found a more austere counter-movement, the Cistercian order.

The carved capitals survived a fall of thirty meters when the columns they rested on were mined; today these splendid works are exhibited in the vaulted thirteenth-century refectory. The forty-minute obligatory tour of the great church's remains (open daily 9-11:30am and 2-6pm; 7F, 4F with student ID) can be confusing and uninspiring. To grasp the extent of the Abbey's grandeur and influence, go first to the **Musée Ochier,** housed in the fifteenth-century Palais Jean de Bourbon, and containing artifacts and detailed historical explanations. Open daily 9:30am-noon, and 2-6:30pm; admission 2F. You can get a magnificent overview of the Abbey and the valley by climbing the **Tour des Fromages,** which is open 9:30am-noon and 2-6:45pm; enter through the syndicat d'initiative, 2F. Try to see the humble twelfth-century **Church of St. Marcel** (its steeple was added in the sixteenth century) and also the **Church of Notre-Dame,** built in pure thirteenth-century Burgundian style. After all the sightseeing, you can stop off for a free glass of Beaujolais at the *caves* in the ancient tower **Barabans,** off the place de l'Abbaye on rue K-J Conant (open only in July and August). Walk off your wine on rue de la République, which is lined with Cluny's oldest houses, many dating from the twelfth century.

South of Cluny is the magnificently situated castle **Berzé-le-Châtel,** overlooking the abrupt slopes and crags of the Bois Clair Pass. A few kilometers down the road (N79) is **Berzé-le-Ville** with its **Monks' Chapel** and notable twelfth century frescoes. (Open Easter-Nov., daily 9:30-noon and 2-6pm; closed Tues. afternoons and Sun. morning.) Twelve kilometers south of Cluny on D22 is the **château St. Point,** home of the poet Lamartine, which houses a small museum. Nearby **Lac St. Point-Lamartine** has sailboat rentals and year-round camping.

Lyon

Lyon has been unjustly maligned by tourists who pause here merely to change trains on their way south. Lyon is worth a visit; the frightful industrial sections visible from the highway are more than offset by the charming vieille ville, striking views, and gourmet food. The motorway which now carries travelers through at an alarming rate was preceded by a Gallic chariot road that the Romans rebuilt when they developed the site as a trade center. Roman legions and later Crusaders marched along the two ancient roads flanking the Rhône. The rivers are still very important to the economy of the city and region for the transport of materials and finished goods.

Practical Information

La Saône and **Le Rhône** cleave Lyon into three parts. The train station and **place Bellecoeur** are centrally located on the tongue of land between the rivers. The Renaissance quarter unfolds on the right bank of the Sâone. The University and the ultra-modern **Part-Dieu** occupy the grid of streets on the left bank on the Rhône. Part-Dieu houses the largest shopping mall in Europe, and is the gleaming commercial center of Lyon's multinationals.

Like Paris, Lyon is divided into *arrondissements*. Unfortunately for the short-term guest, there is no apparent method to the madness. Between the Saône and the Rhône are the 2*ème*, 1*er*, and 4*ème* arrondissements. The 5*ème*, 8*ème*, and 9*ème* are up in the hills on the right bank of the Saône, while the 7*ème*, and 3*ème*, 6*ème*, all lie on the left bank of the Rhône.

The orange *Plan Guide Blay* is expensive (18F), but it will greatly facilitate sightseeing and Métro use. The new Métro is open 5am-midnight, with connections every three to ten minutes. Tickets cost 14.50F to 21F for a *carnet* of six. Distances, however, are not vast between major sights. The funicular prices are a rip-off; a brief, no-view ride from place St.-Jean to the Théâtres Romains or the Basilica costs 4.50F (running every ten minutes, until 8pm). In July and August, guided tours cover different parts of Lyon and finish with a *dégustation* (tasting) of Beaujolais in the *vieille ville* (2:30pm and 8:30pm every day from the Office de Tourisme, Bellecour, 18-50F). Headphones and maps are also available for self-guided tours, 30F includes use of railway and funicular.

Office de Tourisme: place Bellecour, behind the flower market (tel. 842-25-75). Contains an accommodations service. Also provides a free map of the city and an accommodations list. Open 9am-7pm in summer, 9am-12:30pm and 2-6pm in winter. Another office at the train station has a money exchange, cours de Verdun (tel. 842-22-07), and another in Villeurbanne, 25, cours E. Zola (tel. 889-64-42).

Centre Regional d'Information pour Jeunes, 9, quai des Celestius (tel. 837-15-28). A youth bureau which posts lists of study programs and university restaurants.

Student Train Tickets: Agence Wasteels, 40, cours de Verdun, 2*ème*, (tel. 837-01-79) and at the train station.

Post Office: place Antonin-Poncet, opposite place Bellecour. Open all day and night for telephone calls and telegrams. Regular post service and Poste Restante weekdays 8am-7pm, weekends 8am-noon.

American Express: 6, rue Childbert, 2*ème* (tel. 837-40-69). Mail service; shorter lines than you'd expect for a large city. Open Mon.-Fri. 9am-noon and 2-7pm.

Train Station: In Perrache (SNCF information tel. 892-10-50). This sleek conglomeration of stores, bars, restaurants, and agencies also has an *accueil*, offering information and possible dormitory lodgings if you're stranded. Open daily 7am-midnight, open 24 hours in summer. There is a branch of the office de tourisme and a bus station downstairs (bus information tel. 842-27-39).

Laundromat: 19, rue Ste. Hélène, 2*ème*.

English Book Store: Librairie Lavandier, 5, rue Victor Hugo, has a large assortment of English books.

Hitching: For Paris, the autoroute approaches are difficult to hitch on; take a bus (#2, 5, 19, 21, 22, or 31) out and stand past the Pont Monton at the intersection with the N6. For Grenoble, take bus #39 as far as the rotary at blvd. Pinel. Sad to say, but we have heard tales of three-day waits for rides out of Lyon. So if you've been breathing fumes a few hours already, give up and take a train (or try asking for rides as people stop for gas at the first gas station outside of town).

Airport: Aeroport Lyon-Satolas (tel. 871-92-21), 27km from Lyon. 25F bus ride from train station every twenty minutes from 5am-9pm.

Police: place A. Poucet (tel. 892-49-91). **Medical Emergency:** Hôpital Edouard Herriot (tel. 853-81-11).

All-Night Pharmacy: 55, rue Auguste-Comte (tel. 837-07-04). Near station and pedestrian zone.

U.S. Consulate: 7, quai Général-Sarrail, 6ème (tel. 824-68-49). Open Mon.-Fri. 9-11am and 2-4pm.

Telephone Code: (7).

Accommodations

The office de tourisme will find you a room for a 5F fee. Information is also available from the *accueil* bureau in the station. For longer stays during the summer, contact **CROUS**, 59, rue de la Madeleine, 69365 Lyon (tel. 872-55-47) for information on lodgings in student dormitories *(cités universitaires),* as well as details on lodgings with families. The best quarters in which to look for hotels yourself are Perrache and Bellecour.

Auberge de Jeunesse (IYHF), 51, rue Roger-Salengro, Vénissieux (tel. 876-39-23) is a modern hostel by a superhighway and a supermarket, 4km from the station. Take bus #23 or #35. 22.50F per night, breakfast 7F.

Centre International de Séjour, 46, rue du Commandant-Pegoud (tel. 874-18-94 or 876-14-22). This youth *foyer* has 75 beds in singles (70F), doubles or triples (50F), and quads (38F), breakfast included. Meals available for 30F.

Résidence Benjamin-Delessert, 145, ave. Jean Jaurès (tel. 872-86-77). Open all year, this *foyer* has 350 singles at 30F per night, less for longer stays. Breakfast extra.

Hôtel Alexandra, 49, rue Victor-Hugo, 2ème (tel. 837-75-79), on the pedestrian zone by place Ampère between the train station and place Bellecour. One of the many hotels near Perrache with clean rooms and a friendly proprietress. Stair-wells are dingy and no breakfast is served. Try to get a room on the courtyard side for quiet. Singles from 40F; doubles from 80F. Multiple accommodations in some doubles. Showers in almost all rooms, otherwise, 10F. Parking garage in hotel. Reservations advisable all year.

Hôtel du Théâtre, 10, rue de Savoie, 2ème (tel. 837-67-36). 18 rooms; singles from 35F, doubles from 40F. Breakfast 11F.

Hôtel St.-Vincent, 9, rue Pareille, 1er (tel. 826-67-97). Has color TV and currency exchange bureau. 31 rooms; singles 30F, doubles from 35F. Breakfast 9.50F.

Camping: Porte de Lyon, 69570 Dardilly (tel. 832-27-05) is a huge four-star site on the N6, 10km outside town. There is nothing closer. By car, take the motorway north toward Limonest Porte de Lyon. Take bus #44 toward place St.-Paul, change to bus Planche (direction Villefranche), and get off at Maison Carrée. A 1km walk.

Food

Lyon is renowned not only for its *haute cuisine,* bus also for its *grands cuisiniers* (great chefs). Some of France's best cooking schools are based in this gastronomic capital of the nation. The traditional Lyonnaise restaurant is known as a *bouchon.* A great range of restaurants, with *menus* from 40F and up, can be found in charming Vieux Lyon. **Rue Marroniers,** centrally located near the place Bellecour, is saturated with restaurants, many of which offer very reasonable menus. Three large open markets are held every morning at the Quai St.-Antoine (on the Saône), quai V. Augagneur (on the Rhone) and on blvd. de la Croix Rousse. Culinary specialties include *quenelles* (fish balls), *salade fonds artichaut* (salad made with artichoke hearts), *foie gras* (goose-liver paté with truffles), and the delicious local beaujolais wines.

Le Petit Placard, 36, rue de l'Arbre Sec, 1*ère,* off the rue de al Republic. A very fine family-run restaurant with a generous 26F *menu.* For desert, try their *clajoute aux cerises.* Closed Sat. and Sun.

Titi Lyonnais, 2, rue Chaponnay, 3*ème,* on the left bank of the Rhone by Pont Wilson. Popular with locals, serving Lyonnaise cuisine and a 38F *menu.* Closed Mon. evening and Tues.

Opéra Bouffe, 4, rue Bodin; from place Croix Rousse follow rue Montée St.-Sebastian 2 blocks. Run cooperatively, this lively place has *plats du jour* at 16F and live music every Thurs. evening. Closed Sat. and Sun noon.

Le 21, quai Romain Rolland. A genuine *bouchon lyonnais.* Walk through the bar and kitchen to reach the restaurant. Plan on spending 50F.

A La Clef de St.-George, place St.-George, a cooperative endeavor, half French and half Californian. A vegetarian *menu* for 26F, music on Sun. nights at 8:30.

La Queue de Cochon (the Pig's Tail), 1, rue Mulet, 1*ère,* off rue de la Republique. A 42F *menu;* try the *Cochonaille Chaud* (plate of regional pork specialties). Closed Mon. and in June.

Sights

Start at the place Bellecoeur, where shops and flower stalls cling to the edges of the spacious square, and are dominated by an equestrian statue of Louis XIV in the center. The office de tourisme, the major cafe district, and the post office are all nearby. Radiating from the square, the **rue Victor-Hugo** contains bookshops and clothing stores, and the **rue de la République,** stretching north to the place de la Comédie, has several cinemas.

A brief walk across the Saône leads to the most intriguing part of town, **Vieux Lyon,** a showcase of Renaissance architecture along ancient, dark cobblestone streets. The area consists of the St.-Paul, St.-Georges, and St.-Jean quarters. Note the mullioned windows and the many curious details, such as the smirking gargoyle at 11, place Neuve St.-Jean, and the spiral staircase at 32, rue Doyenne. The atmosphere that surrounds these doorways is as Gothic as the ogival arches. Many of the hallways in the buildings lead to passages *(traboules)* which connect the buildings. These were used by members of the Resistance during World War II. This is not a place to meander after dark. Instead, come by day armed with the brochure which takes you on a walking tour, available at the office de tourisme.

From the **Fourvière esplanade** above Vieux Lyon you can gaze down on the urban sprawl. On the summit of the hill rises the extravagant nineteenth-century **Basilique de Fourvière,** as over-stuffed as the confections in the *patis-*

series below (open daily till 7pm). On the descent you will pass the remains of a Roman theater and the **Musée Gallo-Romain** (open Wed.-Sun. 9:30am-noon and 2-6pm, admission free with student ID). The rest of the descent to the river is steep and picturesque.

A particularly interesting church in the St.-Paul quarter is the **Cathédrale St.-Jean**, in the Bourguignon style. It is noted for its strongly articulated nave and flamboyant rose window. Don't miss the fourteenth-century *horloge* (clock) in the north transept. Best seen from across the river, the Cathedral rises up amid red tiles and gray stone, oblivious to the passing barges.

There are twenty-six museums in Lyon, so pick up a list at the syndicat and let your interests be your guide. The **Musée des Beaux Arts** in the Palais St.-Pierre houses a large and very exciting collection of paintings and sculpture. If pressed for time, go straight up to the galleries on the second floor. The collection includes Spanish and Dutch masters (El Greco, Zurbáran, Rembrandt, and Ruysdael); two good Impressionist rooms (Manet, Monet, Morisot, Sisley, Renoir, Degas, Van Gogh), and several rooms of excellent early twentieth-century canvases (Picasso, Matisse, Dufy, and more). The sculpture and Oriental art downstairs is certainly worth your time as well. Open daily 10am-noon and 2-6pm, closed Tuesday; admission free.

For an extraordinary collection of silk and embroidery ranging from Coptic to Oriental, visit the **Musée Historique des Tissues,** 34, rue de la Charité. The museum also exhibits Louis XI's original order to bring the silk trade to Lyon. Open daily 10am-noon and 2-6pm, closed Monday; admission 5F. The **Musée Lyonnais des Arts Decoratifs,** down the street, has reassembled salons of porcelain, silver, and tapestry to illustrate the styles of various periods in the history of French furniture (same hours as the Musée Historique). **La Maison des Canuts,** 10-12, rue d'Ivry (tel. 828-62-04), demonstrates the actual weaving techniques of the *Canuts Lyonnais,* best known for their velvet and silk workmanship. Open daily except Sunday 8:30am-noon and 2:30-6:30pm; admission 1F. The **Musée des Marionettes,** Hôtel Gadagne, exhibits the famous Lyon puppets as well as an international collection. When urban fatigue sets in, leave the city noises behind for awhile in the rose gardens of the **Parc de la Tête d'Or,** Lyon's botanical garden. Open daily 6am-11pm in summer, 8am-8pm in winter.

Entertainment

Lyon hosts a variety of resident theaters as well as an opera company, but the highlight of all its cultural activities comes in June with the **Festival International de Lyon.** In 1981, this cultural smorgasbord offered drama (Racine, Euripides, and the works of young unknowns), music (the Leningrad Philharmonic, opera, and jazz), cinema, and dance. An award is given annually for the best new play written in French. For information, write in care of the Hôtel de Ville, 6968 Lyon (tel. 827-71-31), or get the schedule from the tourist office. The first weekend of September, you can see big puppet parades and little puppet theaters at the **Festival des Marionettes de Lyon** at Le Part Dieu (call the Petit Theatre (tel. 62-90-13) for information).

At the **Cafe-Théâtre de la Graine,** place St.-Paul, you can sip your coffee while the waiters and waitresses enact plays, many of their own creation. The place is popular among students, and shows start around 9pm.

Each December 8th, the Lyon windows light up with candles in the evening, and the streets fill up with parades and carousers for the **Fête de la Vierge.** The **Festival Hector Berlioz** is just that—a week of his music, performed and discussed. For information, contact Auditorium Maurice-Ravel, 149, rue Garibaldi, 69003 Lyon (tel. 860-85-40).

Franche-Comté

Franche-Comté ascends like an enormous stairway from the plains of central France into the mountains of Switzerland. Also known as the Jura, this is an area of steep mountains, clear lakes, and magnificent waterfalls. **Besançon,** nestled in a valley of the Doubs river, is the region's major city. It is a university town, a watch-making center, and a gateway to the half-French, half-Swiss Jura mountain range. **Belfort,** an industrial city on the border of Alsace, . is a good base for visiting the famous modern chapel designed by Le Corbusier in **Ronchamp.** West of Belfort lies **Vesoul,** a historic battleground with many fortresses, and museums. **Ornans,** to the south, has a splendid Courbet Museum, and **Arbois,** the regional capital, offers samples in its splendid wine *caves.* Near the peaceful community of **Lons-le-Saunier** are the grottoes of **Baume-les-Messieurs,** huge caves of petrified rock, and the **Cascades du Hérisson,** where water falls in beaded curtains over weirdly beautiful rock formations. Jura abounds in natural wonders, and most areas are easily accessible to train or bus from Besançon.

Besançon

Besançon is a striking city, a pleasant surprise hidden in the mountainous terrain of the Jura. Spilling over the hills, in and around a horseshoe bend in the River Doubs, Besançon is a city of water, flowers and above all—far above all—it is the city of the **Citadelle,** a fortress which has dominated the area from a high crag since Roman times.

Today, the Citadelle houses a wealth of different city museums. Most of Besançon's sights are located in the old town, within the bend in the river, while the rest of the city extends in all directions over the hills of the opposite bank. There is a good bus system to help you navigate the sprawl. It costs 3.80F to go anywhere on the route, and the tickets are good for an hour after you punch them on the bus. Buy them from the conductor, or at a reduced price in *carnets* from a tabac. Buses stop running at midnight. The train station is located above the valley, so you'll probably want to take the mini-bus (3.80F) to the center of town. The annual **Festival International de Musique** occurs in the first two weeks of September, and the **International Film Festival** occurs in October. In 1982, the **Nouveau Théâtre de Besançon** launched its inaugural at the Centre Dramatique National de Franch-Comté, a company which promises to be innovative and demanding.

Practical Information

Bureau de Tourisme: place Armée-Française (tel. 80-92-55). Walk down the hill from the Train Station on ave. Maréchal-Foch, then follow ave. d'Helvetie to the Pont de la République. The friendly office, on the banks of the Doubs in a beautiful glass building, provides helpful information on regional excursions and good accommodations service. Closed daily from noon-2pm, and Sun.

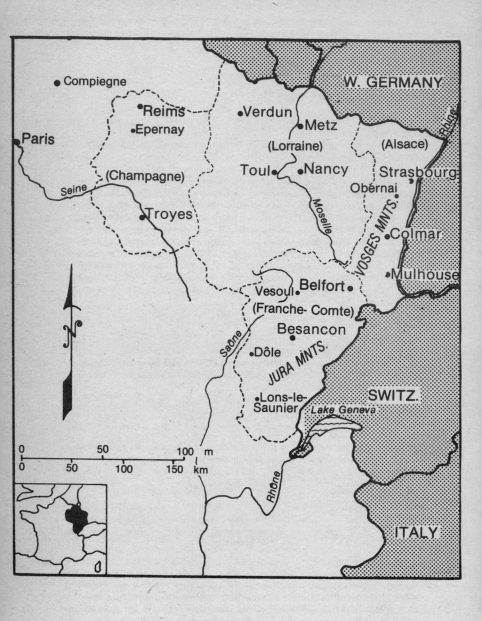

Post Office: rue de la République. Open Mon.-Fri. 8am-7pm, Sat. 8am-noon. This is not the main post office in Besançon. If you want *poste restante* delivered here, address it Poste Restante, Rue Proudhon, 25000 Besancon. (The main office is way out in the new town and hard to reach.)

Train Station: ave de la Paix. For information (tel. 53-50-50).

Police: (tel. 17); **Medical Emergency and Ambulance:** (tel. 81-13-12).

Telephone Code: (81).

Accommodations

Hotels in Besançon are generally expensive, but the CROUS service for University residences is good.

CROUS, Service d'Accueil d'Etudiants Etrangers, 36, rue Megevand (tel. 82 23 79). From July through September, rooms available at the **Cité Universitaire** 30F per night, meals available for 12.20F, Breakfast 6F. Come to the office Mon.-Fri., 9-11:30am, 1:30-6pm. They will give you a map of the Cité and instructions. Or take Bus #7 to the Université stop and head for Building F5 (ask a student— it's not far) where you pay and get a room at the *secrétariat*. After 5pm, you can go directly to the residence, building A-B; get a room from the attendant in the lobby and settle the next day at the *secrétariat* (the general telephone number for the residence buildings is 50-26-88. Use this if you are trying to call someone staying at the Cité.) The CROUS offices can also arrange longer stays in university housing.

Foyer International, 19, rue Martin du Gard (tel. 50-07-54). Closed in summer 1981; call for information and prices. Take bus #7. (30F in 4-6 bed room, 35F in two bed, 50F in single). Near the University. Often closed, so call first.

Foyer des Jeunes Filles, 18, rue de la Casotte (tel. 80-90-01) Women only. Single room 22F, in 2 bed room 18F, 3-4 bedroom 15F. (8F for sheets and a hostel arrangement) Breakfast 5F, meals about 20F.

Hôtel de Lorraine, 5, ave. Maréchal-Foch (tel. 80-13-44). Across the street from the Train Station; a serviceable one-star spot, a 15-minute walk from the center of the old town. Singles 48F, doubles 70F. Breakfast 12F, 6F shower.

Hôtel Paris, 33, rue des Granges (tel. 83-36-56). A bit luxurious and in a central location. Singles at 45F, doubles start at 67F. Breakfast 12F, showers.

Hôtel Family, 13, rue Le Courbe (tel. 81-33-92). Probably the only hotel in the old town that still charges 43F for a single, 53F for a double. Breakfast 11F, showers 5F. Large, clean rooms and friendly management.

Food

The **rue des Boucheries** offers a good selection of restaurants. Try the **Pub de L'Etoile**, Place de la Revolution, which is usually full of young *bisontins* (the name by which natives are fondly labelled). On Wednesday, Friday, and Saturday, visit the **outdoor market** in Place de la Revolution, and sample *Comté*, a cheese resembling *gruyère* (try the sweet variety). Wash it down with *Arbois* or *Jaune* (or both), two wines which taste like sherry. (**Nicolas** in the *place* has a fine selection). For a picnic, buy some *jambon de Haut Doubs* (smoked ham) in one of the *charcuteries* that line rue des Granges.

Le Ronchaux, 29, rue Ronchaux. A place of dark wood and red tablecloths, where 33F will give you a great meal, including such French concoctions as *pampiettes* *de veau.* Closed Mon. Directly across the street from *Le Ronchaux* is *L'Auberge,* 1, rue Chifflet. They have *menus* at 35 and 46F and 12-17F salads and 10-15F omelettes.

Le Tonneau de Jura, 20, rue Charles-Nodier. A real local's local place. Open for lunch only (the bar is open in the evening). Enjoy the hearty 30F *menu.* Here a small carafe of wine costs 2.50F.

Le Grand Café du Commerce, 31, rue des Granges. With its fine 1860 decor, considered the most beautiful cafe in Besancon. A literary and historical monument, Stendhal's Julien Sorel in *Le Rouge et le Noir* spent time here. Don't be fooled by the polished plastic exterior; the fine interior has been preserved.

Sights

The **Citadelle,** built by Vauban on the site of an ancient Gallo-Roman acropolis, rises from sheer rock over the green mountains and the winding Doubs. Open 9am-6:30pm daily during the summer and 9am-5:30pm in the winter; admission, a high 10F. Climb to the top of the walls for a magnificent view of the old town. The buildings within house a variety of museums (all closed Tues.): **the Museum of the Deportation and Resistance** presents a painfully detailed documentation of the French Resistance movement and the Vichy government. The **Musée Folklorique Comtois** displays the arts and crafts native to the region. At the base of the citadel stands the **Cathédrale St.-Jean,** a strange, double-asped building with no main facade and with an amazing clock of 30,000 parts: at noon every day a puppet Christ leaps from his tomb as figures ring bells and Mary turns toward Faith and Charity. (Presentation at ten minutes before the hour; admission 4F, 2F for those under 25 years.)

Pass through the **Port Noire,** the remains of a second-century Roman triumphal arch, to the elegant Renaissance **Palais Granvelle,** built for the chancellor of the Emperor Charles V when Spain ruled these parts. The courtyard is the site of summer concerts. The Palas Grainvelle now houses museum of Besançon's history, at 96, Grande Rue. Open daily 9-12am, 2-6pm, closed Tues; admission 5F for adults, students and children free. Besançon's principle attraction, the **Musée des Beaux Arts,** displays one of the finest collections of paintings in France, with major works of painters including Bellini, Matisse, Courbet, Renoir, and Picasso. It also contains artifacts from Besançon. Open daily except Tues., 9am-noon and 2-6pm. Admission 6F, free with student ID and on Sun.

Near Besançon

Besançon is the ideal base from which to make forays into the **Jura.** The syndicat is well stocked and helpful, and most of the inter-urban buses stop here. Train service will not necessarily get you where you want to go in the Jura, so even railpass holders may have to ride buses, hitch, or cycle.

Once you are out, the variety of attractions is stunning. There are dozens of grottoes and underground rivers to explore on your own, or you can take part in some of the organized activities such as the guided walks in the National forests of **Poligny** and **Pontarlier** or the kayaking courses on the Doubs. These are available to the neophyte as well as the expert; for information contact Roland Dodane Les Hautes Vues, rue du Stade 25130 Villers-le-Lac (tel. (81) 67-19-23).

At the syndicat, pick up a guide to the **route de Belvederes,** and follow one of the paths towards the picturesque towns, mountains, and valleys typical of Franche Comté.

Alsace/Lorraine

Alsace and Lorraine have served France and Germany as political pawns since the third and fourth centuries, when barbarian tribes first swept westward into these regions. They have been invaded repeatedly ever since, more recently during the Franco-Prussian War of 1870-71 and during both World Wars. Although Alsace and Lorraine have endured over a millenium of shifting political fortune together, they remain separate in many fundamental ways. Alsace presents a fascinating hybrid of French and German characteristics, while Lorraine has a less colorful personality, dominated by industrial sites and battlefields.

You'll have no trouble identifying the German influence in **Alsace.** It's reflected everywhere, in the half-timbered Bavarian architecture, in the cuisine, where sauerkraut and sausage accompany French bread, and in the language, where they swear bilingually. Bounded by Germany in the northeast and Switzerland to the south, Alsace suffers a geographic vulnerability responsible for much of its historic identity crisis. Although it spent half of the last century under German rule, parts of Alsace today are strongly nationalistic and patriotically French.

The hillsides of Alsace are crowned with ruined castles, testaments of feudal fiefdoms and foreign counts. Most spectacular is the reconstructed **Chateau du Haut-Koenigsbourg,** the former seat of the Hohenstaufens which was restored by Emperor Wilhelm II. The **route du Vin,** a string of vineyards and picturesque wine-producing villages, runs along the eastern slopes of the Vosges for about 140km from Marleheim to Thann. The low mountains of the **Vosges**— where wooded hills slope down to sunlit valleys and deep, blue lakes— encourage hiking, camping, and cross-country skiing in an unspoiled setting. Hundreds of miles of trails with overnight refuges (or *fermes auberges*) along the way have been marked out; maps and guides are available from **Club Vosgien,** 4, rue de la Douane, Strasbourg (tel. 32-57-96), or at the tourist offices.

The international city of **Strasbourg** is the administrative and cultural center of Alsace, as well as the seat of the Council of Europe. **Colmar,** a tourist center and site of an annual summer wine fair, has a lovely quarter, La Petite Venise, and the Unterlinden Museum. Near **Belfort** (an industrial city), in **Ronchamp** is Le Corbusier's **Notre-Dame-du-Haut,** a stunning modern chapel set on a mountain crest.

The province of **Lorraine** lies to the west of Alsace and derives its name from the Frankish Emperor Lothair. In 843 A.D., the Treaty of Verdun divided the mighty Carolingian Empire into three kingdoms among Charlemagne's grandsons, and the boundaries still have some political validity today. Charles the Bald received an area roughly corresponding to modern France, Louis the German got Germany, and Lothair was granted a "middle kingdom," including Lotharingia, or Lorraine. Annexed to France in 1766 with the death of Stanislas, its last duke, status of the duchy once again became uncertain during the Franco-Prussian War a century later.

Lorraine is the country of Joan of Arc, France's patron saint, born in **Domrémy** in 1412. A tower is all that remains of the church in which she was baptized. In Domrémy you can see the garden where she heard voices for the first time and visit the **chateau de Baudricourt** (now in ruins) where she worshipped.

Yet despite such a rich history, Lorraine today is home to little besides heavy industry and war memorials. **Nancy,** the capital of the former duchy of

Lorraine, offers very little to the visitor, save the magnificent place Stanislas. To the east of Nancy is **Lunéville,** with a decayed chateau built by Duke Leopold of Lorraine to resemble Versailles on a smaller scale. Its grounds were planned by Stanislas, along with the groves of the **parc des Bosquet.** Lorraine is the home of several specialties, the most illustrious of which is *Quiche Lorraine.* The food here is hearty; the bread is heavier than most and potatoes are served with almost every dish. Try the *Potée Lorraine,* a thick vegetable stew.

Strasbourg

Strasbourg is a stately city located right on the German border, with wide boulevards and narrow medieval streets, spacious squares, and covered bridges. The German presence in Strasbourg, from 1870 to 1918 and from 1940 to 1944, did not defeat the natives' intensely patriotic spirit. The French national anthem, the *Marseillaise,* was composed here in 1772 by Rouget de Lisle in an inspired mood after a dinner party. The song was called the *Chant de Guerre de l'Armée du Rhin* until some Provençal southerners, singing it while storming the Bastille in 1789, gave it its simpler name. Strasbourg is now the seat of the nineteen-nation Council of Europe. Serving also as Rhine port, a large university town, and a cultural center, the city handles its duties with grace and a certain Franco-German charm. Border crossings are fairly hassle-free, making a day-trip to Germany a convenient possibility.

Practical Information

Strasbourg has no less than three *offices de tourisme,* but there is one located across the street from the station. All three sell small, clear maps of the city for 2F, which are well worth picking up. The old city is virtually an island in the center of Strasbourg, bounded on all sides by a large canal. From the station go straight on the rue du Marie-Kuss and over the bridge to the Grand'-rue which leads directly to the city's three main squares. Use the large, ornate Cathedral as your landmark and you won't get lost in the old city.

To hitch to Paris, take bus #2, 12, or 22 to route des Romains: for Colmar, try bus #3, 13, or 23 to blvd. de Lyon, and then follow the signs for Colmar to the ramp of the highway. Or, try **Allostop** (see listing below).

A network of bus lines makes up the city transportation system. A ticket for 3.90F allows unlimited changes in one direction of travel for up to one hour (tickets can be bought on the bus or in discount *carnets* at banks or *tabacs* with the sign CTS).

Offices de Tourisme: Directly opposite the station (tel. 32-51-49): main office 10, place Gutenberg (tel. 32-57-07); and at the German border, Pont de l'Europe (tel. 61-39-23). Runs its own tours. Accommodations service 5F (plus a 20F deposit on the room). Central office open daily 8:30am-7:30pm in summer; in winter, week-days 9am-noon and 2-6pm, Sat. 9am-noon, closed Sun.

CROUS: 1, quai du Marie-Dietrich, 67084 Strasbourg (tel. 36-16-91). Lodgings placement service and student travel office selling Transalpino reduced train tick-ets. Open Mon.-Fri. 9-11:45am and 2-4pm. The **Center d'Information Jeunesse Alsace** (youth information Office), 7 Rue des Ecrivains, (tel. 37-33-33) has informa-tion on sporadic trips to surrounding areas.

Post Office: Main office at 5, ave. de la Marseillaise. Open weekdays 8am-7pm, Sat. 8am-noon.

Train Information: place de la Gare (tel. 22-50-50).

Allostop: 5, rue du Général Zimmer (tel. 37-13-13). Near the University off blvd. de la Victoire. Pre-arranged rides to a variety of cities for a small fee. You can also pick up a Youth Hostel card here. Open Mon.-Wed. 2-6pm; Thurs., Fri., 10am-noon.

Police: 11, rue de la Nuée-Bleue (tel. 32-99-08), or place de la République (tel. 32-99-00); **Red Cross:** (tel. 61-05-23).

Medical Emergency: tel. 18 or 36-09-93.

U.S. Consulate: 15, ave. d'Alsace, next to the John F. Kennedy Bridge. Open 9:30am-noon and 2-5pm. Telephone 35-31-04 for information and emergency.

Women's Crisis-S.O.S. Femmes: (tel. 35-25-69) from 2-7pm only. Rape and assault counseling.

Open Market: Wed and Fri., 7am-noon in the Marche St.-Marguerite, four blocks south of the train station.

Library: Bibliotheque Nationale et Universitaire, 6, place de la Republique (tel. 36-00-68). Second major collection in France after Paris.

Laundromat: 100, Grand'rue, open Mon.-Fri., 8am-noon and 2-7pm Sat., 8am-noon. 9F for 5 kilos of wash.

Telephone Code: (88).

Accommodations

There are a few relatively inexpensive hotels in Strasbourg, but they fill up quickly in the summer. While there are several budget hotels near the train station, the area is not the safest at night.

Auberge de Jeunesse (IYHF), 9, rue de l'Auberge de Jeunesse (tel. 30-26-46), 2km from the station; take bus #3, 13, or 23. Functional and clean, though without much charm, Two hundred beds. Optional breakfast.

Hôtel Victoria, 7-9, rue Maire-Kuss (tel. 32-13-06). A large, decent hotel near the station on a busy street. Singles 44-48F, doubles 57-61F. Breakfast included; showers 8F.

Hôtel Weber, 22, blvd. de Nancy. Four blocks south of the train station in one of the dingier parts of town, but the rooms are clean. Singles 46-49F, doubles 51-53F, triples with shower 84-90F. For a better feel of the city, you might want to be closer to centre ville.

Hôtel au Cycliste, 8, rue des Bateliers (tel. 36-20-01). Near the Eglise Ste.-Madeline, across from the old town. A pleasant hotel in a good location. Singles 43-45F, doubles 50-55F. Breakfast 9F, bath or shower 5F.

Hôtel Savoy, 7, rue de Zurich (tel. 35-12-76). Near Hotel au Cycliste, on the opposite bank from the Cathedral. Fairly run down and dark, but a decent budget place. Singles 45-47F, doubles 51-67F. Breakfast 9F, showers 9F. (During the high season-late July-Aug.-weekends are actually better than weekdays.)

Hôtel Patricia, 1a, rue de Puits (tel. 32-14-60). A good location, in the old town behind the Eglise St.-Thomas. The management is particularly untrusting, and can be difficult. Two singles at 46F, doubles 51-69F, with shower 74-82F. Payment required in advance. Breakfast 9F, showers 9F.

Hôtel Michelet, 48, rue du Vieux-Marche-aux-Poissons (tel. 32-47-38). Basic budget hotel on a busy thoroughfare in the middle of the old city. It has one star but probably doesn't deserve it. Singles 53F, 63F, doubles 63-120F. Breakfast 11F, shower 7.50F.

Hôtel Central, 10, place de March-aux-Cochons-de-lait (tel. 88-32-03-05). The location can't be beat (a little hard to find on the way, but not on foot-50 yards from the cathedral at the end of Rue du Maroquin). Management not the pleasantest. Rooms start at 59F for a single, breakfast included (double same room and price plus 10F for a second breakfast). Room with shower 90F. No shower if there isn't one in the room.

Hôtel Elisa, 3, rue Goethe (tel. 88-61-17-84). Near the Botanical Gardens and old university. Very pleasant and quiet, but almost always full in advance in the summer. A little more expensive, but probably worth the difference. Most of the hotel has been redone, the rest about to be, though they have a few cheaper rooms in the second building. Singles for 45F, doubles 55F. Rooms for 2 and 3 at 100F. Breakfast plus 13F. For summer, reserve at least 2 months in advance.

Camping: La Montagne Verte, Terrain municipal, rue du Scknokeloch (tel. 30-25-46), is a large four-star site, open March through October. **Place Baggersee,** on the Lac du Baggersee, route de Colmar (tel. 39-03-40) is also excellent; open year-round. Take bus #13 or 23, direction Graffenstaden-Fegersheim, as far as Baggersee.

Food and Wine

Alsace shares culinary traditions with Germany. Among the traditional dishes are *tarte a l'oignon, paté de foie gras, choucroute garnie* (sauerkraut cooked in white wine sauce and heaped with sausages and ham), *coq au Riesling* chicken in a white wine sauce, and *baeckaoffa* (a casserole of marinated beef, pork, lamb, and potatoes which sometimes must be ordered a day in advance). The Alsatian vineyards produce six white wines and one dry rosé called *Pinot Noir. Riesling,* very dry but characteristically fruity, is the "king" of the local wines. *Gewurztraminer* is extraordinarily fragrant. If you order "un quart" of house wine, you'll probably be given *Sylvaner,* the lightest of the wines in the region. Many restaurants virtually double their prices during the tourist months, and others close down in either July or August. Avoid the over-priced restaurants around the Cathedral and with La Petite France.

Au Pont St.-Martin, 13-15, rue des Moulins. You won't miss this enormous, three-tiered riverside restaurant in the picturesque La Petite France, catering to tourists and locals alike. The volume of business keeps their prices a little lower than their neighbors and the portions are generous. It's often easy to strike up a conversation with table mates. Dinner menu at 36F, three-course lunch menu 25F. Closed Sun. noon.

Restaurant D'Quetsch, 6, rue du Faisan (tel. 36-31-01). On a side street between the Cathedral and place St.-Etienne. Not cheap, but serves excellently prepared regional food to a young and sophisticated crowd. Menu for 40F, but you can eat just as well à la carte. Try the *tarte flambées.* Closed Wed. and in August.

Au Vieux Strasbourg, 5 rue du Maroquin. Located in the pedestrian zone between the Cathedral and the river. Try one or two *petits plats* (9-18F) such as *salade de cervelas* (sausage) or *salade mixte* and enjoy the *winstub* atmosphere.

Hôtel-Restaurant Pax, 24-26, rue du Faubourg-National. This two-star hotel near the train station serves a good vegetarian menu for 35F and a *plat du jour* at 25F. Open noon-1:45pm and 7-9pm every day, closed Sun. off-season.

Student Restaurants: FEC, place St.-Etienne, is the best student restaurant. Tickets cost 9F from the office or 4.50F if you buy one from a local student. The other student restaurants are **Paul Appel,** 10, rue de Palerme; **Gallia,** 1 place de l'Université; and **Louis Pasteur,** rue de Faubourg-National. Inquire at CROUS to find out which one is open during the summer.

During the summer, cafes spill out onto all of Strasbourg's sidewalks and squares. Try those on the place du Marché-aux-Cochons-de-Lait, the place Gutenberg, or in La Petite France. You'll have no trouble finding one, but make sure you check the prices first. The following two cafes are popular with students (don't let the names throw you off; they are cafes): **The Cafeteria** on the Place de l'Universite and **le Cafet,** 12, rue des Freres, behind the Cathedral. Both have outdoor seating.

Sights

Strasbourg's ornate Gothic **Cathédrale** was constructed from rose-colored Vosges sandstone between the eleventh and fifteenth centuries. Its famous single-towered silhouette is practically a trademark for the city. The Cathedral houses the enchanting **L'Horloge Astronomique** (astronomical clock), across whose face marches a parade of apostles (guided visits at 12:30pm daily, admission 2F, tickets sold at the tourist office). While waiting to see the clock's display, you can scrutinize the **Doomsday Pillar** *(pilier des anges)* rising in the middle of the interior and decorated by an anonymous thirteenth-century master from Chartes. The same artist also sculpted the statues flanking the south portal which portray the Church and the Synagogue as two beautiful women. The Cathedral's 142-meter tower has long made it the highest monument in Christendom. If you climb the tower for a superb view you will be following in the footsteps of the young student Goethe who suffered from acute acrophobia and would climb up regularly as a measure of self-discipline. The Cathedral is undergoing renovation because of recently discovered structural problems, but you can still enter at the south portal.

The museums are all within close proximity to the Cathedral. Don't miss the folkloric **Musée Alsacien** (23, quai St.-Nicolas), where you'll find an interesting display of handicrafts, costumes, furniture, and regional art. The **Maison de l'Oeuvre Notre-Dame,** opposite the Cathedral occupies a fourteenth- to sixteenth-century mansion which contains sculpture, stained glass, and other artifacts from times Romanesque, Gothic, and Renaissance. Strasbourg is also home to the **Marionette Museum** and home to the inventor of the celebrated puppet "Guid."

The palatial **Château des Rohan,** a magnificent eighteenth-century building next door, houses a complex of small museums: archeology, fine arts, and decorative arts. The regional pottery and porcelain exhibits are noteworthy, along with the apartments (entry 4F, good for all exhibits). By the river, the **Ancienne Douane,** or old customs house, shelters the pleasant **Musée d'Art Moderne** with a surprisingly good collection of paintings and sculpture by Klimt, Chagall, Arp, Klee, and many of the Impressionists. All museums are open daily April through September except Tues., 10am-noon and 2-6pm; October through March, 2-6pm, and Sun. morning 10am-noon. Admission is 3F, 1.50F under 25 years.

The **Palais de l'Europe,** composed of Vosges sandstone and oxidized aluminum, was opened by former French President Giscard in 1977 to house the Council of Europe. It is also the meeting place for the European Parliament; the hemicycle inside is stunning. When either organization is in session, you may register at the desk (bring your passport) for a look from the visitor's gallery where headsets translating the debates into several languages are available. Across the street is the peaceful **Parc de l'Orangerie,** with its small zoo, designed by Le Notre, architect of Versailles, in 1692. Unfortunately, the flowers are better cared for than the animals.

Goethe, Napoleon, and Metternich are all alumni of the **University** established here in the seventeenth century. During the academic year, follow the blvd. de la Victoire or the rue de Zurich out to the new university quarters at the esplanade. Today, you will find the seven faculties located in the area known as the Palais de l'Université, between blvd. de la Victoire and ave. du Général-de-Gaulle. The university area, with attractive grounds and buildings, also extends across the blvd. de la Victoire to rue Goethe, and rue de l'Université, where there are beautiful botanical gardens and parks. In the summer, not much goes on in this area, but the student service, **CROUS,** is still open (see the Practical Information section), as are some of the university restaurants.

Entertainment

If you are here during the summer, pick up the brochure *Saison d'Eté à Strasbourg* (summer season in Strasbourg) at the office de tourisme for information of all kinds of free entertainment. In the courtyard of the **chateau des Rohan** there is a series of folk dancing demonstrations in June and July. There are free concerts on Thursday evenings at 8:30pm in the **Parc des Contades.** June brings the celebrated **Festival International de Musique.** Contact the Societé des Amis de la Musique, 24, rue de la Mésange (tel. 32-43-10) for information. In season, the **Orchestre Philharmonique de Strasbourg,** directed by Alain Lombard (who is very popular with locals) performs at the Palais de la Musique et des Congrés behind the place de Bordeaux; presentations of **Théatre National de Strasbourg** are staged at their resident theater on the place de la République, while opera and ballet productions by **Opéra du Rhin** are staged at the opera house on the place Broglie. For tickets and information, check at the opera house and at S. wolf, rue de la Mésange, between the place Broglie and the place Kléber.

From November to December the annual **Festival Mimes et Clowns,** 1, rue du Pont St.-Martin (tel. 32-74-01), is held as well as the **Festival Européen de Cinéma d'Art et d'Essai,** 32, rue du Vieux-Marché-aux-Vins (tel. 32-12-30). From May to September there is also a rousing *son et lumière* show at the Cathedral covering twenty centuries of the town's history (8pm in German, 9pm in French, admission 10F, 5F with student ID).

Near Strasbourg

The back roads connecting the many small towns and extensive vineyards, known as the **Route du Vin,** offer a rich taste of the flavorful character of the Alsace region. The vineyards are interspersed with medieval ruins and charming, if over-touristed, small villages. While the route is easily covered by car, the many hills make bicycling more difficult unless you allow yourself a leisurely pace. Hitching is another alternative, but a slow one. You'll have plenty of time to stop for *dégustations* of various wine *caves;* the tourist offices at Strasbourg and Colmar provide information on specific routes and *caves,* and sponsor weekly bus tours during the summer. Several of the larger towns are accessible by local trains from Strasbourg, including **Molsheim, Dambach-La-Ville,** and **Scherwiller.** If you have time, visit the charming towns of **St. Hippolyte, Obernai,** and **Riquewihr,** where the newer buildings date from the Renaissance. Many festivities take place during the autumn grape harvests;

watch for vine wreaths hung outside establishments where *vin nouveau* is available. During the fall you can make $20-30 per day picking grapes. You can either get specifics in September from the Centre d'Information Jeunesse d'Alsace (see the listing in Strasbourg) or try going straight to the houses of the smaller *vinticulteurs* where you will be provided with meals and lodging in bunk rooms.

Colmar

Colmar is the exemplar of Alsatian life. A beautiful smaller city 30 minutes south of Strasbourg by train, it offers both the old and new of Alsace. Colmar preserves more or less intact the half-timbered-houses, tiled roofs and narrow cobblestone streets dating to the 15th and 16th centuries. As elsewhere in Alsace, you will notice the predominance of German culture. The townspeople will as happily speak German with you as French.

The recently restored tanners' lodgings on **rue des Tanneurs** provide an excellent example of the local architecture: half-timbered houses line the streets, and further on a small canal leads to a quaint area called **La Petite Venise.** The multi-colored decorated roof and amber-colored stone of **St. Martin's Church** is visible throughout the old section. Among the ancient homes concentrated around the rue des Marchands, a particularly beautiful four-teenth-century house with Gothic windows faces the church. Two blocks to the west on place des Dominicains, the **Dominican Church** houses Martin Schongauer's masterful Madonna of the Roses displayed in its choir as well as striking fourteenth-century stained glass windows. (Altar open to view daily from 10am-5pm; admission 3F, 2F with student ID). The extraordinary **Musée Unterlinden,** at place des Unterlinden, contains a large collection of medieval religious art in a former Dominican convent which retains its cloister and chapel. Among its collection is Mathias Grunewald's Issenheim Altarpiece and the Gothic *Crucifixion of the Altar.* When you've had your fill of crucifixes, two refreshingly modern rooms in the basement house stunning modern art by Picasso, Braque, Rouault, Vasarely, Léger, and others. (Open daily 9am-noon and 2-6pm, closes at 5pm and on Tues. off-season; admission 8F, 6F with student ID). If you have time, visit the **Musée Bartholdi,** 30, rue des Marchands, across from the Maison Pfister (a very famous sixteenth-century house). The museum possesses a nicely exhibited collection of memorabilia about Colmar, from the eleventh through the nineteenth centuries. Frédéric Auguste Bartholdi (1834-1904), creator of the Statue of Liberty, was born in Colmar. (Open daily 10am-noon and 2-6pm, closed on Tues. from Nov.-April; admission 5F, students 3F.)

Every Tuesday evening at 9pm from June to September, Colmar hosts a folklore spectacle at the place de l'Ancienne-Douane. There are also many free concerts during the summer. Check the pamphlet "Activitiés de Colmar et de sa région" (available at the **Syndicat**) for information. The annual Alsatian **Wine Festival** is held in Colmar in August with widespread sales of wine, beer, and agricultural equipment. The end of August and beginning of September bring the "Sauerkraut Days", two weeks filled with feasting, dancing, wine and beer and—guess what—*choucroute.*

Practical Information

Office de Tourisme, 4, rue des Unterlinden (tel 41-66-80) across from the Unterlinden Museum. Will provide you with a list of hotels, restaurants, and campgrounds and a helpful map of the city. They also organize tours to the smaller villages in the region. Open July and August, 8am-12pm, 1:30pm-7pm.

Bus Tours: Voyages Pauli, 6, rue Berthe Molly (tel. 41-66-80). This agency offers a variety of bus trips in Alsace and beyond, mostly of the little-old-lady variety, but the trips on the **Route du Vin** and to the **Daubs** might be worthwhile if you don't have a car or bicycle and don't have the time to hitch. (Daytrips about 70-100F) Open Mon.-Fri., 8:30-noon and 2-6pm, Sat. 8:30-noon and 2-4pm.

Post Office: 36-38, ave. de la République. Across the street from a lovely park. Open Mon.-Fri., 8am-7pm, Sat. 8am-noon.

Police: 6, rue du Chasseur (tel. 41-08-00).

Open Market: Every Thursday, 6am-6pm and Sat. noon-6pm on the rue des Seruriers.

Laundromat: 8, rue Turenne, 6F to wash, 1F for 12 minutes of drying. Open daily 7am-10pm.

Telephone Code: (89)

Accommodations

Auberge de Jeunesse (IYHF), 6 rue St.-Niklaas (tel. 41 33 08). About fifteen minutes from the station down ave. de la Liberté away from the center of town (ave. de la Liberté is across the tracks; turn left coming out of the station, cross the tracks and double back on the other side until you reach ave. de la Liberté). Or take bus #1 or #2 from the station to ave. de Paris and walk back along the ave de la Liberté to rue St.-Niklaas. 22.50F per night, breakfast 7F.

Maison des Jeunes (Centre International de Sejour) 17 Camille-Schlumberger (tel. 41 26 87). Probably the best deal in Colmar. Three blocks from the station in a pleasant residential neighborhood, ten minutes from the center of town. TV room, beer and soda (for a price) available in the evening. Rooms with four to six beds, 18F per night (registration after 4pm, though call ahead to reserve a place).

Hôtel du Solei, 7 rue St.-Eloi (tel. 41 40 50). A little ways out in the north end of town, off the rue Vaubon. A six-room hotel with a friendly proprietor. Reservations recommended. Singles 40F, doubles 55F. Breakfast 10F.

La Chaumiere, 74, ave. de la République (tel. 41 08 99). Clean, simple rooms; most look onto a courtyard. Singles 50F, doubles 60-110F. Breakfast 12F, shower 5F. Bar downstairs is a local hangout.

Camping (tel. 41 15 94). A three-star site, about half a kilometer out of town. Take the Route de Neuf Brisach (RN 415) out of town and across the Ill river. Or take bus #1 (direction Wihr) to the Plage de l'Ill stop. Open all year.

Food

An inexpensive restaurant is hard to come by in Colmar, though there are a number of places you probably won't mind emptying your pockets for. There are also several concession stands on the Rue des Clefs which serve quite good *tartes flambees* and pizza (10F).

La Taverne and L'Alcove, 2, 4, Impasse de la Maison Rouge (one block beyond the Rue des Tanneurs). Two pleasant restaurants run by the same management. La Taverne open only at lunch, and L'Alcove open only in the evening. Specialties include various *salades composées* (12-25F) and a fixed lunch menu at 34F (dinner is à la carte but worth it). Open for lunch Tues.-Fri. and for dinner Tues.-Sat.

Caveau Hans Emschnockeloch, 36 rue des Clefs. Located in a cozy cellar with candles and wine racks. Serves decent, if plain, Alsatian specialties; pizza and flambees, 22-29F, salads 18-25F. Open for dinner only.

Restaurant de l'Ill, 8, rue de l'Ill. Located 2km northeast of town on the Route de Neuf Brisach, RN 415 just two blocks beyond the canal. Although a good trek from the center of town, it's definitely worth it for a splurge. This is where locals go for a special night out; the restaurant serves some of the largest portions you'll see in France. Main courses start from 35-65F, but salads, 25-30F, spaghetti 25F. Near the campground; take bus #1 towards Horbourg, stopping at Dornig. Closed Tues. between June 15-July 7.

Self-Flunch on the Ave. de la République at the Place Rapp. A plastic-coated self service, but patronized by locals all the same. Good for a cheap meal. Full dinners from about 20F.

Nancy

Although the smog may turn you off, Nancy is worth a day-trip, if only to see the **place Stanislas.** It is a perfectly proportioned square, embellished by Stanislas Leszczynski, an ex-king of Poland who became the last duke of Lorraine when he married his daughter to Louis XV. The seventeenth-century **Hotel de Ville** is the largest building in the square, and it is decorated with handsome eighteenth-century facades, balustrades, gilt-tipped wrought-iron railings, and the Neptune and Amphitrite fountains. The square is at its most spectacular at night during the *son-et-lumière* presentation around 10pm. (The Bastille Day celebration here is fabulous, rivaled only by the festivities in Paris.)

The **Musée des Beaux-Arts,** 3, place Stanislas, has an impressive collection of seventeenth-century paintings and a good selection of modern works by Matisse, Modigliani, and Dufy. (Open 10am-noon and 2-6pm; closed Mon. morning and Tues.; admission 5F, 3F with student ID.) Pass under the **Porte Royale,** the finest of Nancy's seven triumphal arches, and descend to the **Parc Pépinière,** a form of English garden which is the site of frequent summer concerts and an outdoor cafe. Around to the left is the **Palais Ducal,** housing the **Musée Lorraine,** an extraordinarily varied collection from two thousand years of history in this crossroads province; it includes paintings, sculpture, Roman artifacts, costumes, and furnishings. Note the fine tapestries from the Ducal Palace and the standard of Henri II, reputedly the oldest French flag in existence. (Open daily except Tues. 10am-noon and 2-6pm in summer; admission 7F, 5F with student I.D.)

The **syndicat d'initiative** at 14, place Stanislas (tel. 335-22-41) will find you a room in the city free of charge, but you probably won't want to stay in Nancy. Budget hotels tend to fill up quickly in this large, industrial, and rather unpleasant town. The nearby **Camping Municipal de Brabois** (tel. 355-08-88) is a two-star site in Villier-les Nancy, reachable by the N74 or take bus #6 and walk. In town, the **Maison des Jeunes et de la Culture,** 27, rue de la République (tel. 327-40-53) is a good deal at 35F for a single with breakfast (less in multi-bedded rooms). Other budget hotels can be found on rue Jeanne-d'Arc, a noisy thoroughfare not far from the train station.

The cafes on place Stanislas are expensive, but everybody goes there and the other parts of town have little appeal. Avoid eating a full meal here—just sit over an *espresso* and people-watch. The art-nouveau **Excelsior** on rue Henri-Poincaré is a popular student hangout. **Oxebon** at 85, rue St.-Georges is a busy, local place with a management who likes to make sure you get enough to eat.

Nancy's annual **Festival Mondial du Théâtre** fills the place Stanislas with an international throng of theater-goers. The drama fest includes mime and experimental and traditional theater. Check with the theater festival office, 7, place Stanislas (tel. 337-002-21) for details. In October, the **Festival de Jazz** brings a smaller but equally international crowd of musicians, swinging from dusk to dawn.

Champagne

Champagne is known in America for a single bubbly product, this apparently quiet region has long been the site of a strategic border's disquiet. Champagne saw its day as an important trading center with the great medieval weaving centers and fairs at Troyes and Provins, and the region was a battlefield throughout the Hundred Years' War and later during the wars of reformation. Roman legionnaires fought barbarian tribes here, and thousands died here during the slaughters of World War I and the bombing of World War II. Yet, throughout the turmoil, the grape harvest continued. And when the Second World War ended, and France regained control over Champagne, the champagne flowed freely in the national celebration.

Economist John Maynard Keynes once confessed that his one regret in life was that he had not drunk enough champagne. You can avoid this deplorable fate by visiting Champagne's numerous wine cellars *(caves)*. As each manufacturer will remind you, it is the area's unique combination of altitude, climate, chalky soil and cellars carved from limestone that makes champagne production possible. A good bubbly wine made anywhere else simply isn't champagne. The caves themselves are fascinating historical monuments; some have operated since Roman times, a few stretch along a twenty-mile underground network, and others are decorated with striking bas-reliefs.

If you are traveling by car or hitchhiking, follow any of the "routes de champagne" through the **Montagne de Reims**, the **Marne Valley,** or the **Côtes des Blancs** (tourist offices can provide route maps). Alternatively, you can wander off alone to visit the small villages and lakes dotting the region south and west of Epernay. Camping, official or impromptu, is easy and undisturbed. Trains connect the major towns and buses can bring you to the smaller villages, well off the tourist route.

Reims (pronounced "Rans") is a good base for trips to the vineyards or battlefields. Accommodations are reasonable and plentiful and its cathedral ranks among the finest in France. The smaller and less frenetic city of **Epernay** is the best for visiting Champagne *caves*. Outside Reims, the **Forêt de Verzy**—a curious forest of twisted, umbrella-shaped dwarf beeches *(tortillards)*—and the vast **Forêt de Germaine** are ideal hiking areas. **Troyes,** south of Reims and Epernay, is the ancient capital of the province. Although there are no *caves* here, churches, half-timbered houses, and narrow walkways make it a very pleasant village. There are youth hostels in Epernay, Chalons-sur-Marne, Verzy, and Troyes, and bicycle rentals at the station in Epernay.

Reims

Reims is a spectacular medieval city resurrected phoenix-like from its own ashes. Demolished by vandals, ravaged by fire, and devastated by artillery during the Great War, this proud city is as impressive for its perseverance as for its enduring elegance. Hence, Reims carries a vigorous modern life to the spirit of French history which finds its seat in the Cathedral.

Practical Information

Reims is two hours away from Paris (Gare de l'Est); thirteen trains make the trip each day.

Syndicat d'Initiative: 3, blvd. de la Paix (tel. 47-25-69), will give you a list of *caves* to visit and will book rooms for a 3F fee (plus a 20-50F deposit). Open Mon.-Sat. 9am-6:30pm. A more centrally-located annex on rue Libergier, near the Cathedral, is open during the week in summer until 6pm and on Sun. and holidays 9am-8pm.

Post Office: rue Olivier-Metra, place de Boulingrin (the marketplace). You can make long-distance calls from the second floor here. Open Mon. Fri. 8am-7pm, Sat. 8am-noon.

Train Station: blvd. Joffre, right across from the gardens leading into town (tel. 88-50-50). A tourist office at the station can help you with itineraries. Open Mon.-Fri. 9am-noon and 2-6:30pm, Sat. 9:30am-noon and 2:30-5:30pm.

Bus Service: For local buses (tel. 09-08-86); for regional buses (tel. 85-40-63).

Hitching: For Paris, it's best to follow the N31 via Soissons; take bus B or #2, direction Tinquieux. For Luxembourg, try the N380; take bus B, direction Point de Witry, and get off at the terminus. To hitch a ride on a canal barge, go to the old port on blvd. Paul-Doumer.

Harvest Work: Contact ANPE (L'Agence National pour l'Emploi), 40, rue de Talleyrand (tel. 40-16-16). Harvesting begins in late September, 100 days after the first flowering of the vine, and employment confirmation is usually available after June. Open Mon.-Fri. 9am-noon and 2-5pm. Rates are usually the best in France.

Police: (tel. 88-21-12); **Medical Emergency:** (tel. 06-07-08). **Lost and Found** (87-18-82).

Laundromat: 82 rue du Barbatre.

Telephone Code: (26).

Accommodations

For inexpensive hotels, try the area around the place Drouet-d'Erlon. University rooms are available in July and August (singles 32F, less if you stay longer than three nights). Contact CROUS at 34, blvd. Henry Vasnier (tel. 85-50-16: open Mon.-Fri. 8:30am-noon and 1:30-5:30pm) for information on rooms and on university restaurants. There are two youth hostels a long way out of town; the Foyer Leon Pandovoine (tel. 85-35-09), 1. rue Herduin charges 15F for membership and 20F for meals, but long-term residents are preferred. A list of other foyers is available from the syndicat.

Centre Internationale de Séjour, across the street from parc Leo Lagrange (tel. 40-52-60). A 15-minute walk from the station, but definitely the best place to stay in Reims. Turn right past the gardens and follow blvd. Général-Leclerc until the bridge. Cross the bridge (rue de Vesle) and then take the first left, on Chausée Bocquaine beside the Maison de la Culture. Singles with breakfast 41.50F the first night, then 34F per night; 38.50F first night, 31F thereafter in a double, Breakfast included. Bring a student ID or Youth Hostel card. 11pm curfew, 9am lockout from bedrooms, kitchen facilities, and TV room.

Hôtel Chateaubriand, 57, rue Thillois (tel. 47-50-74). A very nice, cheerful place about a ten-minute walk from the station. Singles 35F, doubles with bath 53F. Breakfast 10F, showers 8F. Down the street at #31, is the Au Bon Accueil (tel. 88-55-74), with big rooms and prices about the same as the Chateaubriand. Singles 31-37F, doubles 38-45F. Breakfast 11F, showers, 8F. The friendly **Hotel Thillois** at #17 (tel. 40-65-65) is closed Sundays, with singles 47-70F, doubles 47-70F, breakfast 10F, showers 7F.

Hôtel Monopole, 28, place Drouet-d'Erlon (tel. 88-04-93). A lively location on the main drag, but correspondingly noisy. Singles 42-76F, doubles 55-86F. Breakfast 12F.

Hôtel Linguet, 14, rue Linguet (tel. 47-31-89). On a quiet residential street, about 10 minutes from the station. Friendly and clean. Singles 42-46F, doubles 52-82F. Breakfast 12F. Shower 7F.

Hôtel d'Alsace, 6, rue Général-Sarrail (tel. 47-44-08). The closest to the station, not far from the sights. Large, simply furnished rooms at 40-50F single, 50-80F double. Breakfast 13F.

Camping: Camping-Airotel de Champagne, ave. Hoche, route de Chalons (tel. 85-41-22). Three-star. Open April-Sept.

Food and Wine

The specialties of the region, cooked in champagne, tend to bubble over budget ceilings, but you may want to splurge. Be sure to try the *brie champenoise*. The place Drouet-d'Erlon is filled with bars and *brasseries*, most of them with a menu for 40-50F. **Colbert** (at #64) has demure, white tablecloths and old-fashioned elegance; **L'Eclaireur** (#85) stays open all night; **La Chouette,** Galerie de Lion-d'Or, has a pretty indoor courtyard, and **Le Sube** (#65) has cheap pizzas to go and a menu at 39F, hamburgers 12F. Many are closed on Mondays. For more out-of-the-way meals and settings, try the rue Gambetta (full of student places) or:

Flamm Steak, 17, rue Libergier, two blocks from the Cathedral. Tasty crepes in many varieties; the candle-lit setting is cozy, even at noon. Try the crepe with bananas and rum. Dinner crepes 15-20F, dessert crepes 8-20F. Crepe menu at 40F. Closed Sept. and Sunday dinner; open daily 10:30am-1:30pm, 6:30-10:30pm.

La Boule d'Or, 39, rue Thiers. Substantial portions in a homey atmosphere. Menus at 36, 46, and 56F. Try the *pate champenois* and *coq au vin blanc*. Closed Mon.

Zorba, 8, rue Colbert. Advertises Greek cuisine, but serves French food. A student hangout with a 35F menu which includes service and wine. Omelette 22F, steak 35F. Closed Sun.

Sights

Since 496 A.D. when Clovis, king of the Franks, was baptized here, bringing the Faith of Rome to the people of France, coronation at Reims has been the *sine qua non* of legitimacy for the French monarch. Joan of Arc's goal was to deliver the indecisive Charles VII to Reims so the French would have a legitimate king to support and drive "Les Goddams"—as the English were dubbed because it was then their most common utterance—back across the Channel. From 1173 until the Revolution, all French monarchs save one were crowned here.

Built from blocks of limestone cut from the caves, begun in 1211 and taking longer than a century to complete, the Gothic **Cathédrale de Notre Dame** stands fully equal to the great coronation occasions, even though it has been frequently destroyed and rebuilt. The present Cathedral is the third to stand in this hexed position. Its west facade contains a spectacular rose window, with the deep blue glass made from semi-precious lapis lazuli. The simple and balanced interior was thought to epitomize medieval philosophies concerning harmony and unity of life. Be sure to examine the tapestries which portray scenes from the *Songs of Songs* and *Christ's Infancy*. Note the Chagall windows in the apse depicting the same events in modern style, linked to the great rose window by the continued use of dark blue hues. The Chagall windows replace 18th century works. The Cathedral must be entered from place de Cardinal Luçon, and is open from 9am-8pm daily. There are guided tours for 12F, 6F students. Hours are by demand.

Next to the Cathedral stands the **Palais de Tau,** the former episcopal palace, given its name because the original floor plan was in the shape of a "T". Today it houses medieval carvings and exquisitely fashioned objects of gold and precious stones. Open daily except Tues., 10am-noon and 2-6pm, till 5pm in winter; admission 8F, 4F for students.

To the east lies the less-visited **Basilique St.-Remi,** a Gothic renovation of a Carolingian Romanesque church reputed to contain the tombs of many of France's earliest kings. Its stained glass is especially delicate. Open 10am-noon and 2-6pm daily except Tues. Adjacent to the Basilica is the **Musée Abbaye St.-Remi,** 53, rue Simon, the new archeological museum of the city, which should be fully open by the summer of 1983. The **Musée de Chaumont,** place du Palais, is full of archeological treasures and sculptures. (Open Mon., Wed., Sat., and Sun. afternoons, admission free.) When walking around the Cathedral near rues Colbert and Carnot, notice the **place Royale,** restored to look as it did during the reign of Louis XV. In the center is a statue of Louis XV by Cartellier (the original one by Pigalle was destroyed during the revolution).

If you get a chance, visit the **Salle de Guerre,** 12, rue Franklin-Roosevelt, the simple schoolroom where the Germans surrendered to the Allies on May 7, 1945. The room remains as it was then, and has map-covered walls as well as a few photographs of the signatories. (Open March-Nov., 9am-noon and 2-6pm daily except Tues. and holidays; admission free.)

Formerly an abbey, the **Musée St.-Denis,** 8, rue Chanzy, displays a diverse collection of paintings and tapestries. The ground floor contains ceramics, enamel works, and other pieces. Upstairs you'll find a set of portrait sketches by Cranach, elder and younger, and a fine collection of French art, from Poussin to Gauguin, including an extensive Corot collection and two rooms of Impressionist works by Pissarro, Sisley, Monet, Dufy, and others. (Open daily except Tues., 10am-noon and 2-5pm in summer; admission free.)

Exploring Reims's *caves* will convince you that wine is virtually a religion to the French. Some were built from chapels, others contain illuminated shrines to St. Jean, patron saint of *cavistes,* and the very man who invented the *methode champenoise* for producing champagne, Dom Pérignon, was a monk. The syndicat d'initiative provides a map with a list of the *caves* open to the public; most firms organize free tours, but few offer free samples any more. Most are open from Mon.-Sat. 9-11am and 2-5pm, but each schedule is listed on the map. Tours in French last between fifteen and forty minutes, and some also give English tours on request. **Piper-Heidseck,** 51, blvd. Henry-Vasnier (tel. 85-01-94) takes you around their cellars on a little electric train. **Taittinger,** 9, place St.-Nicaise (tel. 85-45-35) takes you through some of the eeriest and most ancient *caves,* formerly the crypt of an abbey; if not a bar-hop, their tour is at least a solid lesson in history. **Veuve Clicquot-Ponsardin,** 1, place des Droits-de-l'Homme (tel. 85-24-08; closed weekday mornings) has mediocre tours, but a fine film. Madame Clicquot, "La Grande Dame" of champagne, was one of the important figures in the history of champagne production. On the north side of town, **Heidsieck,** 83, rue Coquebert (tel. 07-39-34; open Mon.-Fri. morning, closed in August) and **Jacquart,** 5, rue Gosset (tel. 07-20-20, by appointment only) have been known to give samples, but are nothing special.

Nightlife

As a university town, Reims is full of effervescent nightlife. For wholesome and imaginative entertainment, visit the **Maison de la Culture,** 3-5, chausée Bocquaine (tel. 47-93-44), which has films, plays, and dances, as well as a good cafeteria. For hot spots, try the **Club 51,** rue de Neufchatel, or the **Club St. Pierre,** 43 Blvd. Général Leclerc, both open all night. **Le Sunshine,** 114, rue du Barbatre, is one of the many clubs with jazz and other entertainment (free weekdays, 50F including dinner on Saturdays). Reims is also very proud of its **Théatre de la Comedie,** 1, rue Eugene-Wiet, which regularly hosts exceptional plays in French (tel. 85-60-00).

Epernay

Epernay is far quieter and more modest than the larger towns of Reims and Troyes. Here, the town's raison d'etre is clearly the business of vine and bottle backing the historical importance of Troyes or Reims. Epernay has relatively few sights, but it has a very pleasant place to stay, and it provides easy access to the routes of Champagne.

The vineyards begin on the rolling hills immediately outside of town. A number of prominent caves including the excellent companies of Malt and Perrier-Jouet, lie within town.

Epernay lies seventeen miles south of Reims, thirty minutes away by train. If you're coming from Reims, stop off at some of the tiny villages en route: **Bar-le-Duc,** an elegant old town with beautiful sixteenth- to eighteenth-century houses gracing its cobblestone streets; or **Ay,** another picturesque town on the main rail line. Visit the nearby **Abbey of Hautvillers,** where, in the seventeenth century, Dom Pérignon first shouted excitedly, "Brothers, brothers, come quickly! I am drinking stars!" and champagne was born.

Syndicat d'Initiative: place Thiers (tel. 51-51-66). Across from the station in a small gazebo in a park. Provides information on the *caves* in Epernay. Open Mon.-Sat. 9am-7pm, Wed. 2-5pm only, Sun. and holidays 9:30am-2pm; in off-season closes at 6pm, and all day Wed. and Sun.

Post Office: rue Cap Deullin. Open Mon.-Fri. 8am-7pm, Sat. 8am-noon.

Train Service: for information (tel. 88-50-50).

Bus Station: Gare Routiere, Place, Notre Dame (tel. 51-92-10).

Police: (tel. 54-11-17); **Medical Emergencies:** Hôpital Auban-Moet, 137 rue de l'Hôpital (tel. 54-11-11).

Telephone Code: (12).

Accommodations and Food

Auberge de Jeunesse (IYHF), 13, rue du Dr.-Calmette, near ave. Foch (tel. 51-36-63 or 51-10-97), 2km from the station. 36 beds, kitchen facilities. 22.50F per night.

Open April-Sept., closed Sat. and Sun. until 6pm. Phone before you come—in 1981 the hostel was closed all year.

M.J.C. Centre International de Séjour, 8, rue de Reims (tel. 51-40-82). A beautiful new building with fine singles and good facilities, about three minutes from the train station. Meals often available. Accommodates long-term guests as well as short stays. Singles 32F. (Show your student ID or IYHF card.)

Hôtel le Progrès, 6 rue des Berceaux (tel. 51-22-07), five minutes from the station, just off the place de la République. Singles and doubles at 43F, 53F with bath or shower. Breakfast 13F.

Hôtel St.-Pierre, 1, rue Jeanne d'Arc (tel. 51-21-22). Set on a quiet street about ten minutes from the station. Singles 42-55F, 45-65F with a shower or bath. Breakfast 10F. Closed Wed. afternoons and Aug. 23-Sept. 9.

For inexpensive and filling fare, sample one of the surprisingly numerous Chinese restaurants. **Le Mandarin,** 19, rue Gambetta, is definitely worth trying for its tasty, budget meals, with a menu at 35F (closed Mon.). The **Restaurant Mekong,** rue du Dr.-Verron, offers a comparable menu for 39F (closed Wed.), **Au Petit Chinois,** just this side of the Mercier Caves of the Ave. de Champagne, is a Chinese red-herring: the restaurant serves hearty local fare only. 29.50F gets you a full meal which varies according to the whims of the chef, no other dishes available. A very local scene (nobody knows why it has its name). For champenois specialties, try **La Terrasse,** 7, quai de Marne, a two-star restaurant with a 37F *menu* (closed Tues. night, Wed., and July 15-31; 37F menu is not available on the weekend); or **La Cloche,** 5, place Thiers, across from the station, with menu for 38F (closed Fri. and Aug. 16-Sept. 9).

Sights

What it lacks in sights, Epernay makes up for in tastes and smells, most appealingly on the sweeping ave. de Champagne, distinguished by its mansions, gardens, and monumental champagne firms. By far the best firm to visit is **Moët et Chandon,** 20, ave. de Champagne (tel. 51-71-11; open Mon.-Fri. 10am-12:30pm and 2-5:30pm, in summer also on Sat. 9:30am-noon and 2-6pm, Sun. and holidays till 4pm). The 45-minute tours are very informative, and end with a free tasting. Moët is the champagne of kings; in the firm's lobby are menus from state banquets, royal bills of sale, and a hat which belonged to Napoleon. **Perrier Jouet,** at 26, ave. de Champagne next door, also offers a free tasting (tel. 51-20-53; open Mon.-Fri. 9am-noon and 2-5pm). Tours by appointment only. Ten minutes down the avenue at #75 is **Mercier** (tel. 51-26-64 or 51-71-11; open Mon.-Sat. 9am-noon and 2-5:30pm, till 4pm Sun. and holidays; closed Dec. 15-March 1). Eugene Mercier's firm has long been known for its flamboyant gestures (the President of France once visited the *caves* driven by four white horses), but the tour is bland and ends without a free sample.

If after all this you're still interested in the subject, visit the **Musée du Champagne et de Prehistoire,** 13, ave. de Champagne, where you can learn more about the vineyards and scrutinize a collection of labels from various bottles. The same complex contains a museum of fine arts and an exceptionally large archeological collection. (Open Mon.-Sat. 9am-noon and 2-6pm, Sun. and holidays 10am-noon and 2-5pm; closed Tues., admission 5F.)

Troyes

Troyes is a small jewel of Champagne, which because of ill-luck, has required many re-settings. But each time, the citizenry has turned the misfortune to good effect. When, in 1524, the city was destroyed by fire for the third time, (first in the 9th and 13th centuries), its artists resolved to practice their design upon the city itself, making it their greatest masterpiece. Now, with its host of churches, its narrow, gabled streets and secret passageways, and its half-timbered Renaissance houses, Troyes is one large historical artifact. Venture through the **Quartier St.-Jean,** a cobblestone pedestrian precinct of tiny shops and galleries, to appreciate the hushed charm of this city.

When it was the capital of Champagne, Troyes was famous for its vast fairs, attended by merchants, fortune-tellers, and nomads from around Europe. Today the city still plays host to a *festival populaire* of music, ballet, theater, and art, from June 20-July 11 each year.

South of Reims, Troyes is reached in 1½-2 hours by train from Paris (Gare de l'Est), but takes 3-4 hours if coming from Reims (via Paris only). From Reims, take a bus (2½-3 hours), or, if traveling by car, take the RN19 from Paris.

Syndicat d'Initiative: 16, blvd. Carnot (tel. 43-01-03), near the station. Open Mon.-Sat. 9am-noon and 2-7pm; closed Sun. and holidays. There is a new syndicat near the Cathedral at 24, quai Dampierre (tel. 72-34-30), open Mon.-Sat. till 9pm, Sun. and holidays 10am-noon and 3-6pm during the tourist season. Local and regional accommodations service (2F for local). They conduct guided tours in the summer (for 10F, students 5F), which leave the quai Dampierre office at 3pm on Tues., Thurs, Sat., and Sun.

Post Office: rue Louis Ulbach. Open Mon.-Fri. 8am-7pm, Sat. 8am-noon. This is the best place to make international telephone calls. There is also a branch of the PIT just opposite the train station.

Police: (tel. 43-22-33), in emergency (tel. 17); **Medical Emergency:** (tel. 43-48-55).

Telephone Code: (25).

Accommodations

There are a number of inexpensive hotels in Troyes, though you may do better at any of the half-dozen foyers in town (list available from the syndicat) if you want to meet French people. Places for short stays available mostly during the summer.

Auberge de Jeunesse (IYHF), 2, rue Jules Ferry (tel. 81-00-65). Located in Rosières, 5km from Troyes. Take bus #6B (direction Chartreux) from the syndicat to the last stop. From here, walk 2.2km down a country road. The hostel, set in an old farmhouse complete with fireplace, garden, and real French country gardener, is well worth the trek. Only 22.50F with student ID. Breakfast 7F. Open all year 8am-noon, 5:30-10pm (or later).

Hôtel de Nevers, 46, rue Roger-Salengro (tel. 72-32-03). The owners no longer serve breakfast, but the sunny courtyard and fresh wallpaper make for a pleasant stay. About five minutes from station. Singles 42-45F, doubles 45 or 65F. No showers.

Hôtel Splendid, 42, blvd. Carnot (tel. 43-25-41). A very tidy, two-star hotel with one-star prices. Three minutes from bus or train station. Singles start at 45F, doubles start at 60F. Extra bed 20F. Breakfast 11F.

Hôtel de Paris, 54-56, rue Roger Salengro (tel. 43-37-13). A stylish two-star hotel with a lovely garden terrace. Singles and doubles 59-66F. Breakfast 12F, showers 13F. Closed Sun. morning and from Dec. 23-Jan. 10. Reservations recommended.

Hôtel Grammont, 7, Bd. Victor Hugo (tel. 43-77-91). One-star with a little bit of sag, but a very pleasant proprietress and an excellent deal for its class. Singles 45F (breakfast included), doubles 61F (both breakfasts included). Not far from the train station.

Hôtel Le Marigny, 3, rue Charbonnet (tel. 43-32-87). A pleasant small hotel in a 16th-century building at the edge of the old town (the interior has been nicely renovated but unfortunately disguises the beams and plaster walls). Singles start at 42F, doubles 47-55F; breakfast 10F, showers 10F.

Camping: On RN60, pont Ste.-Marie (tel. 87-02-64). Closed Dec. 12-Jan. 12.

Food

The best area for food is in the Quartier St.-Jean, which is full of creperies and inviting little restaurants (look on rue Paillot de Montabert and rue Champeaux). For lunch, make yourself a picnic and saunter into the **place de la Libération,** a lovely park with fountains, flowers, and ice-cream vendors.

Le Campus, 25, rue Urbain IV. A friendly restaurant with crepes and a vegetarian menu. Prices à la carte, or menu for 25F. Open noon-2:30 and 7-10pm. Closed Sun. and Mon.

Le Tricasse, 16 rue, Paillot de Montabert. A friendly corner-pub atmosphere with lots of young people. A popular bar in the evenings; Jazz club every Friday night. Salads 14-20F, *plat du jour* 25F. Open 11:30am-2pm and 7-10pm. Closed Sun.

Le Grand Cafe, 4 rue, Champeaux. A stylish place of wood and glass, specializing in crepes (6-10F) and ice cream (10-18F). A two-course menu is 42F. Open daily 8am-12:30am.

Le Ceylan, 27, rue Paillot de Montabert. For a change from the usual cheap restaurant atmosphere and decor. The choice of exotic teas is outstanding (12F for a large pot). *Plat du jour* is 30F. Try the pastry and ice cream with your Lotus Tea. Open Tues.-Sat. noon-2pm and 4-7pm.

Creperie la Tourelle, 9, rue Champeaux. Serving a wide variety of imaginative crepes (7-15F), salads (10-12F), and ice cream.

Sights

The high point of Troyes is its **Cathédrale St.-Pierre et St.-Paul,** built from the thirteenth through sixteenth centuries. It is striking for its kaleidoscope of 112 stained glass windows, and is open daily 9am-noon and 2-7pm (5pm offseason). The adjacent **Treasury** contains the jewels of the counts of Champagne (open 9:30am-noon and 2:30-6pm, afternoons only in off-season). The city's oldest church is **Ste.-Madeleine,** built in 1150, and distinguished by its delicate stone lacework (open daily 9am-noon and 2-7pm).

Next to the Cathedral, at 21, rue Chretien de Troyes, is the **Musée St.-Loup,** a former abbey. This all-purpose museum is an amusing mishmash of exhibits—here a mummy or tomb, there a room full of sculptures in disarray, elsewhere a piano. The closed room on the second floor is a library with over four thousand precious manuscripts (the Public Reading Room is open Mon.-Sat. 10am-noon and 2-7pm). The museum is open daily except Tues., 10am-noon and 2-6pm; admission 4F, students free. The price of admission also gains you entry to two other of Troyes' museums (if you visit them within 48 hours; all have the same opening hours). The **Musée Historique de Troyes,** housed in the sixteenth-century Hotel de Vauluisant on rue du Vauluisant, contains religious articles, documents, and examples of Renaissance Troyen sculpture. In the same complex is France's only **Musée de la Bonneterie,** a collection of gloves, hats, and hoisery commemorating the crafts for which Troyes is famous. Also make sure to visit the **Maison de l'outil et de la pensée ouvière,** a museum devoted to local tools of the region. The building which houses the museum is a marvelously restored 16th century *hotel*. The collection is poorly documented, but the tools themselves are beautiful, noble objects that speak volumes without a text. The museum also has an interesting bookshop with a great many books on antisanry. (The museum is at 7, Rue de la Trinite; open 9am-12pm, 2-6pm daily. Entrance 6F.) Also note the many 16th century buildings in the area in very poor condition, and you will appreciate the extraordinary success at restoration and preservation, throughout Troyes.

Near the Cathedral is the **Musée d'Art Moderne Pierre-Levy,** a previously privately-owned collection of paintings. It includes works by such artists as Pissarro, Cezanne, Gauguin, and Picasso, and it promises to be an outstanding museum when it is completed.

For nightlife, try L'Ecu Disco, rue Carbonnet or Discotheque Voltaire on rue Voltaire. The locals also favor Le KVO, open every evening, on the corner de la Fare (near the train station).

Twenty-five kilometers from Troyes (and forty-five minutes by bus) is the **Forêt d'Orient,** a peaceful wooded area set above a large, clear lake and inhabited by wild animals. The area has an **Auberge de Jeunesse (IYHF)** to make your rural retreat even easier: Mesnil St.-Pierre (tel. 45-27-38), next to the lake. It has only twenty places, but offers meals (open May-Oct., 19F per night). There is also a two-star **campground** on the lakes, Camping de la voie Colette (tel. 45-27-15). Open March 1-Oct. 31, which you might try if the hotel is full.

The North

The memory of war is never far from the towns and villages in the north of France. Cemeteries cover the countryside, reminders of World War I massacres at Arras, the Somme, and Cambrai, and nearly every town bears scars from the widescale bombing of World War II.

A grayness hangs over the entire region, created by an ever-present fog and by a pervading aura of sadness. The north has always been the industrial center of France, and the recent economic crisis in the steel, auto, and coal-mining industries has been acutely felt. Industrial violence has risen along with a disastrous unemployment rate, and in recent years, labor-oriented political parties have made substantial gains and assumed control of several city governments.

Despite the twin ravages of war and industry, the area sees considerable numbers of tourists, many of them en route to England via the coastal ports of

Calais, Boulogne, and **Dunkerque,** making their way to Belgium, or seeking out the great cathedrals. Calais and Boulogne lie in the region known as **Pas de Calais,** traditionally a battlefield for Western Europe and, more recently, a strategic center for the control of the British Channel during World War II.

The best course for a tourist in this region of smog and battle scars bypasses the depressed mining and industrial area around Lille and the overpriced major ports. Instead, make a pilgrimage to the great cathedrals built here during the twelfth and thirteenth centuries. Standing as a testimony to both a devout spirit and a new-found prosperity, **Laon, Noyon,** and **Soissons** were the first towns to erect great churches with arching vaults; their constructions led to heroic efforts in a mature Gothic style at **Reims** and **Amiens.** All these cathedrals have somehow survived numerous wars and remain impressive. From its commanding hill-top location, the homes and cathedral of **Laon** prove particularly inspiring.

The north is well-serviced by frequent trains, but many of the smaller towns, such as Laon, are difficult to reach. Auto routes make for easy driving but somewhat frustrating hitching. The flat terrain makes bicycling a good option, especially between cathedral towns, but trucks and frequent rains can be a nuisance.

Unfortunately, the north has become the most expensive area of France. While cheaper than in Paris, both food and accommodation will cost you dearly here. Nor is the North of France renowned for its cuisine, although the area does offer some intriguing Flemish specialties. Try the *paté de canard* (duck paté) or a *ficelle picarde* (a cheese, ham, and mushroom crêpe), and *ouillette* (a particularly slimy type of sausage). Wash it down with one of the local beers.

Calais

Ever since Richard the Lion-Hearted and his Crusaders arrived here in 1189 on their way to Jerusalem, travelers have chosen Calais as the major crossing point between England and the Continent. Today, Calais sees over 15,000 visitors and as many as 160 channel crossings daily. Calais is not a pretty town, having been completely rebuilt during World War II, but it is more appealing than the other Channel port cities. Its most interesting building is the **Hotel de Ville,** a twentieth-century construction in Flemish renaissance style. In front of the hotel, the famous Rodin sculpture, the *Burghers of Calais,* commemorates a dramatic event in the final year of the Hundred Years' War when England's king, Edward III, agreed to hang the mayor and several prominent citizens rather than slaughter all the city's inhabitants. The heroic burghers, who decided to sacrifice their lives for their townsfolk, were saved by the impassioned intervention of Edward's French wife, Philippia. Across the street is the pleasant **Parc St.-Pierre** with its **World War II Museum.** The museum is housed in a blockhouse which served as the German communications center for northern France during the occupation. Open 10am-6pm from June 1st-Sept. 15th; admission 6F, students and children 3F.

Practical Information

There are two train stations in Calais: the Gare Calais-Ville and the Gare Calais-Maritime near the ferry and hovercraft ports. The city is divided by a central canal, with the Calais-Ville station in the center.

Syndicat d'Initiative, 12 blvd. Clemenceau (tel. 96-62-40). About a block away and across the street to the left of the Calais-Ville station. Open in summer 9am-10pm

(9:30am-12:30pm and 2:30-6:30pm off season). They will provide a map and an accommodations list, and book reservations for 5F.

Post Office: (main office), place d'Alsace (tel. 36-43-13), also at place de Rheims, behind the Eglise Notre Dame. Open Mon.-Fri. 8am-7pm, Sat. 8am-noon.

Police: place du Lorraine (tel. 34-37-00).

Ambulance and Medical Emergency: SMUR (tel. 96-72-19). 24-hour emergency service.

Laundromat: corner of rue des Thermes and rue des Pretres; open 6am-10pm.

Money Exchange: (tel. 96-67-75). 24-hour teller at the hovercraft port.

Hitching: For Paris, try on the Boulevard Gambetta or the Boulevard Victor-Hugo, which leads to the motorway A26. Good luck.

Telephone Code: (21).

Accommodations and Food

Maison Familiale des Jeunes Travalleuses, quai du Rhin (tel. 34-36-62). Around the corner from the syndicat. For women only. A little strict, but only 25F a night.

Hotel du Cygne, 32, rue Jean-Jaurès (tel. 34-55-18). Conveniently located across from the Hotel de Ville. Singles and doubles 40-62F. Breakfast 9F. Two other similarly-priced hotels on the same block.

Au Mouton Blanc, 44, rue du Vauxhall (tel. 34-71-52). Off the blvd. Jacquard, four blocks from the Calais-Ville station. Small, fills up fast, with three rooms at 40-45F, several for 55F (with shower). Breakfast 8.50F. The restaurant downstairs has a good menu for 26F.

Camping: Municipal Campground is right on the coast (follow rue Royale). Tents are packed together, but the sites are well-maintained. The weather is often windy and rainy here. 4.70F per place and 3F per person.

Calais bombards the visitor with *"friteries,"* but most restaurants are short on value. Try **Le Laëtitia** on place Crèvecoeur off the blvd. Lafayette; it has good Italian fare with menus at 24F, 31F, and 39F.

Boulogne

Smaller than Calais, Boulogne transcends the tourist trade. A busy port town in Roman times, Boulogne was Julius Caesar's base for his conquest of England. Perhaps in emulation, Napoleon chose it as his base for an intended invasion of England in 1803. Itself invaded by modern tourists on their way to or from England, Boulogne preserves a life of its own, and you'll find your attempts to speak French much appreciated. In mid-July, the city hosts a fête du Poisson, with nightly dinner spectacles at the casino on the quai Gambetta. Even if you're only waiting for the ferry, make time to visit the beautiful, domed **Cathédrale de Notre Dame,** which crowns the fortified, medieval *ville haute.*

A list of hotel accommodations is posted outside the syndicat d'initiative, place Frédéric-Sauvage at the corner of the quai de la Poste and the bridge Pont Marquet (open daily 10am-7pm July 1-Sept. 15; shorter hours off season; tel. 31-68-38). Most of the hotels in Boulogne fill up quickly and are overpriced to boot. If you must stay overnight, try the **Hotel l'Esperance,** 62, rue Amiral-

Bruix (tel. 31-45-17), behind the place Frédéric-Sauvage. The hot water is a little erratic, but the nice proprietor and the comparatively low prices (40F single, 55F double; breakfast 8.50F) make it the best deal in town. The small but well-maintained **Auberge de Jeunesse (IYHF)** is at 36, rue Port-Gayole (tel. 31-48-22), a fifteen-minute walk from the Gare Centrale; take a right on blvd. Voltaire, walk one block, then turn right on blvd. Daunou to rue de Brequerecque; turn left and go up the hill (open from Oct.-April, 7:30-10am and 6-11pm).

Most restaurants in Boulogne cater to the newly arrived British tourists, easing their transition to French soil with menus of fish and chips and other more expensive fare. If you're eating out, you're probably best off ordering the catch of the day. Several restaurants cluster around the place Dalton; or try **Vie Claire,** 22 place des Victoires, which offers a 32F vegetarian lunch menu. On Wed. and Sat. mornings, the place Dalton is the site of an excellent open-air market. For cheese, hit **Le Fromagerie,** 43 rue Thiers, which has over 200 varieties in stock.

Boulogne is accessible by rail or ferry. The ferry port is a twenty minute walk from the town center. There are two train stations: the Gare Maritime is closest to the port, but most trains stop at the Gare Centrale.

Lille

A gray city with over one million inhabitants, Lille is a thriving commercial center where much of France's steel is melted and much of its beer is brewed.

Lille originally belonged to the Duchy of Flanders, and even today much of the city has a Flemish air. The **Vieille Bourse** (Old Stock Exchange) on the place de Gaulle is a masterpiece of the Flemish Renaissance style. Several fine medieval houses can be found on the old **rue Esquermoise** and along the **rue de la Monnaie,** which is lined with many tall, narrow Flemish townhouses. Just off the rue de la Monnaie is the **Cathédrale de Notre Dame de la Treille,** a neo-Gothic church begun in the last century and left unfinished. Despite the unappealing brick of the west facade, the church contains some lovely chapels and an interesting choir masonry.

The ancient and imposing star-shaped **citadelle** in the north part of Lille was restored in the seventeenth century by the Marquis de Vauban, as were many of the fortresses in this area. To get over the moat and inside (it is still used as an army base), you must either sign up for a group tour at the office de tourisme or convince the guard that you're a member of the French army. The exquisitely maintained **Jardin Vauban** across the street is also worth a stroll. Other sights include the triumphal **Paris Gate** and, near the station, the **Eglise-Ste.-Anne,** a five-aisled church in the Flemish *hallerkirk* style. Noteworthy for its collection of regional art and artifacts is the **Musée de l'Hospice Comtesse** at 32, rue de la Monnaie. Originally a hospital (dating from the fifteenth century), the museum houses a collection of beautiful Flemish tiles. Open daily 10am-12:30pm and 2-5pm.

But perhaps the best way to spend time in Lille, however, is to visit the **Musée des Beaux Arts** on the place de la République (open daily except Tues., 10am-12:30pm, 2-5pm, admission 3.50F), with its fine collection of Flemish tapestries and many works by Van der Weyden, Rubens, Fordaens, and the Impressionists.

Practical Information

Though the area around the train station can be relatively sleazy, the bustling squares with their distinctly Flemish flavor can be quite lively.

Office de Tourisme: place Rihour (tel. 30-81-00), is housed in the last remaining fragment of a fifteenth-century palace. Provides information on Lille and the region; organizes group tours of the city. Open Mon.-Sat. 10am-12:30pm, 2-7pm. There is also a small information center at the train station that can give you a list of accommodations. If you plan to stay in Lille for a while, pick up the excellent student-oriented *Guide de Chtimis* (*Chti* is slang for a Lille resident) for 9.50F. The office also maintains a women's information and referral service.

Post Office: The central post office is at 7, place de la République; another major post office sits in back of the old stock exchange on the place de Gaulle. Both locations have Poste Restante and telephone and telegraph service.

Police: rue de Tournai, one block left from the train station (tel. 52-74-92).

Train Station: down the rue Faidherbe from the place de Gaulle (tel. 55-68-71).

Allostop: in the Palais Rihour with the tourist office (tel. 52-96-69). Matches riders with drivers.

Laundromat: Lavanova, 70, rue de la Barre.

Telephone Code: (20).

Accommodations

Decent hotels are expensive in Lille; the hotels clustered around the train station are generally grungy. Check with the tourist office about university housing during the summer.

Auberge de Jeunesse (IYHF), 1, ave. Julien-Destrée (tel. 52-76-02). Down the rue Tournai from the train station, take the pedestrian underpass beneath the motorway then cross the parking lot. Old building, but well-maintained. 22.50F per night, open 7-10am and 5:30-11pm (closed Dec. 10-Jan. 4).

Hôtel Chopin, rue de Tournai (tel. 06-35-80 or 55-34-50), across the street and to the left of the train station. Some singles 60.50F, doubles 74F, breakfast included.

Hôtel le Coq Hardi, 34, place de la Gare (tel. 06-05-89). A very basic place. Singles 45F, and some doubles 59F. No breakfast.

Hôtel le Floréal, 21, rue Ste.-Anne (tel. 06-36-21). Lovely little hotel one block from the station. The six rooms for 58F are always filled, so make reservations in advance. Nice proprietor; sagging beds. Other doubles to 95F. Breakfast 15F.

Hôtel Central, 91, rue des Bouchers de Perthes (tel. 54-64-63), off the rue Nationale. Clean, nice rooms with marble fireplaces. 55F for one bed, 75F for two. Showers are free, and there is no breakfast.

Food and Entertainment

Lille has a large immigrant population, and therefore some of the best deals are in non-French food. Try **Pizza Saint-Germaine,** 4, rue des Tanneurs off the rue Bethune, which serves pizza for 11-25F until midnight, and has a F34 menu.

Le 421, 32, rue des Sarrazins, off the place de la Nouvelle Aventure. Fries with everything, but plenty of food—cheap and good. A student hangout. Menu 25F, drink, but not service included. Couscous F18-34. Nearby, try the more working class **Aux Bretons,** rue Colbert, across from the market, which has a 27F *menu* featuring traditional veal, rabbit, and horse plates.

Pinocchio, 22*bis*, rue de Roubaix, a few blocks north of the train station. Excellent pizza and spaghetti for 11-25F plus service, complete with candlelight, old bricks, and disco music.

Aux Moules, 34, rue de Bethune. Mussels and fries for 28F, and inexpensive a la carte offerings from 6-12F. Open daily till 10pm.

New China, 22, rue Royale, still has an incredible if not quite filling menu for 14.50F. You can really eat on the 22.50F or the 32.50F *menu.* Single main dishes hover around 15F.

La Crêperie de Beaurepaire, 1, rue St. Etienne, parallel to rue Nationale, two blocks from the place de Gaulle. Salted crêpes 6-19F, dessert crêpes 4-12F.

Although the modern university is several kilometers outside the city, most of its students live in Lille, supporting an active city nightlife. Unfortunately, much of it is either too expensive or too sleazy; your best bet might be a cafe or bar on or near the place de Gaulle. Several cafe-theaters have a delightful atmosphere. **Au P'tit Saint-Thomas,** 20, rue des Bouchers is one of the best (tickets 50F). Or check out the very funky club-cafe-restaurant **La Boîte à Musiques,** 8, rue de la Justice, in the student-artist-working class neighborhood of Wazemmes. Don't expect to understand too much, since even ardent Francophiles will need a knowledge of Flemish to catch the subtleties (tickets 40F). For information on student activities, check at the tourist office.

South of Lille

Although **Arras** is a name usually associated with twentieth-century trench warfare, the town dates from the twelfth century and the era of Spanish dominion. Badly damaged during the Revolution and again in 1914-1915, Arras has retained a few traces of its active medieval life. The spacious **Grande Palace** is a square flanked by four tall fifteenth-century façades in the Flemish style, whose basements were originally used to shelter inhabitants during a siege or bombardment. The eighteenth-century **Palais de St. Vaast,** almost totally destroyed during the bombardment and fire of 1915 but now reconstructed, houses the **City Museum,** filled with paintings by local artists, with one Delacroix and one Corot (open daily except Tues., 10am-noon and 2-5:30pm). entrance 3.50F.

Work on the brooding **Cathedral** began in 1783 but, interrupted by the Revolution, was not completed until 1833. The façade features an *escalier monumental* leading down to the sunken rue des Teinturiers. Like the Palais de St. Vaast, the Cathedral retains the scars of war.

The fifteenth-century **Hotel de Ville,** on the place de Héros, was destroyed by fire in 1914 but has been painstakingly restored. The magnificent belltower, crowned by the statue of a lion, is the town's central landmark. You can climb the belltower by special arrangement with the sacristan.

The **syndicat d'initiative,** 11*bis*, rue Gambetta (tel. 51-26-95) is open in summer 9:15am-12:15pm and 2:15-6:15pm daily, except Sunday 10:15am-12:15pm. There is an **Auberge de Jeunesse** at 59, Grand Place (tel. 21-07-83). The **municipal campground** is located on the rue de Temple (tel. 21-55-06).

The bustling city of **Douai** was originally the Roman settlement of *Duacum,* and has undergone several metamorphoses through the centuries, including reconstruction by the celebrated seventeenth-century military architect, the Marquis de Vauban. Its central attraction is the splendid bell tower rising out of the Hotel de Ville and topped by a sculpted lion. The *carillon* (bells rung in concert) is played each weekend, and if your knees have recovered from the

Arras ascent, you can climb Douai's belltower by permission of the concierge. (Open Mon.-Fri. 10am-12:30pm and 2:30-5:30pm; Sun. 2:30-5:30pm; admission 5F). Of the old city walls, only the gates have been preserved: the **Porte d'Arras** and the **Porte de Valenciennes** date from the fifteenth century.

The sixteenth-century **Chartreuse**, on the rue des Chartreux, houses the **Musée de Douai** with some interesting sixteenth-century Dutch and nineteenth-century French art, and fine leaded windows in the Gothic cloisters. (Open daily except Tues. 10am-noon and 2-5pm).

The **syndicat d'initiative**, 70, place d'Armes (tel. 87-26-63) is open Mon.-Fri. 9am-noon and 2-6pm; Sat. 2-6pm. There are a few hotels around the place Carnot, three blocks north of the train station on ave. Clemenceau.

Amiens

On the banks of the Somme, Amiens is a lively commercial center and the major town of the Picardie region. Although much of the old town has been buried by modern expansion, one magnificent Gothic structure remains: the **Cathédrale de Notre Dame.** When the leaders of Amiens decided to rebuild their Cathedral in 1220, they sought to outdo the achievements at Laon and Chartres by making theirs even higher and more ornate. Finished within fifty years and remarkably well-maintained through the wars, Amiens Cathedral presents the Gothic style in its purest form. The west facade, with its surprisingly short towers, presents an astounding complexity of statuary and sculpted detail. The central portal depicts Christ surrounded by a worshipping universe, flanked by scenes from the lives of the saints. The interior is remarkable not only for the clean and weightless arches, but also for the ornate sculpture and painting around the choir. From every angle, inside and outside, Amiens Cathedral presents an image of intricate unity rivaled by few other buildings. (Open daily 7:30am-noon and 2-7pm.)

Other sights in Amiens include the **Eglise St.-Leu** and the **Eglise St.-Germain,** both Gothic churches, and some of the old townhouses around the Cathedral. Amiens is also a university town, and at night the area around the rue Ernest Calvin, dotted with cafes and cinemas, becomes quite lively.

Practical Information

Amiens is served by frequent trains from Paris' Gare du Nord and is not far from the A-1 autoroute. The train station lies at the east end of town.

Syndicat d'Initiative: rue Jean-Catelas, in the Maison de la Culture (tel. 91-79-28). A long walk down the rue Noyen (keep straight, although the road changes names). Provides helpful information on the town and a map of the North. Open daily 10am-noon and 2-7pm. During the summer there is another office outside the Cathedral at 20, place Notre Dame open daily 12:30-6:30pm June-Sept. Both offices can book hotel reservations.

Transalpino: at the Agence GGP, place Alphones Fiquet (tel. 92-40-55). Offers reductions on train tickets to persons under age 26.

CIJ, 45, rue des Otages (tel. 91-21-31), houses an Allostop agency and provides information on temporary employment.

CROUS, 10, rue des Majots (tel. 98-49-50). Although doesn't offer lodging, does provide university restaurant tickets (IIF) and a babysitting service.

Post Office: rue des Vergeaux. Open Mon.-Fri. 8am-7pm, Sat. 8am-noon.

Hospital: place Victor Pauchet (tel. 71-80-51). Emergency (tel. 18).

Police: rue des Jacobins (tel. 91-08-81). Emergency (17).

Bus Station: one block to the right of the train station.

Laundromat: 20, rue Jean-Catelas, across from the syndicat.

Telephone Code: (22).

Accommodations and Food

Many hotels surround the train station, but most are expensive. University housing is available from July 1-Sept. 30. Check with **CROUS,** 13, rue des Majots (tel. 91-84-33; open weekdays 9am-5pm).

Auberge de Jeunesse (IYHF), a small Hostel about 1 km from the station along the blvd. d'Alsace-Lorraine (tel. 91-35-96). Next to the campground in a peaceful setting by the Somme. Strict Proprietor. Kitchen facilities. 22.50F per night. No breakfast. Curfew at 10:30pm. Closed mid-Dec.-mid-March.

Hôtel le Milford, 64, rue de la République (tel. 91-32-87). Good location by the Prefecture and the Cirque; follow blvd. de Belfort from the station. Rooms for 42F; closed last two weeks in August.

Hôtel du Cirque, 24, blvd. Jules-Vernes (tel. 89-35-79). In the same area, but a little fancier. Six rooms with one bed at 50F. Breakfast 12F, showers 5F.

Hôtel aux Touristes, 22*bis,* place Notre Dame (tel. 91-33-45). If you don't mind the name and the unfriendly management, this hotel boasts a beautiful location across from the cathedral. One single at 44.50F, several one-bedded rooms 49-61F, double beds 115F. Breakfast 9.50F. Hotel-bar closes at 8pm, although you can get the key.

Camping: Municipal de l'Etang St. Pierre, beside the Youth Hostel. A great view of the Cathedral and well-maintained. 2.50F per person, children under seven 1.30F, 1.30F for tent. Open 7am-noon, 2-10pm.

For eating out, try **La Soupe a Cailloux,** 16 rue des Boudis (tel. 91-92-70), a charming vegetarian restaurant by the river with entrees 15-17F, desserts and cheese 15-18F, and main dishes like felaffel, and cauliflower casserole 24-27F. Closed Sun., Mon. and August. Also try **La Corne du Boeuf** at 30-36 rue de Bauvais. The *crudités* (raw vegetables) for 11F and *menus* at 17.30F, 26.50F and 28.20F can't be beat (closed Sun.). **La Mangeoire,** 3, rue des Sargents, offers crêpes and *gallettes* from 5-12F. Have a bowl of cider and soak in the atmosphere (closed Sun. and Mon.).

Laon

Laon is one of the little-known jewels of northern France. Like Assisi and Urbino on the plains of Tuscany, it is a hill town in the midst of flat land, an unexpected *butte* crowned by a magnificent cathedral, coming suddenly and spectacularly into view as the traveler approaches from the west.

Laon's history goes back to Roman times and includes a spell as capital of France under the Carolingian kings. It was the birthplace of Charlemagne's legendary companion, Roland, and in modern times of Father Marquette (early European explorer of the Mississippi). Napoleon lost the Battle of Laon to the Prussians in 1814, and his abdication soon followed.

The natural advantage of the site, an easily defended and fortified position, has resulted in Laon's architectural heritage: the *haute ville* is completely surrounded by medieval ramparts, pierced only by the city gates, and commands a spectacular view of the countryside for a radius of thirty miles. Laon's centerpiece is the **Cathédrale de Notre Dame**, one of France's earliest great cathedrals. Sturdy Romanesque pillars support the light Gothic vaulting above; constructed from 1155-1225, the Cathedral foretold the Gothic triumph over the earlier style. Also noteworthy are the stained glass windows in the east and west ends.

Most striking about Laon's Cathedral are the four lavish towers. Each sequence of ornamentation is based on the number eight, and the sculpted cows' heads supposedly commemorate the oxen that helped haul the stone to the plateau. Visitors are sometimes allowed to climb the towers, but only as part of a guided tour.

Practical Information

Laon is served infrequently by trains from Paris' Gare du Nord and from Amiens. Once outside the station you'll see why the city has rarely been attacked, but don't let the cog railway tempt you—it hasn't been used for years. You can either climb the 260 steps to the *haute ville* or wait for the occasional #3 bus.

Syndicat d'Initiative: Opposite the Cathedral gates (tel. 23-45-87) and is open daily 9am-noon and 2-7pm June-Nov., closing at 5pm the rest of the year. The pleasant staff is eager to help with finding accommodations and sightseeing. Guided tours on Sun. at 3pm and other times by arrangement, range from 9F for 2 hours to 24F for a day-long tour.

Comité Departemental du Tourisme, 1, rue St. Martin (tel. 23-24-53), open Mon.-Thurs. 8:30-noon and 1:30-6pm, Fri. 8:30-noon and 1:30-5pm. Provides masses of information on the Picardy region.

Post Office: In the *haute ville* at the corner of rue des Cordeliers and rue Pourier; in the *ville basse* at the place de la Gare. Open Mon.-Fri. 8am-7pm, Sat. 8am-noon.

Police: blvd. de Lyon, a block to the left of the train station (tel. 79-23-82).

Hospital: by the Eglise St.-Martin in a beautiful seventeenth-century building (tel. 23-29-30).

Telephone Code: (23).

Accommodations

The *haute ville* is a lovely place to spend the night. Try:

Hôtel le P'tit Quinquin, 9, place St. Julien off the rue St. Jean (tel. 23-09-09). Part hotel and part private home with a friendly proprietor, eight rooms: five for 50F. Breakfast 8F, no showers. Closed in July.

Hôtel-Restaurant la Paix, 52, rue St. Jean (tel. 23-21-95). A bit fancier and the restaurant is more expensive (fixed menus at 36.80F, 50F, and 73.50F). Singles and doubles 53F and 74F with shower. Breakfast 13F, showers 8F. Closed in August.

Hôtel des Chevaliers, rue Serurier (tel. 23-43-78) is indeed a splurge, with one-bedded singles and doubles at 80F (with shower) and breakfast 14F, but the rooms are charming, the management exceptionally friendly.

Maison des Jeunes, 20, rue du Cloitre (tel. 23-25-80). The nearest thing to a youth hostel and your best bet in Laon. Thirty beds available for 35F, breakfast included. Cafeteria serves meals for 19F all week long.

The hotels in the *ville basse* are clustered around the station. Try:

Hôtel le Carnot, 16, ave. Carnot (tel. 23-02-08). A few singles for 50F. Breakfast 13F.

Near Laon

Compiègne makes an easy daytrip from Laon or from Paris. The town has been historically important as the country residence of French monarchs, from the time of Louis XV, who had a splendid palace built there. Restored under Napoleon, the palace at Compiègne remains a favorite tourist attraction. The rooms of the palace have been reconstructed in both First and Second Empire styles, and the tour guides feed you an inexhaustible supply of anecdotes and background information. The palace can be visited every day except Tuesday, from 1:30-6pm; the guided tour 9F, 4F students; less expensive on Sundays and holidays) lasts 45 minutes and is obligatory. The **Parc du Palais** is beautifully maintained and makes a great picnic spot.

The Gothic **Hôtel de Ville** in the central place of the same name has a magnificent belltower in which fourteenth-century sculpted figures strike bells with hammers to mark the hours. The Hotel also houses the **syndicat d'initiative** (tel. 440-01-00) which has information on all aspects of the town (open daily 9am-12:30pm and 2-6pm). They will also rent bicycles for 17F a day and change your money during office hours. Not far from the center of town is an **Auberge de Jeunesse,** 6, rue Pasteur (tel. 440-26-00) with twenty beds and kitchen facilities (22.50F per night). Surrounding Compiègne is the verdant **forêt de Compiègne,** long the hunting grounds of kings and now a wonderful place for biking.

Soissons has as long and distinguished a history as Laon, but the approach through industrial suburbs gives little promise of anything of special interest except the cathedral, visible in the distance. Like the rest of the region, Soissons suffered heavily in World War I, and its **Cathédrale St.-Gervais et St.-Protais** was almost totally destroyed. Restoration was undertaken from 1920 until 1931, but the facade has remained curiously asymmetrical, with only one of two towers rebuilt. An exhibition of photographs in the nave reveals the extent of war damage.

The former **Abbaye de St. Jean des Vignes,** on the edge of town (enter from blvd. Jeanne d'Arc) has not been restored since the war, and all that remains of the original church are the twin spires rising hauntingly over the town.

The **syndicat d'initiative** 1, ave. de Général-Leclerc (tel. 53-08-27), by the botanical gardens and one block from the place de la République, can provide you with a map and list of hotels. If you plan to stay overnight in Soissons, the **Hôtel de la Gare,** place de la Gare (tel. 53-31-61) is across from the station and has singles and doubles for 55F (closed in August). **Hôtel du Nord,** 6, rue de Belleu (tel. 53-12-55) has singles and doubles at 55F, 65F for two beds (closed in July). **Camping** is possible at sites on the ave. du Mail about 1 km from the center of town (tel. 53-12-00).

A PARTING WORD

If you're wondering how *Let's Go* came to be, the series is as old as just about any of its recent staff members. In 1960, a group of enterprising Harvard undergraduates put together a pamphlet of humorous tips for the student traveler. These first editions included the helpful advice that women should pack "one pair slacks or Bermudas (though Europeans don't approve of pants on women)." While France in these first guides received four-page coverage, it has now blossomed into a four-hundred-page regional book of its own. At present there are six books in the *Let's Go* family, and *Let's Go: Europe* has ballooned to include Egypt, Israel, Morocco, Tunisia, and Turkey.

Although the books are newly researched by different students every year, each new edition draws on the fabric woven by past generations of *Let's Go* researchers and editors. The team of twenty-odd researchers spends a hectic summer laying the groundwork for the latest edition. Equipped with notebook, scissors and paste, aspirin, and resourceful determination, the *Let's Go* undercover agent sets out on the road to adventure or hardship or both. Abandoning concern for personal comfort, the route of a researcher can often be a mad dash from Tuscan hillside village to Turkish mosque to London laundromat.

While the researchers are gathering ingredients on the road, the editorial staff sits back at headquarters concealed in a dormitory dungeon in Cambridge, eagerly awaiting the arrival of each day's overseas produce. The editors-cum-chefs combine this newly-gathered "copy" with the stock of the old books, and add spices of their own.

3122 cups of coffee and six birthday cakes later, after 25,000 sheets of paper and 68 typewriter ribbons have become as exhausted as the ten-person staff itself—the books are ready.

We hope they whet your appetite for travel as much as they have ours.

INDEX

SEND US A POSTCARD

We'd like to hear your reaction.
Did you make any discoveries?
Did we steer you wrong?

Let us know.